Digital Rhetoric and Global Literacies:

Communication Modes and Digital Practices in the Networked World

Gustav Verhulsdonck
University of Texas at El Paso, USA

Marohang Limbu
Michigan State University, USA

A volume in the Advances in Linguistics
and Communication Studies (ALCS) Book
Series

Information Science
REFERENCE
An Imprint of IGI Global

Managing Director:	Lindsay Johnston
Production Editor:	Jennifer Yoder
Development Editor:	Austin DeMarco
Acquisitions Editor:	Kayla Wolfe
Typesetter:	John Crodian
Cover Design:	Jason Mull

Published in the United States of America by
Information Science Reference (an imprint of IGI Global)
701 E. Chocolate Avenue
Hershey PA 17033
Tel: 717-533-8845
Fax: 717-533-8661
E-mail: cust@igi-global.com
Web site: http://www.igi-global.com

Copyright © 2014 by IGI Global. All rights reserved. No part of this publication may be reproduced, stored or distributed in any form or by any means, electronic or mechanical, including photocopying, without written permission from the publisher. Product or company names used in this set are for identification purposes only. Inclusion of the names of the products or companies does not indicate a claim of ownership by IGI Global of the trademark or registered trademark.

Library of Congress Cataloging-in-Publication Data

Digital rhetoric and global literacies : communication modes and digital practices in the networked world / Gustav Verhulsdonck and Marohang Limbu, editors.
     pages cm.
  Includes bibliographical references and index.
   ISBN 978-1-4666-4916-3 (hardcover) -- ISBN 978-1-4666-4917-0 (ebook) -- ISBN 978-1-4666-4918-7 (print & perpetual access) 1. Communication--Technological innovations. 2. Rhetoric. 3. Digital media. I. Verhulsdonck, Gustav, 1975- II. Limbu, Marohang, 1965-
  P96.T42D536 2014
  302.23'1--dc23
                                2013039902

This book is published in the IGI Global book series Advances in Linguistics and Communication Studies (ALCS) (ISSN: pending; eISSN: pending)

British Cataloguing in Publication Data
A Cataloguing in Publication record for this book is available from the British Library.

All work contributed to this book is new, previously-unpublished material. The views expressed in this book are those of the authors, but not necessarily of the publisher.

For electronic access to this publication, please contact: eresources@igi-global.com.

Advances in Linguistics and Communication Studies (ALCS) Book Series

ISSN: pending
EISSN: pending

MISSION

The scope of language and communication is constantly changing as society evolves, new modes of communication are developed through technological advancement, and novel words enter our lexicon as the result of cultural change. Understanding how we communicate and use language is crucial in all industries and updated research is necessary in order to promote further knowledge in this field.

The **Advances in Linguistics and Communication Studies (ALCS)** book series presents the latest research in diverse topics relating to language and communication. Interdisciplinary in its coverage, ALCS presents comprehensive research on the use of language and communication in various industries including business, education, government, and healthcare.

COVERAGE

- Computer-Mediated Communication
- Computational Linguistics
- Dialectology
- Discourse Analysis
- Forensic Linguistics
- Graphic Communications
- Language Acquisition
- Language and Identity
- Language in the Media
- Non-Verbal Communication
- Interpersonal Communication
- Semantics
- Sociolinguistics
- Media and Public Communications
- Cross-Cultural Communication
- Youth Language

IGI Global is currently accepting manuscripts for publication within this series. To submit a proposal for a volume in this series, please contact our Acquisition Editors at Acquisitions@igi-global.com or visit: http://www.igi-global.com/publish/.

The Advances in Linguistics and Communication Studies (ALCS) Book Series (ISSN pending) is published by IGI Global, 701 E. Chocolate Avenue, Hershey, PA 17033-1240, USA, www.igi-global.com. This series is composed of titles available for purchase individually; each title is edited to be contextually exclusive from any other title within the series. For pricing and ordering information please visit http://www.igi-global.com/book-series/advances-linguistics-communication-studies/78950. Postmaster: Send all address changes to above address. Copyright © 2014 IGI Global. All rights, including translation in other languages reserved by the publisher. No part of this series may be reproduced or used in any form or by any means – graphics, electronic, or mechanical, including photocopying, recording, taping, or information and retrieval systems – without written permission from the publisher, except for non commercial, educational use, including classroom teaching purposes. The views expressed in this series are those of the authors, but not necessarily of IGI Global.

Titles in this Series

For a list of additional titles in this series, please visit: www.igi-global.com

Communication and Language Analysis in the Corporate World
Roderick P. Hart (University of Texas - Austin, USA)
Information Science Reference • copyright 2014 • 435pp • H/C (ISBN: 9781466649996) • US $215.00 (our price)

Communication and Language Analysis in the Public Sphere
Roderick P. Hart (University of Texas - Austin, USA)
Information Science Reference • copyright 2014 • 580pp • H/C (ISBN: 9781466650039) • US $190.00 (our price)

Digital Rhetoric and Global Literacies Communication Modes and Digital Practices in the Networked World
Gustav Verhulsdonck (University of Texas at El Paso, USA) and Marohang Limbu (Michigan State University, USA)
Information Science Reference • copyright 2014 • 309pp • H/C (ISBN: 9781466649163) • US $180.00 (our price)

www.igi-global.com

701 E. Chocolate Ave., Hershey, PA 17033
Order online at www.igi-global.com or call 717-533-8845 x100
To place a standing order for titles released in this series, contact: cust@igi-global.com
Mon-Fri 8:00 am - 5:00 pm (est) or fax 24 hours a day 717-533-8661

Editorial Advisory Board

Jeff Grabill, *Michigan State University, USA*
William F. Hard-Davidson, *Michigan State University, USA*
Matthew McCool, *Independent Researcher and Scholar, USA*
Barry L. Thatcher, *New Mexico State University, USA*

List of Reviewers

Meagan Kittle Autry, *North Carolina State University, USA*
Dilli Bikram Edingo, *University of Guelph, Canada*
Mike Edwards, *Washington State University, USA*
Julie Faulkner, *Monash University, Australia*
Jorge Gomez, *University of Texas – El Paso, USA*
Nicholas A. Hanford, *Rensselaer Polytechnic Institute, USA*
Chris Ingraham, *University of Colorado – Boulder, USA*
Ashley Rose Kelly, *North Carolina State University, USA*
Demetrious Jason Lallas, *Wagner College, USA*
Ben Lauren, *Florida International University, USA*
Jennifer Helene Maher, *University of Maryland – Baltimore, USA*
Casey McArdle, *Michigan State University, USA*
Brad Mehlenbacher, *North Carolina State University, USA*
Nonny de la Peña, *University of Southern California, USA*
Mª Pilar Milagros García, *Koç University, Turkey*
Curtis R. Newbold, *Westminster College, USA*
Rajendra Kumar Panthee, *University of Texas – El Paso, USA*
Rich Rice, *Texas Tech University, USA*
Mike Ristich, *Michigan State University, USA*
Martin van Velsen, *Carnegie Mellon University, USA*

Table of Contents

Foreword xv

Preface xviii

Acknowledgment xxviii

Section 1
Historical, Theoretical, and Conceptual Perspectives on Digital Communication

Chapter 1
Digital Rhetoric and Globalization: A Convergence-Continuum Model 1
Gustav Verhulsdonck, University of Texas at El Paso, USA

Chapter 2
Engagement Design: Toward a Holistic Model for Digital Communication Design 41
Curtis R. Newbold, Westminster College, USA

Chapter 3
Toward an Algorithmic Rhetoric 62
Chris Ingraham, University of Colorado at Boulder, USA

Chapter 4
Decoding What is Good in Code: Toward a Metaphysical Ethics of Unicode 80
Jennifer Helene Maher, University of Maryland, Baltimore County, USA

Chapter 5
The Data Machine: Identification in the Age of Data Mining 97
Nicholas A. Hanford, Rensselaer Polytechnic Institute, USA

Chapter 6
The Persuasive Language of Action: Interaction in the Digital Age 113
Martin van Velsen, Carnegie Mellon University, USA

Section 2
Practices of Digital Communication across Cultures in Digital and Global Contexts

Chapter 7
Digital and Global Literacies in Networked Communities: Epistemic Shifts and Communication
Practices in the Cloud Era...131
    Marohang Limbu, Michigan State University, USA

Chapter 8
Developing Intercultural Competence through Glocal Activity Theory Using the Connect-Exchange
Study Abroad App 154
    Rich Rice, Texas Tech University, USA
    Ben Lauren, Florida International University, USA

Chapter 9
Inviting Citizen Designers to Design Digital Interface for the Democratization of Web Online
Environments 174
    Rajendra Kumar Panthee, University of Texas at El Paso, USA

Chapter 10
Social Media in an Intercultural Writing Context: Creating Spaces for Student Negotiations...........191
    Mᵃ Pilar Milagros García, Koç University, Turkey

Chapter 11
Digital Literacy Instruction in Afghanistan 209
    Mike Edwards, Washington State University, USA

Section 3
Emerging Digital Communication in Digital and Global Contexts

Chapter 12
Considering Chronos and Kairos in Digital Media Rhetorics 227
    Ashley Rose Kelly, Purdue University, USA
    Meagan Kittle Autry, North Carolina State University, USA
    Brad Mehlenbacher, North Carolina State University, USA

Chapter 13
A Match Made in "Outer Heaven:" The Digital Age Vis-à-Vis the Bomb in Guns of the Patriots....248
    Jorge Gomez, University of Texas at El Paso, USA

Chapter 14
"A Genuine Moment of Liberation for Me": Digital Introductions as Powerful Learning.................283
    Julie Faulkner, Monash University, Australia

Chapter 15
On the Condition of Anonymity: Disembodied Exhibitionism and Oblique Trolling Strategies.......296
    Demetrios Jason Lallas, Union County College, USA

Chapter 16
Embodied Digital Rhetoric: Soft Selves, Plastic Presence, and the Nonfiction Narrative 312
    Nonny de la Peña, University of Southern California, USA

Compilation of References 328

About the Contributors 360

Index 366

Detailed Table of Contents

Foreword xv

Preface xviii

Acknowledgment xxviii

Section 1
Historical, Theoretical, and Conceptual Perspectives on Digital Communication

Chapter 1
Digital Rhetoric and Globalization: A Convergence-Continuum Model 1
Gustav Verhulsdonck, University of Texas at El Paso, USA

Digital rhetoric has been discussed by many theorists as comprising a marked shift from ancient rhetoric's focus on persuasion. For some of the earlier theorists, digital rhetoric defined a novel relationship between literacy and the mechanics of text as computer-mediated communication and changed relationships between consuming, producing and engaging with discourse as information on a screen. Later digital rhetoricians argue different approaches and definitions that are more inclusive of the different types of discourse facilitated by multimodal, interactive, immersive, and computer-mediated communication as semantic discourse at the interface level and encoded through computer programming language, servers, and networks. This chapter focuses on the different modes of digital rhetoric in the context of globalization through a convergence-continuum model approach. The model presented approaches rhetoric and discourse from various levels as loosely based on the models of activity theory, multimodality intercultural theories of globalization and integrates them into a continuum model ranging from global, public modes to individual, personal digital rhetorical modes and practices. Instead of being prescriptive, this model is descriptive in recognizing the fluid natures of digital rhetorical interactions whereby global and local, public and private, group and individual, production and consumption, human and technological, physical and virtual and other discourse contexts merge.

Chapter 2
Engagement Design: Toward a Holistic Model for Digital Communication Design 41
Curtis R. Newbold, Westminster College, USA

Evolutions in digital communications since the beginning of the century require information designers to think about the possibilities that digital technologies present and the boundaries they allow communicators to appropriately bend or even subvert. Arguing for a more holistic and humanistic approach to digital communications, this chapter approaches the subject with a proposed theory for "engagement design," a design process that integrates the expedience of usability, utility, and cognition with human experience, rhetoric, and emotion.

Chapter 3
Toward an Algorithmic Rhetoric 62
Chris Ingraham, University of Colorado at Boulder, USA

Insofar as algorithms are digital problem-solving operations that follow a set of rules or processes to arrive at a result, they are constrained by the rules that determine their parameters for operating. While an algorithm can only operate according to its instructions, however, the potential rules that might govern an algorithm are inexhaustible. An algorithm's design thus makes rhetorical choices that privilege the importance of some information or desired outcomes over others. This chapter argues for a way of thinking about algorithmic rhetoric as macro-, meso-, and micro-rhetorical. Along these lines, it would be beneficial to think more about algorithms as digital rhetorics with terrific power to sway what counts as knowledge, truth, and material reality in the everyday lives of people across an astonishing range of global communities in the twenty-first century.

Chapter 4
Decoding What is Good in Code: Toward a Metaphysical Ethics of Unicode 80
Jennifer Helene Maher, University of Maryland, Baltimore County, USA

Programming benefits from universal standards that facilitate effective global transmission of information. The Unicode Standard, for example, is a character encoding system that aims to assign a unique number set to each letter, mark, and symbol in the world's various written systems, including Arabic, Korean, Cherokee, and even Cuneiform. As the quantity of these numerical encodings grow, the differences among the written systems of natural languages pose increasingly little consequence to the artificial languages of both programmers and machines. But the instrumental, technical effects of Unicode must not be mistaken as its only effects. Recognized as a metaphysical object in its own right, Unicode, specifically, and code, generally, creates a protocol for the actualization of moral and political values. This chapter examines how Microsoft's inclusion and then deletion of the Unicode encodings U+5350 and U+534D in its Office's Bookshelf Symbol 7 font illustrates how technically successful coding can be rhetorically buggy, meaning that they invoke competing ethical values that, in this case, involve free speech, anti-Semitism, and Western privilege.

Chapter 5
The Data Machine: Identification in the Age of Data Mining 97
Nicholas A. Hanford, Rensselaer Polytechnic Institute, USA

Kenneth Burke warned of the trends of behaviorism in *A Grammar of Motives* as he found them to be a reduction of the human condition. In the current digital landscape, data mining aims at reducing the human user to characteristics and re-presenting those characteristics, through online advertising, to the user they were collected from. Due to these processes, rhetoricians are forced to take a deeper look at how the audience is constituted within digital situations. This chapter discusses the effects of data mining on Burke's work, providing an example for the contextualization of rhetorical theory in new media environments. By contextualizing Burke's concepts, this chapter allows for these ideas to be used more seamlessly within digital rhetoric and any medium where data mining is a consistent practice.

Chapter 6
The Persuasive Language of Action: Interaction in the Digital Age 113
Martin van Velsen, Carnegie Mellon University, USA

Besides the visual splendor pervasive in the current generation of digital video games, especially those where players roam simulated landscapes and imaginary worlds, few efforts have looked at the resources available to embed human meaning into a game's experience. From the art of persuasion to the mechanics of meaning-making in digital video games and table-top role playing games, this chapter investigates the changes and new opportunities available that can extend our understanding of digital rhetoric. Starting with a breakdown of the role of choice, workable models from psychology and the untapped body of knowledge from table-top role playing games are shown to allow game designers to enrich their products with a deeper human experience.

Section 2
Practices of Digital Communication across Cultures in Digital and Global Contexts

Chapter 7
Digital and Global Literacies in Networked Communities: Epistemic Shifts and Communication Practices in the Cloud Era..131
Marohang Limbu, Michigan State University, USA

This chapter explores how the concept of literacy, digital literacy, and global literacy is shifting; how technologies (YouTube, Facebook, Skype, blogs, vlogs, and Google Hangouts) and digital literacies facilitate cross-cultural and intercultural communication and global cultural understandings; how technologies engage global citizens to share, collaborate, cooperate, and create their narratives; and how people become able to address local and global socio-cultural and political issues through various global digital engagements. Finally, this chapter investigates how knowledge is produced, disseminated, and consumed across global cultures in digital contexts.

Chapter 8
Developing Intercultural Competence through Glocal Activity Theory Using the Connect-Exchange Study Abroad App 154
Rich Rice, Texas Tech University, USA
Ben Lauren, Florida International University, USA

This chapter lays a theoretical foundation for the development of an emerging model of studying intercultural communication through problem-based study abroad pedagogy. At the center of this model is a new computer tool called the Connect-Exchange App, which is meant to facilitate transactional learning between users with varying cultural backgrounds. To research how different audiences might use the app, the authors draw upon activity theory to guide their iterative design process to facilitate users' deepening glocal, intercultural competence. Developing intercultural competence is a process of iterative experiences connecting, exchanging, and filtering information.

Chapter 9

Inviting Citizen Designers to Design Digital Interface for the Democratization of Web Online
Environments 174

Rajendra Kumar Panthee, University of Texas at El Paso, USA

Web online environments are supposed to create unifying spaces where diverse societies, cultures and
linguistics as well as literacies and knowledge associated with them merge together as negotiated in
neutral space. However, these online environments are not culturally neutral or innocent communication
landscapes. They may alienate the users from marginal/periphery social, cultural, and linguistic
background and experience because of their disregard to their social, cultural, and linguistics norms and
values in the digital contact zone. Acknowledging the social, cultural, and linguistic limitations of these
technologies that aim to provide agency to their users in this chapter, this chapter proposes to invite
citizen designers to design the interface of web online environments in general and Learning Management Systems (LMS) in particular because this process can transform online environments into democratic platforms. Citizen designers, who have democratic sentiments for the creation of a just society,
are composition students in general and students with periphery cultural and linguistic experience in
particular. Doing a cultural usability test of Blackboard 8, the author argues that current web interface
design is not democratic and inclusive, and proposes to invite citizen designers to re/design interface of
online environments for their democratization so that they would include people from different cultural
and linguistic backgrounds and enhance writing students' writing powers.

Chapter 10

Social Media in an Intercultural Writing Context: Creating Spaces for Student Negotiations...........191

Mª Pilar Milagros García, Koç University, Turkey

The current research study is part of a larger project that aims to analyze ways in which first year intercultural writing students interpret/understand the impact of social media on their composition practices,
critical thinking processes and knowledge negotiations processes. In particular, the current chapter attempts to understand how first year intercultural writing students reflect on and assess the ways social
media has helped them practice and or/acquire more critical thinking skills.

Chapter 11

Digital Literacy Instruction in Afghanistan...209

Mike Edwards, Washington State University, USA

This chapter uses the American military's purchase of a $5.6 million contract to supply the National
Military Academy of Afghanistan with laptop computers as the occasion to investigate the complex and
overdetermined intersections of digital, administrative, and literacy technologies. These intersections
and the challenges they produced for the author as a Western mentor working with Afghan postsecondary instructors in ESL and digital literacies reveal the problematic homogenizing Western economic
and cultural assumptions and the intense naturalization of administrative technologies that accompany
the denaturalized use of digital and textual technologies in global contexts. The connections of those
challenges to recent scholarship in rhetoric and composition highlight the limitations of that scholarship's conception of political economy in a global digital context and also offers new possibilities for
imagining hybrid multilingual digital literacies on a global scale.

Section 3
Emerging Digital Communication in Digital and Global Contexts

Chapter 12
Considering Chronos and Kairos in Digital Media Rhetorics 227
Ashley Rose Kelly, Purdue University, USA
Meagan Kittle Autry, North Carolina State University, USA
Brad Mehlenbacher, North Carolina State University, USA

Any account of the rhetoric of digital spaces should begin not with the provocation that rhetoric is impoverished and requires fresh import to account for new media technologies, but instead with a careful analysis of what is different about how digital technologies afford or constrain certain utterances, interactions, and actions. Only then might one begin to articulate prospects of a digital rhetoric. This chapter examines the importance of time to an understanding the rhetoric of digital spaces. It suggests that rhetorical notions of kairos and chronos provide an important reminder that it is the rhetorical situation, along with rhetorical actors at individual to institutional levels, that construct the discursive spaces within which people participate, even in digitally-mediated environments.

Chapter 13
A Match Made in "Outer Heaven:" The Digital Age Vis-à-Vis the Bomb in Guns of the Patriots....248
Jorge Gomez, University of Texas at El Paso, USA

The stealth-action videogame Metal Gear Solid 4: Guns of the Patriots features the tired heroics of Solid Snake (also known as Old Snake), a retired, legendary soldier whose services are demanded one last time by a world in perpetual war. This epic game, containing almost ten hours of cutscenes alone, delineates the consequences not only of nuclear proliferation, but of mass (re)production in a digital age. In this fourth and final entry in the Solid Snake saga the two go hand-in-hand: a nuclear age exacerbated by advanced technology, advanced technology proliferated under the banner of a post-Cold War war economy. In this chapter, Kenneth Burke's rhetoric of rebirth and Slavoj Žižek's ideological criticism, along with several ludological frameworks, are adopted to show how various multiliteracies can be unearthed from this artifact of digital rhetoric. The chapter closes with implications for digital rhetoric studies.

Chapter 14
"A Genuine Moment of Liberation for Me": Digital Introductions as Powerful Learning.................283
Julie Faulkner, Monash University, Australia

This chapter argues that participation in a digital self-presentation has the potential to challenge inscribed approaches to learning and teaching. It draws from a study of preservice teachers at an Australian university, who were invited to create a digital introduction as part of their English teaching method course. Such a task offered students opportunities to experiment with shifting semiotic forms in ways unavailable to written introductions. Students were asked to critically reflect after the presentation on aspects of technology, representation and learning that were brought into focus in and through their presentations. A semiotic analysis offers insights into the potential of multimodality, as the digital introduction pushed the participants out of familiar territory, often producing creative and stimulating texts. Using Kress's concept of synaesthesia, the chapter explores innovations possible in the creation of new possibilities in a multimodal space.

Chapter 15
On the Condition of Anonymity: Disembodied Exhibitionism and Oblique Trolling Strategies.......296
    Demetrios Jason Lallas, Union County College, USA

The ambiguity of identity in disembodied communities poses unique challenges in the flow of digital rhetoric. Online anonymity can lead to disinhibition, enabling the practice of trolling: the effort to derail discussion for attention, mischief, and abuse. This chapter examines this phenomenon in various social media contexts, exploring effective practices in recognizing and harnessing trolling.

Chapter 16
Embodied Digital Rhetoric: Soft Selves, Plastic Presence, and the Nonfiction Narrative 312
    Nonny de la Peña, University of Southern California, USA

A new embodied digital rhetoric emerges when using nonfiction narratives built in fully immersive virtual reality systems that take advantage of the plasticity of our sensations of presence. The feeling of "being-in-the-world" as described by phenomenologists, including philosophy of mind, film, and virtual reality theorists, is part of the adaptability that humans show in their relationship to technological tools. Andy Clark's "soft selves" and our "plastic presence" merge as the high resolution graphics of the latest virtual reality goggles and robust audio captured at real events tricks our minds into having an embodied connection with the stories portrayed in these new spaces. By putting people into news or documentary pieces on scene as themselves, opportunities for persuasive and effective rhetoric arise. This chapter cites theory, psychology and virtual reality research as well as the author's specific case studies to detail the potential for this new embodied digital rhetoric that allows us to pass through the screen and become present as witnesses to a nonfiction story.

Compilation of References 328

About the Contributors 360

Index 366

Foreword

When digital rhetoric first emerged as a discipline in the 1990s, its initial objects of study were situated strongly in the English language and the Global North. Hypertext fiction, electronic poetry, and websites from corporations, candidates, and taste-makers were situated in familiar frames of cultural, linguistic, and political reference. The work of Richard Lanham, Jay David Bolter, Michael Joyce, and other early practitioners within niche realms of academia did little to promote a truly World Wide Web. As digital rhetoric continues to become a recognized subfield, those asked to define it, such as Doug Eyman, Cheryl Ball, and Jentery Sayers seem to often steer clear of subaltern discourses, even if queer and disabled rhetorical contexts are slated for inclusion by Jonathan Alexander and Melanie Yergeau respectively (Digital Rhetoric Collaborative, 2012).

Although anonymity could create disquieting acts of verbal, visual, or procedural rhetorical violence in the earlier digital rhetoric model, as in the case of the behavior of the aggressor described in Julian Dibbell's 1993 "A Rape in Cyberspace" or Mark Dery's pathological subjects jockeying for attention and mastery in his 1994 *Flame Wars,* such conduct resisted interpretation rather than defied comprehension. Even critics who took hoax, parody, or fraudulent websites at face value understood the rhetorical appeals that had initially grabbed their attention and had encouraged their credulity.

However, after the founding of Flickr in 2004, YouTube in 2005, and Twitter in 2006, the presence of other kinds of global content-creators in very different rhetorical contexts became more obvious, and the boundaries of nation and language in the cyberspaces of everyday life (Nunes, 2006) were redrawn with the rise of new region-specific platforms far away from the familiar discourses of either Silicon Valley or DIY subculture. Sites such as Weibo in China, Cyworld in South Korea, and Orkut in Brazil soon had hundreds of millions of users. As Geert Lovink has pointed out the era of the English-dominated Internet has probably ended even in Europe.

Certainly the increasing internationalization of online video remixing and sharing on many other competing sites has made decoding the provenance of digital objects of study notably much more complex. The language of new media at work in what Lev Manovich has called "database cinema" may draw on literally hundreds of sources in just a few minutes of rapidly changing video clips, and global online remix videos make too many cultural references for a critic in another country to unpack. Furthermore the songs, films, and cultural allusions chosen by many transnational video remixers can reflect a unique orientation of multiple understandings of citizenship. If classical rhetorician could assumes citizenship to be a relatively stable category of subjectivity, digital rhetoricians today can make no such assumptions. Whether it be transnational videogame fan films (Losh, 2010) or human rights music video remixes from the Arab Spring (Gregory & Losh, 2012), digital content-creators are appropriating, mashing up, and crowd-sourcing new forms of digital rhetoric that require new modes of interdisciplinary collaboration.

Remixed images, video, and sound may need to be "unmixed" (Losh, 2012) to be comprehensible for purposes of academic analysis as copies and originals become scrambled.

This is not simply a challenge facing scholars of the rhetorics of visual culture, those working with verbal rhetorics and procedural rhetorics (Bogost, 2007) must also think about questions of internationalization as new forms of digital capital come into play, and new economics oriented around reputation, membership, or attention reorder the social relations in which performative utterances function. For example, how might an SMS mobile money transfer of an earnings remittance in Kenya in the "financial inclusion assemblage" of "subjects, technics, and rationalities" (Shwittay, 2010) be understood as a rhetorical activity? Or how might the labor of a gold farmer in the massive online game *World of Warcraft* (Nakamura, 2010) be staged within existing conventions of deliberation, celebration, and judgment as rhetorical actors assume new online roles? What sense can we make of cybervigilanteeism in India (Shah, 2010) or Internet activism in South Korea that connects mad cow disease associated with meat imports from abroad to ideals of racial purity at home (Chun, 2009)?

Furthermore, as we approach understanding our own participation in the "Internet of things" – as mobile and ubiquitous computing technologies disseminate around the globe, the design of sensors and screens transforms subject-object relations, and more sophisticated machine learning algorithms, data mining approaches, semantic web technologies, and AI chatbots are developed – the very notion of "literacy" is changing as computers become able to read and write and speak in new ways. For example, what should digital rhetoric make of QR codes or RFID devices in considering how we are situated as rhetorical actors in particular rhetorical scenes?

This volume represents a fundamentally new approach to digital rhetoric and global literacy that puts forward a collection of distinct theoretical frameworks that can be used by contemporary rhetoricians to understand these hybrid and heterogeneous case studies from around the world, which challenge the possibilities that our always-already mediated discourse can ever exist in a single, unified, and coherent Habermassian public sphere or that persuasion as it is conventionally understood should be the main focus of our inquiry. It also seriously engages with the category of infrastructural messiness to show the complexities of glocalization and the failures of a techno-missionary agenda epitomized by One-Laptop-Per-Child. Verhulsdonck and Limbu bring knowledge to this project from vibrant scholarly communities both in the study of games and virtual worlds and in digital pedagogy and multimodal composition. They also bring the perspectives of their own complex literacy narratives, which are informed by their own experiences of transnational citizenship, technical expertise, and interdisciplinary research. The book is organized in a way that makes current trends in the field visible and represents the shift in digital rhetoric toward serious engagement with 1) computer science, 2) international studies, and 3) user-centered design. Those working in more traditional rhetorical contexts will appreciate the fact that a number of the articles are still grounded in familiar frameworks of literary study, classical oratory, or mass communication, but – be warned – this is not a book for armchair theorists. Journalists, programmers, and teachers discuss how they are applying theory to practice and readers should be prepared to cross the "yacking/hacking" divide with them. After all, digital rhetoric is a mode of being and doing for all of us, since we all are participant observers.

Elizabeth Losh
University of California – San Diego, USA

Elizabeth Losh *is the author of Virtualpolitik: An Electronic History of Government Media-Making in a Time of War, Scandal, Disaster, Miscommunication, and Mistakes (MIT Press, 2009) and the forthcoming The War on Learning: Gaining Ground in the Digital University (MIT Press). She is the co-author of the forthcoming textbook Understanding Rhetoric (Bedford/St. Martin's, 2013) with Jonathan Alexander and is co-editor of Tweeting the Revolution: Networked Media, the Rhetorics of Activism, and Practices of the Everyday with Beth Coleman. She is Director of the Culture, Art, and Technology program at Sixth College at U.C. San Diego and a blogger for Digital Media and Learning Central. She writes about new forms of learning, institutions as digital content-creators, the discourses of the "virtual state," the media literacy of policy makers and authority figures, and the rhetoric surrounding regulatory attempts to limit everyday digital practices.*

REFERENCES

Blog Carnivals. (2012). *Digital rhetoric collaborative*. Retrieved February 12, 2014, from http://www.digitalrhetoriccollaborative.org/blog-carnivals/

Bogost, I. (2007). *Persuasive games: Videogames and procedural rhetoric*. Cambridge, MA: MIT.

Chun, W. H. K. (2009, April). *Where's the beef: Cyworld versus Faceboo*. Paper presented at the Communications Department Colloquium. Amherst, MA.

Dery, M. (1994). *Flame wars: The discourse of cyberculture*. Durham, NC: Duke University Press.

Dibbell, J. (1998). *My tiny life: Crime and passion in a virtual world*. New York: Holt.

Gregory, S., & Losh, E. (2012). Remixing human rights: Rethinking civic expression, representation and personal security in online video. *First Monday, 17*(8). doi:10.5210/fm.v17i8.4104

Losh, E. (2011). The seven million dollar PowerPoint and its aftermath: What happens when the house intelligence committee sees "terrorist use of the internet" in a battlefield 2 fan film. In M. Nunes (Ed.), *Error glitch, noise, and jam in new media cultures*. New York: Continuum. Retrieved from http://public.eblib.com/EBLPublic/PublicView.do?ptiID=655513

Lovink, G. (2011). *Networks without a cause: a critique of social media*. Cambridge, UK: Polity.

Nakamura, L., & Chow-White, P. (2010). *Race after the internet*. London: Routledge.

Nunes, M. (2006). *Cyberspaces of everyday life*. Minneapolis, MN: University of Minnesota Press. Retrieved from http://site.ebrary.com/id/10180210

Schwittay, A. (2011). The financial inclusion assemblage: Subjects, technics, rationalities. *Critique of Anthropology, 31*(4), 381–401. doi:10.1177/0308275X11420117

Shah, N. (Ed.). (2010). *Digital AlterNatives with a cause?* Hivos & Centre for Internet and Society.

Preface

INTRODUCTION

Rhetoric as a discipline has existed for at least 2500 years, if not longer. Aristotle defined it as the ability to persuade an audience under various circumstances. Rhetoric informs various disciplines and is useful in grounding technological processes by asking valid questions about purpose, context, and audience. Current digital technologies, such as Web 2.0, social networks, cloud computing, mobile apps, video games, and virtual worlds, use rhetorical principles to engage, inform, instruct, persuade, and (inter)act in novel ways. These expressions of new digital modes and practices form a new digital rhetoric that extends traditional ancient rhetoric.

Rather than persuasion, digital rhetoric uses information processes that require different modalities and practices that happen across global contexts and create novel literacies. The inspiration for this book came from two different important developments, namely 1) the New London Group's (2000) call to see English studies as a global pedagogy and increasingly mediated by technology and 2) the call to investigate the "multiliteracies" required as a result of the changed nature of how knowledge, information, and communication are mediated through digital technologies (Hawisher & Selfe, 2000).

Digital rhetoric is different from traditional rhetoric because it emphasizes information and interaction in human-computer-human and human-computer interaction contexts. In so positioning digital rhetoric, we are informed by the theories of Winograd and Flores, who defined human-computer interaction as based on facilitating "communication and interaction" in interface environments (Rogers, Preece, & Sharp, 2007). Scholarship in computers and composition has highlighted how the "strange bedfellows" of composition, rhetoric, and human-computer interaction share similar traits in that both are directed towards an audience and end-user in making decisions or taking actions (Cummings, 2006; Rosinski & Squire, 2009). Similarly, next to this disciplinary merging, we have witnessed a "convergence" on multiple levels, such as the merging of previously separate media into multimedia, the increased integration of technology in life spheres, the collective production of information through "smart mobs" wherein technology and social action converge (Jenkins, 2006).

Given this convergence of media, social processes, and social behavior, we think digital rhetoric can help expand our understanding of the new communication modes and practices, which have slowly been integrated over the last 20 years or so through networked communication. As originally invented by Lord Byron's cousin, Ada Lovelace, through her idea for optimizing weaving processes, computer science has grown tremendously in the last few decades. Networks and the augmenting of human intelligence by offsetting human cognitive processes and creating a way to learn from past mistakes through computation was developed through the visionary work and organizational efforts of Department of

Defense (DoD) researchers Vannevar Bush, Theodore Nelson, Douglas Engelbart, and Ivan Sutherland. After World War II, these researchers had grown tired of the use of technology to destroy human lives and wanted to avoid mistakes from the past by creating ways of augmenting human intelligence (commonly known as Intelligence Augmentation [or IA] as distinct from the later idea of Artificial Intelligence [AI], which was developed by brilliant mathematician and cryptographer Alan Turing at Bletchley Park in the United Kingdom).

Next to these researchers working under the direction of DoD, it was not until Rand Corporation researcher Paul Baran came up with the innovative packet switching network technology that differed from AT&T's direct line network that the Internet came to be built (Lessig, 2001, p. 31). Along with packet switching came another radical idea by network architects David Saltzer, Jerome Clark, and Reed in 1981 in the form of the "end-to-end argument" or E2E argument (cf. Saltzer, Clark, & Reed, 1984). Their idea was simple – essentially push the content to the edges of the network at the user end, while keeping the network based on the simple task of transmitting information efficiently. The changes in creating this type of network can only be seen in retrospect as an enormous change in how information was distributed, consumed, and produced through a network that encouraged innovations in software design, collaborative interaction, and deflected control and centralization of information sharing. Through the principle of network neutrality and prioritizing the users at the end by protecting them with unique dynamic session-based network addresses that changed after each session, the E2E principle has created ripples in our media landscape and created an information culture where information sharing, media convergence, and human innovation are characteristics of an ever-changing media environment based on platforms, networks, and ever-evolving media ecologies.

Combined together, packet switching and the E2E argument prevent a centralized control system for content, since the network carries the information but the end-user can innovate and use the programs to exchange information, as opposed to being constrained by a provider's decision to put limitation on a network (cf. Lessig, 1999, 2001). The end-to-end principle has had a tremendous effect ever since Tim Berner Lee's proposal for CERN to create various protocols (such as ftp, http, etc.) of communication for the World Wide Web has changed from its tentative start of researchers exchanging information over phone lines into wireless networks guided by newer wireless protocols and packet switching and various encryption protocols. Together with the principle of Moore's law (every couple of years a doubling of processing speed), computing has become smaller and faster.

Our desktops slowly have given way to tablets and mobile phones capable of processing information just as fast, connecting us to our loved ones, colleagues, and the world in one technological network. Along with this has come an ideology of "the wisdom of crowds" (or "Smart Mobs," as Howard Rheingold [2003] would have it), where socializing, intellectual property, and information sharing has created an ideology of Peer-to-Peer (P2P) networks, new collaborative forms of working, playing, and socializing through technological networks (Johnson-Eilola, 2005). Indeed, illustrative of this collective "smart mob" ideology are various political upheavals in various countries where people have used mobile technologies to gather and protest against oppressive regimes.

At the same time, not all of the above should be interpreted from a naïve, instrumentalist perspective as technology creating "progress" (Selfe, 1999). Rather, we have seen a proliferation of information and the prediction by Alvin Toffler (1970) that we would suffer from "information overload" (sometimes referred to as "information glut"), an increase in forms of electronic discourse and genres (such as SMS-ing, social networking, using message boards, etc.), but we have not seen a Habermasian (1981) increase in public, political discourse leading us toward greater democratization. Instead, we have seen a more complex world where a greater need of information literacy is demanded of our students, as well as a deskilling and reskilling asked of us by constant technological updates, interfaces, new software, hardware, and practices of computing as interaction and communication, along with ubiquitous monitoring, privacy issues questioning the role of government in such affairs.

We have seen a long line of dominant models of rhetoric characterized as broad epistemic shifts from the Sophist tradition, Aristotle's technical rhetoric, current-traditional rhetoric, cognitive rhetoric, expressivist rhetoric, social-epistemic rhetoric, to our notion of digital rhetoric as integrating many new literacies, modes, and practices and principles of communication and interaction in new ways (Daniell, 1999; Losh, 2009). Rather than insist that digital rhetoric (or "digital rhetorics," for that matter, since we see no solitary grounded definition) replaces these models, our aim in this collection is not to make such a claim. We would rather not fall for a *reductio ad absurdum* of technology as equating progress and greater prosperity.

Rather, we see digital rhetoric as another way of looking at the use of technology in critically informed ways, whereby older definitions of rhetoric are still operational, but form part of a larger network of digital rhetorics (Zappen, 2005). We use the word "network" here in the loosest sense possible—to indicate a system of relations dependent upon each other, but not intrinsically hierarchical—in order to not ground our definition of digital rhetoric in a static, non-dynamic form. Rather than be "blinded" by the newness of technologies (Selfe, 1999), we want to understand how processes of computation in digital media (and we use Janet Murray's definition of digital medium versus "new media") operate and can enrich rhetoric as a discipline in dynamic ways. Briefly, Murray (2012) rejects the term "new media"—which highlights "newness" as a dominant mode—in favor of "digital medium"—the principles of computation underlying each mode—which she roughly divides into four guiding principles: 1) encyclopedic modes; 2) participatory modes; 3) spatial modes; and 4) procedural modes inherent in any medium or interface. For instance, if we consider computation as underlying the Internet, we can see these four modes as part of: 1) its ability to provide us with in-depth information on just about any topic; 2) allowing us to share information and comment upon it, refine it using social interaction with other humans; 3) to inhabit different roles of consumption and production, as well as literally traverse through spatial environments via video games or virtual worlds; and 4) to adopt and interact with information and computer interfaces in ways that are highly procedural.

Rather than focus on some idea of writing "the" definition of digital rhetoric and so ground the discipline, we are inspired by Richard Rorty's (1979) notion of pragmatism in philosophical inquiry – rather than attempt to define digital rhetoric once and for all, we simply want to change the questions we ask of ourselves as a discipline. Instead of asking ourselves about what these new media "mean" to our discipline (a question which is loaded with assumptions about the function of rhetoric as a mode of making sense of the world and rooted in protecting existing models of rhetoric as a discipline) and how we can best study them, we simply accept digital media as modes and practices that create global and local human-computer-interaction and human-to-human interactions that sometimes approximate, but are also different from our prior distinctions of orality, literacy, and print culture. We continue to practice orality and literacy and utilize print culture, but our relationship to them has been changed, as has the role of digital technology in our lives, as so often happens when new technologies "remediate" (Bolter & Grusin, 1999; Ong, 1982; Zappen, 2005) our relations to older technology. Herein lies another reason why we are reluctant to adopt a "replacement" model of "digital rhetoric" – old and new media still exist and are used, but our relationships and attitudes toward them have changed as we come to understand some of the older technologies as prototypes for newer technologies or, in some cases, as requiring new modes of production and consumption, information creation, and global/local literacies.

Therefore, it is important to understand these new digital modes and practices. In the fields of rhetoric, technical and intercultural communication, information science, human-computer interaction, systems theory, and computer science, there is a need for an edited collection of articles focusing on theories, modes, practices, and emerging areas for professionals, scholars, researchers, and educators, who have been grappling with this change and are not so much worried about how to integrate technology in existing frameworks, but rather want to study them as part of larger cultural patterns that are perceived in society.

OBJECTIVE OF THE BOOK

This book will aim to provide relevant theoretical frameworks, current practical applications, and emerging practices of digital rhetoric. As mentioned above, we do not intend to provide an ultimate definition of "digital rhetoric," but rather we see an interesting trend and need to study technology beyond the interface level. Though some may equate this with the work of computer science, we hope to create the understanding that next to end-users and audiences, built-in modes and practices, operating systems, or to use Benkler's (2006) distinctions between physical, code, and contact network layers, these are all part of a rhetorical process of design, use, and architecture wherein structures influence human behavior, decision-making, and actions. The purview of digital rhetoric, hence, is to look beyond the surface and at the semiotic modes of communication from a perspective wherein the user and computation can either or both be studied.

This book will do so by developing new key principles and understandings of the underlying modes, practices, and literacies of communication brought about by digital technologies. Its aim is to provide a robust framework of digital rhetoric, a historical grounding of some of these technologies, theoretical/practical approaches, and studies of emerging practices from a medialogical perspective as forming newer global literacies. In addition, the book aims to strengthen the basis for digital rhetoric research by encouraging multi-disciplinary discussions between rhetoricians, educators, programmers, information developers, game theorists, virtual reality designers, and other practitioners with media and information in general. The importance of this book lies in its ability to clarify, synthesize, and prepare useful strategies, modes, and ideas, and so bring forth a solid understanding of digital rhetoric as an important developing discipline.

TARGET AUDIENCE

The target audience of this book will be composed of professionals, scholars, researchers, and educators working in rhetoric, technical/professional and intercultural communication, information science, human-computer interaction, systems theory, and computer science. In bringing together such diverse perspectives, it aims to show that interdisciplinary perspectives will help inform, clarify, and enrich this burgeoning area of research in digital rhetoric.

TOPICS

As the title indicates, our interest is two-fold in that we are looking at the intersection of digital rhetoric and global literacies. We hope to clarify the two elements as part of a continuum rather than two static entities. For convenience's sake, we provide two working definitions as adopted within this book for these concepts. As mentioned above, we have no desire to anchor our research or that of others down to these definitions, as we realize to do so would be to arbitrarily set up borders and boundaries that are counter-productive in our current undertaking.

Digital Rhetoric

Digital rhetoric studies the increasing convergence of human life and computer technology with a focus on their communication and interaction. Since digital rhetoric is uncharted territory to a degree, our contributors come from diverse backgrounds but are people who are interested in Human-Computer Interaction (HCI), Interaction Design (ID), Computer-Mediated Communication (CMC), Interface Design, Computer Programming, Virtual and Augmented Reality, Computer Code, Algorithms, and Interactive Narratives. As such, this book seeks to investigate how the above may enrich our understanding of rhetorical (communicative) modes, given or emerging communication practices, and underlying human or computer efforts to interact, inform, instruct, persuade, or simply act upon information.

Global Literacies

Global literacies involve how meaning and knowledge is produced, disseminated, and consumed across cultures in various domains utilizing digital technologies (cf. Hawisher & Selfe, 2000). In compiling the book, we were specifically interested in what contributors saw as the key underlying communication and meaning-making practices behind global communication processes. Yet, as is so often the case when attempting to cover a specific area, we quickly recognized that digital rhetoric and global literacies were connected in intricate ways that made for a challenging tension between technologies, local and global contexts, and varying literacies. The below section will provide a brief overview of the topics that will be discussed in each chapter per section.

SECTION 1: HISTORICAL, THEORETICAL, AND CONCEPTUAL PERSPECTIVES ON DIGITAL COMMUNICATION

Section 1 was originally set up as a theoretical framework from which to understand modes of rhetoric, technical communication, digital multimodal principles of communication, and various kinds of computer-mediated communication. Our initial principal goal was to establish a historical overview of the research on digital rhetoric and to come to a more accurate definition. Luckily, we realized that in order for us to approach it from the right perspective, we needed to see both digital rhetoric and globalization as part of the same equation.

In chapter 1, "Digital Rhetoric and Globalization: A Convergence-Continuum Model," Gustav Verhulsdonck provides a brief historical overview of digital rhetoric's emergence, before moving on to discussing Richard Lanham's idea of spectrums of motivation and purposes and extending his ideas to an over-arching convergence-continuum that combines digital and global rhetorical prosumption (production and consumption). Rather than try to define digital rhetoric, Verhulsdonck argues that it exists alongside other earlier definitions of rhetoric, but simply asks other questions regarding interfaces, platforms, networks, code, as co-constructing rhetorical contexts in a convergence continuum.

In chapter 2, "Engagement Design: Toward a Holistic Model for Digital Communication Design," Curtis Newbold theorizes how digital communication can be facilitated by incorporating the idea of Russian psychologist Csikszentmihalyi's "flow" – a heightened state of being "in the zone" where play, work, and design intermingle to create better digital communication. Borrowing from game theory, Newbold argues that we can develop more effective technologies that are more functional because they capitalize on the human need for engagement.

In chapter 3, "Toward an Algorithmic Rhetoric," Chris Ingraham provides us with a fascinating and cogent argument as to why algorithms are inherently rhetorical by making us see human actions as based on procedural logic in the same way that algorithms formalize those human actions. Ingraham's division of algorithms from macro-meso-micro perspectives provides a useful way of looking at the impact of these fascinating data structures that make many applications work, and creates an exciting direction for digital rhetoric to investigate how things work based on procedural (rules-based logic).

In chapter 4, "Decoding What Is Good in Code: Toward a Metaphysical Ethics of Unicode," Jennifer Helene Maher continues her inquiry into the politics and morality of software. Noting the implicit and explicit political and moral quandaries of the Unicode standard, Maher problematizes any neat categorical ideas we might have about software standards in her rhetorical analysis of the political implications of Unicode, which makes for a problematic standard, which poses for Maher important ethical and meta-physical questions on the valorization of certain systems of standards that might at times be unquestion-ingly adopted by programming communities. Similar to Selfe and Selfe's (1984) seminal article on "The Politics of the Interface," Maher identifies the political, material, ideological, and moral quandaries that arise when certain assumptions are codified and used in computer programming.

In chapter 5, "The Data Machine: Identification in the Age of Data Mining," Nicholas Hanford investigates the implications of data mining in light of rhetorician Kenneth Burke's work on identifica-tion as well as adopts Paul Virillio's idea of a Vision Machine to create a "Data Machine" that uses algorithms to make assumptions about its audience. As Hanford argues, such algorithms function to create an audience that is based on user actions, but also complicates the notion of audience for digital rhetoric by noting how such actions do not comprise a dialogue or conversation with that audience that is meaningful. Moreover, Hanford's use of Burke's concept of consubstantiation makes him question the function of data machines and code, which we may want to anthropomorphize, but which operate in completely different procedural ways. Most importantly, Hanford notes in this process how users become decontextualized points of data, while the task of gathering such data is becoming increasingly codified through practices of data mining. For this purpose, Hanford asks rhetoricians to be flexible in adopting new terminologies and approaches in studying digital rhetoric.

In chapter 6, "The Persuasive Language of Action: Interaction in the Digital Age," Martin van Velsen takes up Hanford's call for using different terminologies and approaches by looking at the interactions generated by table-top role playing games. Seen as a precursor to today's popular, turn-based Massively Multiplayer Role-Playing Games (MMORPGs), van Velsen deftly uses the concept of player choice, attention, and Csikszentmihalyi's "flow" to investigate the action-reaction mode of narrative interaction in tabletop game mechanics. In introducing the cognitive schemas posited by gestalt theory and relat-ing them to tabletop gameplay experiences such as narrative backfill, collaborative detail, inattentional blindness, and asymmetric digital rhetorical gameplay dynamics that allow players to "fill" narrative details as part of their experience during or after a table top game, van Velsen demonstrates how digital rhetoric will need to reconsider its study frameworks and account for how such game elements, when tied to ever-increasing interaction challenges, persuade people to engage in complex symbolic action-reaction patterns.

SECTION 2: PRACTICES OF DIGITAL COMMUNICATION ACROSS CULTURES IN DIGITAL AND GLOBAL CONTEXTS

Section 2 addresses practical issues that arise from practicing in digital and global contexts. Chapters are a mix of theory and practice and are also comprised of qualitative (case studies, ethnographies) and quantitative (experimental, controlled) studies and will use methodological or practical approaches to investigate concerns in various contexts as described below.

In chapter 7, "Digital and Global Literacies in Networked Communities: Epistemic Shifts and Communication Practices in the Cloud Era," Marohang Limbu explores how the concept of literacy, digital literacy, and global literacy is shifting over time; how technologies (YouTube, Facebook, Skype, blogs, vlogs, and Google Hangouts) and digital literacies facilitate cross-cultural and intercultural communication and global cultural understandings; how technologies engage global citizens to share, collaborate, cooperate, and create their narratives; and how people become able to address local and global socio-cultural and political issues through various global digital engagements. Finally, Limbu's chapter investigates how knowledge is produced, disseminated, and consumed across global cultures in digital contexts.

Chapter 8, Rich Rice and Ben Lauren's "Developing Intercultural Competence through Glocal Activity Theory Using the Connect-Exchange Study Abroad App," lays a theoretical foundation for the development of an emerging model of studying intercultural communication through problem-based pedagogy. Rice and Lauren's emerging model facilitates transactional learning between users with varying cultural backgrounds. Furthermore, by drawing upon activity theory, the authors explore how different audiences use apps to guide their iterative design process to facilitate users' deepening glocal as well as intercultural competence.

In chapter 9, "Inviting Citizen Designers to Design Interface for the Democratization of Web Online Environments," Rajendra Panthee examines how online environments are supposed to create unifying spaces, such as societies, cultures, languages, and literacies, and how they merge together as negotiated space of neutral space. In his chapter, Panthee argues that these online environments are not culturally neutral communication landscapes, but may alienate participants from marginal social, cultural, and linguistic backgrounds because of their disregard for their social, cultural, and linguistics norms and values in digital contact zones. In this chapter, the author proposes to invite citizen designers to design interfaces that can transform online environments into democratic platforms.

In chapter 10, "Social Media in an Intercultural Writing Context: Creating Spaces for Student Negotiations," Maria Pilar-Milagros states that her current research study is part of a larger project that aims to analyze ways in which first year intercultural writing students in Turkey understand and interpret the impact of social media on their composition practices, critical thinking processes, and knowledge negotiations processes. Pilar-Milagros's chapter aims to understand how first year intercultural writing students reflect and assess on how social media help them practice and acquire more critical thinking skills.

In chapter 11, "Digital Literacy Instruction in Afghanistan," Mike Edwards sees the American military's purchase of a $5.6 million contract to supply the National Military Academy of Afghanistan with laptop computers as the occasion to investigate the complex and over determined intersections of digital, administrative, and literacy technologies. These intersections and the challenges they produced for the author as a Western mentor working with Afghan postsecondary instructors in ESL and digital literacies reveal the problematic homogenizing Western economic and cultural assumptions and the intense naturalization of administrative technologies that accompany the denaturalized use of digital and textual technologies in global contexts. The connections of those challenges to recent scholarship in rhetoric and composition highlight the limitations of this scholarship's conception of political economy in a global digital context. Furthermore, Edwards also offers new possibilities for imagining hybrid multilingual digital literacies on a global scale.

SECTION 3: EMERGING DIGITAL COMMUNICATION IN DIGITAL AND GLOBAL CONTEXTS

Section 3 addresses emerging technologies and uses of digital communication in multiple areas, and it also seeks to observe emerging development of digital communication and interaction beyond what we were/are practicing at present. The chapters concentrate on the current practices, potentials, and issues, as well as future possibilities/perspectives in newer ways by demonstrating novel ways of thinking about computer-mediated communication.

In chapter 12, "Considering *Chronos* and *Kairos* in Digital Media Rhetorics," Ashley Rose Kelly, Meagan Kittle Autry, and Brad Mehlenbacher argue that the rhetoric of digital spaces should begin not with the provocation that rhetoric is impoverished and requires fresh import to account for new media technologies, but instead with a careful analysis of what is different about how digital technologies afford certain utterances, interactions, and actions. In so doing, these authors argue, we begin to articulate prospects of a digital rhetoric. Overall, their chapter examines the importance of time to understanding the rhetoric of digital spaces. The authors suggest that rhetorical notions of *kairos* and *chronos* provide an important reminder that it is the rhetorical situation, along with rhetorical actors at individual to institutional levels, that construct the discursive spaces within which we participate, even in digitally mediated environments.

In chapter 13, "A Match Made in 'Outer Heaven': The Digital Age Vis-à-Vis the Bomb in Guns of the Patriots," Jorge Gomez analyzes the stealth-action videogame *Metal Gear Solid 4: Guns of the Patriots*, and delineates the rhetorical consequences not only of nuclear proliferation, but of mass (re)production in a digital age. In this chapter, Gomez draws upon Kenneth Burke's rhetoric of rebirth, Slavoj Žižek's ideological criticism along with several ludological frameworks that are adopted to show how various multiliteracies can be unearthed from a video game as an artifact of digital rhetoric.

In chapter 14, "'A Genuine Moment of Liberation for Me': Digital Introductions as Powerful Learning," Julie Faulkner argues that participation in a digital self-presentation has the potential to challenge inscribed approaches to learning and teaching. It draws from a study of pre-service teachers at an Australian university, who were invited to create a digital introduction as part of their English teaching method course. Such a task offered students opportunities to experiment with shifting semiotic forms in ways unavailable to written introductions. Students were asked to critically reflect after the presentation on aspects of technology, representation, and learning that were brought into focus in and through their presentations. A semiotic analysis offers insights into the potential of multimodality, as the digital introduction pushed the participants out of familiar territory, often producing creative and stimulating texts. Using Kress's concept of *synaesthesia*, or the condition wherein sensory stimuli are equated with symbols, the chapter explores innovations possible in the creation of new possibilities in a multimodal space.

In chapter 15, "On the Condition of Anonymity: Disembodied Exhibitionism and Oblique Trolling Strategies," Demetrios Lallas demonstrates that the ambiguity of identity in disembodied communities poses unique challenges in the flow of digital rhetoric. Online anonymity can lead to disinhibition, enabling the practice of trolling: the effort to derail discussion for attention, mischief, and abuse. This chapter examines this phenomenon in various social media contexts, exploring effective practices in recognizing and harnessing trolling, and provides interesting perspectives on how trolling can be taxonomized as strategic ways of approaching computer-mediated discourse from a performative (or perhaps, ludic) perspective.

In chapter 16, "Embodied Digital Rhetoric: Soft Selves, Plastic Presence, and the Nonfiction Narrative," Nonny De La Peña, whose background as an award-winning journalist informs her approach to virtual reality as embodied digital experience, shows how virtual experiences are innately tied to emotional experiences that are lived and felt deeply. In her multimedia pieces, De La Peña shows how virtual experiences are somatic, immersive experiences that challenge Cartesian notions of mind/body division, from which "soft selves" and "plastic presence" emerge as examples of the ways in which virtual reality environments persuade or have effects on us in immediate, sensory ways. In ending our book on digital rhetoric with this essay, we hope to continue with the questions in which notions of virtual embodiment and disembodied experiences can still have a strong effect on us by way of virtual delivery. We see digital rhetoric as questioning these Cartesian divisions and asking us to rethink the way we see and experience ourselves, space, and technology. Rather than see the spectre of Donna Haraway's Cyborg in which human identity is subsumed or merged with technology, we see networks and multiplicity creating new spaces and landscapes for exploring the ways in which interaction and communication take place in global, digital contexts.

Gustav Verhulsdonck
University of Texas at El Paso, USA

Marohang Limbu
Michigan State University, USA

REFERENCES

Benkler, Y. (2006). *The wealth of networks: How social production transforms markets and freedom.* New Haven, CT: Yale University Press.

Bolter, J. D., & Grusin, R. (1999). *Remediation: Understanding new media.* Cambridge, MA: MIT Press.

Cummings, R. (2006). Coding with power: Toward a rhetoric of computer coding and composition. *Computers and Composition, 23*, 430–443. doi:10.1016/j.compcom.2006.08.002

Daniell, B. (1999). Narratives of literacy: Connecting composition to culture. *College Composition and Communication, 50*(3), 393–410. doi:10.2307/358858

Habermas, J. (1981). *Theory of communicative action volume one: Reason and the rationalization of society*. Cambridge, MA: MIT Press.

Hawisher, G., & Selfe, C. (2000). *Global literacies and the world wide web*. London: Routledge.

Jenkins, H. (2006). *Convergence culture: Where old and new media collide*. New York: New York University Press.

Johnson-Eilola, J. (2005). *Datacloud: Toward a new theory of online work*. Creskill, NJ: Hampton.

Lessig, L. (1999). *Code and other laws of cyberspace*. New York: Basic.

Lessig, L. (2001). *The future of ideas: The fate of the commons in a connected world*. New York: Random.

Losh, E. (2009). *VirtualPolitik*. Cambridge, MA: MIT Press.

Murray, J. (2013). *Inventing the medium: Principles of interaction design as a cultural practice*. Cambridge, MA: MIT Press.

New London Group. (2000). A pedagogy of multilteracies: Designing social futures. In B. Cope, & M. Kalantzis (Eds.), *Multiliteracies: Literacy learning and the design of social futures* (pp. 9–37). London: Routledge.

Ong, W. J. (1982). *Orality and literacy: The technologizing of the word* (T. Hawkes, Ed.). New York: Methuen. doi:10.4324/9780203328064

Rheingold, H. (2003). *Smart mobs: The next social revolution*. New York: Basic.

Rogers, Y., Preece, J., & Sharp, H. (2007). *Interaction design: Beyond human-computer interaction*. New York: Wiley.

Rorty, R. (1979). *Philosophy and the mirror of nature*. Princeton, NJ: Princeton University Press.

Rosinski, P., & Squire, M. (2009). Strange bedfellows: Human-computer interaction, interface design, and composition pedagogy. *Computers and Composition, 26*, 149–163. doi:10.1016/j.compcom.2009.05.004

Saltzer, J. H., Reed, D. P., & Clark, D. D. (1984). End-to-end arguments in system design. *ACM Transactions on Computer Systems, 2*(4), 277–288. doi:10.1145/357401.357402

Selfe, C. (1999). Technology and literacy: A story about the perils of not paying attention. *College Composition and Communication, 50*(3), 411–436. doi:10.2307/358859

Toffler, A. (1970). *Future shock*. New York: Random.

Zappen, J. (2005). Digital rhetoric: Toward an integrated theory. *Technical Communication Quarterly, 14*, 319–325. doi:10.1207/s15427625tcq1403_10

Acknowledgment

The editors would like to thank the following people: The ever-encouraging and inspirational Dr. Elizabeth Losh at The University of California, San Diego, for her support of this project. To know that the person who knows more about digital rhetoric than anyone is supportive of what you do was an encouragement and inspiration throughout this project for both of us as scholars. Next to her busy publication, conference, and research schedule, Dr. Losh was kind enough to write a foreword for this book and no doubt will be influencing and producing more on the topic. We look forward to her groundbreaking work in this area and are humbled by her kind words about this project. We would also like to thank Dr. Kirk St. Amant at East Carolina University for supporting our project and providing us with practical tips on how to deal with the editing process of this book and for always being a resource of knowledge and wisdom. We also would like to thank Dr. Barry Thatcher at New Mexico State University and Dr. Jeffrey Grabill and Dr. Bill-Hart Davidson at Michigan State University for agreeing to be a part of our editorial advisory board. We appreciate your support.

We would like to thank the various contributors for their hard work and courage in writing in this exciting research area, and for always responding in kind to our queries and demands on their no doubt busy schedules. You created this book with us, and without you, it would not exist. We are excited to have been part of your scholarly journeys, and to have so many different types of scholars enthused about our book topic was exciting. We are excited to see so many new perspectives and new roads travelled in this particularly understudied and hard-to-define scholarly area. Finally, we would like to thank our publisher, IGI Global, who helped us go through the process and were there for us during every step of the process, and all of our colleagues at the University of Texas at El Paso and Michigan State University.

Namaste.

Gustav Verhulsdonck
University of Texas at El Paso, USA

Marohang Limbu
Michigan State University, USA

Section 1
Historical, Theoretical, and Conceptual Perspectives on Digital Communication

Chapter 1
Digital Rhetoric and Globalization:
A Convergence–Continuum Model

Gustav Verhulsdonck
University of Texas at El Paso, USA

ABSTRACT

Digital rhetoric has been discussed by many theorists as comprising a marked shift from ancient rhetoric's focus on persuasion. For some of the earlier theorists, digital rhetoric defined a novel relationship between literacy and the mechanics of text as computer-mediated communication and changed relationships between consuming, producing and engaging with discourse as information on a screen. Later digital rhetoricians argue different approaches and definitions that are more inclusive of the different types of discourse facilitated by multimodal, interactive, immersive, and computer-mediated communication as semantic discourse at the interface level and encoded through computer programming language, servers, and networks. This chapter focuses on the different modes of digital rhetoric in the context of globalization through a convergence-continuum model approach. The model presented approaches rhetoric and discourse from various levels as loosely based on the models of activity theory, multimodality intercultural theories of globalization and integrates them into a continuum model ranging from global, public modes to individual, personal digital rhetorical modes and practices. Instead of being prescriptive, this model is descriptive in recognizing the fluid natures of digital rhetorical interactions whereby global and local, public and private, group and individual, production and consumption, human and technological, physical and virtual and other discourse contexts merge.

DOI: 10.4018/978-1-4666-4916-3.ch001

Copyright © 2014, IGI Global. Copying or distributing in print or electronic forms without written permission of IGI Global is prohibited.

The Spectrum: the entire range of wavelengths of electromagnetic radiation.

Continuous spectrum: an emission spectrum that consists of a continuum of wavelengths. (The Oxford English Dictionary)

Convergence does not mean ultimate stability or unity. It operates as a constant force for unification but always in dynamic tension with change.... There is no immutable law of growing convergence; the process of change is more complicated than that (Ithiel de Sola Pool, Technologies of Freedom)

INTRODUCTION: AN OVERVIEW OF DIGITAL RHETORIC, KEY TERMS AND SCHOLARS

A cursory glance of the scholarship on digital rhetoric displays that no consensus exists on its definition and that staking out a definition of digital rhetoric is a difficult task due to the ever-changing nature of its object of study: the increasing convergence of human life and technology. In this introduction, I will introduce some of the key scholars involved in digital rhetoric and describe why digital rhetoric should not strive for a static definition. As a discipline or field of study, rhetoric itself is notable for its lack of a coherent definition. Considering that rhetoric itself has no universally agreed upon definition, it is not surprising that digital rhetoric has yet to gain a foothold or stable definition. If digital rhetoric comprises everything digital, whether this means a spectrum of actions performed within digital media or physical actions conveyed through digital media as human experience, it becomes difficult to speak of a definition that tries to capture these continuous pulsing signals and forms of energy that are a combination of human life and technology through various descriptive elements of movement, text, animation, music, symbolic, visual, aural, spatial,

temporal and physical interaction and communication. Similarly, if we see computer interfaces as both a mirror and a window, as some scholars have suggested, we start to see the mimetic and autopoietic properties of a medium that mimics but also metastasizes and evolves alongside with us. Yet, in a similar way that rhetoric may be seen as a sort of meta-discipline that incorporates discourse, linguistics, and various forms of communication as well as techniques and principles of generating arguments and knowledge, this chapter argues that digital rhetoric can be seen as a meta-discipline that extends its focus on such a continuum of digital and technologically mediated human behavior and actions. In other words, digital rhetoric studies the implications of how our use of technology impacts, reflects, represents, guides, and co/re/creates evolving forms of digital human action, behavior, communication, logic and knowledge.

This chapter will limit its focus on how digital rhetoric can study human language and computer language and how it can deal with the issue of mediation and human-computer co-creation in creating meaning and knowledge in computer-mediated communication processes. While we may now have a larger palette of digital technologies and interfaces for symbolic manipulation and meaning-making activities to create multimodal arguments through text, visuals, music, video, animations, and for capturing embodied, kinetic information, behind these digital technologies the programming languages of computers are busy passing their own arguments to help us create such arguments digitally, or, as is increasingly the case with the advent of artificial intelligence and data mining, making their own arguments to help inform humans about reality.

To give an example of how imbricated human life and technology are, in our everyday lives many of us rely (perhaps unwittingly) already on various computer technologies to inform us in making decisions, finding knowledge, and generally facilitating different types of understanding. In these contexts, human decisions are informed by how computational processes describe or mediate a particular context or reality to us, which are informed by programming techniques, algorithms, databases, platforms, interfaces and artificial intelligence and pattern matching in order to communicate information to us and with us. A common example of computation as persuasion can be given by the way global positioning systems (GPS) pass on weather information, re-route our driving destinations to avoid traffic congestion, or how recommender systems in e-commerce make estimated guesses on what may also be of interest to us based on tracking our prior buying behaviors. These are all representations of reality that are digital, mediated and inform and may persuade us to act in certain ways. So beyond looking at these representations, digital rhetoric asks how such semantic content is created by various rules in computer language and code. Language as mediated "text" or computational strategy, in other words, is equally interesting for digital rhetoric, and studying the interaction between the semantic multimedia "texts" represented on our interfaces as well as the coding protocols and programming underlying them can enrich our understanding of the field of rhetoric with the vast arrays of technology that are used by most people on a daily basis to make decisions and get specifics views of reality.

This chapter is organized in the following manner: after a short history and overview of the term digital rhetoric, and keeping in mind the ever-changing nature of digital rhetoric and globalization, this chapter tentatively operationalizes digital rhetoric as the study of human and computer interaction and communication, where technologies are globally created and used in multiple ways and so instantiate practices and understandings that can be termed global literacies. As technological developments continue to evolve and develop, trying to pin down "digital rhetoric" on particular instances of technology use is not only counter-productive, but also futile in light of the evolutionary principles of modern day technolo-

gies that require more robust frameworks. Rather than define digital rhetoric, this chapter proposes a continuum model, based on distinguishing the underlying modes and practices that support the complex interactions between ever-increasing convergences of human life with digital technologies. Inspired by Richard Lanham's (2006) four-fold model of various spectrums of motivation of the "at/through" oscillation mode of digital rhetoric, this chapter hopes to extend Lanham's work by proposing a continuum model of convergence, relying on tying digital rhetorical practices as a *continuum* of signals encompassing all forms of human action, behavior, kinesics, communication and interaction from a macro-level of global production to that of a micro-level of individual, private rhetorical communication practices. Rather than prescriptive, the model used is descriptive and focuses on how digital rhetorical practices and global literacies merge together in a convergence continuum that is process-based, evolutionary, and organic rather than static.

In the first section, a broad history of the origins of digital rhetoric is provided with a discussion of some of the key scholars and theories, along with explanations of the various new layers and contexts in which communication takes place. The second section provides a discussion on how digital media all share certain modes and practices based on computation and so provide a common framework of study for digital rhetoric. The third section discusses how computer-mediated communication (CMC) and rhetoric have in common an interest in facilitating the study of how digital media provide certain affordances for communication and interaction and thus create further frameworks of study for digital rhetoric. After this section, activity theory, which focuses on processes rather than static entities, is used to explain how evolving aspects of technology and mediation are part of new digital rhetorical contexts. The section following this discusses how theories of multimodality and multiliteracies help to distinguish digital rhetoric from earlier models of rhetoric by factoring in globalization and intercultural theories that help us frame communication practices as happening on *both* a global and local scale and contexts. The next section lays the groundwork for the main argument of this chapter by combining preceding definitions of digital rhetoric and globalization through a brief history of the various definitions of convergence. The following section articulates how a proposed convergence continuum model could help describe not only digital rhetoric, but also global literacies, by looking at practices from a macro to a micro level and seeing these layers not from a hierarchical point of view, but from a continuous point of view. The conclusion connects the previous paradigms of rhetoric to digital rhetoric as part of a larger continuous network of a convergence continuum that may function as a framework for future rhetorical analysis in combining digital rhetoric and global literacies.

A HISTORY OF DIGITAL RHETORIC

The term digital rhetoric was first introduced by Richard Lanham in his seminal "Digital Rhetoric: Theory, Practice and Property" (1992) before he expanded upon the concept in his book *The Electronic Word: Democracy, Technology and the Arts* (1993). In his work, Lanham questioned rhetoric's focus on books and print culture through the practical effects of hypertext. In this and later work, Lanham (2004, 2006) criticizes the idea of a bounded, linear textual space where writer and reader relations are set. Instead he sees the "electronic word" and specifically, hypertext, as changing the dynamic between consuming and producing a text. Lanham remarks that digital literacy constitutes a process of oscillating between older principles of print literacy which sees texts as flat, linear, and clearly bounded by separate writer-reader relations and the virtual, three-dimensional space of the computer, which combines orality and literacy by blurring distinctions between readers, writers, and writing space and uses multiple modes of communicating textual, visual, verbal, non-verbal and spatial communication modalities.

Lanham's work originated in his interest in the mechanics of mediated texts and the implications of technology on the humanities and the ensuing disciplinary paradigm shifts in academia. Lanham's focus on early forms of computer-mediated communication (or CMC), led him to develop an interest in the mechanics of the computer as a medium that represents but also *alters* the textual experience by virtue of different representation. Lanham's phrase for this altering of textual mediated experience, the "AT/THROUGH bi-stable oscillation", indicates a key distinction for digital rhetoric between semantic content (text) and the mechanics of mediation (hypertext) which provide another semantic context and which Lanham would continue to develop in his work. Simply put, Lanham's distinction represents the oscillating between reading *at* the surface of traditional texts versus reading *through* the text and playing with the underlying mechanics of the mediated experience. In using oscillation as a term, Lanham uses a term from physics and signals theory, which he goes on to develop in more advanced ways.

In his later work *The Economics of Attention* (2006), Lanham continues to address the "At/Through" dichotomy by creating a spectrum of *signal*, *perceiver*, *motive* and *life* as a means of addressing how information overload (too much data) has severely impacted our consumption of media (not enough time) where attention is a commodity (pp. 157-169). Rather than a staid dichotomy, Lanham sees the At/Through oscillation as various rhetorical spectrums asking fundamental questions regarding human *motives* and *purposes* and how at times mediation asks us to oscillate *between* spectrums consisting of style/substance, form/function, reality/dramaturgy and game/play (pp. 157-169). A common example is how a website invites us to read its text through design, a case of visual style before substance (text), and form preceding function. Next to this, a website may interact with us in playful ways or simply be demanding we put in crucial information bearing out over our lives (consider a website where one can find casual games versus a government website that requires us to fill out information that is demanded of us). Likewise, websites may represent different epistemological approaches to reality by the way information is framed and positioned in relation to other discourses.

Masterfully using computer science history, economics, mathematics, art, font aesthetics, game theory, cryptography, code breaking, and the aforementioned signals theory, Lanham convincingly argues that the At/Through oscillation brings us to fundamental aspects of digital rhetoric, the human attention activities in perceiving, producing, and playing with rhetorical meanings through various digital technologies. Lanham uses using Shannon and Weaver's (1963) mathematical theory of communication by using their signals theory where communication is encoded by a sender, becomes a signal (with noise factors) and is then received and decoded by a receiver, who can choose to look at the signal as prima facie signal, or look for deeper meanings or inconsistencies through interpretation.

Although outdated in terms of modern computer protocols, signals theory provides a way for Lanham to articulate how humans themselves use technologies to encode, transmit, and interpret signals, using various aesthetic modes and mechanics in digital contexts in order to convey various motives and purposes. In other words, Lanham uses signals theory to discuss how humans use technology for a spectrum of *rhetorical* purposes *as signals* that allow other humans to process and interpret information in various ways. On the signal spectrum, Lanham addresses how "text, image, or sound" can be produced as pure signal but also can be looked through for meaning (and hence received as pure information but also analyzed for deeper meaning); likewise, on the perceiver spectrum, they can choose to look *at* or *through* images, sounds or texts. In the motives spectrum that asks about the motives in

producing a signal or perceiving it, he sees the desire of humans to find purpose through game or play in producing such signals or perceiving them. Lastly, in the life spectrum, Lanham sees human perception of reality and life as oscillating between the epistemological perspectives of information and drama.

In describing these spectrums, Lanham creates a theory of motivation and purpose that describes how digital media produces communication and interaction that is signal-based and provides this at/through oscillation between looking *at* an interface or electronic medium or looking *through* that interface or medium. Most importantly, Lanham mentions the developments of computer science by Alan Turing (1988; the father of Artificial Intelligence) and Johan von Neumann (1944, 1959; father of game theory) who drove innovations in game theory (for simulations and war-scenarios) and informatics; whereas the personal computer has created "the first generation of hackers" playing with symbolic-meaning making – and drives home the point that digital rhetoric operates along all of the above-mentioned spectrums in mediating the frequencies of human actions as signals that are received and perceived (p.172). In so doing, Lanham revitalizes Kenneth Burke's (1969) idea of a "rhetoric of motives"– that we engage in meaning-producing, semiotic *actions* which give us agency because we identify with particular motives for producing them.

Although Lanham's work is ground-breaking, his term of digital rhetoric has not been embraced widely, perhaps due to the fact that his work is of exceptional width and richness in a day and age in which people, as he aptly notes, are asked to make quick judgments in an "attention economy" of style and substance. Depending on which side of the spectrum one is in this attention economy, Lanham's work is enlightening or simply too difficult to encapsulate into neat categories, yet ground-breaking in its explication of digital rhetoric as not a staid mode of rhetorical-meaning making, but an activity encompassing a full spectrum of energy - human actions based on motives and purposes. For the purposes of this chapter, it provides an important bridge to the convergence-continuum model presented at the end of this chapter.

Digital rhetorician Liz Losh (2009) provides a historical perspective on digital rhetoric's development by noting how cultural and critical academic debates on the "canon" in the 1980s and 1990s influenced the reception of Lanham and other pioneers such as George Landow (1993) and his work on hypertext, and predecessor Gregory Ulmer's (1989) work on television as a grammatological technology (Losh, 2009, pp. 82-86). According to Losh, in this environment, digital rhetoric was received in a reluctant manner as it was seen as a "triple threat by traditionalists" in that it 1) emphasized media studies rather than the dominant study of print culture and literature; 2) invited new "practitioner-theorists" that combined print and media; and 3) invited "unconventional collaborative procedures" (from disciplines such as media studies, computer science, psychology and theater) that threatened novel and established academic English programs and practices under institutional scrutiny (p. 83). In addition, Losh mentions how the deconstructionist theories of continental theorist (and Losh's mentor) Jacques Derrida (1967), as well as the establishing of various programs in rhetoric as a discipline made digital rhetoric an unwelcome addition as discussions on the "death" of the author, literature, stable meanings, "texts", and the traditional canon of literature and other elements dominated academic discourse (p. 83). Moreover, coupled with Lanham (1993) and Landow's (1993) call for a re-imagining of academic institutions and curricula in light of the development of digital developments, digital rhetoric's inception was seen as adding fuel to the flames, threatening English and rhetoric as an academic discipline.

Indeed, while the term digital rhetoric was thus engulfed in disciplinary turf wars during this time, various terms were employed to indicate studies that looked at texts from a medium perspective and were interdisciplinary in their approach. Many of these studies were housed in English Departments or Communication Departments and went under various monikers such as new media studies, digital media studies, media studies, or the more well-known the digital humanities. Buried under a barrage of new terms, digital rhetoric was not picked up until Zappen's (2005) article "Digital rhetoric: Towards an integrated theory" which refocused its definition by making a more explicit connection to traditional rhetoric.

Zappen (2005) makes a crucial distinction between traditional rhetoric and digital rhetoric by emphasizing how: 1) digital rhetoric extends traditional rhetoric and should be disassociated with Aristotle's constrictive definition of "the art of persuasion"; and 2) digital rhetoric uses digital spaces where collaboration between participants allows them to create novel rhetorical techniques for communication. Zappen (2005) defines digital rhetoric as the study of "how traditional rhetorical strategies function in digital spaces and suggest how these strategies are being reconceived and reconfigured within these spaces" (p. 319). In his view, rhetoric has been associated with "persuasion" for too long during its history, and digital rhetoric encompasses new modes and practices of communication and interaction that extend ancient rhetoric. For this reason, Zappen claims digital rhetoric should be "conceived not as a mode of persuasion, but as a testing of one's own ideas, a contesting of others' ideas, and a collaborative creating of ideas—[which] is possible in any medium: oral, print, digital" (pp. 320-321). Zappen's idea of digital rhetoric as a mode of collaboration and interaction in any type of medium is important for pointing to the different dimensions in which digital rhetoric resides, and moves us away from debates on orality, literacy, print culture, hypertext, and into the novel realm of digital media where such distinctions are becoming cumbersome and non-descript. Next to Lanham's pointing out of the importance of semantic content and mediation as part of a full spectrum of human motives and purposes, Zappen's contribution to digital rhetoric lies in his insistence of widening the scope of digital rhetoric and including collaborative communicating through any type of medium.

Digital rhetoric, as a field of inquiry has been discussed by different scholars, whether through direct addressing of the term "digital rhetoric", or indirectly by engaging with the issues of communication, power, access, literacy and mediation through interfaces and networks as reshaping the discipline of rhetoric, composition and teaching (cf. Porter, 2009; Selfe & Selfe, 1994; Selber, 2004). Critical approaches have ranged from critiquing the implicit assumptions of dominant metaphors of interfaces as reifying corporate culture as well as tentative redefinitions of how certain elements, such as delivery – embodiment – need to be reclaimed for the digital, spatial environments created by video games and virtual worlds (Fleckenstein, 2003; Selfe & Selfe, 1994; Porter, 2009). Research in journals such as *Computers and Composition* and *Kairos* touch upon various aspects of digital and multimodal composition and provide a prism of views from different scholars but do not offer a clear signpost of digital rhetoric research (at least not so far as to calling it "digital rhetoric"), but all are united in dealing with associated issues which fall under the purview of digital rhetoric in dealing with the "messy" business of how to deal with technology, mediation, rhetoric and communication and our assumptions about them as scholars, researchers, and teachers of rhetoric and communication in multimedia. In other words, while there is a lot of work done in digital rhetoric in various disciplines, not many scholars confidently take on the terminology *and* the issues at the same time.

Indeed, work under the moniker digital rhetoric got a boost when a number of scholars, (mostly located at the University of California San Diego, or so it seems) started addressing digital rhetoric more clearly around 2008-2009 in very different ways. In their work, UC San Diego researchers such as Ian Bogost (2007) and Elizabeth Losh (2009) clearly address digital rhetoric in very different ways. Under the name of digital rhetoric and looking at it from a computer science perspective, Bogost's research has focused on distinguishing digital rhetoric from classic models of rhetoric by providing "procedural rhetoric" (programming-based arguments that create models of the world) as an alternative to existing paradigms of rhetoric. Using a more classical lens of rhetoric, Losh (2009) has engaged in examining the digital expressions of various discourses of digital technology and their public impact in wide variety of areas including government websites, instantiations and rejections of techno-ideology, the use of technology to justify wars, various public debates conducted over the internet, as well as the rhetoric of video games. In so doing, both Bogost and Losh signal the importance of the term and importance of research in digital culture and a renewed focus on the disciplinary branch of rhetoric that investigates technology, mediation, rhetoric and communication between people using networks of information for public and private purposes.

Earlier work by Lev Manovich (2001) may have spurred these scholars in staking out new territory for digital rhetoric as a field of inquiry. In line with Bolter and Grusin's (2000) argument of remediation, Manovich (2001) argues that new media "remediate" elements of older (analog) media, such as cinema, where the newer medium's characteristics affect communicative properties of the older media (by for instance, incorporating it as a mode of representation in the newer medium) and how this changes the range of human behavior and expression in significant ways. In this, Manovich's argument centers around how digital media engender changes in our modes and practices of writing and communication and so form a "new language" of new media with new characteristics. According to Manovich (2001), the language of new media is based on that of the logic of the computer:

- **Numerical representation:** Representation is done through data and numbers, such as binary code.
- **Modularity:** Each element is independent from other elements and functions independently.
- **Automation:** Modification of mediated texts happens automatically without direct human intervention.
- **Variability:** Media exist in multiple versions rather than one single version.
- **Transcoding:** Computer logic influences modes of representation and idea of self. (Manovich, 2001, pp.64).

Manovich is taking to task the (perhaps) reluctance of the humanities to deal with computer science by clearly indicating the way "texts" are seen from a computer perspective. Rather than see new media as "works of art" as part of a discourse community, or as part of the familiar rhetorical Aristotelian triangle of writer, audience, text, he sees them as encoded in binary numbers, functioning in modular elements independently from each other and in automated ways with multiple copies that are in a constant state of flux. For Manovich, borrowing Walter Benjamin's (1968) formulation, the work of art in the age of computerized reproduction is distributed across various media, platforms, networks, etc., and perhaps most importantly, the logic of computers influences our notions of text, representation(s) of the world and the self rather than any inherent material aspects of one unique artifact (as is the case for Benjamin). Manovich's last point involves human communication taking on "cultural categories and concepts [that] are substituted, on the level of meaning and/or the language, by new ones which derive from the computer's ontology, epistemology and pragmatics" (pp. 64-65). For some in rhetoric as a traditional discipline situated within the humanities, re-conceptualizing communication as a process of computation and coding may be too radical a notion. However, language use and argumentation can also be seen as human "code" we acquire and "computational" neurolinguistic processes that can also be formalized through computer programmers when writing code.

In this chapter, however, Manovich's categorical emphasis on the ontology of the computer is used to show how cultural and computerized forms of communication and discourse can be seen as part of a convergence continuum where human-computer interactions co-create discourse. As opposed to replacing other narratives of literacy that describe dominant paradigms of rhetoric (cf. Daniell, 1999), where discourse is part of current-traditional, individualist-expressivist, cognitive, social-epistemic definitions of rhetoric, this chapter posits that digital rhetoric encompasses these as part of a network of relations which co-exist concurrently. In other words, we should not see digital rhetoric as simply replacing these formulations of rhetoric as part of a naïve progressive narrative wherein technology stands for progress. Instead, there will always be practices and ideas which recombine elements of these earlier paradigms in electronic environments, at the same time that digital rhetoric creates new paradigms in capturing the various spectrums and frequencies of human action through communication and interaction afforded by computation and mediation.

In keeping with Manovich's focus on the ontology of computers, digital scholar and video game researcher Ian Bogost (2007) makes a clear case for a form of digital rhetoric that is founded upon the logic of computers: procedural rhetoric. As many computer scientists may know, in programming, computers follow rules of behavior that are "procedural" – based on clearly defined arguments that tell the program what to do given a particular situation. A simple example of procedural principles that is taught in most beginning computer science classes is how to create a program that first asks one's name as input and then returns a value of "Hello [your name], welcome!" as output. The procedural aspects require considering the situation as a whole before the interaction takes place, and instantiating the variables with identifiers such as input.name, as well as creating rules of behavior (procedures) for the computer to exhibit and elicit the required response for input. Hence, in computer science to "pass an argument" means to run a particular defined value as input during a particular instance of a procedure to gain an outcome or specific output. In the example above, the input of the name was gathered by a pre-encoded query "Please type your name", then stored in the memory of the computer as input, and passed successfully as an argument when the welcome line appeared as output with the person's name. Such a process, most would argue, is far from persuasive, or intelligent, and I would agree. However, when looking beyond this, we can recognize how current digital technology uses our input in advanced ways as output to create states or representations of reality.

It is clear that such procedural arguments here take on a different meaning than traditional rhetoric, where according to Aristotle such arguments can be based on knowledge (*Sophia* – knowledge derived from the ability to discern reality (*Nous*) or learned knowledge (*Episteme*)) and where rhetoricians may use proofs that are artistic or inartistic (*Pisteis*) based on their individual qualities as orators or writers. Rather than discard these notions, digital rhetoric utilizes *different* forms of logic *in addition* to those developed in traditional Aristotelian technical rhetoric. As will be argued below, rather than see digital rhetoric as displacing traditional forms of rhetoric, we may see it as part of the larger palette for human expressive behavior and purpose as part of a continuous spectrum.

However, procedural rhetoric is fundamentally different from traditional rhetoric. For this reason, Bogost criticizes other scholars in digital rhetoric in basing their definitions of digital rhetoric on inadequate criteria, promoting advocacy or disciplinary agendas that fundamentally misunderstand the logic of computers and so misconstrue digital rhetoric. Their characteristics are criticized by Bogost as overly simplistic and reliant upon user-centered ideas of computer as mere "tools" for communication, whereas Bogost's notions of procedural rhetoric are based upon the unique criteria underlying the procedurality and dialogic nature of coded arguments (p. 25). Bogost clarifies his claim of procedural rhetoric as part of digital rhetoric to be based on arguments similar to that of previously occluded disciplines such as visual rhetoric as part of a larger area of investigation for rhetoric:

Procedural rhetoric is the practice of using processes persuasively, just as verbal rhetoric is the practice of using oratory persuasively and visual rhetoric is the practice of using images persuasively. Procedural rhetoric is a general name for the practice of authoring arguments through processes. . . . Procedural rhetoric is a subdomain of procedural authorship; its arguments are made not through the construction of words or images, but through the authorship of rules of behavior, the construction of dynamic models. In computation, those rules are authored in code, through the practice of programming. . . A theory of procedural rhetoric is needed to make commensurate judgments about the software systems we encounter every day and to allow a more sophisticated procedural authorship with both persuasion and expression as its goal. Procedural rhetorics afford a new and promising way to make claims about how things work. (p. 29)

The implications of Bogost's points are far-reaching in that it extends digital rhetoric to the realm of computer-coding, where other rules and practices of logic, classification and authorship exist. In the example above, one can see the simple programming exercise underlines various elements that exist and are used also by humans in communicating with computers and with each other. For instance, object-oriented programming (OOP) requires the creation of classes of objects, which can then can contain certain specifics and values, and can be in turn nested as part of a larger object (hence object-oriented). Next to creating various forms of digital technology, programmers author such elements and pass specific arguments which extend the focus of rhetoric in new directions. In addition to Lanham's focus on mediation as experience and design, Zappen's inclusion of collaborative forms of CMC and widening the scope of digital rhetoric beyond just persuasion, Bogost's argument resounds in that it focuses on what lies beyond mediation and interface – authorship based on procedural, rule-based computer logic. Interestingly, he argues for these processes to be *persuasive* – and thus undoes some of distancing done by Zappen's definition as digital rhetoric as being removed from the process of persuasion.

Digital rhetorician Elizabeth Losh's work has also yielded many breakthroughs in combining various aspects of the practices of digital rhetoric in addition to creating a sense of history of digital rhetoric as a discipline by connecting many of the dots between scholarship in traditional rhetoric and digital rhetoric. In her work *VirtualPolitik* (2009), she boldly interrogates the various forms of governmental, political, electronic communication practices disseminated through government websites, powerpoint presentations, propagandist use of technology for war purposes, as well as various internet sites, video games, simulations, artificial intelligence, virtual humans, embodied conversational agents, intelligent tutoring systems, and older technologies that all fall under the umbrella of digital rhetoric as historical, situated practices.

Her book is a key work in the history of digital rhetoric and combines many deep discussions on digital rhetoric in light of rhetorical history and connecting them to various technologies.

Losh also defines digital rhetoric in a multifaceted definition, and in so doing, underlines the point that with so many competing definitions, digital rhetoric itself is difficult to define. According to her, digital rhetoric is hindered by an insistence upon "attention to the mechanical responses of the computer to input rather than the theories behind the design and continuing evolution of digital media and networked systems" (p. 47). Such a perspective would include looking at how computers are coded to communicate with us, but more importantly to her, also at how evolving practices (both human and computer-based) create emergent forms of communication and interaction. Losh's operational definition for digital rhetoric is concise:

1. *The conventions of new digital genres that are used for everyday discourse, as well as for special occasions, in average people's lives*
2. *Public rhetoric, often in the form of political messages from government institutions, which is represented or recorded through digital technology and disseminated via electronic distributed networks.*
3. *The emerging scholarly discipline concerned with the rhetorical interpretation of computer-generated media as objects of study*
4. *Mathematical theories of communication from the field of information science, many of which attempt to quantify the amount of uncertainty in a given linguistic exchange or the likely paths through which messages travel. (Losh, 2009, pp. 47-48)*

In looking at Losh's definition of digital rhetoric (which she mentions as being not all-encompassing), some patterns emerge. Definitions one and two can be placed in traditional Aristotelian categories of rhetoric. Namely, definition one follows that of epideictic (ceremonial or special occasion) rhetoric, whereas definition two follows deliberative (public/political) rhetoric as defined by Aristotle in *On Rhetoric* (Kennedy, 2006). Definition three extends traditional Aristotelian rhetoric by including computer-mediated media as objects of study in themselves (and seems to follow Manovich's call for seeing the "ontology of the computer" as important to study). Lastly, definition four focuses on computer-based natural language processing analysis and algorithmic processing creating responses based on artificial intelligence (quantifying uncertainty in linguistic exchanges implies a semantic interpretation) and relies on Lanham's use of Shannon and Weaver's (1963) mathematical theories of communication where signals are exchanged between a sender and a receiver with medium noise determining communicative strategies and routing.

Similar to Bogost, Losh criticizes the manner that various efforts in rhetoric are focused on studying the surface of forms of digital discourse, "but [that these studies] too rarely consider the epistemological implications of contemporary information science for networked, digital communication, which may operate with some fundamentally different assumptions about systems of signification than do natural language models" (p. 48). As discussed above, arguments take on a different form whether one talks with a rhetorician versus a computer programmer, as they will have different definitions of them, but make use of them for specific, similar purposes – to enact some form of outcome or action.

Bogost and Losh's criticisms are valid to the extent that all too often the same familiar arguments seem to appear in articles dealing with aspects of rhetoric, technology or digital culture when these are framed from a pedagogical perspective in studies of composition or literacy. For example, some of these perspectives can be summed up as:

- **Digital rhetoric as a warning:** Liberatory advocacy perspectives which warn about the impending danger of giving human autonomy away to computer technology in pedagogical contexts.
- **Digital rhetoric as political agenda:** Political perspectives which see computer technology from a pro- or anti-technology view and push an agenda of seeing technology from an instrumentalist, determinist, replacement, progressive, or critical framework. By pushing this agenda, digital rhetoric is encompassed in frameworks that state technology is a mere tool to be used, an inescapable reality, an ideology which threatens to leave behind many of us, or progress, or should be, in the meantime, critically investigated to determine whether its effects are good or bad.
- **Digital rhetoric as current technology under investigation:** Incomplete and obsolete contemporary perspectives that see current digital technologies as constituting digital rhetoric but which become outdated and obsolete as soon as newer digital technologies are accepted and disseminated.
- **Digital rhetoric as textual analysis:** Literary perspectives that try to "read" digital artifacts/ new media and criticize them from a textual framework or emplace them into existing medium frameworks.

Part and parcel of digital rhetoric is dealing with digital technology beyond its surface as semantic medium, and approaching and realizing that evolution and progress is inherent in any process (human, natural, and technological), not just technology, and recognizing the incredible social, cultural, and cognitive effects created by our use of such technology and that descriptive, rather than prescriptive, models are necessary in light of the adoption and dissemination of various technologies.

In both Losh and Bogost's critical approach to digital rhetoric, they stress the importance of the multi-layered underlying principles of digital rhetoric, which include procedural computer logic (among other elements) rather than consist merely of "semantic" interfaces and end-user experiences. While a valid criticism of rhetoric as a discipline (wherein many are not well-versed in computer programming code or procedural languages), both signal the need for broader perspectives to be included in digital rhetoric as a discipline. Indeed, in a blog post where she attempts to refine her definition, Losh argues that digital rhetoric is "both rhetoric *about* the digital and rhetoric *conveyed* by digital platforms, interfaces, and code" (2012). Whether rhetorical action takes place on the human and computer code level seems to be the contention here, and both Bogost and Losh make a valid point that various perspectives that influence our communication and interaction are crucial for digital rhetoric in shifting its focus away from print culture or seeing digital technology as a medium that only conveys semantic content to us that we then study. Instead, we should move towards more complex, multi-layered understandings of digital rhetoric as a *continuous process* and as will be argued below, as a continuum of human actions as a continuous spectrum of varying frequencies and contexts.

DIGITAL MEDIA AND COMPUTATION AS OBJECTS OF STUDY IN DIGITAL RHETORIC: WHAT WE TALK ABOUT WHEN WE TALK ABOUT DIGITAL RHETORIC

The main reason for this section is to clarify digital technology as guided by basic, computational principles and to introduce the common term of digital medium and computation as grounding digital rhetoric. This is done in order to increase the understanding of various technologies as singular artifacts of study combined under the guise of common, core digital rhetorical principles inherent in rhetorical argumentation (aka human communication and interaction) and procedural arguments (aka computer communication) that are inherent in our experiencing of digital media and the use of computation in these media.

While an enormous amount of research exists on the rhetoric of new media, remediation, the mechanics of hypertext, the semiotics of multimodality, and various studies of computer-mediated communication have been done that provide an enriching perspective for rhetoric, a lot of this research has approached technology from a variety of perspectives and definitions that are difficult to summarize due to competing terminologies and diversity of technologies such as hypertext, websites, mobile computing, video games, virtual worlds, etc. that are studied under the banner of digital scholarship (cf. Aarseth,1997; Bolter & Grusin, 2000; Gurak, 2001; Hawisher & Selfe, 2000; Fleckenstein, 2003; Kress, 2003; Kress & van Leeuwen 2001; Manovich, 2001; New London Group 2000; Johnson-Eilola, 2005; Selber, 2004). The reason for the difficulty in summarizing this research is not so much the amount of it (though a great deal exists in journals such as *Computers and Composition*, *Kairos*, *Technical Communication Quarterly*, various *Institute of Electrical and Electronics Engineers (IEEE)* and *Association for Computing Machinery (ACM)* journals dealing with the design of communication and human-computer interaction), but also the different types of technology as artifacts that are studied and are used to make claims about new media, digital media studies, or the digital humanities.

A further complication is separating *artifact* – the object itself – and the mediating *functions* of the artifact – its computing capabilities and the underlying software providing those capabilities - that provide it certain characteristics, modes and practices, that can then be studied. A simple model that illustrates this issue is provided by Yochai Benkler, who separates the network capabilities as based upon separate spheres of physical, code and content network layers (cf. Lessig, 1999), such as physical infrastructures (computers as hardware), operating systems (software) and the transmission of information (networks). Using physical, code and content layers, we can then make further semantic distinctions based upon the impacts of each layer. For instance, on the content layer we can utilize Shannon and Weaver's (1964) seminal mathematical formulation of communication, in which sender, signal, medium, noise, and reception form a communication network. The difficulty for digital rhetoric is therefore to make sense of some of these semantic distinctions while at the same time paying attention to the various layers and characteristics that alter our communication principles. Turnley (2011) has suggested using Régis Debray's model of "mediology" to give a seven-dimensional network to analyze media from the perspective of technological, social, economic, archival, aesthetic, subjective and epistemomological frameworks as material, aesthetic, knowledge-making, aesthetic and socio-technological aspects that impact the experience of various media. Another example of the layered and (nested) nature of digital media is the Open Systems Interconnection (OSI) Basic Reference Model, consisting of *applications* running on networks, *presentation* of information/ data using encryption, *sessions* that establish connections between different computers and servers, *transport* of data, *network* routing which packages the data, *data links* which arrange bits from physical hard drives into computer-logical sequences, and *physical* elements that are used to create the infrastructure (Murray, 2012, p. 131). As is obvious from the above, there are many spatial, semantic layers involved, and many elements to be discerned if we are to look at digital rhetoric as a process of various layers involving many modes and practices of production and transmission.

Since many different terms are used by different disciplines to study the same elements, it makes sense to combine these terms under one umbrella term and to look below what combines each digital technology in terms of modes and practices of communication from a human and computer perspective. We may talk about investigations in computerized communication in general, CMC, human-computer interaction (HCI), interaction design (ID), interface design, computer coding, or investigating emerging principles and modes in video games, virtual worlds, mobile computing, or focus on the specific practices in the study of computer coding and languages. If digital rhetoric is to study all these disparate elements, common terms need to be used so we can continue to investigate this crucial territory in the interactive space between user-interface-content-computer code. Unless we are willing to accept that our studies are all connected by a connecting factor, the study of digital rhetoric might as well be housed under these various different disciplines. So what makes the "digital" in digital rhetoric so special and why should we study it? What do we talk about when talk about digital rhetoric?

A fascinating discussion developing over the years have been the debates between theorists on the role of attendant digital media such as video games, which play a large role in disrupting our idea of "stable" media of books, films, and music. During the video game debate in the late nineties, a variety of different perspectives, among which literary and discourse analysis (Gee, 2003), dramaturgical theories (Laurel, 2003; Murray, 1998) and play-based (ludological) frameworks (Juul 2005) argued that games have specific game-play elements that are distinctly non-narrative while providing narraive and dramaturgical experiences for video game players. All these discussions demonstrate that digital media cannot be emplaced in the same old (literary, dramaturgical, play-based) categories and that we should avoid simply applying existing frameworks as digital media elide familiar cultural frameworks by remediating and incorporating modes and practices into newer contexts and networks of relations.

Similarly in digital rhetoric, we may need to adopt newer frameworks for what we study when dealing with digital media. For instance, where a computer scientist may be interested in optimizing their code through debugging or writing a more efficient or elegant algorithm or just simply see if their code works, a rhetorician may be wondering what the effects of the code are, what its effects are, or how it came to fruition, etc. A third viewpoint, that of digital rhetoric, may involve investigating all of the above elements from the perspective on both a computer and human-level as semantic content, code, decoded and encoded, sent and received and developed over time. Moreover, as Cummings (2006) has argued, the parallels between computer programming and composition are surprisingly similar, as both are focused on constructing an envisioning an audience before writing, but operate on somewhat different principles based on notions of concrete, binary code or more fuzzy meanings (the former language the unforgiving logic of computer code which works or does not work; the latter more forgiving but no equally fraught with social, cultural contextual "code" of everyday language through which meanings are constructed by an audience).

At issue for digital rhetoric here is capturing the object of study itself, and how a common term can be applied to study the same artifact (or object of study) to highlight rhetorical modes and practices. As different paradigms inform different disciplines and divide them based on various points of view, for digital rhetoric it becomes paramount to bridge the disciplinary differences between computer science (and its subdisciplines) and rhetoric and look for commonalities in its objects of study. For this chapter, it is important that the artifacts of digital rhetoric are defined and proper frameworks are utilized that help to create an understanding of digital rhetoric as a dynamic process of networked relations.

Hence, one prime aspect is the need of clarification in confusing terminology, which needs to start with replacing the term new media itself with digital medium and use computation as the combining factor for objects of study. Even though new media is used to describe various media that are computer-based and great strides have been made in defining characteristics of computers as new media (cf. Bolter & Grusin, 2000; Manovich, 2001), computer scientist Murray (2012) rightly contends that the term "new media" obscures the profound changes introduced by computers behind an emphasis on "novelty [as] the salient property of these phenomena" (p.8). In other words, Murray (2012) claims we need to get rid of such notions to get at the common modes and practices that underlie each medium, which are based upon the principles of computation.

Adopting the term digital medium is crucial for digital rhetoric, because it removes the idea that we continuously need to focus on the "new" elements that may appear on our screens or the "new" characteristics of a medium. As Bolter and Grusin (2000) pointed out, some new medium characteristics are reworkings of older characteristics, wherein a good example could be how we can now see the keyboard as a remediation of the typewriter, or how hypertexts are a reworking of older texts such as the *Talmud* or how computer-based interactive narratives were preceded by the *I Ching* which functioned similarly using some form of mathematical computation to arrive at a narrative path. Further, new media as a term does nothing to address the fact that media will always be updated, and if we decide to cling on to researching "new media" as part of digital rhetoric, we may engage in a futile game of playing catch-up when the next new technology appears on the horizon. Hence, a term needs to be used that underlines the common, historical, rhetorical practices and modes that underlie computerized media and their unique properties that extend beyond being "novel".

In line with Murray (2012) then, this chapter argues that the term *"digital medium"* is adopted for digital rhetoric's object/artifact of study, along with *"computation"* as the functions and characteristics of its objects of study, to see the unique properties of various digital technologies where computation functions to construct emerging and evolving media combining and remediating all of our older media and their common functionalities. For Murray (2012), digital media are connected by the common factor of being involved in a process of convergence based on the connecting factor of *computation*:

Focusing on computation allows us to see all of these disparate artifacts – games, web pages, cell phones, music players, interactive shows – as belonging to a single evolving medium, in which formats that we once thought of as fixed and separate, like spoken and written messages, books and games, movies and file cabinets, television and telephones are being deconstructed into their component parts and reconfigured for interactivity. (Murray, 2012, p. 9)

For rhetoricians, who speak about human communication and interaction, and have developed frameworks centered on human communication as precipitating human action, computation may be problematic for a number of different reasons. However, if we consider that interactivity or interaction involves communication and action, a subtle shift is made in emphasis where human-computer interaction forms a nexus for digital rhetoric by way of seeing communication as interactivity (or communication using various functions) that creates *agency* between humans and computers and vice versa.

For Murray, this shift to computation and the central role of human-computer interactivity requires embracing novel terms borrowed from HCI. Hence, replacing the term "user" with interactor, replacing the term "content" with information design, and replacing the oft-used but confusing term "interactivity" with agency is one of her suggestions (Murray, 2012, p. 12). Interestingly, while Murray's approach is informed by computer science, for digital rhetoric the above terms also

have corollaries in traditional rhetoric – namely the writer/speaker as interactor, text/speech as information design (as rhetorical principles precipitate a product meant to create an communicational effect), and the audience as interactivity/agency. Yet, as Murray (2012) points out, "interactivity" is not the same as "agency" as a computer may deny one's agency by, for instance, not allowing one to level up in a game or by the elements of interface design, which may allow or disallow/constrain certain actions for procedural reasons (p. 13). Furthermore, because digital media afford us a collaborative space to do this in – whether by projecting our thoughts, communicating with others, interacting, playing, or learning- we are really talking about interactor space, information design space, and interactive (designed) or agency (experienced) space.

Further, due to the continuous shifts in software, computational power, interaction design practices, platforms, looking at digital genres as static is counter-productive as these are ever-changing cognitive schemas we acquire and reshape. A common example in computer environments is the switch from the dominant cognitive framework of WIMP (Windows, Icon, Mouse and Pointing) to that of gestural touch-screens, motion sensing, immersive and haptic environments which introduce new cognitive framework and interface genres. For this purpose, Murray (2012) proposes embracing a more abstract notion of genre as seen from a systems-perspective of "artifacts, environments, applications, devices, systems and so on" in order to avoid semantic confusion in investigating the ever-changing design of applications like video games or mobile phones with those of the artifact as we initially were introduced to as being a video game or mobile phone (p. 13).

To sum up, using Murray's succinct terminology and clear points, digital rhetoric may avoid a lot of semantic confusion. At the same time, digital rhetoric gains the rhetoric of computation by recognizing that these consists of several systemic levels and layers of meaning-making where we not only distinguish the objects of digital media, or their computational functions, but also look at the mediated, evolving environments they create, the applications which run these functions, which devices use them, on which operating systems they run, and so forth.

As these layers complicate our simple perspective of digital rhetoric as embracing a human and computer level understanding, in the below section, layers of a digital medium in CMC specifically will be outlined before activity theory is introduced, which this chapter will use for underlining how the study of digital rhetoric can be done on the basis of understanding shared actions based on Burke's (1966; 1969) notion of human motive and purpose (and identification) as framing digital communication modes and practices. Given the above shift from rhetoric as communication to rhetorical interactivity and agency (both human and computer-based processes where levels of autonomy differ in interaction, as we have seen), activity theory also provides a robust framework for studying digital medium and computation from the basis of outcomes of actions while looking at it from a networked perspective wherein technological innovation is seen from an evolutionary view as comprised of Bakhtin's (1973) perspective of heteroglossia of human discourse and material design practices that are embedded in CMC.

Having operationally defined digital rhetoric as the study of human interaction with and through any digital medium that uses computation, it is important to realize that digital rhetoric deals with the changing circumstances of technologies. It does this by looking at a digital medium from a variety of different perspectives that take into account digital artifacts as featuring objective, ecological, sociocultural, mediation and development dimensions over time and space rather than static, bounded media. Further, digital rhetoric's purview increases when one takes into account the various perspectives that can inform it when using digital medium and computation as combining terms for its artifact and object of

study. In so doing, digital rhetoric can combine divergent perspectives from traditional rhetoric, computer science and its various sub-disciplines of interaction design, HCI, CMC, interface design, as well as the semiotics of various ethnographic, qualitative and quantitative studies of networked computerized communication in workplace, business, scientific, or educational settings.

MEDIATION: COMPUTER-MEDIATED COMMUNICATION AND DIGITAL RHETORIC

As mentioned above, it is important to take into account the developments of CMC while developing digital rhetoric as comprised of a human and computer side where varying levels of autonomy and agency exist in interaction in the way a design gives access or denies certain functions on the interface, or more concretely, the crucial territory in the interactive space between user-interface-content-computer code. CMC has long studied how computer mediation impacts communication and provides a good overview of how media provide or disallow certain actions from a human-computer communication perspective. If the above section discussed how humans and computers both interact with each other, this section focuses on how mediation impacts human communicative functionalities and how humans adapt and evolve to such functionalities through a variety of communicational strategies.

A crucial development in digital rhetoric requires we understand that any digital medium changes how we communicate and strongly influences our behavior when using CMC. McLuhan's (1964) well-known "the medium is the message" succinctly states how a medium influences our rhetorical behavior in *how* we convey a message. We know, for instance, that brevity, clarity and succinctness are better communication techniques in a medium emphasizing timeliness such as chat or mobile sms-ing than long epistolary techniques.

Throughout history, it is evident that human modes of communication are impacted by the invention and dissemination of new technologies as these require specific competencies and literacies for their use. From the pen, the Gutenberg Press, morse code, gramophone, long wire radio-transmission, telephony, radio, television, the Internet, mobile computing, and now, wireless fidelity; we have a long and storied history of (mass) media communication techniques that have impacted the way information and discourse are disseminated and transmitted and received by us (Kittler, 1999). Each new technology requires that we pay attention to its particular strengths and weaknesses and asks us to modify our behavior to achieve optimum efficiency and learn the intricacies of that medium. For some of these media that allow us to communicate, it is crucial that we learn how to use it in communicating with each other through that medium, lest we break down our communication (and interaction) with the other person.

The etymology of the word "medium" derives from the Latin "medius" – or middle. While some may see a medium as just that which "mediates" in communicating their intended message and facilitating the reception of that message to the intended recipient(s), as is evident from McLuhan's maxim, a medium is not solely transparent and does impact *how* we communicate. Indeed, a specific argument could be made that a medium is never transparent and always-already affects our rhetorical modes and behavior, because it asks us to take into account the medium when we address the other person, or, in case of communicating with a computer, what input we need to provide in order to get the response/output/outcome we need.

This element of understanding the language of computers is crucial in CMC, because as some theorists have argued, CMC can only approximate how humans have evolved over time to communicate through direct face-to-face communication. As is evident, face-to-face communication has so many implicit elements of communication due to elements that are second nature to the human senso-

rium. Next to listening to someone's verbal speech, we have developed subtle ways to read social cues such as body language and orientation, posture, hand-and arm gestures, facial expressions, gaze, interpersonal distance, as well as voice pitch, tone, cadence as well as prosody – to infer information and meaning beyond *what* is said verbally and into *how* it is said in its physical context (cf. Sproull and Kiesler, 1992; Kock, 2005; Verhulsdonck, 2007). Not only is CMC different in richness of such social cues, it is also vastly different in various characteristics, requiring that we unpack the idea of a digital medium in its involvement when mediating human communication.

Indeed, one of the important strides in medium studies was made by Weaver and Shannon (1963) in their seminal *The Mathematical Formulation of Communication*. In this work they focused on the networked nature of communication by defining it as a process between a sender, medium and a receiver as well as the "cost" of communicating using a medium. They define communication as a process of decoding and encoding a message between a sender and receiver that is conducted through various channels which constitutes a network. A simple diagram can thus suffice to display that communication constitutes of linear lines of communication that constitutes a loop between sender and receiver as reception of a message is indicated or adjustment is needed (see Figure 1).

Shannon and Weaver's model is succinct in clarifying that any medium contains "noise" inherent to the medium and that any communication comes at a "cost" when mediated. As they note, in mediated communication there is a communicative "cost" through transmitting and a loss or potential adjustment that needs to be made in order for a message to come across, whether this loss is caused by the medium carrying the message itself, or the person communicating having to adjust what they say or how they communicate it in order for the communication to be successfully received. For instance, we move closer to people if ambient noises interfere in us commu-

Figure 1. Shannon and Weaver's mathematical model of communication

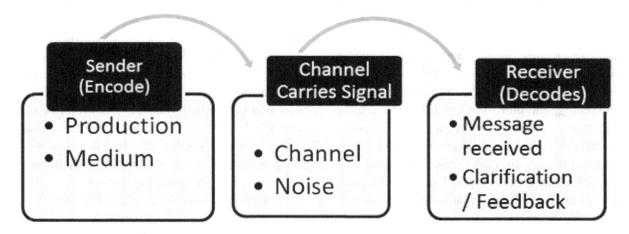

nicating our message to the other person. In a medium, we adjust the channels we know are necessary for getting across to the other person, for instance, when voice chatting, we know voice volume is important, when video chatting, our verbal and non-verbal (facial expression) performance becomes also important as the other person can see us when we speak. The importance of this work for digital rhetoric lies in seeing communication as a *system* and *network of relations* wherein modes and practices are affected by medium characteristics and various states of synchrony or asynchrony.

As any medium has constraints, it is important to understand how a networked digital medium facilitates and alters communication practices. Some of these studies have uncovered the profound effects of CMC networks' ability to "flatten" hierarchical corporate structures and introduce changes in perceptions and practices of work, power, individuality, groups, culture, identity, and communication styles in organizations and underline not only the effects of a medium on communication, but also on human behavior, culture, and organizations by their ability to facilitate or impact a person's "social presence" when com-

municating (cf. Short, Williams, & Christie, 1976; Hiltz & Turoff, 1978).

Social presence theory (Short, Williams, & Christie, 1976) has been the predominant model to study various media and their effects on communication. Many researchers indicate correlations between style and ease of communication in a media environment based on 1) medium richness as related to face-to-face communication or relative lack of medium channels available as based on the human sensorium (eyes, hearing, touch, feel, smell, etc.) affecting communicative behavior 2) the social presence afforded by a medium in giving those communicating the ability to provide extra-linguistic semantic information about one's personality, status, or appearance during communication 3) the ability to use non-verbal social cues such as body language, facial expressions, hand and arm gestures to provide backchannel information that provides important information about the communication progress itself and provides turn-taking 4) how medium familiarity influences our ability to communicate through it in an effective manner and 5) the ability of a medium to provide the channels of communication we have evolved to prefer evolutionarily or that we deem appropriate to certain tasks (Clark &

Brennan, 1994; Daft & Lengel, 1984; Dennis & Valacich, 1991; DeSanctis & Poole, 1994; Fulk, Steinfield, Schmitz & Power, 1987; Kock 2005; McGrath, 1991; Sproull & Kiesler, 1992). Other researchers have downplayed the model of medium channels by positing that medium constraints allow for more intimate, measured impression formation by conscious rhetorical exchanges through, for instance, email, and lead to a greater form of intimacy due to the effect of not having to represent the physical self (Postmes, Spears & Lea, 1999). Perhaps most interestingly, based on evolutionary theory, medium-naturalness theory (MNT) posits humans evolutionary prefer face-to-face communication due to increased levels of physical arousal, experience of immediacy and presence of the other person that create a more "natural" experience of communication (Kock, 2005). However, MNT incorporates Shannon and Weaver's model of communicative cost by conceding that other media may be adapted to at a cognitive load cost, where communicating is less natural but where we evolutionary adapt to a digital medium's characteristics (Kock, 2005).

As is obvious, many of the above medium theories attempt to describe how the way we communicate is affected by the constraints of a medium, and how we adapt and evolve to the constraints of a medium and alter our rhetorical strategies in an evolutionary manner. The above perspectives from studies in CMC are fascinating examples of how digital rhetoric can be enriched by exploring how meaning is created through a systemic view of human social behavior and digital medium characteristics as they evolve. As mentioned above, while we may have the various layers of human and computer networks in digital rhetoric, keeping in mind the constant changes in human behavior and interface design as modes and practices also helps to realize that these elements need to be seen from an evolutionary, network perspective as interdependent through their constant interactivity.

In addition to this evolutionary perspective on human-computer interaction, it is also important to break down the amount of layers that exist in CMC where information is exchanged and how meaning is received. One of the best models is that of Clark and Brennan (1991), defining various medium characteristics that involve human communication based on informational elements supported in computer-mediated contexts. Based on their model, semantic elements can be carried by a medium's ability to facilitate various channels such as:

- **Copresence:** Shared space - A can see what B sees
- **Visibility:** Seeing the other person – A sees B
- **Audibility:** Speaking directly to the other person – A can talk to B and vice versa
- **Cotemporality:** Shared transmission and reception time between participants – A and B can interrupt each other
- **Simultaneity:** Ability to share and receive messages at the same time – A and B can send and receive messages at the same time)
- **Sequentiality:** Turn-taking required of participants – A and B cannot send and receive messages at the same time
- **Reviewability:** Reviewing messages of the other person – A and B can see and review each other's messages on screen
- **Revisability:** Revising messages of the other person - A and B can revise messages of each other and so collaborate (Clark & Brennan, 1991, p. 141-142).

While face-to-face communication provides many of these modes, and we utilize them as second nature without thinking about it, in CMC these elements can all be present, or partially be present. In defining medium characteristics of CMC and comparing it to face-to-face communication, it becomes evident that a digital medium provides communication environments that are both *more* than and *less* than face-to-face communication. Moreover, in their model of "grounding" in communication, Clark and Brennan (1991) expand on Shannon and Weaver's model of communication by demonstrating how in face-to-face contexts, humans use various strategies to exchange verbal information and demonstrate the progress on how the communication is going – whether the message encoded has been decoded, perceived and received. Similarly, especially in human-computer-human interaction, such strategies are important for semantic purposes and help explain human behavior when it is done through a digital medium.

To recap, digital media may provide reviewing, revising or sharing of simultaneous semantic content in visual, textual and symbolic ways (for instance, by sharing screens and audiovisual sharing), but they also constrain communication by asking people to communicate through a medium that has no 1:1 relationship to face-to-face communication (as communication happens through a screen, social cues such as spatial orientation, non-verbals, proximity, etc. are difficult to convey or need to be performed consciously). In highlighting these medium characteristics, as well as the various social, historical and evolutionary factors influencing our use of a digital medium to communicate, these studies complicate our understanding of digital communication and interaction as being comprised simply of the interaction between computers and humans. As shown above, many layers and communicational affordances exist beyond human and computer. These layers can be defined as social, evolutionary on the human side in adopting elements of a digital medium, but are also comprised of the networked relations existing between evolving "artifacts, environments, applications, devices, systems and so on" (Murray, 2012, p. 13) – the flipside of what we see on the screen but which mediate our actions through coding and communication protocols.

Indeed, various theorists have described this duality where technology influences human development and in turn, humans influence technological practices. Gidden's (1984) duality theory of structuration holds that in using environments, people *interpenetrate* and are *interpenetrated* by their environment. Likewise, according to De Certeau (1984), people appropriate *spaces* and make these *places* by repurposing them to their actions, which in turn has led computer scholars to define this interactive dynamic in computer-mediated spaces (cf. Harrison & Dourish, 1996). Like our mediated environment in a digital medium, our use of public spaces is dependent upon the affordances it provides us with, which we can use and constrain and define our use of these spaces, but also provides us opportunities to alter them by us finding new ways of interacting with such spaces. For instance, whereas a regular person may see a bench that affords them a place to sit, it may also function as a skateboard site for skateboarders where the bench affords them to do tricks like boardslides, noseslides, tailslides, or any other trick combination leading up to a slide off of the bench. In other words, the activities, and the cognitive schemas people bring to look at structures and their affordances and the way they interact with a structure, provide different ways of using an environment whereby people may alter its use. To relate this back to digital rhetoric, if we are to study digital artifacts as objects of study, we will need to deal with the shifting nature of this dynamic between humans and computers as digital artifacts that are constantly changing in use and interpreted in different ways by people.

From this perspective, it is therefore important to note how digital rhetoric can utilize distinctions made in interface design for dealing with the shifts and evolving uses and conventions of use and design in digital media. In *The Design of Everyday Things* (1988), computer scientist Donald Norman coined the phrase "affordance" as a term that "[refers] to an attribute of an object that allows people to know how to use it" by the design of a graphical user interface (GUI) providing important indications (or "cues") as to the ways it can be used (Sharp, Rogers & Preece, 2007, p. 33). A distinction is made between "real" and "perceived" affordances based on physical objects like the handle of a door allowing for "real" affordances, and those widgets in virtual interfaces which are essentially perceived by humans and learned through use and experience. An example of the distinction between real and perceived affordances is the use of mouse button providing a "real" affordance (that of clicking either left or right mouse button) versus the perceived hand icon which functions as an interface metaphor in a GUI that indicates we can click on the item and so interact with it. The importance of using affordances are that they function at the interface level to connect humans with the underlying procedural framework and that affordances change incrementally based on how people use a digital medium and create existing cognitive schemas through their developed understanding and experience with common design metaphors. For instance, when adopting an operating system, different metaphors are used if say, one were to use Window (Windows), Mac (Docking station), Linux (Command line interface), Android/iOs (Touch screen) etc.. At the same time, these metaphors change through constant user use and refinement, requiring for updates of the Operating System (OS) and addressing different evolving ways of doing things based on how people use these technologies or how software companies are re-constructing them to new models for monetizing their platforms. For digital rhetoric to study a digital medium, it needs to be aware not only of how human and computer practices change and evolve constantly based on interaction principles and are expressed in affordances where human agency and computer-determined interactivity differ, but also how interface metaphors and

metonomy function to represent discrete actions or sets of data in ever changing ways.

In order to articulate this constant shifting of relations based on material (real) and semiotic (perceived) conditions, Latour (2005) speaks of Actor-Network Theory (ANT) where human and non-human structures both influence each other as part of a network. The revolutionary idea of ANT is that *like* humans, the notion that non-human structures are also *actors* in a network or system of relations. In a clarification on this concept, Latour (1989) describes how actor-network theory is not a strictly mathematical or engineered network due to its malleable nature and set of relations between human and non-human elements:

A network in mathematics or in engineering is something that is traced or inscribed by some other entity -the mathematician, the engineer. An actor-network is an entity that does the tracing and the inscribing. It is an ontological definition and not a piece of inert matter in the hands of others, especially of human planners or designers. It is in order to point out this essential feature that the word 'actor' was added to it. (par. 14)

Further, Latour (1989) notes that ANT's level of analysis is not based on spatial metaphors, but where "one is asked to think in terms of nodes that have as many dimensions as they have connections" where several levels of analysis exist that go against existing paradigms and frameworks for analysis (par. 5). As examples of existing spatial paradigms that constrain analysis, Latour mentions that ANT "allows us already to reshuffle spatial metaphors that have rendered the study of society-nature so difficult: close and far, up and down, local and global, inside and outside. They are replaced by associations and connections" (par. 13). The importance of ANT is not so much that it provides an alternative way of analyzing relations in terms of a network (although useful for our operational definition of digital rhetoric), but that it makes room for human and non-human elements as part of a network whereby spatial relationships are reconfigured into nodes of relations.

If digital rhetoric is to investigate each digital medium and use the umbrella principle of computation, it needs to at least acknowledge how human-computer interaction is part of actor- network relations where such hierarchical, spatial concepts are made obsolete (especially when considering the global nature of CMC). That is, digital rhetoric needs to recognize digital modes and practices as both embedded in material, socioeconomic and semiotic affordances, and conducted through a process of interactivity where practices and modes of communication evolve in nodes of human and non-human elements. Yet, at the same time ANT seems to create new frameworks for analysis of greater granularity. At the end of this chapter, I will explain how some reconfigured distinctions (particularly local and global) can be useful in framing digital rhetoric and globalized communication practices in a continuum framework.

In order to investigate how networks function and how humans and computers as actors influence material and semiotic structures, the next section will introduce activity theory. Activity theory holds that in order to frame any activity, it is important to look at how common outcomes and shared goals create activities that are meant to accomplish an outcome or goal. As activity theory is a robust theory to investigate and frame human-computer interaction from a practical perspective, the next section will provide some background and unpack activity theory and its relevance to studying artifacts of digital rhetoric before this chapter turns to how novel modes of communication introduced by digital media and computation inform and help define digital rhetoric from a convergence-continuum model.

HOW ACTIVITY THEORY FACILITATES THE STUDY OF DIGITAL RHETORIC

Altering Winograd's (1997) definition for interaction design, this chapter operationalizes digital rhetoric as the study of human and computer interaction and communication, where technologies are globally created and used in multiple ways and so instantiate practices and understandings that can be termed global literacies. In order to support this definition, it is important to not only define digital medium and computation as its central object of study, but also to see how layers of different affordance exist, as well as how the interactivity between humans and computers creates a network of enacted relations requiring further study. Furthermore, for this definition it is important that the modes and practices of digital rhetoric as used in global technologies in creating new communication practices, knowledge and literacies can be studied and a robust theoretical framework is adopted that incorporates the evolving nature of each digital medium. The study framework used for proposing the convergence model continuum in this chapter is based on activity theory, which is suitable for digital rhetoric because of its emphasis on various relationships as continuously evolving from a networked approach based on actions that are performed to achieve certain outcomes.

According to Aristotle, rhetoric can be defined as "an ability, in each particular case, to see the available means of persuasion" (Aristotle *Rhetoric* I.1.2, Kennedy 2006, p.37). In *A Rhetoric of Motives* (1969), rhetorician Kenneth Burke defined rhetoric as a way for people to "identify" points of view and hence emplaced it under the banner of *identification*. Taken together, both definitions of rhetoric can be seen as ways in which language can be used to persuade people to identify with each other's point of view and so create motivated, purposive action through common understanding. More importantly, as digital rhetoric studies digital media and computation as a process that evolves, so activity theory is used to study dynamic processes between groups of people, technologies as artifacts, and the various social factors that bind these together in pursuit of a common goal. As a study framework for digital rhetoric, where humans and computers interact towards specific goals in specific ways, activity theory may be useful in highlighting the dynamic in the relationship in human-computer interaction.

Digital rhetoric also needs to take into account how it can study practical processes when these artifacts are used over time. Whereas ANT may seem suitable for mapping out nodes and relations, the evolving nature of digital media requires we look at their practical use over time and the developing modes of global communication, for which activity theory is much more practical and useful. Originally seen as contradictory to ANT because it focuses more on subjects and originally did not focus on non-human actors, activity theory nonetheless provides an interesting framework for digital rhetoric precisely because it allows for the use of various analytical positions in framing actions and activities. This section will provide a brief historical overview of the emergence of activity theory in studies of CMC, and will follow this up with how it incorporates technology as part of studying complex processes in fully contextualized ways, along with other social, environmental and structural factors in order to articulate its importance for digital rhetoric as a field of study.

Activity theory originates in work done in the Soviet Union in the 1920s by psychologist Vygotsky (orig. 1929, 1978) and further developed by Leont'ev (orig. 1947, 1981). Their model was focused on creating a framework for human learning as a process of the human mind internalizing knowledge through activities or actions. Based on their view, human learning is facilitated by activities and actions where we share tools with other humans and so create formative experiences that we then internalize as knowledge and whereby learning is facilitated through activities and tools. In other words, activity theory holds that actions and material conditions facilitate human learning and practice by providing us the use of tools for specific outcomes and modes of production. In this framework, it is crucial to distinguish that as outcomes change, so do tools needed and the goals of a group of humans. Activity theory thus looks at how each element changes in relation to each other as motives and purposes are changed by action through changing practice and modes of production.

Bødker (1989, 1991) introduced activity theory to human-computer interaction studies by looking at how human activities were mediated and facilitated by computer interfaces. Research in interaction design and human-computer interaction has further embraced activity theory and developed a more coherent framework to study mediated communication and interactivity (cf. Engeström, Miettinen & Punamäki, 1999). Recent work in technical communication (e.g. Spinuzzi, 2013) has already shown it to be a robust framework for studying computer-supported group interaction.

Research in sociology and activity theory has defined computer-mediated environments as "information ecologies" where various human outcomes are based on shared actions and tools wherein digital media function as both spaces that create various forms of interaction and places that are used for individual or collective reflection and are highly ecological in nature (De Certeau 1984; Nardi & O'Day, 2000; Norman, 1988; Preece, Rogers & Sharp, 2007). Activity theory studies interactions between technological systems as mediating artifacts and groups of humans across time and space as these emerge as an ecology and evolve and so structure each other's interactions (Cole & Engestrom, 1991) (see Figure 2).

In applying activity theory to HCI, Nardi (1996) defines the aim of activity theory as "understanding the interpenetration of the individual, other people, and artifacts in everyday activity" (p. 8).

Figure 2. Activity theory explains human actions as influenced by multiple factors (adapted from Cole & Engestrom, 1991)

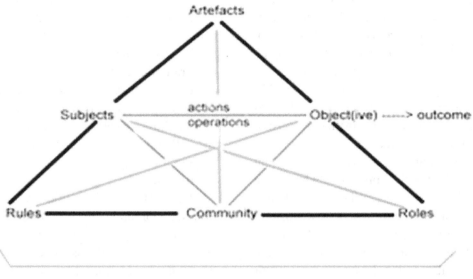

The importance of activity theory for digital rhetoric is that it may provide a different "rhetorical triangle" for capturing activities wherein writer/speaker, audience, text (and context) are reshaped as part of a mediated environment, where the role of writer/speaker is replaced by (inter)actor, audience is replaced by the environment of the design space comprised of rules, roles and communities co-created by mediation and human social interaction, and text and context are replaced by agency and interactivity by technological artifacts of various kinds through the various actions and operations performed by subjects in a temporal environment (see Figure 3).

According to Kaptelinin (1996), activity theory operates from five inter-related perspectives which should be seen as one continuum: 1) the objective, 2) the ecological 3) the sociocultural 4) mediation and 5) development (pp. 107-109), which will be explained below. The objective perspective is object-oriented and takes into ac-

count the properties of objects and the social, cultural and historical understandings (or cognitive schemas) we bring to various objects by which we determine how we interact with them. The ecological perspective sees "motives, goals, and conditions" influencing "activity, actions, and operations" (Kaptelinin, 1996, p. 108). Importantly, a change in a motive, goal or condition creates a different state of activity, actions or operations as people no longer identify with the goal or motivation and thus may cease their mode of production. The sociocultural perspective sees consciousness and knowledge as creating situated cognition, where the mind connects to reality through activities that frame understanding and learning. The mediation perspective sees "the combination of natural human abilities with capacities of external components –tools - to perform a new function" or to do older activities in a more efficient manner (Kaptelinin, 1996, p. 109). The development principle is "to understand a phe-

Figure 3. Re-contextualizing of activity theory in terms of digital rhetoric

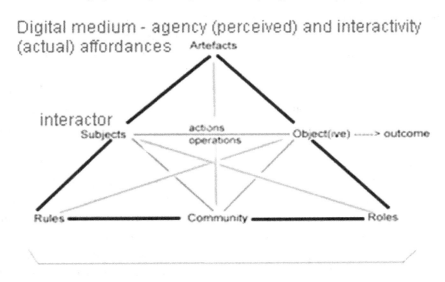

nomenon [and] … to know how it developed into its existing form" – which relies on organic understandings but also provides room for empirical analysis (Kaptelinin, 1996, p.109). In other words, activity theory gives us an evolving perspective on how human-computer interaction is a process of modes and practices that are part of a continuum of object-oriented, ecological, sociocultural, mediological and developmental (evolutionary) factors.

Digital rhetoric, in studying the modes and practices of digital artifacts as digital media that are united under the process of computation, could do well to follow the theoretical framework of activity theory, especially since with some modification, it creates effective ways of distinguishing how interfaces should be read based on their ability to provide perceived agency but also restrict that in terms of interactivity, and how the operations and procedures of computation influence the environment of the digital medium and so influence the mediation and social human interaction. Hence, in adopting this modified model of activity theory for

digital rhetoric, we start looking at digital media and take into account computation, along with the various object-oriented, ecological, sociocultural, mediological and evolutionary factors involved.

By looking at a digital medium from an object-oriented perspective, we ask about the rhetoric of everyday objects and interfaces and our use of them as they afford us different interactions from a human and computer-code perspective. When using an ecological perspective, we ask about the rhetoric of the motives, goals and conditions that unite human-computer interaction through activities, actions and operations. In looking from the sociocultural perspective, we ask about the rhetorical nature in which we internalize and externalize knowledge through the use of digital artifacts and in turn how these digital artifacts may gain knowledge by providing us with internalized input and externalized output and display emergent behavior not unlike humans. In using the mediological perspective, we look at the rhetoric of how technologies may be effective or not effective in mediating and creating knowledge and processes of learning, discovery and invention. Lastly, the development perspective gives us the rhetoric of how media continue to evolve alongside our understanding and use of them in imbricated ways in the synthesis of activity, use, and continuous restructuring of human and computer. In situating all of these perspectives as part of a continuum, activity theory provides a robust framework for studying rhetorical interactions between humans and computers as social actors involved in knowledge generation and activities.

After introducing activity theory as a robust model for studying interaction processes across time within digital rhetoric, the next section will briefly discuss how next to studying digital media and computation as a process that is imbricated with human motivations and helps us communicate and interact, our uses of digital media have also consequences because we do so in increasingly multimodal, intercultural and global ways with other human beings. Hence, next to providing a tentative digital rhetorical triangle for studying interactions on a human and computer level from various angles, the next section will introduce the various contexts of communicating with these technologies and so introducing the continuum model of convergence as contexts for digital rhetorical inquiry.

HOW MULTIMODALITY, GLOBALIZATION AND INTERCULTURAL THEORIES FACILITATE DIGITAL RHETORIC

If rhetoric has been defined in its early stages by the debate surrounding orality (speech) and writing (literacy) (cf. Havelock, 1963; Ong, 1982), the technologizing of the word and the move from print to pixel culture has led to a shift in the definition of literacy. Various definitions have made literacy a word that evolved from individual competencies to "competing narratives of literacy"

where "literacy- the term and concept – connects composition, with its emphasis on students and classrooms, to the social, political, economic, historical and cultural" (Daniell, 1999, p. 393). Instead of competencies ("being literate"), literacy in various scholars' work took a "political turn" in that it was seen reconfigured from a symbol of oppression where writing was an instrument of power to literacy as a corrective instrument engendering socioeconomic and cultural criticism where no innocent position could be taken and power relations themselves were examined. Added to this definition was a call in the field of rhetoric by Faigley (1986) to start paying attention more to "examine the relations between spoken and written language which are emerging in the hybrid forms of electronic literacy" (Daniell, 1999, p. 407). This shift in defining literacy for electronic texts has evolved to even more complex contexts when discussing digital rhetoric and global literacies as various intercultural frameworks come into play alongside specific technology use in material, socioeconomic contexts (Hawisher & Selfe, 2000; Sullivan & Porter, 1997; Thatcher, 2005). This context is more complicated by the way various modes and media converge creating questions and portmanteaus instead of rigid definitions that separate modes and media of communication computers and writing, even going so far that Hart-Davidson and Krause (2004) felt the need to create a "multivocal textumentary" utilizing scripting techniques and metaphors of film-pans that was followed by a similar conversation piece by Walker et al. (2011) that asked where computers and composition as an area of rhetorical inquiry was headed and in need of redefinition and re-integration of different perspectives. Nonetheless, many in the field have taken up Selber's (2004) recommendation that we approach technology from a perspective that involves positioning the self as sole consumer, producer, but also as a critic of technologies and so avoid taking any narrative or material technology at face value.

Due to the processes of globalization and technology creating "Englishes", literacy has been redefined as "multiliteracies" – where multiple modes of literacy need to be developed- as multiple modes of communication conveyed through a digital medium are used to signify meaning (New London Group 2000; Kress & van Leeuwen, 2001). At issue for this definition of multiliteracies is new semiotic modes of conveying meaning "in any and every sign, at every level, and in any mode" and involving issues of "discourse, design, production and distribution" (Kress & van Leeuwen, 2001, p.4). To clarify, multiliteracies exist because of the powerful capabilities of digital media to put in the hands previously separate production and design modes to be used in communication or creating discourse, text or meaning through multiple modes. Rather than one dominant mode (for instance, orality/literacy or speech/writing), digital media provide us multiple modes and media, to communicate in textual, aural, visual, animated, spatial, gestural, and kinesthetic ways. For the conveying of meaning, we need to develop literacies in these multiple modes of technological literacies, in which processes of *discourse* (what medium/media), *design* (what design processes are involved), *production* (which affordances will allow for the best production of discourse) and *distribution* (selection channels for production) all come into play as connected layers of meaning-making for digital rhetoric (Kress & van Leeuwen, 2001).

A good example is the difference between writing an essay with text and visuals versus designing a multimodal three-dimensional environment comprised of spatial elements, ambient sounds, text, textures, primitives, that is meant to have certain interactive effects (for instance, a video game level) on a person – such as motivating them to play on, interacting with non-playable characters (NPCs), learning game rules, pacing, segmentation of gameplay elements (cut-screens, mission explanations, side-missions, main-missions), camera angles, and of course, narrative engagement, we

are approximating the difference in literacies. Not only are multiple elements vying for the attention in the latter, but also there are different ways to "read" and "experience" the environment that go beyond the textual experience and go into human psychology, behavior, gameplay, flow and engagement, three-dimensional environments, multiple ways of engaging the human sensorium and multiple "readings" through interaction. As a result, we can see that "electronic literacy", as a term, does not do justice to the multifaceted aspects of multimodality where multiple considerations of medium choice, design, production and distribution are elements that need to be considered when analyzing or producing discourse from digital media where a digital rhetorical continuum of multiple frequencies of meaning exists.

In addition to multimodalities (i.e. the increase in semiotic layers of expression through various mediological ways mentioned above), a second reason multiliteracies are important for digital rhetoric is that digital media are used in global contexts. Two important points for digital rhetoric are how technology networks create a) globalized communication contexts and b) how the increased semiotic modes of production dissolve the line between consumption and production of media. In the former, Bhaduri (2008) has remarked how local contexts are merged with global contexts, requiring an awareness of what he terms "glocalization" – being aware of both local and global contexts when communicating or working through networks. As most of us are aware of, many companies now operate on a global scale, and require the ability to work in distributed teams located in several separate locations and time zones and negotiate differences of culture. In this sense, the ability to glocalize is important for digital rhetoric in that many CMC and workplace communication and production is now happening on a global level and is a necessary part of professional contexts for intercultural proficiency.

As for the second point, where multiliteracy and multimodality widen the semiotic strata of design and means of being able to communicate, we can now speak of a global context in another way when looking at the means of distribution introduced by the Internet and various network protocols. Through the use of various forms of social networks on the Internet and free software allowing us to create multimedia, the ease of using production methods which previously were restricted to a small amount of trained professionals, multimedia production and distribution has now widened to such a degree that we can now speak of "prosumers" – people producing and consuming multimedia at the same time (Anderson, 2003). Hence, we have witnessed the evolution of the Internet as a medium with its own evolutionary organisms such as memes (popular ideas, jokes, etc.) which are passed on and modified and filtered back into popular mass-media culture such as television at times. For instance, several applications allow one to create comic strips with avatars of oneself, and so chronicle one's life, make jokes, etc. that can then be shared with friends, while requiring no modicum of talent in drawing (the application itself provides this). Likewise, other applications provide one the ability to make "machinima" – a portmanteau of "machine cinema" by providing one an environment to manipulate and film animations with music and sound, or to simply use editing software and create real-life movies with self-created dialogue, environments, camera angles, and special effects added. It should be clear that for digital rhetoric, the consumption of meaning in digital media is only half the picture, as we are now also involved in the study of "prosumers" capable of not only consuming media, but also creating, producing, distributing and choosing media for distributing messages in increasingly advanced ways.

For digital rhetoric to study digital media and computation, it therefore needs a proper framework to study these types of interactions and contexts and develop a framework for studying how not only multiliteracies and multimodalities function in our lives, but also how how intercultural, global

contexts and our changed prosumption of digital modes and practices affect our communicative abilities. The next section provides a history of the term convergence, which helps to capture some of these large-scale changes and provides an understanding of not only the contracted terminology of glocalization and presumption (which displays convergence at a lexical level), but also helps to frame the study of various production modes/practices and contexts in which we now communicate.

CONVERGENCE: A HISTORY OF THE TERM

A key term to be employed in describing modes of digital rhetoric is convergence. Current digital environments, such as web X.0 already display our update-model of various digital media, and show the continuous evolution of social networks, cloud computing, mobile apps, video games. Instead of seeing media as transparent, digital rhetoric sees technology altering human communication and thought processes in a variety of ways by converging human life by "designing spaces for human communication and interaction" (Winograd, 1997, p. 160) and positing that communication and interaction is co-created by technological processes and evolving material and socioeconomic practices. As mentioned earlier in this chapter, the dominant artifact of study in digital rhetoric is a digital medium, which can mean an actual technological physical object, but also its interface, its coding, the interactions a user has with the device, its design, its history and evolution, etc. Further, by making the principle of computation central to digital rhetoric, we have combined these digital artifacts by their ability to compute and so provide output or feedback to humans, whether this is in a process of human-computer interaction or CMC in human-to-human communication.

In digital rhetoric, convergence is the process of merging of various separate mediated experiences in a unified environment that provides various strata (layers) of communication and production. As should be clear to any person entering any social establishment where wireless fidelity is provided and people are staring at their touch-screen mobile phones, technologies have an innate ability to intricately entwine with human processes, perhaps even to the level of creating evolving social etiquettes where some humans, waiting for someone in a physical spot and perhaps out of shyness, now prefer to look at the screen of their mobile phones than engage in social interaction with other humans. This is just a simple example of convergence between human life and technology.

Convergence happens at several contexts, which can be defined, briefly, as happening on the level of 1) production of media contexts 2) semantic modification and understanding of physical contexts 3) digital socialization contexts 4) and virtual symbolic interactionism (digital person-to-person contexts). Convergence can be witnessed in the way digital technology asks us to learn to produce content via on-the-go online web interfaces that combine various modes and media in ever-evolving interfaces. It can also be seen in semantic understanding of physical contexts when we use wireless fidelity and cloud computing networks to aid us in making decisions in physical contexts via on-the-go apps such as global positioning systems (to locate where we are or need to go) or social recommendation services (seeing ratings for restaurants or establishments). Further, we can see digital socialization convergence of physical and digital contexts in the way we learn the social etiquettes of social networks and form physical or virtual relations with people across the globe, where conversations or status updates in online contexts are now part of offline contexts as we exist both on/offline through these social networks. Lastly, we can also see virtual self-representation convergence when we engage in video games to learn how to play and continue playing through ever-increasing challenges or so-

cialize with other humans located across the globe and pursue game challenges together and so learn to represent and experience the physical self in increasingly embodied, textual and performative manners through an avatar (a "virtual" physical representation of the self) in a virtual context. In this sense, the latter convergence is that of the body as interface coupled to a computer, where we represent ourselves in a symbolic manner and engage in symbolic interaction as we perform a "Second Self" in a textual, visual, aural, gestural and non-verbal, physical manner (Goffman 1967; Turkle 1995).

In addition to the above convergence contexts, attention should also be paid to the ability to perform the "self" in various social network contexts, where a digital medium can create communication contexts that can be either strictly private, public or socially filtered (and thus a combination of private and public). Indeed, a point can be made that unless one secludes the self physically, our mobile communication are not socially filtered in the everyday world as others overhear fragments of our conversation. Likewise, social networks are similarly public in that content is easily reshared in other contexts outside of one's network. Physical and virtual communication represent similar spheres of public and private communication contexts, but should not be deemed to be private in any way or shape. Moreover, digital technologies create a "commons" of convergence of symbolic activity where medium, place, time and location cohere to create and influence human-to-human or human-computer interaction. Digital rhetoric hence sees these digital media technology converge with human life in *physical and digital* contexts.

Convergence has a profound influence on the way we interact, produce, consume and exist in the world due to the novel means of production and consumption of information that creates new global, digital literacies and contexts for digital rhetoric. Hence, an examination of the term yields an interesting way to help outline convergence in the form of 3 elements, namely: 1) convergence as production mode 2) convergence as technological medium merging and 3) convergence as a term for novel forms of human interaction due to technology.

Earlier, futurologist Alvin Toffler (1970; 1980) used the term convergence to characterize what he saw as major developments in human production. He described three major economic production transitions as a result of technology – the Agricultural Revolution, the Industrial Revolution and the Information Revolution – where the latter revolution featured increasingly globalized media, commerce and information converging as dominant means of production.

The concept of media convergence, as Jenkins (2006) has noted, originates from Ithiel de Sola Pool (1983) who defined convergence in his work *Technologies of Freedom* as a process involving a tension between "unification" and "constant change" in various separate media industries such as newspapers, print, and telephony. These industries were now confronted with changing democratization of the modes and practices of media production and the increasing role of diversification and participation in the media market. For this purpose, *divergence* and *convergence* are noted by Jenkins to have been understood by Pool "as two sides of the same coin" (p. 19). Pool's model thus creates the idea of a constant evolution and change in technology in refiguring media production as material practices and industry.

In his work *Mediamorphosis*, Fidler (1997) defines convergence as the ability of previously separate technologies (text chat, voice chat, video chat, data applications) to blend in a synergistic manner in order to produce a seamless way of interaction. If we look at the developments in mobile touchscreen phones and recognize their ability to compete with previous mobile phones, desktop computers, cameras, music players, artificial intelligence through intelligent agent devices, global positioning technologies (GPS) and geographic information systems (GIS), and their seamless integration with e-commerce and video games, one can recognize that this convergence of many media modes into single artifacts has taken place and will continue.

Further developing the concept of convergence in terms of technology and culture, Henry Jenkins (2006) notes that convergence also functions to blend human-computer activity in novel ways. In this, he mentions there are vast changes how we interact, create, consume and produce. In the introduction to his visionary *Convergence Culture* (2006), Jenkins mentions that his definition encompasses three different visions of "media convergence, participatory culture, and collective intelligence"(p.7). His book is prescient in that he takes a different approach to the argument of media as merging together argument, and instead talks about media economies where "convergence represents a cultural shift as consumers are encouraged to seek out new information and make connections among dispersed media content [and the] work—and play—spectators perform in the new media system" by seeking out and recreating content (p. 8). In addition, Jenkins' definition of "participatory culture" is linked to his notion of "collective intelligence" – he recognizes that as prosumers of media, we are not bound to "passive" media (television), but are engaged with interactive media (video games, the Internet, etc. etc.) that invite our participation and action. The culture which comes from this he terms "participatory culture" – with consequences for our relationship to intellectual content, intellectual property rights, consumptions and production of media, and media corporations. Since we now participate in our mass-media (for instance, by way of update bars that relay our thoughts through social networks on live television), Jenkins' prescient vision (along with Lanham's) is to see that we deal with an economy of attention characterized by information glut – there is so much information to be found on any topic on the Internet, that we simply "buzz" about it and media companies "feed" off this – our participation and reflection on this information – which Jenkins terms "collective intelligence" and defines as the following: "None of us can know everything; each of us knows something; and we can put the pieces together if we pool our resources and combine our skills. Collective intelligence can be seen as an alternative source of media power" (2006, p.9). Jenkin's definition of "convergence culture" thus makes place for incorporating new ways of collective producing of information and media, our changed roles as prosumers of media, and the collective ways of reflecting and communicating with each other through mass media (and predating notions of "trending topics" on social networks or important news topic bubbles or word maps displaying frequently used words on a social website). All of the above perspectives provide the idea that convergence can be applied as a concept on the scale of socioeconomic production developments, mediological developments, and human social interaction.

As is clear, from a practical perspective, the modes and practice of convergence is a part of digital rhetoric. Further, social interaction is complicated by increasing means of converging communication modes and practices. In using social networks, virtual worlds, video games, mobile computing, location-indicator services, we co-exist in spheres of now merged local/global (glocal), private/public (or a combination through social filtering), and physical/virtual (presence and telepresence) networks. In order to display the above various forms of convergence, and to represent the various spheres in which digital rhetoric can now investigate various contexts, below this chapter will outline a continuum – (a continuous sphere of human frequencies and signals of mediated communication) – convergence model.

CONVERGENCE AS A CONTINUUM MODEL FOR DIGITAL RHETORICAL CONTEXTS

For purposes of clarity, the model of convergence presented in this chapter is multifaceted and focused on production, spatial, mediological, social, personal, and rhetorical convergences as a result of the merging of human life and technology. Convergence is defined in terms of a continuum model of global production practices to local practices to physical, social, individual, rhetorical communication practices. The continuum model fits with approaching the way that digital rhetoric and globalization now function together and blend (or in the words of Liz Losh, "remix") various modes of communication together and where absolute demarcations are artificial. As multiple levels and layers of interaction exist in digital rhetoric in human-computer interaction and CMC between humans, so our digital rhetorical interactions exist in this continuum context model as part of ever-evolving shifting modes and practices (see Figure 4).

The convergence-continuum model presented here is not prescriptive, but rather descriptive in addressing the multi-faceted contexts in which human communication and interaction take place. Rather than focus on the discussion above on the interactions that happen between several layers and across networks, this model limits itself to the activity of human meaning-making as part of a continuous process. The following distinctions are made in the model:

1. **Prosumption convergence:** The merging of means of production and consumption by way of our changed relation to information-sharing as a mode of collective intelligence, information sharing, and intellectual production, socialization, work and play through computerized information sharing on a global and local scale via networks.

2. **Physical-semantic convergence:** The merging of physical space with semantic information conveyed through interfaces physically or virtually, as represented in the emergence of "smart mobs" (Rheingold, 2003) utilizing mobile technology and global positioning systems (GPS) to effect political change through social networks and on-the-go information sharing. Also, this type of

Figure 4. Convergence continuum for digital rhetorical contexts

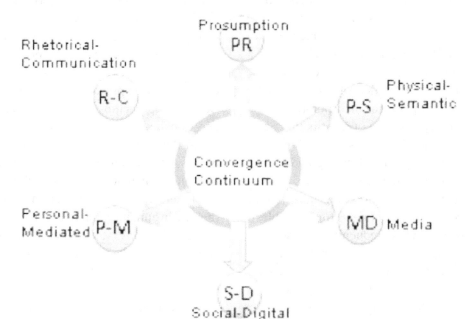

convergence can be seen in augmented reality applications wherein physical locations are layered with semantic information, such as location-aware recommender systems.

3. **Media convergence:** The merging of earlier separate technological media production (audio, video, text, animations, analog, digital etc.) in advanced integrated manners affecting communication, production, and interaction practices.

4. **Social-digital convergence:** Increasing convergence in the changing patterns in the social human-to-human interaction and communication due to digital, networked technologies, as seen in the new social etiquettes created by the convergence of human life spheres with the spheres of technology.

5. **Personal mediated convergence:** The ability (and at times, necessity) to function in networks locally and globally, privately and publically, physically and virtually at the same time in our everyday/professional lives across a multitude of platforms, networks, and mediated communication and interaction modes and practices.

6. **Rhetorical communication convergence:** Merging of modes and practices associated with orality (speech), literacy (writing/reading) with those of digitality (digital artifacts) and the logic of computer-mediated communication as discourse, production, and distribution mode and medium.

As is obvious, convergence means new digital modes of expression extending rhetoric into newer directions and activities beyond mere writing or speaking. A word of caution is needed here to emphasize that the above convergence-continuum focuses on communication contexts, and does not rely on what Henry Jenkins (2006) calls a "black-box" fallacy - one medium that combines all media. Such a convergence would not only be antithetical to the spirit of the above model in which evolving aspects of communication are used, but also be unrealistic given the varied media environments where there are new expressions and modes of thought created by different people. The development of technologies through market forces, new inventions, socioeconomics, developments and human motivations are too great and diverse to sustain such an idea. Hence, there is a strong need for developing understandings of the study of digital rhetoric in these various contexts.

A wide variety of terminology has been utilized to describe the various contexts of digital rhetoric: new media, digital media, web media, multimedia, cybertext, hypertext, persuasive technology, and digital humanities are some of the terms employed in different ways attempting to describe the purview of digital rhetoric. Based on the above perspective, digital rhetoric can be operationalized as interaction and communication in digital contexts that develops literacies through global communication technologies and sees our media landscape as one characterized by the principles of evolutionary media networks and various kinds of convergence. Studying the elements of digital rhetoric means looking at digital medium modes and practices, understanding the principles of computation, various layers of semantic meaning-making, as well as the increased physical, virtual and coded contexts, networks, platforms, interfaces, and medium affordances that provide prosumption, transmission, coding, decoding and encoding of information as human life spheres and technology converge in ever-multifaceted ways.

CONCLUSION

In conclusion, digital rhetoric is not as easily defined by simply saying that computer science needs to be added to rhetoric, or that we need to pay attention to the coded elements below the interface. There are various issues introduced by such an undertaking, among which are how to incorporate visual rhetoric where the primacy of images overpower text due to our visual senses (Arnheim, 1956; Handa, 2004). Another issue

digital rhetoric needs to address is the semiotics of multimodality introduced by various interfaces that ask us to rethink how we read multimedia "texts" as these present us with different ways of consuming and reading texts consisting of multiple images, animations, sound, gestures, and other elements based on new design practices (New London Group 2000, Kress 2003; Kress & van Leeuwen 2001). Further, the issue of spatial rhetoric asks us about the constraints and affordances of public and digital spaces, where space itself can be seen as a rhetorical construct in allowing or disallowing us certain actions in physical and virtual or computer-mediated spaces (Tuan, 1977, De Certeau, 1984) Digital rhetoric also needs to address the issues introduced by the rhetoric of embodiment and identity when using a virtual representation of the self (an avatar) where discourse is impacted by relative disclosure or anonymity through performance of the self, whether in a textual or virtual manner (Turkle 1995; Goffman, 1967). In social network interaction, digital rhetoric also needs to articulate and investigate how different cultures can meet up in computer-mediated spaces, requiring articulating the influence of cultural differences in the experience of time, space, communication styles, as well as valorizing of verbal and non-verbal interaction in digital interactions (Hofstede, 1980, 2001; Thatcher, 2011; Trompenaars & Hampden-Turner 1997).

Another issue introduced by digital rhetoric and global literacies are interactions of glocalized (global and local) discourse communities wherein principles of localization and globalized practices are merged to form their own unique discourse, behavior and etiquettes (Bhaduri, 2008). These can engender new terminology, etiquettes and standards of communication that are all impacted by increased frequency of interaction between cultures, technologies, evolving interface design practices, and should be considered from an evolutionary perspective rather than from a standards perspective. Intercultural perspectives thus inform digital literacies and practices as these continue to evolve and change as a result of intercultural interaction and help inform digital rhetoric (Thatcher, 2011). Further, digital rhetoric needs to consider critical insights from the rhetoric of technology, which has created a greater understanding of how technology itself is built-in with human intentions and is rhetorical itself. These critical perspectives provide digital rhetoric with an important touchstone on how to investigate, study, and possibly help create technologies that take into account the consequences of the design and dissemination of technologies for human purposes in ethical ways (Bijke, 1997; Feenberg, 1991; Heidegger, 1982). Further, digital rhetoric needs to consider the rhetoric of science, which argues science as inherently a rhetorical practice dominated by research paradigms guided by metaphor and rhetorical practices, as it provides a bridge to sciences which have heretofore been ignored or deemed as not related to rhetoric, such as has been argued in this chapter, the study of computer science (Kuhn, 1962; Latour & Woolgar, 1986). Taking into account the rhetoric of science's bridging of rhetoric with science, this chapter uses novel insights drawn from computer science, human-computer interaction (HCI), interaction design, and computer-mediated communication (CMC). These provide an important bridge for digital rhetoric in investigating and articulating some of the above issues and studying them from various ethnographic, design, communication and computer science perspectives to form a more fully developed idea of the directions that digital rhetoric can take us.

Hence, digital rhetoric should focus on digital environments where discourse functions in terms of symbolic actions (rather than spoken or written language). Only by seeing rhetoric as *interaction* do we embrace the way digital technologies provide new symbolic ways of communicating in textual, visual, gestural, or physical ways in mediated environments. Further, from a systems perspective, digital rhetoric adds several different layers to communication by adding computer-mediated communication where various elements influence creation, transmission, noise and reception of semantic meanings. Rather than focus on human verbal action as originating discourse, digital rhetoric is comprised of all actions that happen – whether human or computer initiated and functions on the spectrum of the "At/Through" elements mentioned by Lanham, and as this chapter argues, needs to be extended to a convergence-continuum to study the contexts in which digital rhetorical interaction and communication take place. As has been argued in this chapter, while our interfaces may appear to us as transparent windows for us to make our utterances, they are social constructs supported by an infrastructure that influences communication and interaction by both interpenetrating and structuring our actions as well as allowing us to interpenetrate and re-structure digital by our actions. For this purpose, this chapter speaks of digital rhetoric as characterized by various evolving convergence contexts based on how we produce, consume, explore space as physical element or semantic information, how we deal with media changes, how we incorporate digital technologies into our social lives, how we perform ourselves through mediation in public and private spheres, and how we use rhetorical techniques for communication and interaction in our public and private life.

Lastly, the use and continuous innovation and adaption of novel digital technologies requires that we look beyond the human as a speaking subject and look at how digital artifacts help, interact, guide, constrain, and extend our capabilities into newer dimensions in order for us to continue their use in ethical and productive ways. This requires us to define an ethics of digital rhetoric, as we are utilizing and designing technologies for the above communication purposes, we need to think about how these technologies are implemented and used for utilitarian purposes, provide transparency where needed and foster ecological guidelines for sustaining human life on this planet. For this purpose, it is better to speak of digital "rhetorics" wherein newer evolutionary principles are included to form a more coherent view on how humans may utilize digital technology in more informed ways as well as be informed by these technologies.

ACKNOWLEDGMENT

This chapter is dedicated to Jan Verhulsdonck, M.D., and my lovely wife Jennifer Gomez. The author would like to thank Dr. Eugene Cunnar and Dr. Matthew McCool for their insights and help in creating this chapter, as well as the faculty and staff of the Rhetoric and Writing Studies Department at the University of Texas at El Paso for allowing me to teach a course which touched upon a lot of the above concepts.

REFERENCES

Aarseth, E. (1997). *Cybertext—Perspectives on ergodic literature*. Baltimore, MD: Johns Hopkins University Press.

Anderson, D. (2003). Prosumer approaches to new media composition: Consumption and production in continuum. *Kairos: A Journal of Rhetoric, Technology, and Pedagogy, 8*(1).

Aristotle, . (2006). *On rhetoric* (G. Kennedy, Trans.). Oxford, UK: Oxford University Press.

Arnheim, R. (1956). *Art and visual perception*. London: Faber.

Bakhtin, M. (1973). *Marxism and the philosophy of language*. Cambridge, MA: Harvard University Press.

Barthes, R. (1977). The death of the author. In R. Barthes (Ed.), *Image, music text* (pp. 90–99). London: Fontana.

Benjamin, W. (1968). The work of art in the age of mechanical reproduction. In H. Arendt (Ed.), *Illuminations* (pp. 214–218). London: Fontana.

Bhaduri, S. (Ed.). (2008). *Negotiating glocalization: Views from language, literature and cultural studies*. Delhi, India: Anthem.

Bijke, W. (1997). *Of Bicycles, bakelites and bulbs. Toward a theory of sociotechnological change*. Cambridge, MA: MIT Press.

Bødker, S. (1989). A human activity approach to user interfaces. *Human-Computer Interaction, 4*.

Bødker, S. (1991). *Through the interface: A human activity approach to user interface design*. Hillsdale, NJ: Lawrence Erlbaum.

Bogost, I. (2007). *Persuasive games: The expressive power of video games*. Cambridge, MA: MIT Press.

Bolter, J. D., & Grusin, R. (2000). *Remediation: Understanding new media*. Cambridge, MA: MIT Press.

Burke, K. (1969). *A grammar of motives*. Berkeley, CA: University of California Press.

Burke, K. (1966, 2001). Language as symbolic action. In P. Bizzell & B. Herzberg (Eds.). The rhetorical tradition (2nd ed.) (pp. 1340-47). Boston, MA: Bedford/ St. Martin's

Clark, H. H., & Brennan, S. (1991). Grounding in communication. In L. Resnick, J. Levine, & S. Teasley (Eds.), *Perspectives on socially shared cognition* (pp. 127–149). Washington, DC: American Psychological Association. doi:10.1037/10096-006

Cole, M., & Engeström, Y. (1991). A cultural-historical approach to distributed cognition. In G. Salomon (Ed.), *Distributed Cognition* (pp. 1–47). Cambridge: Cambridge University Press.

Cummings, R. (2006). Coding with power: Toward a rhetoric of computer coding and composition. *Computers and Composition, 23*, 430–443. doi:10.1016/j.compcom.2006.08.002

Daft, R. L., & Lengel, R. H. (1986). Organizational information requirements, media richness and structural design. *Management Science, 32*(5), 554–571. doi:10.1287/mnsc.32.5.554

Daniell, B. (1999). Narratives of literacy: Connecting composition to culture. *College Composition and Communication, 50*(3), 393–410. doi:10.2307/358858

De Certeau, M. (1984). *The practice of everyday life* (S. Rendall, Trans.). Los Angeles, CA: University of California Press.

Dennis, A., & Valacich, J. (1999). Rethinking media richness: Towards a theory of media synchronicity. In R. Sprague (Ed.), *Proceedings of the 32nd Hawaii International Conference on Systems Science* (pp. 48-57). Los Alamitos, CA: IEEE Computer Society.

Derrida, J. (1967). Structure, sign and play in the human sciences. In J. Derrida (Ed.), *Writing and difference* (pp. 278–293, 339). (A. Bass, Trans.). Chicago: University of Chicago Press.

DeSanctis, G., & Poole, M. S. (1994). Capturing the complexity in advanced technology use: Adaptive structuration theory. *Organization Science, 5*(2), 121–147. doi:10.1287/orsc.5.2.121

Engeström, Y., Miettinen, R., & Punamäki, R. (1999). *Perspectives on activity theory.* Cambridge, UK: Cambridge University Press. doi:10.1017/CBO9780511812774

Faigley, L. (1986). Competing theories of process: A critique and proposal. *College English, 48*, 527–541. doi:10.2307/376707

Feenberg, A. (1991). *Critical theory of technology.* New York: Oxford University Press.

Fidler, R. (1997). *Mediamorphosis: Understanding new media.* Newbury Park, CA: Sage.

Fleckenstein, K. S. (2003). *Embodied literacies: Imageword and a poetics of teaching.* Carbondale, IL: Southern Illinois University Press.

Fulk, J., Steinfield, C. W., Schmitz, J., & Power, J. G. (1987). A social information processing model of media use in organizations. *Communication Research, 14*(5), 529–552. doi:10.1177/009365087014005005

Gee, J. P. (2003). *What video games have to teach us about learning and literacy.* New York: Palgrave Macmillan.

Giddens, A. (1984). *The constitution of society: Outline of the theory of structuration.* Berkeley, CA: University of California Press.

Goffman, E. (1967). *Interaction ritual.* New York: Pantheon.

Gurak, L. (2001). *Cyberliteracy: Navigating the internet with awareness.* New Haven, CT: Yale University Press.

Handa, C. (2004). *Visual rhetoric in a digital world.* Boston, MA: Bedford/ St. Martin's.

Harrison, S., & Dourish, P. (1996). Re-place-ing space: The roles of place and space in collaborative systems. In *Proceedings of the 1996 ACM conference on Computer Supported Cooperative Work* (pp.67-76). Boston, MA: ACM Press.

Hart-Davidson, B., & Krause, S. D. (2004). Re: The future of computers and writing: A multivocal textumentary. *Computers and Composition, 21*, 147–160. doi:10.1016/j.compcom.2003.08.008

Havelock, E. (1963). *Preface to Plato.* Cambridge, MA: Harvard University Press.

Hawisher, G., & Selfe, C. (Eds.). (2000). *Global literacies and the World-Wide Web.* New York: Routledge.

Heidegger, M. (1982). *The question concerning technology, and other essays*. New York: Perennial.

Herring, S. C. (2001). Computer-mediated discourse. In D. Schiffrin, D. Tannen, & H. Hamilton (Eds.), *The Handbook of Discourse Analysis* (pp. 612–634). London: Blackwell.

Hiltz, S. R., & Turoff, M. (1978). *The network nation: Human communication via computer*. Reading, MA: Addison-Wesley.

Hofstede, G. (1980). *Culture's consequences: International differences in work-related values*. Beverly Hills, CA: Sage.

Hofstede, G. (2001). *Culture's consequences: Comparing values, behaviors, institutions and organizations across nations*. Thousand Oaks, CA: Sage.

Jenkins, H. (2006). *Convergence culture: Where old and new media collide*. New York: New York University Press.

Johnson-Eilola, J. (2005). *Datacloud: Toward a new theory of online work*. Creskill, NJ: Hampton.

Juul, J. (2005). *Half-real: Video games between real rules and fictional worlds*. Cambridge, MA: MIT Press.

Kaptelinin, V. (1996). Activity theory: Implications for human-computer interaction. In B. Nardi (Ed.), *Context and consciousness: Activity theory and human-computer interaction* (pp. 103–116). Cambridge, MA: MIT Press.

Kittler, F. (1999). *Gramophone, film, typewriter*. Palo Alto, CA: Stanford University Press.

Kock, N. (2005). Media richness or media naturalness? The evolution of our biological communication apparatus and its influence on our behavior toward e-communication tools. *IEEE Transactions on Professional Communication, 48*(2), 117–130. doi:10.1109/TPC.2005.849649

Kress, G. (2003). *Literacy in the new media age*. London: Routledge. doi:10.4324/9780203164754

Kress, G., & van Leeuwen, T. (2001). *Multimodal discourse: The modes and media of contemporary communication*. London: Arnold.

Kuhn, T. S. (1962). *The structure of scientific revolution*. Chicago, London: University of Chicago.

Landow, G. (1993). *Hypertext 3.0*. Baltimore, MD: Johns Hopkins University Press.

Lanham, R. A. (1992). Digital rhetoric: Theory, practice and property. In M. C. Tuman (Ed.), *Literacy online: The promise and perils of reading and writing with computers* (pp. 221–243). Pittsburgh, PA: Pittsburgh University Press.

Lanham, R. A. (1993). *The electronic word: Democracy, technology and the arts*. Chicago, IL: University of Chicago Press. doi:10.7208/chicago/9780226469126.001.0001

Lanham, R. A. (2006). *The economics of attention: Style and substance in the age of information*. Chicago, IL: University of Chicago Press.

Latour, B. (1998). *Actor network theory: A few clarifications*. Retrieved from: http://www.nettime.org/Lists-Archives/nettime-l-9801/msg00019.html

Latour, B. (2005). *Reassembling the social: An introduction to actor-network-theory*. Oxford, UK: Oxford UP.

Latour, B., & Woolgar, S. (1986). *Laboratory life: The construction of scientific facts*. Princeton, NJ: Princeton University Press.

Laurel, B. (2003). The six elements and causal relations among them. In N. Wardrip Fruin, & N. Montfort (Eds.), *The new media reader* (pp. 564–571). Cambridge, MA: MIT Press.

Leont'ev, A. (1981). *Problems of the development of mind*. Moscow, Russia: Progress Press.

Lessig, L. (1999). *Code and other laws of cyberspace*. New York, NY: Basic.

Losh, E. (2009). *VirtualPolitik*. Cambridge, MA: MIT Press.

Losh, E. (2012) Defining digital rhetoric with 20-20 hindsight. *Digital Rhetoric Collaborative*. Retrieved from: http://www.digitalrhetoriccollaborative.org/2012/06/25/defining-digital-rhetoric-with-20-20-hindsight/

Manovich, L. (2001). *The language of new media*. Cambridge, MA: MIT Press.

McGrath, J. E. (1991). Time, interaction, and performance (tip): A theory of groups. *Small Group Research*, *22*(2), 147–174. doi:10.1177/1046496491222001

McLuhan, M. (1964). *Understanding media: The extensions of man*. New York: Signet.

Murray, J. (1998). *Hamlet on the holodeck: The future of narrative in cyberspace*. Cambridge, MA: MIT Press.

Murray, J. (2012). *Inventing the medium: Principles of interaction design as a cultural practice*. Cambridge, MA: MIT Press.

Nardi, B. A. (1996). Activity theory and human-computer interaction. In B. Nardi (Ed.), *Context and consciousness: Activity theory and human-computer interaction* (pp. 7–16). Cambridge, MA: MIT Press.

Nardi, B. A., & O'Day, V. (2000). *Information ecologies: Using technology with heart*. Cambridge, MA: MIT Press.

New London Group. (2000). A pedagogy of multiliteracies: Designing social futures. In B. Cope, & M. Kalantzis (Eds.), *Multiliteracies: Literacy learning and the design of social futures* (pp. 9–37). London, New York: Routledge.

Norman, D. (1988). *The psychology of everyday things*. New York: Basic Books.

Ong, W. J. (1982). *Orality and literacy: The technologizing of the word* (T. Hawkes, Ed.). New York: Methuen. doi:10.4324/9780203328064

Pool, I. (1983). *Technologies of freedom*. Cambridge, MA: Harvard University Press.

Postmes, T., Spears, R., & Lea, M. (1999). Social identity, group norms, and deindividuation: Lessons from computer-mediated communication for social influence in the group. In N. Ellemers, R. Spears, & B. Doosje (Eds.), *Social identity: Context, commitment, content* (pp. 164–183). Oxford, UK: Blackwell.

Preece, J., Rogers, Y., & Sharp, H. (2007). *Interaction design: Beyond human-computer interaction*. New York, NY: John Wiley & Sons.

Rheingold, H. (2003). *Smart mobs: The next social revolution*. New York: Basic.

Selber, S. (2004). *Multiliteracies for a digital age*. Carbondale, IL: Southern Illinois University Press.

Selfe, C., & Selfe, R. (1994). The politics of the interface: Power and its exercise in electronic contact zones. *College Composition and Communication*, *45*(4), 480–504. doi:10.2307/358761

Short, J. A., Williams, E., & Christie, B. (1976). *The social psychology of telecommunications*. New York, NY: John Wiley.

Spinuzzi, C. (2013). *Topsight: A guide to studying, diagnosing, and fixing information flow in organizations*. Austin, TX: Self-Published.

Sproull, L., & Kiesler, S. (1992). *Connections: New ways of working in the networked organization*. Cambridge, MA: MIT press.

Sullivan, P., & Porter, J. (1997). *Opening spaces: Writing technologies and critical research practices*. Greenwich, CT: Ablex.

Thatcher, B. (2005). Situating L2 writing in global communication technologies. *Computers and Composition*, 22(3), 279–295. doi:10.1016/j.compcom.2005.05.002

Thatcher, B. (2011). *Intercultural rhetoric and professional communication: Technological advances and organizational behavior*. Hershey, PA: IGI-Global Press. doi:10.4018/978-1-61350-450-5

Toffler, A. (1970). *Future shock*. New York: Random.

Toffler, A. (1980). *The third wave*. New York: William Morrow.

Trompenaars, F., & Hampden-Turner, C. (1997). *Riding the waves of culture*. New York, NY: McGraw-Hill.

Tuan, Y. (1977). *Space and place: The perspective of experience*. Minneapolis, MN: University of Minnesota Press.

Turing, A. (1988). Computing machinery and intelligence. In D. R. Hofstadter, & D. C. Dennet (Eds.), *The mind's eye: Fantasies and reflections on self and soul* (pp. 53–67). New York: Bantam.

Turkle, S. (1995). *Life on the screen: Identity in the age of the internet*. New York: Simon & Schuster.

Turnley, M. (2011). Towards a mediological method: A framework for critical engaging dimensions of a medium. *Computers and Composition*, 28, 126–144. doi:10.1016/j.compcom.2011.04.002

Ulmer, G. (1989). *Teletheory: Grammatology in the age of video*. New York, NY: Routledge.

Verhulsdonck, G. (2007). Issues of designing gestures into online interactions: Implications for communicating in virtual environments. In D. Novick, & C. Spinuzzi (Eds.), *Proceedings of Special Interest Group Documentation and Online Communication (SIGDOC) 2007* (pp. 26–33). New York: ACM Press. doi:10.1145/1297144.1297151

von Neumann, J. (1959, orig.1928). On the theory of games of strategy. In A. W. Tucker & R. D. Luce (Eds.), Contributions to the theory of games, vol. 4 (pp. 13- 42). Princeton, NJ: Princeton University Press.

von Neumann, J., & Morgenstern, O. (1944). *Theory of games and economic behavior*. Princeton, NJ: Princeton University Press.

Vygotsky, L. (1978). *Mind in society: The development of higher psychological processes*. Cambridge, MA: Harvard University Press.

Walker, J. et al. (2011). Computers and composition 20/20: A conversation piece, or what some very smart people have to say about the future. *Computers and Composition*, 28, 327–346. doi:10.1016/j.compcom.2011.09.004

Weaver, W., & Shannon, C. E. (1963). *The Mathematical theory of communication*. Chicago, IL: University of Illinois Press.

Winograd, T. (1997). From computing machinery to interaction design. In P. Denning, & R. Metcalfe (Eds.), *Beyond calculation: The next fifty years of computing* (pp. 149–162). New York: Springer-Verlag. doi:10.1007/978-1-4612-0685-9_12

Zappen, J. (2005). Digital rhetoric: Toward an integrated theory. *Technical Communication Quarterly*, 14(3), 319–325. doi:10.1207/s15427625tcq1403_10

KEY TERMS AND DEFINITIONS

Affordance: Key concept by Donald Norman for design elements that we can borrow from everyday contexts to create cognitive schemas that will allow end-users of an interface to quickly grasp the uses of an interface element by clear use of metaphor.

Convergence: The process of converging human life with media; the various contexts of communication that take place on a continuum.

Computation: The process by which older media are incorporated into computer code and become modes of signification and discourse, by for instance, filters to make movies look older than they really are.

Computer-Mediated Communication: The study of group and individual communication processes across various computer media such as chat, instant messaging, etc.

Continuum: A whole spectrum of frequencies encompassing kinesthetic, gestural, aural, audio-visual, symbolic, textual, visual, spatial actions are performed.

Digital Medium: Term used by Janet Murray to incorporate "new media" under the study of digital media – which reconfigures older print media into computer code.

Digital Rhetoric: The study of human and computer interaction and communication as co-constructive acts involving multiple networks, platforms, contexts, processes of encoding/decoding wherein interactivity reconfigures rhetorical actions.

HCI: Human-computer interaction studies the way processes can be optimized by using guidelines from the real world. See Interaction Design.

Interaction Design: An overarching discipline that combines Human-Computer interaction, Ergonomics, Social Psychology, Architecture, Computer-Mediated Communication and other disciplines, to make sound design decisions on creating computer interactions that are meaningful and useful for humans.

Mediological: The process of looking at modes and media from a perspective involving seeing these practices as evolving, material, and ever-changing.

Chapter 2
Engagement Design:
Toward a Holistic Model for Digital Communication Design

Curtis R. Newbold
Westminster College, USA

ABSTRACT

Evolutions in digital communications since the beginning of the century require information designers to think about the possibilities that digital technologies present and the boundaries they allow communicators to appropriately bend or even subvert. Arguing for a more holistic and humanistic approach to digital communications, this chapter approaches the subject with a proposed theory for "engagement design," a design process that integrates the expedience of usability, utility, and cognition with human experience, rhetoric, and emotion.

INTRODUCTION

In an emergent, design-centric economy, the time has officially arrived for those in science- and technology-oriented disciplines to peer out from the shadows of communication protocols, grammars, and methods traditionally brought to us from long-standing cultural paradigms. Historical Western practices of communicative precision and expedience in the sciences date at least as far back as the 17th century to the development of the Royal Society of London, where communication protocols were established to diminish rhetoric's "parasitic" influence on technical and scientific texts. This ancient establishment of conventions and methods may be labeled as one of the primary catalysts for the wedge that divides the humanities from the sciences today; it is also an antiquated standard that restricts instrumental communications from holistically engaging and instructing its recipients.

DOI: 10.4018/978-1-4666-4916-3.ch002

Copyright © 2014, IGI Global. Copying or distributing in print or electronic forms without written permission of IGI Global is prohibited.

In the modern era, a "digital age," procedural and grammatical approaches to argumentation (as in the Introduction-Method-Results-Discussion [IMRD] format of the scientific method) have not only continued, but in many disciplines have been refined, systematized, and methodically integrated into higher education's communication curricula—frequently at the expense of ethical awareness and humanization. As the new millennium unfolds, a continued march in this direction can only, sadly, perpetuate the issues raised in Steven Katz's (1992) important article on the ethics of expedience, where human beings seem mechanically removed from communications in order to promote efficiency or, worse, shroud ethical consequences of science and technology.

Fortunately, the crescendo of digital rhetoric as a field of inquiry in the past two decades has provided an exceptional opportunity to re-evaluate the communication practices and pedagogies that have placed a longstanding chokehold on disciplines that Moore (1996) has labeled as *instrumental* (where the communication's intention has typically been to "govern, guide, control, and help people execute physical actions"—usually communication fields related to education, science, technology, engineering, and math). For those who work or teach in such instrumental disciplines, communication design (and by "design," I mean the confluence of the visual, the textual, and/or the interactive) is often awkwardly pitted between two historically conflicting ideologies: rhetoric and objectivity. On the one side, instrumental communicators are being told to be more humanistic, to use creativity, values, and cultural judgment to effectively and ethically persuade their users; on the other side, instrumental communicators are being told that communication is like a "window pane," clear and unambiguous and that objectivity, cognition, and expedience should reign (Miller, 2004).

Moore, in 1996, identified the growing problem: the search for humanism in instrumental communications moved disciplines away from objectivity and closer to rhetoric at the expense of, well, instrumentalism. Fighting off the "expedience" stigma, the goal for practitioners and academics, of course, was to "make it more palatable to themselves and to other academic audiences" (p. 100) by championing humanism. Yet the reality then, as is now, is that industry still has a pressing need: clarity-driven communications that appropriately guide users toward intended actions. They need communications that promote expedience—cognition, usability, and clarity.

Into the new millennium, scholarship and pedagogical philosophies have largely advocated for rhetoric, but the practicality of instrumental communications coupled with industry and societal needs has pressed textbooks and classroom assignments to perpetuate the rigidity of rules, formats, guidelines, rubrics, and protocols. To complicate the matter, in a digital and global era, the design of communication is rarely isolated to writing. As such, we have seen similar restrictive approaches to writing bleed into visual communication. Information design in instrumentally-oriented disciplines have frequently been treated as if they could be reduced to a universally applied grammar (see Kress and van Leeuwen, 2006) and have even been compared to mathematics, "not tied to unique features of a particular language or culture" (Tufte, 1990). Such perspectives are not without merit, of course—they provide productive insight into the fundamentals of visual literacy. But it does not take much imagination to recognize the limitations of such formulaic (and simplistic) approaches to information design.

Such restrictive, non-rhetorical methods of communication design inhibit holistic approaches (not simply left-brained, analytical, but also inclusive of right-brained, conceptual) and engaging viewing and learning experiences (Daniel Pink's [2005] wonderfully insightful exposition on this in *A Whole New Mind* is worth mentioning here). Conversely, extreme favoritism of rhetorical and emotive approaches precludes the need to actually make communications function well in practical settings—such as in education, or technical communications, or wayfinding design, for example. What is needed is an integrated model of communication design. Modern technology has provided enormous potential for immersing—and *engaging*—communication participants and we have an obligation to take advantage. One only needs to look to Harvard University's animated *Life of Cell* (2006) series (an innovatively artistic approach to cell biology instruction through mesmerizing computer graphics and music) to see the instructive *and* experiential value in integrating rigorous science with aesthetic rhetoric.

At least this much is evident: digital technologies are providing new opportunities to converge scientific rigor with artistic manipulation in such a way that the design of communication has a much more holistically humanistic potential. In the following pages, I evaluate how we can design communications through the confluence of method and human experience in what I label as "Engagement Design." This chapter is devoted to establishing a theory and strategy for understanding and employing engagement into communication design, particularly in instrumental disciplines. The theory of engagement design that follows explores complex, humanistically intrinsic faculties—*pleasure*, *enjoyment*, and *play*—as they relate to human instinct, desire, and experience. Furthermore it integrates what I label as the extrinsic factors, *usability* and *cognition*, that must be balanced against the intrinsic. I further establish a definition and heuristic for engagement that might be used to break down the effectiveness of the design of digital communications. Finally, I establish a direction we may wish to go next as we consider further research and evaluation of a theory of engagement.

RHETORIC AND ENGAGEMENT

In his provocative 2001 declaration about the meaning of experience design, Nathan Shedroff (2001) helped pave the avenue for a rethinking of the way in which we engage in (or design engagement for) communication. In some of his opening remarks in *Experience Design*, Shedroff pronounced a truism perhaps so simple that we often overlook it when designing instrumental communications: "At the very least," he says, "think of an experience as requiring an *attraction*, an *engagement*, and a *conclusion*" (p. 4, italics mine). Shedroff further quotes John Dewey: "Everything depends on the *quality* of [an] experience" (qtd. in Shedroff, p. 5). These are carefully selected terms. And even though these terms express a sense of narrative, Shedroff is talking about more than a beginning, middle, and end—more, we might infer, than an experience or a happening, something much more akin to persuasion and invention. That "quality" is framed within the level of engagement, the level at which the user is productively seduced by the information, sensing personal satisfaction, grasping and retaining new knowledge, and immersing herself within the context of the information—so much so that learning is attainable and experiential value is achieved. This perspective is a far cry from the traditional instrumental model, where outcomes seem so paramount that attraction and engagement are left entirely out of the communication equation.

The instrumental communicator is faced with the concept (or perhaps enigma) of engagement every time he or she approaches the construction of a digital communication. The sad—and offensive—stigma, of course, placed on instrumental communicators, has been that they are trained grammatologists (in the most perfunctory, mechanical sense of the word) whose job it is to strip language of its rhetoric and communicate, windowpane style, in the clearest language possible. They are, as the stereotype goes, trade professionals, inverse-pyramid copywriters, ink slingers, and wordsmiths. Instruction about the *design* of information in professional and academic settings has perpetuated the stigma. "Engagement," and "experience," are terms that traditionally have had a more ancillary, backburner, or even, to some, a non-existent role in instrumental communication. "Usability," "clarity," and "efficiency," do not just steer the communication design discussion, they typically commandeer it. Consider the following statement in a widely used technical communication handbook:

When you plan, write, and design a piece of communication…you are creating a communication product. Like any other product, people will use it only if they can find what they need, understand the language, follow the instructions, and read the graphics. In other words, communication products must be usable. Usability means that 'people who use the product can do so quickly and easily to accomplish their own tasks.' (Gurack and Lannon, 2007, p. 35)

"Quick," "easy," usable," "readable," "understandable." No doubt, these terms have value and a respectable status within the disciplines. But are they *all* that matter? Will pulling away from or adding rhetoric and design to these domineering characteristics somehow infect, distort, or diminish the communication? Such a fear is likely rooted in a philosophy engendered by Francis Bacon: "Words plainly force and overrule the understanding, and throw all into confusion, and lead men away into numberless empty controversies and idle fancies" (*Novum Organum* section XLIII). It is a conundrum similar to what Walter Gropius faced when establishing the Bauhaus movement in architecture: when utility reigned,

designers were pigeonholed into an ideology (where aesthetics were considered superfluous) that created very functional but equally ugly and static spaces. The Bauhaus philosophy was to unite utility with meaning in order to improve the overall human experience. Similar ought to be the goal of communications in an era where technology conveniently allows for much more dynamic construction of content and form.

It seems that the age-old rift between science and art has, in instrumental communication disciplines, morphed into a schism that doesn't allow for the imbrication of both usability and aesthetics. The former, after all, resists rhetoric; the latter embraces it. Isn't there a contradiction, the argument goes, between clarity, conciseness, and functionality and creativity-prone ambiguity, art, innovation, fantasy, and persuasion? In the emerging field of information design, where discussions about creativity seem more common, there is still often a clear split the art-science dichotomy; in clear, if not blatant resistance to the methodical design ideologies proposed by those in Tufte's (2010) corner, the opponents follow Mike Cooley's (2000) admonition: information design should foster "intuition, subjective judgment, tacit knowledge, dreams, imagination, and purpose" (p. 60). Engagement design, as a proposed theory for effective and humanistic communication in the digital era, suggests that there is no reason why the seemingly discordant perspectives cannot and should not harmonize.

Arguing in favor of Brenda Dervin's (2000) assessment that human beings make sense out information by designing it rather than simply finding it, I propose engagement design as a model that embraces the ontology of human understanding with the psychology of human action. That is to say, engagement amalgamates the rhetorical canons (invention, arrangement, style, memory, and delivery) with cognitive science. In rhetoric, we talk about *ethos*, *pathos*, *logos*, and *kairos* as the communicative pillars for affecting response and understanding. In psychology, world-renowned researcher Donald Norman (2004) identifies the pillars as *visceral*, *behavioral*, and *reflective* reactions to design that determine how any given design speaks to us. From either perspective, it's hard to deny that communication and understanding happen within an intrinsic, ontological sphere (affected by our culture, upbringing, and general worldview) balanced against the extrinsic nature of design practicality. Richard Saul Wurman (2001), grandfather of information design theory, put it this way: "Interest defies all rules of memorization" (p. 84). What a theory of engagement design allows for is a repurposed way of approaching communication design as a holistic endeavor. In other words, design with engagement in mind rhetorically persuades us to think and act idiosyncratically as human beings do while (simultaneously) physically and cognitively placing purposeful boundaries around interpretation and experience in order to direct understanding toward the desired outcome.

In a time where the production of nearly everything we make and study—architecture, molecular organisms, even nuclear testing—is mediated through a computer screen, our humanistic role in creativity and design is becoming more and more blurred. Digital technologies have only exacerbated the ideological impasse that comes with simulation. As Sherry Turkle (2009) so expertly argued in her work *Simulation and Its Discontents*: "The more powerful our tools become, the harder it is to imagine the world without them" (p. 8). We, especially those raised in the PC era, have become so accustomed to creating (designing, building, sculpting, framing) with a monitor, mouse, and keyboard, that it is hard to believe that engineers and architects actually used to design (draw up) and calculate by hand. Users, likewise, are accustomed to learning in much the same way—through some kind of mediated instruction, banking-method style, rather than through self-discovery. Of course, this inundation of simulation burdens our cultures with a generational divide that argues between the values of the "old way" versus the new.

Disciplines that deal directly with instrumental communications cannot avoid this design conundrum. Most professionals that are required to design something, whatever that might be (in disciplines from biology to physics to marketing), will be faced with the repercussions and benefits of mechanical reproduction. Some will continue to argue that something very human is lost in the designing and using of technologies where simulation is present. And, many (see Paul Virilio's [1994] *Vision Machine* or Baudrillard's [2010] *Simulation and Simulacra*) will have very compelling arguments. Yet the computing power of technology creates such incredible exhilaration for possibility that there is no denying it is here to stay. The expedience that comes with technologies that calculate, code, and shape the user's world is both economically efficient and fascinating. It suggests a human potential to build and create at a pace never before witnessed. The ability to replicate, reproduce, and distribute images of the real world at a precision of subatomic proportions or at light year distances extends to infinity the human potential to learn and to build. It also means that technology is replacing the human senses, tactile experiences with the real world, emotions, a sense of ownership over design, and, ultimately, the ability to be creative.

Thu, we must ask ourselves: is it possible to use design technology in such a way that the expedience of simulation and the ethics of humanism can both be, harmoniously, preserved? Can what has been lost (or is being lost) be regained through concerted efforts to employ *engagement* in such communications? If the inevitability of mechanical reproduction is an obvious fact of life for communicators and the users for whom they design instrumental communications, then the ability to engage the user is not just a question about a quality experience, it is about an ethical choice to help the user to learn, to remember, and to enjoy the experience. Otherwise, instrumental communicators might find that their approaches to communication design are falling into an undesirable category—a functional one but one that doesn't inspire the overall human condition. As Patrick Jordan (2000) has argued, "Usability-based approaches…encourage a limited view of the person using the product. This is—by implication if not intention—dehumanizing" (p. 7).

Instrumental communication disciplines are, of course, moving in the right direction. In 1979, Carolyn Miller (2000) published a seminal article in the field of technical writing that began moving technical communication away from expedience, towards a richer understanding of what the field might and should look like. She argued for a more cultural, rhetorical, communal understanding of technical writing. "The teaching of technical or scientific writing," she says, "becomes more than the inculcation of a set of skills; it becomes a kind of enculturation" (p. 22). Instrumental communication has been moving in that "humanistic" direction ever since. Thirty-plus years after Miller's arguments, it may seem that we have made progress indeed. Most instrumental communication textbooks balance an understanding of a user-centered approach and usability. Few would now argue that rhetoric and user-centeredness don't play an important role in the disciplines. But we have not arrived yet where we need to be. One of the greatest challenges, it seems, is that our communication design instruction and praxis has been guided, at best, with fuzzy roadmaps. We haven't had a communication design framework from which to build our pedagogy and practice; put another way, we have needed an exoskeleton of both utility and meaning that we can work together to flesh out. That is the, admittedly, challenging but necessary scope of the pages of this chapter that remain.

As it may be inferred from the above paragraphs, engagement is not a superficial application that can be easily applied to instrumental communications. Rather, it is complexly associated with human faculties that encourage learning and define meaning. As such, it must be pointed out that a truly representative theory of engagement design ought to be influenced and informed by the many disciplines that study human understanding in the digital era: rhetoric and communication yes, but also human-computer interaction, educational psychology, cognitive science, social science, art, environmental design, and others. Because it is unlikely that any scholar is well-versed in each of these diverse fields, myself included, the model that follows is meant to be viewed as a Burkean discussion-starter in a very multidisciplinary parlor.

The framework for a model of engagement design, based on the discussion above, must be viewed as an amalgamation of the often-polarizing perspectives of human understanding: meaning (where the communication recipient interprets and values a message) and utility (where the recipient makes logical sense out of and can act upon a message). Meaning, from this perspective, seems ontological, intrinsic to human experience with the world and affected by individual idiosyncrasies such as personality, taste, and culture. The model of engagement design explores three fundamental *intrinsic* faculties: pleasure, enjoyment, and play. These intrinsic faculties are then further framed within an *extrinsic* shell, the communication paradigm that frames how information is represented; these extrinsic elements are communication design protocols designed intentionally to affect cognition and response—usability, logic, and environment.

INTRINSIC HUMANISTIC DESIGN

Communication design elements that affect intrinsic response—pleasure, enjoyment, and play—may at first seem non-rhetorical and thus outside the instrumental communicator's purview (aren't they, after all, uniquely tied to a person's inalterable worldview, values system, and personality?). But conscious awareness of how communication design causes physiological and emotional reactions to information is undoubtedly an important part of understanding one's audience. As Aristotle taught us, all communicators are equipped with available means to persuade another to act or think differently. Researchers and theorists have taught us that certain communication design elements (images, colors, typography, and so forth) make experiences with information more affective, memorable, and worthwhile. Using their available means to evoke pleasure, enjoyment, and play, instrumental communicators have the ability to strengthen a given communication's effectiveness. A commonly referenced phenomenon in psychology, after all, is the *aesthetic-usability effect*. The nicer something looks, the more positively it affects our instrinsic reactions, and the better it seems to communicate.

Donald Norman has suggested that, perhaps more powerful than the usability of a product, is our emotional response to its aesthetic design. Using his terms, he suggests that people have visceral, behavioral, and reflective reactions to designs and that designers ought to be cognizant of each. Pleasure is much like the visceral reaction—a non-logical, fleeting and emotional response to design. Enjoyment is much like the behavioral reaction—once involved with a design, we determine if we like using it (is it easy to look at or does it feel nice while using it?) Play is a component of Norman's reflective reaction—it makes us like a design because it tells a story, or gives us something to talk about. We reflect on the design because it was fun, playful, or otherwise unique and memorable. Lidwell, Holden, and Butler (2003) put it this way: "Always aspire to create aesthetic designs. Aesthetic designs are perceived as easier to use, are more readily accepted and used over time, and promote creative thinking and problem solving" (p. 20). Aesthetics, the collective composition of visual elements of design, affect how pleasurable, enjoyable, and playful a communication design is.

Pleasure

Because of its ability to immediately grab attention and affect personal taste and gut reactions, pleasure stands paramount to effective design decisions.

Pleasure encourages users to continue observing and participating with a design because it suggests to him her that their biological (it "feels good," and is "pleasing to look at") and social (it's very "sleek" and "professional") communicative needs are being met. Thus, pleasure emerges in one's experience with a design when they are somehow moved by its aesthetic and physical appeal. Or, put another way, users have a pleasurable experience with a communication design because their personal tastes, cultural expectations, and physical responses to them trigger desirable emotions. Designing to incite pleasure, thus, idiosyncratically encourages users to participate with a design in the first place.

Mihaly Csikszentmihalyi (1990), in his influential work *Flow: The Psychology of Optimal Experience*, argues that pleasure is a critical component to making an experience enjoyable. While his work is intended to improve our understanding about what enhances the quality of life, he argues that the quality of experience is first necessary. To improve the quality of experience, one must consider both pleasure and enjoyment— the former a biological and social need, the latter a more personal sense of self accomplishment. Pleasure typically precedes enjoyment because it is almost always instantly acquired and satisfied. Pleasure might be considered those things that people typically think of as making them happy momentarily, but not for long periods of time— things like good food, good sex, or the comforts that money can buy. Csikszentmihalyi defines pleasure as "a feeling of contentment that one achieves whenever information in consciousness says that expectations set by biological programs or by social conditioning have been met" (p. 45). As this definition suggests, pleasure isn't entirely biological. Csikszentmihalyi continues: "Resting in the evening while passively absorbing information from the media, with alcohol or drugs to dull the mind overexcited by the demands of work, is pleasantly relaxing. Traveling to Acapulco is pleasant because the stimulating novelty restores our palate jaded by the repetitive routines of everyday life, and because we know that this is how the "beautiful people" also spend their time" (p. 46).

Pleasure, then, is both a sensation of biological needs being met and of novelty, of relaxation, and a sense of feeling "cool" or accepted or admired by society. Pleasure comes from recognition by outsiders but also by (even if internally fabricated) feelings of importance and social admittance. While biological needs can ostensibly be met with digital communications (consider ergonomics or tactile design for comfort of computers and other hardware devices) and socially constructed sensations of inclusion and recognition are becoming more prevalent with social media and Web 2.0, perhaps more common opportunities for pleasure in instrumental communications would come from relaxation and from novel experiences. Donald Norman's (2002) idea that "attractive things work better" has significance here (p. 41). The novelty of attractive and beautiful design conjures pleasure because it is unfamiliar yet aesthetically desirable to the user, much the same way Acapulco is novel to a native of New England who doesn't travel often. This might also explain why aesthetically conscious companies like Apple Corp. and Mini have seen so much success in their pleasurable product designs.

In a much less abstract explanation of pleasure, Patrick Jordan (2000) argues that pleasure has three distinct benefits:

- **Practical**: Which "accrue from the outcomes of tasks for which the product is used" (such as when a washing machine delivers the practical benefits of clean, fresh clothes)
- **Emotional**: Which "[pertain] to how a product affects a person's mood" (such as a product or service that is interesting, fun, or confidence-boosting like a video game or new dress)

- **Hedonic**: Which "[pertain] to the sensory and aesthetic pleasures associated with products" (such as the beauty or physical sensation of touching something like a well-designed chair)

Jordan continues by saying that, indeed, pleasure can seem like a "catch-all" term that makes products better. "Pleasure-based approaches to product design," he argues, "can be seen as approaches that consider all of the potential benefits that a product can deliver" (p. 12). Similar to the way in which Csikszentmihalyi explains pleasure, Jordan further breaks down the concept into four distinct kinds of pleasures: physio-pleasure (touch, taste, smell, and sensual); socio-pleasure (relationships and a sense of social interaction); psycho-pleasure (cognitive and emotional reactions); and ideo-pleasure (values and ideologies).

While Norman uses the term "visceral" and Jordan uses the term "hedonic," the idea is the same: aesthetically pleasing designs enhance experience. If the design involves communication, we might infer that participants with the communication are being affected in a way that makes information more palatable. In a recent publication on infographics, authors Lankow, Ritchie, and Crooks (2012) made this perspective immediately relevant to the instrumental communicator: "Even if your goal is to present information for a purely analytical objective…it is still beneficial to have aesthetic appeal. Design," the say, "is to data as cheese sauce is to broccoli" (p. 40). Even for those who like broccoli plain, the metaphor suggests something even more appetizing is happening when the communication is designed pleasurably and, thus, it is more likely to be consumed.

Though he didn't use the term "pleasure" in direct connection with paying attention to images, important French thinker and photography and film theorist Roland Barthes (1981) suggested that *studium* in visualizations affects pleasurable response. *Studium*, he says, is "that very wide field of unconcerned desire, of various interest, of inconsequential taste: *I like/I don't like*." He says that it is by *studium* "that [he] is interested in so many photographs" (p. 26). When people look at a given design, cultural and idiosyncratic characteristics—colors, shapes, imagery—seem to protrude from the communication and "speak" to their tastes, desires, and interests. Through *studium*, viewers are lured in, captivated by a personal connection to it. The design element may simply be something new or unique (perhaps an image of a new technology), or it may have historical significance (like the iconic "Hope" poster of Barack Obama during the 2008 presidential election), or it may simply reflect a cultural value (like "simplicity is the ultimate sophistication"). Regardless, *studium* is an appeal, a pleasurable and visceral reaction to elements of a visual communication that speak to the viewer's background, culture, and even current frame of mind within a given context.

What these pleasurable sensations do for the user-viewer of an instrumental communication is provoke opportunity for meaning-making. Using pleasure as a metaphor, we might even suggest aesthetically pleasurable communication designs increase its ability to "massage" meaning into the participant. Marshall McLuhan (2001), talking more broadly about digital media (and not just about photography like Barthes was, or about products as was Jordan), shapes his own understanding of what pleasure might mean for the observer. For McLuhan, pleasure isn't necessarily "inflicted" on the user like Barthes would argue, but rather pleasure would be "massaged" into the user. He boldly states that media "leave no part of us untouched, unaffected, unaltered. The medium is the massage. …media work as environments. …media are extensions of some human faculty—psychic or physical" (p. 26). If we can be comfortable in suggesting that the design of a communication has the ability to change the genre of its medium, then the design itself

functions as a communicative environment in which meaning "massaged" into our physical and psychological experiences. Just as pleasure from physical environments (like when we eat or have sex) "massages" meaning into our physiological and emotional experiences, pleasure from design environments (like when we are using a website or reading an infographic) massages meaning into our emotional and physiological understanding.

Communication design, in other words, effectively shapes our understanding through components that symbolically shape our understanding. If media are, as McLuhan suggests, extensions of our human faculties, then their constituents—their texts, images, colors, sounds, physical spaces and limitations, and even their hardware and physical housing—are what evoke feelings of pleasure (or remove or fail to offer opportunity for pleasure) in the user. If pleasure isn't effectively applied to the appropriate design elements, some aspect of meaning in the human experience is likely to be lost.

Key to the instrumental communicator is the role pleasure plays in experience design. The novelty, aesthetic appeal, or *studium* that penetrates the user might easily fall into Shedroff's (2001) "attraction" (the attention-grabber) component of an experience. But it ought also fall into the body or bulk of the experience in iterative and refreshing new ways. Pleasure maintains user interest by evoking feelings that satisfy needs. We might infer from this discussion that pleasure is the first of many collections of "available means" whereby the communication designer can rhetorically persuade a reader to pursue the information being presented. The superficial (albeit crucial) components that make up the pleasure collection include what is immediately visible, audible, and tactile: colors, typography, images, graphics, videos, icons, shapes, sounds, product quality, and so forth. The communication designer uses this rhetorical collection to frame the content in such a way that the viewer experiences pleasure upon approach (see Figure 1).

Figure 1. Designing for pleasure

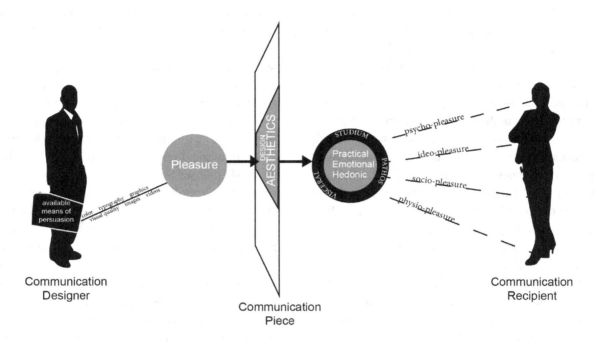

Enjoyment

Evoking pleasure, however, is only the first stage. Pleasure is superficial, provisional, and fleeting. As pleasure needs are being met by the user, the next goal of the instrumental communicator in engagement design is to ensure enjoyment. Enjoyment is about sustained retention in the communication piece where users are fully immersed and even "lose" themselves in the experience. Often, the ability to sustain effective enjoyment requires a certain level of ambiguity designed into the piece. Ambiguity allows for wandering, exploration, curiosity, or puzzles, which lead to discovery and problem-solving. Each of these are proven factors that relate to enjoyable experiences. Much of ambiguity and the ability to discover will be further explored in the next section on play. For now, though, let it suffice to say that instrumental communicators might think in terms of museum design—where ambiguity and discovery are key to enjoyment—when approaching digital com-

munication designs. As C.G. Screven (2000) has noted, in museums, "visitors do not have to pay attention but are free to attend, ignore, or distort the messages being communicated. In such situations, it is immensely important to design information systems that not only reflect the needs and characteristics of audiences but also attract and hold their attention" (p. 131). The key term here is to "hold" attention. While affecting pleasure throughout a communication piece is necessary, enjoyment must move beyond that somewhat superficial experience.

Instrumental communications must, just like a museum, walk a fine line here. Screven (2000) continues: "Dazzling graphics, participatory components, and scholarly accuracy are not as important as the ability connect exhibit experiences…to visitors' worlds or to suggest that exhibit content has personal value for them" (p. 142). Additionally, museum experiences pose many problems for visitors:

Uncertainties about what to see and how to get there, a poor knowledge base for exhibit content..., pervasive misconceptions..., variations in thinking styles, physical and psychological fatigue, social and visual distractions, and the pressures of time" (p. 132).

There must be a clear understanding of both what the user needs to know and wants to know. Allowing the user to selectively sift through what matters to him or her most will ultimately make for a more enjoyable experience because she won't be bogged down or worn out by irrelevant material. "Mindless activities at razzle-dazzle displays," Screven continues, "are often amusing, [but] this kind of fun is usually transient and is likely to diffuse attention rather than focus it" (p. 142). When the user is able to select the relevant information to him or her, learning is much more likely and the experience becomes that much more enjoyable.

Considering that there is substantial room for ambiguity, discovery, and the ability to be selective learners, digital communication designers are left with challenging decisions about what makes information enjoyable. Csikszentmihalyi (1990) provides an excellent framework for understanding just how to create optimum enjoyable experiences. His concept of "flow" suggests that challenges

and skills need to work through and against the human emotions of anxiety and boredom in order to maximize an experience's potential. In other words, every activity we encounter presents us with possible challenges. However, if our skills or knowledge far supersede the requirements of the challenge, we experience boredom. On the contrary, if our skills are far too underdeveloped to reach the demands of the challenge, we become too anxious and often give up on the task. Csikszentmihalyi conceptualized a "flow channel" that designates how and when we are experiencing the optimum enjoyment, or when we are in "flow." See Figures 2 and 3.

The idea here is that as our skills or knowledge improve, we need to be given more challenges. The new challenges make us slightly anxious, but push us to learn and develop. It is this continual progression that pushes us in and out of flow (but always upward toward more difficult challenges and greater skills sets) that allows for enjoyment in an experience. Of the people studied (which included thousands of people over several years) Csikszentmihalyi (1990) explains his findings:

We found that every flow activity, whether it involved competition, chance, or any other dimension of experience, had this in common: It

Figure 2. Flow channel

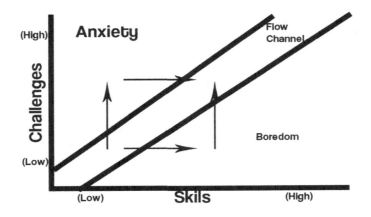

Figure 3. Challenge vs. skill

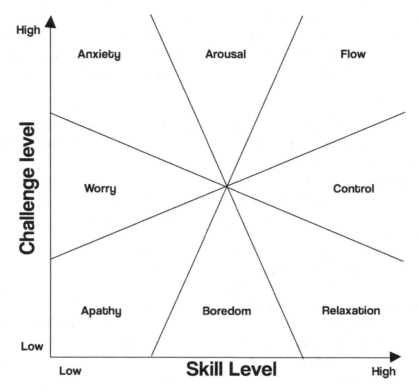

provided a sense of discovery, a creative feeling of transporting the person into a new reality. It pushed the person to higher levels of performance, and led to previously undreamed of states of consciousness. In short, it transformed the self by making it more complex. In this growth of the self lies the key to flow activities. (p. 74)*

This growth of the self is also part of the ethical dimension of incorporating enjoyment into instrumental communications. Understanding how to design experiences that challenge and build skills and understanding at an appropriate pace for the user is paramount to creating experiences that are fully engaging. Csikszentmihalyi (1990) explains eight dimensions that he found almost always are included in enjoyable experiences:

1. The experience or task must have the *chance to be completed*. In other words, there must be a clear finish in sight. Going back to Shedroff's (2001) idea that there must be an attraction, an engagement, *and* a conclusion, it is imperative that throughout the experience, the user knows where she is and what she is working toward. Without a sense of completion (or at least working towards a completion) it is difficult to fully immerse oneself into the task.

2. The participant must be able to *concentrate* on what she is doing. Concentration is affected by many internal and external factors. However, as we consider numbers 3 and 4, it becomes easier to conceptualize designing an experience that allows for full concentration.

3. There must be *clear goals throughout* the experience. Every experience is built by a series of tasks and decisions. If the user has a clear idea of what each small goal is and how it relates to the larger goal, he will be more likely to concentrate and enjoy it.

4. Each task within the experience must provide *immediate feedback*. If a person shoots a basketball, she knows immediately whether or not the shot went in. She knows if it was too short, too long, wide to the right, etc. Similarly, a user working through an instrumental communication needs to know whether or not progress is being made and how she might adjust to improve.

5. The participant must be *deeply but effortlessly involved* so that they are removed from awareness the frustrations of everyday life. Effortlessness often comes from functionality of the design. This is where usability would fall in a communication piece. If the interface design, hardware, speed, terminology, and so forth, seem clunky or confusing to the user, she will not be able to effortlessly engage in the tasks. Rather, she will feel bogged down and frustrated by the poor construction of the elements of the communication. Much like Norman's concept about behavior, the design itself must functionally work well so that user and design respond well to each other, much like a dance.

6. The participant must feel a *sense of control* over her actions. She must feel that the decisions she is making are the decisions that are building toward the ultimate goal. If she begins to feel in a simulation or a website, for example, that the software of the programs are forcing her to make decisions she would otherwise not, her sense of control is diminished.

7. *Concern for the self must disappear.* Csikszentmihalyi (1990) claims that "in everyday life we often feel threatened" (p. 62). Perhaps worried or concerned what others might think, what our own abilities and attributes are, we fail to maximize our potential. Effective engagement design helps the user to feel as though nothing else matters. For that time, she is enjoying using or experiencing the software and the rest of the world and concerns about her role in it disappear.

8. The *sense of time is altered*; hours pass by in minutes, and minutes can stretch out to seem like hours. Perhaps the most difficult component to design into an instrumental communication, the ability to make the user lose a sense of time can help improvement. Like baseball, Csikszentmihalyi (1990) claims, most flow experiences "have their own pace, their own sequences of events... without regard to equal intervals of time" (p. 66).

Clearly, not all eight of these elements of enjoyment are possible or appropriate for all communications all the time. But the larger the number of these elements that are incorporated, the higher the likelihood that the user will sense enjoyment from the experience. The incorporation of these eight principles comes after the information designer considers the pleasure benefits associated with the user. While the planning and development of a communication piece may follow a very different model, communication design and meaning-making land on a continuum where enjoyment follows pleasure. The designer, after constructing a pleasurable experience through aesthetic rhetoric, is tasked with making a communication piece enjoyable. The rhetorical collection of available means in this step becomes content-centered (rather than form-centered), and is thus more abstract. It involves content complexity, style, arrangement, usefulness, relevance, and clarity (See Figure 4).

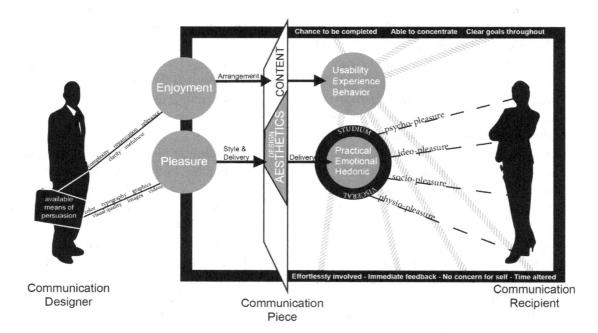

Figure 4. Designing for enjoyment

Participation

Participation is a complicated concept and it is closely tied to enjoyment. When designers of digital communications consider how to keep a user involved with complex information, they are expected to incorporate ways in which the user interacts with, plays with, challenges, and works within an environment of prescriptive ambiguity—where frameworks are in place, but choice and opportunity are possible.

Play is an ambiguous concept. Play theorists consistently wrestle over its diversity, complexity and pervasiveness. Theorist Brian Sutton-Smith (1997) reminds us that play can be found in just about anything from tourism and television, to sexual intimacy and gossip. "There is little agreement among us," Sutton Smith says of those who try to pinpoint play's role in humanity, "and much ambiguity." Yet, this very ambiguity is what makes play so important, so pervasive, and so successful. Ambiguity signifies the unknown, but also the

possible, the potential. The potential to win or lose a game, to feel exhilaration, disappointment, accomplishment, pleasure, or pain. The ambiguity is what drives the motivation to continue playing—to discover what exists in that ambiguity. So it is within this ambiguity that I think it best to begin the discussion of incorporating play into instrumental communication design.

Ambiguity might seem a strange term for technical communicators. Isn't ambiguity what we are trying to avoid! Jim Gasperini (2000), in his article "The Role of Ambiguity in Multimedia Experience," makes a clear statement about the way we perceive ambiguity in communication: "In some forms of writing (e.g., technical writing, journalism), the opposite of *ambiguous* is *precise*. In creative writing the opposite of *ambiguous* is *dull*" (p. 304). But there is more to ambiguity than a lack of precision or excitement. There is an opportunity for instruction far more influential than denotative directives. To be clear, ambiguity, as Gasperini argues, to be used effectively, must still have purpose and structure. The designer must ask—what is it I expect or hope the user to learn from engaging in exploration? What can multiple endings and open possibility do for the user? Gasperini calls this "structural ambiguity," or ambiguity with a purpose. Of course, limitless ambiguity isn't always preferred, nor is it feasible in many communication designs.

As Csikszentmihalyi (1990) argued as his first point of enjoyment—all experiences hoping to fall within the flow channel must have some kind of conclusion. And while infinite conclusions can certainly be designed into some digital media (consider open-ended social media video games like World of Warcraft) and instructional simulations (like a simulation for driving cars where there might be infinite possibilities but no specific ending point), specific endings will be necessary for many others. Gasperini (2000) addresses this dichotomy by defining the one side of structural ambiguity as closed-ended and the other as open-ended. Each has a role, but the important thing is that each presents opportunity for uncertainty and discovery. Such is where play falls—a concept that is, in fact, rule-bound or structured, yet open to new opportunities to improve skills and engage in information.

Play is a concept that is gaining a great deal of traction in both the workplace and in academia. Corporations such as Google and Adobe (only two of many large companies) present themselves as workplace environments where employees are encouraged to explore new ideas, to discover, and, literally, to play games during work. Images and video on their websites show employees playing foosball, surfing, biking, and playing basketball. Academia has seen an incredible growth in serious games colloquia and educational gaming experiments and play pedagogies. Ken McAllister (2001), author of *Game Work: Language, Power, and Computer Game Culture*, and co-director of the Learning Games Initiative at the University of Arizona, argues for the educational benefit of games and play:

There are games that appeal to payers' desires to hunt, solve, maneuver, and plan; the scenarios in which these desires are met are sometimes life-like and sometimes fantastic. Despite all of these variations, however, one fundamental concept ties them together: play.... And play, it is important to remember, is also always instructive. (p. 68)

The attention that play is receiving in disciplines across the academy and in the workforce may come as no surprise. Play has proven to be educational and to increase morale (and thus over-all experience) when designed into workspaces, classrooms, and even instructional technologies. Perhaps, though, one of more important reasons why play is gaining traction in education is that play is innate to human behavior. Humans desire to play in order to discover.

Johan Huizinga (1950), perhaps the most widely recognized mastermind behind play theory, has argued that play is doubtlessly fundamental to the human character. What we have been able to accomplish as a civilization can be traced to our inherent nature to play:

[Play] produces many of the fundamental forms of social life. The spirit of playful competition is, as a social impulse, older than culture itself and pervades all life like a veritable ferment. Ritual grew up in sacred play; poetry was born in play and nourished on play; music and dancing were pure play. Wisdom and philosophy found expression in words and forms derived from religious contests. The rules of warfare, the conventions of noble living were built up on play patterns. We have to conclude, therefore, that civilization is, in its earliest phases, played. (p. 173)

We are a species founded on principles related to play. And while some may argue that play is simply a diversion, unrelated to the "important" tasks of day-to-day life, it is hard to argue that play doesn't instruct and motivate people to achieve and improve. From early chess players to Greek athletes, we have seen the potential of the human mind and body increased through play. And as free and ambiguous as play often seems, it perhaps oddly is almost always rules-bound. Perhaps this is why it is possible to improve through play—there are guidelines and goals involved. Humans naturally fall into play as a means to explore what they are capable of, to engage in competition (even if only with the self) to discover what they didn't know they could know or do before. Over the past century, as play has worked its way into academic and institutional environments, the definitions and understandings of play have varied considerably. Karen Stagniti (2004) in her article "Understanding Play," summed up some of the most prominent play theorists and came up with an emerging consensus about why we might consider as components of play today. She says that play

- Is more internally than externally motivated.
- Transcends reality as well as reflects reality.
- Is controlled by the player.
- Involves more attention to process than product.
- Is safe.
- Is usually fun, unpredictable, pleasurable.
- Is spontaneous and involves non-obligatory active engagement. (p.5)

These guidelines for play are useful when trying to incorporate them into TIPS communications. The information designer can determine what the goals of the piece are and then plan for play accordingly. Perhaps most important from the list above, though, that a TIPS communicator must think about is that play must be controlled by user and must make the user feel safe. Much like Csikszentmihalyi's (1990) arguments that enjoyable experiences require that the participant have a sense of control and that they must not feel self-conscious. Play must be designed so that the user feels like they are working towards something that is rewarding and free from serious conse-

quence. One of the great benefits of play is that it can simulate reality, yet transcend it, offering opportunities to discover with penalties much less severe than what would be experienced in reality.

The discussion of play to this point might seem very similar to the discussion of enjoyment. Yet, they are definitely different. In the trajectory of the information design process, play comes third because it is informed by the previous two. The components of play—the areas of the design where the user is allowed to play (whether that be through a game, a quest of sorts, or a diversion, or something else), must be built upon the principles of pleasure and enjoyment. Pleasure and enjoyment might be considered the theoretical components of the design whereas play would be the praxis of design. Once the design process dart has penetrated the pleasure bulls-eye and transcended the enjoyment principles spectrum (while carrying the baggage of what has been obtained), it can then systematically place them into the design of ambiguity and play to ensure optimum engagement. See Figure 5.

SCIENTIFIC DESIGN, USABILITY, AND COGNITION

Once the designer has implemented the humanistic components of the instrumental communication, namely the pleasure, enjoyment, and play principles (an extremely important precursor to the actual building or coding of any online instrumental communication), he or she is only now ready implement the components that typically affect usability and functionality. In this article, I am arguing for the implementation of engagement design as an ethical means to better humanize the communication piece (and hence the user). Because of this, not much real estate is devoted to the considerations of usability. This is not to say, however, that usability and scientific design do not have ethical implications. But TIPS communicators have understood these principles

Figure 5. Designing for play

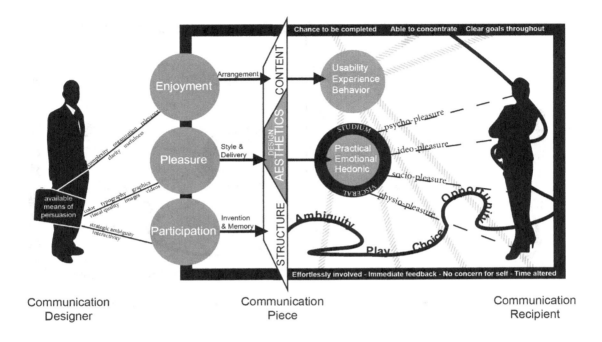

Communication Designer   Communication Piece   Communication Recipient

of usability for quite some time. In the past, it seems to have only been marginally considered, something more of an afterthought. Engagement doesn't supersede or subvert the principles of usability, but rather strengthens them, reinforces their purpose in a new humanistic and ethical light. Strict rules and functionality, no doubt, are critical to effective design.

However, usability is often easily (at least, much easier than more humanistic problems) fixed, particularly in TIPS communications. Usability tests can discover where glitches or miscues happen or where language is unclear or misleading. Often, these problems can be solved with a change in terminology, layout, or organization. In digital technologies, this is a coding, wording, or layout problem. While the overhaul of usability, sense-making, and wayfinding problems may be cause for serious concern in architecture and landscape design (such as in a museum or amusement park), they are much less serious of a problem—at least in terms of fixing the problem—than in the com-

munications that TIPS communicators are more typically required to produce: users manuals, books, websites, tutorials, simulations, modules, and the like. For these reasons, I place usability at the end of the engagement design process. Once pleasure, enjoyment, and play are effectively considered and designed into the structure of the communication piece, usability can be placed around it. Online usability (in all its connotations from computer processing speed to broken links to complexity of language), then, functions as a sort of exoskeleton to the core of the design. See Figure 6.

You can see at the conclusion of the Engagement Design flowchart where the user effectively reciprocates feedback to the designer. This is an iterative process, never to be fully completed. It is the important role of the designer to constantly engage in the user's needs and concerns. In a civilization of constant change, it is important that we contextualize the new potentials for engagement before the old methods become stale,

Figure 6. Engagement Design

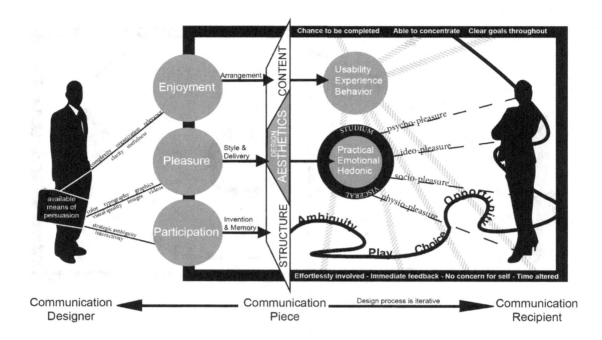

and therefore less pleasurable. Perspectives change as the contexts of communications fight against the ebb and flow of a world that Brenda Dervin (2000) calls "both ordered and chaotic." Sense-making, she says, (or perhaps a better term would be *experience-making*) "focuses on how humans make and unmake, develop, maintain, resist, destroy, and change order, structure, culture, organizations, relationships, and the self" (p. 45). This in a world that, a decade and a half ago (1998), *Wired* magazine claimed

We're talking about a world where people talk with their brains instead of their hands. A world in which communications technology creates global competition.... A world in which innovation is more important than mass production. A world in which investment buys new concepts or the means to create them, rather than new machines. A world in which rapid change is constant. (qtd. in Kline et al., p. 10)

Over 15 years later, the change is perhaps more constant, more rapid. As digital media hit the global fan at the dawn of the millennium with the advent of blogging, YouTube, Facebook, Google, and others, people have become more and more accustomed to (and even expecting) social presence in their media experiences. TIPS communicators will, no doubt, be faced with ever growing challenges to understanding how engagement will play an even more crucial role in TIPS communications. Usability and cognition will work against not just functionality but against an imbrication of technology, culture, marketing, economics, and socially constructed ways of knowing.

What I would like to emphasize with this chart is that usability testing must reach deeper than discovering cognition and output results. It must consider engagement as a crucial component to knowledge and sense-making, discovery, and desire to repeat the experience in a world inundated with divergent ways of learning. Because pleasure and enjoyment play a significant role in interest, the designer, when employing a usability test, must further question the level to which pleasure, enjoyment, and play improved or hindered the *overall* experience of the user.

CONCLUSION: DEFINITION AND THE FUTURE OF ENGAGEMENT

To conclude where we started, I propose the question: what exactly is "engagement?"

Engagement Design, in a sentence, might be: "The design of an experience or communication piece that holistically considers the humanistic components of pleasure, play, and enjoyment *as well as* the scientific components of usability and cognition." Considering what has just been discussed in terms of ethics and expediency, TIPS communicators can use "engagement" as a concept to bridge the dichotomy that exists between usability and aesthetics, science and art, or strict rules and creativity. This bridge, I propose, puts the field in a more ethical position to be more humanistic, and hence more effective, in our communications. The ubiquity of digital media technologies and their ever-growing functionalities not only make engagement design more possible now than at any time in our history, but it also makes it more necessary. Considering theories about cognition and learning (like schema theory, wayfinding, and sense-making); emotional and psychological experience; and design and aesthetics; with a bit of creativity and innovation, technical communicators can learn to incorporate engagement into their designs to make them more humanistic, ethical, and effective.

But the definition is only the beginning. *Engagement Design* requires a taxonomy and rubric that clearly (but complexly) imbricates the concepts of pleasure, enjoyment, play, usability, and cognition. This rubric, as I see it, would be built upon principles related to Csikszentmihalyi's *Flow* diagram, the Yerkes-Dodson law (which guages a person's attention, memory, and problem solving capabilities against physiological or mental arousal) and an inverted likert scale which places a middle score as most important (too much or too little, in other words, of any of the engagement principles is less desirable). The rubric, tested against a corpus of instrumental communication pieces, would determine the level to which the humanistic principles of art and the usability principles of science need to be implemented in a given piece. It is conceivable, for example, that tutorial communications require a different level of aesthetic appeal and usability features than, say, a simulation. Once that is determined, however, we can begin incorporating a more ethical approach to TIPS communication design.

REFERENCES

Anderson, C. (2009, June). The new new economy. *Wired.* 98 – 121.

Bacon, F. (2011). *The new organon: Or true directions concerning the interpretation of nature.* Retrieved 2 April 2012, from http://www.constitution.org/liberlib.htm

Barthes, R. (1975). *The pleasure of the text* (R. Miller, Trans.). New York, NY: Hill and Wang.

Barthes, R. (1977). *Image/music/text* (S. Heath, Trans.). New York, NY: Hill and Wang.

Barthes, R. (1981). *Camera lucida* (R. Howard, Trans.). New York, NY: Hill and Wang.

Baudrillard, J. (2010). *Simulacra and simulation* (S. F. Glaser, Trans.). Ann Arbor, MI: U of Michigan P.

Caillois, R. (2001). *Man, play, and games* (M. Barash, Trans.). Chicago, IL: University of Illinois Press.

Chertoff, D. B. et al. (2008). Improving presence theory through experiential design. *Presence (Cambridge, Mass.)*, *17*(4), 405–413. doi:10.1162/pres.17.4.405

Cooley, M. (2000). Human centered design. In R. Jacobson (Ed.), *Information design*. Cambridge, MA: MIT Press.

Csikszentmihalyi, M. (1990). *Flow: The psychology of optimal experience*. New York, NY: Harper & Row.

Dervin, B. (2000). Chaos, order, and sense-making: A proposed theory for information design. In R. Jacobson (Ed.), *Information design*. Cambridge, MA: MIT Press.

Gasperini, J. (2000). Structural ambiguity: An emerging interactive aesthetic. In R. Jacobson (Ed.), *Information design*. Cambridge, MA: MIT Press.

Gurak, L., & Lannon, J. (2007). *A concise guide to technical communication* (3rd ed.). New York, NY: Pearson.

Huizinga, J. (1950). *Homo ludens*. London: Routledge & Kegan Paul.

Jordan, P. (2000). *Designing pleasurable products*. Philadelphia, PA: Taylor & Francis.

Katz, S. B. (1992). The ethic of expediency: Classical rhetoric, technology, and the holocaust. *College English*, *54*(3), 255–275. doi:10.2307/378062

Kline, S., Dyer-Witherford, N., & de Peuter, G. (2003). *Digital play: The interaction of technology, culture, and marketing*. Montreal: McGill-Queen's University Press.

Kress, G., & van Leeuwen, T. (2006). *Reading images: The grammar of visual design* (2nd ed.). New York, NY: Routledge.

Lankow, J., Ritchie, J., & Crooks, R. (2012). *Infographics: The power of visual storytelling*. Hoboken, NJ: Wiley & Sons, Inc.

Lidwell, W., Holden, K., & Butler, J. (2003). *Universal principles of design*. Beverly, MA: Rockport Publishers.

McAllister, K. S. (2001). *Game work: Language, power, and computer game culture*. Tuscaloosa, AL: University of Alabama Press.

McLuhan, M., & Fiore, Q. (2001). *The medium is the massage*. Corte Madera, CA: Gingko Press.

Miller, C. R. (2004). A humanistic rationale for technical writing. In J. M. Dubinski (Ed.), *Teaching technical communication* (pp. 15–23). Boston, MA: Bedford/St. Martin's.

Moore, P. (1996). Instrumental discourse is as humanistic as rhetoric. *Journal of Business and Technical Communication*, *10*(1), 100. doi:10.1177/1050651996010001005

Norman, D. (2002). Emotion and design: Attractive things work better. *Interactions Magazine*, *9*(4), 36–42. doi:10.1145/543434.543435

Norman, D. (2004). *Emotional design: Why we love (or hate) everyday things*. New York, NY: Basic Books.

Pink, D. (2005). *A whole new mind*. New York, NY: Riverhead Books.

Screven, C. G. (2000). Information design in informal settings: Museums and other public spaces. In R. Jacobson (Ed.), *Information design*. Cambridge, MA: MIT Press.

Shedroff, N. (2001). *Experience design*. Indianapolis, IN: New Riders.

Stagnitti, K. (2004). Understanding play: The implications for play assessment. *Australian Occupational Therapy Journal*, *51*, 3–12. doi:10.1046/j.1440-1630.2003.00387.x

Sutton-Smith, B. (1997). *The ambiguity of play.* Cambridge, MA: Harvard University Press.

Tufte, E. (1990). *Envisioning information.* Cheshire, CT: Graphics Press.

Turkle, S. (2009). *Simulation and its discontents.* Cambridge, MA: MIT Press.

Virilio, P. (1994). *The vision machine.* Indianapolis, IN: Indiana UP.

Wurman, R. S. (2001). *Information anxiety 2.* Indianapolis, IN: QUE.

KEY TERMS AND DEFINITIONS

Engagement Design: A holistic, theoretical model for communication design that encourages judicious awareness of the entire human experience for a communication recipient. Engagement design integrates thoughtful design choices that affect user response, including pleasure, enjoyment, play, participation, ambiguity, usability, and cognition.

Enjoyment: Sustained, positive retention in a communication piece, where a person becomes fully immersed and "loses" him/herself in the experience.

Instrumental Communication: Communication designed with a specific intention to govern, guide, control, and help people execute physical actions. Instrumental communication is frequently found in in communication disciplines related to education, science, technology, engineering, and math.

Intrinsic Humanistic Design: Design elements that affect intrinsic, or emotionally internalized, response to a communication, including pleasure, enjoyment, and participation.

Participation: The way a person interacts with a communication piece, how they play with, challenge, and work within an environment of prescriptive ambiguity—where frameworks are in place, but choice and opportunity are possible.

Pleasure: Experiential and emotional responses of a person that encourages him/her to continue observing and participating with a design because the design suggests to him/her that their biological and social communicative needs are being met.

Structural Ambiguity: Prescribed and purposeful ambiguity strategically built into a communication design in order to foster engagement.

Usability: Communication design perspective that places emphasis on a scientific approach to communication experience, namely cognition, retention, performance, and expedience.

Chapter 3
Toward an Algorithmic Rhetoric

Chris Ingraham
University of Colorado at Boulder, USA

ABSTRACT

Insofar as algorithms are digital problem-solving operations that follow a set of rules or processes to arrive at a result, they are constrained by the rules that determine their parameters for operating. While an algorithm can only operate according to its instructions, however, the potential rules that might govern an algorithm are inexhaustible. An algorithm's design thus makes rhetorical choices that privilege the importance of some information or desired outcomes over others. This chapter argues for a way of thinking about algorithmic rhetoric as macro-, meso-, and micro-rhetorical. Along these lines, it would be beneficial to think more about algorithms as digital rhetorics with terrific power to sway what counts as knowledge, truth, and material reality in the everyday lives of people across an astonishing range of global communities in the twenty-first century.

THE QUINTESSENTIAL DIGITAL RHETORIC

Suppose that, as I was typing this sentence, I'd misspelled the word "misspelled." It wouldn't much have mattered. No sooner would the wrong letters have materialized on my laptop's screen than they would have morphed at once into the accepted, proper spelling. This phenomenon is called auto-correction, and it's a common feature now of most all word processing software, from text messaging on a cell phone to plonking keys on a computer. Auto-correction—which fixes common spelling or grammatical errors when you type—and auto-completion—a related function that predicts the word or phrase you're typing so to spare you the Herculean labor of having to type the rest yourself—are now commonplace on virtually all digital interfaces, whether conducting a web search, writing an email, or editing source code. These technologies are powered by algorithms: those often hidden sets of instructions that intervene in organizing our world in astonishing ways.

DOI: 10.4018/978-1-4666-4916-3.ch003

Copyright © 2014, IGI Global. Copying or distributing in print or electronic forms without written permission of IGI Global is prohibited.

As algorithms go, Autocorrect and Auto-complete are relatively benign operations. They offer a modern convenience, albeit with some corresponding complications that might best be described as *communicative*. Under the sway of auto-completion, for instance, a text message might say, "Boil the pirates," when what it really means is, "Boil the potatoes." This can make for some funny exchanges, typically but not always harmless. In a widely reported incident in early 2012, the Hall County, Georgia police department placed West Hall schools on lockdown for two hours because someone had received a text message saying, "gunman be at west hall today." The sender had tried to type "gunna" as shorthand for "I'm going to," only for Autocorrect to change the word to one it found more appropriate (Gleick, 2012). While algorithms make possible innumerable minute operations that dapple our daily lives in ways we may not notice or regard as especially consequential, they nevertheless do often have stakes with real repercussions for what matters in how people come to understand, communicate, and negotiate the complex realities of our global communities today.

Indeed, in the twenty-first century, algorithms have become an outright pervasive force in our social world. From stoplights to stock tickers, sporting events to search engines, algorithms now are everywhere. Yet, scholars of communication, and of rhetoric in particular, have largely neglected to give the algorithm the attention it deserves. This neglect can certainly not be justified on the grounds that algorithms are neither communicative nor rhetorical. These digital problem-solving operations, which follow a set of rules and automated processes to arrive at a result, can reasonably be called the quintessential manifestation of digital rhetoric in the world today. How that might be so, and what to do about it, are the general inquiries guiding this chapter.

The closest precedent in the scholarly record for thinking about algorithms as rhetorical comes from Ian Bogost's (2007) work on what he calls the "procedural rhetoric" of video games. "Procedural rhetoric," Bogost says, "is the practice of persuading through processes in general and computational processes in particular" (p. 3). Procedurality, for Bogost, refers to the fundamental way software works: through the encoding of rules designed to execute processes that, when followed, represent the world in a particular way. He regards such procedurality as "the principle value of the computer, which creates meaning through the interaction of algorithms" (p. 4). Bogost is interested in the manifestations and consequences of procedural rhetoric in video games, and not in algorithms *per se*. But his idea of a procedural rhetoric—at base, the notion that the computational procedures powering video games are persuasive—nevertheless begins to indicate how something similar might be said at the level of algorithms themselves.

Algorithms can be seen as rhetorical insofar as they exert a persuasive influence upon what is held to be important or true in our social, cultural, political, and economic interactions. And certainly they do, as the example of something so commonplace as a web search reveals. It's algorithms, after all, that enable search engines to guide us through vast amounts of information toward what they hold to be relevant and significant, potentially limiting our intellectual purview based on how they do so. In a more complex sense, then, algorithms are best understood as rhetorical if we consider that their outcomes are not empirically inevitable but rather the product of a particular set of parameters designed strategically to lead toward a particular kind of result. In other words, algorithms implicitly make a rhetorical argument for what factors matter in order to persuade their "audience" that their resultant outcome is the best, truest, or most important. The simple observation that different search engines will often generate different results when given the same search terms illustrates the extent to which algorithms operate rhetorically in this way. Because the rules programmed into the proprietary algorithms that power respective search engines are unique, each one privileges certain factors over others, making results vary between them and hence forwarding different cases for what matters most. Of course, search engines make just one example of this phenomenon. All algorithms perform rhetorically in more or less the same way.

Nevertheless, as programmatic operations reliant upon the automated execution of binary code, algorithms may seem to be grammars more than rhetorics. They may seem "objective" or coolly disinterested. And to a degree, they are. At least, once they're coded and operationalized they remain remarkably consistent. Algorithms take input data, pinball it through a decision-tree of filtering mechanisms, and turn it into an output result. Theoretically, as long as the filtering mechanisms remain the same, the exact same input will yield the identical output every time. But as the input changes, depending on how the code's rules value that input's nuances, the results likewise change, sometimes considerably. Thinking about algorithms as rhetorical thus means recognizing that they are neither infallible nor disinterested, but rather motivated by quite specific epistemic standards that can radically delimit what counts as valid or meaningful in various spheres of our intellectual, social, and material world.

The issues surrounding a rhetorical understanding of the algorithm are many. What is an algorithm's audience? How can bots persuade? Are programmers, quants, and hacks the new guardians of culture and power? What's the relationship between algorithms and all this talk about *information* and *information technology*? Is it algorithms that lead to so much narrowcasting on the web? Does that mean publics have now gone digital? Could algorithms be changing the way we think? What metaphors best help us understand how algorithms work? Is it reasonable to understand them as *arguments*? *Instructions*? Unknowable *black boxes*? How did automation become so ubiquitous in the first place? Have computer technologies finally pushed out the hu-

man? Do algorithms have agency? In fact, what does it even mean anymore to be technologically literate? Is *expertise* now obsolete? And what about our political economy? Surely the spread of automation influences that, too. *Right*?

Endeavoring to answer all these questions, at least most of them, is thankfully not the project of the pages ahead. But I do want to suggest that before we can make sense of the increasingly powerful role algorithms play in our daily lives, we will need to understand them better as the communicative and rhetorical operations that they are. Accordingly, my goal in this chapter is modest: I aim to advance the preliminary claim, introduced briefly above, that algorithms are rhetorical. By looking closer at how that's the case and what it might mean for our engagement with the changing world around us, we may then begin to develop appropriate methodologies and critical strategies to become more engaged members of a world where algorithms rule the roost. Indeed, as algorithms and automation become more pervasive forces in our world, understanding algorithmic rhetoric will correspondingly become a more urgent task both for scholars of communication and those invested in evolving conceptions of global literacy.

WHAT ARE ALGORITHMS?

It might help to begin with the basics. What are algorithms? Fortunately, one need not be a math prodigy or computer scientist to understand at least their fundamental concept. Consider an assortment of definitions. Algorithms have been called:

- "A procedure or set of rules used in calculation and problem-solving; a precisely defined set of mathematical or logical operations for the performance of a particular task" (Oxford English Dictionary online, n. d.)

- "A precise recipe that specifies the exact sequence of steps required to solve a problem" (MacCormick, 2011, p. 3)
- "An *effective procedure*, a way of getting something done in a finite number of discrete steps" (Berlinski, 2011, p. xvi)
- "Simply a set of step by step instructions, to be carried out quite mechanically, so as to achieve some desired result" (Chabert, 1999, p. 1)
- "A set of instructions to be carried out perfunctorily to achieve an ideal result. Information goes into a given algorithm, answers come out" (Steiner, 2012, p. 54).
- "A finite sequence of instructions" (Dyson, 2012, p. 247)

This isn't a quiz. All these definitions will do. But from this selection some recurrent concepts emerge. *Instructions, steps, results*: these are the fundamentals. Curiously, not one of the above definitions—and others could be marshaled that are pretty much the same—mention *digitization* or *automation* as integral to what an algorithm is or does.

In its widest sense, then, to speak of algorithms is to speak of any set of instructions, with specific steps, that lead to certain results. On this view, a recipe for chocolate chip cookies is as much an algorithm as the directions you give a friend to help her reach your house. Each offers instructions and steps—a procedure—that can be repeated indefinitely to achieve results with the same effectiveness. Along these lines, the arithmetical procedures you follow to multiply large numbers, carrying digits, marking the decimal, and so forth, are likewise algorithms in a basic sense. In fact, mathematical functions were the basis for algorithms in their original form.

The first known algorithm ever recorded came from the ancient Sumerians, living around 2500 BC near what is now modern Baghdad. It consists in a repeatable procedure for dividing grain equally between people, a procedure that would theoretically still work today. They etched this method on clay tablets that depict the algorithm in symbols, indicating its importance (Chaubert, 1999). The Greek mathematician Euclid of Alexandria also gives us algorithms that still work today despite being dated to roughly 300 BC. His book, *Elements*, for instance, was in part so successful because it leveraged an algorithm to find the greatest common divisor of two numbers to help establish a framework for the study of geometry that lasted the next twenty-three hundred years (Gazale, 1999).

But the word "algorithm" as we know it today derives neither from the Sumerians nor the Greeks, but rather from a Persian mathematician from the ninth century named Muhammad ibn Musa al-Khwarizmi. His book on "Calculation by Completion and Balancing," known in its original Middle Persian as *Al-Kitab al-Mukhtasar fi Hisab al-Jabr wa l-Muqabala*, is the first known book about algebra (a word that itself derives from *al-jabr wa* in the book's title). Scholars during the Middle Ages Latinized al-Khwarizmi's name and coined the phonetically similar word "algorism" to describe any automatic and systemic method of arithmetic calculation like those his work tried to develop (Chabert, 1999, p. 2).

Today, thanks to centuries of mathematical advancement, the reach of algorithmic automation has become far more extensive than progenitors of the earliest algorithms ever likely imagined. Fibonacci, Leibniz, Gauss, Pascal, Boole, Turing and others all played significant parts in developing our capacity to automate procedures of enormous complexity. But an investigation of the unique contribution that these and other brilliant minds have made to develop the complexity of algorithms, from the days of stone tablets to these days of microchips, is beyond the reach of this chapter.[1] My sights have rather been on the algorithm as we know it today, in order principally to show that we will not know it as well as we may suppose until we know it as rhetorical.

Accordingly, although a reasonable conceptual definition of algorithms might be framed so to include such phenomena as cookie recipes or driving directions, the algorithm as we know it now is digital, and magnitudes more complex than the example of such simple instructions would make it out to be. Automation has for decades now been so sophisticated that, to reach their desired result, algorithms themselves now execute the very instructions and rules that make them algorithms to begin with. In essence, algorithms don't just provide a *recipe* for cookies; they'll actually bake them. The bots behind Google's self-driving car, for instance, don't just offer a set of road directions to help a person drive someplace, the way a GPS device might. These bots navigate through traffic and do the actual driving on their own, street-legally by 2012 in Florida, California, and Nevada (Fountain, 2012). To give this and other examples more traction, it may help to conceptualize the rhetoric of algorithms metaphorically, as John Jones (2011) has tried to do by suggesting three metaphors for how algorithms work.

Algorithms, Jones says, can be seen as autonomous machines, Rube Goldberg devices, or Mechanical Turks. Regarding algorithms as *autonomous machines* means recognizing that once their rules are made, algorithms operate essentially on their own. Theoretically, these rules could be so complex that they enable an algorithm to process any new input, in effect setting the algorithm in autonomous motion, like a robot. Google's self-driving car makes an obvious example of this metaphorical understanding. But perhaps more frightening are military-industrial trends worldwide toward the armed but unmanned drones used for reconnaissance and weaponry in warfare. Powered by algorithms, drones now are programmed to make ethical decisions in absence of human intervention. They don't just carry out the commands of a human on the ground; they are able to enter potential combat situations and decide, on their own, if lethal engagement is or is not advised (Department of Defense, 2011). The algorithms that underwrite such autonomous machines as drones or self-driving cars are rhetorical operations because their instructions set the rules for how to make decisions in any conceivable (or at least plausible) circumstance. In effect, these rules work rhetorically to make certain factors matter in an autonomous machine's decisions and actions—for instance, by setting what satisfactory ratio of estimated enemy targets-to-civilian bystanders might suffice to justify lethal engagement. Though these machines act on their own, their action is guided by how they have been instructed—indeed, *persuaded*—to act.

Jones's second metaphor for understanding the algorithm is to see them as *Rube Goldberg* devices: kinds of digital contraptions that, let's say, send an egg down a chute, which knocks over a train of dominoes, which flicks a switch, which turns on a fan, which spins some cogs and so on until the egg's been poached, peeled, and peppered. In this metaphor, an algorithm is a series of causal steps to go from input A to output Z. The expression "garbage in, garbage out" comes to bear here insofar as these steps are only as good as the rules by which they're written. If you give the algorithm "garbage" data that the rules can't understand, it gives back "garbage" output that makes no sense. Internet radio providers that play songs for people on demand online work effectively in this way. They break songs into hundreds of component parts and, based on what it knows you like, recommends other songs with similar attributes. While these automated bots listen to the input users give them, they nevertheless act persuasively by processing input in a particular way: a way that unavoidably privileges certain assumptions about what qualities it thinks matter most in order to explain a user's tastes. Though their procedures may be linear and irrefragable, algorithms like this act rhetorically the moment they make these privileged qualities matter.

Finally, Jones suggests a third metaphor that would understand algorithms as *Mechanical Turks*. The Mechanical Turk was a chess-playing machine designed by Wolfgang von Kempelen in the eighteenth century (Robert-Houdin, 1859). It appeared to be an automaton, capable of playing and defeating various opponents in chess, but in fact the machine was a hoax, with a person concealed inside and making all the moves. Conceptualizing algorithms as Mechanical Turks means recognizing their shortcomings and consequent complicity with humans who contribute in generating what they output. Amazon.com, for example, has a crowdsourcing program actually called Amazon Mechanical Turk, which they bill as "Artificial Artificial Intelligence" ("Amazon Mechanical," n. d.). Rather than create algorithms to perfect certain tasks, Amazon pays people to fulfill commissions ostensibly done through an automated process. Calling businesses to find the manager's email address, rewriting sentences, recommending similar movies—these and similar tasks are sometimes performed by humans alongside algorithms, when algorithms appear to be doing all the work.[2]

As all these conceptual apparatuses attest, I am interested here in a broad understanding of what algorithms are and do. While my repeated references to "algorithms" in these pages thus refers to the whole category of automated operations we know by that name, or at least to the basic conceptual apparatus behind algorithmic thinking (remember: *instructions, rules, results*), the specific algorithms of most importance to our changing world—and hence to my argument—are those most technologically of-the-moment: the ones whose hidden automated procedures end up quietly running our new media landscape. These algorithms are powerful, creative, unimaginably fast and, usually, the invisible but driving force behind the technologically mediated aspects of our current human condition.

An argument need not be advanced to show just how technologically mediated our lives and societies have become. By now, that much is self-evident. But if algorithms are the force behind so much, if not all, of today's ubiquitous computer-ized technology—if they're what make "apps" work; make communication possible; grant our access to unfathomably huge stores of information; regulate credit card purchases and trades on the stock market, and so on—then the importance of gaining at least a conceptual understanding of algorithms should also go without saying. Of course, it would be insufficient merely to claim that automated bots are influential these days and to leave it at that. Of crucial significance is not just *that* they matter. What matters is *what* they make matter, and *how* they do so.

MATTERING

Unfortunately, the technical intricacy and specialized programming language behind algorithms can intimidate unversed scholars that might, given the right technical know-how, be more inclined to consider their complex processes and influence. But we need not be scared away. Certainly, I am no expert in math or computer science; indeed, one of the points to my argument is that, notwithstanding the barriers to studying algorithms, there remain some nontrivial ways to approach the topic that merit elaborating. A rhetorical lens and vocabulary are crucial but perhaps not obvious ways to expose the shortcomings and repercussions inherent in what has been described by Steiner (2012) as the coming algorithmic takeover.

To call algorithms rhetorical is not to fixate on a minor aspect of their technology, nor to leverage an obscure definition of rhetoric, anomalous to common understanding of the term. Algorithms are rhetorical by nearly any notion of rhetoric available in the literature. There are plenty to choose from:

- "An ability, in each particular case, to see the available means of persuasion" (Aristotle, 2006, p. 37)
- "The use of language as a symbolic means of inducing cooperation in beings that by

nature respond to symbols" (Burke, 1997, p. 43)

- "The art of discovering warrantable beliefs and improving those beliefs in shared discourse" (Booth, 1974, p. xiii)
- "The symbolic inducement of social cooperation" (Hauser, 1999, p. 14)
- "An art of emphasis embodying an order of desire" (Weaver, 1985, p. 211)
- "A mode of altering reality, not by the direct application of energy to objects, but by the creation of discourse which changes reality through the mediation of thought and action" (Bitzer, 1968, p. 4)
- "The art, the fine and useful art, of making things matter" (Farrell, 2008, p. 470)

Despite their nuanced differences, from this sampling of notable definitions a sort of crowd-sourced sense of rhetoric's contours might be ascertained. Without adding yet another definition to the fray (no doubt in one of these meticulously phrased and conspicuously italicized passages so often found in academic writing), we can at least say broadly that rhetoric concerns the exertion of influence. It may persuade, it may aid identification, it may make things matter, and so on, but rhetoric pertains to various ways of influencing behavior and belief. For present purposes, I'm rather fond of Farrell's definition—that rhetoric is the art of making things matter—because it helps make the point about algorithms most clearly. At a technical level, algorithms function by making certain rules matter in certain ways, and the influence of these choices results in making other things matter in the world. In this sense, the rhetorical nature of algorithms is not just a descriptive quality of these automated procedures, variable from case to case. Algorithms are rhetorical at a structural level. Their rhetoricity is an inherent quality of what they are. No algorithms exist that are not also rhetorical.

These claims already may sound aggressive, but they can go still further. In particular, I argue that if algorithms are engaged in *the art of making things matter*, that is, if they are to be understood as rhetorical, then this requires conceptualizing algorithms along three tiers of rhetorical action. I call these the macro-, meso-, and micro-rhetorical tiers.[3] Each will receive its own attention in the pages ahead. Generally, though, the macro-rhetorical tier might tell us how algorithms themselves have come to gain such power and prevalence throughout the planet. The meso-rhetorical might consider to what extent algorithms play a part in making things matter in our world. And the micro-rhetorical might hope to scrutinize the particularities of those processes whereby algorithms go about doing so.

Only by attending to all three tiers of rhetorical action that surround and infuse the algorithm might we adequately respond to their unique and nonpareil significance in the world today. In short, these three algorithmic rhetorics call us toward three scales of *mattering*: algorithms matter immensely in our world; their operations generate results whose repercussions also matter; and they do so precisely through instructions and rules that have already privileged which factors matter in order to reach a result that matters. Juggling these three rhetorics, then, will ultimately mean investigating to what extent algorithms rhetorically re-circulate and sustain their own rhetorical prowess, perhaps as a concrete instantiation of what Niklas Luhmann (1992) has regarded as the autopoiesis of communicative systems.[4]

One thing is certain: if algorithms are the quintessential digital rhetoric, as I suggested in this chapter's opening section, we would do well to understand more about them as we face a future likely to be increasingly mediated by algorithmic automation. The obstacle of technological literacy need not impede us (though, of course, it can only help to know the algorithmic logic learned through the study of higher calculus and computer science; and, in fact, I argue in this chapter's conclusion that achieving full algorithmic literacy in the coming years will eventually mean acquiring the technical chops to generate algorithms of one's own). For now the rhetorical lens of "making things matter" should suffice as enough of a frame to develop an approach to algorithmic rhetoric in greater depth.

The next section thus considers the three tiers of algorithmic rhetorics (macro, meso, and micro) by articulating them with the rhetorical tradition's basis in ancient Greece. Although what we now call "digital rhetorics" are drastically evolved notions of the rhetorical when compared to the models inherited from antiquity—which were based on a culture of orality that had no inkling of the automation or computer mediated communication that are now such commonplaces[5]—linking algorithmic rhetoric with some aspects of the classical period will show, surprisingly, that even these vanguard technologies are rhetorically less novel than they seem.

TOWARD AN ALGORITHMIC RHETORIC

Approaching algorithmic rhetoric through a model of three concentric tiers means taking a holistic approach toward algorithms and the rhetoricity that both surrounds and pervades them. We can get only so far by saying, "Look, algorithms are rhetorical." Surely that's an important truth. And recognizing as much is a meaningful step toward understanding the communicative implications of these automated processes. But there's critical work to be done if algorithms are the rhetorical procedures they appear to be. Doing such work means recognizing that all algorithms act rhetorically in unique ways. The specifics of these ways are partly a technical matter of the mathematical instructions and code by which they are programmed. But also in play are the axiological and praxeological positions that these programming

choices operationalize. Moreover, and concurrently, there are also rhetorical aspects to the very ways algorithms in general have come to attain the influence that they have in our world. This discourse is larger than the details about how specific algorithms work; it concerns how people and institutions make the case for valuing algorithms *per se*. The holistic, three-tier model assumes that each type of these rhetorical activities is important, and that only by understanding them together will a comprehensive characterization of algorithmic rhetoric be possible.

Still, the three-tier model can be hard to envision, so allow me to diagram its conceptual scheme and to say more about why I have called the three tiers macro-, meso-, and micro-rhetorical instead of something else. To begin with, keep in mind that these three types of rhetoric exist concurrently. Each sustains the other. They surround and pervade the algorithm. It may help to know that the macro-rhetorical might have been called a *meta*-algorithmic rhetoric, because it is interested in those rhetorics that elevate the algorithm to such prominence at the level of society at large. Macro- or meta-algorithmic rhetoric, then, doesn't concern algorithms so much as the discourse *about* them. On the opposite scale, meanwhile, the micro-rhetorical might have been called *mesa*-algorithmic rhetoric inasmuch as "meta-" (meaning "above" or "beyond" in the Greek) has no common antonym, but "mesa-" (meaning "inside" or "within") makes a viable candidate.[6] In this sense, mesa-algorithmic rhetoric would be that rhetoric found within particular algorithms. The meta/mesa model, however, would have left no middle space to attend to algorithms categorically as rhetorical operations at the ontological level of structure. All things considered, the model of macro-, meso-, and micro-rhetorics offers what I believe to be the best way of recognizing that all algorithms are fundamentally rhetorical, though they each behave rhetorically in particular ways, and algorithms *per se* are leveraged as valued technologies on a large socio-cultural scale.

These three tiers of algorithmic rhetoric are meant, though, not only to demonstrate the rhetoricity of algorithms. The three tiers also aim to point rhetorical critics who might wish to think about digital automation as a subject of analysis toward important areas of critical attention. The three tiers then encompass quite different areas, fit for scholars of different dispositions and aptitudes. Not only do their scopes differ; so do their corresponding stakes[7] and critical focus (see Table 1). The macro-rhetorical requires attention to the circulation of discourse that contributes to elevating the status of algorithms as valuable technologies. The stakes here are epistemological, having to do with what count as valid knowledge claims. The meso-rhetorical requires attention to identifying the category of technological operations we call "algorithms" as rhetorically constituted. The stakes here are ontological, having to do with the algorithm's nature. And the micro-rhetorical requires critiquing the repercussions and implications of algorithmic rhetoric in its particular instantiations. These stakes are both praxeological and axiological, as they pertain to the practical ramifications and values algorithms exert on the world they mediate. Each will be elaborated below.

The Macro-Rhetorical

In Plato's *Gorgias*, Socrates famously demotes rhetoric to mere cookery. In doing so he disparages Gorgias and other Sophists who conceived of rhetoric as a reproducible art (*technê*) and taught its principles to citizens for whom a facility in oratory posed major advantages in the direct democracy of ancient Athens. The principle behind at least Gorgias's sophistic teaching maintained pragmatically that those who spoke more persuasively would be able to sway public opinion, and the opinion of the courts, about whatever topic they happened to carry forth. The rhetorical arts were those that cultivated these persuasive, oratorical skills. For Plato, though, rhetoric was a sham. Its tenets, if executed deftly in public speech, may well serve to sway opinion (*doxa*), but Truth was a far different matter. In Plato's view, only the method of dialectic—exemplified through his dialogues in what we now call the Socratic method—can lead to the one universal Truth or knowledge (*episteme*) with which all right-thinking people ought to be concerned. By denigrating rhetoric to mere cookery, then, Plato suggests that rhetoric merely follows a recipe; and, as methods go, it can lead only to belief but not to knowledge.

Many readers here will be well familiar with this common history about the first tensions between philosophy and rhetoric, which continue to trouble scholars today. Nevertheless, foregrounding a discussion of algorithmic rhetoric in so ancient a precedent is useful because it reminds us of the stakes in thinking about algorithms as rhetorical. What counts as a valid truth claim? If I can make you believe something, does that make it true? What does communication have to do with what we might claim to know? Are some methods better than others for arriving at the truth? What are they? And where does the algorithm fit in?

The macro-rhetorical tier of algorithmic rhetoric marinates in these questions. It can be understood as the realm of rhetorical discourse

Table 1. Scopes, foci and stakes

	Macro-Rhetorical	**Meso-Rhetorical**	**Micro-Rhetorical**
Scope	Society	Algorithms *per se*	Algorithm's Components
Critical Focus	Circulation	Identification	Critique
Stakes	Epistemological	Ontological	Axiological / Praxeological
Ancient Basis	*Episteme / Doxa*	*Technê*	The Five Canons

concerned with legitimating the algorithm as an epistemically viable method for intervention in our world. In a sense, then, the macro-rhetorical has nothing to do with how *algorithms* behave rhetorically. The "rhetorical" aspect here is rather found in discourse *about* algorithms and their value for innumerable ends. But such discourse is not just concerned with ends, with *what* algorithms can do or make, predict, discover, or learn. The macro-rhetorical realm is also one in which arguments are made for algorithms as the best, most efficient, appropriate / consistent / reliable / disinterested / precise / and accurate *means* for reaching the various ends to which their automation might be directed. It is the macro-rhetorical that calls us to think critically about how and why algorithms have become so pervasive and commonplace across societies and cultures. Of course, this *how* and *why* have inherently rhetorical explanations.

The work required to explore the macro-rhetorics circulating in public discourse and substantiating the algorithm's claim to supremacy as *the* technological meaning-maker of our time is beyond the scope of this chapter. It is possible, however, to adumbrate here what this work might look like and to situate it in relevant scholarly conversations. At issue is a matter of scale. Macro-rhetorics, as the name suggests, take place at the level of big-D Discourse: they permeate entire politico-economic systems (particularly neoliberalism as described by Harvey, 2007), cultural policies (in Miller and Yudice's conception, 2002), ideological state apparatuses (Althusser, 1971), and more generally, those scientific "paradigms" (Kuhn, 1996) whose epistemic regimes hold a powerful, if invisible influence in global thinking. In other words, the growing ubiquity of digital automation has not been arbitrary, or even the result of technological imperatives, but rather it has developed through the interaction of technology and culture—an argument Thomas Streeter (2010) makes about the Internet in general. Trying to isolate macro-rhetorics on this scale is a bit like catching smoke with a net. But the idea

is to look for those laws, policies, conversations, socio-cultural "trends" and the like that reveal a disposition to entrust computerized automation with responsibilities of growing magnitude.

Consider the U.S. stock market. Our markets are no longer operated by a bustling floor of frenetic traders, waving their arms and papers, shouting out, "Buy! Buy! Buy!" (or even, more grimly, "Sell! Sell! Sell!"). Today, algorithms run the market—quietly, coolly, and faster than you can ever imagine. Sixty percent of all trades now "are executed by computers with little or no real-time oversight from humans" (Steiner, 2012, p. 17). In a global political economy that encourages free market competition, algorithms offer an indisputable advantage, making it possible to execute automated trades both faster than others and based upon the interpretation of enormous data stores. The rhetorical topoi that contributed to this takeover have tacitly mobilized such values as speed, consistency, repeatability, and the logical indubitability of quantification in order essentially to make a case that algorithms are a better, more competitively viable way to operate Wall Street today. The more investment bankers, hedge fund managers, and other powerful industry players utilize algorithmic automation to broker their financial decisions, the more others will have to do so to keep up. In this case, as in countless others, algorithms thus exhibit a built-in capacity to sustain and regenerate their own authority.

But, just as macro-rhetorics dye the very fabric of our institutions and the dominant worldviews that govern them from the top down, macro-rhetorics also pervade vernacular contexts from the bottom up. These vernacular rhetorics are powerful conversations, small-d discourses, circulating among ordinary people in everyday life to shape public opinion and inspire political action (Hauser, 1999). Even if "the algorithm" never comes up explicitly as a topic of conversation in vernacular publics (it remains a fairly specialized subject, after all), citizens with no institutional power still contribute to the macro-rhetorics that position algorithmic technologies as desirable and nonpareil on a variety of measures. Our personal computers, cell phones, tablets, and all the services their applications provide, are made possible by algorithms on which we are increasingly made to depend. When algorithms now write AP news articles; when they help us book a plane ticket, help air traffic controllers map the flight patterns, and help pilots fly the planes; when they navigate our way through customer service calls ("For English press one, para en espanol oprima el numero dos"); when they deliver us customized banner ads on the Internet; when they recommend movies or books we're likely to enjoy; when they predict everything from the weather to *coup d'etats* to the outcome of sporting events—and when we let them do all these things and more, whether we relish their possibilities or are wholly oblivious to their existence, we contribute to the macro-rhetorical realm that sustains the algorithm's influence. Manuel Castells (2008) puts it in terms of technological globalization: "Not everything or everyone is globalized," he admits, "but the global networks that structure the planet affect everything and everyone" (p. 81). The macro-rhetorical invites us to think about how algorithms now "structure the planet" and come to "affect everything and everyone," whether we know it or not.

Attending to what I've called the macro-rhetorics surrounding the algorithm thus means engaging the sorts of concerns that bothered Plato so long ago. It means thinking about algorithms as a particular way of conceiving what counts as truth and what counts as mere manipulation of belief. It means thinking about why algorithms are, by and large, being granted the status of truth-makers as they are implemented, extolled, and faithfully trusted to mediate so many parts of global experience. Finally, attending to the macro-rhetorical tier of algorithmic rhetoric means articulating the convergence of our quotidian personal complicity in vaunting the algorithm's status with the deeper, structurally endemic ways algorithms are valued in the globalized world at large.

The Meso-Rhetorical

Rhetoric is a *techne*, a reproducible art. Certainly the same can be said of the algorithm. After all, today we think of algorithms as technologies (a word that derives from the Greek *techne*) largely because they operate through a strict set of learnable rules and instructions that can be repeated effectively for similar results.[8] Plato, in fact, often listed such algorithmic precursors as calculation or arithmetic among the examples of *technai* he provided in various dialogues (alongside cookery, medicine, carpentry, and so forth). Such skills, though, however reproducible, also require a deft hand, a keen eye, and a measure of genuine artistry. Isocrates, for instance, is said never to have given a speech because he had a weak voice and poor delivery, despite possessing an intellectual mastery of the rhetorical principles that make for effective oratory. As a result, in his school Isocrates would *teach* oratory but never *deliver* it. Instead he had his students practice by creating and performing speeches of their own. Gorgias, meanwhile, was a superior oratorical artist and delivered his own speeches, teaching his students by asking them to imitate his own speechmaking. The point here is that a *techne* requires both a repeatable set of precepts and a level of artistry to be well executed. Rhetoric qualifies. And algorithms do, too: as anyone who writes algorithms will tell you, there is without doubt a real artistry to doing so.

Of course, just because the algorithm and rhetoric alike meet enough criteria to make them *technai* does not mean we have proved that the algorithm is rhetorical. What's curious, and on the surface hints at paradox, is that the surefire way to recognize that algorithms operate rhetorically is to observe that they behave less like ancient notions of rhetorical oratory than like Plato's method of dialectic. In classical dialectic, a philosopher asks his interlocutor questions, receiving answers that then prompt subsequent related questions, and then more answers, and then more questions based on those answers again. In this way, the philosopher channels his questions toward a particular desired result; only by asking the right questions at the right times can the dialectician whittle the input of an interlocutor's answers into the output of a conclusion that the interlocutor may not have been able to reach without the questions guiding the conversation to that end. In effect, the authors of algorithms operationalize this dialectic method into a set of procedures capable of being automated and repeated through digital processes. Thinking again of algorithms as decision-trees brings their similarity to this kind of dialectic into focus.

Imagine, for instance, an algorithm designed to do your laundry.[9] In a sense, it would proceed through a dialectic method by asking questions meant to provide it the input data from which to reach its conclusion. Are these clothes whites or colors? Colors. Is the fabric cotton? No. Is it polyester? No. Is it denim? Yes. How dirty is it? Very. By asking certain questions, the algorithm can draw toward a conclusion about how to do the laundry: using a particular water temperature, a certain spin cycle, an appropriate amount of detergent, and so on. Without asking these questions and receiving understandable answers, it would not be able to reach the conclusion it does and do your laundry without shrinking your favorite shirt or leaving all your whites turned pink.

The trick, of course, is that algorithms ask questions strategically because they bring a set of assumptions to bear on the input they receive in response. It's here where the rhetorical becomes more evident. Knowing that the laundry involves colorful clothes is meaningless data unless the algorithm also knows that colorful clothes typically require cold water. The questions algorithms ask thus look for answers it already knows how to translate into actionable conduct or knowledge. In this sense, they don't arrive at conclusions naively at all; some conclusions are already in place, such as what temperature the water ought to be for different kinds of clothes, or how much detergent is necessary for varying degrees of soil. Because, in this fashion, aspects of an algorithm's results are already predetermined, the procedures for arriving at them are biased toward directing the data in a particular way. This clever directing procedure is rhetorical. That it goes disguised in a technical process whose instructions and rules look a lot like a rhetorical handbook might have looked to Plato, while the rhetorical element in fact plays out in a process far more like dialectic, attests to Aristotle's perspicacity in his *Rhetoric* when he called rhetoric and dialectic counterparts (*antistrophos*).

Of course, the disguise of algorithms is part of what makes them so pervasive and quintessentially rhetorical, and it's what we're concerned to think about when considering the meso-rhetorical level of algorithmic rhetoric. Unlike the macro-rhetorical interest in how algorithms *per se* came rhetorically to acquire such preponderance and trust in society at large, the meso-rhetorical is interested in engendering awareness about how algorithms are themselves rhetorical. This awareness need not proceed to the level of specific rhetorical actions that algorithms sometimes perform, variably from case to case, in their code or programming language. That analysis remains for the micro-rhetorical tier. Meso-rhetorics are those that take place at the categorical level, making ontological claims about the fundamental rhetoricity of algorithms in general. The trope of the disguise is apposite here because algorithms are, more often than not, invisible to human perception. We may know they're working, but they function so quickly and commonly now that we scarcely take notice. To think about meso-rhetorics is, first and foremost, to take notice of algorithms in their context, and to recognize them as the rhetorical operations that they are. Carolyn R. Miller (2010) has argued that rhetoric is fundamentally an art of concealment; its tools must not be named, lest rhetoricity be exposed as artifice and rendered ineffective. I argue that, given the potentially dangerous power we have accorded algorithms today, naming their tools and exposing their concealment is a valuable act.

The Micro-Rhetorical

In *De Inventione*, Cicero's (2001) treatise on rhetoric from around 50 BC, he suggests that rhetoric operates through five canons that together constitute the integral parts of effective speech: invention (*inventio*), arrangement (*dispositio*), style (*elocutio*), memory (*memoria*), and delivery (*actio*). Some 150 years later Quintilian (1980) elaborated on the five canons in his *Institutio Oratoria*, establishing a basis for rhetorical education that lasted at least through medieval times. Although our interpretation of these canons has expanded considerably since then, and will continue to expand as our sense of what counts as rhetorical also grows more universal, the original five canons offer one way to think of the particular ways algorithms work rhetorically.

The micro-rhetorical tier of algorithmic rhetoric asks us to do more than consider how algorithms have come to be accorded such faith as knowledge-producers in our world, and it asks more still than to identify the structural rhetoricity of the algorithm as a *technê*. The micro-rhetorical tier involves the particular rhetorical maneuvers a given algorithm performs to make something matter. Given the technical complexity of the algorithms behind, say, our computer software—which, as best I could tell you, are designed roughly by compiling advanced computer language into executable code and then converting it into binary by an assembler—it may seem that a critical effort to uncover their inherent rhetorical tools would require literacy in higher levels of computer science than many humanists or social scientists might have, myself included. Such a technical approach is certainly valuable. And looking for evidence of the five canons embedded in a bot's operational language offers a method to do it. But approaching these automated processes through the five canons can also help to reveal in a more widely communicable sense just what axiological and praxeological stakes particular rhetorical choices raise for humans as we interact with and are influenced by algorithms in our daily lives.

From a critical standpoint, the difficulty lies in correlating the five canons as they pertain to speech with their commensurate techniques as associated with algorithmic automation. My sense is that not all algorithms we encounter will make manifest all five canons. Unfortunately, the inner-nuances of most algorithms are closely guarded from public scrutiny (often for proprietary reasons but also a host of others) and given this guardedness, critical analysis of what I'm calling algorithmic micro-rhetorics may seem impossible without access to the technical specificities that reveal an algorithm's priorities and procedures. It's not. Focusing on human interaction with computers or other automated processes, and doing so through the lens of the five canons, can still accomplish meaningful critical work. Doing so makes it possible to consider how an algorithm known to exist generally, if not in any technical specificity, can rhetorically advance claims with practical and value-laden implications as we communicate with mixed media technologies on a regular basis.

The algorithm that regulates how customer-submitted reviews are ranked on Amazon.com might make a useful example. Although Amazon holds this algorithm close to its chest, we know it exists because the site ranks its regular reviewers with different measures of status and because product reviews on the site (say, of a book) appear in a particular, non-arbitrary order. Drawing from the five canons, we could consider this ordering a kind of rhetorical *arrangement*. In terms of *style* or *delivery*, the way the reviews appear to visitors on Amazon's website represent another rhetorical element, algorithmic insofar as the design is a result of output determined through dynamic automation instead of a static template.[10] The canon of *memory* in this example involves those inputs the algorithm needs to know and remember in order to arrive at a particular result such as ranking a reviewer in a particular way or placing one review higher than another. For instance, when visitors to the site are asked if a review was helpful, yes or no, their answer provides data for the algorithm to remember, tabulate, and consider among many other factors in ranking a reviewer with particular status. These status attributions say that some reviews and reviewers are better than others—the very act of which suggests that Amazon seeks to cultivate a particular way of reviewing its products. The canon of *invention* comes forth in the algorithm that relegates this status by virtue of its implicit argument for the superiority of certain ways of reviewing. Such factors as the length of a review, its documented helpfulness, the amount of products a reviewer has written about overall, and how long the reviewer has been reviewing on the site thus constitute some of the invented available means of persuasion. Accordingly, their scrutiny can reveal the motivations and logic behind this algorithm's rhetorical impact.

The micro-rhetorical tier of algorithmic rhetoric is one that investigates a specific algorithm's strategies, biases, and assumptions to reveal the values it promulgates and the practical effect these values have. As the case of Amazon's customer-review ranking algorithm indicates, something so innocent as an automated measure of status given to a book review submitted by an anonymous reader can in practice delineate what qualifies as the proper means of critical engagement, aesthetic taste, or discourse about cultural artifacts from literature to blenders. While this kind of analysis can valuably take place at the level of code (see, for instance, the edited collection *From A to <A>: Keywords of Markup*, 2010), it need not be resigned to that level alone. We all interact with algorithms more often than we probably realize, and paying more attention to the ways their intervention in our lives makes claims about what matters will help us to attend more critically to their potentially undesirable repercussions.

DIGITAL RHETORIC, DIGITAL LITERACY

In these pages I have tried both to show that algorithms are rhetorical, and to forward a model for understanding algorithmic rhetoric in a way that situates these automated procedures as key loci of critical attention in the years ahead. Although more scholars are beginning to recognize that digital rhetorics are powerful forces all around us (the chapters in this volume offering several extraordinary examples), attention to algorithms has been largely underdeveloped from a rhetorical standpoint. This may be because of gaps in literacy. While the cybernetic tradition in the study of communication theory as a field is thought to have emerged from a quite mathematical basis among engineers—the seminal work being Shannon and Weaver's *Mathematical Theory of Communication* (1948)—it has come a long way since then. Not all of us who study communication can claim to know much at all about math. The rhetorical tradition in particular has its basis in humanism, which has meant that, as James Aune (2001) puts it, "most rhetoricians became rhetoricians in part because of a math phobia" (p. 174). At the least we can say that the majority of rhetoricians tend not to have the math or computer science to approach the algorithm with confidence. I consider myself in this group. But as I have tried to show, the technological hurdles that might discourage us from studying the rhetoric of algorithmic intervention in our world are not so great as to justify the neglect of these important technologies.

In time, inevitably, algorithmic literacy will rise. It will have to. Cathy Davidson (2012) has gone so far as to argue that that in the twenty-first century's new model of global literacy, it will no longer suffice to learn the "three Rs" of reading, writing, and 'rithmetic, which have been imperative for one's social and cultural capital since the industrial age. Today, she says, in the digital age of Web 2.0, we need to add the 'rithm as a fourth indispensible "R" to our wherewithal in a globalized world where technology is becoming a common language. Algorithmic thinking, Davidson says, "helps to end the false 'two cultures' binary of the arts, humanities and social sciences on the one side, and technology and science on the other." The digital humanities are just one area of inquiry that supports this trend to shatter tired divisions of epistemic cultures.

The digital humanities scholar Stephen Ramsay (2011), for example, advocates for algorithmic criticism mindful of rhetorical implications like those I have tried to draw out here. "To speak of algorithms," Ramsay says, "is usually to speak of unerring processes and irrefragable answers" (p. 18). They are, in other words, strictly constrained within the black box of their own parameters. Algorithms thus fit snugly within the epistemic culture of science that favors objective, quantifiable data. But the choices that determine the nature of an algorithm's constraints are unending. These choices are rhetorical, belonging within the qualitative doxastic culture of the humanities. Ramsay wants scholars to see algorithms "loosed from the strictures of the irrefragable and explore the possibilities of a science that can operate outside of the confines of the denotative" (p. 18). By helping to address the limitations of how knowledge is formed, a call for more algorithmic thinking might become a valuable heuristic beyond the algorithm, wherever different epistemic cultures collide.

It comes as no surprise that similar projects are becoming more commonplace. Nathan Johnson (2012) calls us to look "at infrastructure instead of through it," claiming that "investigating the rhetoric of classifications, standards, protocols, and algorithms is an important part of understanding modern rhetorics" (p. 2). Similarly, Lev Manovich (2002) has suggested that *representation* is a key term for new media. New media, he says, "represent/construct some features of physical reality at the expense of others, one worldview among many, one possible system of categories among numerous others" (p. 15-16). This biased way of representing reality sounds suspiciously similar to the one I have tried to problematize

through the algorithm. Any automated procedure that makes things matter by making some things matter more than others is one we have to regard as rhetorical. And if so, the work then begins for those of us interested in critically exposing how different rhetorical practices delimit particular and invested versions of what matters in our world.

REFERENCES

Althusser, L. (1971). Ideology and ideological state apparatuses. In *Lenin and Philosophy* (pp. 127–177). New York: Monthly Review Press.

Amazon Mechanical Turk. (n. d.). Retrieved from https://www.mturk.com/mturk/

Anderson, J. A. (1996). *Communication theory: Epistemological foundations*. New York: The Guilford Press.

Anderson, J. A., & Baym, V. (2004). Philosophies and philosophic issues in communication, 1995-2004. *The Journal of Communication, 54*(4), 589–615. doi:10.1093/joc/54.4.589

Aristotle, . (2006). *On rhetoric* (G. Kennedy, Trans.). Oxford: Oxford University Press.

Atwill, J. M. (1998). *Rhetoric reclaimed: Aristotle and the liberal arts tradition*. Ithaca, NY: Cornell University Press.

Berlinski, D. (2011). *The advent of the algorithm*. New York: Mariner Books.

Bitzer, L. (1968). The rhetorical situation. *Philosophy and Rhetoric, 1*(1), 1–14.

Bogost, I. (2007). *Persuasive games: The expressive power of videogames*. Cambridge, MA: The MIT Press.

Booth, W. (1974). *Modern dogma and the rhetoric of assent*. Chicago, IL: University of Chicago Press.

Burke, K. (1997). *A rhetoric of motives*. Berkeley, CA: University of California Press.

Castells, M. (2008). The new public sphere: Global civil society, communication networks, and global governance. *The Annals of the American Academy of Political and Social Science*, *616*, 78–93. doi:10.1177/0002716207311877

Chabert, J.-L. (Ed.). (1999). *A history of algorithms: From the pebble to the microchip*Weeks, C., Trans.). New York: Springer. doi:10.1007/978-3-642-18192-4

Cheal, J. (2011). What is the opposite of meta? *Acuity*, *2*, 153–161.

Cicero, M. T. (2001). *On the ideal orator* (J. M. May, & J. Wisse, Trans.). New York: Oxford University Press.

Columbia, SC: University of South Carolina Press.

Davidson, C. N. (2012, January 2). A fourth 'R' for 21st century literacy. *The Washington Post*, sec. Post Local.

Dilger, B., & Rice, J. (Eds.). (2010). *From A to <A>: Keywords of markup*. Minneapolis, MN: University of Minnesota Press.

Dyson, G. (2012). *Turing's cathedral*. New York: Vintage.

Farrell, T. (2008). The weight of rhetoric: Studies in cultural delirium. *Philosophy and Rhetoric*, *41*(4), 467–487. doi:10.1353/par.0.0018

Fountain, H. (2012, October 26). Yes, driverless cars know the way to San Jose. *The New York Times*.

Gazale, M. (1999). *Gnomon: From pharaohs to fractals*. Princeton: Princeton University Press.

Gleick, J. (2012, August 4). Auto crrect ths! *The New York Times*.

Harvey, D. (2007). *A brief history of neoliberalism*. New York: Oxford University Press.

Hauser, G. (1999). *Vernacular voices: The rhetoric of publics and public spheres*.

Johnson, N. R. (2012). Information infrastructure as rhetoric: Tools for analysis. *Poroi*, *8*(1), 1–3. doi:10.13008/2151-2957.1113

Jones, J. (2011, December). *Algorithmic rhetoric and search literacy*. Paper presented at the meeting of the Humanities, Arts, Sciences, and Technology Advanced Collaboratory (HASTAC), Ann Arbor, MI.

Kuhn, T. (1996). *The structure of the scientific revolution*. Chicago, IL: University of Chicago Press. doi:10.7208/chicago/9780226458106.001.0001

Luhmann, N. (1992). What is communication? *Communication Theory*, *2*(3), 251–259. doi:10.1111/j.1468-2885.1992.tb00042.x

MacCormick, J. (2011). *Nine algorithms that changed the future: The ingenious ideas that drive today's computers*. Princeton, NJ: Princeton University Press.

Manovich, L. (2002). *The language of new media*. Cambridge, MA: The MIT Press.

McCorkle, B. (2012). *Rhetorical delivery as technological discourse*. Carbondale, IL: Southern Illinois University Press.

Miller, C. R. (2010). Should we name the tools? In J. Ackerman, & D. Coogan (Eds.), *The public work of rhetoric: Citizen-scholars and civic engagement* (pp. 19–38). Columbia, SC: University of South Carolina Press.

Miller, T., & Yudice, G. (2002). *Cultural policy*. London: SAGE.

Ong, W. J. (2002). *Orality and literacy: The technologizing of the world*. New York: Routledge.

Oxford English Dictionary Online. (n. d.). *Algorithm*. Retrieved from www.oed.com

Plato, . (2004). *Gorgias* (C. Emlyn-Jones, & W. Hamilton, Trans.). New York: Penguin Classics.

Quintilian, . (1980). *Institutio Oratoria: Books I-III* (H. E. Butler, Trans.). Cambridge, MA: Harvard University Press.

Ramsay, S. (2011). *Reading machines: Toward an algorithmic criticism*. Urbana, IL: University of Illinois Press.

Robert-Houdin, J.-E. (2009). *Memoirs of Robert-Houdin* (R. S. Mackenzie, Trans.). Whitefish, MT: Kessinger Publishing.

Shannon, C., & Weaver, W. (1948). *The mathematical theory of communication*. Urbana, IL: University of Illinois Press.

Steiner, C. (2012). *Automate this*. New York: Portfolio.

Streeter, T. (2010). *The net effect: Romanticism, capitalism, and the Internet*. New York: New York University Press.

Streeter, T. (2010). *The net effect: Romanticism, capitalism, and the Internet*. New York: New York University Press.

United States Department of Defense. (2011). *Unmanned systems integrated roadmap, FY2011-2016*. Washington, DC: Department of Defense.

Weaver, R. (1985). Language is sermonic. In R. L. Johannessen, R. Strickland, & R. T. Eubanks (Eds.), *Language is sermonic* (pp. 201–226). Baton Rouge, LA: Louisiana State University Press.

KEY TERMS AND DEFINITIONS

Algorithm: A set of instructions with specific steps that lead to certain results; they are usually performed through automated mechanisms.

Macro-Rhetorics: The largest scale in the rhetorical analysis of algorithms, in which one examines the preponderance of algorithms across society. Macro-rhetorics are keyed toward circulation related to classical distinctions between *episteme* and *doxa*. Their stakes are epistemological.

Mesa-Rhetorics: The middle scale in the rhetorical analysis of algorithms, in which one identifies the presence of an algorithm in different parts of lived experience and engenders awareness about its rhetorical nature. Mesa-rhetorics are keyed toward identification based in the classical concept of *technê*. Their stakes are ontological.

Micro-Rhetorics: The smallest scale in the rhetorical analysis of algorithms, in which one scrutinizes the particularities of those automated processes whereby algorithms behave rhetorically. Micro-rhetorics are keyed toward critique grounded in the five canons of the classical rhetorical tradition. Their stakes are axiological and praxeological.

Procedurality: A term used by Ian Bogost to denote the fundamental way software works by encoding rules designed to execute processes that, when followed, represent the world in a particular way.

ENDNOTES

[1] I have relied heavily for my historical understanding on two books: *A History of Algorithms* (Chaubert, 1999) and *The Advent of the Algorithm* (Berlinski, 2000). Curious readers might also consult these texts for a better and more technically rich account of the rise of algorithms than I am able to provide.

[2] The example of drones works here, too, inasmuch as they are often operated or monitored remotely by invisible humans.

[3] Despite their apparent symmetry with Jones's three metaphors for understanding how algorithms work, the three tiers share no direct correspondence with those conceptual apparatuses. There are innumerable varieties of algorithms and metaphorical

ways to understand them. The three tiers of algorithmic rhetoric offer a way to understand the rhetoricity of algorithms, and not just algorithms themselves, though the two are inherently intertwined.

4   Luhmann is a systems theorist who leverages the concept of autopoiesis as a way to describe a closed system that creates and (re) produces itself. In his vision, communication itself is an autopoietic system in that it's closed from anything but itself, even the human. In other words, for Luhmann, humans don't communicate; "only communication can communicate" (1992, p.251). Algorithms might be seen as autopoietic to the extent they (re)produce their own authority through automated procedures operationally absent of human involvement.

5   Interested readers should see Walter Ong's excellent book, *Orality and Literacy* (2002), in which he traces the shift from oral to print to electronic cultures with an eye toward the rhetorical ramifications of each.

6   For more on this terminology, see Joe Cheal (2011), who has investigated the opposite of "meta" and proposed "mesa" as the best solution.

7   Note that these "stakes" have been mapped along the four metatheoretical standpoints described by Anderson (1996; Anderson & Baym, 2004).

8   For more on *technê*, see Janet Atwill's extended treatment of the term in *Rhetoric Reclaimed: Aristotle and the Liberal Arts Tradition* (1998).

9   For this example I am indebted to Steiner (2012), who uses a hypothetical laundry algorithm to explain his decision tree model, though I extend it for different purposes.

10   For more on the canon of *delivery* as technological discourse, see McCorkle, 2012.

Chapter 4
Decoding What is Good in Code:
Toward a Metaphysical Ethics of Unicode

Jennifer Helene Maher
University of Maryland, Baltimore County, USA

ABSTRACT

Programming benefits from universal standards that facilitate effective global transmission of information. The Unicode Standard, for example, is a character encoding system that aims to assign a unique number set to each letter, mark, and symbol in the world's various written systems, including Arabic, Korean, Cherokee, and even Cuneiform. As the quantity of these numerical encodings grow, the differences among the written systems of natural languages pose increasingly little consequence to the artificial languages of both programmers and machines. However, the instrumental, technical effects of Unicode must not be mistaken as its only effects. Recognized as a metaphysical object in its own right, Unicode, specifically, and code, generally, creates a protocol for the actualization of moral and political values. This chapter examines how Microsoft's inclusion and then deletion of the Unicode encodings U+5350 and U+534D in its Office Bookshelf Symbol 7 font illustrates how technically successful coding can be rhetorically buggy, meaning it invokes competing ethical values that, in this case, involve free speech, anti-Semitism, and Western privilege.

DOI: 10.4018/978-1-4666-4916-3.ch004

Copyright © 2014, IGI Global. Copying or distributing in print or electronic forms without written permission of IGI Global is prohibited.

INTRODUCTION

One of the greatest challenges to global literacy in the digital age has proven to be the diversity that exists among natural languages. Of the approximately 7,000 known living natural languages, approximately 80 also exist as a written system. Consequently, one of the most elemental challenges to the digital transmission of information is the character variation among these systems. To process information digitally necessitates a character encoding systems that allows for the unambiguous translation of not only alphabetic (e.g., Latin), logographic (e.g., Chinese) and syllabic (e.g., Cherokee) characters but also characters necessary for punctuation, ideograms and control at both the level of the human-readable artificial programming languages and the machine-readable binary code of 1's and 0's. But creating a standard character encoding system for even one written language is challenging. IBM computer scientist Robert Bemer described the numerical encoding of the relatively simple, Latin alphabet-based Standard American English in the period before the 1960 development of the character encoding system American Standard Code for Information Interchange (ASCII) as nothing short of "the Babel of internal computer codes."

Certainly the development of ASCII had done much to improve character encoding functionality in the Latin-based alphabetic system. However, as information exchange went global via the Internet, the challenge became not simply how to how to encode characters and symbols within particular alphabetic systems but how to encode across those systems. As Joseph D. Becker (1988), of Xerox Corporation, explained in his seminal paper "Unicode 88":

[T]he people of the world need to be able to communicate and compute in their own native languages, not just in English. Text processing systems designed for the 1990s and the 21st century must accommodate Latin-based alphabets for European language such as French, German, and Spanish; and also major non-Latin alphabets such as Arabic, Greek, Hebrew, and Russian; and also "exotic" scripts of growing importance such as Hindi and Thai; not to mention the thousand of ideographic characters used in writing Chinese, Japanese, and Korean. (p. 1)

To address this need, the non-profit Unicode Consortium was formed in 1991 and described its mission as arising out of a need to develop a set of universal standards and specifications so as to enable "people around the world to use computers in any language." Published in the same year, the *Unicode Standard*, according to the Consortium's website, offered "a unique number for every character, no matter what the platform, no matter what the program, no matter what the language." Although often invisible to non-technical end-users unaware of this standard, the Consortium makes clear the importance of the *Unicode Standard* to the most quotidian practices of the Internet: "Our freely-available specifications and data form the foundation for software internationalization in all major operating systems, search engines, applications, and the World Wide Web."

Unicode is undoubtedly an important element to the successful workings of Internet communication. However, at present, Unicode is too often considered only in terms of a technical standard that maximizes efficiency and effectiveness. The numeric translation of characters and symbols appears to facilitate the boiling down of the means of written communication to its most powerful essence as series of 1's and 0's read by the computing machine, a reduction that frees language from the complex, social politics that circulate through it. To think of language then as essentially just a collection of discreet units of information belies the powerful dynamics that are masked rather than resolved through Unicode. In this chapter, I offer an example of what it means to think of the object of code, generally, and Unicode, specifically as still part of an ancient, human tradition concerned with what is good. Drawing on Aristotle's conception of *phronesis* (practical wisdom) as the ability to discern good from ill from among the range of choices available to humans in the activity of living, I illustrate how the numeric Unicode for two symbols translated as U+5350 and U+534D are not only a useful bridge between human language and machine language but also between technical encoding and rhetorical encoding.

TOWARD A METAPHYSICS OF CODE

According to Giles Deleuze (1992), the "passive danger" of the Internet is "jamming" (p. 6). Left ambiguous by Deleuze, we might best understand jamming as the interruption of a system organized to facilitate the seamless flow of information. By no means limited to the digital, an alphabetic system such as English, offers effective pathways for the coded exchange of characters of information organized according to a set of rules and conventions. But with the distribution of information made possible through the Internet, this one system becomes just one of many such systems nestled within a heterogeneous network. Easily viewed as chaotic, the Internet is essentially just one thing: code. As Lawrence Lessig (1998) explains, code is "the software and hardware that constitutes cyberspace as it is—the set of protocols, the set of rules, implemented, or codified, in the software of cyberspace itself, that determine how people interact or exist in this space" (p. 4). Although variation might appear to exist in the human experience of code as effect, the fact remains that the protocols of code "constrains some behavior by making other behavior possible" (p. 5). Alexander Galloway (2004) builds on code qua protocol to discuss how the distributed network of the digital constitutes a unique kind of protocol. Although protocol has always functioned as "a set of recommendations and rules that outline specific technical standards" (p. 6), the protocol of today is no longer "a question of consideration and sense" but instead "of logic and physics" (p. 7). Rather than deliberation and consideration of how the world ought to be, physics aims to reveal how the world actually is. The human state of being is therefore always already subject to this new kind of scientific, algorithmic protocol. Whereas previous behavioral protocols governed "social or political practices, computer protocols govern how specific *technologies* are agreed to, adopted, implemented, and ultimately used by people around the world" (p. 7). Thus, human protocol are always now subject to digital protocol.

In the protocol hierarchy constructed by Galloway, Unicode, I suggest, does not rate highly. At the top of this hierarchy resides the "link layer" protocol that addresses hardware specifics, then comes the "Internet layer" protocol which is responsible for "actual movement of data from one place to another (pp. 40-41). Next is the "transport layer," which oversees the transference of data from one place to another. Finally, at the bottom of the protocol hierarchy is the "application layer." Galloway, who also describes this layer as the "semantic layer," writes that this element of the hierarchy "is responsible for the content of the specific technology in question, be it checking one's email, or accessing a Web page . . . [I]t is responsible for preserving the content of data within the networked transactions." At the semantic layer is where Unicode functions most explicitly, although Unicode might also be considered an important element to the functioning of the transport layer, as Unicode is integral to the stable transfer of characters from a variety of language systems through a one-to-one mapping between a character and unique number. As Figure 1 illustrates, the Unicode chart for the Basic Latin alphabet includes not only numbers and letters but also control codes necessary to processing this system digitally, such as *space* (U+0020) and *backspace* (U+0008). With approximately 102 alphabetic scripts and "as many as a million" (Unicode Consortium) characters numerically mapped unambiguously in the *Unicode Standard* as of 2012, the protocol

Figure 1. The Unicode Standard, Version 6.2 codes for the C0 Controls and the Basic Latin alphabet. These particular codes were originally developed for the American Standard Code for Information Interchange (ASCII) and later included in Unicode.

C0 Controls and Basic Latin

	000	001	002	003	004	005	006	007
0	NUL	DLE	SP	0	@	P	`	p
1	SOH	DC1	!	1	A	Q	a	q
2	STX	DC2	"	2	B	R	b	r
3	ETX	DC3	#	3	C	S	c	s
4	EOT	DC4	$	4	D	T	d	t
5	ENQ	NAK	%	5	E	U	e	u
6	ACK	SYN	&	6	F	V	f	v
7	BEL	ETB	'	7	G	W	g	w
8	BS	CAN	(	8	H	X	h	x
9	HT	EM	)	9	I	Y	i	y
A	LF	SUB	*	:	J	Z	j	z
B	VT	ESC	+	;	K	[	k	{
C	FF	FS	,	<	L	\	l	|
D	CR	GS	-	=	M	]	m	}
E	SO	RS	.	>	N	^	n	~
F	SI	US	/	?	O	_	o	DEL

of code is easily understood as the essence of not only the digital machine but also the human being communicating digitally. As described by the Unicode Consortium, the *Unicode Standard* offers "a consistent way of encoding multilingual plain text and brings order to a chaotic state of affairs that has made it difficult to exchange text files internationally." Perhaps more importantly, from a human perspective at least, is the constitution by the Unicode Standard of a stable encoding that makes possible the inclusion of natural language systems in computer.

With this shift from human-centered protocol to machine-centered protocol, metaphysics takes on renewed importance. Described by Aristotle (1984a) as a journey in which "[w]e are seeking the principles and the causes of the things that are, and obviously of things *qua* being" (VII 3-4), metaphysics has been increasingly marginalized since the philosophical "linguistic turn" that foregrounds the construction of the world through human language and thought. With what Moritz Schlick (1992) described as the realization that "there is no true system of philosophy" (p. 44), the subjective nature of the word in the constitution of the world was seen to rival, perhaps even supersede, the objective laws of nature. For instance, Jean-Francois Lyotard (1984) identifies the role of narrative in the validation and legitimation of knowledge (p. 31). Science is not simply the discovery of the laws of nature that exist out there in the world, apart from human experience. Instead, science itself is a "language game" (p. 27). In this game, best described by Kenneth Burke (1954), scientist have created a language:

devoid of the tonalities, the mimetic reënforcements, the vaguely remembered human situations, which go to make up the full, complex appeal of the poetic medium. To the scientist's symbols one can respond adequately by looking them up in a book. The very lack of pliancy helps to assist them in avoiding the appeal of pliancy. (p. 58)

Rather than just the discovery and reporting of the positivist state of things, science is a rhetorical activity, full of claims, appeals, and persuasion that work to construct science as an a-rhetorical endeavor. As Lyotard explains, "The scientist questions the validity of narrative statements and concludes that they are never subject to argumentation and proof" because narrative belongs:

to a different mentality: savage primitive, underdeveloped, backward, alienated, composed of opinions, customs, authority, prejudice, ignorance, ideology. Narratives are fables, myths, legends fit only for women and children. At best, attempts are made to throw some rays of light into this obscurantism, to civilize, educate, develop. (p. 27)

But here lies the irony. In arguing so, the scientist participates in the perpetuation of the metanarrative of scientific objectivity that naturalizes Enlightenment values and Western imperialism (Haraway; Harding; Latour; McClintock).

Since the 1990s, a renewed challenge to the identification of reality as essentially the effect of a game—a rhetorical one, too boot!—that privileges the human self as the recurring source, player, winner, loser, and referee in the language game of which all things are made began in conjunction with the idea of Internet protocol. Various, but certainly related, threads in this challenge go by such names as *radical* or *non-naive realism* [e.g., Badiou (2008); Meillassoux (2008); Žižek (2012)] and *object-oriented philosophy* [e.g., Bogost (2012); Bryant (2011); Harman (2002)]. Although its roots stretch all the way back to Plato's Forms, *speculative realism*, as Levi Bryant, Nick Srnicek, and Graham Harman (2011) collectively identify these philosophies, has developed as a response to a dominant epistemology that understands the world as only knowable through human language and thought. Seeking to change the course set by the linguistic turn, Bryant, Srnicek, and Harmon argue that the "tiresome [linguistic] turn" forces upon those who seek to know the world the idea

that "discourse, text, culture, consciousness, power, or ideas . . . constitutes reality" (p. 2)." Consequently, knowing is too often focused upon humanity and thereby allows for nothing more than the formation of "correlations" that first and foremost emphasize the primacy of humans as thinking beings that construct the world and does so at the expense of coming to know "reality itself" (p. 3). To really come to know reality necessitates shifting the emphasis on humanness toward thingness.

DEFINING THINGNESS

What does it mean to know thingness? To know what a thing is? To know its being? Although space dictates brevity, I still think it important to lay out some of answers that have been offered to these questions, even if elementally presented here. To know the thing *qua* being demands, according to Aristotle, to know its substance, which is composed of two elements, "matter and form," as well as the "complex" of these elements as a unity (1984b, VIII 1042a 24-32). Of matter and form, there are four "causes": material, form, source, and end. Martin Heidegger (2003) uses the example of a chalice to slightly modify and illuminate the four causes and does so by using the examples of "chaliceness." A chalice has two causes: the material (e.g., silver) and form (e.g., shape) of its construction. And a chalice has a particular source of meaning tied to its use in a specific activity (e.g., religious ceremony). The effects of these three causes are then brought together by the fourth cause, the silversmith. But it is a mistake to believe that chaliceness owes itself to it the *Dasein*, or Being, of the silversmith. Although certainly one cause, matter too has "potentiality" (i.e., the hardness of metalness made possible the potential for a sword as much as a chalice) and that is always part of what constitutes the "actuality" of chaliceness in phenomenological experience. However, potentiality is easily overlooked. As Heidegger explains, "The kind of dealing which is closest to us is as we have shown, not a bare perceptual cognition, but rather that kind of concern which manipulates things and puts them to use" (1962, p. 95). Because our own immersion in "everydayness," the thing in itself, whether a chalice, doorknob, or hammer, becomes "equipment" in a background against which human intentionality takes center stage. Heidegger identifies this perspective of things as "readiness-at-hand." Only in the disruption of the perspective, one that creates a background and foreground, can a thing come to be known in and of itself; that is, to understand a thing as "presence-in-hand."

One way in which presence-in hand starts to become knowable is through the failure of a thing as a tool. Heidegger writes, "When its unusability is thus discovered, equipment becomes conspicuous. This *conspicuousness* presents the ready-to-hand equipment as in a certain un-readiness-to-hand" (1962, pp. 102-3). The presence-at-hand of a thing becomes, not known (for such ease belies the challenge of coming to know thing *qua* being) but glimpsed in the ready-at-hand. But even so, presence-at-hand must not be mistaken for Being, which is "a "primordial phenomenon of truth [that] has been covered up by Dasein's very understanding of Being" (1962, p. 268). This limited human understanding of Being, what speculative philosophers often refer to as "correlationism," too often results in the continued imprisonment of things as little more than equipment.

Leaving behind the philosophical path taken because of the linguistic turn, speculative and object-oriented philosophers seek to renew the value of such wisdom. Harman (2002), for instance, encourages a reading of Heidegger that "forces us to develop a ruthless inquiry," one "devoid of a theory of human action" and dedicated to the "structure of *objects themselves*" (2002, p. 15). Harman argues that to "break loose from the textual and linguistic ghetto" (p. 16) philosophy

must deal with the "natural physical mass" of "tool-being" (p. 18). To do so demands that objects be recognized as never neutral:

The tool is a real function or effect, an invisible sun radiating its energies into the world before ever coming to view. In this way, the world is an infrastructure of equipment already at work, of tool-beings unleashing their forces upon us just as savagely or flirtatiously as they duel with one another. Insofar as the vast majority of these tools remain unknown to us, and were certainly not invented by us (for example, our brains and our blood cells), it can hardly be said that we "use" them in the strict sense of the term. A more accurate statement would be that we silent rely upon them, taking them for granted as that naïve landscape on which even our most jaded and cynical schemes unfold. (p. 20)

Not through human use as equipment does a thing achieve effect in the world. Rather, tool-being acknowledges the transformative effect that objects have in the world, regardless of human intentionality. As such, the subject/object distinction that pervades philosophical thought and constitutes the world through text implodes.

But what of computer code that has no physical mass. Although brain, blood, cells, and DNA are invisible (mostly), they still have a mass. Though their physicality might be veiled within the body, their physicality is undeniable. Unlike most objects, software's invisibility is not simply a consequence of the failure of most to recognize its presence and effect in everydayness, although this is a state of being that code shares with most objects. In its purest form, code does not have mass; it is a human-invisible communicative exchange of combinations of 1's and 0's among machines. Even if we recognize the algorithmic instructions that constitute code as something more than mere texts because code also constitutes protocols that, in turn, effect the social practices of the human *qua* object, the question still remains: how is software a tool-being. Like Aristotle, Heidegger, and Harman, object-oriented ontologist Ian Bogost (2012) argues that know a thing must mean more describing how a thing works. When applied to computers, Bogost observes, "[F]or the computer to operate at all *for us* first requires a wealth of interactions to take place *for itself*. As operators or engineers, we may be able to describe how such objects and assemblages *work*. But what do they *experience*? What's their proper phenomenology? In short, what's it like to be a thing" (p. 10). In answer to these questions, Bogost offers the example of a program he crafted based on his Latour Litanizer, which generates random page lists from entries in Wikipedia. Using pictures tagged in Flickr with "object," "thing," or "stuff," this visual equivalent of the Litanizer was intended, according to Bogost, "to illustrate the diversity of objects by demonstrating individual examples one at a time" (p. 97). However, when a complaint occurred due to a random user viewing a random picture of a woman in a Bunny suit, Bogost decided to change the randomness of the program through the inclusion of a Boolean limitation on the original search inquiry in order to control the perception of "sexist objectification," even if "unintended" (p. 98). But, in doing so, Bogost argues that he robbed from the visual Litanizer its "ontological power," its ability to demonstrate the diversity of objects. In short, the being of the program *qua* object was impeded. Bogost remarks on this limitation: "This alteration solved the problem, but as the Boolean criteria above suggest, the change also risks excluding a whole category of units from the realm of being! Are women, or girls or sexiness to have no *ontological* place alongside chipmunks, lighthouses, and galoshes? (p. 99)" Although potentially offensive from the perspective of human-oriented phenomenology, his comment highlights the problematic privilege given to human protocol, one that demands the sacrifice of an object's being for the sake of human protocol.

In the case of Unicode, its ontological power stems from its power to reproduce the writing systems of the world without the baggage of the social and political subjectivies embedded in those systems and their respective characters. As described in the *Unicode Standard*, *Version 6.2*, its purpose is:

to provide programmers with a single universal character encoding, extensive descriptions, and a vast amount of data about how characters function. The specifications describe how to form words and break lines; how to sort text in different languages; how to format numbers, dates, times, and other elements appropriate to different languages; to display languages whose written form flows from right to left, such as Arabic and Hebrew, or whose written form splits, combines, and reorders, such as languages of South Asia. These specifications include description of how to deal with security concerns regarding the many "look-alike" characters from alphabets around the world. Without the properties and algorithms in the Unicode Standard and its associated specifications, interoperability between different implementations would be impossible, and much of the vast breadth of the world's languages would lie outside the reach of modern software. (p. xv)

Because of the Unicode encoding system, human language and the processing functions necessary for its digital existence are freed from the ambiguity of linguistic signs and rewarded with a one-to-one correspondence that exists in the being of these characters as objects. Contributing to the protocol that ensures control in the distributed network of the Internet, alphabetic-based human language becomes an effect of this protocol. Although easily understood as the subjugation of human language to machine control, Bogost might argue that this reorienting of human language away from the subjectivity that designates language as the primary source of meaning in the world frees us from "tiny prison of our own devising, one in which all that concerns us are the fleshy beings that are our kindred and the stuffs with which we stuff ourselves" (p. 3). If we are to turn away from the imprisonment foisted upon us because of belief in the primacy of human thought and language, even language must come to be understood differently, as much more than just a sign. A language character itself becomes a thing *qua* being.

BEYOND RHETORIC?

With the shift to thingness, what then happens to rhetoric, which, according to object-oriented philosophy is part of the very problem from which we must free ourselves? The "duty of rhetoric," Aristotle explains in *Rhetoric*, is "to deal with such matters as we deliberate upon without arts or systems to guide us" (1984c, I 1357a2-3). Unlike knowledge or, more accurately since the Enlightenment, scientific knowledge that offers a system that generates demonstrable proof of what is true, rhetoric is occupied with persuasion concerning what is probably. Plato (1997b) warns that the danger of rhetoric is embodied in the sophist who aims to enchant an audience into believing what the sophist would have them believe, even in disregard to what is actually true. Socrates asks, "Is not rhetoric, taken generally, a universal art of enchanting the mind by arguments; which is practiced not only in courts and public assemblies, but in private houses also, having to do with all matters, great as well as small, good and bad alike, and is in all the equally right, and equally to be esteemed?" (261a-b). Plato further argues that rhetoric is like cookery, too easily concerned with producing "gratification and pleasure," so that the skilled orator, like the cook unconcerned with the health of the body, ignores the health of the soul (1997a). But, according to Aristotle, the rhetor who has both skill and character typically persuades based on a belief in what is both moral and just. Ultimately, "What makes a person a sophist is

not his abilities but his choices" (1984c, I 1355b 18-19). Crucial to choosing well is *phronesis*. A person who has phronesis has the ability to "see what is good for themselves and what is good for humans in general" (1984b, 1140b9-11). However, the path to not simply effective but good choice is often full of ambiguity; therefore, the ability to exercise practical wisdom (*phronesis*) during deliberations as to how to act (*praxis*) with the appropriate means (*techne*) to achieve a desired end (*telos*) is often considered a limitation rather than a benefit of rhetoric.

Little wonder then that in the digital age, the scientific endeavor to process the world through algorithmic calculation appears to overcome the limitations of rhetoric. It is not simply that machine language does not affect ambiguity and that its own ontological power resides in the endless analytic processing of information. Just as importantly, rhetoric has become subject to digital protocol. Consequently, it has proven tempting to dismiss the traditional role of rhetoric in light of the new rhetoric of the digital age. To this end, Lev Manovich (2001) contends that through tools such as hyperlinking the "new rhetoric of interactivity" displaces those texts that "instructed, inspired, convinced, and seduced their readers to adopt new ideas, new ways of interpreting the world, new ideologies" (p. 77). These new digital technologies therefore signal "the continuing decline of the field of rhetoric in the modern era" (p. 7). Likewise, Galloway locates semantics, the sister of rhetoric from a different tradition, at the bottom of the protocol hierarchy. And even then, semantics is not semantics in the traditional sense. Instead semantics, and with it rhetoric, is backgrounded in favor of the digital processing of information at the level of program applications. Only by doing so is Galloway able to argue, "Code is the only language that is executable" (p. 165). Unlike "mere writing," only the digital machine has an ontological power to convert meaning into action" (p. 166). In sum, "code = praxis."

But if code is praxis, phronesis must also be considered elemental to code as a tool-being. But what possibility for practical wisdom exists when Internet protocol governs what is possible? Aristotle contends, "The origin of action . . . is choice, and that of choice is desire and reasoning with a view to an end" (1984b, VI 1139a 32-33). By "choice," Aristotle does not mean alternatives among the different ways in which a particular piece of code might be crafted. Although certainly important, this kind of choice is a matter relegated to the art (*techne*) of programming. To constitute praxis, code must also be concerned with ends external to issues of quality or aesthetics. As Aristotle explains, [W]e credit a person with practical wisdom [*phronesis*] in some particular respect when they have calculated well with a view to some good end which is one of those that are not the object of any art" (1984b,1140a 28-30). Good then is the moral and political dimension of life. In light of causes and effects of Internet protocol, the effective functioning of protocol might itself be the only good end. Science and technology as both means and ends is exactly what Jacques Ellul (1964) pointed to in his identification of "autonomous technique" and Langdon Winner (1977) in "autonomous technology." Perhaps the dystopian views of modern technology offered by both Ellul and Winner prophesized the Internet protocols that have catalyzed the recent return to metaphysics. If so, protocol might leave us with nothing more than "moral and political indifference" (Winner, 1993, p. 372).

Yet, Internet protocol as both means and ends is not necessarily the only option in a metaphysics of code. Phronesis as the deliberation about good and ill, morality and immorality, justice and injustice might yet prove to have effect through the thingness of code. Remarking on limitations placed upon an "ethics of objects" because of the limiting perspective of correlationism, Bogost points out the arbitrariness with which the object of meat is assigned by some an ethical identify, while most other objects are denied a moral effect, simply because of their status as things:

Does the tofu muster moral practice when slithering gently in the water of its plastic container? Does the piston when compressing air and petrol against the walls of its cylinder? Does the snowblower when its auger pulls powder from the ground and discharges it out of a chute? Perhaps, although if any do, they do so through a code irrevocably decoupled from the material acts they commit. The ethics of the spark plug are no more clear to us than would be those of the vegan to the soybean plant, in a tasty appetizer of edamame. Worse yet, there might be multiple, conflicting theories of soybean ethics—lest one assume that the noble legume is any less capable of philosophical intricacy than are bearded men. (p. 77)

A speculative ethics necessitates the possibility that things are capable of a kind of phronesis, one specific to the matter and of the thing itself. Of course, how to come to know the ethical code of the soybean is certainly not one that might be grasped—not that that necessarily matters in speculative realism. But for the object at hand, what of a metaphysical ethics of Unicode?

A speculative ethics of things demands recognition of the ways in which objects and humans exists in a whirlwind that actualizes as praxis in a particular moment of confluence. Until that point, actuality is potentiality composed by the elements of humanness and thingness, alike. Bogost points to the concept of "hyperobjects," developed by Timothy Morton (2011), as a way of bringing into the foreground being as the being of objects. Concerned with limitations inherent in environmental sustainability rhetorics, Morton uses the example of the flushed toilet to highlight the problem of backgrounding what we consider "away" from human experience: "When we flush the toilet, we imagine that the U-bend takes the waste away into some ontologically alien realm. Ecology is now beginning to tell us of something very different: a flattened world without ontological U-bends." The "hyperobject" works to upend false distinction between here and away by highlighting the existence of other objects:

"When you approach [hyperobjects], more and more objects emerge." Ecology itself is not just a thing but a collection of things that each must be recognized as beings in themselves. But to do this demands "thinking past meta mode" so that objects become more than "our interpretation of them." From Morton, Bogost argues that ethics itself is a hyperobject: "a massive, tangled chain of objects lampooning one another through weird relation, mistaking their own essences for that of the alien objects they encounter, exploding the very idea of ethics to infinity" (p. 79) Ethics then is infinitesimal because of the infiniteness of things through which ethics is actualized. To offer an example of one such ethics of things, I turn to the actuality of Unicode.

THE CASE OF BSSYM7.TTF

In 2003, Microsoft included Bookshelf Symbol 7 font as part of the library of fonts available in its new Office suite. Unlike more commonly used typefaces, such as Arial Narrow and Times New Roman, Bookshelf converts the natural language, alphabetic system of Basic Latin into a combination of recognizable and unrecognizable symbols (Figure 2). Easily dismissed as the example of an exercise motivated by a programmer's desire to play rather than address an actual need, Bookshelf instead allows for the easy encryption of messages. With the development of artificial typographic systems such as Bookshelf, the crisis of the global Babel created through the heterogeneity of alphabetic systems colliding with one another along the hierarchy of Internet protocols had lessen to such an extent that with the conversion of a text composed though a human-readable natural language system, any non-technical end user could easily encrypt that message for whatever reason she had in doing so.

However, soon after the release of Office 2003, Microsoft made available a "critical update" that included a patch for Bookshelf. Although typically used only to address security vulnerabilities, this critical update also sought to remove Byssm7.ttf from Bookshelf (Figure 3). As the company's tool removal summary vaguely explained, Byssm7.ttf "has been found to contain unacceptable symbols" (Microsoft "Description"). Upon completion of a set of instructions that directed users how to download and install the patch, the utility removed the unacceptable symbols from Bookshelf.

From a functional perspective, Bookshelf Symbol 7 Font executed successfully. The code itself was not in any way technically buggy. In fact, the encoding and decoding involved in Bookshelf lends credence to Galloway's argument that code is the only true symbol because of its ability to execute, unlike natural languages. As illustrated in Figure 4, the *Unicode Standard's* code for U+5350 (left-facing, Normal Swastika) and U+534D (right-facing Swastika) allows a typeface like Bookshelf to include characters from a diverse number of natural writing systems, as well as artificial doodles, and for those characters to encode successfully "no matter what the platform, no matter what the program, no matter what the language" (Unicode Consortium). With the characters encoded in Byssym7.ttf, the *Unicode Standard* allowed programmers to incorporate successfully ideographs from the Han unification composed from the shared characteristics among

Figure 2. Translation of Arial font to Bookshelf Symbol 7, version 1.00 in Microsoft Word

Figure 3. Description of the Bookshelf Symbol 7 Font Removal Tool in Office 2003. (http://support. microsoft.com/kb/833404)

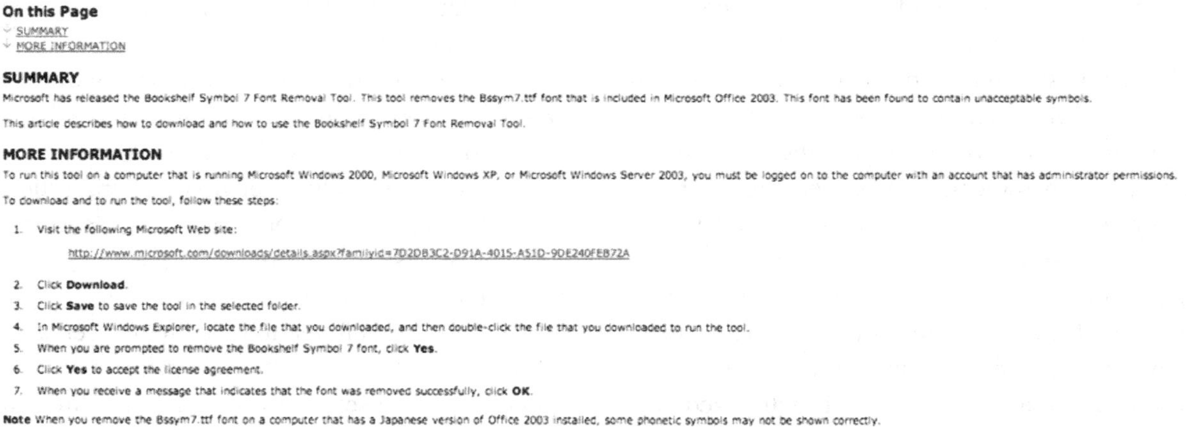

On this Page
˅ SUMMARY
˅ MORE INFORMATION

SUMMARY

Microsoft has released the Bookshelf Symbol 7 Font Removal Tool. This tool removes the Bssym7.ttf font that is included in Microsoft Office 2003. This font has been found to contain unacceptable symbols.

This article describes how to download and how to use the Bookshelf Symbol 7 Font Removal Tool.

MORE INFORMATION

To run this tool on a computer that is running Microsoft Windows 2000, Microsoft Windows XP, or Microsoft Windows Server 2003, you must be logged on to the computer with an account that has administrator permissions.

To download and to run the tool, follow these steps:

1. Visit the following Microsoft Web site:

   http://www.microsoft.com/downloads/details.aspx?familyid=7D2DB3C2-D91A-4015-A51D-9DE240FEB72A

2. Click **Download**.
3. Click **Save** to save the tool in the selected folder.
4. In Microsoft Windows Explorer, locate the file that you downloaded, and then double-click the file that you downloaded to run the tool.
5. When you are prompted to remove the Bookshelf Symbol 7 font, click **Yes**.
6. Click **Yes** to accept the license agreement.
7. When you receive a message that indicates that the font was removed successfully, click **OK**.

Note When you remove the Bssym7.ttf font on a computer that has a Japanese version of Office 2003 installed, some phonetic symbols may not be shown correctly.

Figure 4. The Unicode Standard, Version 6.2 codes for the "unacceptable symbols" removed from Bookshelf Symbol 7 (pp. 35-36)

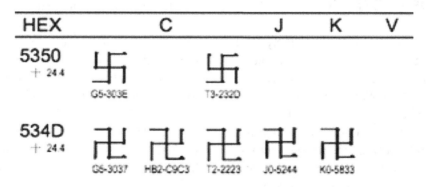

the Chinese (C), Japanese (J), and Korean (K) scripts, collectively referred to as CJK, into the English-language platform of Microsoft Office 2003. In short, Unicode functioned as translator between human language and machine language. For the machine, these symbols encoded and decoded as 11100101100011011000 1101 and 111001011000110110010000; for the programmers, as U+534D and U+5350; and, for the users who choose to use the Bookshelf Symbol as 卍 and 卐. Given the technical success of Byssym7. ttf, why then remove it from Bookshelf, especially given that Microsoft's description of the

font removal tool warned, "When you remove the Byssm7.ttf font on a computer that has a Japanese version of Office 2003 installed, some phonetic symbols may not be shown correctly." If no conspicuousness, to borrow from Heidegger, caused notice of Bookshelf as something more than a typeface, why then did Byssm7.ttf become suddenly presence-at-hand, at least for a moment, and thus something more than just equipment?

Soon after the release of Office 2003, a user voiced complaint about the presence of U+5350 and U+534D in Bookshelf, according to Microsoft product manager Simon Marks (Reuters). Only when decoded by a user, did Microsoft become aware that these symbols, in techspeak, had a "bug," one that also infected the numerical correspondence of this symbol in Unicode. But rather than technical, this bug was rhetorical, because the symbols represented both Nazism and anti-Semitism. In response to consumer complaints, Microsoft Senior Vice President Steven Sinofsky explained in an open letter that inadvertence had led to the swastikas inclusion in the company's software:

Microsoft has learned of a mistake in the Bookshelf Symbol 7 font included in the Microsoft Office System client applications. Due to an unintentional oversight, we failed to identify, prior to the release, the presence of two swastikas within the font. We apologize for this and for any offense caused. Microsoft is taking immediate measures to remedy the issue for all customers. Microsoft has released a utility today for worldwide download that removes the font. Again, we apologize to those who have been offended or upset. We continue to work to improve our processes in order to prevent this type of error in the future. (Sinofsky)

With the announcement of the release of the *bssym7.ttf* tool removal, the Anti-Defamation League (ADL) "praised" Microsoft for alerting the organization to the issue as well for the "detection and removal of two Nazi symbols inadvertently included" in Office (ADL 2003). The ADL's Director Abraham Foxman also thanked the company for its "sensitivity to our concern about the potentially offensive nature of Nazi symbols." But if potential offense were, in fact, the reason for the swastikas' removal, this reasoning does not explain the motivation behind the removal of the third symbol, the Star of David (U+2721), (See Figure 5.)

As a *PC Magazine* pre- and post-update file comparison revealed, Microsoft's critical update also removed the Star of David from Bookshelf

Symbol 7 even though no compliant had been made about the inclusion of the Star of David in the Bookshelf Symbol 7 software (Rupley). Microsoft's use of inadvertence to explain the swastikas' presence in Bookshelf is undoubtedly an effect of the readiness-to-hand of not just Unicode, but software generally. As the mapping of a one-to-one correspondence between textual characters and a unique series of numbers, Unicode is simply equipment that "provides the capacity to encode all of the characters used for the written languages of the world" (Unicode Consortium). As such, there is little need on the part of programmers that utilize Unicode to think of it beyond its technical functionality. In unintentionally including U+5350 and U+534D as part of Office 2003, Microsoft can only be viewed as failing to exercise *phronesis*, which, in turn, denied reflexive action. Resulting then from the exercise of habit, the problem of Byssm7.ttf is hardly surprising. If technology with material presence is denied being, then software, to say nothing of the more elemental character encoding system, is even less likely to be acknowledged as being in its own right because of invisibility.

Of course, the danger of my discussion of Byssm7.ttf thus far is that the power of U+5350 and U+534D is, at some might argue, merely rhetorical, not ontological. The reason that these codes enjoy a moment of presence-at-hand, is because of human interpretation that encodes the symbol of swastika. As described by the ADL:

The swastika was adopted by Germany's Nazi Party. Prior to the Nazis co-opting this symbol, it was known as a good luck symbol and was used by various religious groups. Hitler made the Nazi swastika unique to his party by reversing the normal direction of the symbol so that it appeared to spin clockwise. Today, it is widely used, in various incarnations, by neo-Nazis, racist skinheads and other white supremacist groups. (Anti-Defamation League, "Hate on Display")

Figure 5. Before and after screen shots of Bookshelf Symbol 7 Font in Microsoft Office 2003. Used with the permission of Lester Haines. (http://www.theregister.co.uk/2004/02/11/ms_tears_swastika_from_roof/)

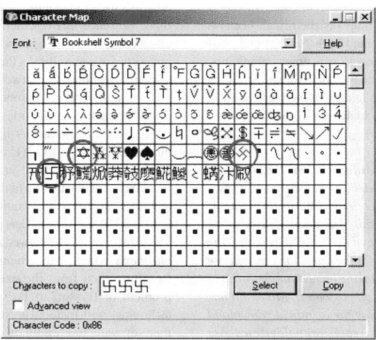

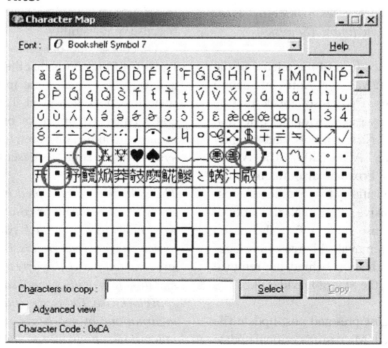

This rhetorical encoding of the swastikas certainly gives powerful meaning to these symbols. And Microsoft's decision to also delete the Star of David through the tool removal signifies a moment of phronetic practice (possibly) in which the company decided to act so as to avoid the possibility that the symbol be actualized as part of anti-Semitic expression. However, the power of these symbols arises solely from humans, not from the things themselves. If the swastikas that prompted the deletion of Byssm7.ttf are to be recognized as things in themselves, this necessitates seeing the way in which Unicode affects human action.

To understand the ontological power of U+5350 and U+534D, as well as U+2721, means to recognize what they effect, even when missing from the Bookshelf Symbol 7 font. Not only does U+5350 and U+534D allow for the encoding of a symbol of Nazism but also a myriad of other rhetorical encodings. As part of *The Report to the U.S. National Museum for 1894*, anthropologist Thomas Wilson noted that so little meaning did this symbol have in America at the time that "the word Swastika did not appear in such works as Worcester's or Webster's dictionaries, the Encyclopaedic Dictionary, the Encyclopaedia Britannica" (p. 763). Wilson traces the swastika's history to its use as a character in ancient Sanskrit, as a sacred symbol in the Buddhist religion, a character in ancient Scandinavian, as ornamentation to symbolize good luck among certain Native American tribes, an ideograph in the Chinese script, and as a symbol meaning prosperity in the Tibetan Bon religion, to name but a few of the swastika's rhetorical encodings. These different rhetorical meanings of the swastika point to the privilege given to the relatively new, Western encoding that arose most prominently with the rise of German Nationalism in the 1930s and 1940s. This decoding reveals the decision to delete Byssm7.ttf in which U+5350 and U+534D was coded as an act of Western privileging. As Christopher John Flynn stated, during a discussion

on the Unicode Consortium's email distribution list unicode@unicode.org, "Banning this ancient symbol would be offensive to Bonpos and many Hindus & Buddhists."

Rather than conspicuousness that signaled unreadiness-to-hand as the reason for the recognition of the thingness of U+5350, U+534D and U+2721, it was the abrupt absence of these codes, at least by those technically knowledgeable of them, that allowed for presence-at hand to occur. As Heidegger explains, "[T]o miss something in this way amounts to coming across something un-ready-to-hand: we also find things which are missing—which not only are not 'handy' . . . but are not 'to hand' . . . at all. Again to miss something in this way amounts to coming across something un-ready-hand" (p. 103). The missing of U+5350 and U+534D does more than just create a technical bug that translates as an absence of functionality or even different rhetorical encodings. Through their absence, the missing codes reveal their ontological power that extends from the code itself to Byssm7.ttf, then to Bookshelf Symbol 7 font, then to Microsoft Office, and right up the protocol hierarchy. Unless one has the power to manipulate these objects of code at the application layer so as to input the numeric character encoding, then the application protocol itself constrains the possibility for human praxis. Although this possibility includes the potential choice to actualize anti-Semitism through the use of the swastika, the presence of these tool-beings also invite the possibility of a whole host of other actualities. Although many might take a bit of pleasure in the hysterics that Microsoft's decision to delete the swastikas from Bookshelf incited on online discussion boards for Neo-Nazi hate groups, the state of things remains that the missing Unicode for both the right- and left-facing swastikas, as well as the Star of David, constitute not only the denial of freedoms of speech and practice of religion but also the continued marginalization of certain cultures and customs.

CONCLUSION

Although correlationism persists in tempting us to focus exclusively on the role Microsoft played in the case of Byssm7.ttf and whether or not the company deserves praise or blame for its inaction and then action, Microsoft is only a small element in the hyperobject of ethics at play in the erasure of U+5350, U+534D, and U+2721 from the Bookshelf Symbol 7 font. For Microsoft no more controls the reality of these codes than does the ADL. Because the ADL decided in July 2010 to downgrade the swastika as a symbol of hate, six years after Microsoft release of the tool removal utility to erase the "unacceptable symbols" from Office, U+5350, U+534D is not suddenly devoid of that meaning. And it is not that other people continue to think of the swastika as a symbol of hate that singularly makes it meaningful. Rhetorical encodings continue to be important; but as an element of the semantic protocol, the code itself constitutes ethics and does so by controlling the possibility for the actualization of rhetorical encodings. But rather than a dystopian wrestling of ethics away from humans, the ethics of code actually provides the opportunity to highlight the diversity of rhetorical meanings that struggle to persist in the digital age.

In the seminal article "What is Computer Ethics?" published in 1985, James Moor wrote, "[C]omputers manipulates symbols but they don't care what the symbols represent" (p. 270). Only through the expected denial to code its existence as a tool-being with moral and political dimensions in its own right could Moor then argue that computer ethics were limited to "the analysis of the nature and social impact of computer technology and the corresponding formulation and justification of policies for the ethical use of such technology" (p. 266). Undoubtedly this understanding of computer ethics continues to dominate the present day. While this perspective certainly contributes to the problematic identification of science and technology as autonomous, it just as

problematically emphasizes the primacy of the human thought and language in the constitution of meaning. With a shift that recognizes the ethics of things like code, the more complex nature of ethics in the digital age start to come into being.

REFERENCES

Anti-Defamation League. (2005). *Swastika/Nazi party flag*. Retrieved from http://archive.adl.org/hate_symbols/neo_nazi_swastika_flag.asp

Aristotle (1984a). Metaphysics. In J. Barnes (Ed.), *The complete works of Aristotle* (Vol. 2, pp. 1552–1728). Princeton, NJ: Princeton University Press.

Aristotle (1984b). Nichomachean ethics. In J. Barnes (Ed.), *The complete works of Aristotle* (Vol. 2, pp. 1729–1867). Princeton, NJ: Princeton University Press.

Aristotle (1984c). Rhetoric. In J. Barnes (Ed.), *The complete works of Aristotle* (Vol. 2, pp. 2152–2269). Princeton, NJ: Princeton University Press.

Badio, A. (2008). *Conditions*. New York, NY: Continuum.

Becker, J. D. (1988, August 29). *Unicode 88*. Retrieved from http://www.unicode.org/history/unicode88.pdf

Bemer, R. W. (1960). *Commentary on survey of coded character representation*. Retrieved from http://www.bobbemer.com/PUBS-ASC.HTM

Bogost, I. (2012). *Alien phenomenology*. Minneapolis, MN: University of Minnesota Press.

Bryant, L. (2011). *The democracy of objects*. Ann Arbor, MI: Open Humanities Press. doi:10.3998/ohp.9750134.0001.001

Bryant, L., Srnicek, N., & Harman, G. (2011). Toward a speculative philosophy. In *The speculative turn: Continental materialism and realism* (pp. 1-18). Melbourne, Australia: re.press.

Burke, K. (1954). *Permanence and change: An anatomy of purpose.* Berkeley, CA: The University of California Press.

Deleuze, G. (1992). Postscript on the societies of control. *October, 59*, 3-7.

Ellul, J. (1964). *The technological society.* New York, NY: Vintage Books.

Flynn, C. J. (2003). *Swastikas to be banned by Microsoft?* Retrieved from http://www.mail-archive.com/unicode@unicode.org/msg20776.html

Galloway, A. (2004). *Protocol: How control exists after decentralization.* Cambridge, MA: MIT Press.

Haraway, D. J. (1990). *Simians, cyborgs, and women: The reinvention of nature.* New York, NY: Routledge.

Harding, S. (2006). *Science and social inequality: Feminist and postcolonial issues.* Champaign, IL: University of Illinois Press.

Harman, G. (2002). *Tool-being: Heidegger and the metaphysics of objects.* IL, Peru: Open Court Publishing.

Heidegger, M. (1962). *Being and time.* New York, NY: Harper & Row.

Heidegger, M. (2003). The question concerning technology. In R. C. Scharff, & V. Dusek (Eds.), *Philosophy of technology: The technological condition* (pp. 252–264). Malden, MA: Blackwell Publishing.

Latour, B. (2002). Morality and technology: The end of means. *Theory, Culture & Society, 19*, 247–260. doi:10.1177/026327602761899246

Lessig, L. (1998). *The laws of cyberspace.* Retrieved from http://cyber.law.harvard.edu/works/lessig/laws_cyberspace.pdf

Lyotard, J. L. (1984). *The postmodern condition: A report on knowledge.* Minneapolis, MN: University of Minnesota Press.

Manovich, L. (2001). *The language of new media.* Cambridge, MA: MIT Press.

McClintock, A. (1995). *Imperial leather: Race, gender, and sexuality in the colonial contest.* New York, NY: Routledge.

Meillassoux, Q. (2008). *After finitude: An essay on the necessity of contingency.* New York, NY: Continuum.

Moor, J. (1985). What is computer ethics? *Metaphilosophy, 16*(4), 266–275. doi:10.1111/j.1467-9973.1985.tb00173.x

Morton, T. (2011). Unsustaining. *World Picture, 5.* Retrieved from http://www.worldpicturejournal.com/WP_5/Morton.html

Plato, . (1997a). Gorgias. In J. M. Cooper (Ed.), *Plato: Complete works* (pp. 791–869). Indianapolis, IN: Hackett Publishing.

Plato, . (1997b). Phaedrus. In J. M. Cooper (Ed.), *Plato: Complete works* (pp. 506–556). Indianapolis, IN: Hackett Publishing.

Reuters. (n.d.). *Microsoft to cut swastikas from fonts.* Retrieved from http://www.reuters.com/newsArticle.html?type=businessNews&storyID=3983750

Rupley, S. (2004). Microsoft's font foibles. *PC Magazine.* Retrieved from http://www.pcmag.com/article2/0,2817,1526828,00.asp

Schlick, M. (1992). The future of philosophy. In R. Rorty (Ed.), *The linguistic turn: Essays in philosophical method* (pp. 43–53). Chicago, IL: University of Chicago Press.

Sinofsky, S. (2003). *An open letter from Senior Vice President Steven Sinofsky*. Retrieved from https://www.microsoft.com/en-us/news/press/2003/dec03/12-12fontletter.aspx

Unicode Consortium. (n.d.). *The unicode standard, version 6.2*. Retrieved from http://www.unicode.org/versions/ Unicode6.2.0/Preface.pdf

Wilson, T. (1896). The swastika: The earliest known symbol, and its migrations, with observations on the migration of certain industries in pre-historic times. In *Report to the U.S. national museum for 1894*. Washington, DC: Government Printing Office.

Winner, L. (1977). *Autonomous technology*. Cambridge, MA: MIT Press.

Winner, L. (1993). Upon opening the black box and finding it empty: Social constructivism and the philosophy of technology. *Science, Technology & Human Values*, *18*, 362–378. doi:10.1177/016224399301800306

Žižek, S. (2012). *Less than nothing: Hegel and the shadow of dialectical materialism*. Brooklyn, NY: Verso.

KEY TERMS AND DEFINITIONS

Equipment: The existence of objects as mere background to the more important human execution of action (see Heidegger).

Metaphysics: Inquiry into the nature or being of things.

Phronesis: The ability to discern good from ill from among the range of choices available to humans in the activity of living; translated by Aristotle as "practical wisdom."

Tool-Being: The existence of objects as things that execute action in their own right (see Harmon).

Unicode: A character encoding system that assigns a unique number set to each letter, mark, and symbol in the world's various written systems.

Chapter 5
The Data Machine:
Identification in the Age of Data Mining

Nicholas A. Hanford
Rensselaer Polytechnic Institute, USA

ABSTRACT

Kenneth Burke warned of the trends of behaviorism in A Grammar of Motives *as he found them to be a reduction of the human condition. In the current digital landscape, data mining aims at reducing the human user to characteristics and re-presenting those characteristics, through online advertising, to the user they were collected from. Due to these processes, rhetoricians are forced to take a deeper look at how the audience is constituted within digital situations. This chapter discusses the effects of data mining on Burke's work, providing an example for the contextualization of rhetorical theory in new media environments. By contextualizing Burke's concepts, this chapter allows for these ideas to be used more seamlessly within digital rhetoric and any medium where data mining is a consistent practice.*

INTRODUCTION

A railroad is approached, not in terms of tracks, engines, roundhouses, repair plants, and working force, but through data as to its capital structure! There it lies, stretched over hundreds or even thousands of miles—yet it is not an actuality, but a prospect. (Burke, 1984, 42)

Meanwhile, if the quantity of information is increasing by 2.5 quintillion bytes per day, the amount of useful information almost certainly isn't. Most of it is just noise, and the noise is increasing faster than the signal. There are so many hypotheses to test, so many data sets to mine – but a relatively constant amount of objective truth. … We love to predict things – and we aren't very good at it. (Silver, 2012, p.13)

DOI: 10.4018/978-1-4666-4916-3.ch005

Copyright © 2014, IGI Global. Copying or distributing in print or electronic forms without written permission of IGI Global is prohibited.

According to their patents, Sony sees the next generation of advertising to be interactive. In a media environment where machines such as Sony's PlayStation Eye and Microsoft's Kinect for the Xbox, both instruments for viewing and interpreting the movements of viewers, it is not too far-fetched that this will be the case. According to their patent, users will be required to shout out the name of the product to skip the advertisement or be prompted with a burger to throw pickles on in order to create a distinct relationship between physical action and consumer product (Ertz, 2012). With these watching machines pervading the media landscape, and the guarantee that they will continue and expand with the introduction of the newest PlayStation and Xbox consoles in 2013, one might believe that we are accelerating towards the surveillance systems of *1984* (Cutlack, 2013). However, online advertising has sped past these proposed connections of sound or motion and memetic imprints. Instead, the online advertisement aims at understanding the human's actions remotely, perceiving the everyday motions of the user to be more rewarding, and profitable, than that of simple response. Online advertising aims to discern the fragmented actions of a human user into patterns that can then be translated into user-specific advertisements. In short, online advertising looks to create a user which can then be fractionally identified with a whole host of products.

Data mining is the process through which these patterns are discerned and users' identities are created. Han, Kamber, and Pei (2012) write, "Data mining turns a large collection of data into knowledge. … Interestingly, some patterns found in user search queries can disclose invaluable knowledge that cannot be obtained by reading individual data items alone" (p. 2). The Internet allows for a massive collection of data and, by its structure, allows for every data point to be associated with a single user. This creates a tremendous potential for discerning an individual's tendencies and patterns of informational, or material, consumption.

All technologies understand a user in various ways (de Vries, 2009). Take, for instance, an elevator. This machine requires simple inputs in order to transport the user to various floors of a building. With specific inputs, it recognizes the floor a user wishes to go to, the floor that user came from, if the user wishes to keep the doors open or close them, and, in case of emergency, if that user is stuck through the use of an alarm or intercom system. However, the elevator is a simple machine in that it cannot discern a user's preferred destination upon entrance or sense people approaching from far away. Perhaps, one day, there will be a "smart" elevator that can discern the body of a particular user upon entrance, either by the use of cameras, weight distribution, or some other tracking device that allows for preferences to be understood for that user. Data mining allows for a vast array of inputs to be understood by the algorithms and for those inputs to then be redirected back at the user in a variety of forms.

The purpose of this chapter is not to argue the moralistic grounds of data mining and its effects on online advertising or the effects on the user. It does not aim at discussing the private and the public and how data mining bridges these through surveillance either. Instead, I look to provide as much antagonism over data mining and its effects on digital rhetoric as I think the two quotes above create. Here we see an early Kenneth Burke pitted against the data wunderkind Nate Silver, both providing an opposite side of the possibilities of data collection and manipulation. Here Burke puts forward the prophets that data bring with them and Silver holds out hope that an abundance of data does not drown out the reality it might bring with it. Instead this chapter looks mainly at defining, and re-defining, instead of chastising.

Internet advertising is driven by what I am calling here the data machine. This concept, derived from Paul Virilio's *The Vision Machine*, aims at understanding the complex sets of algorithms used online as a kind of machine, which requires inputs to create users and then pairs the user with a variety of possible outputs. Alongside my conceptualization of the data machine, this essay will focus on the effects of data mining on Kenneth Burke's concepts of identification and consubstantiation. With a changing understanding of identity – one that is created through associations unknown by the user – there are strong effects on the rhetorical conception of an audience and of identification. When an audience is reduced to the actions of users online, identification becomes a stratified and localized operation, which seeks out a singular and instantaneous transcendence, as opposed to an unending conversation contextualized in the history of the user. This adaptation of Burke's concepts of consubstantiation and identification allow for a medium-specific understanding of this key figure within rhetorical studies.

This medium specificity is the overarching aim of the chapter. In his book, *Lingua Fracta: Towards a Rhetoric of New Media*, Collin Gifford Brooke (2009) writes that the future prospects of digital rhetoric, "depend on our ability to rethink some of our own cherished and unexamined assumptions about writing" (p. 5). This is the overarching theme and the persistent challenge for digital rhetoric that is addressed partly here. For my purposes, data mining is an aspect of new media that can be addressed by previous theories (represented here by Virilio's concepts), but must also be understood to impact existing theories as well (Burke's identification and consubstantiation). With new media environments we must do away with jumps in theory from disciplinary traditions, and instead must respond to the exigency created by new technologies in order to further theory and minimize gaps between old and new.

BACKGROUND

The Vision Machine and the Data Machine

In his book *The Vision Machine*, Paul Virilio (1994) aims at deciphering a number of technologies of perception, from the panorama to the camera to closed-circuit television (CCTV), in order to discern their impacts upon the image and the human. According to Virilio (1994), the vision machine is an optical device, which aims at the "automation of perception" in order for a mechanic foresight to occur (p. 59). In a world where this perception is possible, "The computer would be responsible for the machine's – rather than the televiewer's – capacity to analyse [sic] the ambient environment and automatically interpret the meaning of events," allowing the perceiving human to move away from toiling over CCTV camera feeds (ibid.). The sole purpose of the vision machine is not perception, but prediction. Prediction becomes the end through which perception – and, ultimately, surveillance – becomes a means for various forecasting agents (p. 66).

Virilio (1994) quotes Kipling's notorious saying of "Truth is the first casualty of war" in order to bring this vision machine back to his usual realm of everyday warfare (p. 66). Throughout his seminal work, *Speed and Politics*, Virilio (2006) describes the various ways in which his concept of speed directs societies in capitalist systems towards arenas of total war. Like this total war, which is mainly a spread of military forces for logistical means, the vision machine is a hierarchization of the war of information (p. 66). No longer is the aim of the state to conquer bodies of water, "making oceans a 'vast logistical camp,'" but instead the territory that must be conquered is that of the city and its streets (p. 64). These areas are not conquered through speed in the same way though. Where Virilio stresses the automobile and tank as machines of speed that allow for conquest, it is the camera and the computer that allow for the spaces of human bodies to be overtaken. More importantly, these vision machines become agents not only of prediction, but also of inferring deception, key for the information war machine.

Thus, vision machines are important in their ability to discern the actual from the virtual. Virilio writes about the "fusion of the object with its equivalent image," in discussing the ways that vision machines will be used by future generals on distant battlefields (p. 68). However, this is the essence of the data machine. With the rapid and extensive collection of data online, there is a hope that the object, the human user, will be equivalent to that of their data representation. This fusion will allow for prediction that is more commercially viable and exploitable, particularly when put together in a way that organizes data in terms that are similar to those used by previous audience models. Lest we forget that the creation of an audience is a rhetorical act that is subject to various pressures within the field. Eileen Meehan (1986) reminds us of this aspect of audience analysis, writing on television's rating systems, "Thus, the commodity audience comes to be defined by the dominant rating firm's methodology. And that methodology is itself a function of economic pressures" (p. 450). The human not only becomes a product of this fusion of the user and their data footprint, but of the organization of that user in space and time.

Let us take a step back from the explanation of the data machine's effects on identity creation for the user and instead discuss the shift from the visual to the numerical. How does one come from the vision machine to the data machine? They are, after all, very different mediums that constitute the object in different ways. However, I believe the objective of these two mediums to be very similar. In order for the user in the case of the data machine or the object in the case of the vision machine to be exploited in any way, they must be frozen in time. They both require the object

to transform from an evolving state of becoming to a static state of being. This has long been an issue of creating an audience for their ultimate use as advertising fodder, as the audience created stays in stasis while the audience in the wild may continually change and modify their tastes. For more information on this tension, one should look to Jaron Lanier (2010), who offers some possible directions for users and for the evolution of the Internet and other digital environments.

Virilio (1994) discusses the ways in which Gericault described painting in the early nineteenth century as appropriate for talking at large about photography. Specifically he examines Gericault's use of the Medusa myth in order to talk about the transformation present within painting (p. 38). He writes, "The Medusa is a kind of *integrated circuit of vision* that would seem to bode a future of awesome communication," in discussing this perfect transformation. This awesome communication would allow for a permanent still of the object and all of its parts. The body frozen whole, either in a photograph or as a set of data points, allows for it to be looked over and examined without fear of further transformation.

The data machine aims at constantly capturing the user as if they had just peered upon the Medusa, but a Medusa that strobes over the subject in order to create multiple frozen bodies of data. It purports that these frozen bodies will be better to predict future patterns and actions of the user. Like the vision machine, it assumes that the representation collected from the user, the image in the case of the vision machine, is equal to the totality of the user itself. Instead of the image that is captured by vision machines, there are now acts – clicks, cursor hovers, search queries, the length of time one spends on a page, etc. – that are equated, in sum, to the whole of the user.

In addition to these assumptions made by data machines, it is also important to understand the processes at work within this coded apparatus. Data machines require inputs, yes, but ultimately they are working within themselves. They require the data input of the user to be broken down and stored and then they require the images that advertisers wish to reflect to the user and their related characteristics. However, once the machine has these inputs, all of the actual labor is done by the machine itself. Data machines will examine and organize the user's characteristics in order to match a data point with an appropriate advertisement as soon as the user's webpage loads, creating a single-use, user-specific advertisement embedded within the webpage. This is also an important topic for digital rhetoric to eventually take on. How can rhetoricians study objects which are constantly changing according to the user that opens the website? What does digital rhetoric devolve into when we have texts that are so user- and time-specific that they might only appear once to a user?

Persistent and Single-Input Data

When dealing with data machines, we are dealing with a system requiring several points of data input. Without a critical mass of data, there is a lack of information for the data machine to create more accurate predictions. This is a problem that is not inherent with vision machines, as they look upon an entirety of the body as the whole of data that aims to be projected, instead of the fractional body created online by users. In the case of data machines, it is important to recognize that there are a few kinds of inputs that exist that may effect the machines' outputs in one way or another.

The first that we should look at is the single-input data, which are one-time inputs. This type of data can be anything ranging from a Facebook status update to a Google search query. In addition to these, there are much more basic items of data which are thrust into a user's history every time that they visit a website. This other type of data is persistent data, which a user carries with them throughout the Internet and can be particular to a given site. The user's IP address and their location are usually logged by each website in order to keep a register of who is viewing a site.

Important to note here is that persistent data will change over time with the addition of single-input data types. A Facebook status may be culled for information that will lead to a persistent imprint upon that user's data profile or a cookie left from a particular website might persist in their profile and be re-presented to the user in the form of advertisements. If we take Facebook as an example, once the user creates a profile there is a set of data that is constantly used, including the user's place of living, hometown, education and a multitude of others which are consistently interpreted to match the user with favorable advertisements. However, a single status update could lead to targeted advertising about that status.

MAIN FOCUS OF THE CHAPTER

Issues, Controversies, Problems

Digital Rhetoric and Kenneth Burke

While a lengthy discussion of Kenneth Burke's concepts of consubstantiation and identification occurs later within this chapter, it is important to discuss the reasons for this focus first. If we first look to the title of the field which this chapter is working within, digital rhetoric, we have the choice of emphasis. We can choose to privilege the digital impact on rhetoric or the rhetorical effects of digital environments, just as McGee (1990) understood the divergent understandings of rhetorical criticism. The explication on Burke's concepts that follows is one that privileges the digital impact on rhetoric with the understanding that we are required to adapt our theories for their use in new contexts.

New contexts require new definitions, but Burke's concepts have not always been contextualized. If we look to the source, we can readily realize this call for contextualization. Burke (1969a) writes, "to *define*, or *determine* a thing, is to mark its boundaries, hence to use terms that possess, implicitly at least, contextual reference" (24). It is this sort of definition, with an emphasis on context, that is not always present within the use of Burke within the field. For example, Paul and Philpott's (2009) explication on the formation of a *World of Warcraft* guild simply uses Burke's concept of identification as further complicating the events and texts surrounding this guild, but does not ask how *World of Warcraft* and the online guild affect the concept itself, placing identification into a world without context. Without this contextualization, we create gaps and assumptions that theories are expected to fill in. The remainder of this chapter uses the aspects unique to data mining in order to inform Burke's work and concepts that are still being used today without having been first contextualized.

Consubstantiation and the Data Machine

One of the terms recognized as central to Kenneth Burke's work and impact within rhetorical studies is identification. This process aims at framing rhetoric not as centered around persuasion, but as the unending conversation of identification. Identification is the process through which rhetors aim to recognize the aims and needs of their audience in order to identify them with the motives that they have undertaken and put forth.

The process that is within identification, as its core, is that of consubstantiation. This enveloped procedure is not one that is dealt with by academics with regularity, like that of identification (Day, 1960; Crusius, 1986). Burke (1969a) explains in *A Grammar of Motives* the importance of the etymology of the word substance, the core of this concept that he puts forth. Substance is not simply that which is the essence of what is being looked over, but, more importantly for Burke, that which the object stands upon. He writes, "Yet etymologically 'substance' is a scenic word. Literally, a person's or a thing's sub-stance would be something that stands beneath or supports the person or thing" (p. 22). In order to further explain the inherent difference that occurs when substance is discussed, Burke draws this etymology out further, stating that substance is "used to designate what a thing *is*, [but] derives from a word designating something that a thing *is not*" (p. 23).

What is under attack in the age of data mining is not necessarily identification, as the basic premise of attempting to line up the motives of one party with another is still present within online advertising. Instead, it is a problem of consubstantiation and the assumptions made in the case of substance online. Burke also writes in *A Grammar of Motives,* "[T]he word in its etymological origins would refer to an attribute of the thing's *context*, since that which supports or underlies a thing would be a part of the thing's context" (1969a, p. 23). This context is something that is lost when we refer to the medium of the Internet, if we are even willing to call the Internet as a medium within itself. However, within the structure of online advertising, specifically if we're looking to banner ads (the advertisements that run above or alongside the main content of a website) or pop-up advertisements, we are looking at processes which aim at eliminating context. Online advertising taps into a user's cache of cookies in order to view that user across several websites, dislocating the user from the specific context in which the cookies being relied upon came into existence.

However, let us not divert our attention too far away from the concept that Burke puts forth, consubstantiation. While context continues to be of importance, it is the process itself that offers a dynamism that deals with being tied down too much to context. Burke (1969b) explains consubstantiation as such:

A is not identical with his colleague, B. But insofar as their interests are joined, A is identified with B. Or he may identify himself with B even when their interests are not joined, if he assumes that they are, or is persuaded to believe so.

Here are the ambiguities of substance. In being identified with B, A is "substantially one" with a person other than himself. Yet at the same time he remains unique, an individual locus of motives. Thus he is both joined and separate, at once a distinct substance and consubstantial with another. (p. 21)

The most important thing to note here is the process that occurs in an ideal rhetoric. A and B are not always already consubstantial unless the motives which identify one with the other are put forth, leading to identification. However, this process of consubstantiation is the one that must be acted upon first in order to move into true identification.

When we introduce the data machine to the procedure of consubstantiation, we are confronted with a flattening of this process. Instead of A and B being objects which can be consubstantiated, they are pressed through into a direct consubstantiality through various points of interest, never being separate to begin with. Burke writes that, "To identify A with B is to make A 'consubstantial' with B," pointing to the importance of the evolution inherent here (p. 21). A may be of a similar sub-stance to that of B, requiring that similarity to be brought to the fore, but A is still different than that of B. If we look to the data machine, we are given a process which aims at automatically drawing out connections and patterns in such a way that does not look to bring A to B or B to A, but to instantaneously equates A and B.

This sort of effect is not necessarily new, but it has never been discussed in terms of Burke. If we turn to N. Katherine Hayles (2005), we are able to see that this is an important part of simply dealing with computers. She writes, "Code has become arguably as important as natural language because it causes things to happen, which requires that it be executed as commands the machine can run" (p. 49). In the case of the data machine we must always remember that we are dealing with a machine, which like an elevator, was created in order to fulfill a purpose. However, computers tend to differ from simple machines because of their ability to work within themselves. Hayles also writes that, "Although code originates with human writers and readers, once entered into the machine it has as its primary reader the machine itself. Before any screen display accessible to humans can be generated, the machine must first read the code and use its instructions to write messages humans can read" (p. 50). Here we see the true power of data machines. These programs are ones that use the storehouses of data users have contributed to in order to present an appropriate image or text to the user based on the data in tow and the rules that the machine follows.

Alexander Galloway (2012) takes this discussion one step further, writing on Hayles, "To see code as subjectively performative or enunciative is to anthropomorphize it, to project is onto the rubric of psychology, rather than to understand it through its own logic of 'calculation' or 'command'" (p. 71). While much of this chapter has looked to machina-morphize code into data machines, we cannot staple human psychology upon it so easily. This is why I have couched the effects of the term on rhetoric in consubstantiality, huddled within this humanist theory of rhetoric. Galloway reminds us of an important question, how are we to deal with digital rhetoric if it is always embedded and displayed through the executable language of code?

Effects on Identification

While I would like to keep a majority of the discussion of the effects of data machines on Burke's work within the realm of consubstantiation, it is important that we recognize any effect on consubstantiation will inevitably affect the larger process surrounding it, identification. With identification, Burke aims at establishing a view of rhetoric that moves away from persuasion as the central term for rhetoric and towards this new term as its locus. Identification is the effect of consubstantiation, the joining of two parties that were once divided in order to reach transcendence. Ross Wolin (2001) writes on transcendence, stating, "Although transcendence is not the only kind of transformation Burke analyzes in the *Rhetoric*, it dominates because one of the most common forms of transformation is the creation of a transcendent category to dissolve a dialectical pair" (p. 177). Transcendence is not a category of the divine, but one that allows the viewing of political and social hierarchies that exist, how they exist, and, as Burke hopes, to overcome these hierarchies and divisions.

However, like consubstantiation, we are automatically confronted with the flattening of processes by data machines and their executable language. Burke argues that the only way for identification and eventual transcendence to occur is through the existence of division and the constant challenge to overcome it. Burke writes that there is no identification without division, but when we look at the inner workings of data machines, where does the division exist? Yes, there is a division between the user and the product that is being advertised, but that exists solely outside of the mechanical processes that put forth the rhetorical acts. As described above, the user is always already consubstantiated with other sets of data through the processes of being broken down into characteristics and automatically being assigned to appropriate advertisements. Division in the case of data mining only occurs when we widen the circumference of these rhetorical acts, which is important for rhetoricians in the future to do. However, that division does not occur when we are talking about the intrinsic characteristics of the data machine. Instead we are met with a flattening of transcendence, just as we are confronted with a flattened and automatic consubstantiation. But how is it that this flattening is occurring? The problem ultimately comes down to the importance and centrality of dialectic and dialogue within Burke's work.

Dialogue, Dialectic, and Data Machines

The issue at hand with the flattening of consubstantiation, identification and transcendence extends into other parts of Burke, most importantly into his conceptualizations of dialogue and dialectic. What is lost in an age of data mining is a sense of give-and-take. While users have a history that is brought with them, created and evolving through the use of persistent and single-input data, the data machine is not interested in a dialogizing of its interaction with the user, instead solely capturing the user just as the Medusa captures the body.

The connection between dialog and dialectic is not an explicit relationship that Burke spells out, but if we look to his article "Rhetoric – Old and New" we are able to dispel how this connection manifests itself in his writing. It is here that he writes, "For, if identification includes the realm of transcendence, it has, by the some [sic] token, brought us into the realm of transformation, or dialectic. A rhetorician, I take it, is like one voice in a dialogue" (1951, p. 203). It is in this article that Burke first looks to the shift in rhetoric from persuasion as the central term to that of identification. However, we must realize that key to identification is the idea of cooperative competition, which holds dialogue and dialectic as its central methods.

There might be some rhetoricians who wish to jump ship at the thought of equating dialogue and dialectic, especially when Burke uses dialectic as his term of choice to discuss identification. However, we must look to one of his most famous examples in order to see the connections, the unending conversation. The unending conversation is a dramatic example that describes a parlor conversation that has been going on for so long that no one can recall it in its entirety. It is only through the contextual wrangle that one is able to effectively enter into this shifting and changing conversation. Burke (1974) writes in *The Philosophy of Literary Form*:

It is from this 'unending conversation' (the vision at the basis of Mead's work) that the materials of your drama arise. Nor is this verbal action all there is to it. For all these words are grounded in what Malinowski would call 'contexts of situation.' ... These interests do not 'cause' your discussion; its 'cause' is in the genius of man himself as homo loquax. (pp. 111-112)

This example of the unending conversation is something that Burke draws upon in later works, including the *Rhetoric*, and we can see a distinct link between dialectic, the discovery of contradictions through investigation, and dialogue.

Dialogue is not something that is upheld in the realm of online advertising. The data machine cares not for dialogue, but instead aims to hide itself in the communication acts that occur. Relying upon speed and the rigid structure created between the user and their characteristics, data machines remove dialogue from digital rhetoric for the benefit of advertising. This is not a process which looks to creating a new historiography or a new type of archiving, but a commercial, short-sighted view of the individual user to create instantaneous connections between user and product.

What do we have, then, when dialogue, and to an extent dialectic, is flattened into a sort of computer-mediated monologue? The closest thing that we have present in Burke's work is through the identification of the self and identification in socialization (1969b, p. 39). Burke talks of the self as an important scene of identification where the multiple roles within the human brain compete cooperatively. Burke writes on self-identification, "If he does not somehow act to tell himself (as his own audience) what the various brands of rhetorician have told him, his persuasion is not complete" (p. 39). However, this too is flattened by the concretized processes of data machines.

Robert Wess (1996) writes on Burke's rhetoric stating, "The rhetoric of identification, however, is written in a concrete that is always harden*ing*, never harden*ed*" (p. 200). This is what dialogue is for Burke, a constant hope that there is an evolution present within rhetoric which aims at the transcendence he hopes can exist, and ultimately for the pure persuasion that he imagines. The data machine, however, aims not at becoming, but at always presenting a full being whose times of hardening are overshadowed by those of hardened. The creation of these instantaneous and user-specific advertisements calls upon a subject which has already gone through the steps of hardening and has become hardened in order for a fully viable audience member to be created and sold. This is an issue that Maurice Charland (1987) looks toward when describing constitutive rhetoric and an issue that continues into digital rhetoric. When we take for granted the rhetorics that create a user, we are also relegating that user to become hardened for their use by rhetors as objects of optimistically teleological identification.

Dialogue insists upon an evolving view of the human user instead of a stale set of data that has been organized in a way that provides ample connections to be drawn to consumable products. However, through data machines, online advertising becomes flattened, leaving behind notions of becoming in favor of a more profitable model of a user's being. Charland (1987) writes, "However, rhetorical theory's privileging of an audience's freedom to judge is problematic, for it assumes that audiences, with their prejudices, interests, and motives are *given* and so extra-rhetorical" (p. 133). Rhetoricians are thus required to acknowledge this in the future in a way unlike the data machine. Users must be understood instead as dynamic beings always influenced by previous instances of rhetoric and also evolving in the processes of these rhetorics.

SOLUTIONS AND RECOMMENDATIONS

A Burkean Model of Data Mining

Data mining is not going anywhere in the future of the Internet, as it is a viable and extensive way to create an audience for advertising. Also, without the tools revolving around data mining, we would be without the positive side effects of new connections and a more personalized Internet. Amazon gives us new books that we might want to view based on our interests, which is particularly important for academics. In addition to this, Google created a flu map in order to track the spread of influenza throughout the U.S. based on certain search queries made in certain cities ("Google Flu Trends," n.d.).

With the possible positives and the stability of data mining within the digital infrastructure, we are forced to plunge deeper into the simulacrum that is being constantly created for each Internet user. Software developers and data analysts should look to the everyday in order to more fully grasp the individual through their data. Michel de Certeau (1988) writes on the everyday individual, "Analysis shows that a relation (always social) determines its terms, and not the reverse, and that each individual is a locus in which an incoherent (and often contradictory) plurality of such relational determinations interact" (xi). This definition of an individual is required in order to further data mining for online advertising, and this is what is required of a more Burkean model for data-driven identity formation.

A Burkean model would be sure to look at the individual in the same way that Robert Wess looks at the scientist in his explanation of their existence during the Cold War in the U.S. He writes, "Burke's scientist is a body constituted as a subject in the context of a conjunction of four subject positions: scientist, parent, citizen of a nation, and citizen of the world. ... [T]he reproduction of the subject

in particular intersects with the reproduction of the social formation in general" (1996, p. 195). This model would have to account that the user online is not always a consistent being and is often required to deal with several positions, which may change according to the situation.

Ultimately, the Burkean model for digital identification requires the human to be in conversation with the machine and for dialogue to never take a backseat to instantaneous results. The Burkean data machine must look not to capitalize on every single input by the user, as many inputs might be of no actual relation to the user. Instead, the patterns created for the user must be situated historically according to repetition and the number of the machine's outputs must be expanded in order to gain a higher level of complexity that is inherent in each user. Most important for software developers and data analysts is to recognize that they will never reach the supposed core of the human condition by examining users' movements online. Perhaps simply this recognition will allow for an opening of digital consubstantiation, or at least for a greater humanist perspective in the creation of pragmatic and executable languages.

Burke's Future in Digital Rhetoric

The overarching purpose of this chapter is to continue the challenge to digital rhetoric to adapt the rhetorical theories being used in critique and analysis for the new media environments in which they are being placed. This call for contextualization is not new, but an important challenge that must be constantly emphasized for digital rhetoric's success as a field. Just as Brooke (2009) calls on rhetoricians to embrace different aspects or new conceptualizations of previous theories, Ian Bogost (2007) writes, "In short, digital rhetoric tends to focus on the presentation of traditional materials—especially text and images—without accounting for the computational underpinnings of the presentation" (p. 28).

The preceding analysis of data mining is offered as an example of this contextualization with a focus on the computer and the practices that revolve around it. While this adaptation is new for data mining, other theories of Burke's have been adapted for other digital arenas. Bourgonjon et al. (2011) adapt Burke's Pentad for the unique affordances of video games, hybridizing traditional Pentadic analysis with Bogost's concept of procedural rhetoric in order to offer a new method of analyzing video games. It is through research such as this that allows for the furthering of disciplines and their previous theories in new situations, necessary particularly for digital rhetoric.

FUTURE RESEARCH DIRECTIONS

In the future of the rhetorical study of data mining, and digital rhetoric in general, we are required to constantly adapt and confront older conceptualizations of the digital self. The early works of Sherry Turkle demonstrate a need to reconcile the idea of a liberated-by-technology identity with data mining. Turkle (1995) places the responsibility of identity creation upon the user, writing, "[W]e reconstruct our identities on the other side of the looking glass. This reconstruction is our cultural work in progress" (178). Instead, digital rhetoricians are required to look at the constitutive and procedural rhetorics that are in place to create the identity and the audience of the Internet. In addition to these rhetorics, it is important for rhetoricians to be consistently aware of the executable nature of computational language. These are requirements of any discipline that looks to move from one medium to another. Rhetoricians have attempted this move before (Warnick, 2007; Gurak, 2001), but there continue to be issues of audience within a digital space. While this is particularly interesting within the new media realm, we must also look to how audiences and identities are created with medium specificity in order to have a greater understanding of rhetoric's work within every medium

and communication technology. Going forward, realizing this specificity and adapting previous theories will be invaluable in the understanding of the rhetorical audience within various contexts.

Zappen (2005) writes on digital rhetoric as "an amalgam of more-or-less discrete components rather than a complete and integrated theory in its own right" (p. 323). Instead of attempting to completely bring the history and canon of rhetoric into the digital realm, it might aid digital rhetoricians to looks first at the medium in which they are discussing, as it affords or constricts both audiences and rhetors in their pursuit of communication. Instead of asking how one theorist or rhetorician fits into new media, it is important for rhetoricians to look to the medium first. Rhetoricians will be required to look at media theorists more and more in order to understand the changes from the old to the new and be willing to incorporate their theories in relation with the established philosophies of rhetoric. While maintaining boundaries is important for any academic discipline, it may be required to blur those lines in the pursuit of understanding the vast complexities of the digital landscape.

CONCLUSION

In the small space where Kenneth Burke did much of his writing in Andover, New Jersey, there is a short phrase written in Latin above the window frame reading "potius convincere quam convinciari / ad bellum purificandum." This phrase means "better to debate than to berate / towards the purification of war" (Zappen, Halloran, & Wible, n.d.). Some have taken this to be a fine summation of Burke's work, as it aims to dramatically transform war, Burke's ultimate disease of cooperation, through the logic of dialectic and demonstration. Zappen, Halloran and Wible write, "War, he suggests, may be *purified* through logic or dialectic, that is, through the exercise of the arts of proving or demonstrating our beliefs and actions to others rather than merely reviling or reproaching them." We see here an importance placed on rhetoric as an identifying process that leads to these utopian goals.

However, as has been shown, with the advancement and implementation of data mining, digital identification takes on a different feel than that of Burke's scrawled message. In fact, it appears that instead of *ad bellum purificandum*, we have *ad machinam datam purificandam* – towards the purification of the data machine. Let us break down the Latin a bit more to really get at what is happening in this phrase. According to *Cassell's Latin Dictionary*, *datam*, derived from *datio* – a giving – reveals the practice by which the data machine can work, only through the feeding of inputs into the vast world of data that it has at its disposal (Marchand & Charles, 1892, p. 150). Unlike the war that is to be purified by Burke's work and dialectic, there is no history to these givens, but they are required for the existence of these rhetorical acts.

More interesting are the definitions listed by this dictionary for *machina*. This dictionary lists a few possible translations for the Latin word, including "a machine, any artificial contrivance for performing work, especially a machine for moving heavy weights ... a military engine, a catapult, ballista, etc. ... a platform on which slaves were exposed for sale" (p. 328). We see here all facets of the data machine that have been put forth: the mechanic aspects that create the flattened space of online advertising, the military aspects of vision and data that Virilio warns against, and, most importantly, the essentializing aspect of data machines. Not to equate users with slaves, but when they are within a space such as the physical or digital platform for sale there are a few similarities. They are both viewed for their labor, the slave for their physical labor and the user for their data labor. In addition to this, the ultimate reason for their placement upon this platform is for their ultimate sale. Users are essentialized to their basic characteristics in order to be seen in terms of possible commercial matches instead

of as users who can be seen to be evolving and moving through their actions online.

To bring out this shift, we must take a look at one last example, that of the company that shares the same name as the concept central to this paper, The Data Machine. If we look to their website (n.d.), we are able to see right away the move toward the purification of the data machine. The homepage features examples of what data profiles would look like for specific people, pairing images with central characteristics of those included. We are met with a brunette woman who is identified only as "divorced", "wine aficionado", and "owns a bungalow" – characteristics that all have a high probability of being profitably exploited. We see here the true Latin definition of *machina*, the crane, which excavates these sets of data in order to pick up only the most valuable of characteristics, like the crane in a marble quarry.

What we have instead of the purification of war with logic and dialectic is the flattening of these concepts in order to purify the machine and exploit the vast technological powers available for the sake of creating essential identities, directly in conflict with Burke's purposes and writings. This is precisely what Burke writes against in his war of words with Behaviorism. He writes in the *Grammar* that, "[T]hough nothing is more distinctly 'human' than a scientific laboratory in one sense (for no other species but man is known ever to have made and used one) it is the kind of 'humanity' we get in mechanization" (Burke, 1969a, p. 78). He goes on to write the effect of this mechanization as "lead[ing] consistently to ideals of definition that dissolve the personality and its actions into depersonalization and motion respectively" (p. 79).

Most importantly, we must take away from this chapter that digital rhetoric requires scholars willing to move toward contextualization of both the objects of analysis and of the theories being used to examine them. Just as the user has moved towards being a decontextualized set of data points, the traditional theories and concepts that are being used within digital rhetoric are being concretized in their use. Without constant re-contextualization and re-definition, particularly necessary in a realm that changes as often as the digital, these theories start to create gaps in their use and deny the unique abilities and issues of each medium or practice to fully influence the furthering of scholarship.

ACKNOWLEDGMENT

The author would like to acknowledge the contributions of Gaines Hubbell and Joshua Comer in their tireless support and unending conversations on this subject and many others.

REFERENCES

Bogost, I. (2007). *Persuasive games: The expressive power of videogames*. Cambridge, MA: The MIT Press.

Bourgonjon, J., Rutten, K., Soetaert, R., & Valcke, M. (2011). From counter-strike to counter-statement: Using Burke's pentad as a tool for analysing video games. *Digital Creativity*, *22*(2), 91–102. doi:10.1080/14626268.2011.578577

Brooke, C. G. (2009). *Lingua fracta: Toward a rhetoric of new media*. Cresskill, NJ: Hampton Press, Inc.

Burke, K. (1941). *The philosophy of literary form: Studies in symbolic action*. Baton Rouge, LA: Louisiana State University Press.

Burke, K. (1951). Rhetoric - old and new. *The Journal of General Education*, *5*(3), 202–209.

Burke, K. (1969a). *A grammar of motives* (California Ed.). Berkeley, CA: University of California Press.

Burke, K. (1969b). *A rhetoric of motives* (California Ed.). Berkeley, CA: University of California Press.

Burke, K. (1984). *Permanence and change: An anatomy of purpose* (3rd ed.). Berkeley, CA: University of California Press.

Charland, M. (1987). Constitutive rhetoric: The case of the *Peuple Quebecois*. *The Quarterly Journal of Speech*, *73*(2), 133–150. doi:10.1080/00335638709383799

Crusius, T. W. (1986). A case for Kenneth Burke's dialectic and rhetoric. *Philosophy and Rhetoric*, *19*(1), 23–37.

Cultack, G. (2013, February 12). Xbox 720 may require Kinect to be plugged in, switched on and watching you. *Gizmodo UK*. Retrieved February 14, 2013 from http://www.gizmodo.co.uk/2013/02/xbox-720-may-require-kinect-to-be-plugged-in-switched-on-and-watching-you/

Day, D. G. (1960). Persuasion and the concept of identification. *The Quarterly Journal of Speech*, *46*(3), 270–273. doi:10.1080/00335636009382421

de Certeau, M. (1988). *The practice of everyday life* (S. F. Rendall, Trans.). Berkeley, CA: University of California Press.

de Vries, K. (2009). Identity in a world of ambient intelligence. In Y. Abbas, & F. Dervin (Eds.), *Digital technologies of the self* (pp. 15–36). Newcastle, UK: Cambridge Scholars.

Ertz, S. (2012, August 26). Sony patents an interactive commercial concept. *The Upstream*. Retrieved February 10, 2013 from http://www.plughitzlive.com/theupstream/1925-sony-patents-an-interactive-commercial-concept.html.

Galloway, A. R. (2012). *The interface effect*. Cambridge, UK, Malden, MA: Polity Press.

Google Flu Trends. (n.d.). *Explore flu trends - United states*. Retrieved February 18, 2013 from http://www.google.org/flutrends/us/#US

Gurak, L. J. (2001). *Cyberliteracy: Navigating the Internet with awareness.* New Haven, CT: Yale University Press.

Han, J., Kamber, M., & Pei, J. (2012). *Data mining concepts and techniques* (3rd ed.). Waltham, MA: Morgan Kaufmann Publishers.

Hayles, N. K. (2005). *My mother was a computer: Digital subjects and literary texts.* Chicago, IL: University of Chicago Press. doi:10.7208/chicago/9780226321493.001.0001

Lanier, J. (2010). *You are not a gadget: A manifesto.* New York, NY: Alfred A. Knopf.

Marchant, J. R. V., & Charles, J. F. (1892). *Cassell's Latin dictionary.* UK: Cassell Publishers.

McGee, M. C. (1990). Text, context, and the fragmentation of contemporary culture. *Western Journal of Speech Communication, 54*(3), 274–289. doi:10.1080/10570319009374343

Meehan, E. R. (1986). Conceptualizing culture as commodity: The problem of television. *Critical Studies in Mass Communication, 3*(4), 448–457. doi:10.1080/15295038609366675

Paul, C. A., & Philpott, J. S. (2009). The rise and fall of CTS: Kenneth Burke identifying with the World of Warcraft. In *Proceedings of DiGRA 2009: Breaking New Ground: Innovation in Games, Play, Practices and Theory.* Digital Games Research Association.

Silver, N. (2012). *The signal and the noise: Why most predictions fail but some don't.* New York, NY: Penguin Press.

The Data Machine. (n. d.). *Homepage.* Retrieved February 5, 2013 from http://www.thedatamachine.com

Turkle, S. (1997). *Life on the screen: Identity in the age of the Internet.* New York, NY: Touchstone.

Virilio, P. (1994). *The vision machine.* Bloomington, IN: Indiana University Press.

Virilio, P. (2006). *Speed and politics.* Los Angeles, CA: Semiotext(e).

Warnick, B. (2007). *Rhetoric online: Persuasion and politics on the World Wide Web.* New York: Peter Lang.

Wess, R. (1996). *Kenneth Burke: Rhetoric, subjectivity, postmodernism.* New York, NY: Cambridge University Press. doi:10.1017/CBO9780511552878

Wolin, R. (2001). *The rhetorical imagination of Kenneth Burke.* Columbia, SC: University of South Carolina Press.

Zappen, J. P. (2005). Digital rhetoric: Toward an integrated theory. *Technical Communication Quarterly, 14*(3), 319–325. doi:10.1207/s15427625tcq1403_10

Zappen, J. P., Halloran, S. M., & Wible, S. A. (n.d.). Some notes on ad bellum purificandum. *The Journal of the Kenneth Burke Society.* Retrieved January 10, 2013 from http://kbjournal.org/node/201

ADDITIONAL READING

Ang, I. (2006). On the politics of empirical audience research. In D. Kellner, & M. G. Durham (Eds.), *Keyworks: Media and cultural studies* (pp. 174–194). Malden, MA: Blackwell Publishing.

Aronowitz, S. (2005). Technology and the future of work. In D. Trend (Ed.), *Reading digital culture* (pp. 133–143). Malden, MA: Blackwell Publishing.

Burke, K. (1984). *General nature of ritual. Attitudes toward history* (3rd ed., pp. 179–215). Berkeley, CA: University of California Press.

Burke, K., Rueckert, W. H., & Bonadonna, A. (2003). *(Nonsymbolic) motion / (symbolic) action. On human nature: A gathering while everything flows, 1967-1984* (pp. 139–171). Berkeley, CA: University of California Press.

Carr, N. G. (2011). A thing like me. *The shallows: What the Internet is doing to our brains* (pp. 201–222). New York: W.W. Norton.

Casuri, A. (2008). Data as representation: Beyond anonymity in E-research ethics. *International Journal of Internet Research Ethics, 1*(1), 37–65.

Chung, G., & Grimes, S. M. (2005). Data mining the kids: surveillance and market research strategies in children's online games. *Canadian Journal of Communication, 30*, 527–548.

Cubitt, S. (1999). Virilio and new media. *Theory, Culture & Society, 16*(5-6), 127–142. doi:10.1177/02632769922050908

Galloway, A. R. (2009). The unworkable interface. *New Literary History, 39*, 931–955. doi:10.1353/nlh.0.0062

Herring, S. (2003). Computer-mediated discourse. In D. Schiffrin, D. Tannen, & H. E. Hamilton (Eds.), *The handbook of discourse analysis* (pp. 612–634). Malden, MA: Blackwell Publishing.

Hindman, M. (2009). Political traffic and the politics of search. *The myth of digital democracy* (pp. 58–81). Princeton, NJ: Princeton University Press.

Howard, P. N. (2005). Deep democracy, thin citizenship: The impact of digital media in political campaign strategy. *The Annals of the American Academy of Political and Social Science, 597*(1), 153–170. doi:10.1177/0002716204270139

Hui, Y. (2012). What is a digital object? *Metaphilosophy, 43*(4), 380–395. doi:10.1111/j.1467-9973.2012.01761.x

Hutchinson, W., & Warren, M. (2001). The nature of data: Illusions of reality. *Informing Science* (pp. 262–267). Paper presented at Challenges to Informing Clients: A Transdisciplinary Approach, Krakow, Poland.

James, I. (2007). Virtualization. *Routledge critical thinkers: Paul Virilio* (pp. 45–66). New York: Routledge.

Kirby, A. (2009). Digimodernism and Web 2.0. *Digimodernism: How new technologies dismantle the Postmodern and reconfigure our culture* (pp. 101–123). New York: The Continuum International Publishing Group Inc.

Miller, C. R. (2007). What can automation tell us about agency? *Rhetoric Society Quarterly, 37*, 137–157. doi:10.1080/02773940601021197

Murray, J. W. (2001). Kenneth Burke: A dialogue of motives. *Philosophy and Rhetoric, 35*(1), 22–49. doi:10.1353/par.2002.0004

Pariser, E. (2011). The user is the content. *The filter bubble: What the Internet is hiding from you* (pp. 47–76). New York: Penguin Press.

Pasquinelli, M. (2009). Google's PageRank algorithm: A diagram of cognitive capitalism and the rentier of the common intellect. In K. Becker, & F. Stalder (Eds.), *Deep Search: The Politics of Search Beyond Google* (pp. 152–162). Innsbruck: Studien Verlag.

Ranciere, J. (2009). The future of the image. *The future of the image* (pp. 1–31). London: Verso.

Ruth, A. (2008). Computer mediated learning: applying Burke's pentad. In S. Kelsey, & K. St. Amant (Eds.), *Handbook of research on computer mediated communication* (pp. 73–86). Hershey, PA: IGI Global. doi:10.4018/978-1-59904-863-5.ch007

Sculley, D., & Pasanek, B. M. (2008). Meaning and mining: the impact of implicit assumptions in data mining for the humanities. *Literary and Linguistic Computing*, *23*(4), 409–424. doi:10.1093/llc/fqn019

Striphas, T. (2010). The abuses of literacy: Amazon Kindle and the right to read. *Communication and Critical. Cultural Studies*, *7*(3), 297–317.

Turner, F. (2006). *The shifting politics of the computational metaphor. From counterculture to cyberculture: Stewart Brand, the Whole Earth Network, and the rise of digital utopianism* (pp. 11–40). Chicago, IL: The University of Chicago Press. doi:10.7208/chicago/9780226817439.001.0001

Virilio, P. (1992). Big optics. In P. Weibel (Ed.), *On justifying the hypothetical nature of art* (pp. 82–93). Cologne: Walther Konig.

Virilio, P. (2004). Strategy of deception. In S. Redhead (Ed.), *The Paul Virilio reader* (pp. 209–224). New York, NY: Columbia University Press.

Zittrain, J. (2008). Meeting the risks of generativity: Privacy 2.0. *The future of the Internet and how to stop it* (pp. 200–234). New Haven, CT: Yale University Press.

KEY TERMS AND DEFINITIONS

Ad Bellum Purificandum: Literally, the phrase means "toward the purification of war," but underneath the translation is the sense that Burke was trying to get across in his corpus: that war might be able to be avoided in the purified logic and dialectic.

Consubstantiation: Consubstantiation is the process within the process of identification. This procedure is where the motives of one rhetorical object are joined and made the same as the motives of another object in order for identification to take place.

Data Mining: The attempt to discern patterns from vast stores of user-created data. This process drives most of online advertising and attempts to create a more personalized persuasive space on the Internet.

Dialectic: A process for Burke that is tied with dialogue. This process is the method through which identification can occur, as it is the investigation of contradictions and an attempt to display those contradictions for all to see.

Identification: Identification is seen as the central notion of Kenneth Burke's rhetoric. It is the concept that rhetors look to, matching the motives of one person with the motives of their own in order for transcendence over division.

Rhetoric: For the purposes of this chapter, rhetoric should refer to identification and not to persuasion.

Substance: For Burke, substance is not only the essence of an object, but it is that essence which can only be discerned through its sub-stance, that which it stands upon.

Vision Machine: Paul Virilio's concept, vision machines are machines that see human users in order to move toward the mechanization of perception, specifically of sight. It is important to note here that these are machines that aim to discern the human in order for the purposes of prediction.

Chapter 6
The Persuasive Language of Action:
Interaction in the Digital Age

Martin van Velsen
Carnegie Mellon University, USA

ABSTRACT

Besides the visual splendor pervasive in the current generation of digital video games, especially those where players roam simulated landscapes and imaginary worlds, few efforts have looked at the resources available to embed human meaning into a game's experience. From the art of persuasion to the mechanics of meaning-making in digital video games and table-top role playing games, this chapter investigates the changes and new opportunities available that can extend our understanding of digital rhetoric. Starting with a breakdown of the role of choice, workable models from psychology and the untapped body of knowledge from table-top role playing games are shown to allow game designers to enrich their products with a deeper human experience.

INTRODUCTION

We've seen tremendous technological advances in the visual capabilities of video games. Many available digital products present an almost photo-realistic environment for us to play in. But where does the human experience stand, the sensation that we are interacting with a world as natural and meaningful as our own? Even digital role playing video games known as Massively Multi-player Online Role Playing Games (MMORPGS), where the game play has a strong social aspect, still do not fully connect with our human needs to make meaningful choices. According to Aristotle (1984), "What makes a person a sophist is not his abilities but his choices." In current research in the area of digital story telling the player choices

DOI: 10.4018/978-1-4666-4916-3.ch006

Copyright © 2014, IGI Global. Copying or distributing in print or electronic forms without written permission of IGI Global is prohibited.

and the management of choice outcomes has become the de-facto means by which it is assumed a more meaningful experience can be generated (Riedl & Bulitko, 2013). The reasoning behind this concept is that choice empowers us and gives us more control over the artificial environment. Meaningful decision making can only take place when the structure or seeds for a decision have been well crafted. An assumption in this design is that the fact a choice is available is what makes an experience meaningful. Instead it is better to reformulate the idea of choice and look at the nature of a choice or more specifically the impetus or setup of a choice. For example a choice, or what to do next, is more important when we are the witness to an accident than when we are faced with figuring out what kind of meal to order at a restaurant. We could think of the planning and design of meaningful situations as a form of suggesting possible choice-bearing scenarios. With this assumption in mind the article will mainly focus on the packaging and nature of the signals that pre-empt choices in digital games and give examples of how these signals can be enhanced.

One form of gameplay that accomplishes this goal of allowing players to give a shape and meaning to their choices is called Table-Top Role Play Gaming or Table Top RPGs. This type of non-digital real-life gameplay brings together small groups of players and is known for its complex interaction and storytelling (Van Velsen et al., 2009). The overall approach of the paper is to see how choice generation mechanisms work in table-top RPGs and see how suitable they are for digital video games. It is perhaps an overstatement to define table-top role-playing as a technological achievement; however, the adoption of probability modeling and a long history of rigorous testing and verification have almost given this form of game-play scientific status. Using the results from table-top studies mapped to current methods of interaction in digital games, we can extend our understanding of digital rhetoric. We can then go beyond the traditionally written and spoken forms of rhetoric, which then allows us to describe a more generic model of narrative interaction that forms a potential grounding for procedural rhetoric (Bogost, 2008; Treanor et al., 2012). Before we can investigate any extensions to rhetoric and see how they apply to both digital video games and table-top RPGs, we need to establish how we define digital rhetoric.

Grounding in Digital Rhetoric

With a discussion on digital rhetoric we inevitably arrive at the question of what this term means or what the definition is. Amongst the many existing descriptions and definitions a categorization by Losh (Losh, 2012) stands out, since it acknowledges the wide variety of contexts and purposes of digital rhetoric. Her taxonomy includes two useful definitions:

1. The emerging scholarly discipline concerned with the rhetorical interpretation of computer-generated media as objects of study.
2. Mathematical theories of communication from the field of information science, many of which attempt to quantify the amount of uncertainty in a given linguistic exchange or the likely paths through which messages travel.

These definitions attempt to unpack the complexities involved in digital forms of media that require involved forms of computation to communicate a meaningful message or experience. When we speak of digital forms of media that involve large amounts of computation we mean those digital media where a simulated imaginary environment, complete with artificial characters and narrative, is presented to us through a high fidelity graphical representation. These forms of media are often called digital role playing games.

In this article we go beyond the technical complexities needed to visualize the natural environments in which stories can take place and we will focus instead on the human interaction and narrative aspects those systems afford. More specifically we will try to answer Losh's follow-up question to her categorical inventory of digital rhetoric: "How do we understand forms of invisible labor, and how knowledge is embodied, situated, and co-created?" To answer this question we turn to a tradition of physical and direct interpersonal story based game play or table-top games, specifically those that use storytelling, which are commonly referred to as table-top role playing games. In these games a Narrator moderates and guides players through an imaginary setting and helps the players to invent their own stories and adventures. Using the laws of probability embodied in dice rolls, both the players and Narrator engage in co-constructing a narrative.

A Brief History of Table-Top Role Play Gaming

Table-top role-playing games began when conflict simulations called "war-games" were used to learn tactics and strategies for actual battlefield gain. An example of this is the game *Kriegspiel*, a variant of chess used by officers in the Franco-Prussian war, and the grandfather of modern table-top games. In these games, role-playing was required of players to represent unit actions on each side, but the introduction of negotiations between specific individuals required a referee. Since the inception of the basic mechanics of this form of role play gaming, many table-top games have provided numerous rule-sets to enhance the experience of these interactions, as well as have provided game mechanics to lessen the need for a referee to weigh-in on related outcomes. Table-Top role playing games are a subset of board games, and we are seeing an increase in the popularity of both types. In fact, although digital video games have been and are becoming ever more popular, there are signs that table-top RPGs are also becoming an ever increasing form of game play. Broadly speaking, table-top games can be placed on a spectrum ranging from combat or simulation based gaming to pure narrative and story based play. We will focus on the story oriented variety, where players engage in dialog based interaction with a referee, often referred to as a Game Master (GM), or Dungeon Master (DM), or simply, and for our purposes: a Narrator.

An important aspect of table-top games is that they allow for the use of narrative role playing to be introduced into the game by letting people inhabit a character role (Fine, 2002). Whereas in digital video games the player's appearance of their character role is an important aspect of the experience and embodied in an avatar, in the table-top variety often a player's embodiment is purely up to the imagination. Often, in table-top role-playing games, character points are given to indicate strengths and weaknesses, but character role-playing also helps to determine game outcomes by allowing players to negotiate their actions with the Narrator of the game. It is this negotiation which allows a table-top game to avoid binary choices. In digital video games whenever the player is presented with a choice the narrative branches and one option plays out over another. It is this problem of binary choices that generate a sense of polarized narrative where each turning point halts the story.

AN EXAMPLE TABLE-TOP ROLE PLAYING SESSION

To illustrate the various forms of narrative interaction and to provide an example series of interaction for the rest of the chapter, a constructed game session is provided below. By game session we mean the gathering of a group of people where a game is played in one sitting. Usually a session lasts an afternoon but can also extend to cover a day or more. Only two players, labeled PL-1 and

PL-2, and a GM are included for this example. The imaginary session below is presented as a transcript of the recorded session dialog between players. The interactions are augmented with extra information to signify events or interactions not explicitly said or taken by the participants and is placed in square brackets. Since the players can speak both in-character and out of character we will use the notation convention that anything said or indicated as the actual player is shown in parenthesis, while any dialog or action by the portrayed characters will be without any parenthesis.

GM: *You find yourself in a small dark shop known in the old city for both its rarities as well as its wide variety of useful adventuring goods. It has been owned for centuries by the Mendax family and is now run by the already ancient Kendrik Mendax. As you stand around gazing at all the curious objects you hear a small shuffling in the back of the store. A head peaks out from behind a shelf and looks you two over. You are lucky, the owner himself is present and he bows behind the counter with a flourish of his hand.*

Kendrik: *Can't say I have seen you two here before. If you have not already been informed you have just stepped into the store that has it all.*

PL-1: *Yes yes, we are looking for a small box to store jewels in.*

PL-2: *In case we find any of course.*

Kendrik: *You would be surprised how many adventurers wander in here asking for exactly the same type of item. In fact I might say we rather specialize in just such type of object.*

PL-1: *It must have a lock though.*

Kendrik: *Of course! Did you have any specific size in mind for the box?*

PL-2: *Not too big, maybe something like the size of a cigar box.*

Kendrik: *What about this? (shows a small jewel case). This box is one of our specialties. You just twist open this small seal at the top like so to unlock it. No keys no fuss, a very popular seller.*

GM: *Kendrik shows the two adventurers how to lock and unlock the box by rotating and pressing the cylindrical seal shaped button on the top.*

PL-2: *Perfect! That will do.*

Kendrik: *Let me wrap this up for you and you'll be on your way shortly.*

GM: *The shop owner takes the small box towards the back of the store where he is heard rustling with paper for a lot longer than it should take for such a simple wrapping.*

We break the sample session here for clarity of narrative and pick it up again when the events already discussed become relevant for the discussion.

GM: *After the door to the dungeon slams shut you can only make out a tiny source of light in the distance, otherwise it is completely dark around. You hear no noise. There is no noticeable flow of air.*

PL-1: *Let's go check out that light. Did you bring a torch? I only have flint and steel.*

PL-2: *Yeah I finally remembered to bring a bunch, give it a try.*

GM: *You successfully light two torches and you can now see your immediate surroundings. As it turns out you are not in a dungeon but in an old long dried out sewer system. There is an old almost crumbled door on your left and what appears to be a tunnel stretching out in front of you from where this tiny light source appears to come.*

PL-1: *Let's go see where this leads; I want to know what that light in the distance is.*

PL-2: *Then you can go first.*

GM: *You walk for about five minutes with your heads bent because the ceiling is so low. You reach an old wooden door that looks molded through.*

PL-1: *I kick in the door.*

[Randomly determined outcome by using dice]

GM: You succeed in kicking in the door.

PL-2: I shine a light into the room.

GM: Although your torch would provide plenty of light there is no need to use it. There is a single lantern sitting on a large chest. It appears that the room has been occupied very recently and that there is another way out of this room, a door opposite the one you entered.

PL-1: I remove the oil lamp and try to open the chest.

[Randomly determined outcome by using dice]

GM: You do not manage to open the chest. You notice that there is a seal on the top of the chest that looks remarkably like the seal on the top of your jewel box.

PL-1: I retrieve our jewel box from my bag and open it.

[dice check]

GM: You manage to open the box but it was trapped and a needle poisons your hand.

PL-2: I grab the box but make sure not to touch the needle.

GM: There is a small piece of paper remaining in the box.

PL-2: I read the paper.

GM: The piece of paper says: "please return any found treasure to the Mendax Emporium in this jewel box."

Although the interaction is short there are many aspects of storytelling and narrative interaction compressed into a dense role playing session. This artificial session was constructed from a number of interviews with GMs. Furthermore the session includes typical interactions derived from transcribed live game sessions (Tychsen, 2007). Within this session a number of choices are made by the players through their player characters where the outcome of those choices drastically changed the direction of the game. The nature of choice is important in games where each participant has an influence on the evolving scenario. Our inclination is to see choice-making as the crucial component in any game. We will first look at the mechanics of choice and then show how it can be more important to understand how a GM creates the opportunity for choice and the nature of choice.

THE ROLE OF CHOICE

There is a good case to be made that besides the visual and symbolic supported narrative in table-top role playing, the linguistic constructions being used are not related to classical rhetoric. As in: the Narrator will not argue with the players in order to demonstrate a superior or better formulated plot and experience. This idea of a co-constructed argument is collaborated by Zappen' discussion of digital rhetoric: "where I argue that dialogue — conceived not as a mode of persuasion, but as a testing of one's own ideas, a contesting of others' ideas, and a collaborative creating of ideas" (Zappen, 2005). Instead the game master can only use those linguistic and non-verbal means by which players for themselves construct a meaningful experience. In contrast in digital video games, the means by which the game progresses is by players being offered choices at carefully placed decision points. When players arrive at this decision point they make a choice from a palette of options, and depending on which choice is picked the game progresses or branches in a different direction. Much of this branching mechanism is well established and has been used since the classic "choose-your-own adventure" paperback novels published by Bantum Books (Packard, 1979). Now that we have a sense of the role of choice in general we need to understand its mechanics, in other words: how are choices signaled, understood and acted upon.

The Basic Choice Structure

Digital video games rely on clearly identifiable indicators provided by players to determine how to react. When a player uses a game controller to indicate that he or she wants to open a door, then the game has an unambiguous understanding of the player's intent. There are two reasons why this is important. First of all, the game has a limited amount of options that can occur. The door either opens or it doesn't. If the player wants his or her player character to kick in the door then the game must have that option built-in. Second, the game must indicate that a door is 'openable'. In other words it needs to be able to simulate the physics and appearance of the door opening. Games are presented to us by a computer in which software tries its best to create a realistic depiction of our physical reality. However, there are many aspects of our world's physicality that cannot be provided to us. We cannot probe or interrogate the door's sturdiness or other aspects that could provide us with alternative ways of interacting with it. Superficially this seems to be the reason why digital video games are not as interactive and lively as we might like them to be. However, the problem really starts if we step back and look at the higher-level consequences.

In the example of the virtual door in the game there was vital detail present which we do not have in the grander scheme of things: we knew there was a door. A fundamental issue in digital video games is the problem that we have to show players where the choices are. Consider Figure 1 where we imagine an abstract situation from above where a player starts at location B and walks through a flat space towards location A. The player encounters two walls that diagonally meet at a small opening. Presented with this scenario the player could enter the opening towards A or veer off to the left or right and go towards location B (again). This scenario was chosen because it demonstrates that although four locations are presented the real choice for the player is in fact

Figure 1. Narrative choice

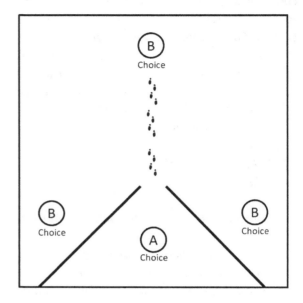

only between A and B. Already with two choices we have a complex situation and one which a game must account for. A game must know what to do in each of these situations and should have content to play or present should the player take that direction.

This is the most basic model of choice we find in every game. Even completely plot-less open ended adventures, sometimes called sandbox games, have both this dilemma and use these setups to engage players. Our implementation or how we deal with the proposed choice model is somewhat different between digital video games and table-top RPGs. Within digital games the computer needs to have a more restricted means of guiding the player to choice points. Digital games achieve this by using the physicality of the rendered worlds. How physicality influences choice is demonstrated in Figure 2.

We still have location A and B but we no longer model the option of the player not entering the choice point. Instead in most games you are physically prevented to go back and re-visit already solved puzzles. One could think of mechanisms like locking a door behind you or collapsing a

Figure 2. Narrative choice model

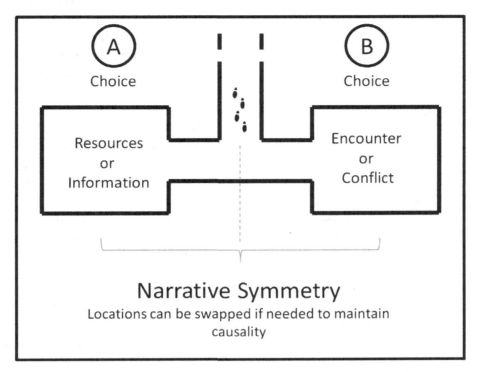

bridge you had just crossed. Instead we now have two clear choices, A and B. One of those choices (in this case A) represents a direction in which information can be found that will explain the larger structure of the game (or the simulated physical environment) and the other choice, here B, poses a hurdle to overcome. We could say that choice A represents new knowledge and B represents new experiences players will have obtained before they progress to the next turning point.

It could be argued that in open ended games the amount of choices at a turning point can be higher than two, which is true. However, the player only evaluates on a pair by pair basis. So for example if there were another choice C, then the evaluation would come down to basic logic, as in: A vs. B, B vs. C and A vs. C. Regardless of the choices available the type of hurdle is still either a form of knowledge/information or an encounter/conflict. To make our choice model complete we should also point out that mapping

choice points to physical game environments doesn't change the player experience. In essence the game or game master could swap the contents of the rooms as seen in Figure 2 and the players would still have a choice of finding resources or going into a conflict situation. How then can a GM provide a means for players to make decisions that they would find interesting or meaningful? One way is to use signposts or messages that inform players of the nature of a choice.

This is Not the Way

Those making digital video games and those who manage table-top role playing games often find themselves in a situation where they have to provide signposts for the players. A signpost is an obvious hint indicating an opportunity for choice. More precisely, it is a way of signaling to players that a decision is required without which the game could not proceed. The problem with using a signpost is that it is an extremely overt means of getting a point across. It would be akin to telling players: "Going left leads to certain doom, whilst going right leads to your ultimate rescue". In extreme cases a signpost tells the players exactly what to do or what steps to take next. If we take the signpost above literally, then no interpretation is required by players and it is this interpretation that is important for the experience. In fact, when confronted with the above signpost players will inevitably conclude many things other than the literal meaning. Player narrative interpretation is one of the mechanisms that can make a game rewarding since a significant outcome rewards the player for making a meaningful choice and further contributes to our sense of Flow (Csikszentmihalyi, 1990). In game studies, the concept of Flow is normally used to describe an ideal state where player actions meet game challenge demands and so create a player's feeling of being "in the zone". The theory of Flow is often used to argue for the pedagogical effects of increased game play on player interactions by letting players increase their ability to successfully meet the cognitive demands of games through their actions (Gee, 2007; Johnson, 2005). How then can games and game masters avoid placing obvious signs along the road, and how can digital video games better promote the feeling of Flow? Much of the rest of this article is about specific high-level mechanisms that can be applied to this problem, however first a few more words on the nature of sign posts. Not only can a sign post indicate the need for an immediate decision, it can also be the indication of a pending or soon-to-arrive narrative juncture. Both table-top and digital forms of storytelling rely heavily on signposts, but it is only the verbal table-top version that uses it when it cannot be avoided. Game masters use signposts as a last resort because it removes a sense of narrative control from the players' experience.

In digital video games there is crucial problem which prevents players' from expressing themselves other than explicitly telling the game what should happen next. What we're up against is the discrete nature of computers and computer software. A game can only react with a well defined and pre-created response, since each response has to be encoded and available within a game at the moment a choice is made. Note that some games allow the usage of template responses which allow parts of a response to be dynamic; however the nature of the response (template) remains the same. In table-top role playing games this issue of choice is somewhat more flexible since the game master can change and alter the game world at will. Regardless of the existence of signposts (because they may be absent as we have seen), sooner or later the players will find themselves in a situation where a choice needs to be made. This choice is a deliberate means by the game master or the video game AI to force the players to select an outcome or narrative path. Although the outcome and management of choices is a complicated and subtle one in the table-top variety and usually the same in the digital, the mechanism of choices are mostly identical.

A major drawback in digital video games, and a non-issue in table-top RPGs, is the fact that players need clear indications of where to go. Even open ended sandbox games provide players with a way to know where on the map and in which direction the next objective lies. Digital video games are bound to this principle because they cannot have players wander aimlessly for hours trying to figure out where to go for the next challenge. Digital video games rightfully emphasize the action portion of their games and/or the puzzle part, where any in between process hinders the player's progress and as such works against the sensation of Flow. Since digital video games do not contain a means of understanding a player's intent they have no choice but to restrict the player's actions by funneling them along pre-defined paths. Giving players many more choices and paths will make players better choice choosers, but it will not give them a more meaningful experience.

ACTION AND REACTION IN THE DIGITAL AGE

Now that we have a good sense of the basic choice structure in games, what place does digital rhetoric have in this framework? Traditionally actions have been regarded as those things players do to move the game forward. More importantly, an action has the association of immediacy, as in: if I (the player) take this action, then there will be an immediate and useful response. Most of these terms, although concrete in reality turn out to be rather vague. For example, what is a 'useful response'?

If we start with the assumption that it is the job of the Narrator or the game AI to present opportunities and overt signposts, then all the narration can do is focus on human computer interaction. In other words, since we cannot alter the nature of choice in games for now, we can work on making the choices more meaningful by adding a layer of human meaning-making. In real life we distill meaning from a situation by finding the salient patterns in the chaos. We clearly see what aspects of a situation have meaning to our own place in context. What we're missing in digital video games is a way for us to know which actions have an immediate consequence in the simulated physical world and which are designed to sort out and elucidate the narrative. We can achieve this by using a number of complementary psychological approaches. First of all we will show how Gestalt Theory allows players to fill in narrative gaps for themselves, and secondly we can use collaborative detail to enforce and re-assure players that their clarification to themselves is a valid one. Seasoned

game masters have been using these techniques for a long time, and we will discuss them in turn to demonstrate the powerful influence they can have.

A Symbolic Approach to Meaning Making

A mostly untapped body of knowledge in the design of role playing based digital video games is Gestalt Theory, a model of human perception going back decades (Humphrey, 1924). Gestalt Theory argues that our minds maintain complete mental models of the physical world, and when presented with seemingly chaotic patterns or broken visual representations of reality, our mind attempts to fill in the blanks to make sense of what has been perceived. Although these overt mechanisms are strongly present in literature (Booth, 1983) and other non interactive media (Chatman, 1980), different mechanisms are needed in interactive environments. One such mechanism of meaning-making is Reification, which is the constructive or generative aspect of perception, by which the experienced percept contains more explicit spatial information than the sensory stimulus on which it is based. For instance, observe the shapes in Figure 3A and you will notice that instead of small fragments of small shapes, larger objects are perceived.

Narrators of table-top role-playing games, with many years of experience, use this artifact of the brain to their advantage when generating interesting puzzles for their players. For instance, see Figure 3B. Players might build a mental model of the narrative in which they are participating based on incomplete information, which is visualized abstractly by the blank center of each square. Intuitively the players, because of Reification, will make assumptions as to the true nature of the events happening to them. For example see Figure 3B, in which the basic principle of Reification is used for three similar boxes. It is our natural in-

Figure 3. Narrative reification model

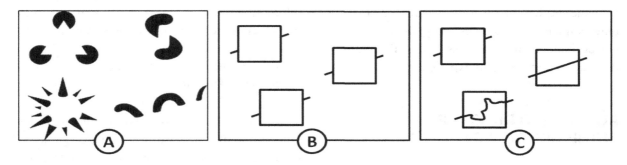

clination to connect the small line fragments and assume this is an indicator of a continuous line running behind what appears to be a white square. After a number of games the players come to the conclusion that the actual lines are how they appear in Figure 3C. Applying Gestalt Reification a Narrator can achieve two goals at once. First of all, the Narrator has a tool that naturally drives players to want to fill in the blanks and therefore continue to search for information. Second, this model can be used by the Narrator to give the players a means to create their own clear explicit description of the true nature of the narrative. It is now completely in the hands of the Narrator to reveal the sequence of events as intended.

We can already begin to see how we can sidestep the choice model problem by using people's natural reaction to benefit the narrative. By using such concepts as Reification we can move the job of meaning-making from the Narrator to the players themselves. No longer is there a need for a discrete choice between an option A or B, but instead we let the players construct what choices exist for them. Digital video games have already started to embrace this concept but haven't had many opportunities to fully take advantage of the mechanisms and instead have mainly played this trump card as the final reveal or conclusion. A powerful version of the Reification narrative control mechanism, but not as widely used due to its complexity, is a phenomenon called backfill. Backfill allows the Narrator to change players' perceptions of already passed events.

Backfill

As consumers of narrative material we have been treated well by having access to a large compendium of works that end in a reveal or surprising conclusion. Perhaps we can think of them better as literary magic tricks where everything you had read or seen should instead be considered in a completely different light. In human directed interactive narrative such as we find in table-top RPGs we find that a succession of smaller reveals or turning points are much more common. Mischler described the effect of turning points best by stating: "Respondents report such events as changing their understandings of their past experiences. They open up directions of movement that were not anticipated by them and could not be predicted by their previous views of their pasts, leading to a different sense of themselves and to changes that were consequential for how they felt and what they did" (Mischler, 2006, p. 39). The narrative experience for the players is that they have constructed their own miniature cliffhangers along the way. All of a sudden they see a complete picture (as in Figure 3) and they have to re-evaluate their own actions as they have played up to that point.

If we think back to the choice model in Figure 2, then what digital games cannot easily do but which Narrators can achieve with ease is to swap the location of the encounter vs. the location of the resources. Not only that, but Narrators can do this at any point in time before players have made a choice either way. From the players' perspective it will seem the way the story plays out is the way it was meant all along. In an abstract way, thinking back to Figure 3B and C, we can say that for a Narrator it is trivial to switch the shape of the lines during play with the players being none the wiser.

To illustrate backfill we can user our example table-top session. When one of the players tells the other players and the GM that his or her character opens the jewel box that has been carried along from the first encounter with the shop keeper, an opportunity exists for the GM to change the outcome of the narrative depending on what is in the box. No matter what object is in the box it can be justified in many ways and can either explain what happened before or drive what will happen next. Similarly when the two players are told they are in a room with two exists it did not matter much which exit was taken; the GM could have easily switched the two locations to suit the narrative.

Collaborative Detail

A more subtle psychological concept, previously not acknowledged as a source for active narrative management, since it is difficult to model and measure, is the notion of collaborative detail. To better illustrate the concept and use of collaborative detail we will first discuss seductive detail. With the advent of powerful graphics capabilities we can now experience perfectly rendered worlds in which every object and character is depicted in glorious seductive detail. However, all this detail can also form a major distracting factor within the overall experience. As we wander through endless landscapes and meet countless simulated people we might wonder: how can we distinguish what is important for the narrative and what isn't? All this lush detail and these perfectly displayed worlds and characters now directly compete with the narrative information that also needs to be communicated to us.

If we change the way we design virtual environments such that each elements plays a narrative role, we can we can then change seductive detail, something that easily leads to cognitive overload (Harp. et al., 1998), into collaborative detail, a concept commonly used in traditional written narrative and more often also in film and television. Collaborative detail is the sense that the movie set and objects in a narrative work are important parts and that they play their own role in telling the story. Using collaborative detail selectively might also lower cognitive load without giving away the answer to critical clues and perhaps further optimize the experience of Flow.

To illustrate how collaborative detail works on a conceptual level please see Figure 4. Here we see what happens when a rectangular magnet is brought in contact with a dusting of metal filings. The filings arrange themselves along the magnetic field and give us a direct glimpse into a physical effect which would otherwise be hidden from us. In many ways this resembles how complex stories play out in many forms of narrative media. Not only do we see what was meant once we have all the information (as in the Reification model), but because of the shape and direction of the 'clues' can we start to get a sense of the overall narrative structure at an earlier stage. Many times, however, what we have at any point in time is a subset of details akin to the inset in Figure 4. A good example of collaborative detail can be found in our example game session, albeit in a simplified form. In the example, there is mention of a jewel box that has a decoration on top in the form of a seal. This visual as presented to the players by the GM re-occurs and cements a story arc that ties together events that happened earlier.

In our example gaming session we see collaborative detail in the scene where the shopkeeper works just a little bit too long in the back of the store to wrap up the purchased jewel box. This is an overt hint to the players that perhaps there is something out of the ordinary regarding

Figure 4. Collaborative detail

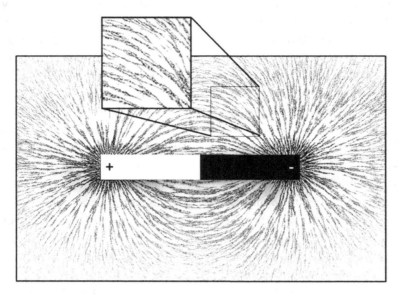

the item they purchased. Indeed later in the scenario it turns out that this detail was a foreshadowing of events to come. There are other such details such as the similarity between seals on the jewel box and the large treasure chest found in the latter part of the scenario. Although subtle, all these details are provided to the players as-is and are not hidden or obscured. There are other mechanisms that operate on a more intuitive level and need further interpretation by players to be understood.

The Psychology of Open Ended Narrative

A final example of a pure psychological decomposition of narrative rhetoric might the phenomenon of Inattentional Blindness (Neisser, 1975; Bredemeier, 2012) (the failure to notice a fully-visible, but unexpected object because attention was engaged on another task, event, or object), which is normally perceived to be an undesired effect, can be used by Narrators and game designers to hide critical clues in plain view. Inattentional Blindness has already been deployed in the literary genre of

detective mysteries, where authors de-emphasize critical clues in the hopes that readers forget these passages until their true meaning is revealed at a critical moment. It is important to mention this rhetorical option since it contains within it the idea that the traditional mapping of oral or written action vs. reaction is no longer applicable in a world where we've become more accustomed to multi-modal stimuli.

If providing narrative hints and clues is complicated in digital video games, it is much more problematic in open ended table-top games. In those forms of narrative a tremendous amount of skill, an even greater need for subtlety and indirect storytelling is needed. If the Narrator said: "and before you, you see a key that will reveal all", then the game is over and the story told. Instead what if we go back to the message on the signpost discussed earlier: "Going left leads to certain doom, whilst going right leads to your ultimate rescue". Any player being confronted with this situation will wonder what the Narrator had in mind and even though the literal meaning is clear the amount of subtext makes an obvious choice nearly impossible. More importantly, even though a choice is posed, it is not clear in which modality the players should respond. A player might roll dice to see what their character might do, or a player might start a negotiation with other players to decide what to do next. We could consider the type of reaction and action to be asymmetrical to the initiating action of the Narrator.

Asymmetrical Digital Rhetoric

There have been some important developments within the video game industry that point to the incorporation of some of the models presented in this article. An important example is the game Portal and even more so its successor Portal 2 (Alessi, 2008). In this game the player plays a character that is forced, by an unseen antagonist, to solve complicated puzzles to survive. The player's assumed reward is the escape from the imaginary testing facility in which she is held. Even though the player character carries what appears to be a weapon, it can only be used to create openings called portals. Portals establish instant pathways between spaces and locations, and they are the main means by which the player can solve the puzzles. Although the choice mechanism is typical for digital video games and follows the models described earlier, the player experiences a strong story element due to the form of asymmetric rhetoric chosen for the game. Interaction between protagonist (you) and the antagonist is conducted through an ongoing action-reaction pattern. Actions in this type of game come in the form of taunts by the antagonist and are either only heard through an omniscient voice or conveyed by an obstacle or hurdle being created before the player's eyes. It is then the reaction of the player that forms a continuous dialog. Portal does not use a traditional rhetoric interaction, where language is used to state an argument and language is used to refute or counter the argument. Instead we see two different modalities (language and action) used both together and against each other

in an effective way. Perhaps it is this difference in modality that allowed the story in Portal to be stronger than in other similar digital games and as such it approaches the same emotional investment end depth of interaction found in table-top role playing games.

Often, the model of Flow as presented in the literature is explained in terms of general player experiences such as challenge, concentration, player skills, immersion, feedback etc. that are offered by challenge within scripted video game environments (Sweetster, et al., 2005; Voskouinsky, et al., 2004). Through such definitions, a general idea is created as to how games can have individual cognitive and pedagogical effects on players through their actions. But there is less of a focus on the interactions of Flow that happen as a result of players that are playing against each other and/or a Narrator. Furthermore, inherent in the existing models and theories is an underlying principle that states that a player's maximum enjoyment of a game is caused mainly by cognitive absorption (Agarwal et al., 2000) with the goal of maximum enjoyment. Perhaps through asymmetric rhetoric, where all forms of interaction modalities are included, can we start to approach cognitive absorption within digital video games.

FUTURE RESEARCH DIRECTIONS

Using some of the principles outlined in this chapter, we can now start to design experiments that will show how players can use mediated storytelling in a way that combines the best of table-top role playing games with the finest from lush digital virtual worlds. A primary question in designing future experiments is: how reliably do players react to the mechanisms described previously? Digital video games are in a tight spot in that respect, since they cannot afford these mechanisms to work only 70% of the time. In order for the game to end or conclude, whatever mechanism is used to guide and steer players, needs to be 100% effective. Studying the effect of the methods described in this article lends itself well to experimentation, since in a way we can think of table-top RPGs as the original form of Wizard of Oz experiment (Kelley, 1984).

CONCLUSION

When working in literary form, an author has limited control over the narrative perception of the reader. In the written and oral form, persuasion works on a linguistic level and thus uses memory and emotion as its main operational mechanisms. In open-ended rhetoric, either in digital form or in group-based table-top RPGs, well-established psychological operational mechanisms can be deployed which utilize the full range of sensory input and human experience. Furthermore, players are not restricted to symmetric rhetoric and can respond with any kind of action they choose to any request or suggestion from the software system or Narrator. There is an inherent tension between the apparent freedoms we have acquired by the multi modal affordances of digital media and the obstacles we now face preventing us from creating fully immersive digital games. This article discussed both the new ways in which we can approach digital rhetoric as a function of action vs. reaction as well as those hurdles still ahead. In conclusion the article demonstrated how a rich set of interaction principles open the door to new forms of persuasive interaction and meaning-making in our digital world.

ACKNOWLEDGMENT

The author would like to thank Josh Williams for awakening the first awareness of the powerful mechanisms in table-top role playing games. Also the author would like to thank Linn Taylor for patiently explaining away all the misconceptions about being a Game Master. Further thanks go out to Gustav Verhulsdonck, Jenna Flohr, Nick Iuppa, director Alexander Singer and screenwriter Terry Borst.

REFERENCES

Agarwal, R., & Karahanna, E. (2000). Time flies when you're having fun: Cognitive absorption and beliefs about information technology usage. *Management Information Systems Quarterly*. doi:10.2307/3250951

Alessi, J. (2008). *Games demystified: Portal*. Gamasutra. Retrieved 2008-08-28.

Aristotle, . (1984). Metaphysics. In J. Barnes (Ed.), *The complete works of Aristotle* (Vol. 2, pp. 1552–1728). Princeton, NJ: Princeton University Pres.

Bogost, I. (2008). *Persuasive games: The expressive power of videogames*. Cambridge, MA: MIT press.

Booth, W. (1983). *The rhetoric of fiction*. Chicago, IL: University of Chicago Press. doi:10.7208/chicago/9780226065595.001.0001

Bredemeier, K., & Simons, D. (2012). Working memory and inattentional blindness. *Psychonomic Bulletin & Review*, *19*, 239–244. doi:10.3758/s13423-011-0204-8 PMID:22222359

Chatman, S. (1980). *Story and discourse: Narrative structure in fiction and film*. Ithaca, N.Y: Cornell University Press.

Csikszentmihalyi, M. (1990). *Flow: The psychology of optimal experience*. New York: Harper & Row.

Fine, G. A. (2002). *Shared fantasy: Role playing games as social worlds*. Chicago, IL: University of Chicago Press.

Gee, J. P. (2007). *What video games have to teach us about learning and literacy*. New York: Palgrave MacMillan.

Harp, S. F., & Mayer, R. E. (1998). How seductive details do their damage: A theory of cognitive interest in science learning. *Journal of Educational Psychology*, *90*(3), 414–434. doi:10.1037/0022-0663.90.3.414

Humphrey, G. (1924). The psychology of the gestalt. *Journal of Educational Psychology*, *15*(7), 401–412. doi:10.1037/h0070207

Johnson, S. (2005). *Everything bad is good*. New York: Riverhead Trade.

Kelley, J. F. (1984). An iterative design methodology for user-friendly natural language office information applications. *ACM Transactions on Office Information Systems*, *2*(1), 26–41. doi:10.1145/357417.357420

Losh, E. (2012) *Defining digital rhetoric with 20-20 hindsight*. Retrieved July 14, 2013, from http://www.digitalrhetoriccollaborative. org/2012/06/25/defining-digital-rhetoric-with-20-20-hindsight/

Mischler, E. G. (2006). In A. De Fina, D. Schiffrin, & M. Bamberg (Eds.), *Discourse and Identity* (pp. 30–47). New York: Cambridge University Press. doi:10.1017/CBO9780511584459.003

Murray, J. (1998). *Hamlet on the holodeck: The future of narrative in cyberspace*. Cambridge, MA: MIT Press.

Neisser, U., & Becklen, R. (1975). Selective looking: Attending to visually specified events. *Cognitive Psychology*, *7*, 480–494. doi:10.1016/0010-0285(75)90019-5

Riedl, M. O., & Bulitko, V. (2013). Interactive narrative: an intelligent systems approach. *AI Magazine*, *34*(1).

Sweetser, P., & Wyeth, P. (2005). *Gameflow: A model for evaluating player enjoyment in games*. ACM Computers in Entertainment.

Treanor, M., Blackford, B., Mateas, M., & Bogost, I. (2012). The micro-rhetorics of Game-O-Matic. In *Proceedings of Procedural Content Generation Workshop*. Raleigh, NC, USA.

Tychsen, A., Newman, K., Brolund, T., & Hitchens, M. (2007). Cross-format analysis of the gaming experience in multi-player role-playing games. In *Proceedings of the DIGRA 2007 Conference*.

Van Velsen, M., Williams, J., & Verhulsdonck, G. (2009). Table-top gaming narratology for digital interactive storytelling. In *Proceedings of the 2009 ICIDS Conference*.

Voskouinsky, A. E., Mitina, O. V., & Avetisova, A. A. (2004). Playing online games: Flow experience. *PsychNology*, *2*(3), 259–281.

Zappen, J. (2005). Digital rhetoric: Toward an integrated theory. *Technical Communication Quarterly*, *14*(3), 319–325. doi:10.1207/s15427625tcq1403_10

ADDITIONAL READING

Aarseth, E. (1997). *Cybertext: Perspectives on Ergodic Literature*. Baltimore, MD: The John Hopkins University Press.

Auerbach, E. (2003). *Mimesis: the representation of reality in Western literature*. Princeton, N.J: Princeton University Press.

Bal, M. (1997). *Narratology: introduction to the theory of narrative*. Toronto, Buffalo: University of Toronto Press.

Bartle, R. (2006). Hearts, clubs, diamonds, spades: players who suit muds. In K. Salen, & E. Zimmerman (Eds.), *The Game Design Reader: A Rules of Play Anthology* (pp. 754–787).

Berne, E. (1964). *Games People Play*. New York: Grove Press.

Bogost, I. (2008). *Persuasive games: The expressive power of videogames*. Cambridge, MA: MIT press.

Core, M. G., Lane, C. H., van Lent, M., Gomboc, D., Solomon, S., & Rosenberg, M. (2006). *Building Explainable Artificial Intelligence Systems*, Proceedings of the Eighteenth Conference on Innovative Applications of Artificial Intelligence (IAAI-06)

Crawford, C. (2005). *Chris Crawford on interactive storytelling*. Berkeley, Calif: New Riders Games.

Forster, F. (1985). *Aspects of the Novel*. San Diego: Harcourt Brace Jovanovich.

Gee, J. (2005). *An Introduction to Discourse Analysis*. New York: Routledge.

Genette, G. (1983). *Narrative discourse: an essay in method*. Ithaca, N.Y: Cornell University Press.

Guthrie, W. (2000). *GameMastering Secrets*. US: Wade Guthrie Press.

Jhala, A., & Velsen, M. (2009). *Challenges in Development and Design of Interactive Narrative Authoring Systems*, a Panel. In proceedings of the 2009 AAAI Spring Symposium.

Juul, J. (2001). *Games telling stories*. Game studies 1 (1) retrieved, April 11, 2008 from: http://gamestudies.org/ 0101/juul-gts/.

Laurel, B. (1993). *Computers as theatre*. New York: Addison-Wesley.

Laws, R. (2002). *Robin's laws of good game mastering*. S.l: Steve Jackson Games.

LeBlanc, M. (2006). Tools for Creating Dramatic Game Dynamics. In Katie Salen & Eric Zimmerman (Eds.), The Game Design Reader: A Rules of Play Anthology, 438-459. Cambridge, MA: MIT Press

Lee, S., Mott, B., & Lester, J. (2011). *Director Agent Intervention Strategies for Interactive Narrative Environments*. In Proceedings of the Fourth International Conference on Interactive Digital Storytelling, Vancouver, Canada, pp. 140-151.

Leitch, T. (1986). *What stories are: narrative theory and interpretation*. University Park, Pa: Pennsylvania State University Press.

Lester, J., McQuiggan, S., & Sabourin, J. (2011). Affect Recognition and Expression in Narrative-Centered Learning Environments. In R. A. Calvo, & S. K. D'Mello (Eds.), *New Perspectives on Affect and Learning Technologies* (pp. 85–96). Springer. doi:10.1007/978-1-4419-9625-1_7

Magerko, B., & Laird, J. E. (2003). *Building an Interactive Drama Architecture*, 1st International Conference on Technologies for Interactive Digital Storytelling and Entertainment, Darmstadt, Germany, March 24 – 26.

Mateas, M., & Stern, A. (2006). Interaction and Narrative. In K. Salen, & E. Zimmerman (Eds.), *The Game Design Reader: A Rules of Play Anthology* (pp. 642–669).

Murray, J. (1998). *Hamlet on the Holodeck*. Cambridge: MIT Press.

Page, R. (2011). *New narratives: stories and storytelling in the digital age*. Lincoln: University of Nebraska Press.

Perlin, K., & Goldberg, A. (1996). *Improv: a system for scripting interactive actors in virtual worlds*. In Proceedings of the 23rd annual conference on Computer graphics and interactive techniques.

Riedl, M., & Young, R. M. (2006). Story Planning as Exploratory Creativity: Techniques for Expanding the Narrative Search Space. In New Generation Computing, Vol. 24, Nr. 3.

Riedl, M. O., Saretto, C. J., & Young, R. M. (2003). *Managing Interaction Between Users and Agents in a Multi-Agent Storytelling Environment.* Proceedings of the 2nd International Joint Conference on Autonomous Agents and Multi Agent Systems, Melbourne, Australia.

Salen, K. (2003). *Rules of play: game design fundamentals.* Cambridge, Mass: MIT Press.

Stern, J. (2000). *Making shapely fiction.* New York: Norton.

Turchi, P. (2004). *Maps of the imagination: the writer as cartographer.* San Antonio, Tex: Trinity University Press.

Tychsen, A., McIlwain, D., Brolund, T., & Hitchens, M. (2007). *Player-Character Dynamics in Multi-Player Role Playing Games.* In DIGRA Conference Proceedings.

Wood, J. (2008). *How fiction works.* New York: Picador.

Young, R. M., & Rivera-Cardona, R. (2011). *Approaching a Player Model of Game Story Comprehension Through Affordance in Interactive Narrative.* In the Working Notes of the Fourth Workshop on Intelligent Narrative Technologies, at the Seventh International Conference on Artificial Intelligence and Interactive Digital Entertainment, Stanford, CA.

KEY TERMS AND DEFINITIONS

Avatar: An avatar is the visual or graphical representation of a user in a computer game or simulation.

Digital Video Game: A video game is an electronic game that involves human interaction with a user interface to generate visual feedback on a video device. In this article the terms video game, digital video game, console game and computer game are interchangeable.

Player Character: A player character is a user's avatar plus all the traits and attributes that make that character unique. It often is the role a player wants to exhibit in a game.

MMORPG: Massively multiplayer online role-playing game (MMORPG) is a genre of role-playing video games in which a very large number of players interact with one another within a virtual game world.

NPC: Non Player Character or any incidental characters other than the player participating in the game or narrative.

RPG: Role Playing Game, a form of a game where players assumed imaginary roles and characters.

Virtual World: A virtual world is an online community that takes the form of a computer-based simulated environment through which users can interact with one another and use and create objects.

Section 2
Practices of Digital Communication across Cultures in Digital and Global Contexts

Chapter 7
Digital and Global Literacies in Networked Communities:
Epistemic Shifts and Communication Practices in the Cloud Era

Marohang Limbu
Michigan State University, USA

ABSTRACT

This chapter explores how the concept of literacy, digital literacy, and global literacy is shifting; how technologies (YouTube, Facebook, Skype, blogs, vlogs, and Google Hangouts) and digital literacies facilitate cross-cultural and intercultural communication and global cultural understandings; how technologies engage global citizens to share, collaborate, cooperate, and create their narratives; and how people become able to address local and global socio-cultural and political issues through various global digital engagements. Finally, this chapter investigates how knowledge is produced, disseminated, and consumed across global cultures in digital contexts.

INTRODUCTION

Technology, without doubt, has brought tremendous changes over the past 20+ years by affecting science, commerce, engineering, and education alike. These changes have revolutionized the twenty-first century cultures and dramatically cultivated the relationship between human, technology, and culture in multiple ways. The advent of digital technologies especially is responsible for this revolution that brought substantial shifts not only at the material levels, but also at the global literacy levels in this digital world. This could be one of the reasons why colleges/universities of the twenty-first century are adopting digital technologies as a practical way of preparing students

DOI: 10.4018/978-1-4666-4916-3.ch007

Copyright © 2014, IGI Global. Copying or distributing in print or electronic forms without written permission of IGI Global is prohibited.

for the local and global cultures. And educators at all levels are integrating computers into their literacy instructions and into their classrooms and professional lives across cultures. And the introduction of digital literacies and technologies complicated the way we traditionally conceived writing and communication across the social and academic institutions.

Since the humanities aligned itself with technology, rhetoric and technology became no longer separate entities, and when technology was formally introduced into the curricula, classrooms, and workplaces, it benefitted students to become tech-savvy human-power for the twenty-first century digital village. Regarding digital literacies, Selfe (1999) contends that an education enriched by technology provided people an equal opportunity to obtain high-paying technology-rich jobs and economic prosperity (p. 135). This situation offers the students of our discipline—rhetoric and composition, English Studies, and professional communication—a profound opportunity to have the equal access for upward social mobility (p.137).

In today's society, people are becoming multi-literate in multiple ways such as culturally, linguistically, scientifically, technologically, and geopolitically literate. Such digital technologies (Web 2.0, cloud, and social media) explicitly or implicitly connect people with other people from diverse cultures, languages, and geographical locations. As Gillen and Barton (2010) state digitally literate people capture an arena of rapidly growing global practices as humans and computers interact in newer ways with innovative purposes (pp. 3-4). The digitally literate people share, collaborate, co-create, and disseminate contents via digital technologies such as Facebook, Twitter, microblogging, LinkedIn, and other cloud/Web 2.0 tools. Furthermore, whatever contents digitally literate people produce will become newer to many other global audiences. From this perspective, digitally literate people always create newer contents in one way or the other, for narratives and stories they create and share in the cloud spaces are culturally and geopolitically dissimilar. Based on the discussion, this chapter investigates how the concept of digital and global literacies is shifting; how technologies and digital literacies facilitate cross-cultural and intercultural communication and global cultural understandings; how technologies engage global citizens to share, collaborate, cooperate, and create their narratives; and how people become able to address glocal (local and global) socio-cultural and political issues through the global digital engagement. At the end, this chapter explores epistemic shifts such as how knowledge is produced, disseminated, and consumed across global cultures in digital and physical contexts.

BACKGROUND INFORMATION

The concept of literacy, in the past was limited; people who could read and write their names were considered literate, and many people still have the same opinion about literacy. So, the way people understand and interpret literacy to some extent is cultural, political, and situated. In this section, I examine the term literacy and technology, for which I will discuss my recent visit to Limbuwan, Nepal such as how different people understand and interpret literacy, and how they engage in digital communication with their local and global colleagues. Last summer (2013), I went to Sungnam and Solma (remote hilly villages of Limbuwan region), Limbuwan that are located in the eastern part of Nepal. During the trip, I got an opportunity to meet and talk to school and college teachers who had advanced college degrees. Likewise, I also met with political leaders, farmers, and students most of them had college degrees. We talked over many topics, among them was "literacy." We discussed what literacy is and what it meant to them. These people had their own understanding and philosophy of literacy and interpreted it in multiple ways. Many of them narrowed down the spheres of literacies. For instance, they considered that people who can read and write their names are literate; others argued that those who can read and can communicate via letters, emails, and social media are literate. One of the local political leaders contended that he was literate because he had a college degree. On the other hand, he mentioned that he did not know how to use technologies (computer and Internet) to communicate with his colleagues. The leader interpreted the meaning of literacy from traditional perspective (one who can read and write is literate). Similarly, I asked many undergraduate and graduate students what "literacy" is and what it means to them. Despite the fact that many of them had a similar concept of literacy like that of the political leader, some other argued that the meaning of "literacy" varies. This demonstrates that the understanding of literacy is not universal.

As I mentioned earlier, I got an opportunity to visit high schools (Ratna Higher Secondary School, Solma and Tinjure Higher Secondary School, Sungnam), Sungnam Village Development Committee Office, and Menchhyayem Radio, Myanglung, Tehrathum. During this visit, I got a great contrast between Limbuwan, Nepal before 2004 and Limbuwan, Nepal of now (2013). For instance, Ratna High School's (RHS) principal, teachers, and students hosted a program to welcome their old student, i.e., me. The school invited school management committee members and parents to attend the program, which started with some announcements and speeches. Some teachers took pictures and videos via their smartphones and posted on Facebook. No sooner had they posted the images, videos, and other information on the Facebook, than immediately Facebook users started commenting about the program from around the world. Before I left for the US for the pursuit of my higher education in 2004, many people in the Limbuwan region did not know about cellphones and smartphones. Without a doubt, they did not know anything about the Internet and social media such as Facebook.

Immediately after the meeting, we, especially alumnae/alumni started communicating over the RHS Facebook page "Ratna Ma. Vi. ka Ratnaharu" (Diamonds of Ratna High School). Through the Facebook page, we proposed to buy some computers as the school was in desperate need of computers and Internet. As soon as we posted the proposal, the alumnae and alumni, including teachers and parents, started donating for the computer project. The reason, I am bringing up this account is that RHS is located in a remote Limbuwan region, and the contributors do not live only in the Limbuwan region and Nepal, but most of them live across the globe such as the USA, the UK, Australia, Hong Kong, Qatar, Korea, Malaysia, Saudi Arabia, and many more. In about two months, the school got sufficient budget, and by the mid of August 2013, the school was able to buy more than a dozen of computers for RHS students and teachers. Despite the fact that people do not live in the same geographical locations, but because of digital technologies and digital literacy, people, in the twenty-first century, live in a tiny global village.

This setting suggests how digital technologies and digital literacies are facilitating our life styles, how an information-based society is transforming human living patterns and cultures, how networked knowledge communities manage knowledge by collaborating, sharing, creating, and finding information, and how networked communication is converging into social capital in the twenty-first century digital village. The background information suggests that digital technology has become a part of networked knowledge communities (NKCs) that enable large numbers of global community members to access knowledge without the necessity for meeting the physical spaces. It also suggests that networked community members have significant access to global networked communication spaces and their online interaction is shifting the way traditional cultures and academia created knowledge. In short, the confluence of global literacies and digital literacies was not necessarily possible since they were not available like that of today. Now, digital communication not only has become newer ways of seeing cultures and people, but also newer ways of connecting and thinking about the world.

DIGITAL LITERACIES, GLOBAL LITERACIES, AND NETWOWRKED COMMUNITIES

The concept of literacy gradually became more fluid, discursive, and complex in the late twentieth and twenty-first centuries. Langer (1991) considered "literacy as the act of reading and writing and ... ways of thinking" and to have "the ability to think and reason like a literate person, within a particular society" (pp. 11, 13), and Langer further substantiates that "[literacy] is the culturally appropriate way of thinking.... Literacy thinking manifests itself in different ways in oral and written languages in different societies" (p. 13). Hiebert (1991) further extends the concept, definition, and understanding of literacy that "represents a profound shift from a text-driven definition of literacy to a view of literacy as active transformation of texts" (p.1). Likewise, Steelman, Pierce, and Koppenhaver (1994) define the meaning of literacy as "to be literate is to be able to gather and to construct meaning using written language" (p. 201).

Similarly, Foley (1994) defined the term literacy to "refer to the mastery of language, in both its spoken (or augmented) and written forms, which enables an individual to use language fluently for a variety of purposes" (p. 184). For Foley "spoken language abilities are closely related to the development of literacy skills in the normal population" (p. 185). Furthermore, Cope and Kalantzis (1998) stated, "[l]iteracy pedagogy ... has been a carefully restricted project—restricted to formalized, monolingual, monocultural, and rule-

governed forms of language" (p. 9). They further extend the idea and scope of "literacy pedagogy to account for the context of our culturally and linguistically diverse and increasingly globalised societies" to interrelate the plurality of texts, and they are that "literacy pedagogy now must account for the burgeoning variety of text forms associated with information and multimedia technologies" (p. 9). Their interpretation of literacy encompasses visual images, their relationship to the written word, "visual design in desktop publishing," and the interface of visual and linguistic meaning in multimedia (p. 9).

In the current networked society, the understanding of literacy is increasingly shifting; the theories and practices of literacy are far beyond the way literacy was understood and interpreted in the past. As I mentioned earlier, the perception of literacy became more fluid, discursive, and complicated, for the term "literacy" now not only refers to understanding of traditional reading and writing, but it also includes the use of digital tools, multimodal tools, and an understanding of global cultures, science, and technologies; it includes the ability to use computers and other mobile technologies (knowledge of digital software and hardware). The concept of literacy has also become "socially and culturally situated values, practices, and skills involved in operating linguistically within the context of electronic environments, including reading, writing, and communicating" (Selfe, 1999, p. 11). In totality, to be literate in the twenty-first century is not limited to the ability of reading and writing, use of technologies (software and hardware), but also understanding of complex local and global communication strategies and socio-political rhetorical practices.

Digital literacy is an understanding of the technological forces that affect culture and human behavior, and it is also a practice of people from various cultural and linguistic backgrounds via digital technologies such as social media, like Facebook and Twitter. The impetuses of digital literacies are pervasiveness of new media technologies, globalization, development of information technology, information economy, and cloud computing technologies, for these factors are like magnets that suck people up in the digital networked spaces whether networked community members are from developing countries or developed countries. In terms of digital literacy, Kress (2010) also states:

Digital literacies are always dynamic in part because technology is perceptively developing so fast in front of our eyes [and] human purpose continue[s] to develop and are reshaped in collaboration. This is the meaning backcloth for the current explosion of creativity in digital literacies that makes this such a fascinating arena in which to work, including in roles in computer science, engineering, education or the digital arts. (p. 8)

This notion suggests that today's digital literacy is different from traditional literacy, for it focuses on human-computer interaction, or human-computer/technology-human interaction (also see Nardi, 1996; Bedny & Karwowski, 2003).

Today's human-technology-human rapport insinuates that digital technologies and humans have a symbiotic relationship, and together they produce contents, meanings, and disseminate them across the global cultures. Digital technologies create an environment where people from diverse cultures collaborate and create knowledge in digital as well as physical contexts. This setting supports digitally networked members to seek ways of sharing, collaborating, and creating cross-cultural contents in newer ways. This situation not only benefits people to understand diverse social, cultural, and political conditions, but also provides them opportunities to create newer epistemologies to meet their needs and expectations. From this perspective, there is not only an urgency to understand the potential of human-technology-human interaction, especially in our field (rhetoric), but there ought to be an utmost need for an ongoing research to create much more global, inclusive, and representational spaces (programs, businesses, and universities) for all global citizens. The research and representational space will play a great role to reduce cultural gaps and promote and expand the meanings of global education, business, and true global comradeship.

Digital literacy comprises both one's ability to use digital software and hardware tools and ability to read, write, collaborate, create, and interact in digital context. Digital literacy is knowledge of using digital skills to research, communicate, create, save, and share in digital environment. It also involves the competencies to create and view texts from critical and philosophical perspective on how diverse digital skills are applied to create meanings, disseminate them, and preserve them. Digital literacy strengthens people's ability to locate, organize, understand, evaluate, and analyze information using digital technologies. In other words, digital literacy facilitates knowledge of current high technology and understanding of diverse technological skills in global and local digital contexts. Cooper (2007) states:

... digital literacies are social practices through which we define meanings and values and discover the effects of our meanings and actions on others. Recognizing the social and theoretical effects of digital literacies is an important goal ... that will enable [people] not only to survive in this world but to create better worlds for themselves and others. (p. 186)

Cooper's notion indicates that digitally literate people are the ones who can communicate and work more efficiently and effectively with their fellow beings (across cultures) by using digital tools and cloud computing technologies (Facebook, Twitter, blogs, vlogs, Wikis, podcasting, Skype, Google drive, dropbox, and iCloud). Digitally literate people can communicate with other global fellow beings in digital contexts by not only creating congenial environment in global and local context, but also by questioning, contesting, and negotiating their spaces. In this process, they together challenge the conservative cultural conditions, political atrocities, and social inequalities (will discuss later). Digitally literate people can also assist other global fellow beings to make their identities visible as well as to solve their social, political problems.

SITES OF DIGITAL GLOBAL LITERACIES IN THE TWENTY-FIRST CENTURY NETWORKED COMMUNITIES

The importance of digital global literacy lies in its contribution to clarifying the emerging discipline of digital global rhetoric. Not only does it aim to clear up a lot of confusing, overlapping discussions, its aim is to provide a solid working definition, a historical grounding, theoretical and practical approaches, and see emerging practices from a beyond-medialogical perspective as forming never global literacies. Moreover, it does so by connecting local digital practices to the global contexts and vice versa by inviting international/transnational contributions by clarifying literacies and by developing them as a result of cross-cultural digital communication practices. Furthermore, the importance of digital global literacy lies in its ability to clarify, synthesize, and prepare useful strategies, modes and ideas in the field such as rhetoric, technical communication, and information science. Global literacies also encompass how meaning and knowledge are produced, disseminated, and consumed across cultures by utilizing digital technologies.

Being a global literate is a way of knowing other cultures, people, and geopolitical conditions by engaging in the digital global networked communities. Among many, such digital global engagement includes communicating with people from diverse geopolitical locations and cultures via social media, blogs, vlogs, and YouTube. As people engage in such social and virtual communication, they start entering into new local and global networked communication atmospheres. Since digital global literacy is more glocal, it invariably facilitates intercultural, cross-cultural, and transnational communications in a larger scale (will discuss in detail later). Global literacy facilitates an awareness of global cultures and awareness of global citizenship where people understand that they are not isolated individual beings, but are global citizens and have both local and global identities and a collective power in this digitally networked village. This setting creates an understanding that global literacy is an extension of information society as it opens up newer global networked rhetorical strategies. In other words, global literacies facilitate people's thinking that they are global citizens and have both local and global voices and identities.

Since global literacy encourages a digital and physical social engagement, global citizens learn from one another. This is one of the reasons why community activists support the promotion and expansion of digital global literacies; they support the proliferation of global (political) civic engagement, and they support the global civic presence in the networked knowledge communities. Globally literate people also find the digital spaces and Web 2.0, social media, and cloud computing tools as learning spaces from both local and global contexts. From this perspective, due to their constant digital engagement, people learn about other cultural conditions, economic situations, and political issues. Additionally, since global literacy is a networked and knowledge-centered, people tend to exchange their global institutional, cultural, and political literacies over cloud tools. Overall, because of the global digital interactions, our way of living and working environment are becoming more global, heterogeneous, and cross-cultural ones in the context of twenty-first century digital village.

As stated earlier, digital global literacies refer to the knowledge of digital skills, digital communication, and critical and philosophical reflection on how diverse digital skills are applied in digital contexts. And global literacy is the knowledge of global digital communication and digital competency via which we understand, evaluate, and analyze global information such as cultural, economic, political, and educational information. Additionally, digital global literacy is functional and transformational that not only refers to literacy in global context, but also denotes to newer ways of seeing the world and speculating about the global cultures. So, there is an utmost need of digital studies to create a sense of belief that we are all global citizens (bottom up approach). Hawisher and Selfe (2000) also state, "[l]iteracy practices are affected by the social and material conditions of particular cultures—we add that this is especially true of literacy practices in media contexts" (p. 4). From this perspective, as I stated in the beginning of this chapter, digital literacy is a social construct that is ideologically determined by individual cultures, and this ideological context is deeply sedimented in a society's understanding and determines, to a great extent, what it means to be literate or illiterate in a particular culture (also see Hawisher & Selfe, 2000, p. 4). Digitally and globally literate people tend to communicate, question, contest, and negotiate their spaces without significant barriers posed by cultural and geopolitical locations, but at the same time, they also understand that people have different individual identities, cultural identities, and linguistic identities.

Digitally literate people are usually globally literate, meaning, digitally literate people always communicate with their local and global audience, and globally literate people trust that they live in a tiny global village. They also believe in global communities and digital global systems such as online business, online education, and online political campaign to mention a few. Global literate people also trust in virtual as well as physical bonds and are prepared to do global virtual transaction; they are willing to undertake global online business such as eBay, Amazon, DealTime, NexTag,

BizRate, Shopzilla, and many other online global businesses. Digitally and globally literate people believe in plastic money (debit/credit cards) and digital money, i.e., digital money and digital virtual transactions on their computer screens, tablet screens, and smartphone screens. Digitally literate people can inform, engage, instruct, and persuade global citizens effectively via digital technologies, and when people are digitally literate, they can collaborate, communicate, and execute business beyond their local cultural, linguistic, and geo-political boundaries. From this perspective, network knowledge society is both local and global, for we do not distinguish any clear benchmark between local and global cultures. Additionally, digitally and globally literate people can prevent Internet hoaxes, email frauds, and phishing, for they constantly interact with other global colleagues and share skills and ideas with their global colleagues. More importantly, due to the dynamism of digital technologies, we cannot predict how social institutions, cultures, business, and academia would look like after a decade.

CLOUD COMPUTING, SOCIAL MEDIA, AND HUMAN-TECHNOLOGY INTERACTION IN THE DIGITAL CONTEXTS

Traditional communication (Web 1.0) used to be point-to-point in which one person would communicate with only another person. This communication pattern limited information sharing processes, collaborative works, and cooperative procedures. The modes and mediums of traditional communication (websites and web-videos, etc.) did not allow audience to participate, especially to comment, critique, and question on the web spaces. It created dichotomy between writers and readers—writers as active producers vs. readers as only passive consumers (Limbu, 2012). As digital technologies have become user-friendlier and especially more interactive, people from diverse cultures and geopolitical locations have started participating in the collaboration and creation of newer contents. This suggests that communication approaches in digital context have developed alongside the various applications of technologies (Cairo, Knobel, Lankshear, & Leu, 2008). As technologies, such as cloud computing tools, are profoundly used in academia, business, and science, as they became a principal means of communication, they significantly changed our personal and professional life styles across the globe. In other words, digital technologies changed the way people communicate, collaborate, and create contents, and they also changed the way people disseminate and consume information in the twenty-first century networked communities. So, it is obvious that "the emergence of new technologies such as Web 2.0 technologies, offers individuals opportunities for new ways of interacting, playing, working, and earning" (Panteli, 2009, p.1). Additionally, the advent of cloud computing confers many user-friendly affordances that serve as technical and psychological tools for sharing and learning within an identified web-based environment (Werstch, 1998).

Cloud computing tools are also popular social networking spaces where people, from around the world, create their contents and readers can comment, critique, and edit them. For instance, "flickr" is a web space for uploading, storing, and sharing digital documents such as pictures, images, and videos. "YouTube" is a web space where people upload, share, and watch videos, and both YouTube creators and their audience comment, question, and answer on the materials they create. This is one of the emerging cloud computing technologies through which people not only share their cultural, academic, and technical thoughts and practices, but they widely question and contest cultural, economic, and political beliefs. This emerging technology significantly empowered people with their local and global voices and identities in digital as well as physical contexts (Limbu, 2013). Similarly, "MySpace" is a social space where people introduce themselves and give information about the type of the music they like and play. MySpace users share, network, interact, and review on the information they upload and store audio and video files.

Cloud computing connects people globally with those who have similar as well as dissimilar social, cultural, and political beliefs. Cloud computing tools allow global citizens to connect with their global colleagues locally and globally via instant messaging and video conferencing such as Google Hangouts and Skype to name a few in which they immerse themselves in virtual networking worlds (also see Hardy, 2002; Kreps & Pearson, 2009). Cloud computing is a public communicative sphere where all communicators (participators-senders and receivers) occupy horizontal and egalitarian digital spaces. That means, cloud computing allows participants to design digital materials, publish their digital contents, and share them with their local and global audience in a digital context. So, cloud computing has aptitude to dialogically and critically engage both writers and readers in digital spaces (also see Kellner & Share, 2007; Lankshear & Knobel, 2008; Lopez, 2008; Luke, 2000). This situation more often than not promotes and expands transcultural and multi-lingual cultural identities that include the promotion of diverse cultural artifacts as well as individual identities. In this digital dialogical process, it also intermingles these elements by disrupting traditional monolithic, hegemonic nature of knowledge and by denouncing the status quo of cultural re/production (Bourdieu & Passeron, 2000; also see Edingo, 2013).

Facebook, as an interactive and collaborative site, mediates the immediate producers' and consumers' worlds and structural social worlds of an individual being, and it establishes a user-friendly environment where the roles of the authors and readers or consumers and producers merge together (Johnson-Eilola & Selber, 1996, 2004; Lundin, 2008; McLoughlin & Lee, 2008). Facebook also invariably tends to create digital democratic, inclusive, and representational spaces where people tend to create their own-networked conduits as authors to their local and global audience (Connor, 1996, 2004, 2008; Sleeter & Tettegah, 2002). Furthermore, the twenty-first century world has become an astoundingly app-centric digital age. For instance, among many, people use Facebook apps such as ads, newsfeed, pages feed, groups, and events to multiply the content sharing and information dissemination processes. Via such Facebook apps, global networked communities can spread their news, information, and discussion across the globe within a few seconds. These digital potentials and possibilities are both transforming the thought processes of global citizens and are transforming the communities, social activities, and political practices across the cultures.

Due to cloud computing, promotion of business, (online) education, politics, religion, and culture has become easier than ever. The human-digital technology interaction promoted web collaboration, document sharing system, content creation and publication, and day-to-day interaction across the cultures. This potential more importantly facilitated digital dialogical engagement such as human-technology-human engagement across the globe in which networked community members get an opportunity not only to interact on issues and seek solutions, but they also get opportunity to observe how people struggle for their survival in different geopolitical contexts. The human-technology-human interaction assists to see how contents are created, how knowledge is shaped, and what strategies people use to disseminate and maintain them in different cultural and geopolitical contexts. Furthermore, due to constant and diverse local and global digital engagement, our private and public spaces and traditional boundaries of cultures and languages are blurred because of the human-technology-human interaction, or because of the human-technology-human interaction, there is not any distinct benchmark that dichotomizes local and global cultures. Additionally, cloud-computing tools are powerful interactive tools,

for they are communicative, collaborative, and user-centered. Above all, cloud computing (Web 2.0) tools have multiple potentials and possibilities to merge the role of writer and reader in virtual and physical spaces, and they have potential to demonstrate what global communication in digital environment is, how they augment our communication skills, and how both the human and technologies exist in symbolic relationship (Graupner, Nickoson-Massey, & Blair, 2009; Johnson-Eilola & Selber, 1996; Lundin 2008; McLoughlin & Lee, 2008; Porter, 2007;).

CLOUD COMPUTING AND GLOBAL LITERACIES FROM THE TWENTY-FIRST CENTURY GLOBAL CONTEXT

Society shapes technologies according to needs and interest of people, and technologies also affect culture and humans; therefore, technology, culture, and humans have interdependent relationships. The computer and human interactions are shifting cultures, academia, and politics in the way people never practiced and have never imagined in the past. From this standpoint what we understand is that the digital networked community is largely and rapidly shaped by members of global communities via the exchanged digital interactions. The exchanged interactions will increase people's ability to produce relevant contents whether that is a simple project paper, or any other scientific inventions, or any social and political thoughts. For instance, Ray Kurzweil (2001) states:

An analysis of the history of technology shows that technological change is exponential, contrary to the common-sense "intuitive linear" view. So we won't experience 100 years of progress in the 21st century—it will be more like 20,000 years of progress (at today's rate). The 'returns,' such as chip speed and cost-effectiveness, also increase exponentially. There's even exponential growth in the rate of exponential growth. Within a few decades, machine intelligence will surpass human intelligence, leading to The Singularity—technological change so rapid and profound it represents a rupture in the fabric of human history.

Technological change is a driving force that affects global communities and transforms individual lives in ways that we might have never thought. As Cairo, Knobel, Lankshear, and Leu (2008) point out how digital technologies have spread, matured, and developed, more people are participating in the creation and collaboration in digital context, and this interactive action changes the global communities as people have never expected 30 years ago.

Cloud computing hence enables people to foster communication skills in using digital tools, not as decontextualized competencies, but as the ways that are connected to other aspects of their learning. So, digital literacies can fruitfully bridge gaps between people's home, workplace, networked community, and school learning lives. Since digital technologies have aptitudes to engage, inform, instruct, and persuade from multiple purposes, cloud computing changes the way people learn, read, perceive, process, create, and disseminate information (i.e., different people attempt to use technologies for their own will to purposes, which results in creation of heterogeneities in the digital age). That is one of the reasons why we should understand that (digital) globalization does not create a homogenous global culture, but heterogeneous ones.

SOCIAL NETWORKING SITES, GLOBAL LITERACIES, AND IDENTITIES

Cloud computing creates digital identity, a psychological identity that prevails in the domains of cloud space. Digital identity is also a set of data that establishes user's cultural, political, and individual identities in the global contexts. For example, social networking tools are digital spaces, which have explicit and implicit impacts on humans and cultures. Hence, as I stated above, with the advent of social networking spaces, people who are digitally connected now have major voices, diverse identities, and agencies, and social networking spaces have become symbol of global and local voices. This notion demonstrates that cloud computing will provide localized and globalized perceptions from contributors who come from all over the world both by informing and altering reader's understanding of digital global rhetoric's as multifaceted practices. Therefore, via such technologies, we can transform societies, institutions, and ourselves, and we can resolve social and political problems and share narratives in digital contexts. In the following section, I will discuss how people use cloud tools such as YouTube, website, blogs, Google Hangouts, and Twitter to create their cultural, political, and individual identities in the global context.

It is obvious that social networking sites tend to enable a subjective, personal, and situated journalism as these sites exemplify a global conversation that is connected through online-networked members, i.e., readers and writers. The online community members foster cross-cultural communication among the networked community members by helping themselves to establish cultural, political, and individual identities. Moreover, social networking sites connect global citizens and also create knowledge that they have different identities; they live in diverse cultural and geographical locations, and they also have different views, but they are global citizens. What I mean by this is in today's society, people from one culture and geopolitical location can constantly network with other global colleagues to interact on political, cultural, and academic issues, and they bring different thoughts and ideas to resolve issues. This particular setting makes people realize that social networking sites and web spaces are mediums through which networked members share their views and reform their cultures and politics as they want.

Furthermore, in social networking spaces, social, cultural, and geopolitical dichotomies are blurred. For instance, audience, readers, and contributors retain a democratic and inclusive playing field, i.e. they have equal access to digital spaces that empower their digital identities and voices. Likewise, concerning the power of social media, activists in China, including in various parts of the world, use social media to learn and promote political debates by sending messages, organizing protests, and changing circumstances in local and global communities (Harp, Bachmann, & Guo, 2012, p. 298). Because of networked communication, many autocratic rulers have been dethroned and dictators are being disempowered around the world. The cultural and political transformations in Libya, Egypt, and Yemen to name a few are some instances how digitally networked people use social networking sites, including other cloud spaces (blog, vlog, and YouTube) to challenge the political hegemonies and atrocities. Hence, social networking communication reveals how people via digital communication can subvert power and politics to meet the needs and expectations of their cultures and community members.

Since social networking spaces establish equal digital and physical space and participation, they can share, collaborate, and co-create contents. What is important about web space like social network is that the revolution of networked communication changes the power relations (for time being); it deconstructs the traditional binary of writers and readers; social networking spaces disrupt the dichotomies between writers and readers. From this perspective, network community does not belong to any specific group of people, but to all (also see Castell, 2005; Edingo, 2013; Limbu, 2013; van Dijk 1991, 2006). As networking space is virtual one, it also tends to affirm people a higher degree of trust and understanding from where people not only critique and question their social

issues, but also contest the political hegemonies and atrocities as mentioned earlier to create their cultural, individual, and political identities in the twenty-first century networked world.

In networking spaces, audience seems to be also more fluid and unpredictable. In other words, audience in social networking spaces are deeply imbricated to both local and global spaces, and audience's thoughts, ideas, and ideologies also keep on shifting as they continuously engage in the digital dialectical communication with people from different cultural, economic, and political backgrounds. Due to such constant digital dialectic interaction, digital network site seems to be a source of cultural and political transformation because in this space, diverse multicultural inquiries and identity issues are brought for dialogues. In so doing, social networked contributors tend to internalize their audience's culture and rhetoric and generate newer synergic discourses to familiarize with audience's expectations from different cultures. So, a person who creates contents in social networking sites is always a creative borrower and contributor, and his/her audience also retain the position of consumer and producer of knowledge. In most of the web spaces, including social networking spaces, audiences are responsible for textual production, collaboration, and consumption. Like Porter (2007) contends writing is an attempt to exercise the will in which we must inevitably borrow codes, traces, and signs from our discourse community (p. 41), in the networking spaces, both audience and writer equally contribute in the production of texts, knowledge, and meanings. From this perspective, both writer and audience in digital contexts are a part of networked communities who share community's interest, knowledge, and assumptions. This concept suggests that social media and cloud discussions are product of networked societies made up of writer and audience. In other words, networked communities are comprised of community activities. This theory implies that audience or readers are not empty souls in the networked communities, but they are the ones who create their own identities, truths, narratives to meet needs and expectations of their communities and community members.

In such digital communication sites, networked community members learn theoretical aptitudes and rhetorical strategies through questioning, argumentation, and interpretation processes. In this process, digital tools and human interactions facilitate heuristics and hermeneutics through which they can construct their own social, cultural, and individual stories. So, digital rhetorical literacies prepare people to use social networking spaces as powerful forces to transform their cultural, political, and linguistic identities because through such digital spaces, people share different geo-cultural rhetorical strategies with their local and global audience. In such spaces, they always reveal how digital and human interactions demonstrate cultural issues, and how they perceive the cultural concerns from their own individual, cultural, and linguistic perspectives. In other words, through diverse digital dialogical engagement, people get an opportunity to enter into different cultural and linguistic spheres of their networked members. In so doing, people realize that social practices are situated and discursive based on cultural conditions and geographical locations. Consequently, social networks direct a new perspective from where networked community members learn that the way they understand, interpret, and create meanings differ not only from culture to culture and time to time, but also from person to person (within a homogeneous culture).

GLOBAL CULTURES AND INTERCULTURAL AND CROSS-CULTURAL COMMUNICATIONS IN THE 21ST CENTURY NETWORKED COMMUNITIES

As mentioned earlier, networked people create contents on web spaces, and they share their cultural, academic, and political experiences in these spaces. As soon as they share the digital contents with their virtual friends, they instantly get their audience's perspectives on the contents. In this regard, Howard (2004) envisioned almost a decade ago that digital communication trend was moving "toward more collaborative writing (abrupt) projects ..., along with the use of online computer conferences, electronic discussion groups, hypertexts multimedia presentations, groupware, and other computer technologies" (p. 398). So, it is obvious that human-computer communication both enhances digital collaboration and co-creation and intercultural and cross-cultural communication in the networked communities in the digital spaces. In the digital spaces, such as vblog, Facebook, Twitter, and YouTube to name a few, both the writer of the text and audience equally contribute in the production of content and knowledge. In this process, we can observe networked community members' participations from different cultural, academic, and geopolitical backgrounds. From this point of view, twenty-first century's networked communities always facilitate, promote, and expand intercultural and cross-cultural interactions.

Currently, in digital communication, networked community members envision and address diverse cultural patterns, political conditions, and academic practices across the globe. And the act of envisioning and addressing issues also includes sharing stories, connecting narratives, commenting, and critiquing on them. This interactive setting makes digital global network move a step beyond the traditional point-to-point communication pattern (because in the traditional point-to-point communication, audience's engagement was not only ignored, but was hierarchical: author vs. audience). Today's interactive cloud computing tools allow people to create voices (of voiceless people); it empowers people to create their identities (by offering equal playing fields on cloud spaces). For instance, people, having Internet access on the computing devices (computers, iPads, smartphones, and tablets), regardless of their geographical locations (e.g., Ratna Second School's computer project from the remote village, Nepal) and geopolitical conditions (e.g., activists from China, Libya, and Yemen to name a few) can record activities and share them with their global audience; then they instantly can discuss the issues and momentarily may come to a resolution. This type of cloud computing and digital interaction process always facilitates intercultural and cross-cultural communication, and via such interaction people get opportunities to understand diverse cultural narratives, political conditions, and cultural norms, values, and practices.

Furthermore, as global networked communication facilitated by cloud (digital) technologies retain intercultural and cross-cultural understanding, "[s]ocial media can become a participatory forum where people with common interests can come together, become empowered, and ultimately join efforts to improve their communities" (Harp, Bachmann, & Guo, 2012, p. 298). In such digital participation, people not only discuss their cultural and individual narratives, practices, and values, people also re/design and reform their cultural conditions, values, and beliefs. From this perspective, mass media, in contemporary digital societies, are the primary human social fields and agencies as these processes and mediation are the primary mechanisms (Fairclough, 2006; Silverstone, 1999; Thompson, 1995; Tomlison, 1999; Virilio, 1997). So, technology and human interactions expose the fact that, within our current network communication system, interactions such as sharing and interacting, are serving as culturally inclusive and representational digital discourse because "[c]omputer interfaces … are sites within which the ideological and material legacies of racism, sexism, and colonialism are continuously written and rewritten along with more positive cultural legacies" (Selfe & Selfe, 2004, p. 431).

Digital communication sparks primarily a new digital and global pedagogical site that channels people's thought processes, lifestyles, and sense of agencies; it energizes a global citizen's

sense of imagination via global digital engagement across the global cultures. In other words, people, via social networking sites and other cloud and Web 2.0 tools, constantly interact with other global fellow beings on diverse cultural and political backgrounds, and such interaction actually prepares them to understand global as well as local life styles, social problems, and political issues. In this regard, Harp, Bachmann, and Guo (2012) believe that "[s]ocial media help people to be active in political and civic arenas and help promote dialogue" (p. 298), which also stimulate their cultural and political movement by questioning and contesting in order to reform their communities and life styles. Furthermore, in the digital interaction whether it is via YouTube, or videos, or vblogs, or social networking sites, people always have something new contents to share with their global networked audience. So, via digital communication, people invariably seem to globalize the local socio-political questions and concerns and localize the democratic global practices. Through such networked communication, people will be able to share their cultural issues and maybe potential solutions as well that will gradually transform their cultural and individual conditions, such as who they are, what they are, and what identities they deserve now and in the future in their cultures. Such cross-cultural communication also gradually edifies them to transform their life styles, cultural conditions, and political situations in meaningful ways. For instance, the Egyptian people (including their networked colleagues) compelled the former President Hosni Mubarak to give up his autocratic rule for which digital technologies (social networking sites) were one of the powerful forces that forced him to renounce his 30-year's autocratic rule. This suggests that local and global digital engagement introduces a twenty-first century digital revolution that significantly results in some social, cultural, and political shifts. So, how culture and people change depend upon how people use cloud computing tools, how people communicate to create cultural and political literacies, and where and in which conditions people should use the power and potential of digital technologies to bring changes in their cultures and communities.

Digital communications demonstrate that cloud tools offer people a sense of entitlement that they not only are important fellow-beings in their community, but they are also fundamental global citizens in this global village, or they also feel that it is their obligation to help each other to globalize their socio-political conditions to become globally visible. So, in a networked community, global citizens can communicate with one another without significant barriers posed by geopolitical locations, language, and culture. This notion promotes intercultural and cross-cultural communication that provides people opportunities to learn other social, economic and political circumstances; they also learn to process and connect their cultural literacies and individual narratives to other cultural and political conditions. Furthermore, through such human-computer-human interaction, people understand that globalization does not homogenize cultures, but people understand the same contents in multiple ways, and globalization heterogenizes global cultures. For instance, Barbara and Nooy (2009) also state:

If new technologies merely connect up people who are unequipped to manage communication appropriately, their potential remains unrealized. While widespread access to the Internet opens up intercultural contact to new groups of users, this ease of access gives the illusory impression that intercultural communication online is similarly unproblematic. We assume that 'they' will just be like us online, ignoring the possibility of cultural variation... we ignore such variation at our peril. (p. 14)

Barbara and Nooy (2009) also argue, "public Internet discussion is a way of getting to know some of the locals in the global village but it will mean doing so not only in their language but largely on

their terms" (p. 189). So, cross-cultural discussion is a way of knowing the locals in the global village, for digital discussion offers learners possibilities to experience cultural differences. In other words, in the networked communities, global citizens communicate about their common concerns, needs, and issues, and they will discuss them to identify ways of solving local as well as global problems. Thus, the intersectionality of human, culture, and technology invite global citizens to the cloud spaces so that they can promote cross-cultural interactions. In so doing, global citizens whoever they are and wherever they live always attain global literacies, which eventually make them recognize what their cultural and political conditions are and what they should undertake to create better communities for themselves. Overall, because of the constant digital global interaction, we are encountering digital epistemic shifts in the twenty-first century cloud era; these shifts include cultural shifts, academic shifts, and technology shifts. For instance, academic institutions are transforming from analog to digital, industrial economy to information economy, and monoculture to multicultures. Nonetheless, we should always understand that global network is endless process, and we do not know how cultures, communities, and communications would look like after 10 years.

Likewise, as I implied somewhere above, globally literate people are a part of massive global networked communities who create such a robust intercultural and cross-cultural communication and global systems that they even trust in global digital bonds, and digital business in digital contexts with the people they have never met. Furthermore, globally and digitally literate people not only trust in digital communication, but they also believe in digital transactions on the computer, smartphone, and tablet interfaces. The reason they trust in such bonds is that digital communication is a system, and they (digitally and globally literate people) tend to understand basic global norms, values, and assumptions such as what constitutes global cultural credibility and validity, and what formal and systemic conventions are followed in the digital context. This global ethos has become a compelling and competing global system that is acceptable within local and global networked communities. That is one of the reasons why people do online business, people shop online (from different geographical and geopolitical locations), and they also take online courses. This suggests that digital technologies are facilitating global literacy, and global literacy is empowering intercultural communication, global commerce and global citizens' rights and responsibilities.

PROCESS OF KNOWLEDGE PRODUCTION, DISSEMINATION, AND CONSUMPSION ACROSS CULTURES

Global literacies refer to working with global citizens across the globe to cultivate understandings of diverse cross-cultural communication patterns. Such cross-cultural practices can fruitfully bridge the gap between people's local culture with that of global cultures. In this bridging process, human-technology-human interaction connects global cultures as well as introduces diverse global literacies, and it furthermore facilitates the construction, dissemination, and consumption of knowledge for the benefits of the networked community members. The interesting part of the knowledge construction, dissemination, and consumption is that though networked community members discuss the same content in the digital spaces, it (content) is always interpreted, reinterpreted, and consumed in multiple ways, for every individual (networked member) perceives knowledge based on the shared beliefs of his/her communities he/she grew up (Bazerman, 1981; Scott, 1967). This theory suggests that there is not such a thing that is absolutely true, for "knowledge is a commod-ity situated in a permanent location, a repository to which the individual goes to be enlightened" (Berlin, pp. 773-74).

Digital technologies also play prominent role in connecting people from across the globe; so, human-technology-human interaction embodies how networked cross-cultural communication facilitated and human-technology-human interaction portrays how glocal truth is generated. From this point of view, networked community members whether they are writer and audience are creators of their own cultural meanings and shapers of realities. This theoretical notion suggests that truths and realities differ from culture to culture, person to person, and time to time. This discussion suggests that knowledge is community generated and a community maintained phenomenon. In short, knowledge production is a networked act; our knowledge originates in the networked communities to which all the networked community members belong, meaning they (networked community members) always incorporate their cultural narratives; they integrate their individual literacies in the discussion and in the production of content.

As I mentioned above, the global digital engagement has tremendously shifted the traditional concept of cultures, people, and geo-political conditions. In this process, as Aneesh, Hall, and Petro (2012) state, "[t]he world is made and re-made through widely distributed and networked spheres of production—across art, media, and social practices;" in such knowledge production "[t]here is no objective, universal, transcendent reality independent of all system of observation. There is [also] no self-identical world out there to be discovered" (p. 3). Aneesh, Hall, and Petro's perspective suggests that knowledge is epistemic, and production of knowledge is pluralistic and relative. Since knowledge is epistemic, pluralistic, and relative, production of realities differs in the way cultures and texts are conceived from local and global contexts. So, the important argument we ought to consider is that prior to the advent of cloud computing, there was a misconception that globalization and technology would totally change cultures, languages, and other social practices into one grand culture (see Selfe, 1999; Barbara & Nooy, 2009). The problem with this conception was that people did not realize that the process of knowledge invention is a social act (LeFevre, 1987), or our experiences and literacies originate epistemology to which the networked community members belong. In other words, knowledge is community generated and community maintained phenomenon, and in global digital engagement people realize that cultures differ from each other in the way realities, audience, and languages are conceived in diverse communities (also see Scott, 1967; Brummett, 1979; Bruffee, 1986).

Additionally, the global digital engagement and global literacies suggest that the epistemological assumptions about truth and language not only differ significantly culture-to-culture, community-to-community, and person-to-person, but even a person changes and contradicts within himself in the course of time. Therefore, global literacies show that global as well as local knowledge production is epistemic, and attainment of global literacy is almost impossible without intercultural and cross-cultural engagement in the networked communities. Therefore, in the current digital networked digital village, global citizens institute cross-cultural networked communities in order to reimagine, redefine, and reconstruct realities in relation to their networked engagement. In this process, the networked communities inform us that digital global engagements—intercultural and cross-cultural communication—as I mentioned somewhere above, do not construct "the homogeneous global culture," but heterogeneous ones. This theory as Barbara and Nooy (2009) point out challenges the traditional concept that "the ever-widening reach of global communications networks will lead to the disappearance of cultural differences over time" (p.186). In the past, people did not realize how digital intercultural interaction and digital dialogical processes can

re/design and re/construct the global communities by creating heterogeneous cultures across the globe. In other words, the traditional notion that globalization, global communication, and global Internet networks will lead to the disappearance of cultural difference is hammered by human-technology-human interaction. Moreover, digital technologies (cloud/Internet) facilitate not only to construct knowledge and disseminate them, but also maintain them in the web spaces in multiple ways. This further suggests that knowledge is local, discursive, and situated, and intercultural communication in digital context forms global literacies by producing diverse contents by disseminating them and by consuming them in multiple ways.

Similarly, the practice of knowledge production, dissemination, and consumption informs global citizens about global cultures, rhetorics, and lifestyles. So, digital literacies construct a concept that digital global interaction proliferates the reconstruction of multiple realities of cultures and people. Digital global literacy, in the global and local contexts, demonstrates that humans live in the world of conflicting claims, and there is no possibility in any matter that determines truth in a priori way. More importantly, in the lack of digital literacy, we can never be certain of any culture, but we act in the face of uncertainty to create situational truth, or digital global literacy is a newer way of knowing the globe; it is a newer way of appreciating cultures and people; it is a newer way of perceiving human affairs both in digital and physical contexts. In a nutshell, digital global literacy advocates not only for diversity of cultures and languages but also for the digital global village. So, in the world of cloud computing, there will not be disappearance of cultures and languages, but new languages (global Englishes) will arise and foreign cultures will be integrated to local cultures. The digital intercultural and cross-cultural communication suggests that new local cultures will arise among subgroups (also see Poster, 2012; Loss, 2013 in the collection).

Likewise, human-technology-human interaction exposes global cultures, people, and geopolitical locations by engaging people in virtual spaces (social media, blogs, vlogs, and YouTube). In this setting, global citizens get opportunity not only to expose cultural individualities, but also to reveal intercultural, cross-cultural communication and cross-institutional rhetorical strategies. Such cross-cultural engagement, collaboration, and cooperation construct knowledge that they are not isolated individual beings, but are global citizens and have global collective power. From this perspective, developing digital literacies in academic cultures means to enable students and teachers to develop their understandings of global cultures and practices. Such practices involving digital literacies and global literacies can fruitfully bridge the gaps between people's cultures and individualities. For instance, Selfe (1998) states:

These perspectives on what [people] are learning when they learn different digital tools suggests why teaching digital literacies is so important. It is not just that learning such digital applications involves acquiring essential skills for workers and citizens in our electronically connected world. Rather, digital literacies are social practices through which we define meanings and values and discover the effects of our meanings and actions on others. Recognizing the social and theoretical effects of digital literacies is an important goal for [people], one that will enable them not only to survive in this world but to create better worlds for themselves and others. (p. 186)

So, the collective conversation in the digital context is the production and management of knowledge, for the production and management transform knowledge into social capital—social economy. Hence, global literacy is knowledge-based global and local economy, and we are at utmost need to pursue intense research to establish how knowledge-based glocal economy rules should be written and rewritten and designed and redesigned; how knowledge and education are human capital; and how knowledge produces information across the globe. Likewise, the current global media culture is multi-centered; its voices, practitioners, and inventors deriving from all corners of the earth, violating assumptions about center and periphery, North and South, first and third worlds, Western and non-Western, and imperial and subaltern. This global knowledge is not promoted by the great powers-that-be like the past, but it is created, disseminated, and consumed by general networked community members (also see Poster, 2012). In other words, humans, cultures, and digital technologies constantly interact and relentlessly create and recreate and consume and reconsume global and local knowledges and disseminate them across the globe.

Conclusively, the way of twenty-first century's knowledge production, dissemination, and consumption is much more complex and different from it was done in the past, for the epistemological sites of contemporary global village and global media are linked to different global as well as local communities. For instance, people like myself are connected to the global networked communities instantly regardless of my race, gender, age, and geographical location. I, via cloud computing tools, can organize webinars with other global networked citizens on social, academic, and political issues, for which it does not matter whether my virtual partners are from Asia, Australia, Europe, North America, and South America (maybe, in the near future, from different planet like Mars). As long as I have the Internet access and have computing devices, I am connected to the global networked community, and I can easily accomplish online video conversation, online chat, and online collaboration. As mentioned earlier in this chapter, Ratna High School's (remote Limbuwan region, Nepal) computer project is a good example to support this theory. Overall, knowledge is constructed and reconstructed and our understanding of global culture is shaped and reshaped through shared digital artifacts as discussed above. The creation of supportive problem-solving communities is therefore important aspects of the educational facilitation of development in the digital world (also see Beetham, McGill, & Littlejohn, 2009).

CONCLUSION AND FUTURE PERSPECTIVE

Digital global literacies, in the 21st century's globalized world, address the unseen and unaddressed issues, for global literacy has a potentiality to coordinate with different global cultures and global academia. If we research and explore more on global cultures, we will be abler to build better global literacies as well as better cross-cultural and political relationships. Such research can also create better manpower who will be abler to better collaborate, cooperate, and create communities, universities, and businesses. When people, including students become digitally and globally literate, they will be able to compete for high-paying jobs and technology-rich jobs across cultures. Such manpower not only works for communities, social institutions, and multinational companies, but they also better understand global as well local cultures. This circumstance also transforms the mono-cultural, monolingual, and ethnocentric settings into more dynamic global cultural understanding by reducing or eliminating economic gaps, racial tensions, and geopolitical misunderstandings that we have been confronting as an enormous issue. Besides, digital global literacy provides a site for transgressive literacy practices that express and value difference such as cultural histories, racial multiplicities, linguistic diversities, and geopolitical locations.

We need to promote global literacies in the areas of culture, language, science, engineering, and local technical communication so that we can provide visibility and easy access to global as well as local audience of the twenty-first century globalized world. Since very little research is done on digital global literacies, there is utmost need of research in the area of global literacies such as understanding cross-cultural communication in order to see how human-computer-human interaction facilitate our business, education, and global relationship. Thus, we have to explore the potential of global literacies in digital and physical context to facilitate communication and information effectively across the global cultures. As Feenberg (1991) long ago stated that we, being technology literate, are becoming what we are by shaping our current and future choices (p. 12). So, these are some factors how local cultures become an integral part of the flourishing science and technology movement at the global context because by collaborating and cooperating in global context, we are creating complex and unpredictable global networks in the fields of rhetoric, science, culture, engineering, and business.

More importantly, students, including global citizens, can develop their critical and analytical uses of digital literacies and global literacies when they engage in constant digital networked dialogues with their local and global partners. We can also virtually engage students from different cultures/nations in diverse research project, writing, and communication. In such contexts, students understand other cultural practices, socio-political conditions, and geopolitical conditions that I hope awakens students and global citizens and will be able to view the twenty-first century's globally shifting epistemologies. They (networking students and global citizens) will be able to connect their local epistemologies to the global level and vice-versa; they will be able to develop a sense of knowing and helping out each other globally by discerning how people live, suffer, and solve their issues across cultures (and also how they have to address such issues for themselves). Such digital engagement and global literacies may call global awareness not only on global friendship, but also may seek for global peace, progress, and prosperity.

Finally, it is obvious that students exposed to digital global literacies can work more effectively, efficiently, and scientifically. In today's cloud era, we can no longer simply educate students to be passive consumers and producers of technology, but also help them become critical thinkers on technologies and global cultures. So, we should demonstrate the relevance of technology and global literacy in our field by making students network critically, work effectively, and scientifically so that they will be address the cultural gaps, academic differences, and political tensions. In other words, as educators, rhetors, and administrators, if we want to leave our intellectual footprints on this earth, we should truly consider redesigning and reconstructing much more democratic and representational programs (including, cultures and institutions) not only for our contemporary global fellow beings, but also for future generations. So, our research in our field (rhetoric) should create inclusive curricula, courses, and academic culture through which students will be able to address their cultural and political issues in local and global contexts. Therefore, this is one of the emerging global pedagogical sites why we should constantly advocate for reimagining, redefining, and restructuring what writing instructions, twenty-first century global rhetorics, technological theories, literacy instructions, and global communication resources should look like, and how they should be used as a newer call for a new orientation in the twenty-first century's cloud era.

REFERENCES

Aneesh, A. Hall. L., & Petro, P. (2012). Beyond globalization: Making new world in media, art, and social practices. New Brunswick, NJ: Rutgers University Press.

Arasaratnam, L. (2011). *Perception and communication in intercultural spaces*. New York, NY: University Press of America, Inc.

Barbara, E. H., & de Nooy, J. (2009). *Learning language and culture via public internet discussion forms*. Great Britain, UK: Palgrave MacMillan.

Bazermann, C. (1981). What written knowledge does: Three examples of academic discourse. *Philosophy of the Social Sciences, 11*, 361–387. doi:10.1177/004839318101100305

Bedny, G. Z., & Karowski, W. (2003). A systemic-structural activity approach to the design of human-computer interaction tasks. *International Journal of Human-Computer Interaction, 16*, 235–260. doi:10.1207/S15327590IJHC1602_06

Beetham, H., McGill, L., & Littlejohn, A. (2009) *Thriving in the 21st century: Final report of learning literacies for the digital age (LLiDA) project*. Retrieved June 10, 2007, from http://www.academy.gcal.ac.uk/llida/

Bourdieu, P., & Passeron, J. C. (2000). *Reproduction in education, society and culture* (2nd ed.). California, CA: SAGE.

Bruffee, K. A. (1986). Social construction, language, and the authority of knowledge: A bibliographical essay. *College English, 48*(8), 773–790. doi:10.2307/376723

Brummett, B. (1979). Three meanings of epistemic rhetoric. In *Proceedings of Speech Communication Association Annual Convention* (pp. 1-9). San Antonio, TX.

Cairo, J., Knobel, M., Lankshear, C., & Leu, D. (Eds.). (2008). *Handbook of research on new literacies*. New York, NY: Peter Lang.

Castells, M. (2005). The network society: From knowledge to policy. In M. Castells, & G. Cardoso (Eds.), *The network society: From knowledge to policy* (pp. 3–21). Washington, DC: John Hopkins Centre for Transatlantic Relations.

Cohen, D. (2006). *Globalization and its enemies* (J. B. Becker, Trans.). Cambridge, MA: MIT Press.

Connor, U. (1996). *Contrastive rhetoric*. Cambridge, MA: Cambridge University Press. doi:10.1017/CBO9781139524599

Connor, U. (2008). Mapping multidimentional aspects of research. In U. Connor, E. Nagelhout, & W. V. Rozycki (Eds.), *Contrastive rhetoric: Reaching to intercultural rhetoric*. Philadelphia, PA: John Benjamins B.V. doi:10.1075/pbns.169

Cooper, M. M. (2007). Learning digital literacies. In G. E. Hawisher, & S. Selfe (Eds.), *Multimodal composition: Resource for teachers, new dimensions in computer and composition* (pp. 181–186). Cresskill, NJ: Hampton Press, Inc.

Cope, B., & Kalantzis, M. (2000). *Multiliteracies: Literacy learning and the design of social futures*. London, UK: Routledge.

Cuonzo, M. A. (2010). Gossip and the evolution of facebook. In D. E. Wittkower (Ed.), *Facebook and philosophy* (pp. 173–179). Chicago, IL: Open Court.

Edingo, D. (2013). Re-evaluation of Nepali media, social networking spaces, and democratic practices in media. In M. Limbu, & B. Gurung (Eds.), *Emerging pedagogies in the networked knowledge society: Practices integrating social media and globalization*. Hershey, PA: IGI Global. doi:10.4018/978-1-4666-4757-2.ch015

Fairclough, N. (2006). *Language and globalization*. New York, NY: Routledge.

Feenberg, A. (1991). Critical theory of technology. New York, NY: Oxford.

Foley, B. E. (1994). The development of literacy in individuals with severe congenital speech and motor impairments. In K. G. Butler (Ed.), *Severe communication disorders: Intervention strategies* (pp. 183–199). Gaithersburg, MD: Aspen.

Gillen, J., & Barton, D. (2010). *Digital literacies* (A research briefing by the technology enhanced learning phase of the teaching and learning research programme). Engineering and Physical Sciences Research Council. Retrieved from http://eprints.lancs.ac.uk/33471/1/DigitalLiteracies.pdf

Gilter, P. (1997). *Digital literacy*. New York, NY: John Wiley & Sons.

Graupner, M., Nickoson-Massey, L., & Blair, K. (2009). Remediating knowledge-making spaces in the graduate curriculum: Developing and sustaining multimodal teaching and research. *Computers and Composition*, *26*, 13–23. doi:10.1016/j.compcom.2008.11.005

Hanna, B. E., & Nooy, J. D. (2009). *Learning language and culture via public Internet discussion forums*. Great Britain, UK: Palgrave MacMillan. doi:10.1057/9780230235823

Hardy, M. (2002). Life beyond the screen: Embodiment and identity through the Internet. *The Sociological Review*, *50*(4), 570–585. doi:10.1111/1467-954X.00399

Harp, D., Bachmann, I., & Guo, L. (2012). The whole online world is watching: Profiling social networking sites and activities in China, Latin America, and the United States. *International Journal of Communication*, *6*, 298–321.

Hawisher, G., & Selfe, C. (2000). *Global literacies and the World-Wide Web*. New York, NY: Routeledge.

Hiebert, E. H. (1991). Introduction. In E. H. Hiebert (Ed.), *Literacy for a diverse society: Perspectives, practices, and policies* (pp. 1–6). New York: Teachers College Press.

Howard, T. W. (2004). Who owns electronic texts? In J. Johnson-Eilola, & S. A. Selber (Eds.), *Central works in technical communication* (pp. 397–408). New York, NY: Oxford University Press.

Johnson-Eilola, J., & Selber, S. (1996). After automation: Hypertext and corporate structures. In P. Sullivan, & J. Daughtermann (Eds.), *Electronic literacies in the workplace: Technologies of writing* (pp. 115–141). Urbana, IL: National Council of Teachers of English.

Johnson-Eilola, J., & Selber, S. A. (2004). *Central works in technical communication*. New York, NY: Oxford University Press.

Kellner, D., & Share, J. (2007). Critical media literacy: Crucial choices for a twenty-first century democracy. *Policy Futures in Education*, 5(1), 59–69. doi:10.2304/pfie.2007.5.1.59

Kellner, D. M. (2002). Technological revolution, multiple literacies, and restructuring of education. In I. Synder (Ed.), *Silicon literacies: Communication, innovation and education in the electronic age* (pp. 152–167). New York, NY: Routlege.

Knobel, M., & Lankshear, C. (2008). Introducing TPCK. In American Association of Colleges for Teachers (Ed.), Handbook of technological pedagogical content knowledge (TPCK) of educators (pp. 3-27). New York, NY: Routledge.

Kreps, D., & Pearson, E. (2009). Community as commodity: Social networking and transnational capitalism. In N. Panteli (Ed.), *Virtual social networks: Mediated, massive, and multilayers sites* (pp. 155–174). Eastbourne, UK: Macmillan.

Kress, G. (2010). The profound shift of digital literacies. In *Digital Literacies* (A research briefing by the technology enhanced learning phase of the teaching and learning research programme). Engineering and Physical Sciences Research Council. Retrieved from http://eprints.lancs.ac.uk/33471/1/DigitalLiteracies.pdf

Kurzweil, R. (2001). The law of accelerating returns. *Kurzwell: Accelerating intelligence.* Retrieved February 24, 2013, from http://www.kurzweilai.net/the-law-of-accelerating-returns.

Langer, J. A. (1991). Literacy and schooling: A sociocognitive perspective. In E. H. Hiebert (Ed.), *Literacy for a diverse society: Perspectives, practices, and policies* (pp. 9–27). New York: Teachers College Press.

LeFevre, K. (1987). *Invention as a social act. Edwardsville and Carbondale.* IL: Southern Illinois University Press.

Limbu, M. (2012). Teaching writing in the cloud: Networked writing communities in the culturally and linguistically diverse classrooms. *Journal of Global Literacies, Technologies, and Emerging Pedagogies*, 1(1), 1–20.

Limbu, M. (2013). Emerging pedagogies in the networked knowledge communities: interweaving and intersecting global communities in the 21st century global village. In M. Limbu, & B. Gurung (Eds.), *Emerging pedagogies in the networked knowledge society: Practices integrating social media and globalization.* Hershey, PA: IGI Global. doi:10.4018/978-1-4666-4757-2.ch003

Lopez, A. (2008). *Mediocology: Multicultural approach to media literacy in the twenty-first century.* New York, NY: Peter Lang.

Losh, L. (2014). Foreward. In G. Verhulsdonck, & M. Limbu (Eds.), *Digital rhetoric and global literacies: Communication modes and digital practices in the networked world.* Hershey, PA: IGI Global.

Luke, C. (2000). New literacies in teacher education. *Journal of Adolescent & Adult Literacy*, 43(5), 424–435.

Lule, J. (2012). *Globalization and media: Global village of Babel.* New York, NY: Rowman & Littlefield Publisher, Inc.

Lundin, R. W. (2008). Teaching with wikis: Toward a networked pedagogy. *Computers and Composition*, 25, 432–448. doi:10.1016/j.compcom.2008.06.001

McLoughlin, C., & Lee, M. (2008). The three P's of pedagogy for the networked society: Personalization, participation, and productivity. *International Journal of Teaching and Learning in Higher Education*, 20, 10–27.

Nardi, B. A. (1996). Activity theory and human computer interaction. In B. A. Nardi (Ed.), *Context and consciousness: Activity theory and human-computer interaction* (pp. 1–8). Cambridge, MA: The MIT Press.

Panteli, N. (2009). *Virtual social networks: Mediated, massive, and multilayers sites*. Eastbourne, UK: Macmillan. doi:10.1057/9780230250888

Porter, J. E. (2007). Foreword. In H. A. McKee, & D. N. DeVoss (Eds.), *Digital writing research: Technologies, methodologies, and ethical issues* (pp. ix–xix). Cresskill, NJ: Hampton Press.

Poster, M. (2012). Global media and culture. In A. Aneesh, L. Hall, & P. Petro (Eds.), *Beyond globalization: Making new world in media, art, social practices*. New Brunswick, NJ: Rutgers University Press.

Scenters-Zapico, J. (2010). *Generaciones' narratives: The pursuit & practice of traditional & electronic literacies on the US-Mexico Borderlands*. Logan, UT: Utah State University Press.

Scott, R. L. (1967). On viewing rhetoric as epistemic. *Central States Speech Journal*, *18*, 9–17. doi:10.1080/10510976709362856

Selfe, C. (1998, April). *Technologies and literacy in the 21ˢᵗ century: The perils of not paying attention* (Chair's address to the conference on College Composition and Communication). Chicago.

Selfe, C., & Hawisher, G. (2004). *Literate lives in the information age: Narrative of literacy from the United States*. Mahwah, NJ: Erlbaum.

Selfe, C. L. (1999). *Technology and literacy in the twenty-first century: The importance of paying attention*. Illinois, IL: Southern Illinois University Press.

Sidney, D., Rice, J. A., & Vastola, M. (2011). *Beyond postprocess*. Logan, UT: Utah State University Press.

Silvertone, R. (1999). *Why study the media?* London, UK: SAGE.

Sleeter, C., & Tettegah, S. (2002). Technology as a tool in multicultural teaching. *Multicultural Education*, *10*(2), 3–8.

Steelman, J. D., Pierce, P. L., & Koppenhaver, D. A. (1994). The role of computers in promoting literacy in children with severe speech and physical impairments. In K. G. Butler (Ed.), *Severe communication disorders: Intervention strategies* (pp. 200–212). Gaithersburg, MD: Aspen.

Thompson, J. B. (1995). *The media and modernity*. California, CA: Stanford University Press.

Tomlison, J. (1999). *Globalization and culture*. Cambridge, UK: Polity Press.

Van Dijk, J. (2006). *The network society: Social aspects of new media*. London, UK: SAGE Publications.

Van Djik, J. (1991). *The network society: Social aspects of new media de netwerkmaastchappij*. Houten, The Netherlands: Bohn Staflen Van Loghum.

Virilio, P. (1997). *Understanding pragmatics*. London, UK: Verso.

Vygotsky, L. S. (1978). *Mind in society: The development of higher psychological processes*. Cambridge, MA: Harvard University Press.

Vygotsky, L. S. (1986). *Thought and language*. Cambridge, MA: MIT Press. (Original work published 1934)

Vygotsky, L. S. (1987). *Thinking and speech* (N. Minick, Trans.). New York: Plenum Press.

Vygotsky. (n. d.). Retrieved from http://psychology. about.com/od/profilesmz/p/vygotsky.htm

Wertsch, J. (1998). *Minds as action*. New York, NY: Oxford University Press.

KEY TERMS AND DEFINITIONS

Cloud Computing: It is used to refer to networked-based services; it is also a concept that involves a large number of computing devices (computers, smartphones, tablets, and iPods/iPads) connected to a synchronous as well as asynchronous communication network (Internet).

Cross-Cultural Communication: It is a form of global communication that seeks to understand how people from different cultures, geographical locations, and geopolitical condition communicate and what kind of rhetorical strategies they use to communicate.

Cultural Literacies: It is a study of culture, such as how modern science, technology, and education is affecting culture, people, and artifacts and how cultures are changing overtime.

Digital Literacies: It is an ability to effectively and efficiently understand, navigate, and evaluate digital technologies, software, and hardware and use them for specific purposes.

Global Literacies: It refers to human ability to understand, evaluate, and appreciate cultures, people, politics, religions, and education systems from across the globe.

Intercultural Communication: It is used synonymously with cross-cultural communication and global communication.

Chapter 8
Developing Intercultural Competence through Glocal Activity Theory Using the Connect-Exchange Study Abroad App

Rich Rice
Texas Tech University, USA

Ben Lauren
Florida International University, USA

ABSTRACT

This chapter lays a theoretical foundation for the development of an emerging model of studying intercultural communication through problem-based study abroad pedagogy. At the center of this model is a new computer tool called the Connect-Exchange App, which is meant to facilitate transactional learning between users with varying cultural backgrounds. To research how different audiences might use the app, the authors draw upon activity theory to guide their iterative design process to facilitate users' deepening glocal, intercultural competence. Developing intercultural competence is a process of iterative experiences connecting, exchanging, and filtering information.

DOI: 10.4018/978-1-4666-4916-3.ch008

Copyright © 2014, IGI Global. Copying or distributing in print or electronic forms without written permission of IGI Global is prohibited.

INTRODUCTION AND BACKGROUND

Workable solutions for communication problems in global societies come from flexible approaches. Such solutions require a high level of *intercultural competence* in order to listen, reason, and debate productively. Intercultural competence is the ability to communicate successfully with people through an understanding of culturally-specific values in order to identify differences related to ethics, politics, religion, literacy, morality, history, geography, and ethnicity. While glocalization is typically defined as the distribution of products or ideas which are dispensed globally yet accommodate users in local markets–essentially micro-marketing (Tharpe, 2001)–glocal thinking following principles of transactional rhetoric can also foster productive dialectical exchange.

We have known for many years that productive transactional models of communication include an information source, transmitter, channel, receiver, and destination. They tackle three categories of problems: technical, semantic, and behavior change (Shannon & Weaver, 1949). James A. Berlin (1987) in *Rhetoric and Reality* points out that culture and experience influences the socially-constructed realities of writers or speakers as they interact with others. For Kenneth Burke, rhetoric is equipment for living, and we can use rhetoric to overcome technical, semantic, and behavioral miscommunication. But learning how to develop intercultural competence in communicative environments facilitating glocal, transactional rhetoric is an enormously complex, context-driven, and ongoing process.

THE NEED FOR INTERCULTURAL COMPETENCE MASHING

Spend a few minutes reviewing recent news media with glocal transactional rhetoric in mind to examine such complexity. We must assume people are in some way connected through communication tools, that we are sender-receivers rather than merely senders, and that we must work to achieve *stasis* or shared recognition of cultural disjuncture or hegemonic forces through a productive level of intercultural competence. As an example, consider a recent debate between Pakistani young girls about nuclear proliferation and "Indian aggression" ("What," 2011). Certainly

Figure 1. What Pakistani girls think about India (http://tinyurl.com/mzlsj3t)

some further understanding of cultural difference, such as characteristics of self-restraint, is necessary in order to more fully understand cross-cultural positioning (see Figure 1). Or, consider an interfaith dialogue at the "Global Future 2045" Congress regarding human problems such as the militarization of neuroscience as weaponry, when religion becomes ideology, arguing for the disarmament of three weapons of mass destruction: poverty, fear, and hate ("Interfaith," 2012). Some level of understanding related to uncertainty avoidance differences across cultures and organizations could aid the conversation (see Figure 2). Or, consider the Obama-Singh 21st Century Knowledge Initiative, designed to "strengthen collaboration and build partnerships" in order to foster mutual understanding, facilitate education reform, and strengthen civil society without threatening cultural identity ("Obama," 2013). One hurdle with the initiative is in understanding how diverse the definition of "civil society" is cross-culturally due to power distance differences (see Figure 3). Finally, consider a recent article outlining former U.S. Department of Justice official John Yoo's views. He is known for his legal justification of President George W.

Bush's "enhanced interrogation techniques" (see Figure 4). During a recent U.S. House Judiciary committee meeting he testified in support of President Obama's approach to the use of drones for targeted killings (Voorhees, 2013).

Many cultural differences complicate accepting or agreeing with U.S. policies worldwide. In *Power Politics*, Arundhati Roy (2001) points out, "The issue is not about Good versus Evil or Islam versus Christianity as much as it is about space. About how to accommodate diversity, how to contain the impulse toward hegemony—every kind of hegemony: economic, military, linguistic, religious, and cultural" (p. 131). Similarly, Gerald Savage and Han Yu (2013) in *Negotiating Cultural Encounters* present workplace case studies involving issues of diversity in global style guide creation. Other case studies include problems transferring technical knowledge across multicultural organizations, problems seeking excellence in cross-cultural communication rather than just removing ambiguity, problems analyzing if documentation from one cultural can be translated with adequate cultural understanding to other cultures, and problems related to English

Figure 2. Interfaith dialogue- The Global Future 2045 Congress (http://tinyurl.com/kyw52wg)

Figure 3. Obama-Singh 21st Century Knowledge Initiative Awards (http://tinyurl.com/d3hvymq)

language instruction in many countries. Indeed, sustainable solutions for citizenry today require complex transactional exchanges that require significant, glocal intercultural competence.

In *The Global Intercultural Communication Reader* Guo-Mong Chen and William J. Starosta (2008) detail the need this way: "The citizens of the twenty-first century must learn to see through the eyes, hearts, and minds of people from cultures other than their own. [...] In order to live meaningfully and productively in this world, individuals must develop their intercultural communication competence" (p. 215). While language proficiency and regional knowledge, of course, is linked to glocal thinking and should be a primary goal, maximizing reflection over interactive experiences with people who share a different cultural ethnicity and background can also aid in understanding difference. This includes knowledge about other cultures and behaviors, empathy for feelings of people from other cultures, self-confidence over strengths and weaknesses, and characteristics of one's own cultural identity. As technical communicators and rhetoricians, we must develop tools and applications that support equitable interaction between people to help determine difference, and

Figure 4. The guy who wrote Bush's torture memos (http://tinyurl.com/l9nx8pm)

we can use scales like Geert Hofstede's (2010) cultural value dimensions of collectivism and individualism, masculine and feminine cultures, uncertainty avoidance scales, power distance, indulgent vs. self-restraint, and structural characteristics to improve transactional communication.

Hofstede reasons culture is "software of the mind," and that we carry with us malleable patterns of thinking, feeling, and behavior when collaborating. Digital environments created to enable glocalized transactional exchanges between users can make use of Hofstede's cultural dimensions in order to develop greater positional understanding. For instance, knowing that people in India often have a greater sense of collectivism than people in America strengthens the cultural competence of those engaged in a transactional exchange. The development of this culturally-specific rhetorical reflection can use activity theory to determine progression of understanding in technical, semantic, and behavioral communications (Pareeti & McNair, 2008). Hofstede's dimensions, in other words, help define cultural characteristics and values in ways that differ from our own identifiers. Interacting to determine difference is an important first step. Knowledge-makers today can cultivate intercultural competence through opportunities for meaningful exchange with communication tools that value glocal interaction design and mash together culturally diverse hybridity and socially complex content (Burke, 2009).

GLOCALIZATION AND STUDY ABROAD

Internationalizing identity in this way, in part to prepare people better for interacting in an era of globalization, is not homogenization. According to Thomas Friedman in *The World is Flat 3.0* (2007), there are three stages of globalization: countries internationalizing, companies internationalizing, and individuals internationalizing. It is imperative that we teach learners how to communicate professionally through connecting the local and global, whether they be from economic (Stiglitz, 2002), cultural (Appadurai, 2001), ideological (Rupert, 2000), or political (Ougaard, 2004) perspectives. The term "glocal" suggests equal consideration to the globalization of the local as well as the localization of the global. In fact, according to Roland Robertson (1995), glocalization is the coexistence of the global and local or the universal and particular. It appropriates professional communication and user experience prac-

tices to recognize how cultural interactions lead to mass degrees of cultural hybridity. According to Robertson (1995), glocalization includes "the creations of products or services intended for the global market, but customized to suit the local cultures" (p. 28). It is the "interpenetration of the global and local resulting in unique outcomes in different geographic areas" (Ritzer, 2004, p. 73), or the immediate real-world application of larger lessons learned. Ultimately, glocalization is a process of retooling cultural products and information to suit one's cultural needs. Literally, it is customization of the software of the mind. And it is in this sharing of ideas, retooling, and reappropriating that people with various local interests–keeping the global in mind–can rethink approaches to information exchange. The process is not homogenization; it is a complex mashing of cultural identity and interests propelled by identifying and respecting difference.

Recognizing difference is imperative in the workplace, in the academy, and as citizens of global societies. Communicators are increasingly expected to support the global distribution of products and services by working in transnational teams, working with an increasingly diverse customer and investor base, generating complex policies that support multinational people with varied interests, and meeting expanding notions of citizenship. Because glocalization is the simultaneity or co-presence of both universalizing and particularizing media types and interests, with regard to teaching leadership, Brooks and Normore (2010) reason it is critical that leaders in the academic world today recognize the need to tailor educational curriculum through experiential glocal learning (p. 52). Strengthening glocal digital literacy, they reason, is imperative, yet there are many obstacles that continue to prevent educational systems around the world from creating sustainable intercultural connections and exchanges that prepare students and teachers for developed, glocal knowledge work. As Starke-Meyerring, Duin, and Palvetzian (2007) suggest, "In collaborating with their increasingly diverse colleagues, technical communicators must be able to build shared virtual team spaces, exploring and weaving together a diverse range of local cultural, linguistic, organizational, and professional contexts in ways that allow for developing trusting relationships and for sharing knowledge across multiple boundaries" (p. 142). And Sir Ken Robinson (2006), in his work on ways in which schools disable creativity, points out the dire need for diverse educational systems across the world to reform education with this divergent learning approach in mind due to economic and cultural changes:

Every country on earth at the moment is reforming public education. There are two reasons for it. The first of them is economic. People are trying to work out, how do we educate our children to take their place in the economies of the 21ˢᵗ century. [...] The second though is cultural. Every country on earth is trying to figure out how do we educate our children so they have a sense of cultural identity, so that we can pass on the cultural genes of our communities. While being part of the process globalization, how do you square that circle? The problem is they are trying to meet the future by doing what they did in the past. And on the way they are alienating millions of kids who don't see any purpose in going to school. When we went to school we were kept there with the story, which is if you worked hard and did well and got a college degree you'd have a job. Our kids don't believe that, and they are right not to by the way. (Robinson, 2010)

We must prepare professional communicators to work with people with diverse backgrounds and interests in digital networks, (re)defining their selves in light of others, expanding their understanding of citizenship in various communities requiring emerging global policies, in highly politicized local realities with increasingly complex stakeholder interests.

Study abroad program work follows the ideas of Robinson, Starke-Meyerring, Duin, Palvetzian, and Brooks and Normore; that is, to increase divergent, glocal thinking in order to increase intercultural competence. In a recent *Inside Higher Education* article, for instance, Elizabeth Redden (2013) discusses disparities involved in international students studying in the U.S. Numbers of international students studying in America are up. American students are typically not comfortable with difference, according to the article, and they have simplistic views of themselves and the world around them. Larry A. Braskamp, President of the Global Perspective Institute, is quoted in Redden's article: "In many ways, international students coming on campus is an opportunity for students, faculty members, and international administrators to take advantage of that difference and that diversity." Furthermore, "in a sample of about 48,000 undergraduates at more than 140 four-year colleges, [Braskamp] found that about one-third report never having taken a course that 'focuses on significant global/international issues or problems' or that 'included opportunities for intensive dialogue among students with different backgrounds and beliefs'" (Redden).

Many networked learning environments are being created to bridge such gaps as well. In "Globally Networked Learning Environments in Professional Communication: Challenging Normalized Ways of Learning, Teaching, and Knowing," Starke-Meyerring (2010) points out significant economic or environmental or social justice issues we have today are often sidelined. She states, "despite their global nature and their far-reaching consequences for local communities, much deliberation and decision making about these issues has been shifted to global economic institutions, presenting new challenges for public participation" (pp. 259-260). She reasons that professional communication programs have a vital role to play in preparing citizens to contribute to these transactional rhetorical situations, and details GNLE learning models as partnerships to "engage faculty, programs, institutions, companies, civil-society organizations, community organizations, or other individuals and entities [...] that transcends traditional institutional, linguistic, and national boundaries" (p. 261). Similarly, in "Online Education in an Age of Globalization: Foundational Perspectives and Practices for Technical Communication Instructors and Trainers," Kirk St. Amant (2007) provides a brief overview of the global market in online education, which seems to be moving toward more glocally-invested transactional rhetoric models, and points out that there are many initiatives supporting international online instruction. According to St. Amant, four of the most significant challenges include access, design, scheduling, and language (p. 18). To work through these and other challenges, in "Building a Shared Virtual Learning Culture: An International Classroom Partnership," Starke-Meyerring and Andrews (2006) encourage faculty considering developing networked partnerships to build a robust collaborative workspace, provide intensive mentoring and instruction on peer review, to begin with on-location visits and videoconferences, and to develop a virtual interaction system, keeping in mind that there are great differences between workplace and classroom contexts.

There are many obstacles. In "Global Partnerships: Positioning Technical Communication Programs in the Context of Globalization," Starke-Meyerring, Duin, and Palvetzian (2007) identify key challenges that educational programs in Technical Communication creating global partnerships, in particular, face (p. 162). The following list comes directly from their research. *Resources* are not often readily available, such as funding for student travel, assistance for visiting students, event planning time, travel to partner sites, staffing, technologies, workload reductions to create time, and leadership and administrator interest. In terms of *quality*, challenges include finding appropriate supervision and mentorship for exchange students, finding high quality international students with the necessary English skills, approving curricula,

supporting students, building a common knowledge set of students in partnerships, addressing the impact of international students on courses, ensuring deep-level experiences in the partnership, and maintaining rigor. Many *cultural differences* abound, such as differences in understanding of time, bureaucracy, teaching and learning styles, the importance of technology and communication tools, and legalities with contracts. Proficiency in *language* and the impact of largely monolingualism of U.S. students is an important challenge. And there are *organizational* issues, such has progressing from "handshake" partnerships to systematic integration, identifying system-wide key players and necessary approvals, and obtaining needed waivers from the university for certain requirements to accommodate needs a partner institution may have. Finally, and perhaps most importantly, there are *political* challenges, such as maintaining trust with partners, obtaining proper visa information, and ensuring student health and safety during exchanges (p. 162). Clearly, we need models of study abroad that embrace a philosophy of divergence, of glocal practice, and of focused academic instruction which scaffolds extended intercultural professional communication relationships. We need to provide practical pedagogical approaches which teach us problem-solving for immediate and long-term issues.

Duke University's Intercultural Skills Development Program (ISDP) is one attempt to teach students more intercultural competence. ISDP has been created because "intercultural skills are paramount to enhance communication and the ability to connect, support and engage those who are different from us" ("Intercultural," 2013). This accelerated summer curriculum teaches students and faculty how to become change agents for self and intercultural awareness, instructing how to see one's own "cultural lens" in order to positively impact cross-cultural interactions that may be had on campus. ISDP uses intercultural encounter and adaptation simulations to acquaint participants with processes international students take prior to joining Duke. The purpose is to build "cultural intelligence," exploring conflict, cultural values, and communication styles in order to build an "intercultural toolbox," such as Burke's equipment for living, and to reflect on "cultural biases in communication and practice problem-solving" in order to deepen the programming of the software of the mind ("Intercultural," 2013). Many universities are developing similar intercultural competency building programs.

Learning to become interculturally competent through social learning was a primary goal of the CEFcult project (see http://www.cefcult.eu), as well. Funded with support from the European Commission, Education, Audiovisual & Culture Executive Agency, the project brought together 12 partners from 8 different countries to increase foreign language proficiency for intercultural professional communication. It used a web-based environment including social media and an ePortfolio artifact storage and assessment tool. The environment integrated assessment of intercultural competences using self-direction through seven specific activities or professional communication processes: project management, quality and evaluation, dissemination, preparation and then development of a web-based learning environment, pilots with language learners, and project transfer. Project researchers found that learners build intercultural competence through performing in intercultural contexts and also through observing and understanding intercultural performance; thus, self-reflection over frequent assessment, in addition to open feedback on individual learner's intercultural performance, is important for growth (Verjans, Rajagopal, & Valentine, 2010). Through this ePortfolio platform users connect and interact with other learners and experts on their individual and shared intercultural performance; the workflow includes a user profile, video samples, a collection of users who share similar characteristics or learning goals, and problem-based scenarios and tasks eliciting intercultural behavior.

THE CONNECT-EXCHANGE STUDY ABROAD MODEL

Similar to this ePortfolio performance support system model, the Connect-Exchange Study Abroad model at Texas Tech University is designed to afford opportunity to a greater number of students and faculty and global citizens by integrating highly interactive learning environments through onsite, online, and mobile modalities. The model is designed to intensify and focus team-teaching and time spent studying abroad for undergraduate and graduate students in Texas and India. It is a flexible and dynamic global networked learning environment, created to better prepare students to solve complex, global problems by deepening intercultural understanding. It follows the teaching philosophy that using mobile technology must be about "learning across contexts anytime, anywhere" (Matias & Wolf II, p. 138). In a section focusing on multiculturalism and new media in *Negotiating Glocalization: Views from Language, Literature and Culture Studies,* Saugata Bhaduri (2008) points out that because globalization defines our era, we must embrace such complexity and change in our learning environments, and that "our aim should be to stimulate new thinking, research and policy work in a domain that remains largely ignored by scholars of education. Millions of youth are growing up in a world where global processes are placing new demands on educational systems that are traditionally averse to change" (pp. 15-16). Similarly, Henry Jenkins (2006) uses the phrase "convergence culture" to describe ways in which people make meaning today. Making sense of the world involves wielding the flow of content across multiple media platforms, bringing together the everyday, and working to combine "technological, industrial, cultural, and social changes" (p. 4). Every story gets told, and students as consumers need to be taught how to participate actively to be prosumers of mass content to participate in these stories through filtering and participating in the economics of attention (Anderson, 2003). Consumption becomes a collective meaning-making process, as seen by the use of databases to prioritize hits on specific content. This is a global economics of attention. And at the root of convergence processes is distribution and intelligent synthesis of divergent content.

The connect-exchange model funnels and appropriates change as quick-paced transactional rhetoric, while fostering individualized cultural rhetorical reflection. Knowledge-makers today make meaning by mashing content together, using mobile tools and quickly uploaded content, including content from various cultures around the world, late-breaking news media and the most immediate controversies worldwide, with tremendous cultural diversity and social complexity in our local communities and hybrid subcultures. Educational paradigms must follow suit in order to graduate *functionally* literate global citizens. For instance, users explain points of view on theoretical topics by connecting daily experiences or trends in their own popular culture music scene. As Lee Rainie and Barry Wellman (2012) put it, "daily life is connected life, its rhythms driven by endless email pings and responses, the chimes and beeps of continually arriving text messages, tweets and retweets, Facebook updates, pictures and videos to post and discuss. Our perpetual connectedness gives us endless opportunities to be part of the give-and-take of networking" (cover). Instead of the traditional four-month study abroad program, student intercultural learning in our connect-exchange model begins with mobile, connected tools users often have readily available. Diana J. Muir (2013) in "An International Perspective on Mobile Learning," points out that connectivity and infrastructure in many countries still has a long way to go, but global literacy is absolutely critical in facilitating this change. Instead of going in to a study abroad experience with relatively little knowledge about how a foreign society works, in the connect-exchange model, students use live and recorded video and audio feeds, a customizable interactive course management system, and

a variety of mobile devices to connect virtually before they physically travel to a new place. Another way of understanding this model is thinking about glocalized thinking; that is, looking at the global through the lens of the local before acting.

Many scholars have examined the impact of this type of transactional rhetoric on shaping global literacies. For instance, Gail Hawisher and Cynthia Selfe (2000) in *Global Literacies and the World-Wide Web* suggest that authoring, designing, reading, analyzing, and interpreting "are shaped, both directly and indirectly, by concrete contexts for language and language use" (p. 3). Assumptions Hawisher and Selfe rely upon, which are critical in all intercultural communication projects, include the belief that the social and material conditions of cultures, especially in media contexts, impact all literacy practices. They also rely on the belief that the nature of literacy is ideologically determined, that literacy practices are shaped by multiple cultural groups for multiple purposes, and that literacy development doesn't necessarily lead to social mobility or educational progress (pp. 4-5). Our interactions online always carry with them literacy practices that recognize difference and that are rooted in historical, cultural, and racial diversity (p. 15). To guide our iterative development of the app, we draw upon activity theory to begin to understand the enormously complex intercultural situation to strengthen our own intercultural competence.

DEVELOPING THE CONNECT-EXCHANGE MOBILE APPLICATION

The Connect-Exchange App immerses members of the study abroad program in user-generated content that represents often overlooked aspects of daily life across different cultures, such as details that can help build intercultural competence and determine difference. Users may choose, for instance, to share multimedia representations of their homes, local grocery stores, workplaces and spaces, places of worship, nightclubs, or local traffic patterns, and they may make comparisons between representations of like content from different cultures. For instance, users might compare how grocery stores or traffic patterns diverge locally, and that unique knowledge can serve several purposes for the study abroad program: to prepare users for studying abroad in vastly different environments, to build cultural competence and determine difference, to facilitate conversations about cultural difference, and to enable reflection about communicating across cultures. These representations make culture the subject of users' interactions with each other. The intended outcome of this exchange is to stimulate meaningful reflection that ultimately produces more reflective thinkers. To develop this intercultural competence-building tool, we composed wireframes based on best practices of mobile interface design and relied on extensive research on popular apps accessed by smartphone users. Most communication and content-sharing apps do not foster the type of reflection needed in intercultural exchange. We turned to activity theory (AT) to help further develop the interface and functionality of the app in order to better understand the types of activities we wanted to support and promote, particularly the navigability and functionality of the interface as it would influence technical, semantic, and behavioral communications of users.

In *Acting with Technology: Activity Theory and Interaction Design*, Kaptelinin and Nardi (2006) discuss several tenets of activity theory in human-computer interaction. They first explain an "emphasis on human intentionality" (p. 10) to determine ways in which users communicate with localized and individualized goals in mind, and how an app can facilitate these goals to meet users' needs and expectations. "The asymmetry of people and things" (p. 10) favors the user over their tools, positioning "intention, imagination, and reflection as core human cognitive processes" (p. 10). This focus on users also ensures that developers substantiate design with human intentionality; that is, that we understand that our audience expects a tool to be useful for goal-oriented exchanges.

Kaptelinin and Nardi further explain that "the importance of human development" must keep developers focused on the changing behavior of users. The app must support emerging use and respond to "how human activity unfolds over time in a historical frame" (p. 10). And the last tenet is "the idea of culture and society as shaping human activity" (p. 10). In other words, communication is often socially produced, and culture influences external and internal comprehension of information, but "these processes take place in part within individuals as people have the capacity to radically restructure cultural conceptions, transcending culture in unpredictable ways" (p. 11). The Connect-Exchange App must allow for external and internal growth, and in educative environments where the goal is to exchange cultural information and knowledge and to learn ways of rhetorically designing productive intercultural communication, the app must respond to users' need for customization as well. Thus, the user is uniquely in control over information access, and the app's interface must empower users while immersing them with significant opportunities for content-exchange and reflection.

We began revising our wireframes by conceptualizing the Connect-Exchange Study Abroad Program as an activity system made up of smaller, constantly transforming assemblages, always expanding and developing in unpredictable ways. Table 1 details how the study abroad program can function as an interrelated system made up of actors, objects, outcomes, tools, rules, stakeholders, and division of labor. The Connect-Exchange App is a tool that is embedded as a part of the total experience of immersing students in different cultures and ideologies. The app enables cultural exchange through multimedia, such as video, sound, text, image, etc. To create this immersive atmosphere we developed two main outcome-based activity systems as a way to understand how users in the study abroad program are likely to use the app. The first activity system we call *connect*, and the second we call *xChange*.

Table 1. Activity theory map of the connect-exchange model

Actors	University students and faculty working together to learn how to communicate across cultures at several universities in different countries and regions.
Object	To transform how people from different countries and cultures communicate and perceive the world, and to provide an overview of how differing worldviews, values, attitudes, and behaviors can influence the work of technical communicators.
Outcomes	To develop audience awareness, critical thinking, diversity and multiculturalism, and to perform effective style and information design in intercultural contexts. Each outcome helps to provide improved cultural understanding and enables actors to develop skills for performing intercultural communication. Also, these outcomes will make actors better prepared for communicating in workplace cultures.
Tools	Physical (classroom), virtual (web-based), and hybridized learning environments. Actors use audio, video, still-image, and text. Common assignments are blogs, video-based biographies and discussions, audio-recorded interviews that can be shared with others, and publishable papers. The connect-exchange app is a central tool of the program.
Rules	Actors are required to engage each other on blogs and in the different learning environments. Participation is graded and attendance is expected. Embedded in the experience is evaluation of student work, so the quality of writing, thinking, and participation must be superior. Students must also represent their respective institutions well, and so their behavior must be professional.
Community Stakeholders	University students, faculty, and administrators. Additionally, workplace audiences have a stake in this work as actors enter the workforce as information designers, usability experts, university faculty, instructional designers, business analysts, and technical writers. Additionally, there is a ripple effect across educational programs and their constituents.
Division of Labor	Actors are engaged in a range of activities collectively and individually that will help to transform their understanding of culture and intercultural communication. For instance, actors may be immersed in service learning opportunities that have them enter into discourse with people from other cultures. Each student-actor is required to perform the same assignments, though they have some agency in choosing their individual focus. Faculty-actors act as guides or facilitators, and learn along with students.

The connect view is an activity stream that details user activities as users share information. The objective for this activity system is for users to interact with other users' original content. If a user uploads a new picture, for instance, the connect page will explain "Ben uploaded a new picture" or "Rich uploaded a new video." Beyond providing these just-in-time notifications, the connect stream tells users who have viewed xChange content and how often (see Figure 5). So, if the connect stream explains that "Ben uploaded a new picture" it will also show how many times the picture has been viewed and what other users viewed or tagged the picture. In this way, the connect stream aggregates how information is accessed, shared, and understood by users, without making it a requirement that the user click on content, giving users agency over navigation. Much like browsing an online newspaper, users can view the connect stream without selecting any or all content. Instead, users browse and select the content that seems most interesting and relevant to their interests or current focus of study. We also encourage users to create tags based on Hofstede's cultural values dimensions to help frame and filter discussions that include difference. Users can choose to tag their own or others' xChange content, but must offer an explanation to support their tags. There are several embedded tags as part of the interface, such as #collectivism or #individualism. Tags can be viewed by all users of the app. Additionally, users can choose to filter the connect stream in order to make the app customizable, but the filters do not hide user activity. Rather, filters are used to strategically sort activity by users, topics, tags, groups, class, university, or region. Filters can allow users to customize what connect activity stream they view, but they do not allow users to hide the content shared in the app. Each user is granted agency to improve his or her experience through tagging and filtering, but not to fundamentally change the desired outcome for using the app (i.e. reflection and dialogue).

The second activity system is the xChange environment (see Figure 5). In the xChange environment users author, share, and tag content. Users can post videos, photos, documents, sounds, and news articles. Users can also contact others through an embedded chat feature that can be used synchronously or asynchronously. Once content is created in the xChange environment, users can immediately select for the information to show up in the connect activity stream or save for sharing later. The content is also stored in the users

profile under My Media for additional editing or deletion (see Figure 2). In the xChange environment, users are provided authoring tools to help support the sharing of content. For instance, the video sharing tool allows users to edit video length, sound, and tint color. The picture sharing tool allows users to straighten, crop, tint color, and enhance photos with presets. Users can also edit sound by editing length, EQ, and volume. Text documents can be authored in the app as well, in our text editor. Each of these tools requires users to think through the rhetorical effects of their messages. Altering color or size of a photo can equally change the message for the receiver of the photo. A video can be edited, actually making the

Figure 5. Connect and xChange activity streams

exchange less authentic. In this way, authors of content must consider the rhetorical design of shared information and its influence across cultures. Once new content has been selected for sharing, a notification goes out to the connect stream that says "Ben uploaded a video." Users can then view, comment on, and tag this content, or use filters to find related content shared through the app. As an activity system, the xChange environment is constantly expanding and contracting in rhizomatic ways as users add, edit, and delete content. Indeed, as users develop content they deem culturally relevant, the crowd-sourced tags create the transactional environment conducive to reflection on shared content and difference.

As Figure 6 also demonstrates, the iterations of the profile pages change a fundamental approach to the app. Originally, we did not want users to create profiles. Instead, we asked users to upload a picture and write a brief biography and description of their affiliations. Once we wireframed the app, we realized that users may want a profile page to help them organize and claim a section of information in the data stream in the app for themselves, but we surmised that the page should be limited and the focus should be on content rather than ownership. After using AT to guide our design, the profile pages changed to allow for customization, emerging use, and internal and external growth. These changes to the profile page were also based on our ongoing understanding that users might interact in certain physical environments, such as media labs, and that those physical spaces may eventually be represented virtually in the app, creating the hybridized thirdspace that is important to program objectives and outcomes. The My Media environment on the profile page, for instance, stores user media so they can update tags, edit content, or delete media they don't want to share. User profiles also allow a view of the connect feed that only logs activities of that specific user. In this way, a user can follow his or her own progress and view how much and what content is being shared, and reflect on his or her own participation in the program and internal growth in ability to communicate across cultures and locate difference. Additionally, users can choose to share content from their own profile pages, allowing for a flexible participatory approach. Lastly, users can choose to create or join different groups to exchange information. These groups can facilitate group or class work and do not function the same as a filter. Groups are the only invite-only area of the app to allow for the sharing of coursework and other classroom-based dialogue. Users of a group, however, can choose to make content public.

AT is useful for conceptualizing ways in which the development of intercultural competency is much like the iterative design process. Just as iterative design requires a recursive process that is ongoing and never ends, so too does the development of intercultural competency. The tools we use to develop our ability to communicate across cultures must be flexible and respond to emerging uses. Our shift from focusing primarily on the interface instead of on the interface's users, to later designing to support multiple assemblages that are constantly expanding and contracting, and also to privilege user agency over interface, helped us develop the app in ways that better support the program's key outcomes of reflection and intercultural competency development to enable a more productive and transactional glocal rhetoric. AT purports that users keep communicative goals in mind, and that often those goals are socially-constructed and the tools we use contain cultural and historical values and ways of seeing and doing. Thus, intercultural communication tools should foster a transactional, glocal rhetoric by focusing on supporting activity with an immediate and relatively transparent interface design that builds a community of user-generated dialogue and exchange.

Figure 6. Iterations of profile pages

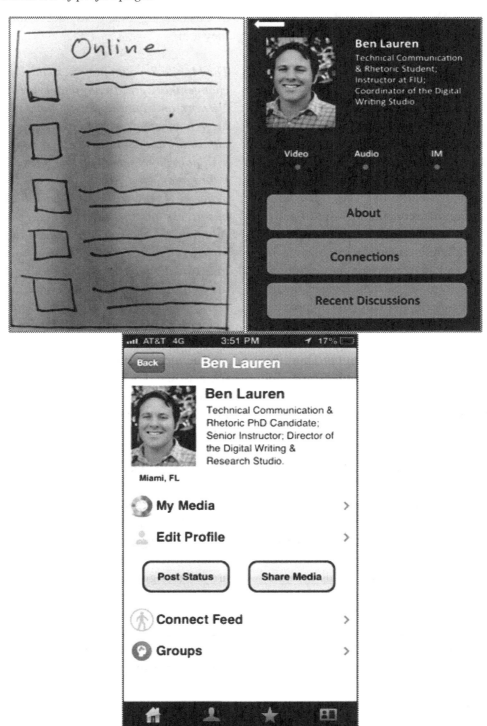

EXTENDING THE CONNECT-EXCHANGE APP TO OTHER USER COMMUNITIES

Manual Castells, et al. (2009), in addition to re-searching differences impacted by age, gender, ethnicity, and socioeconomic status, identify this lens glocalization of intercultural exchange with another complication: increasingly, the use of mobile tools creates a merging of the public and the private or the workplace and the personal or the curricular and co-curricular. They discuss this as a "full-time intimate community." Specifically, because of the increasingly ubiquitous global diffusion of mobile communication, staying in touch anytime and anywhere becomes a cultural hybridity of habit (p. 92). Sustained engagement, and thus an increase in intercultural competence through transactional rhetoric, is possible with mobile connectivity in ways that computer-mediated communication may not be. Thus, the real and virtual, the workplace and personal, and the academic and otherwise, develop an everyday life synergy. And because "mobile-phone users are also found to have high disclosure of their subjective self because mobile subscribers tend to use the technology for close interpersonal relation-ships" (p. 92), the relationships being developed through these connect-exchange intercultural interactions become a high-context intimate community. Effective mobile applications and the use of the Connect-Exchange App in contexts other than study abroad must embrace highly complex networks, in other words, in sustained ways which maximizes reflective interaction.

Rainie and Wellman (2012) in *Networked: The New Social Operating System* trace how increasingly ubiquitous mTechnologies are creating a class called "networked individualism." Through users' connected lives and experiences networked relationships develop, networked family structures are built, networked work experiences generated, networked spaces are created, and networked information is built. We never fully quit all of these networks as they're a sort of "wireless skin," as Castells suggests, easily accessible wherever they are:

The Mobile Revolution has extended the cultural changes that were already underway as the Social Network and Internet Revolutions took hold. A large number of people have emerged who are almost always online or on their mobile phones: available to others, capable of searching for information, and usually able to create online material if they wish. They have built continuous access into their lifestyles and expectations. Additionally, their access nudged them into an internet-first frame of mind, encouraging them to use their smartphones laptops, or desktops to access the internet when they have a question to research or something to publish–a status update, a picture, a video. (Rainie & Wellman, 2012, p. 95)

The virtual and the real transact to become the networked real. In the case of the Connect-Exchange Study Abroad program, this is the interculturally connected real, including information sources, transmitters, channels, receivers, and destinations working on technical, semantic, and behavior differences and problems. The lifeblood of networked societies is immediate access. The Internet in our pockets. We are conditioned to be networked. "In-person encounters" are not the only "meaningful form of social connection"; emails, texts, Facebook posts, tweets, and more are just as significant and natural, as Rainie and Wellman contend (p. 119). The multilayered processes of layered and interwoven media forms and narratives must be somewhat demediated, however, if they're to be analyzed and reflected and retooled to determine intercultural difference. Just because availability is increasingly ubiquitous, increasingly affordable, and increasingly reliable, and just because digital natives are becoming increasingly savvy and interconnected, doesn't mean intercultural competence is easily obtained.

Living applications valuing immediately usable effective transactional rhetoric is needed.

Thus, a significant problem in intercultural communication is in the building of tools that work in local and global settings in tandem to become reliable, transactive spaces where people from multiple cultures can experience simultaneity and co-presence. These tools must interface various Internet access protocols, mobile devices, operating systems, and user experience. One strategy to usability test is to work with multiple cultures abroad as well as locally to begin to examine what is lost in translation within these transactive spaces. But a primary problem with intercultural communication instruction is that we don't know what we don't know, though that does not mean we are left to haphazardly guess about the unknown. A model of learning that embraces communicative intellect mediated through authentic intercultural exchange is vital. The goal is networked habitation in physically and virtually hybridized environments, which we conceive of as a thirdspace that can equitably represent multiple, diverse users and viewpoints.

We use the idea of thirdspace to conceive of hybridized learning environments like the connect-exchange model, where senders and receivers of information can equitably construct and transact ideas: "the study of space offers an answer according to which the social relations of production have a social existence to the extent that they have a spatial existence; they project themselves into a space, becoming inscribed there, and in the process producing the space itself" (Lefebvre, 1991, p. 129). It is important to highlight that social existence is tied directly to spatial existence, which means "it is *concretely represented*–in the social production of social space" (Soja, 1996, p. 46), creating a hybridization of new forms of multiculturalism to bridge and transform cross-cultural relations (Bhabha, 1994). As Homi Bhabha (1994) suggests, "in-between spaces provide the terrain for elaborating strategies of selfhood [...] that initiate new signs of identity,

and innovative sites of collaboration, and contestation, in the act of defining the idea of society" (pp. 1-2). The location of transactional exchange, which is virtual when using smartphones, as a sort of in-betweeness of cross-cultural understanding, can become a hyperreal space. And if we are to extend these concepts further, intercultural communicators and the applications that support them must be open to divergent practices and thinking, to different ways of working and exchanging ideas, and to learning environments that can support what Edward W. Soja (1996) calls "radical openness." Such thirdspaces could exist in various workplaces and exchanges, such as those between citizens and public officials, students and teachers, and colleagues in a variety of disciplines.

CONCLUSION

When developing artifacts to support intercultural connect-exchanges through mobile technologies we must recognize social factors that influence writing, or more broadly, communication: "yet writing (and especially alphabetic writing) is a technology, calling for the use of tools and other equipment: styli or brushes or pens, carefully prepared surfaces such as paper, animal skins, strips of wood, as well as inks or paints, and much more" (Ong, 1982, p. 80). Developing contextualized smartphone apps in particular, as tools to increase intercultural competence, especially in countries where the smartphone is becoming ubiquitous, is critical, precisely because "technology [...] is itself a social process, saturated with the power relations around it, continually reshaped according to some people's *intentions*" (Ohmann, 2008, p. 26). Since writing and communication is a recursive, reflexive praxis, our approach and tools should change over time, altered by experience, interaction, and other forms of corrective behaviors that teach us to be better communicators and make better products.

The Connect-Exchange Study Abroad program and its mobile application seeks to provide a more glocal experience for faculty and students working in the program following principles of transactional rhetoric while fostering productive dialectical exchange. Learning how to create a communicative environment conducive to useful glocal transactional rhetoric to practice digital communication across cultures in order to increase intercultural competence is an enormously complex, context-driven, ongoing process which activity theory can play a role in. We need more in-between spaces to deepen our understanding of cultural difference, and software that we carry around with us can help share our motivations for making sense of the world in sustainable ways.

REFERENCES

Anderson, D. (2003). Prosumer approaches to new media composition: Consumption and production in continuum. *Kairos: A Journal of Rhetoric, Technology, and Pedagogy, 8*(1), Spring.

Appadurai, A. (2001). Grassroots globalization and the research imagination. In A. Appadurai (Ed.), *Globalization* (pp. 1–21). Durham, NC and London: Duke University Press. doi:10.1215/9780822383215-001

Berlin, J. A. (1987). *Rhetoric and reality: Writing instruction in American colleges, 1900-1985*. Carbondale, IL: Southern Illinois University Press.

Bhabha, H. K. (1994). *The location of culture*. London: Routlege.

Bhaduri, S. (Ed.). (2008). *Negotiating glocalization: Views from language, literature and cultural studies*. Delhi, India: Anthem.

Brooks, J., & Normore, A. (2010). Educational leadership and globalization: Literacy for a glocal perspective. *Educational Policy, 24*(1), 52–82. doi:10.1177/0895904809354070

Burke, P. (2009). *Cultural hybridity*. Cambridge, UK: Polity Press.

Castells, M., Fernández-Ardèvol, M., Qiu, J. L., & Sey, A. (2009). *Mobile communication and society: A global perspective*. Cambridge: MIT Press.

CEFcult. (n. d.).Retrieved from http://www.cefcult.eu

Cress, C. M., Collier, P. J., & Reitenauer, V. L. et al. (2005). *Learning through serving: A student guidebook for service-learning across the disciplines*. Sterling, VA: Stylus Publishing.

Daft, R. L., & Lengel, R. H. (1986). Organizational information requirements, media richness and structural design. *Management Science, 32*(5), 554–571. doi:10.1287/mnsc.32.5.554

Engeström, Y., Miettinen, R., Punamäki-Gitai, R. L., & International Congress for Research on Activity Theory. (1999). *Perspectives on activity theory*. Cambridge, UK: Cambridge University Press.

Friedman, T. (2007). *The world is flat 3.0: A brief history of the twenty-first century*. New York: Farrar, Straus and Giroux.

Hawisher, G., & Selfe, C. (2000). *Global literacies and the world-wide web*. London: Routledge.

Hmelo-Silver, C. E. (2004). Problem-based learning: What and how do students learn? *Educational Psychology Review, 16*(3), 235–266. doi:10.1023/B:EDPR.0000034022.16470.f3

Hofstede, G., Hofstede, G. J., & Minkov, M. (2010). *Cultures and organizations: Software of the mind*. New York: McGraw-Hill.

Intercultural Skills Develop Program (ISDP). (2013). *Duke University international house*. Accessed February 15, 2013 from http://studentaffairs.duke.edu/ihouse/trainings-and-workshops/intercultural-skills-development-program-isdp.

Interfaith dialogue (The Global Future 2045 Congress). (2012). *YouTube.* Accessed March 10, 2013 from https://www.youtube.com/watch?feature=player_embedded&v=MudSgPnqBFM.

Jenkins, H. (2006). *Convergence culture: Where old and new media collide.* New York: New York University Press.

Kaptelinin, V., Kuutti, K., & Bannon, L. (1995). Activity theory: Basic concepts and applications. In *Human-Computer Interaction* (pp. 189–201). Heidelberg, Germany: Springer Berlin. doi:10.1007/3-540-60614-9_14

Kaptelinin, V., & Nardi, B. A. (2006). *Acting with technology: Activity theory and interaction design.* Cambridge, MA: MIT Press.

LeFevre, K. (1987). *Invention as a social act (Studies in Writing and Rhetoric). Carbondale, IL: Southern Illinois UP. Leont'ev, A. N. (1978). Activity, consciousness, and personality.* Englewood Cliffs, NJ: Prentice-Hall.

Matias, A., & Wolf, D. F. II. (2013). Engaging students in online courses through the use of mobile technology. In L. A. Wankel, & P. Blessinger (Eds.), *Increasing student engagement and retention using mobile applications: Smartphones, Skype, and texting technologies: Cutting edge technologies in higher education.* Bingley, UK: Emerald Group. doi:10.1108/S2044-9968(2013)000006D007

Muir, D. J. (2013). An international perspective on mobile learning. In Z. L. Berge, & L. Y. Muilenburg (Eds.), *Handbook of mobile learning* (pp. 561–570). New York: Routledge.

Obama Singh 21st Century Knowledge Initiative. (2013). *USIEF: United States-India Educational Foundation.* Accessed March 10, 2013 at http://www.usief.org.in/Institutional-Collaboration/Obama-Singh-21st-Century-Knowledge-Initiative-Awards.aspx.

Ohmann, R. (2008). Literacy, Technology, and Monopoly Capital. In M. Sidler, E. Smith, & R. Morris (Eds.), *Computers in the composition classroom: A critical sourcebook.* Boston: Bedford/St. Martins.

Ong, W. J. (1982). *Orality and literacy: The technologizing of the word.* London: Routledge. doi:10.4324/9780203328064

Ougaard, M. (2004). *Political globalization: State, power and social forces.* Houndmills, UK: Palgrave Macmillan.

Paretti, M. C., & McNair, L. D. (2008). Communication in global virtual activity systems. In P. Zemliansky, & K. St. Amant (Eds.), *Handbook of research on virtual workplaces and the new nature of business practices* (pp. 24–38). Hershey, PA: IGI Global. doi:10.4018/978-1-59904-893-2.ch003

Rainie, L., & Wellman, B. (2012). *Networked: The new social operating system.* Cambridge, MA: MIT Press.

Redden, E. (2013). *Strangers in a strange land.* Inside Higher Ed. Accessed March 1, 2013 at http://www.insidehighered.com/news/2013/03/04/international-educators-consider-challenges-integrating-students-abroad.

Ritzer, G. (2004). *The McDonaldization of society.* Thousand Oaks, CA: Sage.

Robertson, R. (1995). Glocalization: Time-space and homogeneity-heterogeneity. In M. Featherston, S. Lash, & R. Robertson (Eds.), *Global modernities* (pp. 22–44). London: Sage. doi:10.4135/9781446250563.n2

Robinson, K. (2005). RSA animate - Changing education paradigms. Accessed March 10, 2013 from http://www.youtube.com/watch?v=zDZFcDGpL4U&list=PL39BF9545D740ECFF&index=7.

Roy, A. (2001). *Power politics* (2nd ed.). Cambridge, MA: South End Press.

Rupert, M. (2000). *Ideologies of globalization: Contending visions of a new world order.* London: Routledge.

Savage, G., & Yu, H. (2013). *Negotiating cultural encounters: Narrating intercultural engineering and technical communication.* Hoboken, NJ: Wiley.

Shannon, C. E., & Weaver, W. (1949). *The mathematical theory of communication.* Urbana, IL: University of Illinois Press.

Soja, E. W. (1996). *Thirdspace: Journeys to Los Angeles and other real-and-imagined places.* Cambridge, UK: Blackwell.

Spinuzzi, C. (2013). *Topsight: A guide to studying, diagnosing, and fixing information flow in organizations.* Austin: Self-published.

St. Amant, K. (2007). Online education in an age of globalization: Foundational perspectives and practices for technical communication instructors and trainers. *Technical Communication Quarterly, 16*(1), 13–30. doi:10.1080/10572250709336575

Starke-Meyerring, D. (2010). Globally networked learning environments in professional communication: Challenging normalized ways of learning, teaching, and knowing. *Journal of Business and Technical Communication, 24*(3), 259–266. doi:10.1177/1050651910363266

Starke-Meyerring, D., & Andrews, D. (2006). Building a shared virtual learning culture: An international classroom partnership. *Business Communication Quarterly, 69*(1), 25–40. doi:10.1177/1080569905285543

Starke-Meyerring, D., Duin, A. H., & Palvetzian, T. (2007). Global partnerships: Positioning technical communication programs in the context of globalization. *Technical Communication Quarterly, 16*(2), 139–174. doi:10.1080/10572250709336558

Stiglitz, J. E. (2002). *Globalization and its discontents.* New York: Norton.

Sun, H. (2012). *Cross-cultural technology design: Creating culture-sensitive technology for local users.* Oxford, UK: Oxford University Press. doi:10.1093/acprof:oso/9780199744763.001.0001

Tharpe, M. (2001). *Marketing and consumer identity in multicultural America.* Thousand Oaks, CA: Sage.

Verjans, S., Rajagopal, K., & Valentine, C. (2009). *Online CEF-based assessment of oral proficiency for intercultural professional communication.* Education and Culture DG: Lifelong Learning Programme. Accessed March 11, 2013 at http://cefcult.eu/data/Training_material_background-CEFcult.pdf.

Voorhees, J. (2013, March 8). The guy who wrote Bush's torture memos thinks Rand Paul was standing for some extreme position. *The Slatest.* Accessed March 10, 2013 from http://www.slate.com/blogs/the_slatest/2013/03/08/john_yoo_drones_torture_memo_author_sides_with_obama_blasts_paul_rand_s.html.

What Pakistani girls think about India - amazing video! (2011). *YouTube.* Accessed March 10, 2013 at https://www.youtube.com/watch?v=9QwvVFhplkQ.

KEY TERMS AND DEFINITIONS

Convergence Culture: A type of cultural practice currently considered a paradigm shift in society as it is represented by the spread of participatory media across a range of devices.

Glocalization: Typically defined as adapting global products to local use, glocalization can also suggest sharing local culture and cultural artifacts to other or larger cultural or global organizations.

Intercultural Competence: The ability to understand and communicate effectively with people from different cultures.

Problem-Based Learning: PBL, as opposed to concept-based instruction, is a form of self-guided learning where students work to solve a problem and an instructor acts as a facilitator or resource.

Thirdspace: A hybridized environment moving in conjunction with and necessarily beyond a physical location to include both physical and virtual communication.

Transactional Learning: An approach to learning which embraces a dialectical exchange of ideas while deferring judgment in order to synergistically gather momentum toward collective understanding.

Chapter 9
Inviting Citizen Designers to Design Digital Interface for the Democratization of Web Online Environments

Rajendra Kumar Panthee
University of Texas at El Paso, USA

ABSTRACT

Web online environments are supposed to create unifying spaces where diverse societies, cultures and linguistics as well as literacies and knowledge associated with them merge together as negotiated in neutral space. However, these online environments are not culturally neutral or innocent communication landscapes. They may alienate the users from marginal/periphery social, cultural, and linguistic background and experience because of their disregard to their social, cultural, and linguistics norms and values in the digital contact zone. Acknowledging the social, cultural, and linguistic limitations of these technologies that aim to provide agency to their users in this chapter, this chapter proposes to invite citizen designers to design the interface of web online environment in general and Learning Management Systems (LMS) in particular because this process can transform online environments into democratic platforms. Citizen designers, who have democratic sentiments for the creation of a just society, are composition students in general and students with periphery cultural and linguistic experience in particular. Doing a cultural usability test of Blackboard 8, the author argues that current web interface design is not democratic and inclusive, and proposes to invite citizen designers to re/design interface of online environments for their democratization so that they would include people from different cultural and linguistic backgrounds and enhance writing students' writing powers.

DOI: 10.4018/978-1-4666-4916-3.ch009

Copyright © 2014, IGI Global. Copying or distributing in print or electronic forms without written permission of IGI Global is prohibited.

INTERFACE RE/DESIGN BY CITIZEN DESIGNERS AND DEMOCRATIZATION OF WEB ONLINE ENVIRONMENTS: AN INTRODUCTION

Web online environments are supposed to create unifying spaces where diverse societies, cultures and linguistics as well as literacies and knowledge associated with them merge together as negotiated space of neutral space. However, these online environments are not culturally neutral or innocent communication landscapes. They may alienate the participants from marginal/periphery social, cultural, and linguistics background and experience because of their disregard to their social, cultural, and linguistics norms and values in the digital contact zone. Acknowledging the social, cultural, and linguistic limitations of these technologies that aim to provide agency to their users in this chapter, I propose to invite citizen designers to design the interface of web online environments because this process can transform online environments into democratic platforms. Citizen designers, who have democratic sentiments for the creation of a just society, are composition students in general and composition students with periphery cultural and linguistic experience in particular. Also, these citizen designers are mainly the non-expert/historically disfranchised composition students who have democratic impulses/sensibilities for the creation of just/democratic digital environment in the digital contact zone. I propose to invite them to design digital interfaces since interfaces are cultural maps, and it is important to identify the cultural information passed along the online environments. Therefore, it is necessary to rewrite the relationship between center and periphery groups in a society through the re/design of interface of online platforms because this rewriting of the relationship can contribute to the democratization within the culture and educational system through the authentic representation of marginal voice.

I conduct a usability test of Blackboard Learn in order to assess what citizen designers experience in an online environment of Blackboard as well as how it can be transformed into a democratic platform since Blackboard is the most Web tool that writing students use in a cross-cultural digital contact zone situation. My focus in this chapter is will be on the interface re/design of digital platforms used for a cross-cultural collaboration in the contact zone. For this, I invite citizen designers to re/design digital interfaces. I propose to invite them to design those digital interfaces since interfaces are cultural maps, and it is important to identify the cultural information passed along the online environments. Therefore, it is necessary to rewrite the relationship between dominant and marginalized group in the society through the re/design of interface of online platforms because this rewriting of the relationship can contribute to the democratization within the culture and educational system through the authentic representation of marginalized and oppressed voice.

Interface re/design plays a great role in online environments as literacy is figured through the interface. Periphery writing students' participation in its re/design may validate their prior literacy practices besides acknowledging their cultural and linguistic norms and values. Further, interfaces are treated as site of rhetorical practice- "one(s) that open up new possibilities for making meaning" (Kimmehea & Turnely, 2010, p. 33). Interface re/design may be invaluable to periphery writing students to exercise their rhetorical power since they can facilitate different literacy and rhetorical practices that "transcend and yet are embedded in a specific geocultural location" (Pandey, 2007, p. 123). Further, writing in the digital environment demands writing students "a range of critical composing practices, and visual figuration and interactivity offer fruitful starting points for the development of critical, multimodel literacies" (Kimmehea & Turnley, 2010, p. 33).

Most importantly, the act of interface re/design helps users remain active, and it provides them power to intervene through manipulating objects. Similarly, the users can convert these actions into interactions in the new media interface as "new media actively involves and engages the user in using, playing, exploring, experimenting, discovering, and sharing" (Carnegie, 2009, p. 166). In this way, interface re/design helps composition students in general and periphery writing students in particular to make their voice heard through re/design. With this, interface may orient toward user needs by paying special attention to the user and its culture. It necessitates special attention to cultural dimensions while designing interface because they can "provide insight and help designers adjust UIs (User Interfaces) to better serve users" so that the designers can "achieve more compelling and successful solutions" (Marcus & Gould, 2012, p. 342). For this, all design efforts mandate profound understandings of intended users, their individual needs and preferences.

WRITING CLASSROOMS AS CROSS-CULTURAL CONTACT ZONE: AN INTRODUCTION

Because of the globalization of education, US universities have been an international center for higher education for a very long time now. As a result, students all over the world with diverse racial, cultural, and linguistic backgrounds and prior literacy training come to the US, and US universities in general and FYC classrooms in particular have become excellent examples of cross-cultural contact zones. For the convenience of this study, I categorize composition students into two broad categories: students from the dominant culture, those on the center, and students from sub cultures, those in the periphery. When these center/periphery students come together in the composition classroom, periphery students find themselves lacking agency or subjectivity since

the center neither guarantees their rights, nor assumes any responsibilities to recognize their culture to build a cross-cultural community in the contact zone. The periphery students feel alienated when the implementation of curriculum, syllabus, teaching pedagogy and selection of technology and online environments are concerned with a disregard to cultural and linguistic norms and values as well as prior literacies they bring with them. Further, when these different students come together in an online environment of Blackboard (which most US universities use it), periphery students feel further alienated when Blackboard Learn and other online platforms don't recognize their cultural and linguistic norms and values in the online environment.

The contact zone is a complex concept that refers to a situation in which multiple discourse communities with asymmetrical power relations exist in a dynamic relationship with each other (Pratt, 1991; Yee, 2002). Pratt (1991) defines contact zone as "social spaces where cultures meet, clash, and grapple with each other, often in contexts of highly asymmetrical relations of power, such as colonialism, slavery, or their aftermaths as they are lived out many parts of the world today" (p. 34). Her notion of a linguistic contact zone is widely used in academia while talking about asymmetrical power relations or other social struggles for power. It is used to refer to unequal power relations between languages, communication, and culture to name just a few. Similarly, Wolff (2002) describes contact zones as "imaginary spaces where differing cultures meet. Very often the cultures have different languages and certainly different values, and very often one culture will dominate the other as it privileges itself. The 'contact zone' is where the two come together, sometimes in situations of conquest and sometimes in conversation" (p. 241). The dominant culture tries to dominate others in the process of privileging itself in the contact zone. As a result, other minority or periphery cultures are most of the time silenced instead of being encouraged to create a dialogue. It is necessary to have a conversation between different cultures in order to recognize the heterogeneity of contact zone and change it into a creative force for social transformation through conversation. It is important for the writing classroom whether in everyday classroom situations or in the online classroom. Gottschalk (2002) argues that "recognizing heterogeneity can mean recognizing the diverse natures and needs of both students and instructors, rather trying to homogenize their experiences, and, in turn, it can mean welcoming innovation and variation in our choices and plans for courses" (p. 58). Hence, any attempt to homogenize sacrificing the irreducible differences can alienate members who belong to marginal category whether it is that of culture, communication or language. Therefore, Gottschalk (2002) argues that "it is assuredly wise to recognize and take advantage of clashes between differing cultures, values, and disciplines, rather than pretending that they do not exist" (p. 63). Even if the writers mentioned here don't discuss contact zone in terms of digital contact zone, their discussion can be used to discuss the contact zone situation in the digital platforms since the current design of online environments seems to be favoring dominant cultural and linguistic norms and values in the name of creating neutral or universal technology. Rhetoric and Writing Studies (RWS) scholars such as Selfe and Selfe (1994) have already analyzed interfaces, computer interfaces for that matter, as cultural and linguistic contact zones, and I use their ideas in my analysis.

CURRENT DESIGN OF ONLINE ENVIRONMENTS

Current digital technology designs are not serving towards democratization of online environments in the cross-cultural digital contact zone. Most of them are designed from dominant cultural and linguistic perspectives, and they seem to be ignoring the cultural and linguistic norms and

values students from other cultural and linguistic backgrounds bring. As a result, the composition students with periphery cultural and linguistic backgrounds neither are represented in the design process, nor are allowed to customize their interfaces according to their needs and way of life. According to Wysocki (2004), "there is little or nothing that asks composers and readers to see and then question the values implicit in visual design choices, for such design is often presented as having no value other than functionally helping readers get directly to the point" (p. 6). She also agrees that software design has been further influenced by corporate capital and the defense industry, leading to a "logic of computer architecture" (p. 6) that has stifled the environment of student agency and invention, leading to what Lockton (2007) has described as "architectures of control in design" (n. p.). Writing students with periphery cultural and linguistic backgrounds lose agency in these online environments.

Digital technologies used in composition classrooms in the cross- cultural contact zone are dominant culturally and linguistically in their orientations acknowledging dominant cultural and linguistic norms and values. They are more text-centric and position learners as individual, isolated, and creatively inventive in that isolation and learners/users of these technologies are seen as quasi-passive recipients of knowledge in this paradigm, not as active contributors to their own learning and that of their peers (Jonhson-Eilola, 2004; Berlin, 1982). When these digital online environments are created from the profit motive, they keep on ignoring the dynamism of multicultural and multilingualism in the cross-cultural contact zone situation of composition classroom, and as a result, the users will be treated as passive, isolated and individual. Also, they keep on ignoring the spirit of multi-modal composition.

Writing students should be provided with the access to semiotic modes so that they could select from available means of communication as well as develop critical perspective towards communication tools they use in their everyday life. This access to and knowledge of semiotic mode helps writing students recognize the "'interested action' of socially located, culturally and historically formed individuals, as the remakers, the transformers, and the re-shapers of the representational resources available to them" (Kress, 1999, p. 84). This sense of remaking or re/designing helps the designers both reflect individual interest as well as socio-cultural trends since semiotic change is thus "shaped and guided by the characteristics of broad social factors, which are individually inflected and shaped " (Kress, 1999, p. 84). Semiotic systems that refer different means of communications are regularized by different larger factors such as cultural values, social contingencies, and innovations of individual signs and social interactions. These notions of semiotic system and remaking/redesigning help tremendously in the process of transformation. Culture plays a great role in this process by affecting and even structuring social practices of communication. Text productions in the context of multi-modal and multi-media in this age of digital technologies have been very complex. As a result, writers/designers are now seen as the "remakers, transformers, of sets of representational resources- rather than as users of stable systems, in a situation where a multiplicity of representational modes are brought into textual compositions" (Kress, 1999, p. 87). The writers are now more designers than written text producers who don't just critique but create as well. However, the present design of online platforms does not seem to be fostering this sense of remaking/redesigning.

DEVELOPING A CRITICAL PERSPECTIVE TO CURRENT INTERFACE DESIGN

Popular approaches to interface believe that it should be invisible, but this is regarded to be an uncritical approach as Selfe and Selfe (1994) have

already questioned. Wysocki and Jasken (2004) argue that "interfaces are thoroughly rhetorical: Interfaces are about the relations we construct with each other- how we perceive and try to shape each other- through the artifacts we make for each other" (p. 33). Therefore, they argue that teachers of writing need to involve themselves and their students in the redesign of interfaces (p. 46). Similarly, Rosinski and Squire (2009) argue that designing digital interfaces demands writers to make both rhetorical aspects of navigational system as well as technological choices that are rhetorical in nature (p. 158, 162). Therefore, they argue that teachers of writing need to involve themselves and their students in the redesign of interfaces (p. 46). Further, it is equally important to develop critical perspective to look at the current interface design and involve periphery writing students in the design activity in order to let them use their rhetoric to make them heard in terms of re/design activity.

Although interactive technologies also known as Web 2.0 tools are regarded to be the most democratic, they are not so in terms of design principles since their design remains beyond user control. Current Blackboard Learn design can be taken as an example since users cannot design its interfaces the way they like. Hence, Blackboard Learn interface works in an arhetorical way. The user agency is always constrained in the online environment of Blackboard Learn since it does not allow users any customization or re/design opportunities. They deprive users from using their rhetorical power through their design activities. With this particular current Web 2.0 design, it is not for creating a democratic environment empowering students from periphery cultural and linguistic backgrounds and experiences. Therefore, Arola (2010) argues that "it is important for those of us teaching composition to bring a critical lens to the design of Web 2.0" at this point of time when Web 2.0 technologies are dominating our web experiences (p. 13). It becomes a must for both writing instructors in a contact zone situation of FYC and upper level writing classes in U.S. universities to participate writing students in general and periphery writing students in particular to transform online environments into democratic platforms that do not exclude writing students in terms of their cultural, linguistic, and social backgrounds.

INTERFACE RE/DESIGN AND ITS CONTRIBUTION TO PERIPHERY WRITING STUDENTS

The meaning and scope of interface range from place of interaction to developing hardware and software. It is both complex and contested conception. In its most basic level, it refers to means or place of interaction between two parties, systems, or disciplines. Whenever there is an interaction, the notion of interface exists. Carnegie (2009) notes that the interface "is a place of interaction whether the interactions are between user and computer, user and software, computer and software, user and content, software and content, user and culture, and the user and other users" (p. 65). Hence, it can be regarded as the common meeting point and place of interaction for the technological, human, social, and cultural aspects which make up computer-mediated communication and, more specifically, new media. It is a relationship builder between different entities such as human beings, technologies and cultural as well as linguistic backgrounds that human beings belong to. Interface designs are conscious expressions of their designers' or producers' "views of the technology, the users, and the corporate, educational, or entertainment setting in which it will be used" (Mardsjo, 1996, p. 309). Wysocki and Jasken (2004) argue, "interfaces are about the relations we construct with each other- how we perceive and try to shape each other- through the artifacts we make for each other" (p. 33). Interface designs are often motivated by the commercial ambition of their producers.

At the deeper level, interfaces, whether computer or web, are cultural maps that produce or reproduce different cultural norms and values, and it is important to identify the cultural information passed along these interfaces. Talking about computer interface, Wood (1992) argues that the information passed along these interfaces "can serve to reproduce, on numerous discursive levels and through a complex set of conservative forces, the asymmetrical power relations that, in part, have shaped the educational system we labor within and that students are exposed to" (p. 21). Computer and other interfaces are the mappings and remapping of social and educational systems where the sense of ownership and opportunity to access them matter a lot.

Interfaces as cultural maps are linguistic contact zones where cultures meet in highly asymmetrical relations in course of interaction between users, technologies and users' cultures. Selfe and Selfe (1994) argue that it is necessary to understand and identify the cultural information passed along in the maps of computer interfaces since they are "sites within which the ideological and material legacies of racism, sexism, and colonialism are continuously written and re-written along more positive cultural legacies" (p. 484). They argue that primary interfaces "generally serve to reproduce the privileged position of standard English as the language of choice of default, and, in this way, contribute to the tendency to ignore, or even erase, the cultures of non-English language background speakers in this country" (p. 488). These interfaces constantly "name, marginalize, and define differences as the devalued Other" (Giroux, 1991, p. 33). This particular tendency in interface design marginalizes others who don't belong to dominant backgrounds in terms of culture, language and class. As a result, writing students from periphery/ marginal backgrounds feel alienated since they should abandon their cultural and other values while entering cultural and linguistic borderlands of the interface.

Interfaces are also different types of borders as pointed out by Giroux (1991). As borders, they are non-innocent physical, cultural, and linguistic borders (Selfe & Selfe, 1994, p. 495). These borders as cultural formations are "historically constructed and socially organized within rules and regulations that limit and enable particular identities, individual capacities, and social forms" (Giroux, 1991, p. 30). As a result, interfaces and their designs enable those who belong to cultural and linguistic norms and values that these interfaces are designed with whereas others who come from other cultural and linguistic norms and values are certainly limited by these interfaces. In such situations, users/students from periphery cultural and linguistic backgrounds feel excluded in the design process since their cultures and languages are not included in their designs.

USABILITY TESTS AND THEIR RESULTS

I conducted an empirical study with writing students. My research subjects were writing students enrolled in FYC courses and upper level writing courses such as Workplace Writing and Technical Communication. The first level involved the (online and/or face-to-face) execution of a simple survey with screening criteria to determine citizen designers who are composition students in general and composition students with periphery cultural and linguistic background/experience in particular. In this case, citizen designers are The University of Texas at El Paso students who were enrolled in FYC and upper level writing courses at the time of this research. At the second or interview phase, I assessed citizen designers' experience with Blackboard Learn, Wiki and blog interfaces as representative Web tools used in writing classrooms. However, the usability test I conducted was different from other tests of similar nature because it focused more on user experience in those online environments than simply how usable a particular

technology was. Motivated by the cross-cultural technology design, it was more focused on action and meaning making than the usability of online environment. Therefore, the primary method used here was the usability test of Web interface i.e., Blackboard, Wiki, and other interactive website interfaces used for the academic purpose in order to test their user-centeredness and cross-cultural dynamics.

I asked different questions to my research subjects as a part of usability test of Blackboard Learn since it is one of the web tools writing students participate in. To my first question whether he or she was included in the Blackboard design, I received different answers from them. Some of them argued that they were included because the Blackboard has a minimalist as well as neutral design approach. For example, Participant 5 said: "It's not designed for a particular group. It kind of includes everyone in its design." They argued that it was not designed for a particular group of users. That way, they believed that no user was neither included nor excluded. But others argued that they were excluded from the Blackboard design because it did not recognize their culture and language. For example, Participant 7 said that "[i]n my opinion, no. I think it is mainly for English language speakers. There is no option to include other languages." Similarly, Participant 12 said that "[t]here is just an English even if we are in a border city. Even if it is easy for me, it is not for other students because they don't have a good English and the navigation options are not in Spanish. I came to know about it when I did a Web analysis as a part of Technical Writing class." That way, even if Blackboard Learn is intended to be universal and neutral platform, it is not in reality because it is favoring dominant culture and language indirectly.

My second question asked my research subjects what user experience and expertise they required to work on Blackboard interface. Some of the research subjects said that the Blackboard design was very simple and did not require any special skills or training to use it. On the other hand, others said that one should be well versed on Anglo American culture and Standard American language. For example, Participant 1, 8 and 13 said that one should be "well versed on Anglo American culture and Standard American language." Participant 13 said that "[i]f one is not used to setting appointments electronically, one has an issue it with. From this perspective, even if it is not an Anglo, it is American culture for sure." Participant 13 pointed out something important that exists beyond the surface structure, rather, something embedded to the deep structure of cultural difference. As a whole, both types of responses were really helpful for my research. Even if counter Blackboard replies seem to be directly favoring my inquiry, the pro-Blackboard responses are more powerful than counter Blackboard because they explain how web online environments, in the name of making online environments neutral and universal, are ignoring cultural and linguistics norms and values students bring to the cross-cultural contact zones in the design process. It reinforces the danger of cultural and technological hegemony in the technology design.

I next asked whether there were any difficulties, problems, and /or confusions while navigating because of cultural differences. Once again I received various responses. Some research subjects said that there were no problems or difficulties on Blackboard navigation because of cultural and linguistic differences whereas many others said that there were many. For example, Participant 8 said that "I don't know whether they have anything to do with culture or not, but I don't recognize what some of the buttons mean. What would they symbolize? I also notice that the links and buttons are not placed on the right place. I don't understand those buttons, and I get confused. For example, if I am looking for my grades, I don't know where I exactly find them." Almost all of the participants pointed out that they had navigation problems on the Blackboard interface whether because of links and buttons

on the wrong place or due to lack of graphics. Participant 12 said that "[t]he links and buttons are not placed on the right place. For example, I had to look for a page for more than a minute to find a right link. I asked my sisters for help since they were used to it. My sisters informed me that they had the same problems before. May be it is because of difference between Blackboard as a system and me as a user from a different cultural and linguistic background. It is not only the matter of familiarity with the system." Similarly, they said that it was language/written text dominated, and it didn't favor the visual learners. For example, Participant 13 said that "[i]t is undoubtedly very simple, but this simplicity doesn't make it easy. It is dominated by language use. However, many people including myself are visual learners. This too much of language does not help the visual learners. Blackboard is very difficult to navigate through because of symbols that make no sense." Most of the participants expressed their concerns with navigation, and they told that the navigation issues could not be limited to familiarity with the Blackboard system. They were related to cultural and linguistic differences between them as users and Blackboard as a system. They felt that the research subjects were not considered in the design.

The participants also informed me that they became confused with certain words on the Blackboard interface. For example, Participant 5 said: "Some of them are really confusing. For example, I didn't know what "module" and "tools" meant. Also, assessment and assignment sounded same to me. When you click through them, you get the idea. But, for the first time, they confuse users. Some terms such as SCROM are really difficult or confusing. There is definitely a big gap between what these terms mean and our understanding. Users feel little lost at the beginning." Participant 8 said that "I encountered problems due to use of language. I think designers should focus more on the users. I personally can understand what words, links and buttons mean, but other people may not understand them. For example, users, who understand Spanish very well but very little English, may not understand what these words mean. I think same thing happens to people from other cultures." Similarly, Participant 9 said: "I believe that the links and buttons are not placed on the right place. Navigating Blackboard as far as when you like to see your class, upload assignments and so on, it is very problematic. One should begin navigating it afresh as well as you should upload one's assignments once again." Similarly, Participant 14 said: "I have problems or confusions with terms. For example, I mostly get confused with "tools" and "channels." My first language is Nepali and whatever I see, I happen to translate to Nepali. Hence, I happen to translate tools as instrument for doing something and channel for something related to TV channels. But their meanings are different in the case of Blackboard." This particular linguistic difference hindered writing students from successful navigation of Blackboard.

Regarding whether language use and graphics on Blackboard had anything to do with the student learning/writing or not, I received mixed responses. Many of them agreed that an environment had a great role to play in a learning process. Even if some students said it was nothing to do with their direct response, they didn't deny the importance of specific language and graphic use for the creation of a favorable environment in the online platforms indirectly. Many of the subjects said that the use of specific language and more use of graphics were invaluable. Participant 1 said that "language use and graphics play a great role because they help to create a favorable environment so that I can relate them to my everyday life." Similarly, Participant 3 said: "An environment does something to the learning process. When something is easy to follow, it engages students. As a result, they want to discuss the subject at hand, and it is positive to cognitive learning. More people discuss more on Wiki than on Blackboard because Wiki creates a little bit more comfortable environment than Blackboard does." Participant 12: "I would say yes because if you are familiar to an environment,

you will easily learn and learning process will be easier. If it is not, it will be little bit difficult. That way, language use and graphics create a favorable environment so that I can relate them to my everyday life, and they contribute a lot to the cognitive learning. They help you to be familiar with something, and this familiarity helps your learning process." Directly or indirectly almost all of the participants recognized the importance of favorable online environment for an effective learning process, and use of language and graphics played a crucial role for the building up of a positive environment.

To my inquiry whether research subjects would change anything about Blackboard, almost all of them said that they would change parts of Blackboard to create an online environment that helps all participants feel at home. Participant 10 said: "Yes, I would definitely. I think I would make it much more accessible to people different cultures." Similarly, Participant 12 said that she "would change because it would be easier to navigate through for future users. Users can help the design what exactly needs to be done to a particular technology." Their responses spoke volumes about the present design of technologies such as Blackboard. The writing students from periphery cultural and linguistic backgrounds were aware of the exclusion of periphery students from the Blackboard design. They put great emphasis on creating an inclusive environment to all the members in the discourse community in the cross-cultural digital contact zone. They felt the importance of creating a digital online environment where the members in that discourse community feel comfortable as well as at home.

With regard to what they would change, besides language, translation tools and others, almost all of them emphasized the customization opportunity to the users so that they could fix the navigation and other problems. They said that they would re/design or customize the interface according to their needs as well as their way of life. Almost all of the participants said that they would change word choice, install language translation tools, and make it visually appealing. Most importantly, almost all of them gave primary focus to the navigation part. Participant 3 said that she "would work on the navigation and visual side." Similarly, Participant 6 argued that she would "change the navigation because new students find it difficult to navigate Blackboard Learn currently" and she stated that she "would simplify the navigation." In order to simplify the navigation, Participant 9 argued: "Blackboard needs to be made personal i.e., let the users upload something that is related to their cultural and linguistic backgrounds. It makes them more sense to them. That way, we can turn around instead of sticking to one. Have something that pertains to something instead of having that black generic thing." Some of the participants raised some democratic issues such as addressing the needs of discourse community members in the cross-cultural digital contact zone. For example, Participant 12 pointed out: "UTEP is located on a border city, and there are many Hispanic students besides others. I asked some UTEP students to navigate through Blackboard as a part of my Web analysis in order to know whether they had any problems in navigation due to language. I would change the navigation as sometimes the links take me to a totally different place. May be I would put more images as it is just a writing currently. I would more focus on visual aspect as I myself am a visual learner. I would also change the order of the pages as some of them don't open properly." Her views are worth considering in course of technology design in general and Blackboard design in particular for a cross-cultural technology design. Similarly, Participant 14 said that she "would work on navigation, it does not let you open sub-categories on Blackboard. I think it should let students open multiple tabs at a time." On top of it, almost all the participants pointed out that providing an opportunity to customize the interface so that it could solve those navigation issues as well as being inclusive in terms of design.

As a continuation of previous questions related to customization opportunity to the users, I asked my research subjects whether they would let users design the interface according to their needs and ways of life. Almost all of them said it would be very invaluable especially for a cross-cultural digital contact zone. Besides two participants, all others regarded users re/designing invaluable from different perspectives. Participant 1 said that "[e]very user does have different user needs, so, that applies very well because every individual has his or her perspectives and needs. But changing interface by anyone is not a good idea." Similarly, Participant 2 said that she "would let users to design interface the way they like since it helps them reflect their personality, culture and stuff like that." Interface re/design by users contributed to active user engagement. For example, Participant 7 said that "[i]t (was) definitely a good thing for a user to be active because it would create close relationships between students and Blackboard. They would probably get on more, and they would find it easier to navigate when they design in their way. That way, one could add something that belongs to his or her culture. It makes them feel more comfortable, and this sense of comfort makes them do something willingly." Similarly, Participant 10 said that she "would let the users design the way they like." Participant 11 said that she "would let the users design the way they like because certain people organize things differently, so, if you let them design interface they like, it would be like a notebook. Organizing the interface and moving around the modules would be something personal, and it makes the users feel they did it." Participant 12 said that "it would be cool if it lets users design the interface the way they like. It would be personal and it would help me go to the task directly instead of navigating through different pages. If one could design incorporating different cultural norms and values, it would certainly be more welcoming. May be putting some sidebars that give the users something from their cultures so that they would feel included in the design."

Interface design by users also would contribute a lot to the learning process of those visual learners because users could bring some visuals. For example, Participant 13 said that "I would install things that make Blackboard more visual." As a whole, re/designing or customizing technology by users could contribute a lot for making online environment inclusive and user-centered.

Finally, in terms of website/online platforms they prefer, almost all of my research subjects longed for a user-centered interface so that could customize it according to context, their needs and their way of life. They preferred Wiki and other interactive websites to Blackboard because they help them customize according to their needs, at least to a certain extent. For example, Participant 2 said that "[t]hese online platforms would be helpful to people from marginal cultural and linguistic backgrounds. Through their input in the design of these platforms, they help them make themselves culturally and linguistically visible." Similarly, Participant 3 said that "[t]hey help users maintain their cultural and linguistic norms and values through their design, visual appeal and language use. I think that would definitely help the users keep their cultural norms and values through the design. Also, they help them keep themselves visible in a cross-cultural digital contact zone." According to Participant 4, the ability to customize those online environments "would definitely help the users maintain their cultural and linguistic norms and values." Comparing different online environments, Participant 7 said that "[a]s far as things you can do, Wikis and other interactive websites are far better than Blackboard because students can do things their way. It would provide the user more comfort."

To my role of cross-cultural interface design question, they pointed out different issues ranging from making the users visible culturally and linguistically to democratization. They emphasized having equal say through the form as well as the content of the website. Participant 1 said that "[i]t helps create a democratic environment,

and it ensures equal say from people participating cultures." Similarly, Participant 2 said that "your history and who you are today makes it feel at home and everyone and a lot of your culture is your belief. People should hear you, and people learn from that. Some people get inspired by it." In a slightly different way, Participant 4 said that "I guess in sitting down and creating a cross-cultural website, including people of different culture won't make it necessarily democratic. Definitely from the comfort standpoint, feeling comfortable in the online environment would definitely be great as it helps you from not getting intimidated." Participant 5 asserted that "[i]t ensures equal say from people from participating cultures. It is important because if you are already included in the website, you kind of feel more comfortable and acknowledged. When you feel comfortable, you participate more in a discussion and provide your opinion than you are not." Similarly, Participant 12 said that "yes, it is important to make a website cross-cultural according to its users, contexts and purpose. Universities are all very diverse and people from different backgrounds come, so, they need to keep in consideration so the users feel good when they are included in the design of technologies that universities use. This helps them feel comfortable." Participant 13 said that "[i]t is basically related to putting little bit of yourself." All of the participants emphasized feeling comfortable in an online environment among other things such democracy.

To my next question how their participation in the interface design would help them acquire their agency in a cross-cultural digital contact zone. All the participants agreed that participation in the interface design helps the designer acquire his or her agency in the contact zone. For example, Participant 1 said that "[i]t provides me an opportunity to introduce myself as who I really am." Participant 1 puts emphasis on keeping oneself intact in the online environment instead of forgetting oneself and adopting other cultural and linguistic norms and values. Similarly, Participant

3 said that "[i]t provides me a decisive power in the design process. I just like my opinion implemented in the design. I want voice of my opinion reflects who I am, what I believe and so on." Participant 3 added something to what Participant 1 already said. Participant 3 liked to have some decisive power in the design process and have her voiced heard in implementation. Similarly, Participant 12 said that when cultural norms and values were reflected on the design, she would feel "acknowledged and visible." Their views on technology design and their concern about democratic online environment were impressive. They were very mindful of the issues of democracy, and they had a very sound knowledge about creating democratic online environments. In this way, with the participation of citizen designers in the interface re/design process ensures the representation of otherwise unheard voice. With this, interface becomes a cross-cultural platform that includes cultural and linguistic norms and values of members in the composition discourse community.

CONCLUSION

Citizen designers' participation in the interface design will help them express their voice that otherwise remains silent. Similarly, it provides them an opportunity to exercise their rhetoric in the process of interface design. With this, writing students with periphery cultural and linguistic backgrounds will acquire their agency on the one hand whereas they will be a creation of conducive learning environments for students from different cultural and linguistic backgrounds on the other hand. Therefore, Panthee (2012) argues that "[i]nterface design will help writing students exercise their rhetorical power to create democratic online environments whereas culture and language will help them as subject matters for critique and design in their interface design activity" (p. 52). With

these citizen designer acts, the online environments will be transformed into democratic spaces that don't exclude anyone on the basis of cultural and linguistic differences.

FYC students in general and FYC periphery writing students in particular should be involved in re/designing interface in the cross-cultural digital contact zone to deconstruct cultural and linguistic knowledge passed along those interfaces designs and create new cultural and linguistic knowledge for the social change instead of just critiquing the existing designs. It helps them uncover "the cultural horizon under which it was designed" and re-contextualize that can "uncover that horizon, demystify the illusion of technical necessity, and expose the relativity of the prevailing technical choices" (Feenberg, 2010, p. 18). This act of re-contextualizing technological design can lead to the democratization of technology with the finding of new ways to privilege the excluded values. Finally, it will lead to development of educational reform and promotion of "multicultural democracy" (Kellner, 2002, p. 157). Therefore, inviting citizen designers to design interfaces of online environment will be invaluable to make interfaces the complete picture of culture and language in our society. With this, the online environments also will transform into a democratic platforms with the representation of the marginal voice in the interface design. As a result, interfaces of online environments wont disable anyone on the basis of culture and language.

REFERENCES

Arola, K. L. (2010). The design of Web 2.0: The rise of the template, the fall of design. *Computers and Composition*, *27*(1), 4–14. doi:10.1016/j.compcom.2009.11.004

Beauvais, P. J. (2002). First contact: Composition students' close encounters with college culture. In J. M. Wolf (Ed.), *Professing in the contact zone: Bringing theory and practice together* (pp. 21–47). Urbana, IL: NCTE.

Bellamy, R. K. E. (1996). Designing educational technology: Computer-mediated change. In B. Nardi (Ed.), *Context and consciousness: Activity theory and human-computer interaction* (pp. 123–146). Cambridge, MA: MIT Press.

Berlin, J. A. (1982). Contemporary composition: The major pedagogical theories. *College English*, *44*(8), 765–777. doi:10.2307/377329

Berlin, J. A. (1992). Poststructuralism, cultural studies, and the composition classroom: Postmodern theory in practice. *Rhetoric Review*, *11*(1), 16–33. doi:10.1080/07350199209388984

Bowie, J. L. (2009). Beyond the universal: The universe of users approach to user-centered design. In S. Miller-Cochran, & R. L. Rodrigo (Eds.), *Rhetorically rethinking usability: Theories, practices and methodologies* (pp. 135–163). Cresskill, NJ: Hampton Press, Inc.

Bratteteig, T., Morrison, A., Stuedahl, D., & Mortberg, C. (2010). Research practices in digital design. In I. Wagner, T. Bratteteig, & D. Stuedahl (Eds.), *Multi-disciplinary design practices* (pp. 17–54). London: Springer-Verlag.

Braun, M. J. (2008). The political economy of computers and composition: Democracy hope in an era of globalization. In L. Worsham, & G. Olson (Eds.), *Plugged in technology: Rhetoric and culture in a posthuman age* (pp. 95–124). Cresskill, NJ: Hampton Press, Inc.

Buchanan, R. (1995). Rhetoric, humanism and design. In R. Buchanan, & V. Margolin (Eds.), *Discovering design: Explorations in design studies* (pp. 26–66). Chicago, IL: The University of Chicago Press.

Buchanan, R., & Margolin, V. (1995). Introduction. In R. Buchanan, & V. Margolin (Eds.), *Discovering design: Explorations in design studies* (pp. ix–xxvi). Chicago, IL: The University of Chicago Press.

Canagarajah, S. A. (1999). *Resisting linguistic imperialism in English teaching*. Oxford, UK: Oxford University Press.

Carnegie, T. A. M. (2009). Interface as exordium: The rhetoric of interactivity. *Computers and Composition*, *26*, 164–173. doi:10.1016/j.compcom.2009.05.005

Carpenter, R. (2009). Boundary negotiations: Electronic environments as interface. *Computers and Composition*, *26*, 138–148. doi:10.1016/j.compcom.2009.05.001

Cope, B., & Kalantzis, M. (2000). Designs for social futures. In B. Cope, & M. Kalantzis (Eds.), *Multiliteracies: Literacy learning and the design of social futures* (pp. 203–234). New York, NY: Routledge.

Cross, N. (1995). Discovering design ability. In R. Buchanan, & V. Margolin (Eds.), *Discovering design: Explorations in design studies* (pp. 105–121). Chicago, IL: The University of Chicago Press.

Feenberg, A. (2010). *Between reason and experience: Essays in technology and modernity*. Cambridge, MA: The MIT Press.

Giroux, H. (1991). *Border crossings: Cultural workers and the politics of education*. New York, NY: Routledge.

Gottschalk, K. K. (2002). Contact zones: Composition's content in the university. In J. M. Wolf (Ed.), *Professing in the contact zone: Bringing theory and practice together* (pp. 58–78). Urbana, IL: NCTE.

Grabill, J. T. (2003). On divides and interfaces: Access, class, and computers. *Computers and Composition, 20,* 455–472. doi:10.1016/j.compcom.2003.08.017

Hall, S. (1986). On postmodernism and articulation: An interview with Stuart Hall. L. Grossberg (Ed.). Journal of Communication Inquiry, 10(2) 45-60.

Hawisher, G. E., & Selfe, C. L. (2000). Introduction: Testing the claims. In G. E. Hawisher, & C. L. Selfe (Eds.), *Global literacies and the World-Wide Web* (pp. 1–18). New York, NY: Routledge.

Hilligoss, S., & Williams, S. (2007). Composition meets visual communication: New research questions. In H. A. McKee, & D. N. DeVoss (Eds.), *Digital writing research: Technologies, methodologies, and ethical issues* (pp. 229–247). Cresskill, NJ: Hampton Press.

Johnson, S. (1997). *Interface culture: How new technology transforms the way we create & communicate.* New York, NY: Basic Books.

Johnson-Eilola, J. (2004). The database and the essay: Understanding composition as articulation. In A. F. Wysocki, J. Johnson-Eilola, C. Selfe, & G. Sirc (Eds.), *Writing new media: Theory and applications for expanding the teaching composition* (pp. 199–235). Logan, UT: Utah State University Press.

Julier, G. (2008). *The culture of design* (2nd ed.). London: Sage.

Kimmehea, A. C., & Turnely, M. (2010). Refiguring the interface agent: An exploration of productive tensions in new media composing. In C. E. Ball & J. Kalmbach (eds.), RAW [Reading and Writing] New Media (pp. 257-273). Cresskill, NJ: Hampton Press, Inc.

Kress, G. (1999). English at the crossroads: Rethinking curricula of communication in the context of the turn of the visual. In G. Hawisher, & C. Selfe (Eds.), *Passions,pedagogies and 21st century technologies* (pp. 66–88). Logan, UT: Utah State University Press.

Laurel, B. (1990). Introduction: What's an interface? In B. Laurel (Ed.), *The art of human computer interface design* (pp. xi–xiii). Boston: Addison-Wesley.

Marcus, A., & Gould, E. W. (2012). Globalization, localization, and cross-cultural user-interface design. In J. A. Jacko (Ed.), *The human-computer interaction: Fundamentals, evolving technologies, emerging applications* (3rd ed., pp. 341–366). London, New York, NY: CRS Press Taylor & Francis Group. doi:10.1201/b11963-19

Mardsjo, K. (1996). Interfacing technology. *Computers and Composition, 13,* 303–315. doi:10.1016/S8755-4615(96)90019-5

Margolin, V. (1995). The product milieu and social action. In R. Buchanan, & V. Margolin (Eds.), *Discovering design: Explorations in design studies* (pp. 121–145). Chicago, IL: The University of Chicago Press.

Marshall, D. P. (2004). *New media cultures.* New York, NY: Oxford University Press.

McNely, B. J. (2008). *Agency, invention, and sympatric design platforms.*

Miller, R. (2002). Fault lines in the contact zone. In J. M. Wolf (Ed.), *Professing in the contact zone: Bringing theory and practice together* (pp. 121–146). Urbana, IL: NCTE.

Panthee, R. K. (2012). Web 2.0 technologies, cultural and technological hegemonies, and teaching design to deconstruct them in the cross-cultural digital contact zone. *Journal of Global Literacies, Technologies, and Emerging Pedagoies, 1*(1), 38–55.

Porter, J. E., & Sullivan, P. A. (2004). Repetition and the rhetoric of visual design. In C. Handa (Ed.), Visual rhetoric in a digital world: A critical sourcebook, (pp. 290-299). Bsoton/New York, NY: Bedford/St. Martin's.

Pratt, M. L. (1991). Arts of the contact zone. *Profession*, *91*, 33–40.

Raskin, J. (2000). *The humane interface: New directions for designing interactive systems*. Boston, MA: Addison Wesley.

Rosinski, P., & Squire, M. (2009). Strange bedfellows: Humans-computer interaction, interface design, and composition pedagogy. *Computers and Composition*, *26*, 149–163. doi:10.1016/j.compcom.2009.05.004

Russell, D. (1997). Rethinking genre in school and society: An activity theory analysis. *Written Communication*, *14*(4), 504–554. doi:10.1177/0741088397014004004

Selber, S. (2004). *Multiliteracies for a digital age*. Carbondale, IL: Southern Illinois University Press.

Selfe, C. L. (2009). The movement of air, the breath of meaning: Aurality and multimodal composing. *College Composition and Communication*, *60*, 616–663.

Selfe, C. L., & Selfe, R. J. (1994). The politics of the interface: Power and its exercise in electronic contact zones. *College Composition and Communication*, *45*(4), 480–504. doi:10.2307/358761

Sheridan, D., Ridolfo, J., & Michel, A. (2008). The available means of persuasion: Mapping a theory and pedagogy of multimodal public rhetoric. In L. Worsham, & G. Olson (Eds.), *Plugged in technology, rhetoric and culture in a posthuman age* (pp. 61–94). Cresskill, NJ: Hampton Press, Inc.

Skjulstad, S., & Morrison, A. (2005). Movements in the interface. *Computers and Composition*, *22*, 413–433. doi:10.1016/j.compcom.2005.08.006

Spinuzzi, C. (2003). *Tracing genres through organizations*. Cambridge, MA: MIT Press.

Spinuzzi, C. (2008). *Network: Theorizing knowledge work in telecommunications*. New York, NY: Cambridge University Press. doi:10.1017/CBO9780511509605

Spinuzzi, C. (2009). Light green doesn't mean hydrology!: Toward a visual rhetorical framework for interface design. In S. Miller-Cochran, & R. L. Rodrigo (Eds.), *Rhetorically rethinking usability: Theories, practices and methodologies*. Creskill, NJ: Hampton Press, Inc.

Stevenson, N. (2011). *Education and cultural citizenship*. Los Angeles, CA: SAGE.

Stuedahl, D., Morrison, A., Mortberg, C., & Bratteteig. (2010). Researching digital design. In I. Wagner, T. Bratteteig, & D. Stuedahl (Eds.), *Multi-disciplinary design practices* (pp. 3-15). London: Springer-Verlag.

Sun, H. (2012). *Cross-cultural technology design: Creating culture-sensitive technology for local users*. New York, NY: Oxford University Press. doi:10.1093/acprof:oso/9780199744763.001.0001

Turnley, M. (2005). Contextualized design: Teaching critical approaches to web authoring through redesign projects. *Computers and Composition*, *22*, 131–148. doi:10.1016/j.compcom.2005.02.007

Vanhoosier-Carey, G. (1997). Rhetoric by design: Using web development projects in technical communication classroom. *Computers and Composition*, *14*, 395–407. doi:10.1016/S8755-4615(97)90008-6

Wagner, I., Bratteteig, T., & Stuedahl, D. (Eds.). (2010). *Multi-disciplinary design practices*. London: Springer-Verlag.

Watzman, S., & Re, M. (2012). Visual design principles for usable interfaces: Everything is designed: Why we should think before doing. In J. A. Jacko (Ed.), *The human-computer interaction: Fundamentals, evolving technologies, emerging applications* (3rd ed., pp. 315–340). London, New York, NY: CRS Press Taylor & Francis Group. doi:10.1201/b11963-18

Wolf, J. M. (Ed.). (2002). *Professing in the contact zone: Bringing theory and practice together.* Urbana, IL: NCTE.

Wood, D. (1992). *The power of maps.* New York, NY: Guilford.

Wysocki, A. F. (2005). Awaywithwords: On the possibilities in unavailable designs. *Computers and Composition, 22,* 55–62. doi:10.1016/j.compcom.2004.12.011

Wysocki, A. F., & Jasken, J. I. (2004). What should be an unforgettable face.... *Computers and Composition, 21,* 29–48. doi:10.1016/j.compcom.2003.08.004

Yee, C. (2002). Contact zones in institutional culture: An anthropological approach to academic programs. In J. M. Wolf (Ed.), *Professing in the contact zone: Bringing theory and practice together* (pp. 257–273). Urbana, IL: NCTE.

KEY TERMS AND DEFINITIONS

Asymmetrical Power Relations: Relationships between/among people having unequal power dynamism.

Center/Periphery: Center refers to an entity with power, control and resource. It has a decisive power whereas periphery lacks power, control and resources. As a result, periphery lacks decisive power. The periphery is the other of center. Center/periphery can be understood as insider/outsider features of a certain entity.

Citizen Designers: Composition students who come from marginal/periphery social, cultural and linguistic backgrounds. They lack social power, control, and resource. With this, they don't have decisive power in different social as well as virtual spheres.

Cross-Cultural Contact Zone: It refers to a situation when different cultures with unequal power dynamics come together and clash because there is a tendency of favoring one culture over others. In such a situation, the dominant culture also tries to impose its norms and values upon subordinate cultures. FYC in US universities can be taken as an example of cross-cultural contact zone where students from different social, cultural, linguistic as well as different literacy trainings come together.

Cross-Cultural: Cross-cultural is a situation when two or more different cultures come together. It also refers to a multicultural situation where there is an existence of different cultures.

Customize: modify or change according to one's need.

Democratic Platforms: Online platforms that ensure equal say from different cultural and linguistic backgrounds.

Dominant/Subordinate/Marginal: Dominant refers to a group of people such as elites, institutions or groups who exercise social power that results in social inequality. Most of the time it refers to western, white, elite, and non-English speakers. Subordinate/marginal refers to a group of people who are non-western, non-white, and non-English speakers. Subordinate/marginal are the other of dominant.

Interface and its Redesign: Interface can be understood as communication or interaction. In this chapter, interface refers a place of interaction between technologies, users and their cultures. Since interfaces of digital technologies such as Blackboard, Wiki, Blogs, Facebook, MySpace and so on are designed from the perspective of the dominant cultural and linguistic backgrounds because of various reasons such as profitability or power dynamics, they are not serving a democratic goal in our society. This study believes that when digital interfaces are designed by students from periphery cultural and linguistic backgrounds, they can be transformed into democratic platforms. Further, it also believes that this knowledge of interface and design can help students to develop their writing skills.

Invention: It is an act of making something new whether through social participation or through mixing/hybridizing different social, cultural, linguistic norms and values to name just a few.

Multi-Modal Composition: It refers to an act of communication through different modes of communication such as writing, audio/visual and so on.

Negotiated Space: It refers to an online space that is designed compromising differences between different cultures, languages and so on.

Neutral Space: Online space that neither supports one nor rejects other social, cultural and linguistic norms and values.

Student Agency: Student agency refers to student power that helps them make decision or implement their decision.

Text-Centric: It refers to a composing space or environment that prioritizes text production over other means of designing/creating at a time of multi-modal composition.

Unifying Spaces: Online spaces that try to unify the differences among users who belong to different cultural and linguistic backgrounds to name just a few.

Usability Test: a test that asks users whether a particular technology is usable or not.

Web 2.0: It is a read and write web.

Web Online Environments: Online environments created by web technology. Online environments refer to virtual environments created by digital technologies. Blackboard, Wiki, blogs, Facebook or MySpace can be the best examples of online environments.

Chapter 10
Social Media in an Intercultural Writing Context:
Creating Spaces for Student Negotiations

Mª Pilar Milagros García
Koç University, Turkey

ABSTRACT

The current research study is part of a larger project that aims to analyze ways in which first year intercultural writing students interpret/understand the impact of social media on their composition practices, critical thinking processes and knowledge negotiations processes. In particular, the current chapter attempts to understand how first year intercultural writing students reflect on and assess the ways social media has helped them practice and or/acquire more critical thinking skills.

INTRODUCTION

The activities that used social media showed me that the subjects in the articles have their examples in real life as well.

We live in a world in which technology is constantly evolving. Technological advances in general and the internet in particular bring people from very different cultures and socio-economic contexts closer together than ever; in fact, according to Sherry Turkle (1999), "the Internet links millions of people together in new spaces that are changing the way we think…, the form of our communities, our very identities" (p. 643). However, technology is only a medium; it provides us with opportunities to engage in communication exchanges, but does not help us acquire the communicative tools and skills needed to engage in global communications and literacies. Another fact about today's world is that English has become the lingua franca that people from all over the world use to communicate for a variety of purposes with a variety of

DOI: 10.4018/978-1-4666-4916-3.ch010

Copyright © 2014, IGI Global. Copying or distributing in print or electronic forms without written permission of IGI Global is prohibited.

people. Both situations present English language instructors (ESL, EFL, Second Language and composition instructors) with great opportunities; in order for writing instructors to effectively help English language learners, we should encourage them to attain intercultural competence (Byram, 1997) rather than the proficiency level of a native speaker. For that to happen, instructors of English in general and writing instructors in particular need to endlessly reinvent ourselves in the classroom, which, to me, posits a great opportunity or kairos.

As much as our society has changed, our student populations and their needs and learning styles have evolved as well. In the past, I have noticed some reticence among some intercultural writers to participate in class, which could indicate that those students failed to understand the value of the knowledge we, as writing instructors, try to help them acquire. Some of students' seeming reluctance may have stemmed from the fact that they could not establish connections between what they learned in the writing classroom and how they learned outside the classroom, which may, in turn, result in students' apparent lack of interest or motivation. In my opinion, this challenge posits another perfect opportunity for writing instructors who should keep building bridges among those perceived disconnects. By designing classroom activities that promote students' active participation in the learning process, writing instructors may be able to aid intercultural writers learn how to communicate in a global world while they consciously decide how to adopt to and adapt new literacies. Furthermore, we should always create activities that encourage students not only to consume but, most importantly, to produce knowledge while using all the technology that has become an integral part of their lives (George, 2002; Trimbur, 2002).

It is my belief that combining sound theoretical and pedagogical practices in the intercultural writing classroom could be beneficial to both instructors and intercultural writers for three main reasons. Firstly, if writing instructors choose course readings on content that is directly related to our intercultural students' context and interests, they would be familiar with those topics, which could grant a higher participation rate. Secondly, writing instructors should create activities that use various types of social media because that would effectively incorporate and recognize how our students learn and write outside the classroom. Finally, writing instructor should involve their students in classroom assessment activities in which we invite our students to engage in dialogue with us in terms of what is working for them and what could be improved in the class. If writing instructors incorporate those activities in our classrooms, our students' transition into the new academic context and expectations, the writing classroom, may not necessarily be only about compliance but about resistance and negotiation.

This chapter is based on a survey that asked students to reflect on general aspects of their basic writing class (what they had learned so far, what they still needed to work on, and so on), and on specific content-based activities (how activities that used social media helped them with critical thinking, critical writing and knowledge negotiations). In particular, this chapter will report on students' answers to question three in the survey: "How have activities that used social media (YouTube videos, web sites, advertisements, etc.) helped you improve your critical thinking skills?" Many writing instructors and theorists agree upon the fact that technology can help students in the classroom as long as it is used in meaningful ways; furthermore, according to danah boyd (2009), "Educators have a critical role when it comes to helping youth navigate social media. You can help them understand how to make sense of what they're seeing... [T]hey need to understand the structures around them." In an attempt to help intercultural writing students to critically understand and use social media spaces, this chapter will code and analyze my students' answers as they reflected on whether and how class activities that integrate social media had helped them practice and improve their critical thinking skills.

THEORETICAL FRAMEWORK

Much current research in Composition Studies in the United States is based on radical models of instruction which expect students to be participatory in and responsible for their own learning, for, as Brian Huot (2002) asserted, "[w]e have evolved pedagogies that conceive of teaching as a coaching and enabling process" (p. 164). Besides, according to scholars as Catherine McLoughlin and Mark J.W. Lee (2010), "[t]here is a clear imperative for educators and students to move towards a social and participatory pedagogy rather than one based on the acquisition of pre-packaged facts" (para. 8). The word participatory has also acquired different connotations with the utilization of the Web 2.0 platform in the classroom, which includes sites for social networking (Facebook or Twitter); sites where users can share various media (YouTube); or sites where users can upload creative work (podcasts, blogs, etc.) (Greenhow, Robelia, & Hughes, 2009, p. 247). Furthermore, many scholars have also pointed out the advantages of students being more participatory in their own assessment (Black & William, 1998; Boud, 1995; Little, 2005; Nunan, 1988; Oscarson, 1989), mainly because it helps to create life-long learners. However, in academic institutions from other countries, Second Language (L21) and intercultural writers may be part of cultural backgrounds in which those "radical" pedagogies are not such common practices.

Turkey is, to a large extent, perceived as a traditional country with a teacher-centered educational system (Altun & Büyükduman, 2007) where the teacher is conceived as an authoritative figure who passes knowledge to students, who are passive receivers. However, as Altun and Büyükduman (2007) reported in their case study, other researchers, such as Şahin (2001), Tezci and Gürol (2002), among others, have concluded that classes that used social constructivist instructional designs were perceived positively for the most part by both instructors and students. As observed by Professor Hacer Hande Uysal (2007), even if our

intercultural students share cultural backgrounds, or constitute heterogeneous groups, they may still present distinct discrepancies (p. 193). In fact, it may very well be that, in a country like Turkey, where students must pass a highly competitive university entrance exam, some students may consider "constructivist instructional design as 'time consuming,' 'boring,' 'unnecessary,' and 'irrational' because they had to pass their exams having their instruction in an 'untraditional' way" (Altun & Büyükduman, 2007, p. 35); or they may consider that their instructors are trying to assign more work to them (Sener, 2007, p. 7). To me, understanding how students who have already passed that examination understand and view those social constructivist environments represents great possibilities for L2 writing educators. In fact, if we want to respect and promote multicultural and intercultural educational contexts that value students' prior knowledge and experiences, "understanding how [L2 writers] participate in their new academic communities and acquire academic discourses in their second language (L2) has become critical" (Morita, 2004, p. 573).

Writing instructors can engage in various practices in order to help bridge gaps between L2 writers' prior knowledge and academic experiences and the new academic expectations in which those L2 writers may be expected to take on more responsibility for their own learning. For example, we could utilize self-assessment and reflection activities on the one hand and activities that incorporate social media on the other hand in our classrooms as research tools so that we can discover ways in which we can help construct those bridges among perceived disconnects. That entails a deep commitment to our students because, although it is true that "writing academic assignments causes people to 'change their speech', to take on particular identities," (Ivanič, 1998, p. 7) we should ensure that our classroom environments are not alienating our intercultural writing students in the sense that certain identities are preferred and/or more valued and, thus, forced upon them. Furthermore, we need to be careful not to perpetuate cultural myths about others or solely reinforce Western cultural values. As the New London Group (2000) posited, "[h]ow do we ensure that differences of culture, language, and gender are not barriers to educational success? And what are the implications of these differences for literacy pedagogy?" (p. 10) How do we help L2 writers without imposing cultural values that may ostracize them or lead them to pure mimicry so they can fit in?

That emphasis on respecting and promoting multiliteracies and multiple identities has influenced disciplines such as Composition Studies and L2 writing in terms of what is taught in class and whose knowledge counts as valid. In an effort to help students succeed in their academic lives, scholars in the fields of composition studies and L2 writing teach writers to acquire new vocabulary and to adopt new identity features that will help them succeed in the academic world, which is their new discourse community (Bizzell, 1992; Brodkey, 1987; Brown et al., 1993; Bruffee, 1986; Faigley, 1985). Those new tools taught to students will also help them make sense of reality, for rhetoric is, according to Berlin (2003), a way of interpreting the world (p. 719).

Again, composition instructors need to be careful, for if students are simple recipients of knowledge, what is there for them to choose? How can people, who are considered to have no power and who are 'consumers' rather than 'producers,' (de Certeau) enact any agency and exert change? One should not despair, though, for there is hope for students and teachers. In fact, scholars such as Anderson (2003) assert that, nowadays, our students are prosumers, which he defines as people who both consume and produce; in his multimedia essay on prosumers, he asserts that "[e]quipping students to participate in new media discourses empowers them to act in a world in which the knowledge currencies are increasingly digital." Thus, our classrooms need to become spaces where some seemingly strict borders between

concepts and practices such as written and visual texts (Trimbur, 2002; Olson, 2002), and notions of consumer and producer, among others, must be constantly negotiated and blurred. Writing instructors can help their students acquire and negotiate skills to communicate effectively with a global audience in ways that are aligned with their experiences outside the classroom. Thus, if L2 writing instructors design their courses incorporating activities that offer spaces in which our intercultural learners can use and incorporate their prior knowledge (either on a particular topic or on how to compose multimedia texts that are parallel to how our students learn and communicate outside the classroom), our L2 writing classrooms will become a place in which negotiations can happen, and in which multiliteracies and intercultural identities are truly valued and pondered. By incorporating activities that use Web 2.0 as a platform, our classroom may become a space where "knowledge is decentralized, accessible, and co-constructed by and among a broad base of users" (Greenhow, Robelia & Hughes, 2009, p. 247).

It is my belief, based on years of informal observation, that students do enact resistance and power in critical classrooms; one way in which that negotiation can be observed is through self-assessment and reflection activities. According to a synthesis on L2 writing research written by Leki, Cumming & Silva (2008), self-assessment has been used in L2 writing classrooms in three different ways. First, in exams that try to place students based on their ability (Alderson, 2005; Bachman & Palmer, 1999; Ekbatani and Pierson, 2000); secondly, for students to state their own objectives and then check their own progress (Cumming, 1986; Cumming, Busch, & Zhou, 2002; Hoffman, 1998); and thirdly, as part of reflective essays in portfolios (p. 86). Much research in the field of Composition Studies and L2 Writing has praised the value of reflection and classroom self-assessment activities for how they help students to improve their writing abilities (Black & William,

1998, 2006; Black et al., 2003; Butler & Lee, 2010; Daugherty and Ecclestone, 2006; Ekbatani, 2000; Gardner, 2006). However, not much research has focused on other advantages of self-assessment in the classroom to identify how it may help students negotiate among identity features.

Reflection can also be practiced in less formal (non-evaluative) situations and then become part of daily classroom activities, which is an area that has not been widely explored in L2 writing. Reflection is dialectical2 and vital to learning how to write and is, thus, close to current pedagogical practices in critical pedagogy and composition studies, which value students being more involved in their learning process. Besides, self-reflection is also an intrinsic value of some types of social media, such as personal websites or social network profiles because, in those, "authors evaluate how their self-as-presented matches the self they envision to be at their own core. Identity development and self-learning thus operate in tandem" (Stern, 2008, p. 114). Thus, I strongly believe that students' reflection can become pedagogical when it is practiced both in surveys that ask them reflect on what they have learned and they still need to practice more, and in activities that use social media as a space in which they can negotiate among various identities to construct meaning and texts. If writing instructors offer students opportunities to reflect, we will probably observe instances of negotiation (resistance and/or acceptance, among other possibilities), be they of identity traits (good student, student expert, among others), or of power (students sharing some responsibility in their learning process, but also in what counts as valid knowledge). As a consequence, if we do not provide students with opportunities to reflect through self-assessment activities, a great opportunity for them to (learn to) negotiate in their new academic environment may be missing.

At this point, I should acknowledge I do not consider either self-assessment, or technology in general and social media in particular to be

neutral; quite on the contrary, I am aware that the "revolutionary" (postmodernist or not) theories of teaching those tools are based on value Western models (of teaching, of knowledge construction and so on). As a consequence, those theories and practices may unwillingly help to "impose" certain values on students who come from non-Western contexts. According to Chandra Talpade Mohanty (2003), in order for alternative knowledges to be recognized, there needs to be "systemic[atically] politicized practices of teaching and learning" (p. 148). We, as composition teachers in intercultural, multiliteracies, multi identities contexts need to help create spaces that can accommodate diverse populations and carefully draft self-assessment activities that are informed by critical theories and pedagogies. If we resist "in self-conscious engagement with dominant, normative discourses and representations and in the active creation of oppositional analytic and cultural spaces," (p. 148) then we will have created those spaces.

As aforementioned, reflection in self-assessment can lead to negotiations between students and their instructors. Self-assessment activities that encourage students to reflect on their writing and inner selves as writers allow those students to negotiate their knowledge (both prior and acquired) at the same time that they engage with existing (and sometimes preferred) discourses in the academic world. Because students can participate in those negotiations, they can also start acquiring and negotiating different voices that are informed by the identities they inhabit through the various discourses they are acquiring.

METHODS

Research Site and Participants

This chapter is part of a larger study that aims to identify and analyze ways in which first year intercultural writing students in a private university in Istanbul, Turkey, interpret/understand the impact of social media on their composition practices, critical thinking and knowledge negotiations processes. In particular, this chapter attempts to understand how first year intercultural writing students reflect on and assess how activities that use social media have helped them with negotiations of knowledge via critical thinking.

This study has taken place in a private university located in Istanbul; our university caters for various student populations: firstly, many of our students come from rather affluent families, but the percentage of students on a full or half scholarship has been increasing in the past few years; some of those scholarships are for students from remote and economically challenged regions of the country. Overall, our university accepts students who score within the 10.000 highest scores in the national university entrance exam, which in Turkish is called Öğrenci Seçme Sınavı (ÖSS). About 1.5 million students across the country prepare for that examination and compete for one of the 450.000 available spaces.

Upon passing that exam and being admitted to the university, all students must take the TOEFL exam because the language of instruction at this university is English. If students do not obtain the necessary TOEFL entry score, then they need to enroll in language courses at the English language department where they stay until they pass the TOEFL exam. Most students spend an average of one semester taking English classes and one of the reasons why our students may need such a short period of time is that many of them have graduated from an American high school and are used to an English instruction environment, or some other private high school and are also fluent in English. The students who come from low income families and remote areas in the country have attended public high schools and their level of English is lower. On the other hand, students who come from low income families and remote areas in the country have attended public high schools and their level of English may be lower.

Consequently, the level of competence in our students is rather heterogeneous.

Once students pass the TOEFL exam and are admitted to the university, one of the first core courses they need to take is Basic Academic Writing, where we teach students to write analytical summaries and syntheses. COMM101 is a course that aims to teach the same skills and has a common syllabus, but each instructor can tailor the course to a particular content. Personally, I teach a Basic Writing course that focuses on popular culture and new media, and I let my students choose their own research topics. Besides, my COMM101 introduces students to arguments and rhetorical strategies, something no other instructor does. In the spring 2013 semester, I taught four sections of COMM 101 in which a total of 52 students were registered. The day the mid-semester survey was due, 46 students were present.

Social Media in Turkey

Turkey is a market where telecommunications, such as mobile telephony, has thrived in the last few years; on the contrary, social media is a rather new phenomenon. Sites like YouTube have been recently banned due to political censorship. Nowadays, YouTube can be accessed, but other social media such as Twitter and Facebook have been under scrutiny during the past month because, according to Prime Minister Erdoğan, they have been used "to incite and organize collective action" (Rheingold, 2008 p. 225). Ever since a group of peaceful protestors camped at Gezi Park in the center of Istanbul, mostly Twitter, and to a lesser extent, Facebook, have been used to inform people both in Turkey and around the world about the recent political protests against Erdoğan and his politics.

Notwithstanding the current situation in Turkey, this project was conducted before the aforementioned events; thus, when I was trying to obtain information to understand how young people in general and my students in particular use social media in Turkey, none of the students referred to any of the current events in Turkey, for they had not occurred yet. On the day we were discussing social media and activism, I asked three of my groups to write about the types of social media they use and the purposes they use those media for (the fourth group was not included in this activity due to time constraints). As it can be observed in Figure 1, most of the 36 students who were in class on the day we worked on this topic use Facebook; the second most used social medium is Twitter with 21 student answers; the third most popular social medium is Instagram, which students use to share their pictures. Interestingly enough, only four students admitted to using YouTube on a regular basis. Another surprising finding was that four students considered "the internet" as a social medium. Other types of media mentioned were email, newspapers, email, but were only mentioned by a student at a time so they have been labeled as "Other."

Why Young People Use Social Media in Turkey

In my opinion, Internet fulfills everything that I need to learn. I can read daily news, watch TV episodes, listen to music from stations on internet.

Facebook was identified as the most widely used type of social media, and most of the students claimed they use it for entertainment purposes: to have fun. Thus, they post pictures, and chat to friends who do not live in the same city or country. To a much lesser extent (three answers), students use Facebook to be informed about current events and to read about people's opinions on a given topic. On the other hand, fourteen students identified Twitter as their favorite type of social media to follow news and political events throughout the world and in Turkey. They asserted that expediency in Twitter was the most important factor why they choose it to be informed about the latest

Figure 1. Different types of social media my students use

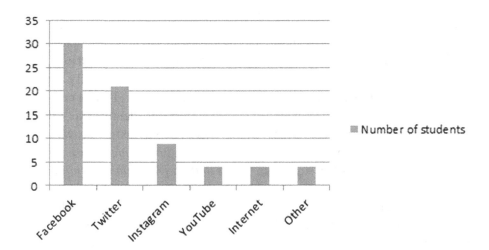

news. However, a few students also noted that Facebook and Twitter provided personal opinions on recent news, and that if they wanted objective portrayals, they read newspapers. Instagram was identified as the third most widely used type of social media, but it was identified as a place to simply share pictures. Only a few students mentioned using YouTube and the reasons why they use that social medium is to share videos. None of the students identified new media or social media as potential learning tools that could be used for learning purposes.

Methods of Data Collection

My overall project aims to understand how intercultural writers at a private university in Istanbul understood/interpreted how social media affects their writing practices, critical thinking and negotiating skills. In particular, this chapter uses only surveys as data, which means no triangulation could be accomplished. Besides, I did not expect to attain replicability; what I wished to accomplish was, and still is, an understanding of how students from a highly privileged institution in a so-called traditional educational system viewed social media in general and in the classroom. To that purpose, I collected two different kinds of documents: a survey that asked students three questions about the class in general and three questions about certain activities in particular; and a paragraph on which students identified what types of social media they used in particular and for what purposes.

Two months into the semester, I asked students to type up the answers to a six-question survey, which was anonymous because I wanted students to be completely honest and practice critical thinking and writing while answering those questions. About two weeks after the first survey we were discussing new media and activism, so I asked students to write about the different types of social media young people in Turkey generally use and the ones each one of them in particular engage

with. They also needed to write about the frequency with which they use social media; finally, I also asked them to inform me about what purposes motivated them to engage with the various types of social media. The latter informal activity is used to describe how social media are used in general in this country and in the research site I have chosen in particular.

Methods of Data Analysis: Analysis of Rhetorical Strategies

I analyzed students' surveys in order to answer research question number three, "How have the activities that used social media (YouTube videos, websites, advertisements, etc.) helped you improve your critical thinking skills? Consequently, I looked for rhetorical strategies students use to negotiate identities and knowledge in self-assessment activities. I read students' answers to self-assessment and started highlighting answers that seemed to fit into patterns of rhetorical strategies, such as making statements, or giving advice. Once I had highlighted all answers, I created a map of answers that I used to see larger patterns, namely identity traits those L2 writers were using and how those patterns related to one another. After creating that map, I reread students' responses trying to identify some cross analysis among categories. Thus, I came up with the five most frequent identity traits these intercultural writers inhabited as they answered self-assessment activities: *social media user/visual learner, self as author, good student, and resisting writer/student*, and *negotiating writer/student*. Interestingly enough, the cross-analysis allowed me to observe that students were switching from visual learner to self as author and vice versa, and that students who started out by resisting certain questions and/or the content of the class, then moved on to engaging in negotiations as to how the class could be improved (see Figure 2 for more detailed relationship among identity traits).

Figure 2. Map of identity traits in survey question number 3

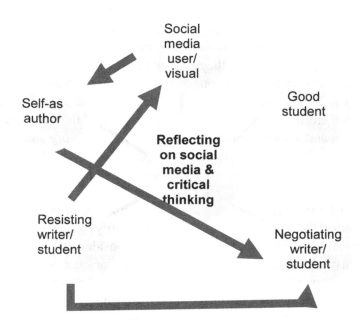

In this research project, I was interested in analyzing whether students utilized acquired knowledge in self-assessment activities, especially because the survey in general asked students to reflect on what they had learned. Thus, in students' reflection of their own writing, I looked for themes that related to: 1) power dynamics or whether students felt they had any power over what was considered valuable knowledge; and 2) evaluation of assignments or how students talked or wrote about how they saw social media. Overall, as Canagarajah (1999, 2002) and Lee (2008) have done in their work, I wanted investigate whether "the hybrid cultural background of the writers has influenced their negotiation of established genres and conventions" (Matsuda et al., 2003, 159).

Research Models

Once I had coded students' answers, I used key concepts from Speech Act Theory, which helped me identify and analyze rhetorical strategies such as asserting, suggesting, requesting, claiming, thanking, inter alia (Searle, Kiefer & Bierwisch et al., 1980). I also used Ivanič's (1998) theories of writing and identity that aided me to categorize students' identity traits when they reflected on whether and how social media in particular had helped them become more critical thinkers. In that sense, Ivanič's (1998) concept of "self as author," (p. 26) or how a writer portrays her/his persona as an authority became a helpful framework. Finally, Turkle's (1995) definition of identity as "a set of roles that can be mixed and matched," (p. 180) also became useful when understanding how students moved from one identity to (an)other. With all those research models in mind, I read what students wrote in order to understand what they were doing while engaging in reflection and self-assessment, namely whether they inhabited or positioned themselves in various identities and, thus, negotiated different roles in the classroom through social media.

RESULTS

This section analyzes students' answers to question three in the survey. Namely, I observed instances in which students used critical thinking as they were reflecting on the activities that focused on social media. In particular, I will categorize how students used various rhetorical strategies to inhabit different identities and, thus engage both in negotiations of knowledge and of various roles in the classroom.

Identities L2 Writers Inhabited to Negotiate Knowledge

As I read students' answers, some themes or identities kept repeating themselves; this section will report on the five most frequently inhabited identities: *social media user/visual learner, self as author, good student, and resisting writer/student,* and *negotiating writer/student.* Each identity is subdivided into various categories that represent the various rhetorical strategies students used to position themselves in those identities.

Social Media User/Visual Learner

In many of their responses, students positioned themselves as learners who value activities that use visual texts and social media. By valuing those activities, they were also able to establish connections between the activities and/or readings and their experiences outside the classroom. In order to position themselves in this particular identity, students used asserting or making statements as a rhetorical strategy. Overall, student responses in this section can be grouped in three themes: Firstly, students valued activities that used visual elements on how much easier it was for them to focus on taught concepts; thus, some of the recorder answers stated that: "visual effects are more effective than the other ones," "while watching videos or advertisements, we have the possibility to see what we talk about," "we can be more attached with the subject with visual elements," or even "[w]hen we watch videos about our subjects, we can easily focus on the topic."

A second theme that emerged was that students were able to identify connections between class activities and their lives outside the classroom. In this subcategory some students asserted that "social media is more related to our lives," or "I can be more focused on the lesson when using social media."

Thirdly, students positioned themselves in this identity by asserting that social media helped them consider a topic from various perspectives and, thus, practice critical thinking. Consequently, some students asserted that "social media appealed us from many aspects," which another student phrased as "I have watched educational videos from YouTube which are about certain topics we focus on in our classes. By watching them, I am able to criticize the topic from different perspectives."

Finally, a group of responses in this identity started out by students positioning themselves as social media users/visual learner, and then transitioned to inhabiting the identity of "self as author." One of the student's response identified the connection between the reading on gender stereotypes, a video we watched about gender in the media, and then concluded that "if I see the similar things in my life, I can apply the critical thinking skills right away."

Self as Author

As I read students' responses to this survey question, it became obvious that, at times, these intercultural writers viewed themselves as writers who already knew or understood how to do certain things in spite of the fact that they were starting to learn how to write effective academic essays. In that sense, this identity feature is a smooth transition from the social media user/visual learner; students could identify the value of class activities that used visual materials and social media, consequently, they could also strongly assert what they had accomplished or already knew how to do. In this identity feature, the most widely used rhetorical strategy was making statements or asserting.

Three different topics emerged in this category. Firstly, students were very assertive in terms of understanding skills related to the process of writing: "When we are watching a video, taking notes on sheets simultaneously improves my perception when I was writing, and it develops my attention, which is extremely low." Other students also showed awareness of rhetorical conventions: "I think those activities helped me to improve my judgment skills on ethos, pathos, and logos approaches. Hence, I can analyze the main purpose and understand the strategy the authors used to give their messages to their audience;" or "[w]e can also easily understand rhetorical context when we do activities that used social media."

Another set of answers focused on how students could establish connections among readings (synthesis), or between readings and life outside the classroom. Here are a few examples: "If I see similar things in my life, I can apply critical thinking," or "the subjects in the articles have their examples in real life as well."

A final common topic I observed had to do with how students were aware of how any topic could be discussed and interpreted from various perspectives (critical thinking) and how that was easily accomplished in activities that used social media. Thus, some students asserted, "those activities all had great influence on me. I need to criticize the topic because I it understand better when I use my correlation between my opinion and their opinion." Another student also stated that those activities "taught me to look on a certain video or [visual] aid from different perspectives and analyze the aim for publishing it and thus more understanding on how I should deal with it."

From Resisting to Negotiating Student

Although less students inhabited this identity in their answers, I have decided to include it before analyzing the identity trait of "good student" because, to me, this category represents a smooth transition for students who positioned themselves as "self as author;" that transition showed that, by knowing what works for them, they could also challenge or resist certain aspects of the class they may have found of little value. Besides, even if these students are still learning how to write academic papers, they are capable of resisting and pushing the norms of English, as Ming-Zhan Lu (1998) has asserted. Finally, according to Canagarajah (1999), not all educational practices have to lead to assimilation; thus, these intercultural writers used reflection in this surveys to resist or even negotiate certain assignments by either proposing alternatives or talking back to instructor.

1. Resisting certain activities and/or readings. The first rhetorical strategy students used to resist certain activities was asserting or making statements. A student claimed that "[s]ome texts give too much theoretical information, but don't show how to use it practically," and another author asserted "when we always read, it's boring."

2. Rejecting the question. Under this theme, I observed that some students asserted that social media had not affected their critical thinking skills in any way. Thus, some of the students' answers were: "they didn't affect me about any skills," "no improvement," or simply leaving the answer blank. By far, one of the most resisting students was rather vocal about his rejection of certain activities. He mostly focused his answers on a video we watched in class, which analyzed how women were generally portrayed as objects in the media and the effects of that portrayal on women. The student strongly opposed that video and asserted that activities that used

social media "haven't helped me at all... I want to add, that video about women being used for commercials, was actually really bad for my nerves. Because the woman making the speech looks at the situation from only one angle. And that angle is a reflection from her feminist side."

3. From resisting to negotiating. In this subcategory, students moved from resisting certain activities or readings to proposing solutions. Consequently, one the most frequently used rhetorical strategies in this category was giving advice on what works better for them. A student said "Visual media is more useful than documented sources for some people;" another answer reported that "[i]t is better to use videos or other visuals."

Good Student

For the purpose of this study, I interpret "good student" as an identity in which students agree with what the instructor asks. Students may inhabit that identity by using this survey question as a space in which they inform their instructor that they have agree with the fact that activities that focus on social media helped them improve their critical thinking skills, and/or they could also thank the instructors. Overall, the answers in this category usually provide few supporting evidence for students' claims and are mostly opinion-based.

1. Agreeing with the instructor's questions. The first rhetorical strategy used in this category was making statements to agree with instructor's ideas. Thus, some of the students answers stated that social media "made the lesson more interesting and got my attention;" other students said "I think that activities that use social media are fun," "they are really helpful;" or "[u]sage of social media, especially videos and blogs, makes it a lot easier to understand the topic."

2. The second theme that emerged in the category of a good student used thanking as a rhetorical strategy. Therefore, a student said: "Thanks to this course I really care about it (trustworthiness of social media) now," another student said that the activities helped him/her "judge the realities I had never thought about before."

3. Recognizing instructor's authority. In this final theme, a student also used making statements or asserting as a rhetorical strategy to inhabit the identity of a good student who recognizes the instructor as the authority in the classroom: "When the professor provided a short clip which was about advertisement, we can directly understand what's the meaning of a stereotype."

DISCUSSION

I believe this research study will contribute to current research on students' reflection in intercultural writing and Second Language (L2) contexts by providing insights on how these students negotiated among various identities in order to ask for their prior knowledge and various learning styles to be recognized. One of my initial goals was to understand how intercultural writers in a context that, educationally speaking, may be deemed as traditional wrote about how they perceived social media's effect on their critical thinking skills.

The conclusions that I can draw from my findings is that this research has explored how students moved from one identity to another and, thus, engaged in an authentic dialogue with their instructor to negotiate not only what they thought worked better for them, but also what they thought should count as valid knowledge and content material. This project has, consequently, explored the intersections between various identity traits (*social media user/visual learner*), *self as author, and resisting writer/students,* and *negotiating writer/student*) and intercultural writers understanding and practice of self-reflection or self-assessment. This section analyzes the main findings; namely, the relationship between rhetorical strategies and identity inhabiting, and the relationship between rhetorical strategies and negotiations of knowledge.

Finding One: Rhetorical Strategies Students Used to Position Themselves in Various Identity Traits

As I started analyzing students' answers, it was clear to me that students utilized various rhetorical strategies to position themselves in various identities. The identities I have identified here are "institutional roles" (Canagarajah, 2004), and focus on student identity features in particular because, after all, this research project focused on intercultural students/writers. Based on the results outlined in the previous section, the most commonly inhabited identities were social media user/ visual learner, self as author, and good student. To a lesser extent, students also positioned themselves as resisting-negotiating student.

The analysis section starts by interpreting why the most used rhetorical strategy was asserting both as students inhabited the identity trait of *social media user/visual learner* and of *self as author*. As it has been mentioned in the methods section of this chapter, most of the students in my classes have graduated from private high schools and have traveled on various occasions to other countries, mostly to England and the United States; consequently, they are very familiar with the English-instruction institutions and certain pedagogical practices and portrayed themselves as very assertive writers. That level of familiarity could be an explanation as to why these intercultural writers inhabited many times the identity trait of self as author. Students at that stage had already appropriated some of the "authoritative discourse" practices. Another plausible explanation would be that our students "have grown up in a technology saturated and an image-rich culture, questions of

communication and composition absolutely will include the visual, not as attendant to the verbal but as complex communication intricately related to the world around them" (George, 2002, p. 32). Therefore, being exposed to and composing texts that combine visual, written and aural media is second nature to them. As my intercultural writers positioned themselves as self as author, they clearly stated their knowledge and understanding of rhetorical conventions, and identified connections between what was being taught in the classroom and their prior experiences outside the classroom. That yielded a very fascinating finding in this project: students clearly engaged in conversations and dialogue of identities. In most of the answers, except those classified under the good student identity, students seem to move from one identity to (an)other, which resonates with Turkle's (1995) theory of "identity as a set of roles that can be mixed and matched, whose diverse demands need to be negotiated" (p. 180). Providing intercultural writers with opportunities to reflect on their own writing can help them engage in dialogue with their instructor.

Another fascinating finding in this research project came from the complexity of and, sometimes, even seemingly contradictory, responses these intercultural writers provided. As a researcher and an educator, it was fascinating for me to see how these intercultural writers sometimes talked about themselves as being almost experts in their own writing. In spite of the fact that self-assessment and reflection may very well be Western concepts, it is also true that English has become a world language; consequently, many L2 writers from other countries are somehow familiarized with those two concepts as well as with some other academic literacy practices.

In addition to these writers' prior experience with English-speaking academic context, as participation in the discourse of self-assessment increased, they appropriated some of that language to show their instructor that they have learned some lessons and could then apply them in their writing. However, some students also portrayed themselves as good students who agreed with everything she said because, after all, she is the authority figure. On the other hand, as students gained more confidence in themselves and their abilities, they seemed to shift toward the identity trait of self as author. However, I do not wish to imply that there is a unique explanation to that, a kind of cause-effect relationship between an increasing participation in self-assessment and a rise in writer's awareness. I did observe, though, that as students participated more in certain discourses, namely self-assessment, they seemed more comfortable in the cultural and social expectations of that genre. It is also true that some students may have been already familiar with self-assessment prior to this class.

Another possible explanation for this seemingly contradictory finding, namely that these intercultural did not want to share authority with the instructor while at the same time they portrayed themselves as assertive writers who knew how to do certain things prior to attending this class, could be that no identity trait is a clearly and distinctly separated from other traits. Quite on the contrary, I would assert that the fact that these L2 writers presented such a range of identity traits shows that our identities as writers are multiple, complex and interconnected.

Finding Two: Rhetorical Strategies L2 Writers Used to Negotiate Knowledge

Although the identity traits of *resisting writer/ student* and *negotiating writer/student* are the least inhabited ones, valuable conclusions can be inferred from students' answers as they positioned themselves in those identity traits, especially because they showed resistance to certain practices. The most fascinating finding in that identity trait was to see how some students used silence as a rhetorical strategy to show resistance. At first, I was puzzled by some students' choice not to answer

that survey question. However, when I stopped looking at the data as a researcher and I looked at it as an L2 and intercultural writer myself, I could identify with the decision of choosing not to answer certain questions. Furthermore, another equally fascinating finding was to see how a student strongly opposed certain activities that used social media. At first, I was shocked because I had assumed that, as a somewhat experienced instructor, I knew what was best for my students; however, that particular student helped me realize that every topic we discuss in class should be analyzed from various perspectives in order for our classrooms to truly embody critical thinking.

Overall, the conclusion I can arrive at is that students' answers show that, when given the opportunity, intercultural writers can engage in negotiations of knowledge with their instructors by asserting that they already possess some knowledge that should be valued and incorporated in the classroom. Resistance was a rhetorical strategy used to engage in negotiations. Thus, providing our students with opportunities to engage in reflection will help them "become prepared for and adapt themselves to the economic challenges of affiliation with globalization, the information society and the knowledge and skills they demand. In other words, they are in the process of negotiation on how to find a proper combination of local and global" (Koç, 2006, p. 41). I would like to add, though, that we should not strive only for adopting but also for adapting certain practices through negotiations.

Furthermore, some of the intercultural writers in my classes presented identity traits that denoted that they were very reassured about what they already knew; even more so, some of those writers, at times, switched roles with their instructor in the sense that they knew what worked for them. To me, identifying instances in which power dynamics were reversed was very illuminating. Although I am conscious of the fact that students' power may only apply to this particular context, the L2 writing classroom as a "linguistic habitus" (Bourdieu,

1991, p. 37), it was nonetheless inspiring to see how some of these intercultural writers were very assertive about their prior knowledge.

I have used Bourdieu's concept of *tabula rasa* to make meaning of these intercultural writers' prior experiences and knowledge. I assert that students do not come to our classes as blank slates on which we can inscribe information; they already have certain knowledge that we, as writing instructors, should honor and respect. Besides, we should create spaces in which we help those students share that prior knowledge with their peers and their instructors. I believe it is in the creation of those spaces (third spaces, according to Homi Bhabha) that we will be able to accomplish what educational settings that are informed by social constructivism purport to do, which is encouraging students to be more participatory in and responsible for their own learning. Writing instructors working in intercultural environments should be flexible enough to accommodate those social constructivist theories that inform their pedagogies to fit students' needs in a given context. Although some research in Turkey has proven that certain student populations did find social constructivist instructional design useful, we cannot and should not assume that all the different populations (different social classes and ethnicities, just to name two) may welcome those practices. In our classrooms, we should combine carefully designed activities that use social media to engage students in knowledge consumption and production, and self-assessment activities that create spaces that promote reflection and negotiations. By combining those tools and activities, our classrooms could become those alternative spaces in which our students can practice how to adopt and adapt to new and global literacies (Mills, 2011).

RECOMMENDATIONS

Limitations of the Study and Suggestions for Further Research

This study only collected one type of data: surveys. Thus, all the conclusions are based on my interpretations (although those are based on theoretical premises) of students' answers. This study could have had a second opinion if I had been able to send my analysis to students so they could check that my interpretations truly mirrored what they were trying to accomplish. However, because the first and foremost objective of the survey was anonymity so I could provide a safe space for my students to honestly "talk back to me," I could not send my interpretations to the students, for I did not know who wrote what. That could be addressed in a future project, which should collect at least three different types of sources. Besides, a future project that wishes to understand the changes multicultural writers undergo should use qualitative methods to collect data (Greenhow, Robelia, & Hughes, p. 246) over a more extended period of time. Thus, in a future project, an instructor could observe class on days in which students are interacting with and writing while using social media; one could also collect students' samples of multimodal and multimedia writing to observe the kinds of negotiations (of knowledge, meaning, and identities) they engaged in as they composed texts using social media that are written for a global audience. Finally, interviewing a purposeful sample of students to ask whether the instructor's analysis seems fair and close to their intentions would grant triangulation and truly involve our students in the process.

REFERENCES

Altun, S., & Büyükduman, F. I. (2007). Teacher and student beliefs on constructivist instructional design: A case study. *Educational Sciences: Theory and Practice, 7*(1), 30–39.

Anderson, D. (2003). Prosumer approaches to new media composition: Consumption and production in continuum. *Kairos, 8*(1).

Berlin, J. (2003). Rhetoric and ideology in the writing classroom. In V. Villanueva (Ed.), *Cross-talk in comp theory* (2nd ed., pp. 717–737). Urbana, IL: NCTE.

Bizzell, P. (1992). *Academic discourse and critical consciousness*. Pittsburgh, PA: University of Pittsburgh Press.

Black, P. J., & Wiliam, D. (1998). *Inside the black box*. London: GL Assessment.

Boud, D. (1995). *Enhancing learning through self-assessment*. London: Kogan Page.

Bourdieu, P. (1991). *Language & symbolic power*. Cambridge, MA: Harvard University Press.

Boyd, d. (2009, April). *Living and learning with social media*. Paper presented at the Penn State Symposium for Teaching and Learning with Technology. State College, PA. Retrieved from http://www.danah.org/papers/talks/PennState2009.html

Brodkey, L. (1987). *Academic writing as social practice*. Philadelphia, PA: Temple University Press.

Brown, A. L., Ash, D., Rutherford, M., Nakagawa, K., Gordon, A., & Campione, J. C. (1993). Distributed expertise in the classroom. In G. Salomon (Ed.), *Distributed cognitions: Psychological and education considerations* (pp. 188–228). Cambridge, UK: Cambridge University Press.

Bruffee, K. A. (1986). Social construction, language and the authority of knowledge –A bibliographical essay. *College English, 48*, 773–790. doi:10.2307/376723

Byram, M. (1997). *Teaching and assessing intercultural communicative competence*. Clevedon, UK: Multilingual Matters Ltd.

Canagarajah, A. S. (1999). *Resisting linguistic imperialism in English teaching*. Oxford, UK: Oxford University Press.

Canagarajah, A. S. (2002). *Critical academic writing and multilingual students*. Ann Arbor, MI: University of Michigan Press.

Canagarajah, A. S. (2004). Multilingual writers and the struggle for voice: Assessing some approaches. In A. Blackledge, & A. Pavlenko (Eds.), *Negotiation of identities in multilingual contexts* (pp. 266–289). Clevedon, UK: Multilingual Matters Ltd.

Faigley, L. (1985). Nonacademic writing: The social perspective. In L. Odell, & D. Goswami (Eds.), *Writing in nonacademic settings* (pp. 231–248). New York: Guilford.

George, D. (2002). From analysis to design: Visual communication in the teaching of writing. *College Composition and Communication, 54*(1), 11–39. doi:10.2307/1512100

Greenhow, C., Robelia, B., & Hughes, J. E. (2009). Learning, teaching, and scholarship in a digital age: Web 2.0 and classroom research: What path should we take now? *Educational Researcher, 38*(4), 246–259. doi:10.3102/0013189X09336671

Huot, B. (2002). Toward a new discourse of assessment for the college writing classroom. *College English, 65*(2), 163–180. doi:10.2307/3250761

Ivanič, R. (1998). *Writing and identity: The discoursal construction of identity in academic writing*. Philadelphia, PA: Benjamins. doi:10.1075/swll.5

Jenkins, H. (2006). *Convergence culture: Where old and new media collide*. New York, London: New York University Press.

Koç, M. (2006). Cultural identity crisis in the age of globalization and technology. *The Turkish Online Journal of Educational Technology*, *5*(1), 37–43.

Lee, H. (2008). Learner agency and identity in second language writing. *International Journal of Applied Linguistics*, *156*, 109–128. doi:10.2143/ITL.156.0.2034425

Leki, I., Cumming, A., & Silva, T. (2008). *A synthesis of research on second language writing in English*. New York, London: Routledge.

Little, D. (2005). The common European framework and the European language portfolio: Involving learners and their judgments in the assessment process. *Language Testing*, *22*(3), 321–336. doi:10.1191/0265532205lt311oa

Lu, M. Z. (1998). Reading and writing differences: The problematic of experience. In Jarratt and Worsham (Eds.), Feminism and composition studies: In other words (pp. 239-251). New York: Modern Language Assocation.

Matsuda, P. K., Canagarajah, S., Ken Hyland, L. H., & Warschauer, M. (2003). Changing currents in second language writing research: A colloquium. *Journal of Second Language Writing*, *12*, 151–179. doi:10.1016/S1060-3743(03)00016-X

McLoughlin, C., & Lee, M. J. W. (2010). Personalised and self-regulated learning in the Web 2.0 era: International exemplars of innovative pedagogy using social software. *Australasian Journal of Educational Technology*, *26*, 28–43.

Mills, N. (2011). Situated learning through social networking communities: The development of joint enterprise, mutual engagement, and a shared repertoire. *CALICO Journal*, *28*(2), 345–368.

Mohanty, C. T. (2003). *Feminism without borders: Decolonizing theory, practicing solidarity*. Durham, NC: Duke University Press. doi:10.1215/9780822384649

Morita, N. (2004). Negotiating participation and identity in second language academic communities. *TESOL Quarterly*, *38*(4), 573–603. doi:10.2307/3588281

New London Group. (2000). A pedagogy of multiliteracies: Designing social futures. In B. Cope, & M. Kalantzis (Eds.), *Multiliteracies: Literacy learning and the design of social futures* (pp. 9–37). New York: Routledge.

Nunan, D. (1988). *The learner-centred curriculum*. Cambridge, UK: Cambridge University Press. doi:10.1017/CBO9781139524506

Olson, G. (2002). The death of composition as an intellectual discourse. In G. Olson (Ed.), *Rhetoric and composition as intellectual work* (pp. 3–31). Carbondale, IL: Southern Illinois University Press.

Oscarson, M. (1989). Self-assessment of language proficiency: Rationale and applications. *Language Testing*, *6*, 1–13. doi:10.1177/026553228900600103

Rheingold, H. (2008). Mobile media and political collective action. In J. Katz (Ed.), Handbook of mobile communication studies (pp. 225–239). Boston: MIT Press.

Searle, J. R., Kiefer, F., & Bierwisch, M. (Eds.). (1980). speech act theory and pragmatics. Dordrecht, Holland: Reidel Publishing Company.

Sener, J. (2007). In search of student-generated content in online education. *E-mentor*, *4*, 1–8.

Stern, S. (2008). Producing sites, exploring identities: Youth online authorship. In D. Buckingham (Ed.), *Youth, identity, and digital media* (pp. 95–118). Cambridge, MA: The MIT Press.

Trimbur, J. (2002). Delivering the message: Typography and the materiality of writing. In G. Olson (Ed.), Rhetoric and composition as intellectual work (pp. 188-202). Carbondale & Edwardsville, IL: Southern Illinois University Press.

Turkle, S. (1995). *Life on the screen: Identity in the age of the Internet*. New York: Simon & Schuster.

Turkle, S. (1999). Cyberspace and identity. *Contemporary Sociology*, *28*(6), 643–648. doi:10.2307/2655534

Uysal, H. H. (2007). Tracing the culture behind writing: Rhetorical patterns and bidirectional transfer in L1 and L2 essays of Turkish writers in relation to educational context. *Journal of Second Language Writing*, *17*, 183–207. doi:10.1016/j.jslw.2007.11.003

KEY TERMS AND DEFINITIONS

Composition Practices: Writing process that includes various stages from brainstorming to final draft and involve thinking, reflecting, revising, and rewriting.

Critical Thinking: Active and willing processes of critically understanding, analyzing and utilizing information, which has been acquired by reading or observation.

Intercultural Communication: Examining exchanges and interactions between individuals and their cultures, but also among people from different cultural backgrounds.

Second Language (L2) Writing: Writing produced by people in a language other than their first language. In this context, L2 writing refers to writing in English by speakers of other languages.

Social Media: Any medium of communication that utilizes technology to engage in various activities that involve sharing and exchanging information and knowledge.

ENDNOTES

[1] Any term used to refer to speakers of languages other than English is contested and controversial. For the purpose of this chapter, I have decided to use L2 writers in the theoretical background section because some of the theories I use come from the field of Second Language Writing. However, I will also use the term "intercultural writers" to refer to the students in the particular context I analyze.

[2] Although self-assessments are written pieces per se, I believe they can become dialectical (in a Bakhtinian sense), for they show how students' multiple voices or heteroglossia and discourses (old, new, authoritative, individual) conflate in those reflective activities.

Chapter 11
Digital Literacy Instruction in Afghanistan

Mike Edwards
Washington State University, USA

ABSTRACT

This chapter uses the American military's purchase of a $5.6 million contract to supply the National Military Academy of Afghanistan with laptop computers as the occasion to investigate the complex and overdetermined intersections of digital, administrative, and literacy technologies. These intersections and the challenges they produced for the author as a Western mentor working with Afghan postsecondary instructors in ESL and digital literacies reveal the problematic homogenizing Western economic and cultural assumptions and the intense naturalization of administrative technologies that accompany the denaturalized use of digital and textual technologies in global contexts. The connections of those challenges to recent scholarship in rhetoric and composition highlight the limitations of that scholarship's conception of political economy in a global digital context and also offers new possibilities for imagining hybrid multilingual digital literacies on a global scale.

INTRODUCTION

When I was preparing to deploy to Afghanistan, one of my West Point English Department officer colleagues trained me up on the required protective gear and body armor. Another officer, a Lieutenant Colonel from Physics and Nuclear Engineer-

ing, briefed me on the benefits I would receive, to include what the Army calls danger pay. "It's good money," he said. "But it's not worth your life." He was right: there is an incommensurability there. For the Afghan instructors I worked with, their jobs were in some way worth their lives: it took considerable bravery for them to allow other Afghans to know they worked with Americans. It took considerable bravery for a female medical student to go to school at the National Military

DOI: 10.4018/978-1-4666-4916-3.ch011

Copyright © 2014, IGI Global. Copying or distributing in print or electronic forms without written permission of IGI Global is prohibited.

Academy of Afghanistan (NMAA) when she knew she risked being sprayed in the face with acid, or for a female interpreter to work with the NMAA mentor team after being called a "whore for Americans" by students from the far provinces. What, then, is an income or an education worth?

A second way to ask that question: in Kabul, after a series of back-and-forth emails, the academic advisors, the training branch, the contracting officers, and the education contractors arranged a face-to-face meeting at Camp Eggers. The Afghans who stood to benefit from the projects discussed in the meeting were not included. For the most part, Afghans seldom do business by email. The Western mentor team held the meeting on the second floor of a building constructed out of transmodal shipping containers. We sat in a semicircle in plastic chairs and discussed the relative merits of the various graduate programs the Afghan instructors might attend, as well as the English-language literacy programs, and how much it might cost, and we talked about funding TOEFL prep programs. TOEFL, the Test of English as a Foreign Language, is one of the primary assessment tools for Afghan literacy instructors. We discussed the debate over using literacy in English as an L2 or second language bridge language rather than performing L1 native language literacy education in Dari or Pashto and then moving to L2 literacy. We performed the immaterial labor of putting together literacy education contracts without involving any of the Afghans in the administrative apparatus that we were planning for them.

This chapter examines how that administrative apparatus formed and forms a significant but often invisible component of digital literacy instruction, and how its constituent technologies when taken in conjunction with the inextricable technologies of language literacy and digital literacy are deeply imbricated in the cultural, religious, and economic systems of local cultures even as those cultures are linked to or alienated from global cultures by those very technologies. Computers

as technological objects, through their links to administrative technologies and technologies of literacy, can serve to reveal those often previously invisible links as points of disruption.

BACKGROUND

In 2011, I was a civilian assistant professor at the United States Military Academy at West Point. I deployed to Afghanistan in January and returned in June of that year, as a member of an advisor team with the mission of helping the Afghans to build their postsecondary National Military Academy (NMAA) into what President Karzai has called in public appearances the "crown jewel" of higher education in Afghanistan. While I understand that anecdotes are not equivalent to evidence, part of my method in this chapter is to use the particularities of individual experience in order to attempt to avoid the totalizing essentialisms and reductive binaries often enacted by Western scholars engaging other cultures (see, e.g., Hofstede, 2001). Our advisor team was constituted under the National Training Mission—Afghanistan (NTM—A) as a part of the International Security Assistance Force (ISAF). We stayed at a base on the ISAF military side of Kabul International Airport, again in those steel shipping containers—my shared room was 9 feet wide by 17 feet long, with a window on one end and a door opening into a hallway on the other. To get to NMAA, the team would take two soft-skinned vans and two up-armored SUVs and drive for about 20 minutes around the perimeter of the airfield over to the Afghan military side, and would pass through four guarded security checkpoints in order to arrive at the complex that formerly served as the Soviet-built Air Academy. Those security checkpoints were guarded either by ISAF forces—Belgians when I was there—or by Afghan National Army soldiers. However, ISAF does much of its work by contracting Afghan and foreign vendors to provide nation-building and security services, and in fact, the ISAF presence distorts the local economy: the best-paying jobs go to the English- and computer-literate Afghans who can work as interpreters with the ISAF forces, to the point where government interpreters earn about $665 per month, while government doctors[1] earn about $220 per month. Many of Kabul's remaining professional corps—doctors, programmers, librarians, professors, lawyers, engineers—who can speak English are working as interpreters, engaging in the immaterial labor of language use. Furthermore, according to my colleagues in the ISAF contracting office, the largest dollar-value contract in Afghanistan was not for providing gasoline for military vehicles, or for building roads, or for equipment maintenance. The largest dollar-value contract in Afghanistan was for literacy instruction.

Afghanistan has a deeply communal and tribal culture, and a deeply religious culture, and Afghan economics is deeply influenced by Islam and by the tribal and social nature of the culture. Afghans generally believe that God is just, and that life is often a matter of chance, dependent on God's will rather than on individual self-determination. Understanding the tribal and group-oriented nature of the culture is essential to working with Afghans. In Afghan students, I saw the same considerable cultural resistance to Western notions of autonomous individualism that has been described by many scholars working in the area of second-language literacy learning. Many Afghan men I encountered were highly skilled orators, but tended to be uninterested in the abstract principles of rational argumentation, instead privileging the reliance on performance and rhetorical commonplaces characteristic of a residual oral culture. It took me a long time in working with Afghan faculty to understand that many face-to-face meetings and interactions were for phatic rather than transactional purposes, for maintaining bonds or reinforcing relationships rather than accomplishing tasks or moving the mission forward, and so required rhetorics entirely different from those privileged by the Western tradition.

According to the CIA World Factbook (2012), more than a third of the population of Afghanistan is unemployed, more than a third of the population lives below the poverty line, and about three-quarters of the population is illiterate. The World Bank (2012) estimates the average per capita income to be $470 per year. In the modern era, the nation has seen various levels of conflict and war in the 30-odd years since December 1979. Electricity in downtown Kabul is intermittent. Most Afghans are polylingual, with at least some proficiency in Dari and Pashto, the two official languages. Balochi, Urdu, Nuristani, and Uzbek are not uncommon. Residual oral cultures like that of Afghanistan place a great deal of importance on memorization, and in Afghanistan there are many Dari and Pashto speakers who memorize the Quran without knowing the Arabic that they memorize. Very few Afghans speak Arabic. A significant number of Afghans speak English.

According to Lieutenant General William Caldwell (January–February 2011), who was commander of NTM-A at the time of my deployment there, English served an important military function as a bridge language among Afghanistan's many dialects and also served as "the accepted language for the international aviation community" (p. 25), and so many Afghans were trained in English literacies. Military and police literacy training in Afghanistan employed over 1000 instructors across the country, and additional civilian literacy instruction programs worked to educate between 300,000 and 400,000 Afghans per year between 2002 and 2007 (Caldwell 2011, p. 25). At the time of my deployment, approximately 85% of NMAA cadets studied English as their required foreign language, using the unfortunately dated Defense Language Institute (DLI) American Language Course (ALC) curriculum. This decades-old curriculum was designed to be administered intensively in daily six-hour blocks of classes, with each book in the course taking 30 hours or roughly one week to complete. The books are poorly written and incoherent, and in the hands of inexperienced instructors often served as impediments to learning: I frequently consulted with instructors and offered them guidance to correct errors, unclear points, and obsolete idiomatic expressions in the books. Furthermore, adapting an intensive language curriculum to a semester-long 45-lesson course teaching two books per semester offered its own difficulties in pacing and in ensuring students received adequate learning reinforcement. As it was designed in 2011, the NMAA adaptation of the ALC curriculum required faculty to assign more work outside of class than they or students were willing to undertake, and its outcomes in terms of the pace and consistency of improving language competence suffered as a consequence. That language competency was a necessary component of the technological competency we were also working with the Afghans to promote.

The World Bank estimates that 30% of Afghans have access to electricity. In 2006, according to the most recent United Nations statistics available (2012), Afghanistan had 0.39 computers per 100 people, the third lowest ratio in the world, more than only Rwanda and Cambodia (UNData). Statistics about internet access differ slightly: according to the CIA World Factbook entry for Afghanistan, in 2009, 1 million out of the nation's estimated 30.4 million population, or roughly 3.2 percent, had internet access; according to Afghanistan Internet Usage and Telecommunications Reports, about 4.2 percent of households in 2011 had access to the internet. Afghan students are very different from the privileged undergraduates described by Berry, Hawisher, and Selfe (2012) who "have known little of a world devoid of communication networks" ("Digital literacies, technological diffusion, and globalization"). My own internet access through Afghan Wireless, a major ISP in Kabul where access is common and reliable enough to be relatively inexpensive, cost $88 USD per month, a significant sum even when compared to the monthly salaries of the relatively well-paid interpreters.

In addition to the material economic concerns that promoting literacy (digital and otherwise) in Afghanistan presented, I would also present concerns relating to what some theorists have characterized as immaterial economic concerns. Michael Hardt and Antonio Negri (2000) defined immaterial labor as "labor that produces an immaterial good, such as a service, a cultural product, knowledge, or communication" (p. 290). For Hardt and Negri, "analytical and symbolic tasks" and "the production and manipulation of affect" (p. 293) are varieties of immaterial labor. The immaterial labor students perform in language and literacy learning, whether L1 or L2, constitutes economically valuable work, but not necessarily valuable in the conventional market-oriented capitalist way we think of value for exchange. During his tenure as the NATO International Security Assistance Force (ISAF) commander, General David Petraeus repeatedly asserted that literacy is both a necessary component of security in Afghanistan and a significant component of the infrastructure ISAF attempted to build over there. There are significant challenges in promoting post-print literacy education in a largely residual oral culture. ISAF's massive nation-building effort was in many ways an educational effort, especially in the focus that General Caldwell, Commander of the subordinate NATO Training Mission—Afghanistan (NTM-A), brought to the project. Caldwell (13 Sep. 2010) wrote that literacy "is a matter of life and death in Afghanistan," and that it additionally serves as "the essential enabler that addresses not only life and death issues, but. . . the ability to enforce accountability, the opportunity to attend professional. . . education, particularly specialized skills taught in technical schools and continued education, and the knowledge to combat corruption."

What happens if we think about literacy education as immaterial labor in relation to General Caldwell's note that in September 2010, "the NATO training mission ha[d] about 27,000 recruits from the Afghan army and police in. . . literacy programs at any given time," and that "[t]hat number [would] grow to. . . 100,000 by June of [2011]"? Can we consider so-called stability operations to be a form of immaterial labor, and if so, what do we consider to be the product—the economic output—of stability operations in Afghanistan?

It depends on how far in the future one looks for the positive economic effects of having a stable government, one might well reply. But economic activity does not exist as economic activity solely because it has an outcome that can at some future point be exchanged on the market for cash value. Economic value must be understood beyond the exclusively market-based perspective we too often rely on in discussing functional and digital literacies in economic globalization, because it forms a significant component of the overdetermined interrelationships among digital technologies, administrative technologies, and literacy technologies in Afghanistan.

PROBLEMS

Digital Technologies

One of the initiatives that the American mentor team undertook in Afghanistan was to provide the Afghan students at NMAA with laptops in order to promote the learning of sustainable digital literacies. This was a $5.6 million dollar contract. The Americans who wrote that contract seemed to have not thought much beyond simply directing technological resources at the problem they perceived: they bought 17 pallets of laptops for the students, apparently believing that the Afghans would easily and swiftly internalize the years of aggregated experience Americans have had in our own technological culture, and failing to see any need for instruction in computer use.

In response to this problem, I led an initiative to integrate computers into NMAA's curriculum and day-to-day administration, classroom instruction, and student classwork and homework. This

initiative built upon the scholarship of Cynthia Selfe (1999) and Patricia Fitzsimmons-Hunter and Charles Moran (1998) that demonstrated the need to attend as much to instructor training and education as to the technology itself. I first developed a survey instrument to poll NMAA faculty and incoming first-year students about their experiences with computers and shared my findings with the American Special Advisor for Computers and Automation Training and Education to the Afghan Minister of Defense, with the intent that we would use those findings to design an education program to instruct faculty in using computers before the students receive theirs. My hope was that the program would ensure that the computers would not go unused, damaged, or sold—a genuine and potentially expensive risk in Afghanistan's education- and resource-poor society.

The instrument surveyed both faculty (almost all of whom responded) and students (about 30% of whom responded). The surveys were administered anonymously in Dari, and included an informed consent notice and space for respondents to sign indicating either their consent or their refusal for their responses to be published in an academic context studying computer use in Afghanistan.[2] The questions asked both faculty and students about their skill levels with computers (Table 1), their use of computers at school or work (Table 2), their use of computers outside school or work (Table 3), and the purposes for which they used computers (Table 4).

Table 1. How skilled are you with computers?

How Skilled are Uou with Computers?	Faculty (N=134)	Students (N=162)
Expert	11	0
Highly skilled	31	6
Somewhat skilled	80	61
A little skilled	9	52
Not skilled	3	43

Table 2. How much have you used computers for work or education?

How Much Have You Used Computers for Work or Education?	Faculty (N=134)	Students (N=162)
Very extensively	57	4
Regularly	44	2
Some	25	20
A little	7	32
Very little or none	0	104

Table 3. How much have you used computers outside of work or school, at home, with friends, or on your own?

How Much Have You Used Computers Outside of Work or School, at Home, with Friends, or on Your Own?	Faculty (N=134)	Students (N=162)
Very extensively	27	20
Regularly	36	18
Some	46	38
A little	13	41
Very little or none	8	45

As the responses indicate, all faculty reported having used computers, and roughly 91 percent of faculty reported having at least some skill with computers. However, I later discovered from one of the translators that faculty who reported having done software or network development mistakenly believed those terms referred to simply using software or networks.

The responses also indicate 26 percent of students had negligible experience with computers, and 84 percent of students had negligible formal schooling with computers. Again, I later found out that first-year cadets take an information technology familiarization course, and this

Table 4. What have you used computers for?

What Have You Used Computers For?	Faculty (N=134)	Students (N=162)
Email	90	31
Web browsing/ internet	87	39
Word processing	81	38
Presentations	70	25
Movies/music	60	66
Software development / programming	46	62
Network/web development	36	15
Database	36	15
Games	32	70
Spreadsheet/ financial	30	5
Graphics/video editing	26	22
I have not used computers	0	39

circumstance was the source of the high incidence of "programming" responses to the fourth question: difficulties in translating relatively unfamiliar terms associated with digital literacies contributed to an initial misrecognition of the level of student skill with computers.

In coordination with the American Special Advisor for Computers and Automation Training and Education for the Afghan Minister of Defense, I used those findings to design an education program to train Afghan faculty in using computers before the $5.6 million procurement contract was to take effect upon distribution of the laptops to students. We developed a plan for training 26 Afghan instructors, to include at least two instructors from each academic department, who would then be able to train their colleagues. We secured a computer laboratory with 26 working and up-to-date computers, with 2 additional computer classrooms available with about 20 seats each, and requested a site survey to help determine whether those additional labs and seats were available for training. Afghan academic instructors were scheduled for training in the afternoons from 24 July (the end of classes and beginning of exams) until 17 October (the day before classes would start), for a total of almost 12 weeks, 2–3 hours per afternoon, Saturday–Wednesday. Our ideal outcome was to have teachers who were sufficiently trained in using computers to be able to help the cadets use their laptops every day in class and every day for homework. The program also sought to ensure long-term affordability for the Afghans by relying on widely-adopted and UNESCO-recommended free and open source courseware and learning management systems.

However, we encountered difficulties with administrative technologies that prevented the timely implementation of the plan before my departure. While we received and stored the computers in a warehouse in April 2011, waiting for the move to the more reliable sustainable power supply and broadband wireless at the new campus in Qargah, that move was postponed by the failure of American logisticians to anticipate that the multi-ton wind turbines that would provide the sustainable power supply required roads far better than those in Kabul, and the failure of those American logisticians to adequately communicate with the Afghan government.

Administrative Technologies

At the National Military Academy of Afghanistan, there are no clocks on the walls. The beginnings and endings of classes are marked by a soldier who stands in a central courtyard and blows a bugle. He tends to blow the bugle anywhere from four to twelve minutes before the classes are actually scheduled to end, and anywhere from three to nine minutes after classes are scheduled to begin. So a 55-minute class can be 34 to 48 minutes

long, which has problematic implications for pedagogy, and for eventual regional institutional accreditation.

The Afghan bugler stands as one example of an administrative technology—timekeeping and its relation to the Carnegie credit and student hour—typically invisible to American educational contexts. Another would be NMAA's use of a homeroom system wherein instructors rather than students shift between classrooms, because of worries about students' lack of familiarity with schooling practices. The Academy required those mobile English instructors to be tested for proficiency, and the speaking comprehension portion of the tests used materials (including audio recordings) published in 1972 by the Defense Language Institute in Lackland, Texas. When I tried to acquire more up-to-date supplemental materials for the Afghan instructors with the assistance of American educational publishers, I was initially prohibited from doing so by copyright and foreign export restrictions imposed by those educational publishers. We then sought the aid of the British contingent in ISAF, who were willing to provide British English instructional materials, as long as they were given input as to what sort of English was taught as a second langue at NMAA, a debate itself complicated by the fact that some Afghan instructors had been taught colonial English in graduate schools in India and Pakistan. ISAF would not fund such regional graduate instruction for newer instructors, however, so we developed a plan for distance learning graduate education via the internet, only to face resistance from the instructors who pointed out quite correctly that the unreliability of electricity and internet access in Kabul would make such education a challenging prospect. These circumstances demonstrate how administrative technologies intersect with computer technologies and literacy technologies in complex and overdetermined ways in global contexts.

Literacy Technologies

The literacy campaign in Afghanistan was a drumbeat from higher command: General William Caldwell noted (January–February 2011) that when he took command of NTM–A, "the overall literacy rate of the Afghan National Security Forces stood at about 14 percent" and "as we assessed training programs for the army and police, it was immediately evident that illiteracy was affecting the speed and depth of instruction. All training has to be hands-on; each skill has to be demonstrated" (p. 23). That drumbeat had material effects: in the Task Order Request associated with literacy training at NMAA, the estimated payroll cost of instruction for teacher salaries for one semester of English literacy training for 842 students was $109,980.00. Four years of English instruction is expected to get students to ninth grade level proficiency at a total cost of $1044.94 per student, not including instructional materials.

As noted before, many of those instructional materials were antiquated and culture-specific, and our attempts to overcome those barriers presented new challenges. The team went into negotiations with the British forces and the Joint Command's training branch to provide copies of a British series military-oriented English language textbooks for the cadets. Debates over how to fund what were effectively foreign military purchases required considerable negotiations with all parties concerned, including the academic publishers.

However, my smaller-scale efforts to help the Afghans build an English language professional development library collection owned and used by Afghan faculty to support pedagogical best practices in the areas of teaching developmental reading and writing and second-language literacy instruction and classroom practice met with more success, because of their smaller scale. The team and the Afghan instructors were able to partner with publishers and with other institutions in the United States to enable the Afghan faculty to continue expanding that professional development library on their own, and such ad hoc non-contract, non-capitalist, non-market solutions seemed to present the greatest possibility for sustainability.

THEORIZING SOLUTIONS

Recent scholarship on language difference in the global influence of composition has offered a strong critique of the hegemonic role of technology-driven transnational "fast capitalism" in that influence. Such scholarship acknowledges the challenges associated with ethnic difference and usefully analyzes the complications associated with language difference within and outside the U.S. in its critique of what Min-Zhan Lu (2004) has characterized as "a world ordered by global capital, … where all forms of intra- and international exchanges in all areas of life are increasingly under pressure to involve English" (p. 16). However, that scholarship fails to acknowledge the implications of economic difference: there is more than one form of economic activity, and much economic activity is non-capitalist or alternative-capitalist. The current situation in Afghanistan makes visible the ways that market-based economic transactions exist in a broader context of feudal, theft, independent, slave, gift, and other forms of transactions and institutions of value.

The ISAF project in Afghanistan carries value in economic contexts beyond the market. Classical economic perspectives identified land, labor, and capital as the three primary economic inputs to the production of value, and examined how those economic inputs could be combined and transformed into other economic outputs. Today, in the information economy's context of immaterial production, the new inputs consist of material-technological capital (mostly computers in their various forms, which have replaced land as the new scene of economic production), immaterial labor, and immaterial capital (often understood as the intellectual property associated with the texts and songs and books and computer software that immaterial labor produces and that gets aggregated itself and reproduced into new forms of immaterial capital or embedded in forms of material-technological capital).

Furthermore, the value produced from those three inputs changes form via three fundamental economic problems.

1. **The Substitution Problem:** Labor can change its value depending upon who performs it, and depending upon who appropriates that value, and at what point in the cycle of production, distribution, use, and re-production. Economist Duncan Ironmonger (1999) detailed the functioning of the substitution problem as manifested in the mis-measure of household labor when calculating Gross Domestic Product: despite the fact that household labor clearly has value inasmuch as we sometimes pay people to do it, we do not include estimations of the value of all the beds made, bathrooms scrubbed, floors mopped, and laundry washed in our calculations of Gross Domestic Product. Why not?

2. **The Transformation Problem:** We know that labor can become capital, and thereby take new forms in its contribution to the cycle of production, distribution, use, and re-production. Consider the person-hours the Afghans have contributed to building and developing NMAA in years past. Some economists would point to the ways their use of two of the factors of production—labor, in the form of their hours of work, and capital, in the forms of the buildings and computers and networks they used—were transformed into a product—the NMAA curriculum—that is itself used as a form of capital and an input absolutely fundamental to the production of the Afghan nation. How does that transformation happen?

3. **The Aggregation Problem:** We know that economists make assertions about how individuals act in ways that we generally characterize as economic, and we also know that economists make assertions about how large groups made up of individuals also act in ways that we generally characterize as economic. The Cambridge Capital Controversy of the 1960s demonstrated that generalizing from one to the other—from the individual to the group—is always going to be problematic, because one winds up comparing many different items (curricula, graduates, literacies) and aggregating them all together as capital. The same phenomenon occurs with labor. Aggregation necessarily implies mis-measurement and bad calculations because in macroeconomic theorizing one will always be lumping together curricula, graduates, and literacies (not to mention beds made, bathrooms scrubbed, floors mopped, and laundry washed, some of which were contributing preconditions to the production of curricula, graduates, and literacies). What happens when we know we cannot accurately use individual behavior to talk about group behavior?

While these three terms and problems are complicated in their own right, they become more so when we examine them in an Afghan context, partly because of the way that culture shapes economy. American economic activity, while diverse, often takes place in a market-based context, whereas the Afghan economic activity outside of the major cities takes place in a largely material-agricultural and often feudal context. In this instance, contra Marx, cultural difference would seem to drive technological and economic difference. Immaterial production as understood in America consists largely of (1) the informatized production of material goods and (2) the market-based production of immaterial goods.

Immaterial production as understood in Afghanistan is very different and involves—to a large degree—the circulation of cultural commonplaces with the purpose of maintaining familial, tribal, and intertribal bonds. Cash-based alternative capitalist transactions such as bribery and graft often function to reinforce tribal and intertribal bonds. Afghanistan usefully illustrates to us the ways that economy often serves cultural purposes rather than the other way around, suggesting that Min Zhan Lu's (2004) concerns with the assumed all-consuming nature of technology-driven global capitalism are problematically exaggerated: the economic activity of immaterial production, like so many other things in Afghanistan, does not align with our expectations.

In all of these challenges, we see deeply material problems compounded by cyclical shortsightedness: we know that literacy itself constitutes infrastructure, as well as the material things like electricity and roads. And a nation requires a literate population to enact the infrastructural changes that Americans tend to associate with prosperity and modernity. My work with the mentor team was built on the expectation was that digital technologies, as material-technological inputs to the process of immaterial production, would provide increased value and increased efficiencies in learning to the Afghan students in the ways that computers substitute capital-intensive processes for labor-intensive processes. But one needs the affordances offered by a material and administrative infrastructure to support the needs of a literate population. The complex and overdetermined local networks of digital, administrative, and literacy technologies exist in a cyclical and temporal cycle of production, distribution, use, and re-production.

ENACTING SOLUTIONS

The mentor team's efforts in literacy and computer literacy education can be seen as ways to jump-start the process of aggregating immaterial knowledge production at NMAA, and to make that process ultimately self-sustaining. We wanted to make ourselves obsolete. But the Afghans' need for computer literacy should remind us that scribal literacy and print literacy are themselves technologies that transform, substitute, and aggregate value in ways that do not always align across cultures, and in ways that are not always in the service of market-based exchange: those modes of aggregation long predate post-industrial capitalism, and can be seen in the contexts of mercantile economics, feudal economics, and Islamic economics. As Richard Ohmann (1985) pointed out long ago, "this age of technology, this age of computers, will change very little in the social relations. . . of which literacy is an inextricable part" (p. 687). Even if the Afghans' material-technological inputs begin to approach Western levels, they will engage the process of production with culturally different forms of immaterial labor and immaterial capital. Some of our expectations and approaches were incommensurable.

The abstract principles of rational argumentation are a form of commensurability in the way we suppose them to transcend context in the interest of transacting. Commensurability is the essence of market capitalism: money dissolves difference in market transactions, and it's too easy to make the mistake of seeing English as a sort of global currency, as something that erases difference by rendering all things commensurable. There exists a deep conceptual link between seeing the market transactions we identify with capitalism as beyond question and seeing notions of a global "standard English" as beyond question. Westerners from developed nations too easily identify all economic concerns as market concerns, ignoring the enormous diverse economy constituted by communal and feudal and independent and gift and alternative capitalist practices, and thereby assuming that far too many language practices are utilitarian and pragmatic and commensurable. Horner, Lu, Trimbur, and Royster (2011) have contended that "notions of the 'standard English speaker' and 'Standard Written English' are bankrupt concepts. All speakers of English speak many variations of

English, every one of them accented, and all of them subject to change as they intermingle with other varieties of English and other languages" (p. 305), pointing toward the importance of acknowledging the incommensurability of language.

At the same time, in Afghanistan's tribal culture, there is a need for commensurability. As Lu (2006) noted, "English is being used in multilingual countries... as a 'link language' for collective struggle against long and complex histories of intra- and international injustices along lines of race, ethnicity, gender, and class" (p. 612). Those injustices have long existed in the ethnic prejudices that privilege Tajiks over Hazaras and reinforce pervasive misogyny, and play out in any number of social effects, from individually and group-enacted violence to economic discrimination, as well as the pervasive corruption described by Sarah Chayes (2007). One hopes that the "translingual fluency" Horner et al. (2011) described "as deftness in deploying a broad and diverse repertoire of language resources, and responsiveness to the diverse range of readers' social positions and ideological perspectives" (p. 308) might help in working against those intracultural injustices and toward self-determination.

In order to work toward such self-determination, Suresh Canagarajah (2006) has argued, "[s]tudents must be trained to make grammatical choices based on many discursive concerns: their intentions, the context, and the assumptions of readers and writers" (p. 610). He noted that "multilingual students will resist [standard English] from the inside by inserting their codes within the existing conventions. This activity serves to infuse not only new codes, but also new knowledge and values, into dominant texts" (Canagarajah, p. 611). In Afghanistan, such activity—what Canagarajah has called "code meshing" (p. 598)—happens not only among students and Afghan instructors but among expert dominant-language users like the multinational workers who would incorporate "Salaam" or "Sobh ba khayr" or "Tashakor" or other Dari and Pashto phrases

into their emails to me. The Afghan translators I worked with used computers supplied by NTM–A running Windows Vista, which did not support Dari or Pashto. In day-to-day work, they used English as their display language and most used a hot-key combination to toggle back and forth between using the Arabic alphabet (to type in Dari or Pashto) and English as the input language. Material constraint, administrative technologies, and digital and global literacies overdetermined a rich and complex array of language practices. Similarly, some Afghans would indicate their linguistic self-determination via such code-meshing in digital communications with their Afghan and multinational counterparts, as well, engaging in Facebook exchanges and emails that interspersed phoneticized Roman-alphabet Dari and Pashto, Arabic characters transliterating Dari and Pashto, and English.

We should understand as well that the bugler-as-timekeeper and the schedule of classes constitute an administrative technology that is part of the deeply complex and overdetermined networks of objects and practices that underpin the work of teaching and that we largely take for granted, but that my experience in Afghanistan made freshly visible to me. To again borrow a formulation from Ohmann, digital literacy "embeds social relations within it" (p. 685), and those social relations look profoundly different across cultures. Those deeply complex and overdetermined networks of objects and practices function in the intersections of technologies, economics and composition, and more specifically in the intersections of composition's process-based attention to work over time and the Marxian attention to labor performed over time and the aggregation and transformation and appropriation of its value. My attention to time, labor, and aggregation here is anti-teleological, though, because it seeks to superimpose a time-based economic model that functions cyclically rather than linearly over those networks. These complex and overdetermined networks of objects and practices, of people, cultures, histories, problems, resources, and technologies all provide the context in which the economic cycle takes place and its accompanying problems of aggregation, substitution, and transformation.

IMPLICATIONS

In the early stages of my work in Afghanistan, I found myself focused on the technologies associated with literacies and computers, because they were familiar to me as objects of study. My cultural unfamiliarity with my Afghan counterparts allowed me to initially see the administrative technologies, as well, but I was still seeing only the technologies: my answer to Bill Hart-Davidson's 2004 question—"Are we so focused on the technology itself that we fail to see the people involved?" (p.148)—would have been a guilty "yes."

One of the books I took with me on the week-long trip from Fort Benning, Georgia to the Ali Al-Salem military air base in Kuwait to Bagram airfield to Kabul was Sarah Chayes' 2007 account of the problems with corruption in Afghanistan after the fall of the Taliban. Chayes used the work of Near Eastern Studies Professor Michael Barry to observe that during times of conflict "leadership among Pashtuns is acquired by a pretender's ability to extract wealth from a lowland power in one of those three familiar forms—plunder or tribute or subsidy—and distribute it among his men" (p. 101), and this use of "plunder or tribute or subsidy" ought to highlight the existence of alternative economic systems in Afghanistan. It would be a fundamental economic mistake to attempt to apply the economics of one space or context to another, and I would argue that Afghanistan currently exists as a technological third space (Bhabha, 1994) in its deployment of digital, administrative, and literate technologies, and in the ways those technologies function within its space.

When I arrived in Afghanistan, I moved freely from my office overlooking the airfield to various classrooms and offices to mentor and observe the Afghan instructors, though that freedom of movement was circumscribed by the boundaries of the small campus, fenced on all sides, accessible only through checkpoints with gates, crew-served weapons, and armed guards. We drove past the airfield to get there: on one side the civilian Kabul International Airport that the Ariana and Kam and Safi jets fly out of with the few wealthy enough to travel on them, and on the other the helicopters and cargo planes of the Afghan Air Force.

I see similarities to the technology-enabled large-scale mobility of the multinational military presence there—the helicopters and cargo planes, flying missions and materiel and personnel beyond, within, and across Afghanistan—in the critique Horner and Lu (2009) offered of the formulation by which "success... is imagined in terms of the extra-territorial mobility achieved: the ability of the few across the world to constantly move, untied by emotion or responsibility to any one territory, identity, or career" (p. 122). Transnational and transterritorial mobility is a marker of privilege, much as in Hawisher, Selfe, Kisa, and Ahmed's deployment (2010) of "the term transnational... to signify a growing group of students who are at home in more than one culture... These students typically speak multiple languages, often including varieties of English from outside the United States, and maintain networks of friends, family members, and other contacts around the globe" (p. 56). Such privilege is embodied as well by what Berry, Hawisher, and Selfe (2012) have characterized as "the linguistic imperialism of English" ("Global digital divide: From Nigeria and the People's Republic of China"). This assumed privilege of mobility (including digital mobility) associated with the American fetish for cars and planes and so-called footloose capital is far different from the tribally and socially connected nature of Afghanistan's deeply local culture.

Some soldiers at the airfield never went outside the gate: the only Afghans they saw were the KBR and Sodexo service workers and the merchants at the bazaar. The provincial reconstruction teams were able to get out and work closely among the Afghans, but that experience was rare, and many kept to their own enclaves, providing security against perceived threats rather than working with local communities, moving from place to place in armored vehicles, extraterritorial in the way they seldom engaged the people who populate and constitute the territory. Borders are by definition local phenomena, and extraterritorial mobility transcends the local in the worst way: by possessing the privilege and the outward security—the technological armor—to ignore it.

Fetishizing that sort of extraterritorial mobility and idealizing globalizations' ability to move across and transcend local borders both strike me as problematic. In my work mentoring faculty and helping the Afghans to develop their own curriculum and pedagogy, I was most productive having tea with Afghan teachers in a tiny, overpacked group office with overflowing bookshelves, battered metal desks, discarded and broken computer monitors and CPUs, and walls badly needing paint. What's important is not the crossing but the places crossed; not the privileged transcendence of mobility that homogenizes space for the traveler but the inability to transcend—the down-in-it-ness—at the borders between heterogeneous technological spaces.

The "translingual approach" advocated by Horner, Lu, Royster, and Trimbur (2011) isn't translingual at all: it does not pass by or transcend borders, but builds a nuanced understanding of how the borders work in their intersections and hybridity. Such an understanding must take the form of a sort of rooted hybridity, and won't necessarily be gained by those wearing body armor and traveling between bases in sealed armored vehicles who like the digital interfaces Selfe and Selfe (1994) have described "enact small but continuous gestures of domination and colonialism" (p. 486). It's understood and made visible on foot, at the gates and borders and crossings between one place and the next. We might well heed Nick Carbone's 2004 observation that "[t]echnologies become invisible quickly" (Hart-Davidson & Krause, p.148), but that invisibility can only happen when they exist as a component of a complex of already-naturalized technologies: changes in one technology disrupt the adaptation or visibility of another.

While one implication of the obstacles and challenges I encountered in Afghanistan would be to direct renewed attention to clearly unresolved issues associated with the global digital divide, another would be to reject the narrative of all-consuming teleological Western economic development as applicable to non-Western economies, and to investigate how practices associated with Islamic economics and other alternative economic spaces might align with global digital literacies. So, too, might the hybrid practices associated with Afghanistan's third-space digital, administrative, and literate technologies illuminate possibilities for border digital literacy initiatives.

CONCLUSION

Much of the American-produced curriculum and materials I initially tried to transport to my Afghan context simply did not work. The workbooks and listening comprehension tests associated with the Defense Language Institute's American Language Course were far too idiosyncratic for Afghan students, and what worked instead were day-to-day observations and interactions and one-on-one mentoring. The ISAF command sought a decontextualized too-easy cross-cultural mobility and commensurability through its enormous market-based Western capitalist expenditures on resources that the Afghans don't currently have the infrastructure to maintain.

The Afghan context I have examined here complicates the privileging of concepts—technology, commensurability, and mobility—central to many of the ways we think about global digital literacies. As I've suggested, I think rhetoric and composition as field has begun to do good work engaging with linguistic heterogeneity in that global context. According to Canagarajah (2006), global Internet users are demonstrating

the mixing of not only different varieties of English but also of totally different languages. To be literate on the Internet, for example, requires competence in multiple registers, discourses, and languages, in addition to different modalities of communication (sound, speech, video, photographs) and different symbol systems (icons, images, and spatial organization). To capture these changes for textual processing and production, scholars have now started using the term multiliteracies... These changes in text construction make it easy to envision that different varieties of English may find a 'natural' place in the evolving shape of the text. (p. 612)

Canagarajah's argument was in reference to the work of Stuart Selber (2004), who has used the term multiliteracies in relation to computers as encompassing a "functional literacy" representing "computers as tools" and "students as effective users of technology;" a "critical literacy" representing "computers as cultural artifacts" and "students as informed questioners of technology;" and a "rhetorical literacy" representing "computers as hypertextual media" and students as "reflective producers of technology" (Contents). My experience with a largely residual oral culture in Afghanistan, and with students and soldiers for whom print literacy was in many cases a relatively unfamiliar technology, showed me that substituting the word "writing" for Selber's "computers" leads to interesting revisions of functional, critical, and rhetorical literacies.

Writing and computers are both technologies that aggregate and naturalize labor-intensive processes (language acquisition and mastery; document production and distribution) into capital-intensive processes (Google Translate; the Web distribution of hybrid Dari-English video mashups), and in doing so call into question the

notion of expertise. It's impossible for Afghans and Americans to be sufficiently polyglot autodidacts in their interactions, so our mutual understanding was necessarily partial, provisional, and in process: the productive aggregation and transformation of knowledge is ongoing in the ways the Afghans are literally inventing the university and reinventing their nation. My mentoring work with the teachers, and the ongoing teaching practica I developed in conjunction with the Afghan English teachers are always acts of code-meshing, and never settled or static or authoritative.

However, many of the arguments scholars in rhetoric and composition make about the presumedly Western and capitalocentric economics of globalization rhetorically shut down the possibility of economic agency and self-determination. In so doing, they ascribe to an imagined technology-driven global capitalism a market-based homogeneity it does not possess. The languages we speak extend and carry value beyond the marketplace, beyond the bazaar, and tracing how they do so is absolutely essential to any hope of promoting the life-and-death matter of literacy instruction in Afghanistan. Performing that tracing can illustrate for our field how the privileged rhetorics of technology, commensurability, and mobility are themselves contingent and necessarily dependent upon cultural and economic context in ways that we might otherwise fail to recognize or value.

I've tried here to offer an examination of digital literacy instruction in Afghanistan as an object or product of the often invisible network of processes that surround it. The various economic problems I've defined—transformation, substitution, aggregation—occur at various stages in that economic cycle of production, distribution, use, and re-production, wherein the economic inputs of immaterial labor (the work of Afghan English instructors), immaterial capital (schedules of classes and timekeeping practices), and material-technological capital (the computers in the warehouse waiting for Qargah) form a complex and overdetermined network that transforms over time.

Computers transform labor-intensive processes into capital-intensive processes, and that's part of my point: immaterial labor and the immaterial capital it produces transform and aggregate over time, so that transistors plus code become computers, and computers plus code become networks, and networks plus administrative technologies plus computers plus the aggregated weight of thousands of years of scholarship and pedagogy become institutions and institutional practices that shape and inform our everyday teaching, and that require our attention.

Lieutenant Colonel John Hartke, a professor in West Point's Department of Physics and Nuclear Engineering, was the sole remaining American mentor to work with NMAA. In Fall 2012, NMAA completed the move from Kabul International Airport to the new National Defense University site at Qargha.

REFERENCES

Afghanistan Internet Usage and Telecommunications Reports. (2012,12 Nov.). *Internet world stats: Usage and population statistics.* Retrieved 19 Dec. 2012 from http://www.internetworldstats.com/asia/af.htm

Berry, P. W., Hawisher, G. E., & Selfe, C. L. (2012). *Transnational literate lives in digital times.* Logan, UT: Computers and Composition Digital Press/ Utah State University Press. Retrieved June 1, 2013, from http://ccdigitalpress.org/transnational

Bhabha, H. (1994). *The location of culture.* London: Routledge.

Caldwell, W. B., IV. (2010, 13 Sep.). Literacy as a matter of life and death. *The Huffington Post.* Retrieved 6 Feb. 2011 from http://www.huffingtonpost.com/lt-gen-william-b-caldwell-iv/post_838_b_714906.html

Caldwell, W. B. IV, & Finney, N. K. (2011, January-February). Security, capacity, and literacy. *Military Review*, 23–27.

Canagarajah, A. S. (2006). The place of world Englishes in composition: Pluralization continued. *College Composition and Communication, 57*(4), 586–619.

Chayes, S. (2007). *The punishment of virtue: Inside Afghanistan after the Taliban.* New York: Penguin.

Fitzsimmons-Hunter, P., & Moran, C. (1998). Writing teachers, schools, access, and change. In T. Taylor, & I. Ward (Eds.), *Literacy theory in the age of the Internet* (pp. 158–170). New York: Columbia University Press.

Gibson-Graham, J. K. (2006). *A postcapitalist politics.* Minneapolis, MN: University of Minnesota Press.

Hardt, M., & Negri, A. (2000). *Empire.* Cambridge, MA: Harvard University Press.

Hart-Davidson, B., & Krause, S. D. (2004). Re: The future of computers and writing: A multivocal textumentary. *Computers and Composition, 21,* 147–160. doi:10.1016/j.compcom.2003.08.008

Hawisher, G., Selfe, C., Kisa, G., & Ahmed, S. (2010). Globalism and multimodality in a digitized world. *Pedagogy, 10*(1), 55–68.

Hofstede, G. (2001). *Culture's consequences: Comparing values, behaviors, institutions and organizations across nations* (2nd ed.). Thousand Oaks, CA: Sage.

Horner, B., Lu, M., Royster, J. J., & Trimbur, J. (2011). Language difference in writing: Toward a translingual approach. *College English, 73*(1), 303–321.

Ironmonger, D. (1999). Counting outputs, capital inputs and caring labor: Estimating gross household product. *Feminist Economics, 2*(3), 37–64. doi:10.1080/13545709610001707756

Lu, M. (2004). An essay on the work of composition: Composing english against the order of fast capitalism. *College Composition and Communication, 56*(1), 16–50. doi:10.2307/4140679

Lu, M. (2006). Living-English work. *College English, 68*(6), 605–618. doi:10.2307/25472178

Lu, M., & Horner, B. (2009). Composing in a local-global context: Careers, mobility, skills. *College English, 72*(2), 113–133.

Miller, R. E. (2005). *Writing at the end of the world.* Pittsburgh, PA: University of Pittsburgh Press.

National Military Academy of Afghanistan. (2011, 2 April). *Task order request.* Nato Training Mission—Afghanistan.

Ohmann, R. (1985). Literacy, technology, and monopoly capital. *College English, 47*(7), 675–689. doi:10.2307/376973

Pennington, M. C. (2003). The impact of the computer in second-language writing. In B. Kroll (Ed.), *Exploring the dynamics of second language writing* (pp. 283–310). Cambridge, UK: Cambridge University Press. doi:10.1017/CBO9781139524810.019

Selber, S. (2004). *Multiliteracies for a digital age.* Carbondale, IL: Southern Illinois University Press.

Selfe, C. L. (1999). *Technology and literacy in the twenty-first century: The importance of paying attention.* Carbondale, IL: Southern Illinois University Press.

Selfe, C. L., & Selfe, R. J. Jr. (1994). The politics of the interface: Power and its exercise in electronic contact zones. *College Composition and Communication, 45*(4), 480–504. doi:10.2307/358761

UNData. (2012, 10 Sep.). *Personal computers per 100 population.* United Nations Statistics Division. Retrieved December 12, 2012, from http://data.un.org/Data.aspx?d=MDG&f=seriesRowID%3A607

World Bank. (2012, October). *Afghanistan overview.* Retrieved December 20, 2012, from http://www.worldbank.org/en/country/afghanistan/overview

World Factbook, C. I. A. (2012). *CIA World factbook—Afghanistan.* Retrieved December 18, 2012, from https://www.cia.gov/library/publications/the-world-factbook/geos/af.html

KEY TERMS AND DEFINITIONS

Administrative Technologies: The processes, know-how, techniques, procedures, and systems of use that accompany a culture's deployment of technological objects and artifacts: rather than computers, automobiles, and photocopiers, think typing skills, driver testing and licensing, and filing systems.

Diverse Economy: The notion from J. K. Gibson-Graham (2006) that our contemporary economy is constituted not only by market-based capitalist transactions and institutions, but by those that would be considered feudal, alternative capitalist, gift, slave, or independent forms of economic activity.

Immaterial Capital: In today's information economy, the counterpart to the classical economists' conception of material capital (factories, heavy machinery) as one of the three inputs (in addition to raw materials) of economic activity: software, intellectual property.

Immaterial Labor: In today's information economy, the counterpart to the classical economists' conception of physical, material labor (assembly-line work, operating heavy machinery and tools) as one of the three inputs (in addition to raw materials) of economic activity: data entry, education, online communication. From Hardt & Negri (2000).

Material-Technological Capital: In today's information economy, the counterpart to the classical economists' conception of land as the site of production and therefore as one of the three inputs (in addition to raw materials) of economic activity: computers and other technological data-processing devices.

ENDNOTES

[1] This information came from an interpreter and former medical doctor who worked with the NMAA team. As for all Afghan sources with whom I spoke directly, I have left him anonymous out of concern for his safety.

[2] Neither NMAA, NTM-A, nor Afghanistan's Ministries of Education or Defense currently have Institutional Review Boards or protocols associated with human subjects research. Signed documents indicating informed consent are available.

Section 3
Emerging Digital Communication in Digital and Global Contexts

Chapter 12
Considering *Chronos* and *Kairos* in Digital Media Rhetorics

Ashley Rose Kelly
Purdue University, USA

Meagan Kittle Autry
North Carolina State University, USA

Brad Mehlenbacher
North Carolina State University, USA[1]

ABSTRACT

Any account of the rhetoric of digital spaces should begin not with the provocation that rhetoric is impoverished and requires fresh import to account for new media technologies, but instead with a careful analysis of what is different about how digital technologies afford or constrain certain utterances, interactions, and actions. Only then might one begin to articulate prospects of a digital rhetoric. This chapter examines the importance of time to an understanding the rhetoric of digital spaces. It suggests that rhetorical notions of kairos and chronos provide an important reminder that it is the rhetorical situation, along with rhetorical actors at individual to institutional levels, that construct the discursive spaces within which people participate, even in digitally-mediated environments.

INTRODUCTION[1]

"So low has Rhetoric sunk," I.A. Richards (1936) writes, "that we would do better just to dismiss it to Limbo than to trouble ourselves with it—unless we find reason for believing that it can become a study that will minister successfully to important needs" (p. 3). More than seventy-five years after Richards characterized an invigorated study of rhetoric as the study of "misunderstanding and its remedies," with substantial interventions shaping the problem space of rhetoric by Burke (1941, 1969), Booth (1961, 1974), and the great European re-visioning of Perelman and Olbrechts-Tyteca (1969), rhetoric is now theorized significantly beyond a solely Aristotelian orientation (p. 3). Ancient rhetoric provided the rill from which

DOI: 10.4018/978-1-4666-4916-3.ch012

Copyright © 2014, IGI Global. Copying or distributing in print or electronic forms without written permission of IGI Global is prohibited.

the river of rhetoric might grow, but through the intervening millennia of erosion and geographical changes to disciplines and to education broadly, ancient rhetoric became but one tributary to a vast river fed also by philosophy, linguistics, philology, psychology, and other disciplines. Accounts of rhetoric as *mere* persuasion, or even elevated notions of persuasion closer to dialectical argument, leave rhetoric firmly located in antiquity.

Our goal in this chapter is to connect complex discussions in historical and contemporary rhetoric with emerging discourses about digital media environments and that necessitates that we immediately address the question in this volume of "digital rhetoric." To do this, we draw on an account by Miller in a recent interview with *Figure/Ground Communication* (Ralon, 2012). Miller suggests that digital rhetoric might, "at this stage," be characterized as "a hypothesis—or maybe a hope" (para. 3). Her justification for this claim is that both the scope and focus of a digital rhetoric currently appear to remain under-theorized and that the intellectual form of rhetoric remains varied, particularly when taken beyond the U.S. context in which rhetoric found its revival in the 20th century.

"So low has Rhetoric sunk," we might say, that we would do better just to dismiss it and find a more contemporary media theory. Communication theorists such as Castells (2000), for example, provide researchers with ways of talking about the relationships, interactions, and contexts that make up our networked society to account for the kinds of discursive utterances, interactions, and actions we are seeing with the rise of digital technologies. Similarly, Engeström (1999, 2000) offers a rich agenda for educators interested in the technological, economic, and cultural dynamics in the modern global workplace. Taylor (2001) offers complexity theory as a way to understand how networks and networked communication has changed the cultural landscape of our society.

Can we find reason for believing that rhetoric can become a discipline that will *minister successfully* to the important changes of late 20th and early 21st century media environments and discursive landscapes? We emphatically argue that rhetoric can. A thoughtful account of the rhetoric of digital environments begins not with the provocation that rhetoric is impoverished and requires fresh import from other disciplines to account for new media technologies but, instead, asks what is different about how new media technologies afford or constrain certain utterances, interactions, and actions. Classic and contemporary rhetorical theory offers us a carefully elaborated language for describing how rhetors, exigencies, discourse, and situation interact both theoretically and practically. Thus human-computer interactions extend from textual interfaces and literacy practices which extend from oral traditions and dialectic.

To examine how rhetoric can minister successfully to our contemporary communication technologies, we offer a study of discourse acts taking place in a micro-blogging space called Twitter. For our purposes, the choice of Twitter is not a reflection of its superiority over other media. Rather, we look to this platform as one commonly used, albeit very popular site, a space that currently has significant purchase with a wide user base. As well, Twitter and some of its features may help us explore particular rhetorical concepts, *kairos* and *chronos*. While these features are not entirely unique to Twitter, they certainly shape much of the discourse surrounding this tool and provide us with some insight into the founder's perception of prospective users' needs. In large, prominent lettering at the top of their "About" page, Twitter thus boasts of being the "*fastest*, simplest way to stay close to everything you care about" and that one of its chief goals is to serve as "a *real-time* information network that connects you to the latest stories, ideas, opinions and news" (Twitter, 2013, emphasis ours). The site's timeliness, global connection of users and usefulness as a tool for business are, therefore, critical to the site's popularity.

Use of Twitter for the purposes of social action has gained considerable attention from communication and education researchers, with many of its features and uses inviting debate and disagreement. Khazan (2013) and Vargas (2011) posit that social media such as Twitter are crucial for sharing international news coverage. Gladwell (2010), inversely, has argued against the power of social media tools as a coordinating instrument for revolutions around the world, including unrest in Moldova, Iran, Egypt, and Tunisia. Similarly, Morozov (2011) and others (Comninos, 2011) have noted that, despite the coordinating and reporting benefits of Twitter, revolutionary activities are more likely to be met with yet more rigid Internet sanctions and surveillance measures. Of course there is Giddens's third way, Lindgren (2013) reminds us, and we might eschew utopic and dystopic technological narratives by instead carefully reviewing the particular. For example, in terms of the particular February 2011 Libyan uprising, Lindgren shows us that many tweets from activists were "directed mostly toward the powerful, corporately controlled news media nodes" (p. 78).

Twitter has also been cited for its role in crisis response, including following major natural disasters and related distress (Acar & Muraki, 2011; Binder, 2012; Doan, et al., 2011; Kelly & Miller, forthcoming; Larsson & Ågerfalk, 2013; Sakaki, 2010; Thomson, et al., 2012) as well as for citizen journalism (Murthy, 2012). Not only has Twitter enjoyed considerable scholarly and media coverage (Collins, 2011; Garber, 2012; Lawn, 2012; Tsukayama, 2012) but, according to Smith and Brenner (2012) of the Pew Internet and American Life Project, Twitter has enjoyed considerable use as well, with 15 percent of online adults use Twitter, up significantly from just eight percent in 2010. Indeed, a recent survey of 1372 respondents indicates that more than 35 percent

of higher education scholars use Twitter (Faculty Focus, 2010), suggesting that this popular micro-blogging space has infiltrated educational settings as well (Lockett et al., 2012).

After Lee and Liebenau (2000) and Leetaru, Wang, Cao, Padmanabhan, and Shook (2013), we are intrigued by the complex and dynamic role of time (and by default, space) in the unfolding of complex and controversial "communicative landscapes." Our case study and analysis thus provides a provocative glimpse into the machinations of these media spaces, but it also distorts the high-speed and long-term development of topics across these spaces, making it difficult to explicitly define duration (at least using traditional notions of duration), temporal location (e.g., where the spaces that we are investigating begin and end), and sequencing (since the discourse threads both interact and occur independent of one another). We acknowledge that the role of time has become increasingly compelling given its relationship with globalization (Walker, 2009), Internet technologies (Kenyon, 2008), and our accelerated society (Gleick, 1999; Leccardi, 2003). We agree with Ancona, Okhuysen, and Perlow (2001) when they assert:

Suddenly, "time" and "timing" are everywhere. Speed, acceleration, just in time, and Internet time are just a few concepts making headlines in the popular press. Academic journals also have seen a proliferation of research papers on time and timing. New terms, metaphors, and theories are emerging (e.g., time famine, entrainment, poly-chronicity, chronos and kairos, temporal lineages, cohort effects) ... As the pace of research dramatically accelerates, ... time and timing have moved from the background to the foreground. (p. 512)

Our analysis carefully attends to temporal unfolding of discursive practices in various media spaces. To advance our discussion of the trends we see through a quantitative temporal analysis, we take a rhetorical stance that contributes to current discussions of two concepts: *chronos* and *kairos*, as they relate to transformational changes in discursive practices through emerging digital communication spaces. This account further serves as a possible example of how digital media environments may be theorized rhetorically.

RHETORICAL CONCEPTIONS OF TIME: *KAIROS AND CHRONOS*

Rhetorically astute speakers and writers carefully consider timing and are opportunistic about moments for achieving their speech goals. Astute rhetors also employ discourse strategies that take careful account of the audience for their speech. Branches of oratory are not surprisingly separated according to specific genres of rhetorical response (forensic, epideictic, deliberative) connected to given times (past, present, or future). Description, praise, or blame are thus accorded different and appropriate times. Particular rhetorical strategies, figures of speech for example, employ strategies for looking forward (prolepsis) or backward (analepsis) in time. Other critical figures include chronographia (detailed description of recurring times), hysteron proteron (disordering time), procatalepsis (anticipating future arguments or events), enallage (manipulating grammatical structures to influence semantic interpretation), and ampliatio (related to epitheton, giving a name to someone or thing prior to its having been given that name) (Burton, "Figures of Time," n.d.).[2] The rhetorical tradition offers two broad characterizations of time: *chronos* and *kairos*. *Chronos* characterizes linear quantitative time, the kind of time we experience through the measurements of clocks and calendars. *Kairos* refers to a special, qualitative kind of time. *Kairos* describes the opportune time to do something and in the appropriate measure and with a complexity that has lead to its extensive study in the rhetorical tradition.

Kairos

Kinneavy is largely responsible for the highlighting the importance of *kairos* for contemporary rhetoric by drawing on the classical tradition. In his "*Kairos*: A Neglected Concept in Classical Rhetoric" (1986), Kinneavy argues that *kairos* has a central place in sophistic, Platonic, and Ciceronian rhetoric. Beginning with Hesiod's "Observe due measure, and proportion [*kairos*] is best of all things," Kinneavy connects *kairos* not only with historical discussions of the rhetorical tradition, but also articulates its ethical, epistemological, and aesthetic implications (p. 58). *Kairos*, then, becomes both the craft of determining the appropriate time and also a means of evaluating the appropriateness of the speech event. Kinneavy sees *kairos* as a powerful construct for college composition teaching as well as anticipating our situated view of discourse production in general. This "*kairos* program in composition" is extended by Baumlin (1987) and Carter (1988) and tied directly to important contemporary social theories of learning and of writing.

The import of *kairos* into contemporary rhetoric was not easy, Miller (1992) reminds us, because it "is one of those ancient Greek terms that doesn't translate simply to contemporary English" (p. 311). There are two general aspects of *kairos* to consider in formulating a definition or description of the term: the temporal and the spatial dimensions. Miller tells us that the first, the temporal dimension, can be considered in terms of a rhetorical situation. Where Bitzer (1968) would posit certain material constraints that afford certain moments a kairotic opportunity, these moments would appear as "exigences punctuating chronos," while Vatz (1968) might oppose, suggesting the ability to socially construct the moment, telling us that "every moment along the continuum of *chronos* has its *kairos*" (Miller, 1992, p. 312). Putting these two perspectives into play, Miller

(1992) describes rhetorical situations as being constituted by the "dynamic interplay between objective and subjective, between opportunity as discerned and opportunity as defined"—this is the complexity of the temporal aspect of *kairos* (p. 312). The spatial aspect similarly raises questions about the objective and subjective nature of discovery versus definition. To help resolve this tension, Miller turns to Swales' "Create A Research Space" (CARS) model as an example of how to "obliterate the distinction between objective and subjective" and, instead, to understand *kairos* as an "opening [that] is actively constructed by writers and readers and is simultaneously accepted as really existing (or not) in a way that matters for subsequent actions" (p. 313). Putting these aspects back together, Miller situates *kairos* as a rhetorical negotiation, where "rhetoric engages the phenomena of concrete experience and itself is engaged by the force of human motivation," but experience is also not determinate and stable; so we are left with an art that "must be an instrument by which one indeterminacy struggles with another" (p. 313).

What Miller's account provides is a more complex way to understand situation through *kairos* because "*Kairos* also holds in productive suspension the apparently objective and subjective dimensions of context" (pp. 322–323). Moving the discussion of *kairos* into a rhetoric of technology, Miller (1994) reminds us of the term's utility in discussing change "as either continuous or discontinuous, evolutionary or revolutionary" (p. 83). Metaphors of technological change rely on the concept of *kairos*, including metaphors of generations, eras and ages, and revolutions (Miller, 1994, p. 86). Examples of this include how technologies have different "generations" (e.g., the third generation iPad) and our references to the digital or information "age."

What we want to underscore too is how powerful notions of *kairos* have been to contemporary rhetoric, including Miller's account of technological changes through the lens of *kairos*. Offering further assessment of the importance of *kairos* to contemporary rhetorical theory, in *Rhetoric and Kairos*, Miller (2002) situates the collection as partially a response to Gaonkar's (1997) challenge to rhetoric and its globalization. Gaonkar contends that rhetoric is "too thin," once again "sunk so low," and that its utility has surely been left behind somewhere in antiquity. Miller (2002) argues that the essays in the collection, "demonstrate the depth, complexity, and untranslatability of the Greek concept of *kairos*" (p. xi). Two decades later, Gaonkar might ask how rhetoric could theorize emergent digital media forms.

Chronos

Chronos is frequently offered in contrast to *kairos* and, in contrast, *chronos* often looks much less exciting as a construct. Where *kairos* is the opportune moment and the correct measure that moment affords, *chronos* is described simply as "linear time" (Sipiora, 2002, p. 2). Yet time (*chronos*) has fascinated communication scholars for centuries, especially fascinating modern communication technology theorists. This is primarily because the technologies we use to create and measure time are so tied up within our communications and discursive spaces (Bluedorn, 2002; Borgmann, 2000). *Chronos*, if there ever was a rhetorical concept wed to the technological contexts and interfaces it describes, is that concept. We move through human temporal accounting from sundials to water clocks into the 13th century with the development of mechanical clocks. Mechanical clocks, not the steam engine, Mumford (1934) tells us are the key-machine of the modern industrial age. The clock's purpose becomes to order society by shifting from individual to communal experience of time passing, and these technologies "transform tasks and create new work and wealth by *accelerating the pace of human association. By coordinating and accelerating human meetings and goings-on, clocks *increase the sheer quantity of human contact*" (McLuhan, 2003, p.

209, emphasis ours). Clocks, effectively, appear to produce a world where "'Time' has ceased, 'space has vanished....'" (McLuhan & Fiore, 1967, p. 63).

Also working with the concept of time and the arrangement of human activities, Enos (2002) describes how the Athenians developed ways to measure minute time with seeming correlation to the development of legal and civil practices. Drawing on archaeological evidence, he writes that Athenians had the ability to measure minute-time by the fifth century B.C. and that the water clock was connected to how the Athenians measured time in legal processes of the day. Legal proceedings, according to him, were sometimes measured according to water clock time, with particular times set for the accuser, the defendant, and the resulting discussion and deliberation (p. 82). The relationship between time and writing, in these contexts, was to stabilize the oration. In their numerous studies of the influence on different technologies on our perceptions of time, these researchers remind us that time is at its heart socially constructed. Indeed, both these discourse communities review the role of time and human action and understanding and our cultural shift from modernity to the post-modernity.

Cultural studies scholars continue to examine how time, communication, and time technologies have an enormous influence on our daily lives (e.g., Burgelman, 2000). Time is constructed through a careful system of measurement and technologies. These technologies, Peters (2009) asserts, are tools for "synchroniz[ing] earth and heaven, culture and nature, and the periodic events of history and astronomy" (p. 6). As well, he reminds us that time-keeping technologies have had a dramatic influence on both political and religious power and that this influence is evidenced in the resistance or subversion of established calendric systems in the French and Russian revolutions. Overall, cultural studies help us understand the ways that humans have historically "cut up" some experience by using technologies. Burgelman (2000) thus insists ours is a society where "... the now,

the globally, instantly available and reachable, the mobile, the live, the just in time, and the virtual dominate." This shapes how we experience the passing moments, how we organize our day, and subsequently our society. They do not, however, provide as much insight into rhetorical motivation or experience of time, the human urge to experience the "before and after" of Aristotle.

Smith (2002) tells us that Aristotle's definition of *chronos* was the "number of motion with respect to the before and the after," but that this definition should be understood as referring to something other than a spatial sense of "motion" (Aristotle 4.II.219b, qtd. in Smith, p. 48). That other sense of motion is through time. Time, argues Aristotle, is not without movement; that is, we notice how time has passed when we notice movement. Thus, he posits, time is a property of movement—a quantity of it, even. Thus time is a number of movements that we recognize in knowing what was before and what came after. A precise definition of the "before" and of the "after" is not provided by Aristotle. Smith, however, provides the following elaboration:

This definition combines the three essential features of chronos: change, a unit of measure, and a serial order that is asymmetrical. There is, first, the element of change, motion, process, of something going on which lasts through or requires a stretch of time. Time, it appears, is not identical with the movement, but cannot be thought apart from the movement. Second, an appropriate unit of measure must be given, so that the elapsed time and the quantity of the movement can be measured or numbered. Third, there is the element of serial order or direction expressed in the term 'before' and 'after.' (p. 49)

Aristotle is essentially defining time as change, measure, and serial order, leading us to our contemporary understanding of *chronos* as an exact quantification of time (Ramo, 1999). Or, if we believe Bostock (2006): "time as a thing numbered, rather than a thing we number with" (p. 141). This conception of time, Smith (2002) notes, "furnishes an essential grid upon which the processes of nature and of the historical order can be plotted and to that extent understood" (p. 49). Thus, we arrive at our current conception of time as something that we count with hour and minute hands or the uptick of digitally-displayed numbers on a screen. For Smith (2002), *chronos* in effect becomes the necessary step-child or the underlying structure for the much more interesting *kairos*, where *chronos* scaffolds the qualitative organizing principle of kairotic opportunism and situational assessment as a quantitative reference point. *Chronos*, in this light, serves more as a time stamp than as a means of explaining or understanding rhetorical speech events. For Smith (2002), then, "both aspects of time are ingredient in the nature of things and both have practical import" (p. 48). Still, as secondary as Smith (2002) views *chronos*, he also outlines the features of *chronos* in a way touches on the most interesting aspects of its rhetorical traditional: "In *chronos* we have the fundamental conception of time as measure, the *quantity* of duration, the length of periodicity, the age of an object or artifact, and the rate of acceleration of bodies" (p. 47). Thus, *chronos* is the day-to-day movement of time from before to after or from past to future (where the present or "now" consists of successive nows measured by seasons, days, hours, minutes, or smaller increments).

And increments continue to become smaller. An example of these smaller units is the second, which the Le Système International d'Unités (SI) defines as "9,192,631,770 cycles of the radiation, which corresponds to the transition between two energy levels of the ground state of the Cesium-133 atom" (National Institute of Standards and Technology, n.d.). Web-based posts have long-reflected measuring in small increments, with IRC logs, many instant messaging services, and web forums, and blogs sharing the date and time to the minute. So too do many ubiquitous digital technologies in our homes, including our ovens,

refrigerators, microwaves, coffee makers. Our mobile phones can track our running time while playing energizing tunes, and our automobiles not only tell us the time, but some may record and time-stamp anomalous events for reporting to mechanics. Reporting bad behavior of automobile drivers too is time-stamped with red light traffic cams. While many of these report to us minutes, they can often also calculate in smaller increments. Twitter shows us these small increments, without digging up log files, to share that someone has posted only a few seconds ago. That will later change from minutes to days, adaptive to the human shaping of temporal progression.

As precise as modern time-keeping devices appear to have gotten (Greenwich Mean Time, Newtonian, or relativistic time), research from various disciplines that emphasize the intimate relationship between human perception and neurological processes continues to confound our assumptions about the pure objectivity of time. Gorn, Chattopadhyay, Sengupta, and Tripathi (2004), for example, have shown how particular web design features (such as the use of chroma and value levels that heighten a sense of relaxation) reduce user impatience with download times. Eraut (2004) describes "crowded" work contexts and how they compel employees to be more selective with their attention and to digest information needed to accomplish tasks more quickly, speaking to decision making and reflective practice. Evans (2004), as well, argues that our estimates of the amount of time that has passed are connected directly by the complexity of the tasks we are undertaking at the time, concluding that "the experience of duration constitutes a physiological response to both self and situations, which is, in principle, independent of any objective temporal attributes of a particular event or situation" (p. 21). Indeed, it may be that sensory-perceptual experience orders our experience of time prior to cognitive processes. Sensory-perceptual experience is first represented as a combination of the time it takes for the cortex to capture the perceptual moment, for the neurons to fire and distribute information, and for the short-term memory to record the end of one event and the beginning of another. Sensory-perceptual experience at the level of our most fundamental physiological operations, thus, marks the smallest grain-size of "time" that humans are able to process (pp. 24–25). Thus, if we now know that our experience of the perceptual moment *now* has an outer limit of two to three seconds (between perceptual attention shifts), then time cannot be viewed as an objective reality. Instead, *now* must be interpreted as a function of our subjective (i.e., constructed) physiological organization of temporal events. In short, time is sensory-perceptual and cognitive as much as it is technologically mediated and socially constructed.

With all of these aspects at work in our perception of time, dramatic changes to any one aspect of our life-times are likely to generate much interest. The Internet and World Wide Web have done just that, with some speculation about what these new technologies mean for our cognitive capacities (Carr, 2010). Gleick (1999) posits that the Internet has produced "new orders of magnitude" that amount to transformed communication realities: "Chaos theorists understand such systems to undergo phase transitions, as water does when it turns coherently to ice or incoherently to steam. The controlling factor here is not heat or energy but pure connectivity" (p. 69). So how do we begin to measure the profound influence of a post-modern world governed by rules that do not want to adhere to the unmoving principles of time and time measurement? Here it is useful to separate the influences of revised definitions of time into several traditional spheres: global, institutional, and individual (where fragmentation, in particular, plays a critical role). Globalizing forces, while promising greater flexibility, accessibility, and growth, also challenge both organizations and individuals to adapt to flexible schedules and to be available both online and in person (Walker, 2009). At the institutional level, time is being transformed by modern conceptions of time (e.g., Mattelart's,

1996, summary of Taylor's style of management as effectively connecting human workflow with the strict measurement of time) and post-modern workplace realities (distributed products and services, global time-scales, company-to-company cooperation, and high-speed telecommunications).

Orlikowski and Yates (2002) argue that, rather than existing independently of human action (i.e., objective) or socially constructed through human action (i.e., subjective), a third perspective is possible. They write, "that time is experienced in organizational life through a process of temporal structuring that characterizes people's everyday engagement in the world" (p. 684). Maznevski and Chudoba's (2000) study of virtual team dynamics supports this argument, showing how teams organize their time around communication patterns related to various tasks (Massey, Montoya-Weiss, & Hung, 2003). On the individual level, our visions of freedom from the constraints of time began in the 1970s when visionaries such as Negroponte (1979, 1996) began describing technological futures that emphasized *my time* versus Prime Time (p. 172). Organizational theorists have spent considerable time and energy investigating how working people spend their time both individually and in groups. Perlow's (1999) study of time use among software engineers working for a Fortune 500 company revealed an interdependent relationship between work content, activity sequencing, and systemic effects of sequences. Time use was enacted frequently by continuous crises (i.e., problems), employee beliefs in high-visibility sacrifice and "heroics" in problem solving, combined with collaboration and team support. Ultimately, Perlow argues that a collective time management approach is required since individual time management strategies often fail in the face of larger organizational and cultural time use.

Through this review of literature on time across disciplines, we have shown that it has become an increasingly important concept in the study of digital technology. How, then, can we incorporate our rhetorical understanding of time, *chronos*, into this discussion? When we move the rhetorical discussion to the digital, we see that time does two things: it tells us about day-to-day events, chronologically, and it also provides us with new views of technology. What Twitter helps us to see is that discourse on social media is not only about the "big" moments. That is, seizing the kairotic moment is not the only function of Twitter. While the website is certainly popular in times of big news moments (such as the Fukushima Daiichi nuclear disaster in March 2011 or the 2012 Presidential election night), the momentous is not the only function of the social media space. Many of the discourse acts that play out online are situated within the quotidian banalities of our lives. The conversation stretches over time, is punctuated by news sources that help drive certain conversations, and allows for widespread participation in discourse. But these discourses and their connection to time are often overlooked. To look a little closer, we examine one case study to uncover some of the complexities in these interactions and conversations.

TRACING TWEETS: A SITE OF INQUIRY

To explore the potentialities of the rhetorical concepts of *kairos* and *chronos* in digital spaces, we present a case study of Twitter use related to a merger between two large utility companies in the U.S. Our case study is part of a larger project that explored the merger (Kelly & Kittle Autry, 2013; Kinsella, Kelly, & Kittle Autry, 2013) and that supported arguments for applying a humanities-based research orientation to developments in social media spaces (Kittle Autry & Kelly, 2011). Using data from Twitter and online local newspapers likely to cover the regional merger, this chapter first uses an analysis of verbal data (Fairclough, 1995) to track trends in Twitter discourse surrounding an energy merger. We address the question of Twitter use in response to the merger with an eye toward changes

across time. It is in this unfolding of information exchange, debate, and argumentation across time that we believe provides rhetoricians with unique opportunities to contribute to a growing social science literature on the importance of temporality to organizational and cultural research. Thus, after Zaheer, Albert, and Zaheer (1999), we were mindful of the novelty of our research approach and paid careful attention to time in terms of the existence interval (time needed for the "event" being studied), the observation interval (time we observed), recording interval (frequency the phenomenon was measured), aggregation interval (time-scale used while recording data and aggregating for analysis), and validity interval (time-scale accounted for by theory). After Larsson and Ågerfalk (2013), we admit that approaches to collecting rich online data are still developing as are the automated tools designed to support them. Because of our focus on the discourse practices of Twitter in relation to online newspapers, we were able to collect extensive data across many days within two time frames separated by several months, a feature of the spaces we were studying and the availability of contributions over lengthy periods of time; as well, the availability of web-based data-collection and analysis tools allowed us to manage and analyze complex data sets without requiring a large research team or expensive technologies (Avital, 2000).

Data Collection and Analysis

We had two data collection periods,[3] the first being in January 2011, when the companies announced their proposed merger, and later in September 2011, as administrative hearings to approve the merger process took place. We used keyword searching to identify artifacts on Twitter and several online newspapers' websites and LexisNexis.[4] Once we had collected this data, we segmented the data[5] so that we would be able to compare the relationship between Tweets and online newspaper articles across time. We next developed a coding scheme to analyze our verbal data. Beginning with the press release announcing the merger, we identified several coding themes. The press release first addressed matters of clean energy and alternative energy developments, gesturing toward *technoscientific* concerns. Second, as a business proposition, significant economic implications warranted attention, which we described as *economic* concerns. These two domains gave us two broad categories for which we developed subcategories. Within technoscientific domain, we identified subcategories concerned with health, safety, and the environment. Economic concerns are applied broadly in our coding, identifying not only the companies' business standpoints, but also public concerns. Therefore, within the economic domain, we coded for *individual concerns* (e.g., people with personal investments, such as stocks in the companies), broader *social concerns* (e.g., job losses), and *business concerns* (e.g., the two companies merging leaving no competitors). A third domain was labeled *informative* and included data that did not fall into the two categories with which we were concerned, such as Tweets that were simply reporting that the merger was announced. All of these coding categories were coded as mutually exclusive.[6]

We then performed a temporal analysis (Geisler & Munger, 2002). A temporal analysis afforded us the opportunity to see patterns revealed in the data that we would not be likely to see otherwise—for example, using close reading—giving us a larger scale of pattern and a point at which to depart and look more closely at the texts to see what was going on. As will be explained in our results, we not only looked for trends within each data set, but we also set up a contrast between our Twitter and newspaper data to explore some possible implications of the trends observed. After identifying major themes in the discourse about the merger, we looked at the Tweets more closely to identify what exactly was being communicated about the merger online and the source of this information. Specifically, we noted relationships between online newspaper articles and Tweets that fit into an agenda-setting model (McCombs & Shaw, 1972). That is, we saw Twitter users taking up discussions made in online newspaper articles and sharing those articles with their followers. These data are not statistically significant but do offer another way to look at our case.

Results

Early Tweets about the merger were less speculative about technoscientific or economic concerns. Instead, Tweets primarily delivered news that the merger had been announced. These kinds of Tweets initially made up 96 percent of the discussion about the merger in the first data collection period. Moreover, these Tweets were often borrowed from newspaper headlines, in both national and local papers. Only 4 percent of the Tweets discussed economic concerns, and none discussed technoscientific issues. As the trend of strictly informative Tweets began to slow, we saw a rise in Tweets about economic concerns, representing 14-15 percent of the Twitter discussion. Those Tweets were related to the projected job losses, proposed rate hikes, and the potential negative financial and philanthropic influence on the city where the subsumed company was headquartered. Technoscientific concerns, such as the state of the subsumed company's nuclear plants, remained marginal across all subcategories (Figure 1).

Our online newspaper data help to contextualize the data provided by the Tweets we collected. Although significantly fewer articles were initially coded as "Informative," a clear initial trend where the articles were providing basic information about the merger existed. Much more quickly than the Tweets, newspaper data turned to economic concerns and speculations. After the initial announcement in January, we saw that 22 percent of the newspaper articles focused primarily on general information reporting on the merger, while 78 percent editorialized on the economic implications for the metro areas where

Figure 1. Tracking informative, technoscientific, and economic concerns about the energy merger on Twitter across two different time periods

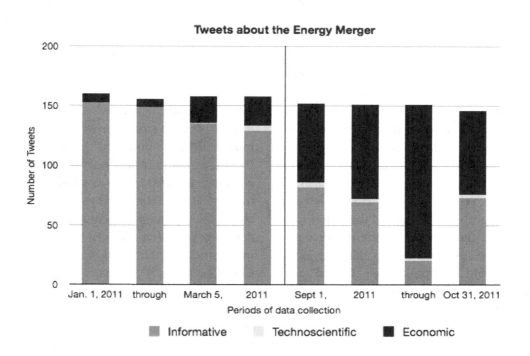

the companies were located as well as the companies' customer bases. None of the articles touched on technoscientific concerns. Given the affordances of the genre, namely length, and the exigence of the enterprise to sell newspapers by providing content publics are interested in, the newspapers' quick turn to economic discussions is unsurprising. Articles expounded on the job losses for employees made redundant by the merger and also speculated about what might happen to philanthropy in the city from which the merged company would eventually be moved. Not long after, the reality of the merger's economic implications, which included rate increases to facilitate site expansion and construction, began to unfold.

Economic concerns grew in both Tweets and newspaper articles during the second data collection period, representing between 43 percent at the beginning and 85 percent of the discussion three quarters of the way through it. Perhaps it would be more precise to say that detailed discussions about economic implications began to shape the discourses occurring in local newspapers and in Tweets about the potential merger. In both the Twitter and the newspaper data, there was minimal representation of individual concerns about the merger's economic implications. A more interesting trend was the discussion, which grew in both the Tweets and online newspaper articles, of the social implications of the merger. Social implications were varied, most often related to job losses, and these social considerations were, interestingly, eclipsed by business concerns. As well, we observed a sharp increase in both Tweets and newspaper articles discussing the implications of the merger in terms of competitiveness. This trend in business concerns coincides with an order from the Federal Energy Regulatory Commission (FERC) conditionally approving the proposed merger, if the two companies could resolve issues of competitiveness.

Most of the Tweets about the merger, in both the first and second data collection periods, were generated by and/or retweeted from news sources such as *The Wall Street Journal*, local newspapers, television news, and business journals, as well as online news reporting sites around the web (Figure 2). Many of these retweets were identical to the original news sources' wording, but occasionally, users would editorialize the information reported when retweeting (sharing) the information. Thus users in front of retweeted information about the merger announcement wrote, "What does that mean for [the company's] employees?" or "is that good news or bad for customers?" One

particularly dramatic Tweet read, "What happens when King Kong marries Godzilla? Apparently we'll find out when [the two companies] merge," referring to the sheer size and potential economic and political power that the newly-merged company. A small percentage did not include any links from news sources and instead simply reflected on the merger. Many of these concerns were economic, such as, "If [the companies] merge... wouldn't that be a Monopoly??? Haven't monopolies been outlawed?" and "[Companies'] CEO's say rate hike necessary to cover severance payments of 2000 employees losing jobs due to merger? R u kidding?" One of the rare tweets about the environmental implications read, "I don't trust this [company's] merger. Still won't make strides in the world of renewables... #No-Coal."

Twitter's function as a platform to disseminate information and potentially facilitate conversations is striking. In the case of the proposed merger between two utility companies, we see how Twitter served in part to amplify the voice

Figure 2. A breakdown of themes in the Tweets about the merger that expressed economic concerns

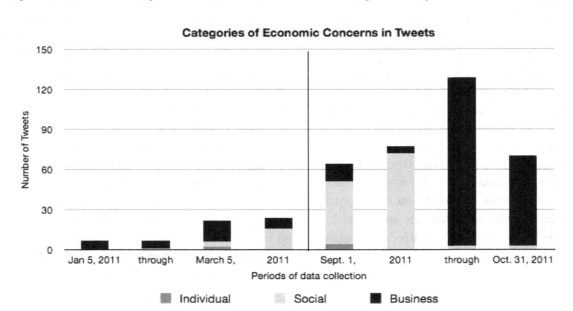

of the newspapers, following in an agenda-setting model. Individual users were quick on the uptake of Tweets from the newspapers, thus expanding the reach of the local papers we studied to a potentially global audience. More to the point, these users also amplified the message of a newspaper when its story was most relevant, when it was first published and Tweeted about by the paper. What becomes an interesting implication, for us, from the interactions between Twitter and online newspapers is that the conversations prescribed by journalists are shared freely. This finding is also supported by existing research that shows Twitter timing follows the timing of major organizational outlets fairly consistently (Binder, 2012; Larsson & Ågerfalk, 2013).

Still, though, we feel almost apologetic about what seems a nonsubstantive conclusion—studies of emerging social media and their relationship to time and timing in communication suggest that we continue to pay attention to our intended audience, the timing of our communications, and our discursive goals for communicating. We anticipate that practice will follow shortly, offering recommendations, principles for action, and methods for analyzing the success of our communication strategies with emerging social media such as Twitter (see, e.g., Hines, 2012)

TIME AND DIGITAL RHETORIC

What we learn from our case study spans theoretical concerns about rhetoric in digital spaces and methodological approaches available to rhetoricians and related scholars invested in the humanistic study of online communication. Differences in the discourses and affordances of the media spaces that encompass the merger event, while not entirely surprising, present certain methodological challenges since it is difficult for researchers to anticipate the particulars of the communication context and the social actions that may result. In both these media spaces, visitors come and go without formal entrance or exit. Also, in addition to the freedom to come and go from the conversational space, the antecedent threads of the conversation isolate and push back against those who come later and wish to join. If visitors stay long enough, conventions of the space invite deeper engagement; thus, hashtags, @replies, and an understanding of supplementary functionality allow for richer conversational exchanges. We are challenged by a digitally-mediated "parlor" that both is and is not what Burke (1941) might have been describing when he described the human condition and our endless conversations.

Chronos offers a rich etymological history that helps us begin to account for various aspects of contemporary technologically-augmented discourses—sensory-perceptual cognitive (mind), technological, and sociocultural—by providing some sense of the global, institutional, and individual constructions and experiences of time, as well as their interaction with one another. In our case study, emerging out of our data we saw three broad domains that we eventually coded. These three domains can be productively theorized with the conceptions of *chronos* we have provided here, with the global conception of *chronos* telling us something of the large-scale economic concerns that were raised. The institutional tells us a great deal about the complex landscape of merging companies, state Utilities Commissions, FERC, and oppositional grassroots organizations concerned with nuclear power and the continued pursuit of dirty energy. Individual concerns about job losses, their own or loved ones', are often undermined by personal uncertainty and ultimately come up against institutional timelines and agendas. Individual concerns are always shaped by and subject to forces beyond their day-to-day experience.

As we watch the reactions, the observations, and associated trends of citizens in our data set, we can see that the larger structures situating them cannot be ignored. Abstracting these structures away from their temporal orientations—announcing the merger, scheduling associated with administrative and regulatory meetings, filing dockets, and so on—we highlight that still all of these structures shape the ways in which the media takes up the issues at hand. Adding another dimension, the media takes up issues on a news cycle, introducing more temporal structuring. This is perpetuated across the Twitter data set that we collected. What this tells us might seem simple, but is critical to keep in mind: the digital spaces wherein discourses occur are always situated within larger structures, spaces, agendas, and timelines.

Not only is it critical for rhetoricians to attend to the temporal affordances of emerging interfaces and communication patterns influencing and influenced by these environments, but we can also benefit considerably by carefully balancing our analyses with the considerable traditions of *kairos* and *chronos*. These traditions account for individual, social, and cultural dimensions of time, timing, and speech events, oral, written, or digitally produced. Our discussion of *kairos* and *chronos* follows arguments that other rhetorical scholars have made in light of discussions about possible "digital rhetorics." Indeed, rhetoric gives us the tools to examine digital spaces with a critical eye. For example, Brooke (2009) "re-visions" the rhetorical canon to give us a framework to study the technological interfaces with which we now work on a daily basis. The canons themselves give rhetorical scholars the tools we need for both analysis and invention; but, Brooke argues, "we must begin to move from a text-based rhetoric, exemplified by our attachment to the printed page, to a rhetoric that can account for the dynamics of the interface" (p. 26). This orientation is not new (e.g., Hill & Mehlenbacher, 1998; Selber, Johnson-Eilola, & Mehlenbacher, 1996), but reminds us that rhetoricians need to remain attentive to the contexts of discourse acts.

This rhetoric that accounts for the interface is one in which the rhetorical theorists have a good understanding of contemporary and emerging technologies and make connections between our historical understanding of the canons and what these technologies accomplish today. Another rhetorical scholar, McCorkle (2012), demonstrates the flexibility of rhetorical theory to account for new technologies as they arise. He argues that the rhetorical canon of delivery is inherently a technological discourse, saying, "theories of delivery have historically helped to foster the cultural reception of emerging technologies of writing and communication by prescribing rules or by examining and privileging tendencies that cause old and new media forms to resemble one another" (p. 5). Delivery has always mattered as a paradigm for acceptance of technology and, thus, asserts McCorkle, it is no coincidence that we find ourselves in a moment where delivery is relevant anew to rhetorical scholars who are once again revisiting ideas about the canon to connect them to digital media that are prominent today.

"So low has Rhetoric sunk," Richards' (1936) words echo, "that we would do better just to dismiss it to Limbo than to trouble ourselves with it—unless we find reason for believing that it can become a study that will minister successfully to important needs" (p. 3). Richards (1936) goes on to outline reasons to be convinced that rhetoric could ultimately "minister" to important issues and needs. And we have followed after him in this chapter, appreciating his statement's timeliness both when he wrote it and today. Most would agree that the number of tools we have to communicate with one another have changed. Communication technologies have developed exponentially, presenting us with a virtual onslaught of new affordances and constraints. But do we need new critical methods to examine the way these tools shape spheres of discourse? "Digital rhetoric" as an approach or theoretical framework would suggest so by its title alone. Perhaps by "digital rhetoric" we simply mean to refer to a subset of environments where discourse acts take place, an increasingly large subset, in which case the question becomes how we might apply our critical tools to have a better understanding of where we may find shortcomings to our traditional methods. For example, *kairos* tells us much about the situation, as Miller shows us. How are situations different in digital spaces? If we understand these digital spaces to be rhetorical spaces, then we ought to be able to devise a compelling argument that the rhetorical concepts we have in our critical toolbox do the job, partially do the job, or do not do the job at all.

We have shown that *kairos* and *chronos*, two conceptions of time, both offer insight into discourses occurring through social media platforms. Twitter is a media wherein discourses that are more broadly situated occur. Twitter acts as a component space of larger conversational spaces that exist across media. Where we as communication scholars often have a somewhat comfortable, although often conflicted, relationship with situating traditional media in larger contexts, social media becomes difficult to place. As Burgelman (2000) reminds us, our "socialisation no longer takes place in one's neighbourhood and identity building is no longer geographically determined" ("What is possible?," para 7). Perhaps what our study demonstrates best is that some preliminary analysis of a particular social media tool within a particular context is essential to understanding what components of the conversational space we are coming to understand in our examination. Instead of dismissing the tool or providing it with undue agency or power, we can more critically situate social media tools in context by approaching them as being situated in larger spheres of discursive and social action.

It should be evident as well from the limited focus of our case study that situation and context are crucial to a rhetorical account of these new technological affordances. Presuming that rhetoric might account for an entire media space under some unified theory would be to take a distinctly a-rhetorical approach. To show how rhetorical theory fails to account for the affordances and constraints of digital media (and specifically social media tools in our case), one must articulate how they change the rhetorical situation so dramatically as to render the vast bodies of rhetorical literature irrelevant. It

appears that, in the case we have examined, many of the same rhetorical constraints—those beyond the technology alone—are at play and shaping the situation. Rhetorical actors bring to new technologies what is in their rhetorical repertoire: we see, for example, how people learn to use news, by reading, suggesting, and sharing.

Our study of *kairos* and *chronos* through discourses taking place on Twitter additionally serves as an important reminder that using the term "digital rhetoric," focusing primarily on the modifier "digital," creates a distinction that we might not want to be making. Not only does it distinguish between "analog" and "digital," but such phrasing also encourages the idea that the technology itself is somehow set apart from the broader historical, cultural, social, economic, legal, and political spheres. Or, to borrow from Miller (1979), "Reality doesn't come in packages clearly marked 'technical' or 'nontechnical'" (p. 613). In her case, she was talking about the matter of technical writing and its position in relation to the humanistic tradition. Quotable as the statement is, it also invokes an important reminder to those interested in a "digital rhetoric." Placing the emphasis on the adjective, "digital," in "digital rhetoric" participates in what Miller aptly describes as reasoning "obscured by a tradition of thought in both the sciences and the humanities, a tradition which has become a tacit understanding, a form of common sense" and this understanding she describes as a "positivist view of science (and of rhetoric)" (Miller, p. 610, 615).

But this time we are not looking through the rhetorical to the scientific—the objective world of facts and reality, a positivist might posit—but we're looking through the rhetorical to the "digital" perhaps. *Chronos* reminds us that the technologies of time-keeping, including the various digital realizations, are still a rhetorical matter. Indeed, they have always been a rhetorical matter if we take rhetoric to be a study of "misunderstanding and its remedies" where "[m]eanings mind intensely" (Richards p. 1, 10). Put another way, looking to *chronos* reminds us that the "digital" in what we wish to call a "digital rhetoric" has antecedent forms—and interacts with antecedent forms such as the newspaper article in our study—and these forms are, we suggest, not the product of material objects alone, but of the human crafting of *techn*ology in material, cultural, social, etc. spheres through rhetorical acts. When looking to the emerging digital spheres for these *ongoing* negotiations and rhetorical efforts we are looking not only to the material technological forms, but we are also, and especially, looking to contemporary discursive spheres and discourse acts, which are partially situated in digital technologies, but entirely situated in the cultural, social, and rhetorical spheres that we all inhabit.

We end here speculating about rhetorical constraints and rhetorical situations with new technologies, an area rich for future research. We are particularly interested in what influence the rise of newly afforded strategies, such as open access and blogging, might have on our consideration of discursive spaces afforded by digital media. Exploring these questions from a rhetorical orientation might proceed by examining highly theorized rhetorical concepts, as Brooke (2009) and McCorkle (2012) do, and as we have gestured toward with *kairos*. Further, undertheorized rhetorical concepts from antiquity may offer crucial sites for further inquiry, as we suggest *chronos* does. The uptake of this concept in disciplines across the social sciences and humanities suggests that there is a certain utility to the term, *kairos*, even though its roots reside in antiquity. This underscores the importance of evaluating how the affordances and constraints of these new technologies, not the technologies themselves, participate in changing rhetorical situations. Conversely, looking to the changing rhetorical situations we encounter ought to afford us fresh perspectives on the technological evolution we continue to watch rapidly unfolding.

REFERENCES

Acar, A., & Muraki, Y. (2011). Twitter for crisis communication: Lessons learned from Japan's tsunami disaster. *International Journal of Web Based Communities*, 7(3), 392–402. doi:10.1504/IJWBC.2011.041206

Ancona, D. G., Okhuysen, G. A., & Perlow, L. A. (2001). Taking time to integrate temporal research. *Academy of Management Review*, 25(4), 512–529.

Avital, M. (2000). Dealing with time in social inquiry: A tension between method and lived experience. *Organization Science*, 11(6), 665–673. doi:10.1287/orsc.11.6.665.12532

Baumlin, J. S. (1987). Decorum, kairos, and the new rhetoric. *PRE/TEXT, 5*, 171–183.

Binder, A. R. (2012). Figuring out #Fukushima: An initial look at functions and content of US Twitter commentary about nuclear risk. *Environmental Communication: A Journal of Nature and Culture, 6*(2), 268–277.

Bitzer, L. F. (1968). The rhetorical situation. *Philosophy & Rhetoric, 1*(1), 1–14.

Bluedorn, A. C. (2002). *The human organization of time: Temporal realities and experience*. Stanford, CA: Stanford University Press.

Booth, W. C. (1961). *The rhetoric of fiction*. Chicago, IL: University of Chicago Press.

Booth, W. C. (1974). *The rhetoric of irony*. Chicago, IL: University of Chicago Press.

Borgmann, A. (2000). *Holding on to reality: The nature of information at the turn of the millennium*. Chicago, IL: University of Chicago Press.

Bostock, D. (2006). *Space, time, matter, and form: Essays on Aristotle's* Physics (Oxford Aristotle Series). J. Annas and L. Judson (Eds.). New York, NY: Oxford.

Brooke, C. G. (2009). *Lingua fracta: Towards a rhetoric of new media*. Cresskill, NJ: Hampton Press.

Burgelman, J. C. (2000). Traveling with communication technologies in space, time, and everyday life: An exploration of their impact. *First Monday*, 5(3). doi:10.5210/fm.v5i3,733

Burke, K. (1941). *The philosophy of literary form*. Berkeley, CA: University of California Press.

Burke, K. (1969). *A grammar of motives*. Berkeley, CA: University of California Press.

Burton, G. O. (n. d.). Figures of time. In *Silva Rhetoricae*. Retrieved from http://rhetoric.byu.edu

Carr, N. (2010). *The shallows: What the Internet is doing to our brains*. New York, NY: Norton.

Carter, M. (1988). Stasis and kairos: Principles of social construction in classical rhetoric. *Rhetoric Review*, 7(1), 97–112. doi:10.1080/07350198809388842

Castells, M. (2000). *The rise of the networked society* (The information age: Economy, society, and culture, Vol. 1). Oxford, UK: Blackwell Publishers.

Collins, D. (2011). *Is Twitter a waste of time?* Problogger, 2 June 2011. Retrieved from http://www.problogger.net/archives/2011/06/02/is-twitter-a-waste-of-time/

Comninos, A. (2011). *E-revolutions and cyber crackdowns: User-generated content and social networking in protests in MENA and beyond*. (Thematic reports of the Global Information Society Watch). Retrieved from http://www.giswatch.org/sites/default/files/gisw_-_e-revolutions_and_cyber_crackdowns_0.pdf

Doan, S., Vo, B.-K. H., & Collier, N. (2011). An analysis of Twitter messages in the 2011 Tohoku earthquake. In *Proceedings of the eHealth 2011 Conference*, (pp. 58–66).

Engeström, Y. (1999). Activity theory and individual and social transformation. In Y. Engeström, R. Miettinen, & R. Punamäki (Eds.), *Perspectives on activity theory* (pp. 19–38). Cambridge, UK: Cambridge University Press. doi:10.1017/CBO9780511812774.003

Engeström, Y. (2000). Can people learn to master their future? *Journal of the Learning Sciences*, 9(4), 525–534. doi:10.1207/S15327809JLS0904_8

Enos, R. L. (2002). Inventional constraints on the technographers of ancient Athens. In P. Sipiora, & J. S. Baumlin (Eds.), *Rhetoric and kairos: Essays in history, theory, and praxis* (pp. 77–88). Albany, NY: State University of New York Press.

Eraut, M. (2004). Learning to change and/or changing to learn. *Learning in Health and Social Care*, 3(3), 111–117. doi:10.1111/j.1473-6861.2004.00073.x

Evans, V. (2004). *The structure of time: Language, meaning, and temporal cognition*. Amsterdam, The Netherlands: John Benjamins. doi:10.1075/hcp.12

Faculty Focus. (2010). *Twitter in higher education 2010: Usage habits and trends of today's college faculty*. Retrieved from http://www.facultyfocus.com/free-reports/twitter-in-higher-education-2010-usage-habits-and-trends-of-todays-college-faculty/

Fairclough, N. (1995). *Critical discourse analysis*. Boston, MA: Addison Wesley.

Gaonkar, D. P. (1997). The idea of rhetoric in the rhetoric of science. In A. G. Gross, & W. M. Keith (Eds.), *Rhetorical hermeneutics: Invention and interpretation in the age of science* (pp. 25–88). Albany, NY: SUNY Press.

Garber, M. (2012, January 31). Be better at Twitter: The definitive data-driven guide. *The Atlantic*. Retrieved from http://www.theatlantic.com/technology/archive/2012/01/be-better-at-twitter-the-definitive-data-driven-guide/252273/

Geisler, C., & Munger, R. (2002). Temporal analysis: A primer exemplified by a case from prehospital care. In E. Barton, & G. Stygall (Eds.), *Discourse studies in composition* (pp. 283–304). Cresskill, NJ: Hampton Press.

Gladwell, M. (2010). Small change: Why the revolution will not be tweeted. *New Yorker* (New York, N.Y.), (October): 4. Retrieved from http://www.newyorker.com/reporting/2010/10/04/101004fa_fact_gladwell?currentPage=al

Gleick, J. (1999). *Faster: The acceleration of just about everything*. New York, NY: Vintage Books.

Gorn, G. J., Chattopadhyay, A., Sengupta, J., & Tripathi, S. (2004). Waiting for the Web: How screen color affects time perception. *JMR, Journal of Marketing Research*, *41*(2), 215–225. doi:10.1509/jmkr.41.2.215.28668

Hill, C. A., & Mehlenbacher, B. (1998). Transitional generations and World Wide Web reading and writing: Implications of a hypertextual interface for the masses. *TEXT Technology*, *8*(4), 29–47.

Hines, K. (2012). An in-depth look at the science of Twitter timing. *KISSmetrics: A blog about analytics, marketing and testing*. Retrieved from https://blog.kissmetrics.com/the-science-of-twitter-timing/

Kelly, A. R., & Kittle Autry, M. (2013). Access, accommodation, and science: Knowledge in an 'open' world. *First Monday*, *18*(6). doi:10.5210/fm.v18i6.4341

Kelly, A. R., & Miller, C. R. (forthcoming). Intersections: Scientific and parascientific communication on the Internet. In A. Gross, & J. Buehl (Eds.), *Science and the Internet: Communicating knowledge in a digital age*. Amityville, NY: Baywood Press.

Kenyon, S. (2008). Internet use and time use: The importance of multitasking. *Time & Society*, *17*(2/3), 283–318. doi:10.1177/0961463X08093426

Khazan, O. (2013, June 12). These charts show how crucial Twitter is for the Turkey protesters. *The Atlantic*. Retrieved from http://www.theatlantic.com/international/archive/2013/06/these-charts-show-how-crucial-twitter-is-for-the-turkey-protesters/276798/

Kinneavy, J. L. (1986). *Kairos*: A neglected concept in classical rhetoric. In J. D. Moss (Ed.), *Rhetoric and praxis: The contribution of classical rhetoric to practical reasoning* (pp. 79–105). Washington, DC: The Catholic University of America Press.

Kinsella, W. J., Kelly, A. R., & Kittle Autry, M. (2013). Risk, regulation, and rhetorical boundaries: Claims and challenges surrounding a purported nuclear renaissance. *Communication Monographs*, *80*(3). doi:10.1080/03637751.2013.788253

Kittle Autry, M., & Kelly, A. R. (2011). A humanistic approach to the study of social media: Combining social network analysis and case study research. In *Proceedings for the 29th ACM International Conference on Design of Communication*. (pp. 257-260). Pisa, Italy: ACM.

Larsson, A. O., & Ågerfalk, P. J. (2013). Snowing, freezing … tweeting? Organizational Twitter use during crisis. *First Monday*, *18*(6). Retrieved from http://firstmonday.org/ojs/index.php/fm/article/view/4294/3688 doi:10.5210/fm.v18i6.4294

Lawn, R. (2012, September 6). Tu and Twitter: Is it the end for 'vous' in French? *BBC News Magazine*. Retrieved from http://www.bbc.co.uk/news/magazine-19499771

Leccardi, C. (2003). Resisting acceleration society. *Constellations* (Oxford, England), *10*(1), 34–41. doi:10.1111/1467-8675.00310

Lee, H., & Liebenau, J. (2000). Time and the Internet at the turn of the millennium. *Time & Society*, *9*(43), 43–56. doi:10.1177/0961463X00009001003

Leetaru, K. H., Wang, S., Cao, G., Padmanabhan, A., & Shook, E. (2013). Mapping the global Twitter heartbeat: The geography of Twitter. *First Monday*, *18*(5-6).

Lindgren, S. (2013). *New noise: A cultural sociology of digital disruption*. New York, NY: Peter Lang.

Lockett, A., Losh, E., Rieder, D. M., Sample, M., Stolley, K., & Vee, A. (2012). The role of computational literacy in computers and writing. *Enculturation, 14*.

Massey, A. P., Montoya-Weiss, M. M., & Hung, Y.-T. (2003). Because time matters: Temporal coordination in global virtual project teams. *Journal of Management Information Systems*, *19*(4), 129–155.

Mattelart, A. (1996). *The invention of communication* (S. Emanuel, Trans.). Minneapolis, MN: University of Minnesota Press.

Maznevski, M. L., & Chudoba, K. M. (2000). Bridging space over time: Global virtual team dynamics and effectiveness. *Organization Science*, *11*(5), 473–492. doi:10.1287/orsc.11.5.473.15200

McCombs, M., & Shaw, D. (1972). The agenda setting function of mass media. *Public Opinion Quarterly*, *36*(2), 176–187. doi:10.1086/267990

McCorkle, B. (2012). *Rhetorical delivery as technological discourse*. Carbondale, IL: Southern Illinois University Press.

McLuhan, M. (2003). *Understanding media: The extensions of man*. Corte Madera, CA: Gingko Press.

McLuhan, M., & Fiore, Q. (1967). *The medium is the message*. New York, NY: Bantam.

Miller, C. R. (1979). What's practical about technical writing? In B. E. Fearing, & W. K. Sparrow (Eds.), *Technical writing: Theory and practice* (pp. 14–24). New York, NY: MLA.

Miller, C. R. (1992). Kairos in the rhetoric of science. In S. P. Witte, N. Nakadate, & R. D. Cherry (Eds.), *A rhetoric of doing: Essays on written discourse in honor of James L. Kinneavy* (pp. 310–327). Carbondale, IL: Southern Illinois University Press.

Miller, C. R. (1994). Opportunity, opportunism, and progress: Kairos in the rhetoric of technology. *Argumentation*, *8*, 81–96. doi:10.1007/BF00710705

Miller, C. R. (2002). Forward. In P. Sipiora, & J. S. Baumlin (Eds.), *Rhetoric and Kairos: Essays in history, theory, and praxis*. Albany, NY: State University of New York Press.

Morozov, E. (2011). *The net delusion: The dark side of Internet freedom*. Jackson, TN: PublicAffairs.

Mumford, L. (1934). *Technics and civilization*. San Diego, CA: Harcourt Brace.

Murthy, D. (2012). *Twitter: Social communication in the Twitter age*. Boston, MA: Polity.

National Institute for Standards and Technology. (2010). *NIST Time*. Retrieved from http://www.nist.gov/pml/div688/utcnist.cfm

National Institute for Standards and Technology. (n.d.). *Unit of time (second)*. Retrieved from http://physics.nist.gov/cuu/Units/second.html

Negroponte, N. (1979). 1996). Books without pages. *SIGDOC Asterisk Journal of Computer Documentation, 20*(3), 2–8. doi:10.1145/235741.235742

Orlikowski, W. J., & Yates, J. (2002). It's about time: Temporal structuring in organizations. *Organization Science, 13*(6), 684–700. doi:10.1287/orsc.13.6.684.501

Perelman, C., & Olbrechts-Tyteca, L. (1969). *The new rhetoric. A treatise on argumentation*. Notre Dame, IN: University of Notre Dame Press.

Perlow, L. A. (1999). The time famine: Toward a sociology of work time. *Administrative Science Quarterly, 44*(1), 57–81. doi:10.2307/2667031

Peters, J. D. (2009, April). *Calendar, Clock, Tower*. Paper given at the Media in Transition 6 conference, Cambridge, MA.

Ralon, L. (2012, July 25). Interview with Carolyn Miller. *Figure/Ground Communication*. Retrieved from http://figureground.ca/2012/07/25/interview-with-carolyn-r-miller/

Ramo, H. (1999). An Aristotelian human time-space manifold. *Time & Society, 8*(2-3), 309–328. doi:10.1177/0961463X99008002006

Richards, I. A. (1936). *The philosophy of rhetoric*. New York, NY: Oxford University Press.

Sakaki, T. (2010). Earthquake shakes Twitter users: Real-time event detection by social sensors. In *Proceedings of the International World Wide Web Conference*, (pp. 851–860).

Selber, S. A., Johnson-Eilola, J., & Mehlenbacher, B. (1996). Online support systems. *ACM Computing Surveys, 28*(1), 197–200. doi:10.1145/234313.234397

Sipiora, P. (2002). Introduction: The ancient concept of *kairos*. In P. Sipiora, & J. S. Baumlin (Eds.), *Rhetoric and kairos: Essays in history, theory, and praxis* (pp. 1–19). Albany, NY: State University of New York Press.

Smith, A., & Brenner, J. (2012). *Twitter use 2012* (Report of the PEW Internet and American Life Project). Washington, DC: PEW Research Center. Retrieved from http://www.pewinternet.org/~/media//Files/Reports/2012/PIP_Twitter_Use_2012.pdf

Smith, J. E. (2002). Time and qualitative time. In P. Sipiora, & J. S. Baumlin (Eds.), *Rhetoric and kairos: Essays in history, theory, and praxis* (pp. 46–57). Albany, NY: State University of New York Press.

Thomson, R., Ito, N., Suda, H., Lin, F., Liu, Y., Hayasaka, R., et al. (2012). Trusting Tweets: The Fukushima disaster and information source credibility on Twitter. In *Proceedings of the 9th International ISCRAM Conference*, (pp. 1–10).

Tsukayama, H. (2012, September 24). Facebook, Twitter and data access. *The Washington Post*. Retrieved from http://www.washingtonpost.com/business/technology/facebook-twitter-and-data-access/2012/09/24/ab8eb0a8-0655-11e2-afff-d6c7f20a83bf_story.html

Twitter. (2013). *About*. Retrieved from https://about.twitter.com/

Vargas, J. A. (2011, February 7). Egypt, the age of disruption and the me-in-media. *The Huffington Post*. Retrieved from http://www.huffingtonpost.com/jose-antonio-vargas/egypt-age-of-disruption-me-in-media_b_819481.html

Vatz, R. E. (1968). The myth of the rhetorical situation. *Philosophy & Rhetoric, 6*(3), 154–161.

Walker, J. (2009). Time as the fourth dimension in the globalization of higher education. *The Journal of Higher Education*, *80*(5), 483–509. doi:10.1353/jhe.0.0061

Zaheer, S., Albert, S., & Zaheer, A. (1999). Time scales and organizational theory. *Academy of Management Review*, *24*(4), 725–741.

KEY TERMS AND DEFINITIONS

Chronos: Often characterized as linear time such as the progress of a clock.

Digital Media: A form of media storage and transmission that relies on discrete representation of information. Playfully, see *Oxford English Dictionary* from Latin *digitus*, digits, fingers for counting.

Kairos: Traditionally has been understood as an opportune moment that might one might seize for rhetorical effect.

Rhetoric: Richards would tell us that rhetoric is the study of "misunderstanding and its remedies" (1936, p. 3).

Social Media: Sometimes characterized by technological affordance, social media describes RSS feeds, blogs, wikis, podcasts; alternatively, social media might be described in terms task orientation, such as identity management, tagging, commenting, real-time sharing, and integration and display of data from other social sites.

ENDNOTES

[1] All authors contributed extensively and equally to this work.

[2] See Silva Rhetorica for further detail on these figures. Burton, Gideon O. "Figures of Time." *Silva Rhetoricae*. Brigham Young University. http://rhetoric.byu.edu

[3] During our first data collection period we used Google RealTime as a source for Tweets. RealTime no longer offered Twitter feeds during the second data collection period. Our second data collection method was to capture Tweets real-time with an RSS feed searching for specific terms.

[4] Our sample consisted of the four key cities for the merger, including the headquarters for both companies and cities that would be affected by future energy infrastructure development. We collected online newspaper articles from eleven newspapers across two states, for a total of 42 articles pertaining to the merger. Several of the newspaper articles were re-published across newspapers owned by the same media company.

[5] Both Tweets and newspaper articles were left as individual segments, meaning that an entire Tweet or an entire newspaper article served as one unit of data in our analysis. Segmenting was divided across eight periods, four for each data collection period, by dividing the number of Tweets for each period. Newspaper articles were then included in the periods determined by the Tweets.

[6] We ran preliminary inter-coder testing, having a coder who was not associated with the project code 30 minutes worth of data. After revising the definitions and examples for the coding scheme, based on the feedback from this first coder, a second coder associated with the project coded more of the data. These codes were tested against a sample of 10 percent of the Twitter data by our second coder and one of the authors, with a resulting inter-coder reliability Kappa coefficient of 0.903 across the three domains.

Chapter 13
A Match Made in "Outer Heaven:"
The Digital Age Vis–à–Vis the Bomb in *Guns of the Patriots*

Jorge Gomez
University of Texas at El Paso, USA

ABSTRACT

The stealth-action videogame Metal Gear Solid 4: Guns of the Patriots features the tired heroics of Solid Snake (also known as Old Snake), a retired, legendary soldier whose services are demanded one last time by a world in perpetual war. This epic game, containing almost ten hours of cutscenes alone, delineates the consequences not only of nuclear proliferation, but of mass (re)production in a digital age. In this fourth and final entry in the Solid Snake saga the two go hand-in-hand: a nuclear age exacerbated by advanced technology, advanced technology proliferated under the banner of a post-Cold War war economy. In this chapter, Kenneth Burke's rhetoric of rebirth and Slavoj Žižek's ideological criticism, along with several ludological frameworks, are adopted to show how various multiliteracies can be unearthed from this artifact of digital rhetoric. The chapter closes with implications for digital rhetoric studies.

DOI: 10.4018/978-1-4666-4916-3.ch013

Copyright © 2014, IGI Global. Copying or distributing in print or electronic forms without written permission of IGI Global is prohibited.

The game is not the experience. The game enables the experience, but it is not the experience (Jesse Schell, The Art of Game Design, p. 10).

INTRODUCTION

Their ludological skeleton notwithstanding, more and more modern videogames embody artifacts of interest in rhetoric, literary, and literacy studies. In fact, as Colby, Johnson and Colby (2013) point out, three academic conversations about videogames currently converge: "the study of games as games, digital games studies, ludology; composition-rhetoric, writing studies, writing pedagogy; and discourse analysis, literacy studies" (p. 1). Through analysis of a particular videogame, my aim here is to show how the medium's multimodal nature lends itself to multidisciplinary approaches that can prove fruitful not only for understanding videogames as a form of digital rhetoric but for understanding multiliteracies. As Colby, Johnson and Colby (2013) state, "By researching video games and gameplay practices, scholars have the opportunity to understand gamers' complex learning and literacy development strategies, practices that carry significant implications for education in general" (p. 1). Aside from analyzing videogames through a rhetorical lens, some of the cards games bring to the table are "genres at least as diverse as literary genres, layers of interactivity, different styles of gameplay, player and player-character identities…procedurality, the rules of gameplay, gaming culture, gaming terminology, gaming history, the gaming industry, theories of design" (Johnson & Colby, 2013, p. 94). Even so, my analysis is at heart rhetorical, treating videogames as rhetorical artifacts, as others have (Bogost, 2008; Boone, 2008; Bourgonjon, Rutten, Soetaert, & Valcke, 2011; Colby, Johnson, & Colby 2013; Garrelts, 2013; Mateas & Stern, 2005; McAllister, 2006; Voorhees, 2009). In my case, I define "rhetoric" as "the art of communication" in order to encompass purposes other than persuading

(e.g., obfuscating), and "rhetorical artifact" as "any sign that communicates."

In presenting language as symbolic action at heart, Burke (1966) broadened the scope of rhetoric to encompass "any use of symbol systems in general," defining humankind as "'the symbol-using, symbol-making, and symbol-misusing animal'" and the "*Inventor of the negative*" (pp. 63, 6, 9). My rationale for employing Burke's (1962) dramatism (the perspective that "treats language and thought primarily as modes of action") for *Guns of the Patriots* is grounded in the idea that videogames, as rhetorical artifacts, are complex systems made up of symbols enacted by the player (p. xxii). Bogost (2008) echoes how Burke birthed the field of visual rhetoric: "In the tradition of oral and written rhetoric, language remains central. But Burke's understanding of humans as creators and consumers of symbolic systems expands rhetoric to include nonverbal domains known and yet to be invented or discovered" (p. 124). Among these domains are videogames as digital symbolic systems, and several scholars have applied Burke's theories to analyze them: Boone (2008) to *World of Warcraft*; Soetaert, Bourgonjon, and Rutten (2011) to *Civilization* and *Heavy Rain*; Bourgonjon, Rutten, Soetaert, and Valcke (2011) to *BioShock*; McAllister (2006) to avatars; and Voorhees (2009) to *Final Fantasy*. As of yet there is no scholarship on any game in the *Metal Gear Solid* saga situated in the wider multiliteracies or applying Burke's theories. Whereas scholars who do apply Burke focus on Burke's dramatist pentad (act, scene, agent, agency and purpose), my focus is Burke's rhetoric of rebirth (within dramatism) as one of several interpretive schema of multiliteracies that helps illuminate the arguments, symbols, and overall narrative of *Guns of the Patriots*. In addition to Burke as theoretical lens, I also adopt Slavoj Žižek's criticism of techno-ideology and deep ecology, and specific to ludology, Mateas and Stern's (2005) definitions of immersion and agency as well as Bissell's (2011) distinction between the framed narrative and ludonarrative.

The role *Metal Gear Solid 4: Guns of the Patriots* serves within the series is not only climactic capstone to the tale of Solid Snake, but "a vindication of Kojima's unique interpretation of the videogame medium," per *IGN UK* (as cited in *Metal gear solid 4*, 2010). The game's elements speak to the genre's affordances employing rhetoric through a multimodal medium, in turn shaping multiliteracies, making *Guns of the Patriots* a salient object of study for digital rhetoric. Specifically, the game's narrative centered around artificial intelligence beset by nuclear weapons comprises a contra-nuclear, contra-technology, and contra-warfare argument that can only be discerned through critical reflection. This argument is only reinforced when Kojima stated his *Metal Gear* saga "has an 'anti-war, anti-nuke' message throughout the series" (Tamari, n.d.). In this chapter, I analyze *Guns of the Patriots* through the lens of Kenneth Burke's rhetoric of rebirth and Slavoj Žižek's criticism of both techno-ideology and deep ecology to elucidate the game's symbolic meaning. First, I define digital rhetoric and multiliteracies and fit videogames within them, then providing an overview of Burke's rhetoric and Žižek's criticism, and reviewing the literature on nuclear games, *Metal Gear*, and nuclear rhetoric. Thereafter, I offer a précis of the game's plot and overall context, describe the game's elements from a rhetorical lens, and derive a number of literacies. Following the rhetorical analysis, I close with implications and future directions for digital rhetoric studies.

BACKGROUND

Digital Rhetoric, Videogames, and Multiliteracies

Before looking at *Guns of the Patriots* as a rhetorical artifact, I would like to define "digital rhetoric" as "the art of bit-modulated communication." This definition would mean digital rhetoric is circumscribed by discrete binary systems (true/false, on/off, yes/no) such as those in computers, programs, websites, social media, email, mobile phones, videogames and new media in general. Delimited this way, one important subset of digital rhetoric would be screen-modulated rhetoric, which in turn could address the "*materiality* of mode [that] holds specific potentials for representation, and at the same time brings certain limitations," or the affordances of conveying information through screens/touchscreens (Kress, 2003, p. 45). As opposed to the logic of writing for example, the screen is organized by the logic of the image, which in turn is spatially arranged and "simultaneously present" (Kress, 2003, p. 20). As Zappen (2005) writes: "Studies of digital rhetoric help to explain how traditional rhetorical strategies of persuasion function and are being reconfigured in digital spaces" (p. 319). Hence, one of the scholarly goals of digital rhetoric should be assessing digital affordances: how does digital communication differ from its analog counterpart, and how do the differences affect the audience, the author, and the text? For instance, how does an online article from the *New York Times* differ from the print-based version, or the mobile version? With videogames (as with other bit-modulated communication), among the various affordances are layers of interactivity (to the point of immersion and simulation of a range of experiences), real-time feedback, and multiple modes of communication (the "multimodal literacy *par excellence*") (Gee, 2007, p. 18). My chosen vantage point for studying these videogame affordances is that of multiliteracies.

By "multiliteracies," I mean literacy in multicultural, multimodal, and multilinguistic meaning-making. As Cope and Kalantzis (2000) outline, multiliteracies imports the need for an "open-ended and flexible functional grammar which assists language learners to describe language differences (cultural, subcultural, regional/national, technical, context-specific, and so on) and the multimodal channels of meaning now so important to communication" (p. 6). From a multi-modal framework this grammar requires "reading across varied and hybrid semiotic fields and being able to critically and hermeneutically process print, graphics, moving images, and sound" (Kellner, 2002, p. 163). As Colby, Johnson and Colby (2013) sum up, videogames "become exemplar multimodal texts, aligning word, image, and sound with the rules and operations constrained by computer technologies but composed by teams of writers, designers, and artists to persuade and entertain" (p. 4). Instead of being "constrained" by bits however, I would contend videogames can lay claim to certain affordances precisely because they are bit-modulated communication. Specifically, videogames *situate meaning in a multimodal space through embodied experiences to solve problems and reflect on the intricacies of the design of imagined worlds*" (Gee, 2007, pp. 40-41). Were we to lose track of how meaning is being constructed in these videogame spaces, "or which rhetorical representations and practices they encounter as they work in and around those games, or what motivates them to teach and learn in these language rich venues," Selfe and Hawisher (2013) warn "we run the risk of ignoring a whole arena of serious language use and play" (p. xviii). Such an arena is only underscored by the fact that videogames are growing increasingly more complex as memory capacity and processing speeds continue to expand.

Videogames are a prime candidate in literacy studies for several reasons. One reason is the ways videogames mirror more than they subvert sociopolitical paradigms of inequality. In multiple literacies we should address, as Kellner (2002) underlines, "how media culture can advance sexism, racism, ethnocentrism, homophobia, and other forms of prejudice, as well as misinformation, problematic ideologies, and questionable values, and in this way we can promote a dialectical approach to the media" (p. 160). Historically, as Selfe and Hawisher (2013) point out, the "language practices—the reading,

composing, and communicating that happen in, around, and throughout computer gaming environments—have been of interest to compositionists since gaming's appearance on early personal computers" (p. xv). Partly because they immerse players into their worlds, there is the notion that learning through videogames is a natural, intuitive yet challenging process (Kress, 2007; Squire, 2006). A videogame's immersive nature can indeed represent "a move away from decontextualised representation and imaginary identification towards participation, communication and co-creation" that is emblematic of multiliteracies (Kress & Van Leewen, 2001, p. 110). Nonetheless, in a mass-market product one cannot discount the potential for inadvertently succumbing to propaganda even when actively co-creating. Multiliteracies therefore plays a critical role in helping learners parse the varied messages embedded in videogames. As Kellner (2002) summarizes:

Media culture teaches proper and improper behavior, gender roles, values, and knowledge of the world. Individuals are often not aware that they are being educated and constructed by media culture, as its pedagogy is frequently invisible and subliminal. This situation calls for critical approaches that make us aware of how media construct meanings, influence and educate audiences, and impose their messages and values. A media literate person is skillful in analysing media codes and conventions, able to criticise stereotypes, values, and ideologies, and competent to interpret the multiple meanings and messages generated by media texts. (p. 159)

In addition to literacy skills pertaining to videogames, Colby (2013) emphasizes that "games should be used in such a way that the gaming literacies players already possess help them bridge more complex academic literacies" (p. 135). Although Colby (2013) observes that these gaming literacies are sometimes gender-specific, what her study found was that "females can enjoy learning with video games as much as males, provided they have access to the gaming literacies that the males have" (p. 136). In terms of the sociopolitical landscape and the role of education, Luke (2000) proclaims that lest "educators take a lead in developing appropriate pedagogies for these new electronic media and forms of communication, corporate experts will be the ones who determine how people will learn, what they learn, and what constitutes literacy" (p. 71). Likewise, Snyder (2002) states that the "print-based industrial model of education needs to be redesigned to take account of the reality that young people are more likely to develop complex literacy repertoires outside educational institutions" (p. 8). Some of these literacy repertoires underscore an awareness of the symbolism behind stories, spaces, and societies in games, an ability to read between the lines and below the surface of things, a skill in reading what is "frequently invisible and subliminal," and a capacity for decoding "stereotypes, values, and ideologies" (Kellner, 2002). Literacy in decoding symbolic meanings is of upmost relevance to multimodal literacy if we assume modes are "semiotic resources" that are "culturally and socially fashioned," considering as well that each mode "carries only part of the informational 'load': no mode fully carries all the meaning" (Kress & Van Leeuwen, 2001, p. 21; Kress, 2003, p. 45, pp. 20-21). Semiotically then, symbols are one of the inner-layer modes of meaning within a given text, irrespective of whether the symbol was intentionally implanted by the author.

Comprehending the symbolic imperatives within games might seem elided by the notion that videogames are to be played and not reflected upon. Yet as Bogost (2008) retorts, whereas videogames are always played, "the sort of play that we perform is not always the stuff of leisure. Rather, when we play, we explore the possibility space of a set of rules—we learn to understand and evaluate a game's meaning" (p. 136). In grasping the meaning of a game, one can find videogames "make arguments about how social or cultural systems work in the world—or how they could work, or don't work…When we play video games, we can interpret these arguments and consider their place in our lives" (p. 136). Nonetheless, while playing videogames might be an organic practice for some players, many of these arguments are not framed explicitly but rather symbolically, with characters, settings, and events standing for ideas that can be strung into broader themes. And since symbols contain much of what is *meaningful* in an artifact and yet are not immediately discernible (as opposed to signifiers), mining symbols from artifacts does not come naturally, it must be taught. To interpret the symbolism in *Guns of the Patriots*, I find the theoretical lens of Burke's dramatism and Žižek's ideological criticism quite apropos.

Kenneth Burke's Dramatism

Before delving into Burke's rebirth rhetoric, it is important to understand Burke's views on dramatism. In short, Burke's (1962) dramatism is the theory that "treats language and thought primarily as modes of action" (p. xxii). To Burke (1966), language is a "species of action, symbolic action," a tool, a device that can help humanity survive or destroy each other, a kind of "fortunate fall," making redemption, one of the key features in rebirth rhetoric, possible (p. 15; Rueckert, 1982). Language is symbolic action in part because, according to Burke (1966), what distinguishes Homo sapiens from other species is that "*Man is the symbol-using animal*" (p. 3). Burke's motto for dramatism is, "By and through language, beyond language" (as cited in Rueckert, 1982, p. 137). This means that through language one can "unify himself and the world," and drive toward perfection "set in motion and fed by the impulse to abstraction [of ideas]" (Rueckert, 1982, p. 137). Burke (1966) believes that inherent to the nature of symbol systems is a "principle of perfection" that together with the view of humankind as the symbol-using animal means "man is moved by this principle," such that humankind is *"rotten with perfection"* ("perfection" used ironically) (pp. 17, 16). Just as well, the "essence of drama [is] moral choice and willed action" (Rueckert, 1982, p. 145). Dramatism thus deals with "agon," the conflict between good and evil (Bobbitt, 2004). In dramatist criticism, the "truly representative case of human motivation must be linguistic," include a "representative anecdote" containing scope, and be a "summation" of the fundamental symbols of conflict in the grander discourse (Bobbitt, 2004, p. 7). I consider *Guns of the Patriots* a case-in-point for this representation.

Burke's Rhetoric of Rebirth

One of the ways in which Burke's dramatism functions is through Burke's drama of redemption, the secular version of the Christian motifs of original sin, salvation, and redemption. Burke (1961) co-opts theological language as "secular analogues that throw light upon the nature of language" (p. 4). With Burke, the scientific account of humankind is "inadequate," since humans are a "moral-ethical animal" at heart, which in turn is something the church exploits (Rueckert, 1982). This essence of humankind caused Burke to come up with its secular variant. Nevertheless, the Christian mythos is significant in that its drama has several "essential truths about the human condition" (Rueckert, 1982, p. 46). The difference however, is that Burke's (1961) secular version reduces theology (a discourse of God) to logology, a discourse of discourses, "words about words" (p. 1). Burke's "religion," put another way, is not meant to save humankind in the next world, but "designed to save man in this world" (Rueckert, 1982, p. 134). From a scholarly perspective, as Bobbitt (2004) points out, Burke's drama of redemption is "much overlooked," although at the same time, it is not wholly present in any of his writings, but rather dispersed throughout. Other names for

Burke's redemption drama are the "pattern of experience…dialectic of the Upward Way, the Mystic Way, the tragic pattern…search for the self…dialectic of the platonic dialogue…grammar of rebirth, [and] the ladder of abstractions" (Rueckert, 1982, p. 107). For my purposes, I will stick with "rhetoric of rebirth."

Burke's rhetoric of rebirth, as seen in Foss, Foss and Trapp (2001), consists of three prime components: pollution, purification, and redemption. As Rueckert (1982) sums up, the "three main archetypal structures are pollution (hell), purification (purgatory), and redemption (heaven)" (p. 104). Pollution is the default state of humankind, the polluted status whereby humans are imbued with guilt, much like the theological concept of "original sin" (Burke, 1966, p. 15). The need for order out of this polluted state in turn "leads to Guilt / (for who can keep commandments!)" and results in the *"spirit of hierarchy"* (Burke, 1961, p. 4; 1966). In other words, "Those 'Up' are guilty of not being 'Down,' those 'Down' are certainly guilty of not being 'Up'" (Burke, 1966, p. 15). Whereas pollution is a state of existence, purification is an act.

Purification is the process that attempts at purging this guilt, either through mortification (which involves inducing oneself to suffer for our collective guilt) or victimage (scapegoating someone else entirely). If either of these attempts is successful, redemption would be the end result. Mortification is a kind of sacrifice in that it is "dying to this or that particular thing" (Burke, 1950, p. 266). A scapegoat can be seen as a "cathartic vessel [residing] in the excessiveness with which he forces us to confront the discriminatory motives intrinsic to society as we know it" (Burke, 1966, p. 94). Thus, Burke (1966) contends that in victimage the scapegoat is offered up for "purgation," whereby the "character that is to be sacrificed must be fit for his role as victim; and everything must so fit together that the audience will find the sacrifice plausible and acceptable" (p. 81). Victimage, moreover, can be either "verbal or…

physical action" (Rueckert, 1982, p. 151). Whether verbal or physical however, "the principle of drama is implicit in the idea of action, and the principle of victimage is implicit in the nature of drama" (Burke, 1966, p. 18). Although redemption is a new state (a new identity), the rebirth triptych does not end: another form of guilt will come about. As Bobbitt (2004) summarizes, using symbols results in a hierarchy, the negative (i.e., the thou-shalt-nots), and the drive for perfection, leading to guilt. No symbolic action is complete without all three components. Further, the purpose of seeking purification is not eternal rebirth, as opposed to Christian doctrine, but *internal* rebirth (Rueckert, 1982). Internal rebirth means rebirth is temporal.

Slavoj Žižek's Critique of Deep Ecology

Deep ecology, in simple terms, is the environmental worldview that is ecocentric as opposed to anthropocentric. Žižek's (1999) critique of deep ecology in an essay entitled "Of Cells and Selves" provides insight into how the extreme form of environmentalism works against its own goals. As Žižek (1999) clearly underscores, deep ecology does not escape the charge it seeks to exterminate: anthropocentrism. "[T]he very demand it addresses to man to sacrifice himself for the interests of the entire biosphere confers on him the exceptional status of universal being" (p. 305). Put another way, if deep ecology asks for humankind to equate its interests with the rest of the flora and fauna, since no other being does so, it posits humankind as a kind of "universal being" which would place a higher status than any other living thing. In a similar fashion, the critical point when humankind will become a "universal cosmic consciousness...'more than human'...a global organism," one of the claims of "New Age techno-ideology," in Kantian terms would not lead to an "ecstatic immersion" of the "noumenal Thing" but rather would make of us "lifeless puppets deprived of human dignity"

(Žižek, 1999, p. 306). This deprivation would bring with it an end to sexual difference as well, bringing to life the "asexual Alien Thing which reproduces itself by direct cloning" (Žižek, 1999, p. 306). What ensues would be an optimization of life in the direction of supreme autonomy, in other words.

Exploring the ethical consequences of cloning humankind, Žižek (1999) brushes through the cycle of every technological advancement: moral fear, confusion, and subsequent "normalization." Normalization involves the advancement being assimilated into our lives, and "we get used to it, invent new norms of conduct with it" (p. 307). Cloning is unique however, in that the kernel of free will is at stake. Nevertheless, Žižek (1999) concludes that there is no argument against cloning, because either our genome does not encapsulate fully who we are, which would mean cloning would not affect us, or it does, in which case we would just be "avoiding the inevitable," trying to delimit science by pointing toward a false freedom. In analyzing the nature versus nurture debate, Žižek (1999) likewise highlights how the Self would dissolve if we were try to look "behind the screen," only finding "neuronal, biochemical...processes" (p. 312). Ergo, in defining the role of the genes as opposed to the environs one overlooks the "*interface* which...delimits the Inside from the Outside" (Žižek, 1999, p. 312). Seen together, one can see how cloning would not reproduce the "self-referential loop," one's own subjectivity. What *would* be problematic however, is not the prospect of doubling the human body, but of "doubling my unique Soul" (Žižek, 1999, p. 316). Of course, the soul need not be a spirit but rather consciousness.

Literature on Nuclear Games, *Metal Gear,* and Nuclear Rhetoric

From Atari's 1980 arcade game *Missile Command* to 1985's *Raid Over Moscow* and the first *Metal Gear* (released in 1987), in the Cold War's twilight it is not surprising to find nuclear warfare a subject of interest in the rapidly-growing console game era. Interestingly enough, the opening epigraph in *Metal Gear Solid 2: Sons of Liberty* quotes the National Museum of American History exhibit "Information Age: People, Information and Technology" as stating: "Scientists had to make thousands of calculations to create the (atomic) bomb and determine its effects…Computers and atomic bombs…both products of World War II, grew up together" (2001). Recently, along with the extant *Metal Gear* franchise (which includes console games, mobile games, handheld games, trading-card games, print adaptations, a radio drama, a digital graphic novel and a motion picture currently in pre-production), real-time strategy games such as the *Civilization* series, the *Command & Conquer* series and *Spore* (2008), as well as first-person and third-person shooters such as the *Call of Duty* series, *Fallout 3* (2008) and *Mass Effect 3* (2012) have incorporated nuclear arms into either their narratives (e.g., a cutscene shows a nuclear detonation), their gameplay (e.g., a nuke is one of the available weapons in multiplayer gaming), or both (List of *Metal Gear* media, 2013). In regard to literature addressing nuclear elements in games, Schulzke (2009) and Pichlmair (2009) discuss the post nuclear apocalypse game *Fallout 3* in terms of moral choices and the hostile post-apocalyptic world, respectively.

In regard to the *Metal Gear* saga in particular, White (2009) observes that the first *Metal Gear* for the MSX2 spawned the stealth-action video-game genre, whereas Deen (2011) presents the *Metal Gear Solid* series of the franchise as forms of "interactive film." Similarly, as an example of framed narratives (the story framing the game that is typically not interactive but rather expository) both Crogan (2002) and Newman (2002) cite the first *Metal Gear Solid*. Aside from the game's visual affordances, Quijano-Cruz (2009) offers *Metal Gear Solid* as a videogame specimen with high sociocultural valencies, while Ouellete (2008) notes the game's thematic concern of

government-cover-ups and state conspiracies are likewise evident in the games *Half Life*, *Deus Ex*, and *Resident Evil*. Highlighting the prevalence of text in console and computer role-playing games of the mid-1980s, Garrelts (2013) underscores the first *Metal Gear* released in 1987 as an action game with similar levels of text in its menus, narration, and dialogue and thus co-opting the text-heavy trademark of RPG games.

In a paper studying ruin imagery in games and its relation to gender, Watts (2011) highlights *Metal Gear Solid 2: Sons of Liberty* (a prequel to *Guns*) as demonstrating "society's increasing reliance on information technology and the subsequent feared loss of our humanity," a dystopian view of the digital world that concludes *Sons of Liberty* and runs deeper in *Guns* (p. 250). More specifically, Watts (2011) points out that Arsenal Gear (the nuclear-armed-and-mobile fortress) being in ruins at the end of *Sons of Liberty* signifies "liberation from technological dependence, which literally catapults the player-character back to the basic roots of American society, symbolized by Federal Hall [the place where Arsenal Gear ends up]" (p. 250). This return to American ideals is an idea that can be nicely juxtaposed with the AIs in *Guns* codenamed after presidential leaders etched onto Mt. Rushmore. Indeed, the name "The Patriots" itself is emblematic of *Sons'* digital (albeit flawed) reproduction of American values (Watts, 2011, p. 250). Similarly, Conway (2010) considers the fourth wall broken in *Sons of Liberty* "technological corruption" induced by the AIs, while noting that *Guns* "blur[s] the boundaries between the gameworld and the physical world" (pp. 149-150). In effect, the person you take orders from in *Sons of Liberty* is revealed to be an AI posing as colonel, making the game a case of an unreliable narrator in that part of the game's missions are exposed as virtual simulations. In terms of the philosophical implications of artificial intelligences such as The Patriots, Andersen (2013) frames such consequences as "existential risks," risks threatening our existence and comprising AI, nanotechnology, and biotechnology. In *Guns*, the existential risks inherent to AI, when coupled with the military-industrial complex, are disastrous to the human population.

Aside from literature on nuclear games, certain scholarship on nuclear weapons through a rhetorical lens is quite relevant. Historically, nuclear criticism arose in the 1980's as "a high-theory movement encapsulated by Derrida's designation of nuclear weapons as 'fabulously textual,'" a movement that was rendered "obsolete" once the Cold War ended (Lynch, 2012, p. 347). Thereafter, what emerged were studies of nuclear colonialism, the "siting of nuclear mining and storage on lands disproportionally occupied by indigenous persons," a post-Cold War discourse that includes "the behavior of would-be nuclear states and terrorists" (Lynch, 2012, p. 341; Taylor, 2010, p. 3). In a paper on the "technoaesthetic" nature of the bomb, Masco (2004) underscores how in lieu of actual weapons tests, post-Cold War Los Alamos veered toward modeling nuclear arsenals through computer simulations in a program called the "Science-Based Stockpile Stewardship" that led to "each nuclear device [being] purified of its destructive potential…in ways that free its aesthetic possibility from its destructive potential, finally allowing the bomb to cease being a bomb at all" (p. 358). Not unlike a videogame in other words, Masco (2004) shows how these simulations include "virtual-reality gloves and goggles (needed to interact with the nuclear simulation)" that come to represent a "virtual embodiment" of the bomb (p. 365). As far as implications of these bomb simulations, Masco (2004) points out that such an orientation precludes "any visceral understanding of the power of the U.S. nuclear arsenal, replacing it with sophisticated material science questions and a virtual spectacle, which together offer only complexity and aesthetic pleasure" (p. 367).

Analyzing weapon gerontology of the post-Cold War US nuclear program in particular, Masco (2004) illustrates the salience of using birth analogies and gendered language in describing the maintenance of nuclear stockpiles, citing how Gusterson's study of Lawrence Livermore National Laboratory titled "Nuclear weapons testing: scientific experiment as political ritual" highlights "the connotative power of words to produce—and be produced by—a cosmological world where nuclear weapons tests symbolize not despair, destruction, and death but hope, renewal, and life" (as cited in Masco, 2004, p. 359). In another work studying post-Cold War rhetoric of nuclear weapons, Taylor (2010) observes how science fiction imagines a scenario wherein "humans rhetorically detached from their visceral, nationalist identification with a genocidal technology [choose] instead to envision different futures that encouraged the development of a more peaceful coexistence," comparable to the counter-nuclear narrative that emerges in nuke-ridden world of *Guns of the Patriots* (pp. 19-20). When framed as teleological perfection, what according to Brummett (1989) Burke considers the God term and the Devil term in language, the bomb is ultimately a representation of "*negative* vocabularies" (pp. 93-94). According to Burke (1962), if God-terms are "names for the ultimates of motivation," then the bomb would be the apotheosis of the negative drive (p. 74). Other fictional counter-nuclear and nuclear-disaster narratives are discussed by Dowling (1987) and Mannix (1992).

Guns of the Patriots Summary and Context

Guns of the Patriots begins in 2014, five years after the events in *Metal Gear Solid 2: Sons of Liberty* (2001). In *Guns*, the initial antagonists are The Patriots, a furtive organization originally actual people but now a set of five artificial intelligences

(AIs) running the world. For instance, The Patriots secretly rig presidential elections and control the media. As with the first and second game in the series, you play as Solid Snake, a legendary soldier who has single-handedly saved the world from nuclear catastrophe numerous times. Solid Snake is himself a clone of a previous war hero known as Big Boss. As a result of genetic manipulation, Snake is now the victim of accelerated aging (and is thus referred to as "Old Snake") and of a retrovirus (by the name of FOXDIE) implanted by The Patriots engineered to kill people around him, friend or foe. Liquid Ocelot, the person whom you as Solid Snake have to stop, directs five armies of private military companies (PMCs) under a mother company by the name of Outer Heaven. In addition to the five PMCs, Ocelot commands the U.S. Armed Forces through his own AI (named GW, short for "George Washington"). Ocelot's goal is to usurp the mother artificial intelligence (named JD, short for "John Doe") with which The Patriots rule society's public spheres. Just like GW, the other AIs are named after Mt. Rushmore presidents: TJ (Thomas Jefferson), TR (Theodore Roosevelt), and AL (Abraham Lincoln). At the end of the game, Snake defeats Ocelot and The Patriots. Because the FOXDIE virus makes Snake into a biological weapon, Snake attempts suicide but ultimately cannot pull the trigger. Thereafter, Snake meets Big Boss in a graveyard, but due to the virus Snake possesses, Big Boss dies in his arms.

Aside from Liquid Ocelot, The Patriots' former founders include Big Boss and his commanding officer Major Zero (who appears as a vegetable at the end of *Guns*). Big Boss' epithet "Big" was bestowed by the U.S. government for succeeding Boss, his female mentor, as war hero. This succession occurs at the end of *Metal Gear Solid 3: Snake Eater* (which is chronologically first in the series and is set during the Cold War) once Boss (serving as a U.S. soldier) defects to the Soviet Union at the beginning of the game. In *Snake Eater*, you as Big Boss (codenamed "Naked Snake" at first) are ordered to defeat Boss to prevent a

nuclear war from erupting. Upon defeating Boss you find out she was only following CIA orders and acting as U.S. spy in the Soviet Union, making her death a kind of martyrdom you as Big Boss feign ignorance about with your commanding officers. Indeed, much of the overarching theme of the *Metal Gear Solid* saga is that behind wars there are furtive political machinations at play, and therefore the public is purposefully and strategically misled about the reasons governments engage in warfare with other nation-states or ideologies.

As the fourth installment of the saga, *Guns of the Patriots* (2008) is owned by the Japanese game developer Konami Corporation, created by game designer, Hideo Kojima, and released for the PlayStation 3. The *Metal Gear* franchise was launched with the release of the two-dimensional *Metal Gear* for the MSX2 Japanese computer in 1987, but exploded in popularity with the release of the cinematic, three-dimensional *Metal Gear Solid* for the PlayStation console in 1998 (selling millions of copies since). Since its release, *Guns of the Patriots* has sold 4.75 million units as of March 2009, making it one of the top-selling video game for the PlayStation 3 (Konami, 2009; List of best-selling video games, 2010). All together, the *Metal Gear* franchise sold more than 26.5 million units in its more-than-twenty-year existence, making it the 40th best-selling video game franchise of all time, including PC and consoles (List of best-selling video game franchises, 2010).

Just like the other three games in the *Metal Gear Solid* series, *Guns of the Patriots* belongs to the stealth genre of videogames and is played from a third-person perspective (the player can see the character he or she controls), although the player is given the option of toggling into first-person point-of-view. Released in 1998 for the PlayStation console, the first *Metal Gear Solid* is recognized as the first 3D stealth game, and could be seen as the most prominent in the genre (Stealth game, 2013). Every game in the series carries the subtitle Tactical Espionage Action as a way of denoting the genre in a way that is more specific to the story. As a sub-genre, the stealth game (characterized by sneaking around enemies as opposed to directly confronting them) generally falls under the much broader action-adventure game genre (characterized by a narrative to play out, real-time action, and puzzles to solve). Well-known action-adventures games include the *Tomb Raider* and *Grand Theft Auto* series. The direct prequel to *Guns of the Patriots*, *Metal Gear Solid 2: Sons of Liberty* has been called "the first example of a postmodern video game" (*Metal gear solid 2*, 2013). Weise (2003) claims *Sons* harbors "a multi-faceted ideological argument." Further, *Sons of Liberty* is regarded as the first 3D postmodern game due to the fact the game 1. refers to itself as a game (breaks the "fourth wall"), and 2. questions the nature of reality through the emergence of artificial intelligence known as The Patriots (*Metal gear solid 2*, 2013).

DIGITAL RHETORIC OF *GUNS OF THE PATRIOTS*

Before analyzing *Guns of the Patriots*, what follows is a bird's-eye overview of the videogame as an artifact of digital rhetoric. As hinted in my epigraph, the experience of any game is comprised by but is not limited to its elements. The game's elements include the player, the interface, the narrative, the mechanics, and the aesthetics. Aside from screenshots, to further clarify the terminology I will also offer some relevant definitions.

The Player

The only person you control in the game is Solid Snake (referred to as "Old Snake" in the in-game interface), the legendary war veteran who must once again save the world even in old age (albeit old through advanced aging). As Snake, you have various real-world weapons (such as the M4) at your disposal. When unarmed, you can use close-quarters combat, and to further enhance character fidelity (how realistic the character is), you can smoke, eat and drink. To emphasize stealth action as opposed to direct action against enemies, Snake wears an "OctoCamo" sneaking suit that is a state-of-the-art, octopus-inspired camouflage that mimics the pattern and color of any surface it comes into contact with (Figure 1). In addition to Snake, you can also remotely control a miniature

Figure 1. OctoCamo in full effect

Metal Gear robot called Mk. II (and III) that can be used for reconnaissance. Mk. II was created by Otacon and is very similar in function to the *Star Wars* R2D2 droid (e.g., it can access computer terminals).

The Interface

In defining the "interface" as everything between the player and the game world, Schell (2008) highlights a controller as *physical input,* the screen as *physical output,* and in-game menus/displays as a *virtual interface,* myself focusing on the virtual interface (see Figure 2). (pp. 223-224).

The virtual interface seen above shows the life and psyche bars in the top-left corner below the name "Old Snake." The top-right corner shows radar that detects nearby enemies in red (aware of your location) or yellow (unaware), and gives the percentage of OctoCamo active (the higher the percent the more camouflaged). The bottom-right corner shows your equipped weapon and ammo, and the bottom-left shows your equipped item (in this case the "Solid Eye" goggle with radar, night vision, and binocular capabilities among other things). Weapons and

items are toggled, described and selected in a drop-down-and-sideways interface (see Figure 3).

In order to receive information and guidance on a given mission, a staple of the *Metal Gear Solid* story has been the Codec, a radio transceiver (see below) with which you communicate with Otacon (real name: Hal Emmerich) and others on your squad. While some Codec transmissions are automatically shown on a subtitled virtual interface, most transmissions are optionally sent by the player calling Otacon (or any other squadmate). Communication through the Codec ranges from mission debriefings, tips for fighting bosses, and background on your enemies and your current surroundings. Codec communication is thus highly context-specific (Figure 4).

Another relevant virtual interface is the "Virtual Range," a virtual reality simulator created by your mission aide (and geek) Otacon to train using various weapons (including guns, knives). Aside from being a virtual shooting range, the Virtual Range also discloses a history of each of the weapons. The weapons themselves can be upgraded and customized through the game's Drebin Points system, named after the gun launderer Drebin who sells the upgrades.

Figure 2. In-game player interface

Figure 3. The item selection interface

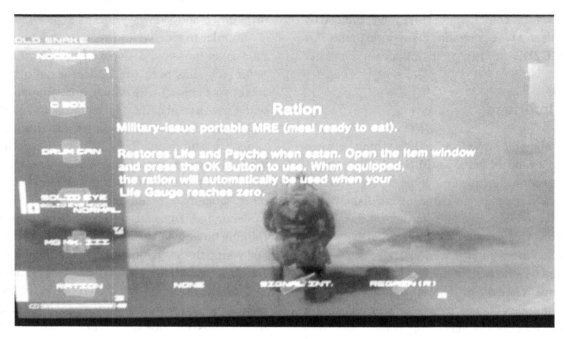

Figure 4.Otacon through the Codec interface

The Narrative

The game's narrative can be defined as the "sequence of events" that are either "pre-scripted" and "linear" or "emergent" (Schell, 2008, p. 41). The narrative structure includes scripted cutscenes (with the option of subtitles) that can be considered a "framed narrative" in that such a narrative cannot be (significantly) altered by the player (Bissell, 2011, p. 37). *Guns of the Patriots* holds the Guinness World Records for the longest uninterrupted cutscene (27 minutes) between levels and the longest sequence of cutscenes (71 minutes) in the game's ending (Longest cutscene in a video game, 2013). The "emergent" narrative that involves the story advancing through real-time player controls can also be considered the "ludonarrative," in that the ludonarrative entails the story advancing through gameplay, is "unscripted and gamer-determined…and usually amounts to… getting from point A to point B" (Bissell, 2013, p. 37). The ludonarrative is also important when considering the affordances of videogames in telling stories. Not only are stories in videogames told through the equivalent of a film, but through interaction with the story through the ludonarrative. While the framed narrative for *Guns of the Patriots* has been outlined earlier, the ludonarrative includes things under the player's control such as in how much time the game is completed, how PMC soldiers are evaded or bosses are defeated (which weapons are used), and which routes are taken to get from point A to point B (the gaming world allows some freedom so as to not feel on rails). The main bosses the player confronts are the Beauty and the Beast unit composed of four cyborgs who once defeated are revealed to be female soldiers suffering from PTSD. The final boss is Liquid Ocelot, and the battle is a seamless blend of framed and ludonarrative in that the player controls certain portions but other parts are pre-ordained by the grander frame.

The Mechanics

We can define the "mechanics" as "the procedures and rules" of a game (Schell, 2008, p. 41). Considering the game's emphasis on stealth strategy,

Figure 5. Briefing on playing possum

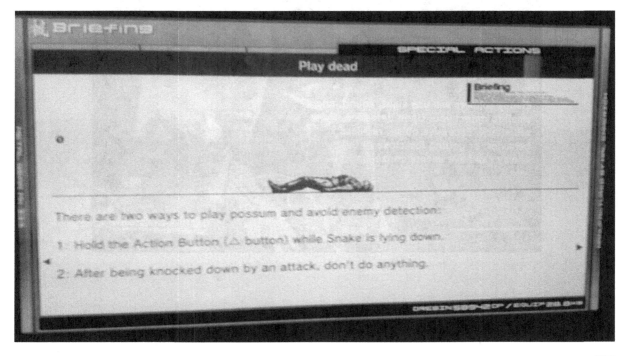

much of the player's actions are meant to avoid being seen or heard by enemy combatants. To this end, the game provides a neatly organized tutorial ("Briefing" in Figure 5) that animates numerous stealth and combat strategies. Among these are crawling, walking while crouched, and using weapons. Your psyche gauge monitors your stress in combat situations, impacting your aim, for instance. More, you can attach suppressors (silencers) on weapons and even use anesthetic rounds. Unlike games where enemies need to be killed to advance the game, you can theoretically complete the game by only tranquilizing enemies (including bosses). Unlike role-playing games, you as Snake cannot engage in dialogue with characters you encounter in your environs (although you can converse with squadmates through the Codec). There are five difficulty levels, from "Liquid Easy" to "Boss Extreme." Other than conforming to player competence, the variation in difficulty levels provides replay value in that numerous titles (or emblems) are bestowed on

the player upon completion of the game. All but two of the emblems are names of animals (such as "Raven" or "Fox"), with the highest emblem of "Big Boss" given for not being detected by enemies (and not killing any of them) and not using any "Continues" or rations (for regaining health). Aside from rations, noodles and other food and drinks can be used to regain health. And while smoking reduces health, it can also be used to detect infrared security beams and increase psyche.

The Aesthetics

How the game "looks, sounds, smells, tastes, and feels" is the game's aesthetics (Schell, 2008, p. 42). Specific to *Guns of the Patriots*, the game's aesthetics includes the sound effects, the soundtrack, and the visual fidelity (how realistic the game looks). All characters in the game are voiced by voice actors, the soundtrack is scored in part by the well-known composer Harry Gregson-Williams, and, given stealth relies on silent movement, just

Figure 6. Load screen tips

about every action or interaction with the environment carries with it a realistic sound that varies in volume. In fact, one of the tips during the load screen summarizes the role senses play in relation to enemies (see Figure 6). Given the fidelity to the real-world (as opposed to cartoon-like games), it is also not surprising to know the game aims for photorealism, and missions are set in the Middle East, Eastern Europe, and South America as well as fictional locations like Shadow Moses island (the setting of the first *Metal Gear Solid*).

The Literacies

From these game elements, several kinds of literacies can be extracted. In relation to the player, if learning is to take place it is important for a game to offer a playable character with a strong sense of values and yet feel imbued with a sense of control over the character. As Gee's (2007) "identity principle" states: "Learning involves taking on and playing with identities in such a way that the learner has real choices (in developing the virtual identity) and ample opportunity to meditate on the relationship between new identities and old ones" (p. 222). The choices one has as player-Snake are to customize his OctoCamo with different color suits, upgrade weapons, and to either kill or avoid enemies altogether. These choices allow for a wide range of experiences when playing, from earning a different emblem at the end of the game to having a more difficult playing experience. Nevertheless, the player bears witness to Snake's heroic persona, in such a way that ludonarrative choices will not change Snake's framed narrative (e.g., Snake attempts suicide in every playthrough). While the lack of player agency might seem to take away from the playing experience, it is a stout individual that can carry more meaning and make for a "good" videogame. Gee (2007) highlights Solid Snake as an example of a robust character, noting that "Good video games offer players strong identities...players learn to view the virtual world through the eyes

and values of a distinctive identity (e.g., Solid Snake in *Metal Gear Solid*)" (p. 216). By seeing the world through the eyes of Snake in other words, the player not only brings in her own lifeworld into the ludonarrative (e.g., choosing to tranquilize enemies), but absorbs Snake's views on the nature of war and justice and in so doing might see the current world differently. In effect, identifying with a strong character might lead to increased retention of the character's worldview and might modulate empathy (Cohen, 2006; Peng, 2008). Additionally, the player learns about Snake's own cultural background. For instance, even though Snake is a clone of Big Boss (himself a Caucasian character), we are told in the framed narrative that the fertilized egg came from a "healthy Japanese woman" (Kenichiro & Kojima, 2008). In a very real sense then, Solid Snake is a hybrid character of multicultural identity upon whom the fate of the world depends.

Given the self-evident lack of minority characters in videogames, Snake as a cultural chimera means not only that "blood from the East flows within your veins," but that when combined with an altruistic nature positively representing a minority character might change player perceptions of the Other (Kenichiro & Kojima, 2008). It has been shown that playing prosocial (voluntary behavior meant to benefit others) videogames increases empathy in the player (Greitemeyer, Osswald, & Brauer, 2010). The reverse has also been shown to be true, insofar as a study found that the greater the empathy experienced while reading the greater the likelihood of engaging in prosocial behavior (Johnson, 2012). Although *Guns of the Patriots* is not prosocial in the sense that it allows for violence as a solution to problems, the fact that Snake does not express pride in his heroism let alone pleasure in his violence does at least make the player consider the moral value of his violent acts. There is then a current of anti-heroism in Snake when he frames his own valiant acts in such a way that he considers himself "no hero...never was...I'm just an old killer...hired to do some wet work" (Kenichiro & Kojima, 2008). The player is subsequently implicated in this wet work to reinforce the notion that war driven by politics is ultimately immoral. There is nothing heroic about it, and someone like Snake just happens to be the right man for the job. In this manner it could be said that the game is prosocial insofar as the violence is not endorsed by the main character, and insofar as the violence only comes about for a greater good (and even then might not be justified). In players who are already empathetic, unjustified violence in a game has been found to produce guilt in the player (Hartmann, Toz, & Brandon, 2010). Whether unjustified or not, the violence in *Guns* is situated within a specific geopolitical context (The Patriots, and soldiers with nanomachines).

When it comes to the various interfaces, one form of literacy pertains to the way in which visual information is processed. As Appelbaum, Cain, Darling, and Mitroff (2013) summarize in reviewing the psychonomic literature, action videogame players "exhibit enhanced performance in a number of sensory, perceptual, and attentional domains, as compared with individuals with limited-to-no action video game experience" (p. 1). Although Appelbaum et al.'s (2013) own study did not look at a *Metal Gear Solid* game in particular, the interfaces in *Guns of the Patriots* certainly require a degree of visual dexterity inherent to its action game identity. The in-game display showing different information in the screen's four corners, when combined with the game world requires the player to manage ammo, health, stress, enemy positions, camouflage levels, and player location almost simultaneously. In firefights resulting from being spotted, the player must oscillate between each of these interfaces in real-time. As Kress (2003) notes, the literacies required for reading multimodal texts such as videogames include "differentiated attention to information that comes via different modes, an assessment constantly of what is foregrounded now, assessment about where the communication load is falling, and where to attend now" (p. 174). Thus, oscillating

between the various in-game displays and the gaming world translates into processing (reading) information of differing eye-levels (e.g., top left or bottom-right), differing signifiers (gauges, blips on the radar, characters, and surroundings), and differing purposes (combat, survival, evasion, reconnaissance). While this might seem like a visual overload, Appelbaum et al. (2013) found in their study that action videogame players possess greater visual sensitivity to information that allows them to accumulate such information and be able to make quicker decisions than non-action videogame players. It should then go without saying that gamers inexperienced with action or stealth videogames might struggle, as "the forms of reading necessary to play at least some of the games successfully become more subtle and demanding" (Kress, 2003, p. 160). Other than the in-game interfaces, the Codec interface requires the player to read text as it scrolls up. When it comes to written text as it comes up on the screen, one form of reading gamers practice involves "notions of 'information as it is supplied,'" as opposed to "notions of 'completed text'" (Kress, 2003, p. 163). In addition to the written text on screen the player also hears the Codec speaker's voice, and sees the speaker's gestural language. Hence, the information simultaneously comes in through different modes and the player must process all modes according to their learning styles.

In terms of the Virtual Range, one important literacy relates to learning the original context of things and acquiring multicultural awareness. As opposed to experiencing things in a vacuum, through the Virtual Range the player can learn about the history, culture and overall context of all of the weapons the player has unlocked from the game. These weapons include pistols such as the Chinese Type 17 Mauser (see Figure 7), rifles such as the Russian Mosin-Nagant, and submachine guns such as the Czech Škorpion vz. 83. As information about the selected weapon scrolls, the player learns not only about the original context of the weapons but in doing so learns about the

Figure 7. Type 17 Mauser information

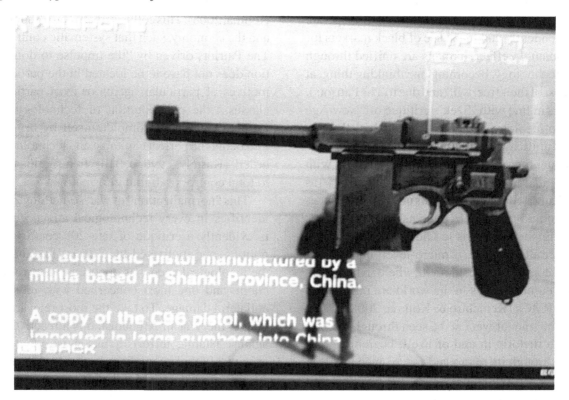

history and culture of the country of origin. Considering that there are about 50 different weapons, the information is given in the technical communication genre as opposed to filtered through one of the character's points-of-view. What results is a kind of mini *Wikipedia* article the player might not have otherwise read. The affordance for learning then is that players "are not always overtly aware of the fact that they are 'learning,' how much they are learning, or how difficult [or unfamiliar] it is" (Gee, 2007, p. 124). It should be mentioned that the player could also learn such information through Codec conversations with squadmates, since the conversation changes just about every time a squadmate's frequency is reached. Regardless, for the player to adopt such multicultural artifacts, coupled with the fact Snake is a multicultural character, might foster greater feelings of global citizenship. A study by Bachen, Hernández-Ramos, and Raphael (2012) tangentially supports this, inasmuch as it found that a simulation game affords young people the ability to "live the lives of people in other countries could induce students' identification with culturally and geographically distal characters, increase students' sense of global empathy, and boost their interest in learning more about the countries in which their characters live" (p. 452). Although *Guns of the Patriots* is not a simulation game per se, the game certainly situates the player in various geographical areas across the world while supplying equipment that cuts across cultures and contexts.

Žižek and the Patriots

The state of perpetual war in *Guns* also means private military company (PMC) soldiers are controlled by the Patriots through the use of "nanomachines" in order to optimize effectiveness against rebel factions (which still operate independently and make use of black markets for weapons). In effect, humans are unified through nanotechnology, becoming one thinking thing, at the cost of their free-will (and due to The Patriots). This is in line with Žižek's critique of "New Age techno-ideology": where one would think that this grand unification of humanity would bring a new enlightenment that merges digital technology with the human mind to bring about a singularity (as Ray Kurzweil anticipates), this unification reduces humankind to "lifeless puppets" subject to AIs. As Campbell explains to Old Snake, the system in place allows not just "micro-level" but "macro-level" control of the battlefield, where sixty percent of all combat forces in the world are made up of these PMCs (Kenichiro & Kojima, 2008).

This state of war can be seen through Burke's rebirth rhetoric in and of itself, beginning with how, through its micro and macro-management, it reduces "civilian casualties and human rights violations," a purification process. Though this be true, Snake notes the "war economy" creates "war orphans" and "child soldiers" (Kenichiro & Kojima, 2008). More important, war itself, self-perpetuating, self-driven, is so normalized that the field is not one driven by a desire for peace, but for power, of "PMC versus PMC," creating what Campbell aptly labels a "quagmire of war" (Kenichiro & Kojima, 2008). As Solid Snake keenly observes: "War has changed. It's no longer about nations, ideologies, or ethnicity [but] an endless series of proxy battles fought by mercenaries and machines. War, and its consumption of life, has become a well-oiled machine" (Kenichiro & Kojima, 2008). This allows war to perpetuate itself, and war itself is thus a kind of guilt machine, the status quo for the Orwellian control it provides, where the age of deterrence becomes an "age of control." As Snake says: "Genetic control. Information control. Emotion control. Battlefield control. Everything is monitored and kept under control…and he who controls

the battlefield…controls history" (Kenichiro & Kojima, 2008). This collusion between technology and the economy, such that systematic control by The Patriots driven by "the impulse to domination does not have to be located in the particular motives of particular agents or even particular classes.…the collaboration of technology and capitalism seeks to complete itself by bringing into being the perfect capitalist and technological order" (Kastely, 1996, p. 313). In turn, this leads to total control of digital information.

This "normalization" of war, something Žižek identifies in every technological advancement, is evidently a critique of late 20th century war politics, one motivated by a desire to vanquish the ideological enemy as opposed to a territorial claim, and one most concerned with reducing collateral damage. To take the most relevant example, the War in Afghanistan is a reactive war against Islamic terrorism meant to counteract growth of fundamentalism in the Middle East. At the same time, Middle Eastern geography makes micro-level warfare remain small scale, employing Predator drones and special-ops work for reconnaissance. In its efforts to reduce civilian deaths, the U.S. hits the bull's-eye at the wrong target—while the U.S. focuses on putting in place a technological system that makes war what Snake calls a "cleaner, safer battlefield," the U.S. fails to ask itself why it fights a war in the first place. Just as well, the U.S. neglects the number of non-combat casualties, subsequent orphans and other affected family relations. In a speech on drone policy and the continuing war in Afghanistan, Pres. Obama (2013) acknowledged that a state of "perpetual war…will prove self-defeating". This is analogous to the PMCs in *Guns* optimizing battlefield conditions, largely through micro and macro-level control, all the while losing track not only of war as an immoral state of affairs, but of war as a means to an end. So pervasive then, war in *Guns* can be seen as a form of "collective guilt" since there can be a "collective conscience," or a "collective identity" (Bobbitt, 2004). In this case it the conscience of The Patriots and the guilt of everyone else.

No advancement in the field of battle has been more destructive than the atom bomb. In *Guns*, this advancement becomes available in the black market through the production of the Metal Gear Ray units, a bi-pedal, computer-controlled machine able to store nuclear warheads among its armament. As Williams (1989) shows Burke "work[s] under the nuclear shadow in…elaborations of…theory," this alternate reality is not far from what Burke (1966) demonstrates is a result of language, "the instrumental value in developing atomic power [that] now threatens the survival of the language-using animal" (p. 15). In the case of *Guns*, it is *digital* language (i.e., binary code) and its advancement, propagation, and eventual domination over other languages by The Patriots that brings this threat to fruition. Undoubtedly, the videogame presciently describes the increasingly digitized nature of 21st century warfare (drones, the PRISM online surveillance system, grid networks and digital information systems, nanotechnology that includes adaptive camouflage and nanorobots, and animal-like robots such as those being developed by the Defense Department's research wing known as DARPA).

Snake's Rebirth

Guns of the Patriots is a "representative anecdote" for analysis from a dramatist perspective in that it is linguistic in its features, it possesses scope of human drama, and it is a "summation" of symbolic conflicts, as will be shown. The irony for the game's hero, Solid Snake, is that in devoting his entire life trying to stop nuclear annihilation, he becomes a "doomsday device," as the designer of the FOXDIE virus, Dr. Naomi Hunter, tells Snake, becoming "indiscriminate" about who it kills and eventually causing an epidemic (Kenichiro & Kojima, 2008). Snake is thus the postmodern representation of the "walking biological weapon" *par excellence*: short of taking his own life, he has

no control over the FOXDIE virus he was injected with by The Patriots as part of a plan to kill those who were trying to overthrow them. Both Liquid Snake and Liquid Ocelot, for instance, die from that same virus embedded into their DNA (Kenichiro & Kojima, 2008). In this sense Snake represents the epitome of what it means to lack free will, given that his life, from birth on, has been fully determined by his genetic code.

Nevertheless, at the end of the game Snake finds out through Big Boss that the "new FOXDIE is uprooting the old [one]," and thus, that he need not kill himself to save humankind (Kenichiro & Kojima, 2008). This revelation makes Snake's rebirth apparent, as Big Boss suggests in an uplifting fashion: "Don't waste the life you have left fighting. That new world is yours to live in, not as a snake, but as a man" (Kenichiro & Kojima, 2008). Ergo, for the first time in his life, Snake is no longer Snake, the hero who saves the world, but just another human being out to "see this age off" (Kenichiro & Kojima, 2008). Snake is "the tragic protagonist [who] comes to knowledge of his pollution, acknowledges…reaffirms… and dies [or is fated to]" (Rueckert, 1982, p. 108). Snake is not only reborn, but as Kenneth Burke's rhetoric of rebirth demonstrates, undergoes pollution, purification, and redemption through his old FOXDIE virus, the fact he is a clone, his iconic status, and the new FOXDIE.

Although as Burke notes, pollution is the default state, in Snake pollution is a unique state. He is one of three clones of the legendary soldier codenamed Big Boss. But unlike the other two clones, Liquid Snake and Solidus Snake, he is the only one who feels guilty about it, to the point where he reluctantly accepts the fact his genes are determining his need to save the earth (the gift of combat prowess) while he does not consider what he is doing in any way glorious. As he himself says, "I'm no hero…never was…I'm just an old killer…hired to do some wet work" (Kenichiro & Kojima, 2008). Given the fact that he has saved the world several times by the time he is now "Old" Snake, and the fact everyone else considers him a legendary hero, this confession illustrates Snake's deep sense of guilt deriving from his fated life, fated by his Big Boss genes. And as Rueckert (1982) shows, "outpourings, such as confession" are characteristic of symbolic change (pp. 104-105). His confessions then, illustrate purification.

This altruistic heart also makes Snake worthy of sacrifice through "poetic justice." Per Burke (1974), Snake is a vessel "too good for this world," and "the *most perfect* sacrifice" (p. 40). Snake's guilt however, is compounded learning that the old FOXDIE injected by Dr. Hunter, whom herself was following orders from The Patriots, fates him to kill those around him, friend or foe, all according to The Patriots' plans. In this sense, Snake could be seen as a scapegoat, as the scapegoat is the "sacrificial animal upon whose back the burden of…evils is ritualistically loaded," and in this case the "evils" are those The Patriots see fit to destroy (Burke, 1974, pp. 39-40). As Snake relates to his combat partner Raiden as Snake removes a bandage where his face was burned: "I have no future. In a few months, I'm going to be a weapon of mass destruction" (Kenichiro & Kojima, 2008). As his purification process exemplifies though, there is a difference between embracing fate and giving in to it. Comparably, given Snake's identification as a weapon of mass-destruction, a human time-bomb outdated for the field of modern warfare, the post-Cold War humanizing discourse of the atom bomb reconceived "an image of the masculine bomb-body as senior citizen, so aged and weak as to be unable to perform. No longer the 'baby boy,' the bomb…now structurally positioned at the end of its life course, as the 'old man,' struggling against the progression of time and failing faculties" (Masco, 2004, p. 360). Such a binary identification fits since the scapegoat is the dialectical figure that merges "the contrary principles of identification and alienation" (Burke, 1950, p. 140). We as players positively identify with Snake, yet we cannot help but gain a sense of distancing when thinking about how Snake's genes are sui generis in their destructive capacity.

Nonetheless, in light of Žižek's cloning analysis, Snake's fate sheds light on the nature versus nurture debate. To begin with, Snake's fate seems to be determined by his genes, given that he is destined to a life of "fighting" because he is the figurative Brother of the legendary Big Boss, and his literal clone (through a genetic military experiment by The Patriots). In this sense, humankind has been able to double the "unique Soul" Žižek points out as the real danger of cloning, for Snake is not just a double of Big Boss, but evidently carries the same combat proficiency and will. Big Boss, before he turned into a villain when he co-founded The Patriots, fought on the side of justice, for his country, the U.S., just like Snake. Similarly, Big Boss saved the world during the Cold War by taking down his own mentor, Boss. Then Snake in turn did the same when he took down Big Boss when Big Boss plotted world domination through the Metal Gear unit. Coupled with Snake's own guilt, and the lack of an adequate hero to take his place, Snake has no choice but to fight and mimic Big Boss by being the big hero. In keeping with dramatism, Snake is a "marked man [containing] a personal flaw" (Burke, 1974, p. 40). Snake's fatal flaw to be exact, is genetic in origin.

Whether genes determine human nature or not is determined by Snake, as his reluctance to accept the label of "hero" is what Žižek calls "avoiding the inevitable," accepting the fact that our genes do in fact fully encapsulate who we are. In other words, as much as Snake dodged the label of "hero," he could not dodge the essence of heroism delineated by his soldier genes, giving him the ability to overcome the greatest odds, as Dr. Hunter says, "an ordinary man wouldn't even be standing by now," referring to his ability to survive the FOXDIE virus while everyone it infects does not (Kenichiro & Kojima, 2008). Philosophically, Snake's case shows that it is our genes that control us, not the other way around, that we do *not* "have the power to turn against our creators," something Dawkins (2006) (who placed the gene as the engine of evolution but stressed human capacity to surpass evolutionary drives) would disagree with (p. 201). In short, Snake is precluded a basic notion of free will—he is trapped by his genes to a life of war, no matter how hard he tries to fight his fate, although this does not mean that Snake represents the doubling of Big Boss' unique subjectivity, the "self-referential loop" Žižek would contend is not reproducible even through cloning. However, everything else that is the essence of Big Boss, Snake is. As Liquid Ocelot, who is the mental doppelganger of Liquid Snake (Revolver Ocelot grafted Liquid's arm once his was lost in the first *Metal Gear Solid* and eventually Liquid's psyche usurped Ocelot's mind), the other Big Boss clone, tells Snake: "The Patriots saw fit to create us, and in doing so became our only raison d'être" (Kenichiro & Kojima, 2008). Regardless, as we find out in the game's conclusion, Snake's figurative rebirth allows him to break from this reason for being, and forge a new identity, despite the fact that he has "no genes, no memes" to pass on "to the next generation," according to his partner and tech expert Otacon, but not before he finds out through an extreme form of mortification that showcases attempted suicide and self-inflicted suffering (Kenichiro & Kojima, 2008). Of course, since Snake is still alive at the end of the game Otacon might not realize the extent to which Snake will influence subsequent generations by the example that he set. Kojima himself stated that *Guns of the Patriots* "main theme has been what we should and ultimately do pass on to future generations" (Tamari, n.d.). In this sense, as word spreads Snake will pass on his memes of heroism, resilience, and redemption. For a game showcasing the consequences of genetic engineering, it certainly does not occlude the memetic power of ideas when considering that includes passing on both the "sins of the fathers" (Big Boss and the Patriots) as burdens on Snake as well as Snake's own resilient nature on future heroes.

The purification process that seeks to purge the guilt can occur through mortification or through victimage. Snake "require[s] purification as peculiar and private as his burden," his burden being uniquely genetic in nature (Rueckert, 1982, p. 104). With Snake, mortification is the chosen avenue, as he decides not to assign blame to The Patriots for his state (although he would be justified in doing so), but instead adopts a suffering of the self in various ways. One way is seen in his reluctance to accept his power to save the world not despite, but *because of* his genes, his unique state. Instead, Snake chooses to cast himself down as unworthy of even something like companionship, as he tells Raiden: "I'm a shadow, one that no light will shine on. As long as you follow me, you'll never see the day" (Kenichiro & Kojima, 2008). This view leads to Snake eventually volunteering to be the one to stop Liquid Ocelot by shutting down his AI, GW, a venture that entails suicide since GW is protected by microwaves that can "evaporate any living person within range" (Kenichiro & Kojima, 2008). Snake at this point already has his left eye burnt off. But when the matter is brought up, a darkly cynical Snake responds: "A giant microwave oven. You'd have to have a death wish to go in there. Sounds like the perfect job for me" (Kenichiro & Kojima, 2008).

The irony however, is that it *is* the perfect job for Snake, but not because of his death wish, his evident mortification, but because as the genetic descendant of Big Boss, he is the one most capable (in an evolutionary sense, "fittest"). "This is my fight, my destiny," Snake claims, in a not-so-tacit acceptance of the fated narrative (Kenichiro & Kojima, 2008). As Rueckert (1982) notes, the "ideal kind of mortification is free," and Snake's brave assertion shows how his mortification is "self-willed" (p. 148). Further, Snake being scorched again by the microwaves illustrates Burke's looking at "fire and the chemical processes of purification and organic change produced by fire," and Snake's ritualistic purification (chunks of his OctoCamo uniform and Solid Eye come off) through searing burns (a form of "cleansing") can be juxtaposed with the simultaneous attempt at infecting the head AI with a virus that will restore the world to its natural state (Rueckert, 1982, p. 105; Burke, 1966, p. 97). One other way to look at this climactic level of the game is through Buell's (2001) notion of "toxic discourse," defined as "expressed anxiety from perceived threat of environmental hazard due to chemical modification by human agency," and Heise (2008) suggests it is "a crucial trope by which writers and filmmakers explore the porous boundaries between body and environment, public and domestic space, and harmful and beneficial technologies." (p. 31; p. 161). Yet, Snake's self-sacrifice is representative of how mortification can be seen as "dying for a cause, negating one's own life in order that others may live" (Rueckert, 1982, p. 150). And Snake's cause is certainly for the greater good.

Snake is ultimately successful in his "fight," bringing down GW along with Liquid Ocelot, but agonizes over microwave radiation, seizures, bullet wounds, stab wounds, a charred left eye, a beating, and is closer to death than life. This signifies, on the one hand, how purification is "usually painful," how both "physical and psychological suffering" takes place, and how "the doer himself...suffers most" (Rueckert, 1982, p. 108). On the other hand, the player controlling and yet *witnessing* Snake's agony as he slowly progresses through the giant microwave oven illustrates how mortifications *must* be witnessed; they are evidence, presented to an invisible divine audience" (Burke, 1950, p. 222). In reality, because we not only witness Snake but also control him, ours is a form of "vicarious victimage" (Burke, 1966, p. 97). And this cathartic act that Snake experiences in this climactic scene is truly a form of "catharsis by scapegoat" (Burke, 1966, p. 18). Yet his destiny does not end there. In the graveyard where Boss, the soldier who trained Big Boss, is buried, Snake tries to kill himself with his own gun, realizing his FOXDIE fate will only bring more deaths.

Figure 8. Snake attempts suicide

This attempted suicide is the culminating form of his mortification, one that ends with Snake in a sweat, unable to pull the trigger, to purge the gene-driven guilt from his veins (Figure 8). In light of Burke (1974), the fact he is unable to commit suicide is significant in that suicide is "the act of rebirth reduced to its simplest and most restricted form," and that the "symbolic slaying of an old self [evident in the death wish] is complemented by the emergence of a new self" (p. 39). Snake's purification process, in other words, is anything but "simple," and as Rueckert (1982) observes, is always "a process of moving from one thing to another...from one self to another...from negatively charged to positively charged" (p. 105). In Burke's view, rebirth is "not instantaneous...not achieved through the acts of others...not sent from on high...not a matter of mere motion [but] a tearing down and a building up...a (lengthy) process involving regression as well as progression; and its success depends upon the individual in whom it works" (Betts Van Dyk, 2006, p. 48). Snake is quite literally torn down, as well as psychologically torn asunder.

Snake's redemption process begins when his suicide attempt, his mortification, ends. As Big Boss tells Snake, "Time for you to put aside the gun...and live" (Kenichiro & Kojima, 2008). Immediately, Snake's first reaction is shock, since Big Boss is supposed to be dead by the hands of Snake himself in the very first *Metal Gear* game. If we recall that Snake is the clone of Big Boss, the killing of Big Boss by Snake would mean that the "symbolic parricide [is] simply an extension of symbolic suicide, a more thoroughgoing way of obliterating the substance of one's old identity," in this case the "sins of the father" that gave Snake his genetic guilt (Burke, 1974, p. 41). Yet, Big Boss relates that he was never dead, just kept in a state of "eternal sleep" by The Patriots, freed once The Patriots were destroyed by Snake (Kenichiro & Kojima, 2008). Once the shock subsides, Snake finds out that because the new FOXDIE is preventing the old FOXDIE from reproducing, he will not become the doomsday weapon he thought he would, hence transforming from being "negatively charged to positively charged," as Rueckert (1982) notes. As Big Boss says his own final words before he himself dies (from the old FOXDIE that kills those with the target genes), despite the fact that Snake is man-made, Snake is finally able to live as a man free from the initial guilt. And freedom, Burke (1966) relates, is "the most 'positive' of all experiences," and it is what entices Snake, having saved the world one last time, to, as he himself says, "see this age off…as a beast…a shadow of the inside…of the old age" (p. 435; Kenichiro & Kojima, 2008). Snake does as Kastely (1996) claimed Burke urged us to: "live with our disease by making peace with its symptoms" (p. 311). At this point, "a new [self] is born…equipped with some knowledge he did not previously have" (Rueckert, 1982, p. 109). This in turn reifies his internal rebirth since he goes beyond the "old age" and into the new one.

Snake seems to transcend his fate at this point. Put another way, transcendence is "the building of a *terministic bridge*, whereby one realm is *transcended* by being viewed *in terms of* a realm 'beyond' it" (Burke, 1966, p. 187). The realm Snake transcends is that of The Patriots, since in destroying them he moves "beyond" their "control" (Kenichiro & Kojima, 2008). At this point a new guilt emerges, as Burke claims, in the form of the new FOXDIE virus Big Boss claims will eventually "become a threat" if he manages to live "that long," although he does not specify how long "that long" is (i.e., although Snake no longer has the "old" guilt to worry about, a "new" guilt has taken its place) (Kenichiro & Kojima, 2008). At least, this guilt does not coincide with The Patriots remaining active (The Patriots having been found by Big Boss himself, along with Ocelot and Zero). Here, Snake's identity fundamentally changes, noting that such a change requires the *"obliteration of one's whole past lineage"* (Burke, 1974, p. 41). Snake's lineage, as clone, is inherently genetic, and through FOXDIE and the death of Big Boss, and Ocelot along with Zero, all past lineages one way or another are expunged from the record. If we consider that "a thorough job of symbolic rebirth would require the revision of one's ancestral past itself," Snake is symbolically reborn at the end of the game (Burke, 1974, p. 41). Snake's genetic guilt is *"transformed, transcended, transubstantiated*, by incorporation into a wider context of symbolic action" (Burke, 1974, p. 52). Hence, Snake transcends his initial state, changing his genetic lottery at the end of the game.

World Reborn

Adding to Snake's own mirroring of Burke's rebirth rhetoric are The Patriots themselves. The Patriots spawned out of a desire for order in the world, which is in line with the "drive for perfection" and need for a sense of order (which subsequently brings guilt) Burke (1966) mentions, a form of digital purging through the creation of norms, and their destruction by Old Snake its new "blank slate," as Big Boss calls it (Kenichiro & Kojima, 2008). Out of an honest desire for global peace, The Patriots were initially led by Major Zero, Big Boss' former commanding officer. At its core though, "[a]ny…utopia's apparent positives would be, in fact, disguised negatives-reversals, projections, and reformulations of our failed institutions" (Kastely, 1996, p. 310). The Patriots were created "to manage and control the American state," based on Zero's desire to create "an orderly world, one governed by rules" (Kenichiro & Kojima, 2008), yet according to Žižek (1997), this form of techno-utopia

conceals its exact opposite: an unheard-of imposition of radical closure. This, then, is the Real awaiting us, and all endeavours to symbolise this Real, from utopian (the New Age or 'deconstructionist' celebrations of the liberating potentials of cyberspace) to the blackest dystopian ones (the prospect of the total control by a God-like computerized network . . .) are just that: so many attempts to avoid the true 'end of history,' the paradox of an infinity far more suffocating than any actual confinement. (p. 154)

With the rise of digital technology that included "the internet, and genetics" however, The Patriots' power "grew immense," becoming "the proud police of the world" (Kenichiro & Kojima, 2008). As Rueckert (1982) shows, both victimage and mortification can be "monstrously perverted," as Zero did. As Big Boss says, the one man who started it all, "that one man's [Zero's] desires grew huge, bloated....we realized too late....we had created a beast" (Kenichiro & Kojima, 2008). More specifically, Zero developed a network of AIs to make the decisions for the organization, building the four distinct AIs: GW, TJ, TR, and AL, and the core AI, JD, out of his goal of spawning a "unified world state," which proved unsuccessful since it only brought forth war (Kenichiro & Kojima, 2008). Through the establishment of control and the creation of norms, AIs become the symbolic purging of the chaos in the world, as Big Boss explains: "The Patriots were those norms, a neural network reduced to its simplest form. That's what they really represented, uniformity without individual will, without change" (Kenichiro & Kojima, 2008). As with the AIs, the perpetual

war itself can be seen as a symbolic purging of humankind's crusade toward perfection, as Burke (1974) illustrates:

War is cultural. It does promote a highly cooperative spirit. The sharing of a common danger, the emphasis on sacrifice, risk, companionship, the strong sense of being in a unifying enterprise--all these qualities are highly moral, and in so far as the conditions of capitalistic peace tend to inhibit such expressions, it is possible that the thought of war comes as a 'purgation,' a 'cleansing by fire.' (p. 319)

Likewise, the drive toward perfection evident in The Patriots having autonomy over legal, political, and financial spheres can be seen as a kind of "Hellhaven," Burke's term for when "rational attempts to eliminate a set of current problems lead to a bleak and inhuman future" (Kastely, 1996, p. 310). Hellhaven can also be paralleled with Outer Haven, the name for Liquid Ocelot's submarine which safeguards GW with numerous nuclear-armed Metal Gear units and the setting for Solid Snake's final boss battle. "Outer Haven" is itself a portmanteau of Outer Heaven (the military sanctuary free of ideology or national allegiance that Big Boss created) and data haven (an environment for unregulated networks). Aside from illustrating how the framed narrative in the game illustrates Burke's rebirth rhetoric, I will next illustrate how the interplay between the framed narrative and the ludonarrative can produce other forms of literacy.

Immersion and Agency

One of the most significant literacies can be gleamed from the ways in which the ludonarrative interacts with the mechanics and is shaped by the framed narrative. Specifically, the game's ludonarrative and mechanics deliver a sense of both immersion and agency. Here I adopt Mateas and Stern's (2005) definitions of immersion as "the feeling of being present in another place and engaged in the action therein," and agency as "the feeling of empowerment that comes from being able to take actions in the world whose effects relate to the player's intention" (p. 649). Given *Guns'* serious subject matter and the fact the game is the fourth in the series, the player at this point has at least built a familiarity with Solid Snake. Germane to immersion though, several ludonarrative moments can truly make the player feel present within the gaming world. It is important to underline that the ludonarrative offers more opportunity for immersion than the framed narrative because it is in the ludonarrative that the player is in control and can thus exert influence over the narrative.

Perhaps the most emotionally engaging moment is when Snake goes on the suicidal mission toward the end of the game and the player guides Snake through the giant microwave oven. Dramatically, the scene is certainly the climax of the game (set in the Outer Haven submarine). For one, Snake's squadmate Raiden (a cyborg ninja now lacking limbs) must hold off an army by wielding a sword with his teeth. In another room, your squadmates Meryl and Johnny fight back outnumbered against another army of elite soldiers. With a Gothic-like chant as background music and split-screens showing your squadmates struggling, you as Snake first walk through the tunnel that leads to the AI you must implant a virus in. Due to the microwave radiation though, you are forced to crouch, are slowed to a crawl, all the while your OctoCamo and Solid Eye sear off little by little and your health depletes.

Moving inch by inch, there comes a moment when it seems you simply won't make it, and Snake will die along with his squadmates. And it is at the point where it seems Snake simply cannot go on any further and yet, keeps inching closer, because *you* the player keep inching closer that you come to understand the nature of resilience and sacrifice for a greater good. Indeed, as Kress

(2007) declares, through immersive experience videogames can "challenge players' taken-for-granted views about the world" (p. 145). Specific to Snake's worldview, a survey by Qin, Rau, and Salvendy (2009) found that the degree of immersion in computer games is correlated with feelings of empathy. This finding (that immersion is an affordance for empathy), has been confirmed by studies of the effects of reading fiction (Bal & Veltkamp, 2013; Johnson, 2012; Mar, Oatley, Hirsh, Paz, & Peterson, 2006). Because you know that Snake will probably not survive the mission, one cannot help but be moved by Snake's heroism in its full glory, and as consequence fully immerse themselves into Snake's character at this stage of the narrative. It is here that we partake of one of the prime affordances of videogames: being able to "*situate meaning in a multimodal space through embodied experiences to solve problems and reflect on the intricacies of the design of imagined worlds*" (Gee, 2007, pp. 40-41). The meaning created here is the meaning of Snake's altruistic ethos: Snake has already saved the world from nuclear destruction four times before and yet has never been paid for his services by the government and has actually been associated with a terrorist organization by the media at large. This moment then, when we see Snake exert his last breaths to lift up the world one last time is unquestionably the "full-body experience" Bissell (2011) describes upon playing *Mass Effect*:

you lose track of your manipulation of it, and its manipulation of you, and instead feel inserted so deeply inside the game that your mind, and your feelings, become as seemingly crucial to its operation as its many millions of lines of code. It is the sensation that the game itself is as suddenly, unknowably alive as you are. (p. 126)

The other relevant experience that comes about through the game's ludonarrative is a sense of agency, of empowerment over the gaming world. According to Mateas and Stern's (2005) neo-Aristotelian theory of interactive drama, agency involves a balance between "material" and "formal" constraints, wherein material constraints are actions that can be taken by the player (the ludonarrative) and formal constraints are based on plot (the framed narrative) (p. 654). Thus, the ludonarrative and framed narrative must complement each other in order for the player to experience any agency in the game. On one side of the spectrum, games can value the ludonarrative over the framed narrative, resulting in an "open-ended story without a clear point of view [that] may disrupt the plot structure too much, thus disrupting agency" (Mateas & Stern, 2005, p. 657). On the other side of spectrum, games with an overshadowing framed narrative might make the player feel as though they are only observers in the action as opposed to actual participants. Nonetheless, when games lack agency the issue is not a lack of ludonarrative choices, not in other words "a lack of options of things to do [but] having insufficient [framed narrative] to decide between choices" (Mateas & Stern, 2005, p. 654). When looking at games lacking agency this way, *Guns of the Patriots'* interplay of ludonarrative and framed narrative is in sufficient harmony so as to allow the player to feel empowered, to feel co-author of a meaningful experience. One way this agency is realized is in the aforementioned microwave scene where the player comes to empathize with Snake's desire to overcome a great obstacle. Even though Snake's framed narrative illustrates his resilience, it is ultimately the player who takes hold of Snake through the ludonarrative and helps him succeed in the mission by rapidly mashing the button in the controller to the point of exhaustion, an exhaustion shared with Snake. Simply put, if the player fails, Snake fails, not the other way around, and the player must try again. Notably, a study found empathy to contribute to a greater sense of agency in videogames (Peng, 2008). I would contend that empathizing with

Snake's courageous yet humble ethos is partially responsible for the agency felt in ludonarrative moments such as this one.

One other way this agency is achieved is by softly enforcing upon the player the need for stealth and evasion from enemy forces as opposed to the traditionally fast-paced confront-and-shoot scenarios in action games. By thinking before acting, patiently practicing misdirection over direct confrontation, the player is encouraged to "explore thoroughly before moving on, to think laterally, not just linearly, and to use such exploration and lateral thinking to reconceive one's goals from time to time" (Gee, 2007, p. 217). The lateral thinking on display here results in the player observing enemy routes, distracting enemies with noises, and making use of the OctoCamo to camouflage oneself in the surroundings. If the player impatiently confronts the enemy time and again, they will radio for backup and the cavalry will show up to illustrate the strategic disadvantage of a Rambo-like ego. Considering the preponderance of first-person shooter games that contract the player to kill without question, the stealth-action genre offers a chess-like response to conventional game mechanics. The ludonarrative then, is multifaceted enough to force the player to think things through, to strategically weigh the options between advancing in a given level and incurring health damage. Partaking of the ludonarrative therefore "becomes itself a kind of narrative—the embodied actions by which players push forward toward the game's end" (Journet, 2013, p. 206). Whatever the ludonarrative choices taken will translate into a different emblem at the end of the game, different amounts of Drebin Points to upgrade weapons and an overall different playing experience (e.g., calm, stressful).

Yet through cutscenes and scripted Codec transmissions (the player is from time to time called through the Codec) the framed narrative gently reminds the player what the goals of the mission are so as to avoid venturing into the open-world genre where the player is free to pursue sidequests at the expense of the framed narrative (in some games the player is not actually required to return to the framed narrative). Actually, other than collecting various trophies there are no sidequests in the game that allow a free-range of movement through the gaming world. As can be surmised, the story in *Guns of the Patriots* is grand enough so as to engross the player into finishing the framed narrative, and missions are short enough so as to show long cutscenes between gameplay that illustrate the importance of the grand frame. "You get control and are controlled," as Bissell (2011) puts it (p. 39). In short, with a fairly careful oscillation there is no illusion of player agency: the ludonarrative is there to allow a wide variation between getting from point A to point B to point C, and the framed narrative is there to make sure you do not miss the best portions of the game. As player one cannot but sympathize with Snake's will to triumph once and for all, and yet, because he is visibly aged, almost come to pity Snake's cough fits, occasional failures at aiming properly, and cursed genes that kill everyone around him. Because of the game's levels of immersion and agency, what results for the player are not "surrogate experiences, but actual experiences" of what it means to be a veteran soldier in a battlefield where evil is driven by a lust for power more so than pure evil, and good is driven by altruistic forces that expect no princess at the end of the castle (Bissell, 2011, p. 182). I would nevertheless be remiss if I did not mention how the *Metal Gear Solid* series is known for such lengthy cutscenes that some players feel there is not enough ludonarrative in the game to even out the framed narrative. I find this to be a valid argument if it were not for the fact that cutscenes can be skipped (a genre convention), that the adventure genre expectations are in line with the amount of framed narrative, and

that the framed narrative is fairly engaging (even if one enters the series out of order).

As a whole, there are a number of salient implications for these literacies. One implication involves looking at how games as complex symbol systems of bit-modulated communication can change the very nature of rhetorical claims (such as symbols). As Bogost (2013) posits, "because games are systems, they offer a fundamentally different way for characterizing ideas. They can inspire a different kind of deliberation than we find in other forms of media, one that considers the uncertainty of complex systems instead of embracing simple answers" (p. 143). The way that *Guns of the Patriots* reifies abstract ideas allows the player to directly experience not only those ideas, but the *consequences* of things such as violence, war, altruism, and technology run-amok through the digital affordances of immersion, agency and symbolism. The value then, is in seeing how videogames "always situate ('show') the meanings of words and show how they vary across different actions, images and dialogues. They don't just offer words for words ('definitions')" (Gee, 2007, p. 218). Such a view is grounded in the multimodal notion that knowledge "changes its shape when it is realised in the different modal material" (Kress, 2003, p. 50). The meanings of words such as "war," "government," and "heroism" are therefore complicated by the game's ethos and presented in a light different from the mainstream. This ideological reframing is in turn significant when considering that, as Squire (2006) notes, "games have been taken up most stridently in the military, which is largely charged with training those who have fallen through the cracks of the American educational system" (p. 27). The most well-known example of this is *America's Army*, a videogame developed by the U.S. Army that as a form of "militainment" has been shown to be an example of propaganda (Nieborg, 2009; Ottosen, 2009). Therefore, as entities such as the military and corporate interests use games "to spread their ideologies, it is crucial that educators with an interest in democracy and K–12 education examine the medium's potential to spread their influence" (Squire, 2006, p. 27). A game such as *America's Army* is worth studying in order to understand *how it is* that the game, as a bit-modulated artifact, can enact propaganda without the player construing the message as such. This endeavor becomes all the more important when considering that *America's Army* has been used as a recruitment tool in schools (*America's Army*, 2013).

FUTURE RESEARCH DIRECTIONS

Future research could address how rhetoric in other videogames, or how other forms of digital rhetoric such as tablet apps illustrate multiliteracies through the interplay of the ludonarrative and framed narrative, or by imbuing the player with varying levels of immersion and/or agency. Likewise, in its treatment of violence *Guns* could be juxtaposed with highly-popular first-person shooters such as those from the *Call of Duty* series, the *Medal of Honor* series, the *Halo* series, and the *Battlefield* series. Aside from *Guns*, subsequent research could examine how other videogame protagonists undergo Burke's cycle of redemption (most notably the *God of War* series and the *Assassin's Creed* series), in order to determine whether the motif functions the same way in other games, and if not, to see how the mechanisms behind the symbol systems in other videogames function.

CONCLUSION

Given the various literacies someone who plays *Guns of the Patriots* will be exposed to, it befits digital rhetoric studies to incorporate *Guns* and other videogames (both mainstream and independently developed) into the "wider context," the context "of the larger realm," the wider playing field inviting multidisciplinary collaboration between rhetoricians, literacy scholars, game designers literature scholars, and scholars within the social sciences (e.g., sociologists and psychologists) and the hard sciences (e.g., computer scientists and ecologists). What I have elucidated is the *"functional specialisation"* of videogames as objects of immersion, agency, and symbolism (Kress, 2003, p. 46). If we think of games as ludo-rhetorical "possibility spaces" (places where, depending on the player, differing outcomes are possible) moreover, "then researchers need to account for how players inhabit them and the mechanisms by which meanings become interpreted from these experiences" (Squire, 2006, p. 20). To that end, I have provided Burke's dramatism, Žižek's ideological criticism, Mateas and Stern's (2005) notions of immersion and agency, and Bissell's (2011) distinction between the framed narrative and ludonarrative as theoretical methods for uncovering fertile meanings from the player's gaming experience. We as theorists of digital rhetoric must therefore contend with the fact that as "more of our cultural attention moves from linear media like books and film to procedural, random-access media like software and video games, we need to become better critics of the latter kind" (Bogost, 2008, p. 136).

Put another way, if we don't take videogames seriously as rhetorical artifacts, as possibility spaces, as ludological settings, and as bit-modulated environments in need of critique, then we preclude ourselves from extracting the multiliteracies deeply embedded within the medium. In recognizing that the challenge in multiliteracies is "to make space available so that different lifeworlds flourish; to create spaces for community life where local and global meanings can be made," videogames can answer the challenge if they are immersive, imbue agency, and create multifaceted meanings out of their ludonarrative and framed narrative (New London Group, 2000, p. 16). Such meanings are likewise contingent on and constantly molded by the player's own lifeworlds (cultural, historical, political, religious, socioeconomic) that they bring in, because as Bissell (2011) proclaims, to "interact with any creative work, whether a video game, an album, a book, or a film, is, in a very real sense, to be its co-creator, to pull from its core your own personal meaning and significance" (p. 226). Upon inspection artifacts like *Guns of the Patriots* only show how games can "let players be producers, not just consumers" of information and meaning (Gee, 2007, p. 216). When we play by pressing and mashing buttons, one wonders whether the buttons also push us, motivate us and further submerge us into the game world. Considering Burke's (1966) question about the nature of language, we could even ascribe such a question to our interactions and relationships with games: "Do we simply use words, or do they not also use us?" (p. 6). Do we simply use games then, or do they not also use us? Just as well, while we can say that we invented language, if Burke (1966) suggests "it might be more accurate to say that language... 'invented' man" (p. 9) inasmuch as thinking about the ways language frames and encapsulates our thoughts and actions, might we also ponder the degree to which games, through their ludological and rhetorical worlds, "invent" us?

REFERENCES

America's Army. (2013). In *Wikipedia*. Retrieved from https://en.wikipedia.org/wiki/America's_Army

Andersen, R. (2013). Omens. *Aeon*. Retrieved from http://www.aeonmagazine.com/world-views/ross-andersen-human-extinction/

Appelbaum, L. G., Cain, M. S., Darling, E. F., & Mitroff, S. R. (2013). Action video game playing is associated with improved visual sensitivity, but not alterations in visual sensory memory. *Attention, Perception & Psychophysics*, *75*(4), 1–7. doi: doi:10.3758/s13414-013-0472-7 PMID:23709062

Bachen, C. M., Hernández-Ramos, P. F., & Raphael, C. (2012). Simulating REAL LIVES: Promoting global empathy and interest in learning through simulation games. *Simulation & Gaming*, *43*(4), 437–460. doi:10.1177/1046878111432108

Bal, P. M., & Veltkamp, M. (2013). How does fiction reading influence empathy? An experimental investigation on the role of emotional transportation. *PLoS ONE*, *8*(1), e55341. doi:10.1371/journal.pone.0055341 PMID:23383160

Betts Van Dyk, K. K. (2006). From the plaint to the comic: Kenneth Burke's *Towards a Better Life*. *Rhetoric Society Quarterly*, *36*(1), 31–53. doi:10.1080/02773940500403611

Bissell, T. (2011). *Extra lives: Why video games matter*. New York, NY: Vintage Books.

Bobbitt, D. A. (2004). *The rhetoric of redemption: Kenneth Burke's redemption drama and Martin Luther King, Jr.'s I have a dream speech*. Lanham, MD: Rowman & Littlefield Publishers.

Bogost, I. (2008). The rhetoric of video games. In K. Salen (Ed.), *The ecology of games: Connecting youth, games, and learning* (pp. 117–140). Cambridge, MA: The MITPress.

Bogost, I. (2013). Exploitationware. In R. Colby, M. S. S. Johnson, & R. S. Colby (Eds.), *Rhetoric/composition/play through video games: Reshaping theory and practice of writing* (pp. 139–148). New York, NY: Palgrave Macmillan. doi:10.1057/9781137307675.0019

Boone, G. W. (2008). *A Burkean analysis of World of Warcraft: Identity work in a virtual environment*. (Master's thesis). Retrieved from ProQuest Dissertations and Theses. (AAT 1454169) Berkeley, CA: University of California Press.

Bourgonjon, J., Rutten, K., Soetaert, R., & Valcke, M. (2011). From counter-strike to counter-statement: Using Burke's pentad as a tool for analysing video games. *Digital Creativity*, 22(2), 91–102. doi:10.1080/14626268.2011.578577

Brummett, B. (1989). Perfection and the bomb: Nuclear weapons, teleology, and motives. *The Journal of Communication*, 39(1), 85–95. doi:10.1111/j.1460-2466.1989.tb01021.x

Buell, L. (2001). *Writing for an endangered world*. Cambridge, MA: Harvard University Press.

Burke, K. (1950). *A rhetoric of motives*. New York, NY: Prentice Hall.

Burke, K. (1961). *The rhetoric of religion: Studies in logology*. Boston, MA: Beacon.

Burke, K. (1962). *A grammar of motives*. Berkeley, CA: University of California Press.

Burke, K. (1966). *Language as symbolic action: Essays on life, literature, and method*.

Burke, K. (1974). *The philosophy of literary form: Studies in symbolic action* (3rd ed.). Berkeley, CA: University of California Press.

Cohen, J. (2006). Audience identification with media characters. In J. Bryant, & P. Vorderer (Eds.), *Psychology of entertainment* (pp. 151–181). Mahwah, NJ: Lawrence Erlbaum.

Colby, R., Johnson, M. S. S., & Colby, R. S. (Eds.). (2013). *Rhetoric/composition/play through video games: Reshaping theory and practice of writing*. New York, NY: Palgrave Macmillan. doi:10.1057/9781137307675

Colby, R. S. (2013). Gender and gaming in a first-year writing class. In R. Colby, M. S. S. Johnson, & R. S. Colby (Eds.), *Rhetoric/composition/play through video games: Reshaping theory and practice of writing* (pp. 123–138). New York, NY: Palgrave Macmillan. doi:10.1057/9781137307675.0017

Conway, S. (2010). A circular wall? Reformulating the fourth wall for videogames. *Journal of Gaming and Virtual Worlds*, 2(2), 145–155. doi:10.1386/jgvw.2.2.145_1

Crogan, P. (2002). Blade runners: Speculations on narrative and interactivity. *The South Atlantic Quarterly*, 101(3), 639–657. doi:10.1215/00382876-101-3-639

Dawkins, R. (2006). *The selfish gene* (3rd ed.). New York, NY: Oxford University Press.

Deen, P. D. (2011). Interactivity, inhabitation and pragmatist aesthetics. *Game Studies: The International Journal of Computer Game Research, 11*(2). Retrieved from http://gamestudies.org/1102/articles/deen

Dowling, D. (1987). *Fictions of nuclear disaster*. Iowa City, IA: University of Iowa Press.

Foss, S. K., Foss, K. A., & Trapp, R. (2002). *Contemporary perspectives on rhetoric* (3rd ed.). Prospect Heights, IL: Waveland Press.

Garrelts, N. (2013). The pencil-shaped joystick: A synoptic history of text in digital games. In R. Colby, M. S. S. Johnson, & R. S. Colby (Eds.), *Rhetoric/composition/play through video games: Reshaping theory and practice of writing* (pp. 25–32). New York, NY: Palgrave Macmillan. doi:10.1057/9781137307675.0009

Gee, J. P. (2007). *What video games have to teach us about learning and literacy*. New York, NY: Palgrave Macmillan.

Greitemeyer, T., Osswald, S., & Brauer, M. (2010). Playing prosocial video games increases empathy and decreases schadenfreude. *Emotion (Washington, D.C.), 10*, 796–802. doi:10.1037/a0020194 PMID:21171755

Hartmann, T., Toz, E., & Brandon, M. (2010). Just a game? Unjustified virtual violence produces guilt in empathetic players. *Media Psychology*, 13(4), 339–363. doi:10.1080/15213269.2010.524912

Heise, U. K. (2008). *Sense of place and sense of planet: The environmental imagination of the global.* New York, NY: Oxford University Press. doi:10.1093/acprof:oso/9780195335637.001.0001

Johnson, D. R. (2012). Transportation into a story increases empathy, prosocial behavior, and perceptual bias toward fearful expressions. *Personality and Individual Differences, 52*(2), 150–155. http://0-dx.doi.org.lib.utep.edu/10.1016/j.paid.2011.10.005 doi:10.1016/j.paid.2011.10.005

Johnson, M. S. S., & Colby, R. (2013). Ludic snags. In R. Colby, M. S. S. Johnson, & R. S. Colby (Eds.), *Rhetoric/composition/play through video games: Reshaping theory and practice of writing* (pp. 83–98). New York, NY: Palgrave Macmillan. doi:10.1057/9781137307675.0014

Journet, D. (2013). Afterword. In R. Colby, M. S. S. Johnson, & R. S. Colby (Eds.), *Rhetoric/composition/play through video games: Reshaping theory and practice of writing* (pp. 205–206). New York, NY: Palgrave Macmillan. doi:10.1057/9781137307675.0024

Kastely, J. L. (1996). Kenneth Burke's comic rejoinder to the cult of empire. *College English, 58*(3), 307–326. doi:10.2307/378714

Kellner, D. M. (2002). Technological revolution, multiple literacies, and the restructuring of education. In I. Snyder (Ed.), *Silicon literacies: Communication, innovation and education in the electronic age* (pp. 154–169). New York, NY: Routledge.

Kenichiro, I., & Kojima, H. (Producers). Shuyo, M., & Kojima, H. (Directors). (2008). Metal gear solid 4: Guns of the patriots [Videogame]. Japan: Konami.

Konami Corporation. (2009, May 14). *FY2009 financial results.* Retrieved from http://www.konami.co.jp/en/ir/ir-data/meeting/2009/0514.pdf

Kress, G. (2003). *Literacy in the new media age.* New York, NY: Routledge. doi:10.4324/9780203164754

Kress, G. R., & Van Leeuwen, T. (2001). *Multimodal discourse: The modes and media of contemporary communication.* London, New York: Arnold, Oxford University Press.

List of. *Metal Gear* media. (2013). In *Wikipedia.* Retrieved from http://en.wikipedia.org/wiki/List_of_Metal_Gear_media

List of best-selling video game franchises. (2010). In *Wikipedia.* Retrieved from http://en.wikipedia.org/wiki/List_of_best-selling_video_game_franchises

List of best-selling video games. (2010). In *Wikipedia.* Retrieved from http://en.wikipedia.org/wiki/List_of_best-selling_video_games#PlayStation_3

Longest cutscene in a video game. (2013). *Guinness World Records.* Retrieved from http://www.guinnessworldrecords.com/records-5000/longest-cutscene-in-a-video-game/

Luke, C. (2000). Cyber-schooling and technological change: Multiliteracies for new times. In B. Cope, & M. Kalantzis (Eds.), *Multiliteracies: Literacy, learning, and the design of social futures* (pp. 69–91). New York, NY: Routledge.

Lynch, L. (2012). We don't wanna be radiated: Documentary film and the evolving rhetoric of nuclear energy activism. *American Literature, 84*(2), 327–351. doi:10.1215/00029831-1587368

Mannix, P. (1992). *The rhetoric of antinuclear fiction: Persuasive strategies in novels and films.* Lewisburg, PA: Bucknell University Press.

Mar, R. A., Oatley, K., Hirsh, J., Paz, J., & Peterson, J. B. (2006). Bookworms versus nerds: Exposure to fiction versus non-fiction, divergent associations with social ability, and the simulation of fictional social worlds. *Journal of Research in Personality, 40*(5), 694–712. doi:10.1016/j.jrp.2005.08.002

Masco, J. (2004). Nuclear technoaesthetics: Sensory politics from Trinity to the virtual bomb in Los Alamos. *American Ethnologist, 31*(3), 349–373. doi:10.1525/ae.2004.31.3.349

Mateas, M., & Stern, A. (2005). Interaction and narrative. In K. Salen, & E. Zimmerman (Eds.), *The game design reader: A rules of play anthology* (pp. 642–669). Boston, MA: MIT Press.

McAllister, K. S. (2005). *Game work: Language, power, and computer game culture*. Tuscaloosa, AL: University of Alabama Press.

Metal gear solid 2: Sons of Liberty. (2013). In *Wikipedia*. Retrieved from http://en.wikipedia.org/wiki/Metal_Gear_Solid_2:_Sons_of_Liberty

Metal gear solid 4: Guns of the patriots. (2010). In *Wikipedia*. Retrieved from http://en.wikipedia.org/wiki/MGS4

Newman, J. (2002). The myth of the ergodic videogame: Some thoughts on player-character relationships in videogames. *Game Studies. The International Journal of Computer Game Research, 2*(1).

Nieborg, D. B. (2009). Empower yourself, defend freedom! Playing games during times of war. In M. van den Boomen, S. Lammes, A.-S. Lehmann, J. Raessens, & M. T. Schäfer (Eds.), *Digital material: Tracing new media in everyday life and technology (MediaMatters)* (pp. 35–47). Amsterdam, The Netherlands: Amsterdam University Press.

Obama's speech on drone policy. (2013, May 23). *The New York Times*. Retrieved from http://www.nytimes.com/2013/05/24/us/politics/transcript-of-obamas-speech-on-drone-policy.html?pagewanted=all

Ottosen, R. (2009). Targeting the player: Computer games as propaganda for the military-industrial complex. *Nordicom Review, 30*(2), 35–51.

Ouellete, M. A. (2008). I hope you never see another day like this: Pedagogy & allegory in post 9/11 video games. *Game Studies. The International Journal of Computer Game Research, 8*(1).

Peng, W. (2008). The mediational role of identification in the relationship between experience mode and self-efficacy: Enactive role-playing versus passive observation. *Cyberpsychology & Behavior, 11*, 649–652. doi:10.1089/cpb.2007.0229 PMID:18954275

Pichlmair, M. (2009). Assembling a mosaic of the future: The post-nuclear world of Fallout 3. *Eludamos. Journal for Computer Game Culture, 3*(1), 107-113. Quijano-Cruz, J. (2009). Chopin's dream as reality: A critical reading of eternal sonata. *Eludamos: Journal for Computer Game Culture, 3*(2), 209–218.

Qin, H., Rau, P., & Salvendy, G. (2009). Measuring player immersion in the computer game narrative. *International Journal of Human-Computer Interaction, 25*, 107–133. doi:10.1080/10447310802546732

Schell, J. (2008). *The art of game design: A book of lenses*. Burlington, MA: Morgan Kaufmann.

Schulzke, M. (2009). Moral decision making in Fallout. *Game Studies. The International Journal of Computer Game Research, 9*(2).

Selfe, C. L., & Hawisher, G. E. (2013). Foreword. In R. Colby, M. S. S. Johnson, M. S. S., & R. S. Colby (Eds.), Rhetoric/composition/play through video games: Reshaping theory and practice of writing (pp. xv-xviii). New York, NY: Palgrave Macmillan.

Snyder, I. (Ed.). (2002). *Silicon literacies: Communication, innovation and education in the electronic age*. New York, NY: Routledge.

Soetaert, R., Bourgonjon, J., & Rutten, K. (2011). Video games as equipment for living. *CLCWeb: Comparative Literature and Culture, 13*(3). doi: doi:10.7771/1481-4374.1794

Squire, K. D. (2006). From content to context: Video games as designed experiences. *Educational Researcher, 35*(8), 19–29. doi:10.3102/0013189X035008019

Stealth game. (2013). In *Wikipedia*. Retrieved from http://en.wikipedia.org/wiki/Stealth_game

Tamari, E. (n.d.). Hideo Kojima interview. *Konami*. Retrieved from http://www.konami.jp/mgs4/uk/interview/03.html

Taylor, B. C. (2010). A hedge against the future: The post-Cold War rhetoric of nuclear weapons modernization. *The Quarterly Journal of Speech, 96*(1), 1–24. doi:10.1080/00335630903512721

The New London Group. (2000). A pedagogy of multiliteracies: Designing social futures. In B. Cope, & M. Kalantzis (Eds.), *Multiliteracies: Literacy, learning, and the design of social futures* (pp. 9–37). New York, NY: Routledge.

Voorhees, G. (2009). The character of difference: procedurality, rhetoric, and roleplaying games. *Game Studies. The International Journal of Computer Game Research, 9*(2).

Watts, E. (2011). Ruin, gender, and digital games. *Women's Studies Quarterly, 39*(3/4), 247–265. doi:10.1353/wsq.2011.0041

Weise, M. (2003). *How videogames express ideas*. Retrieved from DiGRA: Digital games research association Web site: http://www.digra.org/dl/db/05150.07598.pdf

White, M. (2009). The senescence of creativity: How market forces are killing digital games. *Loading..., 3*(4).

Williams, D. C. (1989). Under the sign of (an) nihiliation: Burke in the age of nuclear destruction and critical deconstruction. In H. W. Simons, & T. Melia (Eds.), *The legacy of Kenneth Burke* (pp. 196–223). Madison, WI: University of Wisconsin Press.

Wright, E., & Wright, E. (Eds.). (1999). *The Žižek reader*. Oxford, UK: Blackwell Publishers, Ltd.

Zappen, J. P. (2005). Digital rhetoric: Toward an integrated theory. *Technical Communication Quarterly, 14*(3), 319–325. doi:10.1207/s15427625tcq1403_10

Žižek, S. (1997). *The plague of fantasies*. New York, NY: Verso.

KEY TERMS AND DEFINITIONS

Aesthetics: The sensory modes of a videogame: taste, feeling, appearance, sound, and smell.

Affordance: The limits and potencies of a mode.

Agency: A sense of empowerment resulting from being able to exercise one's will and effect action as a player in the videogame, either through the ludonarrative or the framed narrative.

AI: Artificial intelligence.

Artifact: Any sign that communicates.

Deep Ecology: An environmental philosophy that emphasizes ecocentrism.

Digital Rhetoric: The art of bit-modulated communication.

Dramatism: The theory that views language as symbolic action.

Framed Narrative: The expository story in a videogame, usually static and therefore unchangeable by a player.

Immersion: A sense of existing in another world resulting from the interactions and experiences with such a world.

Interface: The spaces between a player and the gaming world, including a virtual interface (menus/displays) that the player sees but is not actually existent in the gaming world.

Ludology: The study of games (including videogames), and methods of play.

Ludonarrative: The narrative of a videogame effected through gameplay and hence varying according to the player.

Mechanics: The rules and methods of a videogame.

Mode: A semiotic material for communication.

Multiliteracies: Multicultural, multimodal, and multilinguistic meaning-making.

Multimodal: Comprised of multiple modes.

PMC: Private military company.

Rhetoric: The art of communication.

Rhetoric of Rebirth: A secular form of the Christian archetypes of pollution, purification, and redemption, a kind of symbolic action stemming from guilt, with rebirth as its goal.

Chapter 14
"A Genuine Moment of Liberation for Me":
Digital Introductions as Powerful Learning

Julie Faulkner
Monash University, Australia

ABSTRACT

This chapter argues that participation in a digital self-presentation has the potential to challenge inscribed approaches to learning and teaching. It draws from a study of preservice teachers at an Australian university, who were invited to create a digital introduction as part of their English teaching method course. Such a task offered students opportunities to experiment with shifting semiotic forms in ways unavailable to written introductions. Students were asked to critically reflect after the presentation on aspects of technology, representation and learning that were brought into focus in and through their presentations. A semiotic analysis offers insights into the potential of multimodality, as the digital introduction pushed the participants out of familiar territory, often producing creative and stimulating texts. Using Kress's concept of synaesthesia, the chapter explores innovations possible in the creation of new possibilities in a multimodal space.

DOI: 10.4018/978-1-4666-4916-3.ch014

Copyright © 2014, IGI Global. Copying or distributing in print or electronic forms without written permission of IGI Global is prohibited.

INTRODUCTION

Bill Green (2001), speculating on the implications for subject English in the 21st century, points to 'the proliferating phenomenon of techno-textuality' (p. 249). Yet, research also suggests that in many classrooms, much textual study remains print-based (Papert, 1992, Lankshear & Knobel, 2006, Morris, 2010). If digital technologies are used in a classroom, it often occurs in a Web 1.0 environment where print material is merely uploaded. Limited interactivity and agency are demanded from the learners, who often 'power down' (Warschauer, 2003) to meet school demands, becoming disengaged from formal learning in the process.

Working in the second decade of the century, it is timely to reflect on such changes and whether shifts from print culture towards a digital culture have led to a substantive rethinking of educational practices. Narrowing the focus, debates over the past two decades argue how far digitally-based technologies have effected change in literacy pedagogies (see Green & Bigum, 1993, Bigum, 1995, Lankshear, 1997, Lankshear, Snyder & Green, 2000, Kress, 2003, Gee, 2008, for example). The possibilities for new kinds of writing afforded by digital technologies and social media now permeate digital worlds, if not English classrooms. A dimension of this shift has been the opening up not only of new kinds of content, but also of form, in terms of what can now be authored. It is the disruption and expansion of form that this study explores, and how the writers of the new technologies see the process as inclusive of literacy elements such as technology, identity and representation. I argue that the study, albeit small in scope, has resonances that extend beyond the English classroom environments, and even classrooms per se. The implications can be transferred to other settings where Information and Communications Technologies can be used as provocations for new kinds of writing.

The purpose of the project was to position preservice teachers as active and discerning participants within this digital way of knowing so that they could investigate these connections for themselves. Many school learners own a number of digital devices, and by virtue of having grown through various eras of computing and information technology, adapt to the shifting topography of digital life. Understandings from the digital activities could then be transferred by preservice teachers to local school settings as authentic practice, being both rooted in children's own textual play as well as in sound literacy pedagogy.

In this project, I created a digital introduction task to replace a traditional written student introduction, beginning a 12 month class in teaching method. The task required students to represent aspects of themselves digitally, present this representation to me and their peers and then critically reflect on the practices and technologies involved. One aim of the interaction was to push students into a less comfortable space. This space was created through their need to learn new technological skills, understanding the expanded capacity of the chosen technology to shape their purposes, as well as the choices they needed to make to characterize themselves for a peer audience. These 'pedagogies of discomfort' (Boler, 1999) were in turn constructed by me as generative learning conditions in which students might be thrust out of habituated print text practices. Meanwhile, the immersive possibilities of being engaged in processes of digital self-representations offered learning as demanding and pleasurable. Students were required to work at the outer edge of their expertise with ICT, keeping notes on their efforts and responses. The only instruction they were given was to minimize print and oral commentary as far as possible, allowing their chosen images to carry the weight of meaning (Kress, 1995).

The task was structured as an open-ended 'problem', grounded in a literacy concept. The framework I chose as the best fit for the task was Bill Green's (1988) 3D literacy model, which describes three interrelated dimensions of literacy: operational, cultural and critical. Green's model appealed because it argues these dimensions of practice are not hierarchical, but always interconnected and simultaneous. Like digital play, apprehension and skills develop interchangeably and contingently. Operationally, students had to understand and use digital technologies, employing a repertoire of (multi)literate practices strategically and appropriately for their audience (the cultural dimension). Introducing themselves to a new cohort of peers constituted a 'literacy event' (Buckingham 2003) which engaged social and deliberate meaning-making. To participate in the critical dimension, students were encouraged to explore the self reflexive, or constructed nature of identity and representation through responding to a number of guided questions.

BACKGROUND

Universities and schools are increasingly populated with learners who are shaped by their relationships with information and communication technologies (ICT) in ways unimaginable to many current educators (Green & Bigum, 1993). These students are adept at multitasking, sophisticated in their uses of electronic technologies, and used to a trial and error approach to solving problems, contrasting with a more logical, rule-based approach by previous generations (Oblinger, 2003; Oblinger, Martin & Baer, 2004). Formal learning practices which decontextualize ways of knowing increasingly lead to student disconnection with school learning.

One commentator notes:

[It is] no surprise that when we incarcerate teenagers of today in traditional classroom settings, they react with predictable disinterest [...] They are skilled in making sense not only of a body of content, but of contexts that are continually changing. (Economist.com, n. d.)

While the extent to which teenagers are skilled in making sense of a body of content could be argued, their understanding of popular texts is always situated practice. Differences within ways that school and out-of-school literacies are organized have been usefully analyzed by Bernstein (1999). While schooling values vertical, segmentally structured discourses of knowledge, popular (and digital) ways of knowing to which everyone has potential or actual access can be described as 'horizontal'. They are 'likely to be oral, local, context-dependent and specific, tacit, multi-layered and contradictory across ... contexts' (p. 8). Young people pick up valued knowledge by word of mouth and there is a rapid turnover of what is required to be a participant within and across a number of cultural contexts. Students as readers and producers of Green's techno-textuality thus need to disembed themselves from familiar, and increasingly multiliterate ways of thinking, in order to immerse themselves successfully in formally-constructed knowledge, knowledge which continues to privilege print forms of language. Moreover, while pre-school learners naturally discover the world in multimodal ways, the balkanization of school curriculum serves to fracture and isolate approaches to learning (Kalantzis & Cope, 2012).

Under the new knowledge economies, however, not only has the conceptualization of literacy undergone significant evolution, but also how we learn and practice multimodal forms of communication. Multiliteracies call for understandings of complex relationships among visuals, space and text and interpreting a range of symbols in critical and culturally appropriate ways (the New London Group, 1996). Arguing that we are now experiencing a 'visual turn', Kress (1995) examines the cognitive shift from print to illustrative text. Syntactic demands on print language have lessened as visual material becomes more complex and abstract. While the move away from print has been resisted by traditionalists, Kress sees the increasingly sophisticated emphasis on visual material as adding force to a rich rescripting of what we mean by 'literacies'. Bernstein's call for attention to horizontal discourse in schools maps onto our new economic/global realities.

Given these tensions, how is education negotiating the new capacities, forms of knowledge and skills demonstrated in our contemporary learners? The theory of multiliteracies (the New London Group, 1996; Cope & Kalantzis, 2000) takes fresh reconceptions about literacies in a technologized, globalized environment and overlays them onto more established notions of situated practice. Through building the theory, a semiotic, or multimodal understanding of meaning-making enables creative and re-visioned practices.

To what extent are these concepts and new approaches found in contemporary classroom practice? Anlayzing patterns in organizational culture, Christenson (1997) argues that most changes undertaken are sustaining innovations; changes that better support a present system and make it more effective. Christenson advocates far more radical change that he terms 'disruptive innovations'. Innovations of this kind are systemic and dramatically alter the existing culture. Senge, Scharmer, Jaworski and Flowers (2004) support Christenson's views and suggest that the processes most organizations undertake are fundamentally flawed because they continue to seek to impose 'old frameworks on new realities.' (p. 84)

NEW SEMIOTIC POSSIBILITIES

How then might 'new realities' be more effectively conceptualized and put into practice, in this case, as part of a teacher education course? I have argued that digital technologies, supporting Kress's visual turn, have afforded expanded resources for making meaning. The rules and norms of cyberspace create a different, and distinctively sense of spatial awareness, involving a 'fracturing of space' (Lankshear & Bigum 1999 p. 457). We can now shift back and forth between different modes of meaning, creating new design

patterns. Space is no longer closed and intention-specific, but 'open, continuous and fluid' (Knobel & Lankshear, 2007 p.11).

Kress (2003) calls the ways that we can purposefully mobilize these resources *synaesthesia*, or the remaking of semiotic resources *within* modes (transformation) and *across* modes (transduction). While multimodality is not new, through rapidly-changing technologies, we can, and increasingly do, deploy faster ways, in terms of production and sharing to overlay image, word, gesture, image, sound and space. Three dimensional space opens prospects for cognitive reshaping of texts, which are, Kress (1997) argues, resources. In this sense, the producer's relationship with the text has become something more generative and creative. The processes which drive this shifting meaning-making create qualitatively new forms of meaning from those that have previously existed. Users of previously static systems have become remakers, or transformers, of representational resources.

These expanded technical capabilities have an accompanying mindset. Knobel and Lankshear (2007) argue that what makes literacies 'new' is the 'ethos stuff' that accompanies the digitality. Without these dispositions around collaboration, production and distributed expertise, technical innovation changes little to alter sedimented literacy practices. It is not the act of remixing and authoring in new ways that is important per se, but 'how it enables people to build and participate in literacy practices that involve different kinds of values, sensibilities, norms and procedures and so on from those that characterize conventional literacies'. (p.7)

Kalantzis and Cope (2012) discuss these processes as design, or 'the study of form and structure in the meanings we make' (p. 182). Linking all representation and communication to multimodality, they argue that we constantly re-represent written language when we shift modes, imagining how things might look and feel as we cross over from reading and writing. Within each mode exist different systems, or organizing logics (Kress, 2003) which affect the ways that the semiotic elements are integrated or 'braided' (Mitchell, 1994).

The practice of exploring how parallel, or complementary modes of meaning are composed, juxtaposed and transposed explodes narrow conceptualizations of literacy. Moreover, such an approach offers possibilities for deep learning argue Kalantzis and Cope, as we invite learners to shift between modes to extend understanding. Burke and Rowsell (2009) claim that reading is now coterminous with hybrid writing practices:

Digital texts ... require a semiotic understanding on the part of the reader. Online reading trajectories offer multiple genres and cross-genres, often extended through the creator's distribution of the site. (p. 117)

Nelson (2006), moving from digital reading to writing, goes beyond explicit representation in describing how we make new meanings. He claims that:

the potential for authorship, authentic expression of an authorial voice, lies not so much in the words, images, sounds, etc. that we employ, but rather in between them, in the designing of relations of meaning that bind semiotic modes together. (p.57)

I sought to understand how (and if) students would use digital technologies to forge meanings in new ways. If synaesthesia, or shifting back and forth between modes were evident, how might students conjure up and recombine elements from available resources, representing differently?

A CRITICAL MULTIMODAL APPROACH

In exploring whether and to what extent my participants exploited the potential of digital technologies to create innovative, synthesized

forms of authorship, related questions emerged. Awareness of communication and representation on the part of the creators is integral to confident literate practice. As a way of heightening media awareness, the written reflections would, I hoped, detail the combinative approaches the authors used, simultaneously developing appreciation of the creative processes involved. Burn and Durrant (2008) argue that critical understanding is more accessible when students have some grasp of how media texts are actually produced.

It was a demanding set of task expectations but one which I framed as strongly motivated, in the sense of Papert's (2002) 'hard fun'. Multimodal texts offer high levels of engagement for young people, who are generally expert readers of their complex semiotic worlds (Kress & van Leeuwen 2001; Johnson-Eilola 1997). However, while young people make discriminations about and within their chosen texts, they do not always consciously evaluate or articulate the criteria they use (Buckingham 1993; Doecke & McCleneghan 1998). Self reflexivity, or a critical knowledge of the constructedness of students' own texts, is integral to the process of writing the technologies. I wanted to investigate how far students' reflections suggested understanding of Green's (1988) critical dimension of literacy. The critical reflections and student use of metalanguage, along with the introductions themselves, contributed to the data from which I drew the findings.

THE STUDY

This study explored changing forms of textual practice using new technologies and asked whether participation invited a critical awareness of (self) representation. In asking students to create a digital innovation, I also wanted to discover pedagogical resonances, or the 'disruptive' possibilities for re-imagining routinized teaching practices. The small-scale study was, then, loaded as an exploration of how students used the technologies for rhetorical purposes and the pedagogical potential of the task for more critically reflective literacy practice.

Twenty-four education students of various ages completed the introductions as part of their English teaching specialism course at an Australian university. The introductions were prepared as students' first task in the first semester of a year-long course. Students arrived from an undergraduate degree to complete their Diploma of Education unfamiliar with the university, me or their peers. The university is located in a very culturally-diverse suburb of a large city, and the English specialism class reflected both cultural and economic mix in student background.

They constructed and presented a 5 minute digital introduction to me, as course lecturer, and their fellow postgraduate teaching method students. The purpose of the elements of the task was to introduce students to a new cohort, extend their current knowledge of ICT from where it currently stood (Green's 1988 notion of 'operational' literacy) and to consider the potential of the software for their purpose and audience ('cultural' dimensions of literacy). More critically, students were asked to link their self-representational processes to literacy theory from their readings and then to think reflexively on what they had learned (the critical dimension) and the implications that the learning held for their teaching practice. To guide their reflections, I suggested the following questions and recommendations:

- What were the opportunities and limitations of the software you chose?
- Link your introduction to ideas in literacy theories and frameworks to theorize your practice (e.g., Green, 1988; Freebody & Luke, 1990; Hull & Nelson, 2005)
- What choices did you make during the process of your presentation in relation to the 'version' of yourself you chose to communicate to us?

- Reflect on what you have learned during the process (about yourself, your capacity with digital technologies, your choices about the ways you chose to represent yourself) and the implications of the task for you as a literacy teacher

Moreover, I created a digital introduction myself as a teacher-participant to explore the creative and reflective processes involved. My own field notes added to the data collection.

I sought preservice teachers' permission to use their introductions and reflections as data for investigation of my research questions. I also invited written responses to follow up questions asked. Extended survey responses were followed up in further directed discussion

I used Kalantzis and Cope's design analysis approach (2012, p. 200) to analyse the data, in conjunction to my own questions directing student critical reflections. Design analysis includes consideration of elements of design and their interrelationships, point of view, generic borrowings, inclusions and exclusions, as well as consideration of the ways that the content is mediated by the technology.

I then highlighted, grouped and regrouped different patterns of response, cross referencing and refining themes and categories. Exploring gaps and assumptions in the writing, I investigated multimodal features and prevailing discourses in students' texts, and linked these to the relevant concepts in the literature.

DISCUSSION

The preservice teachers' interview data, their reflections and the digital introductions provided a number of insights into the research questions. My central question asked whether, and how far, students took up the affordances offered by new technologies to create new kinds of texts.

The introductions ranged from limited, in terms of exploitation of form, to rich and generically innovative. At the limited end, the presentations used the task as a kind of digital scrapbook, posting photos of friends, family and pets, following a chronology from baby to university student, occasionally supported by a favourite music track. The visual and audio resources in these cases mimicked print resources of self-representation; they tended to be linear in structure and drew upon known conventions such as photo albums.

However, other students consciously wrestled with the 'messiness' of ICT (Bigum, 1995), producing conceptually and visually spectacular introductions. Working at the edge of personal digital expertise, their range of programs included iMovie, Prezi, xtranormal, Movie Maker, Power-Point, Google earth, websites and blogs. A number of reflections outlined hours spent on learning new software to serve their communicative aims.

In some cases, authors 'bent' genre conventions as they played with identity constructions. This was done from a distanced perspective and, often, with knowing humor. Amy, for instance, filmed people playfully talking about her and talking 'as' her – at no point did she ever either appear or reveal anything substantial about herself. Employing documentary and vox pop techniques, Tom edited clips of his family and friends discussing him posthumously, with one brother struggling to remember he even had a brother.

Another introduction engaged an animation program with computer generated, HAL-type voices, to satirize aspects of his decision to become a teacher education student. He chose a Napoleonic war scenario to request safe passage to the outer suburb where he would commence his teacher education qualification (Xtranormal, n. d.). Richard's reflection allows insight into the ways he set up his introduction, and how it enabled a range of playful options more difficult to achieve through linear print text:

I wanted to play with the possibility of becoming a teacher being set up in opposition to the 'glory' of fighting an animated Napoleonic war. I thought this might reflect the common prejudices against the profession of teaching (it being 'unmasculine' etcetera) while [the outer suburb] could become territory that required armed escort. The ironic tone of the digital introduction was intended to interest the audience and at the same time, the irony also required the audience to act as 'text participants' so they could understand, for instance, the stereotype of the drunk and quarrelsome authority figure, or the self-conscious and historically displaced authority figure.

Perhaps this highlights the critical dimension of Green in particular; there was no attempt to make the digital introduction appear 'natural' or 'normal' at all, and indeed, the awkwardness of the technology's limitations ended up being as much a feature of the presentation as the message itself.

Invoking McLuhan's (1964/1994) 'medium as message', Richard calls upon a number of tropes and technological juxtapositions to explore the reverberations of his chosen resources. The symbiotic relationship between mode and meaning argued by McLuhan pre digital technologies has become an innate feature of digital writing as design. Similarly aware, a Singaporean student, Koh, constructed an on screen digital jigsaw puzzle with his name written in the centre piece. Other digital pieces contained hyperlinked identity features (a Google map link to his street, satay recipes, a trailer to a favourite television series). Clicking and dragging the pieces to the centre section completed his personalized jigsaw, which formed a map of Singapore, a design not previously apparent.

Liam filmed himself in profile, speaking. He then stood opposite his interactive screen profile and conducted a conversation with himself. The use of an inner dialogue made social in this way suggests the space *between* spoken words and images that Nelson (2006) alludes to. The transposition enabled a 'synthesis of form and meaning' (Hull & Nelson, 2005, pp. 238-9) through the binding of modes and ideas. It created for Liam a more complex and telling expression of authorial voice.

Matt created on Google Earth an annotated tour of the history of his relationship and work with a Japanese tent theatre company. He uploaded to Google Earth photographs and notes of events that took place in Tokyo and Melbourne linked to his ongoing collaboration, 'flying' us to Tokyo and pasting theatre photos on relevant points of the map. Similarly to Liam's dialogue with himself, two dimensional space could not replicate the topography Matt wanted to create as an architectural layer to his photographic images.

The level of 'orchestration' (Kress, 2003) in these examples was high, as students borrowed and experimented with combinations. This was not, however, an effortless process, as evidenced by Gert:

I felt a bit scared as I know my ICT smartness is not exactly fed every day by trying out and using new technologies (but I think it should be, if only to keep up with what some students might know about or like to use.) Also, a sense of playfulness kicked in pretty quickly, connected to the challenge to organize one's life into a 5 minute digital show.

Caroline noted the communicative shift, argued by Kress (1995) and Mitchell (1994), from print to the visual:

A very real challenge for me was to 'let the images do the talking'. I observed some of my peers make extensive use of the spoken and written word, which did make me consider how easy it might be to fall into the trap of providing the students with too much of a teacher's voice and not allowing them to develop their own.

Caroline's connection between 'telling' and teacher voice suggests an intuitive understanding of Lankshear and Knobel's (2006) 'ethos stuff', where producers of digital material, not the instructors, define the learning map as 'folksonomies'.

David demonstrated understanding of the potential of digital technologies to move beyond 'reframing what is'. He constructed the shifting between modes – Kress's 'synaesthesia' – as alternative pathways to learning:

The digitally-based problem solving that the introduction exercise provided was extremely important, as it provided the impetus to think creatively with new media, and to use it as an instrument of alternative pedagogy ... Some people see the digital medium as a way of reframing what is ... Others seem far more willing to manipulate space, image, sound, and notions of interactivity and clusters of disparate media - and they seem to handle it with far greater success.

This semiotic movement ('fluency of information flow') is linked by Matt to increased deeper power of exploration:

The point is that these technologies are only special in as much as they allow us to see pictures, hear sounds and read text close to instantaneously, and from places that might usually have taken a week to order through libraries. It is this fluency of information flow that allows questions to be researched more deeply.

Whether heightened information flow does invite depth is consistently argued in digital learning discourse. As an embryonic teacher, Matt believed that shifting to Web 2.0 approaches does offer qualitatively different kinds of pedagogies:

[I have visions that] the smart board should be up and running and the students logged in (using solar panels and wind energy to run it of course, with a meter to the side to gauge if the school has

uploaded any electricity to the grid this month). Instead of the teacher handing the student the WB marker to write up headings as to where the class left off last time, the student navigates the whole class to a folder of student offerings on their web page/wiki/FB page. Further questioning surrounding the headings found, YouTube selections shown, Google Earth models downloaded so that, in an analysis of Australian xenophobia, the architecture of the Twin Towers can be studied, copies of the Quoran distributed bookmarked at the page that states that... (paraphrasing) 'If a person disagrees with Islam, a safe harbour should be found for them and the means given for them to travel there (speaker on Radio National Encounter 14/09/11). Pull up sites on the demonstration of fear-mongering in Australian politics with links to Australian Bureau of Statistics showing not one refugee boat arrival was ever found to have links to terrorism of any kind. In this example, many types of technologies, hardware, software and networks are used to illuminate deep social mores ... mythologies.

The point is that these technologies are only special in as much as they allow us to see pictures, hear sounds and read text close to instantaneously and from places that might usually have taken a week to order from stack. It is this fluency of information flow that allows questions to be researched more deeply. For the very same reason news flies around the globe – we watched the killings in Tehran via Facebook/YouTube uploaded from mobile handsets because the state censored any real coverage. Instantaneous – so that some diplomatic response comes quickly and protestors can subvert oppressive censorship.

Artists should use their digital tools like political analysts. Actuaries should use charts using video examples from the floods in Pakistan from last night's news; Mathematicians should be projecting live forming fractal visualizations. Scientists should have their lab computers keyed in to the world wide search for extra-terrestrial life (SETI at home).

Linking his digital introduction and reflection to more complex understandings, Matt reflected on the potential of the task to develop critical perspectives:

The creation of a digital introduction was an interesting process because it forced me to examine perceptions of my own identity. It required that I construct a version of myself and my story for a particular context and audience. Beyond instances of fact, considerations of 'truth' are relatively constructed. Upon reflection I understand, to a greater extent than I did before, the role of my ideological viewpoint in constructing a discourse that is not universally shared. I think this is important for a prospective teacher to understand.

Matt's appreciation of knowledge as contingent is taken further by David, as he articulates the significance of the introductions for rethinking learning and teaching approaches. David claims:

The digital introductions were an immediate challenge (digital media being largely dismissed as lacking in academic rigour or pedagogical value). The digital introductions immediately legitimised digital spaces as valuable and dynamic sites of classroom activity. With the structural and aesthetic possibilities presented by the task, it was remarkable to see the potential of a multiliteracy approach manifesting through my classroom experiments with digital media ... The digital introduction was a genuine moment of liberation for me – it gave me a sense that 'English teaching' was a far richer and more exciting a vocation than I had initially believed, and would allow me to accurately represent the digital culture that I had grown up with.

Lankshear and Knobel's 'ethos stuff' (2007) entails a mindset that is oriented to collaboration and building knowledge from the ground up. Kirk's reflective comments reinforce this disposition, and, like David, rues its uneasy fit with traditional schooling:

Teens today appear to learn far more intuitively and laterally by using forms of ICT, than if they were expected to learn exclusively through methods of rote learning, engagement with paper-based (static) texts, or through physical face-to-face socialisation. As I see it, digital technology actively encourages contemporary learners to explore new ways of visual, auditory, kinaesthetic and meta-cognitive representation. Learners are provided with a new channel through which to socialise, interact and collaborate, and it constantly changes and regulates itself in response to the collective needs of those who use it. Digital technology invites content creation from its users in such a way that a hierarchical, top-down, unitary or "classical" model of teaching and learning has become increasingly invalid or inapplicable to teenagers' lives.

Not all students reflected in such depth and detail, some of which was drawn from further voluntary interview questions, post-reflection. However, these data suggest that the task invited levels of meta-awareness. There was, among many comments, a central focus on reconceptualized communication and representational interrelationships, which could be further built upon in future explorations.

IMPLICATIONS

The digital introductions offered much in terms of the power of the digital medium to create expanded spaces for creativity. Moreover, animating new challenges through ICT enabled reflexivity in relation to our own framing (Green, 2001)

and thus provided agency to think critically and creatively about 'doing school'.

My digital introductions aimed to move authors and readers beyond the 'confinement' of one mode (print text) into alternative pedagogical spaces, drawing both from conventional autobiographical writing and open-ended multimodal possibilities. Some student responses surpassed anticipation, serving to reiterate significant aspects of the learning process, not the least including Papert's (2002) 'hard fun' of immersive technologies. Student critical reflections revealed long hours of work to extend their personal knowledge of unfamiliar programs, seeing it as a means towards 'rich and more exciting' learning (David). Moreover, the reflective work which followed the presentations served as 'traces of practice' (Pahl and Rowsell (2012), illuminating elements of emerging understanding.

Presentations pushed identity conventions into innovative technological spaces – the mode in this case 'reformulating' and expanding the content possibilities. The 'braiding' of modes (Mitchell 1986) was often in evidence, as authors interknit various visual, aural and written genres to achieve meaning. The ways that the students approached the open-ended task always demonstrated, to some extent, Kress's synaesthetic qualities made available through multimodality. Further directed learning could exploit this affordance more deliberately, pushing students even further outside their technological and creative comfort zones.

FUTURE RESEARCH DIRECTIONS

As high stakes testing regimes embed themselves more trenchantly into educational policy and practice, questions continue over what kinds of knowledge and skills are currently being identified and assessed, and for what purposes. Kress (1997), discussing the concept of design, sees curriculum as 'a design for the future' (p. 78). If design comprises agency, creativity, innovation and collaboration, then these features are rarely valued in the growing policy emphasis on standardized testing. What McClenaghan and Doecke (2010, p. 224) refer to as the 'psychometric mindset' sits uneasily with the kind of dispositions that Knobel and Lankshear (2007) argue accompany new literacies. Curriculum, or future design, should be a research priority in times of surveillance and accountability to tap new literacy practices central to contemporary learners' lives.

If this study is indicative, the role of the teacher in authentic learning remains significant. While agency is fundamental in meaning-making, some learners (and teachers) will take up new invitations, while others remain cautious. The expanding body of research should provide impetus for changed practice in the classroom, confronting the narrowing effects of compliance.

There are now numerous studies of teachers' work with digital authorship in the classroom (see, for example, Ohler 2008, Carrington and Robinson 2009, Pahl and Rowsell 2012, Robin 2008). Encouraging new ways of understanding through creative interactions with digital resources should be integral to every educator's purview. The value of using curriculum and assessment as vehicles for preservice teacher creations and discussions of the digital media is demonstrated through increasing numbers of research studies. Thinking differently about digital rhetorics and being reflexive about the ways we frame our texts (Green, 2001) re-imagines an expansive pedagogy for future classrooms.

REFERENCES

Bernstein, B. (1999). Vertical and horizontal discourse: An essay. *British Journal of Sociology of Education*, 20(2), 157–173. doi:10.1080/01425699995380

Bigum, C. (1995). Schools and the Internet: Reinventing the 1980s?. *Incorporated Association of Registered Teachers of Victoria (IARTV) Seminar Series, no. 47*.

Boler, M. (1999). *Feeling power: Emotions and education*. New York, NY: Routledge.

Buckingham, D. (1993). *Children talking television: The making of television literacy*. London, UK: Falmer Press.

Buckingham, D. (2003). *Media education: Literacy, learning and contemporary culture*. Cambridge, MA: Polity Press.

Burke, A., & Rowsell, J. (2009). Reading by design: Two case studies of digital reading practices. *Journal of Adolescent & Adult Literacy*, 53(2), 106–118. doi:10.1598/JAAL.53.2.2

Burn, A., & Durrant, C. (2008). Media education: A background. In A. Burn, & C. Durrant (Eds.), *Media teaching: Language, audience and production* (pp. 11–25). Adelaide, Australia: Wakefield Press.

Carrington, V., & Robinson, M. (Eds.). (2009). *Digital literacies: Social learning and classroom practices*. California: UKLA.

Christenson, C. M. (1997). *The innovator's dilemma: When new technologies can cause great firms to fail*. Boston: Harvard Business School Press.

Cope, B., & Kalantzis, M. (2000). Multiliteracies: The beginnings of an idea. In B. Cope, & M. Kalantzis (Eds.), *Multiliteracies: Literacy learning and the design of social futures*. London: Routledge.

Doecke, B., & McCleneghan, D. (1998). Reconceptualising experience: Growth pedagogy and youth culture. In W. Sawyer, K. Watson, & E. Gold (Eds.), *Re-viewing English* (pp. 46–57). Sydney, Australia: Clair Press.

Economist.com. (n. d.). 'From literacy to digiracy: Will reading and writing remain important?' Retrieved May 18, 2008, from http://www.economist.com/science/PrinterFriendly.cfm?story_id=11392128

Freebody, P., & Luke, A. (1990). Literacies programs: Debates and demands in cultural context. *Prospect: Australian Journal of TESOL, 5*(7), 7–16.

Gee, J. P. (2008). *What video games have to teach us about learning and literacy.* Basingstoke, UK: Palgrave Macmillan.

Green, B. (1988). Subject-specific literacy and school learning: A focus on writing. *Australian Journal of Education, 32*(2), 156–179. doi:10.1177/000494418803200203

Green, B. (2001). 'English teaching, 'literacy' and the post-age. In C. Durrant, & C. Beavis (Eds.), *P(ICT)ures of English: Teachers, learners and technology.* South Australia: AATE.

Green, B., & Bigum, C. (1993). Aliens in the classroom. *Australian Journal of Education, 37*(2), 119–134. doi:10.1177/000494419303700202

Hayes, T. (2011) Finding a place for Falstaff: Language and creativity in the English curriculum. In *AATE Conference Notes December 3-6, Melbourne.* Retrieved January 22, 2012, from http://www.vate.asn.au/aateconference2011/component/content/article/10-about-aate-conference-2011.html

Hull, G., & Nelson, M. E. (2005). Locating the semiotic power of multimodality. *Written Communication, 22,* 224–161. doi:10.1177/0741088304274170

Johnson-Eilola, J. (1997). Living on the surface: Learning in the age of global communication networks. I. Snyder (Ed.), Page to screen: Taking literacy into the electronic era (pp. 185-210). Sydney, Australia: Allen and Unwin.

Kalantzis, M., & Cope, B. (2012) Literacies. Port Melbourne, Australia: Cambridge.

Knobel, M., & Lankshear, C. (2007). *A new literacies sampler.* Retrieved April 15, 2012, from http://everydayliteracies.net/files/NewLiteraciesSampler_2007.pdf

Kress, G. (1995). *Literacy or literacies: Thoughts on an agenda for the day after tomorrow.* Unpublished paper.

Kress, G. (1997). Visual and verbal modes of representation on electronically mediated communication: the potentials of new forms of text. In I. Snyder (Ed.), *Page to screen: Taking literacy into the electronic era.* Sydney, Australia: Allen and Unwin.

Kress, G. (2003). *Literacy in the new media age.* London: Routledge. doi:10.4324/9780203164754

Kress, G., & van Leeuwen, T. (2001). *Multimodal discourse.* London: Edward Arnold.

Lankshear, C. (1997). *Changing literacies.* Buckingham, UK: Open University Press.

Lankshear, C., & Bigum, C. (1999). Literacies and new technologies in school settings. *Pedagogy, Culture & Society, 7*(3), 445–465. doi:10.1080/14681369900200068

Lankshear, C., & Knobel, M. (2006). *New literacies: Everyday practices in classroom learning.* Berkshire, UK: OUP.

Lankshear, C., & Snyder, I. with Green, B. (2000). Teachers and technoliteracy: Managing literacy, technology and learning in schools. Sydney, Australia: Allen and Unwin.

McLuhan, M. (1994). *Understanding media: The extensions of man.* Cambridge, MA: MIT Press. (Original work published 1964)

Mitchell, W. J. T. (1986). *Inconology: Image, text, ideology.* Chicago, IL: University of Chicago Press.

Morris, D. (2010). Are teachers technophobes? Investigating professional competency in the use of ICT to support teaching and learning. *Procedia – Social and Behavioural Sciences 2*(2), 4010-4015.

Nelson, M. (2006) Mode, meaning and synaesthesia in multimedia L2 writing. *Language learning and teachnology, 10*(2), 56-76.

Oblinger, D. (2003). Boomers, gen-Xers and millenials: Understanding the new students. *EDUCAUSE Review, 38*(4), 37–47.

Oblinger, D., Martin, R., & Baer, L. (2004). *Unlocking the potential of gaming technology.* Paper presented at National Learning Infastructure Initiative Annual Meeting. San Diego, CA.

Ohler, J. (2008). *Digital storytelling in the classroom: New Media pathways to literacy, learning and creativity.* Thousand Oaks, CA: Corwin Press.

Pahl, K., & Rowsell, J. (2012). *Literacy and education* (2nd ed.). Thousand Oaks, CA: Sage.

Papert, S. (1992). *The children's machine: Rethinking school in the age of the computer.* New York: Basic Books.

Papert. S. (2002). *Hard fun.* Retrieved March 21, 2012, from http://www.papert.org/articles/HardFun.html.

Robin, B. (2008). Digital storytelling: A powerful technology tool for the 21st century. *Theory into Practice, 47*(3), 220–228. doi:10.1080/00405840802153916

Senge, P., Scharmer, C. O., Jaworski, J., & Flowers, B. S. (2004). Presence: Human purpose and the field of the future. Cambridge, MA: The Society for Organizational learning, Inc.

The New London Group. (1996). A pedagogy of multiliteracies: Designing social futures. *Harvard Educational Review, 66,* 60–93.

Warschauer, M. (2003). *Technology and social inclusion: Rethinking the digital divide.* Cambridge, MA: MIT Press.

Xtranormal. (n. d.). Retrieved from http://www.xtranormal.com/watch/12353479/rmit-english-digital-intro-2011

KEY TERMS AND DEFINITIONS

Communication: Creating meaningful and effective messages.

Digital Introductions: Introductions presented through digital technologies.

Disruptive Pedagogies: Teaching approaches that aim to shift the learner to critically understanding habituated ways of seeing the world.

Literacy/Literacies: The capacity/ies to make and participate in meanings that will enable effective and fulfilled engagement in society.

Mode: An organized, regular means of representation and communication, such as through speech, writing, gesture, music etc.

Multimodal: Combinations of different modes.

Preservice Education: Undergraduate or postgraduate teacher education degrees.

Representation: Ways of seeing and thinking to make meaning.

Semiotics: The study of how we use signs in meaning-making.

Synaesthesia: Mode-shifting between visual, gestural and spoken modes.

Chapter 15
On the Condition of Anonymity:
Disembodied Exhibitionism and Oblique Trolling Strategies

Demetrios Jason Lallas
Union County College, USA

ABSTRACT

The ambiguity of identity in disembodied communities poses unique challenges in the flow of digital rhetoric. Online anonymity can lead to disinhibition, enabling the practice of trolling: the effort to derail discussion for attention, mischief, and abuse. This chapter examines this phenomenon in various social media contexts, exploring effective practices in recognizing and harnessing trolling.

INTRODUCTION

Responding to the US National Security Agency's Planning Tool for Resource Integration, Synchronization, and Management "PRISM" surveillance project, Lawrence Lessig (2013) reiterates his longstanding concern about the freedom of computer-mediated communication. He writes of a condition of constant surreptitious monitoring of digital expression that he believes has since come to pass: "Gone would be simple privacy, the relatively anonymous default infrastructure for unmonitored communication; in its place would be a perpetually monitored, perfectly traceable system supporting both commerce and the government."

Whether or not we ever were or are truly anonymous online, the social identity model of deindividuation effects (SIDE) has posited that our experience of CMC is a performance of our impression that we participate online without direct consequence to our face-to-face identities if we so desire. Certainly the frisson of quasi-anonymous performativity in computer-mediated communication is well-documented. Deindividuated intimations of anonymity in the virtual crowd exhilarate posters unburdened by

DOI: 10.4018/978-1-4666-4916-3.ch015

Copyright © 2014, IGI Global. Copying or distributing in print or electronic forms without written permission of IGI Global is prohibited.

physical face-to-face identity categorization, language, typography, and chronemic information alone the limit of digital expression (Walther & Parks, 2002). Deindividuation theory proposes that behavior becomes socially deregulated under conditions of anonymity and group immersion, as a result of reduced self-awareness (Diener, 1980; Postmes & Spears, 1998; Prentice-Dunn & Rogers, 1989; Zimbardo, 1969). Further, the hyperpersonal theory of SIDE posits a concentration of expressive capacity as individuals reallocate cognitive resources from spatial environments to message construction in CMC (Walther, 2007). Feeling like bricoleurs of identity, we shuffle multidimensional roles online in constant simultaneity, leading us to feel more like our "true self" when decked out in an array of virtual masks (Turkle, 1995). This benefit goes both ways, in reception as well as production. As deindividuated posters: "We read in ways that allow us to ignore the privileges accrued by virtue of having a 'normal' subjectivity" (Jung, 2007, p. 165).

Yet with the creeping suspicion that no CMC is truly anonymous, the potential for indeterminacy of identity to open spaces liable to provoke miscommunication is exacerbated. We could never take everything online at interface face value, as Sherry Turkle taught us, and it is important to consider to what extent deindividuation coincides with a corollary anxiety that one's performance of anonymity reflects an impression of potential recording and disclosure. This chapter will review traditional theories of the disembodied disinhibition that accompanies deindividuation, adding speculation that the performance of anonymity may be inflected by presentiments of audience and surveillance as represented by the intensity of insult in online trolling as representing a "scramble for recognition" and in Michael Conley's novel investigation of the rhetoric of insult. The practical results and application of the potential cross-purposes between anonymity and a scramble for recognition that belies attention-seeking insult will be the focus of the final section of this chapter.

THE JEOPARDY OF ANONYMITY

Judith Donath was among the pioneers in researching the habit of online anonymous trolling. Her 1999 study, "Identity and Deception in the Virtual Community," is the first to use the term "troll" in serious critical analysis. Status enhancement, she claims, not amusement, motivated early trolls (Donath, 1999). Her study of Usenet chatgroups identifies a poster named Ultimatego, about whom "some readers were intimidated by her intimations of upper-crust social knowledge; others were infuriated by her condescending remarks" (Donath, 1999). Donath introduces the term "trolling" in a quote from a poster regarding Ultimatego's antics: "Are you familiar with fishing? Trolling is where you set your fishing lines in the water and then slowly go back and forth dragging the bait and hoping for a bite. Trolling on the Net is the same concept – someone baits a post and then waits for the bite on the line and then enjoys the ensuing fight" (Donath, 1999).

As with intention, rank and authority diffuse online, where all anyone "is" is signs on a screen. Couple this cypherality with constant instant updating, oftentimes in several media, under multiple screen names, and the line between informing and performing, porous enough face-to-face, becomes even more tenuous online. Diminished auras of authenticity and presence in digital correspondence approximate absence; the mocking tendency Erving Goffman (1959) labels "The Treatment of the Absent" tends to creep into digital discussion, in a sense, a performance of "real" conversation. Goffman writes:

When the members of a team go backstage where the audience cannot see or hear them, they very regularly derogate the audience in a way that is inconsistent with the face-to-face treatment that is given to the audience. In service trades, for example, customers who are treated respectfully during the performance are often ridiculed, gossiped about, caricatured, cursed, and criticized when the performers are backstage. (p. 170)

When everyone is performing, everywhere is backstage.

John Suler (2004) describes the disembodied disinhibition that results. He reminds us, "The traditional Internet philosophy holds that everyone is an equal, that the purpose of the net is to share ideas and resources among peers" (p. 324). Remoteness relaxes correspondents: "People don't have to worry about how they look or sound when they type a message. They don't have to worry about how others look or sound in response to what they say. Seeing a frown, a shaking head, a sigh, a bored expression, and many other subtle and not so subtle signs of disapproval or indifference can inhibit what people are willing to express" (p. 322). When anonymous, people may not feel accountable 'in real life' for their online communication, free to disclose information more intimate than what they may disclose face to face (Hollenbaugh and Everett, 2013). Suler (2004) lists five habits of mind that characterize chronic disembodied disinhibition:

- **Invisibility:** "In many online environments, especially those that are text-driven, people cannot see each other. When people visit web sites, message boards, and even some chat rooms, other people may not even know they are present at all—with the possible exception of web masters and other users who have access to software tools that can detect traffic through the environment, assuming they have the inclination to keep an eye on an individual person, who is one of maybe hundreds or thousands of users. This invisibility gives people the courage to go places and do things that they otherwise wouldn't." (p. 322)

- **Asynchronicity:** "In e-mail and message boards, communication is asynchronous. People don't interact with each other in real time. Others may take minutes, hours, days, or even months to reply. Not hav-

ing to with someone's immediate reaction disinhibits people. In real life, the analogy might be speaking to someone, magically suspending time before that person can reply, and then returning to the conversation when one is willing and able to hear the response." (pp. 322-23)

- **Solipsistic Introjection:** "Absent face-to-face cues combined with text communication can alter self-boundaries. People may feel that their mind has merged with the mind of the online companion. Reading another person's message might be experienced as a voice within one's head, as if that person's psychological presence and influence have been assimilated or introjected into one's psyche." (p. 323)

- **Dissociative Imagination:** "If we combine the opportunity to easily escape or dissociate from what happens online with the psychological process of creating imaginary characters, we get a somewhat different force that magnifies disinhibition. Consciously or unconsciously, people may feel that the imaginary characters they "created" exist in a different space, that one's online persona along with the online others live in an make-believe dimension, separate and apart from the demands and responsibilities of the real world. They split or dissociate online fiction from offline fact." (p. 323) and

- **Minimization of Status and Authority:** "While online a person's status in the face-to-face world may not be known to others and may not have as much impact. Authority figures express their status and power in their dress, body language, and in the trappings of their environmental settings. The absence of those cues in the text environments of cyberspace reduces the impact of their authority." (p. 324)

Suler (2004) writes: "Rather than thinking of disinhibition as the revealing of an underlying 'true self,' we can conceptualize it as a shift to a constellation within self-structure, involving clusters of affect and cognition that differ from the in-person constellation" (p. 321). Anonymity ranks as a "principle factor" that creates the disinhibition effect:

When people have the opportunity to separate their actions online from their in-person lifestyle and identity, they feel less vulnerable about self-disclosing and acting out. Whatever they say or do can't be directly linked to the rest of their lives. In a process of dissociation, they don't have to own their behavior by acknowledging it within the full context of an integrated online/offline identity. The online self becomes a compartmentalized self. In the case of expressed hostilities or other deviant actions, the person can avert responsibility for those behaviors, almost as if superego restrictions and moral cognitive processes have been temporarily suspended from the online psyche. In fact, people might even convince themselves that those online behaviors "aren't me at all." (p. 322)

The minimization of status and authority in CMC compartmentalized selves who "aren't me at all" provokes rudeness: "Online, in what feels more like a peer relationship — with the appearances of authority minimized — people are much more willing to speak out and misbehave" (p. 324). Further, never before have writers of underprivileged economic status had such access to publishing their thoughts free of social status markers (McKee & DeVoss, 2007). The irreverence and disdain for authority that characterizes those without traditional face to face authority combines with the compartmentalization of self online to provoke intensity of invective seldom experienced offline.

The proliferation of rudeness, of the insults that characterize anonymity, render corners and comment sections of the internet veritable pasquinades of vituperation. The carnival of quasi-anonymity that can sometimes ensue belies true anonymity, in that the hyperpersonal insults that fly bespeak a sense of audience that would not factor into true anonymity. In other words, if conditions were truly anonymous, one might expect the jockeying for reputation leading to rudeness and insults to lessen, not amplify. Michael Conley (2010) characterizes insult as a "scramble for recognition" (p. 122). Discussing Aristotle's *Rhetoric*, he writes:

Honor and Reputation are among the most pleasant things through each person's imagining that he has the qualities of an important person." The Greek word we have translated "imagining" is telling—phantasia; and "important person" is the English for the Greek spoudaios—"one who deserves to be taken seriously." Insults would constitute a threat to that "fantasy"—that is, a threat to what is properly referred to as "self-esteem." But if we are talking here about self-esteem as a fantasy, one entertained even by those who are high up in the ranks of society, then perhaps their philotimo [honor] is less justifiable than they think. Bearing that possibility in mind might act as a reminder to those who feel insulted not to take themselves so seriously as to be offended even when no offense was intended, and it might also act as a check in the mind of the insulter, insofar as the insulter is arrogating to himself or herself a "fantasy" of deserving to be taken seriously. (p. 124)

This last positive aspect of insult—of keeping in check people who take themselves too seriously—is one that is often lost in discussions of deindividuation, disembodied disinhibition, and the compartmentalization of self. Much CMC that seems on the surface to be flaming can actually reflect more ironic, hyperbolic, or playful forms of communication rather than being aggressive; many instances of "flames" perform the positive aspect of insult Conley identifies that a more decontextualized analysis might misrecognize as offensive

(Spears, Postmes, Lea, & Wolbert, 2002). Flaming may reflect the operation of undocumented norms that vary widely between newsgroups, Websites, intranet cultures, and dominant social media like Facebook (Lea, O'Shea, Fung & Spears, 1992; Walther, Anderson, & Park, 1994; Underwood, Kerlin, & Farrington-Flint, 2011). Anonymity associated with CMC, far from undermining the social dimension of the self and behavior, can strengthen its very basis (Spears et al., 2002)

DISEMBODIED EXHIBITIONISM

Having discussed the positive and negative effects of anonymity, we turn to examine instances of actual performance. Trolling can display an ambivalence that transcends deindividuation and injects an element of self-consciousness that is alert to performativity. For example, anonymous poster "mimicking regular benevloent (sic) users' names (President Keyes)" on popular message board I Love Everything, theorizes rather archly about his own performance:

when we troll, we create our own reality. And while you're studying that reality—judiciously, as you will—we'll troll again, creating other new realities, which you can study too, and that's how things will sort out. We're history's trolls ... and you, all of you, will be left to just study what we do. (5/23/13)

Here we see a self-mockery spiking what is a succinct trolling manifesto. But however arch, there is pride of performance here. Internet comedians like Andrew Aurenheimer, Adrien Chen, Jason Fortuny, and David Thorne post fake ads to mislead others, then post the results on their blogs. (mclol.com, 2010) Posters delight in crashing entire discussion sites, as Boxxy did the lively

prankster and social-jamming 4chan /b/board. (Johnson, 2009)

The rise of A$AP Rocky, recent recipient of a $3 million record deal with Sony, RCA, and Polo Grounds Music, is an example of masterfully self-aware anonymous trolling. A$AP Mob member A$AP Yams created a blog on Tumblr with the pseudonym "Eastside Steve." Yams, a founder of the A$AP crew, never disclosed that he and the Tumblr were associated with Rocky. As Eastside Steve gathered cache, Yams used his niche as a strategic tool to promote Rocky in the marketplace. Rocky describes Yams' branding strategy: "He'd put old-school stuff on that, like old-school Dipset, old-school Roc-a-Fella, old-school Wu-Tang, old-school Pimp C, old-school DJ Screw shit — and then he'd mix, like, one Rocky song in there, and people would be like, man, who is this kid? This shit is kinda dope. It got to a point where he stopped putting out music for a while, and he got people hitting him up, like: 'What happened to that Rocky kid? That "Houston Old Head" track is crazy. That "Been Around the World" track is crazy.' So by the time we dropped "Purple Swag," European kids was already waiting on me. That's when Tumblr went crazy." (Sunderman, 2013)

Beyond pride in performance and aesthetic ambition there is certainly an erotic element to anonymous trolling. In "A Rape in Cyberspace," Julian Dibbell explains the pleasure of non-physical pseudonymous digital eroticism:

For while the facts attached to any event born of a [. . .] strange, ethereal universe may march in straight, tandem lines separated neatly into the virtual and the real, its meaning lies always in that gap. [. . .] Amid flurries of even the most cursorily described caresses, sighs, and penetrations, the glands do engage, and often as throbbingly as they would in a real-life assignation – sometimes even more so, given the combined power of anonymity and textual suggestiveness to unshackle deep-seated fantasies. And if the virtual setting and the interplayer vibe are right, who knows? The heart may engage as well, stirring up passions as strong as many that bind lovers who observe the formality of trysting in the flesh. (Dibbell, 1993)

Indeed, explicit sexual language typifies the insulting rhetoric of many trolls. Intrigued by the persistence of a comment-section troll on his website, Paul Lukas of Uniform-Watch.com posted a plea and then managed to convince a regular who goes by the pseudonym Joe "Big Cock" Johnson to agree to speak on the phone, provided that no identifying information would be shared. Lukas characterizes Joe's seven-year string of comments as "mostly about his 12-inch penis and the massive loads of semen that spew from it". An extended excerpt of the interview is quoted below, as Joe's responses not only cohere with Suler's taxonomy of disembodied disinhibition, but affirm Conley's thesis about the insulter as one whose abuse is meant in part to prevent an identified authority from taking himself too seriously.

Uniform-Watch: *When and why did you decide to create the Joe Johnson persona, and to start posting under that identity?*

Joe Johnson: *Um, yeah, that's a good question. I don't remember exactly when I started, but it was definitely early in the blog's existence. The identity was random. Obviously, I wasn't gonna use my real name. Once I came up with this identity and posted a comment, and then you or another commenter referred to it or responded or whatever, then it seemed obvious to stick with it, so I did.*

UW: *But what led you to do it in the first place? Like, why post abusive, trolling commentary? What was the motivation?*

JJ: *Really just to amuse myself. I still have a very sophomoric, immature sense of humor. I've always found cuss words to be funny. I find it particularly amusing when there's*

a lot of shock value. Like, if you're in front of a bunch of old people, or people from another generation, and you say something shocking, I find that amusing. And that's a character flaw, I'm sure. But nevertheless, it was mostly about shocking people, mostly with vulgarities. When people see "cunt" or "twat" or something like that, those go beyond the typical "fuck" or "shit."

UW: *Right, they're more transgressive. And you like that.*

JJ: *Yeah. I think that's funny, to think about someone's reaction. I never intended to be malicious, although I'm sure I said some things that sounded that way. But it was never my intent. And then you would sometimes respond in a way that gave me the impression that you were at least somewhat amused by what I was doing, so I figured I wasn't, you know, injuring you or anything like that. But I don't know, maybe I was. That was never my intent, though.*

UW: *You said the name "Joe Johnson" was random, but is Joe's whole persona based on anyone in particular?*

JJ: *No. Again, it was just based on amusing myself.*

UW: *Had you ever done anything like that before, acting as a troll on a web site?*

JJ: *Yeah, absolutely. I used to do it a lot. I don't so much anymore. Uni Watch is really the end of it, the last one...Like there's this site, ApartmentRatings.com, and I would review apartments by saying things so outlandish, so over the top, that nobody would ever believe it. I wasn't trying to stop anyone from living in a particular apartment, but it was just fun to say, "There's a prostitution operation being run out of this apartment" or whatever, and I took great amusement in going back and seeing if someone had responded to it. (http://www.uni-watch.com/2013/04/19/an-interview-with-uni-watchs-most-prominent-troll/)*

Granted the juvenile language and sense of humor, and the rhetorical aggression hints at "the full deadly force of 'nobodiness'" Lynn Worsham (1998) warned us about (p. 213). In post-modern communication in general, there is also a self-consciousness at work in the exchange, and a seeming delight in performance for the sake of performance, as though here, in anonymous trolling, a relatively new aesthetic form of expression is being delineated. As with "mimicking regular benevloent (sic) users' names (President Keyes)", "Joe Johnson" is in his own way 'creating other new realities', where there is no authority beyond the capacity to convince others of what one wants them to believe, and the capacity of others to identify that hallmark of trolling.

This impulse is inherently political, and trolling abounds in anonymous political discourse. A discussion on Drew Curtis's news aggregator Fark.com dramatizes an unmasking endgame, where a "Joe Johnson"-type is called out for a bad performance. Here "Somedude210" condemns "Elzar" in a spirited debate about President Obama's performance in office prior to his 2013 State of the Union Address. First "Somedude210" quotes "Elzar"'s insult-laden message in italics:

its [sic] funny to watch all the libby libs try to explain away Obama's towers of failure. They whine and complain and seek aid benefit and handouts claiming that 0bummer was setup and it was an inside job hatched by GWB and Dick Cheney. Today's conservative politician is twice the man of yesteryear and like Governor Christie has said, 'You people disappoint me on Tuesday, you don't do what you're supposed to for Mitt Romney on Tuesday - I will be back, Jersey-style, people. I will be back'

So have fun with your witty headlines libtardmitter, just don't blame us when you find yourself in a concentration camp without your guns.

"Somedude210" follows this quotation with a point-by-point response, equal parts accusation that "Elzar" is not the poster he pretends to be, with tips on how to step up his trolling technique:

Couple of things about this I need to talk to you about.

1. *What failures are you talking about that we're deflecting for Obama and what inside job are you talking about*
2. *Christie? Are you shiatting me? He's a North-east Republican. He's a RINO to you lot. Clearly, you're trolling*
3. *If subby is a libtard, why would he have guns? I thought libby lib libs are so liberal that they don't believe in guns at all? So how would they have guns to lose when they go to these concentration camps?*
4. *And finally, what the hell are you smoking and where can I get some, because that's some strong shiat man. /yes, I know you're trolling, but I'm making sure you fix it to be a better troll next time*

In a similar unmasking, Chris Mooney charts the insulting rhetoric of scientifically-minded trolls. He notes, "They're predominantly climate deniers, and they start in immediately arguing over the content and attacking the science — sometimes by slinging insults and even occasional obscenities" (Mooney, 2013). In this there seems to be a purpose beyond "Joe Johnson"'s anarchic impulses and "Elzar"'s antipathy toward President Obama. A recent study regarding this phenomenon in the *Journal of Computer-Mediated Communication* found that rudeness contributes to polarization of an issue. They discovered that those who are exposed to uncivil deliberation in blog comments are more likely to perceive science as risky than those who are exposed to civil comments (Anderson et al., 2013). Cypherpunk activists exploit people whose guard is down both for their own amusement and to advance their political agendas. Following the 14 December 2012 Sandy Hook Elementary School shootings, a poster on Encyclopedia Dramatica uploaded a video game called "Bullet to the Head of the NRA" that prompted significant outrage: exactly the outcome the stunt was designed to elicit. In its entry on the game, Encyclopedia Dramatica features a section titled "Hannity Gets Trolled." Alex Pareene observes about the controversy: "Now ED is its own anonymous community of dedicated trolls. Trolls, despite the way the term is usually used these day, aren't just 'jerks.' They're people who seek to provoke extreme reactions — outrage, usually — in other people, for lulz" (Pareene, 2013).

Further complicating the indetermination of online intention is the potential profitability of anonymous CMC. Beginning in the late 1990s, the CEO of Whole Foods, John Mackey, posted 1100 messages under the alias "rahodeb" (an anagram of his wife's name) on Yahoo! Finance's bulletin board, often attacking Whole Foods' competitors, such as Wild Oats, as in this 28 March 2006 hit piece:

OATS has lost their way and no longer has a sense of mission or even a well-thought-out theory of the business. They lack a viable business model that they can replicate. They are floundering around hoping to find a viable strategy that may stop their erosion. Problem is that they lack the time and the capital now. (Martin, 2007)

Mackey's temporary trolling success may also be seen in coordinating brand identity protection services and online reputation enhancement agencies such as iProspect and eModeration, with clients ranging from BBC Worldwide and MTV to Sony, HSBC, and Seagram's, which bespeak the malleability of online content and amplify doubts about digital forum sincerity, since one can never be sure if the opinion of another poster is sincere or sponsored. Even the popularity of one's following can be bought, as the Twitter account scandal of

the Romney for President campaign attests (Coldewey, 2012). A UK social media management company, eBuzzing, builds followings, offering social video advertising, sponsored conversation, and Facebook fan recruitment services:

We get your video viral views by distributing them through our network of social publishers. Propel your content into the heart of social media, Facebook and onto the YouTube homepage.

We identify influencers relevant to you [sic] brand and we help you to get them actively involved in your marketing campaigns.

We recruit active fans for you [sic] Facebook pages and we entirely manage registration and the engagement process. You only pay for a guaranteed number of registered fans and applications installed.

Taken to extremes, brand management becomes digital propaganda, promoting an atmosphere of cynicism, where accusations of "paid troll" fly, and sockpuppet confessions abound. George Monbiot describes a "whistleblower" who contacted him:

He was part of a commercial team employed to infest internet forums and comment threads on behalf of corporate clients, promoting their causes and arguing with anyone who opposed them. Like the other members of the team, he posed as a disinterested member of the public. Or, to be more accurate, as a crowd of disinterested members of the public: he used 70 personas, both to avoid detection and to create the impression that there was widespread support for his pro-corporate arguments. (Monbiot, 2011)

Another anonymous astroturfer owns up to a career of "meme-patrol" duties: "These strategies included various forms of personal attacks, complaining to the forum moderators, smearing the characters of our opponents, using images and icons effectively, and even dragging the tone of the conversation down with sexual innuendo, links to pornography, or other such things." He (his only identification is through personal pronouns) calls his work "stir[ring] up page clicks," "making my living lying and heckling people who come online to express their views and exercise freedom of speech" (*Conscious Life News*, 2013). That much of the comment section to this article is given to doubting the veracity of the anonymous self-styled "paid internet shill" demonstrates how doubt ramifies online.

TROLL PATROLLING

An effective tactic to counteracting overbearing disembodied exhibitionism, amateur and professional alike, is community moderation. Formspring allows users to block others from asking questions. Reputation systems, like Fark's, update usenet's killfile solution to include not only ignore lists but upvoting and downvoting of pseudonymous posters by attribute – "funniest" and "smartest" – to enable peer pressure to police behavior and affiliates of regular posters to ferret out trolls. Posters on Reddit.com recently went so far as to name names, rebelling against the site's anything-goes ethos, by discovering and releasing the real names of the posters behind a creepy "Predditor" board, and alerting campus and law enforcement authorities to the worst offenders (Hess, 2012).

Facebook and Google would do away with anonymity altogether. During a Marie Claire round table discussion on cyberbullying and social media, Facebook's marketing director Randi Zuckerberg explained how using real names online could help curb bullying and harassment: "I think anonymity on the Internet has to go away. People behave a lot better when they have their real names down. I think people hide behind anonymity and they feel like they can say whatever they want behind closed doors" (Protalinski, 2011). This is a significant problem, as *Consumer Reports* found that in 2011, 800,000 minors were bullied or harassed on Facebook (Bazelon 2013). For its part, Google+ seeks to make connecting with people on the web more like connecting with people in the real world: "Because of this, it's important to use your common name so that the people you want to connect with can find you."

Unless the anti-anonymity concerns prevail, however, trolls will continue their quasi-anonymous posting among us for the foreseeable future. Regardless of the pitfalls of anonymity, pseudonymity has proven a boon to the internet (Figure 1). To lessen disembodiment is to lose page clicks. While venerable and popular blogs like Andrew Sullivan's Daily Dish generate so many hits that Sullivan can afford to turn comments off entirely, avoiding thereby all the "cacophony, vitriol, and ghastliness […] of flame artists" (Sullivan, 2011), that is an increasingly unique luxury, and most blogs and media sites depend on robust anonymous comment sections to augment interest and retention. Indeed, comment moderation platform development firm Disqus reports that 61 percent of commenters use pseudonyms, 35 percent choose to be anonymous and only 4 percent use their "real identity," verified by Facebook. The report also finds pseudonymous posters make the best comments (Sonderman, 2012). Contrary to Disqus's findings, though, TechCrunch.com recently endured an exodus that sparked a return to anonymity:

It was early 2011 and TechCrunch's comment section was overrun with trolls. Bullies and asshats were drowning out our smart commenters. We hated our commenters because, well, they hated us. So we rolled out Facebook Comments in an attempt to silence the trolls — by removing their anonymity.

But we eventually discovered that our anti-troll tactic worked too well; The [sic] bullies and as-shats left our comments sections, but so did everyone else. Now, several years later, after dozens of endless meetings and conference calls, we've decided we're going to try out Livefyre instead of Facebook Comments.

Frankly, our trial with Facebook Comments lasted way too long at too steep of a cost. Sure, Facebook Comments drove extra traffic to the site, but the vast majority of our readers clearly do not feel the system is worthy of their interaction.

And we want our commenters back. (Burns and Blisener, 2013)

Indeed, resentment toward moderation is a popular form of comment section message, as we can see in "Inbound_the_Ball"'s response to a May 6, 2013 "True Hoop" blog post on ESPN. com:

I see ESPN deleted my comment about how whether Miami wins or loses... ESPN is profiting.

ESPN lets the spammers post a million of those smileys all over the place without doing something... but when someone says one word about how ESPN loves all the haters and trolls and is pandering to them... that's when you delete comments. Amusing.

Further, trolls discuss methods to beat moderators, by changing names and IP addresses. On Tina Brown's Daily Beast, the website *Newsweek* became, posters "FourDiedRiceLiedHillaryCriedThePreezyWasAWOL" and "The Ghost of Nixon Present" discuss, in tones reminiscent of Beckett characters, account migration:

FourDiedRiceLiedHillaryCriedThePreezyWasAWOL @The Ghost of Nixon Present: *Yes, but I can't remember which name you were using. I could probably figure it out though. So many names, so little time...*

Figure 1. The perpetual traffic machine

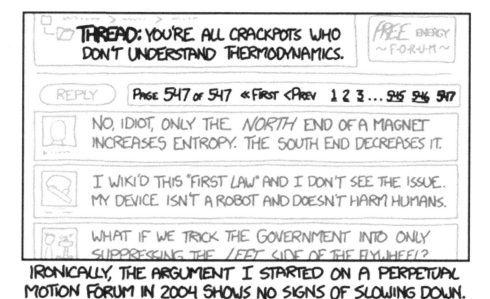

The Ghost of Nixon Present @FourDiedRiceLiedHillaryCriedThePreezyWasAWOL @ The Ghost of Nixon Present: *Yeah I know the censors wreck [sic] havoc*

FourDiedRiceLiedHillaryCriedThePreezyWasAWOL @The Ghost of Nixon Present: *It used to annoy the hell out of me to get banned. But then I set up a system where it didn't really matter. Names are like pants now.*

Negotiating the hyperpersonal quasi-anonymity / heightened critical awareness of CMC, where names are increasingly like pants, is made easier with working knowledge of oblique trolling strategies. First generation cypherpunks Deborah Natsios and John Young, proprietors of Cryptome. org, a pioneering open source document clearinghouse, adapt a COINTELPRO infiltration guide to contemporary strategic and domination trolling, cyberbullying and harassment. Identifying the traits of the professional disinformationalist, they outline a five-step site invasion process that advances through concerted consensus cracking, forum sliding, topic dilution, information collection, and anger trolling to gain full control (Natsios and Young, 2012). Earnest posters might want to be on guard for others prone to exhibiting these and the seventeen rhetorical patterns characteristic of hype and spinstorms Cryptome lists, detailed in Table 1.

Recognizing these patterns heightens hyperpersonalization; knowing one is performing anonymity even when suspecting the encounter of trolly surveillance, requires more critical awareness than during face-to-face communication. As taxing as disembodied exhibitionism can be, exacerbated by heightened vigilance against trolling, nevertheless it makes us better readers online, more discerning of information we process and its sources online and off.

CONCLUSION

Even without Lawrence Lessig's justifiable concerns about how truly anonymous we are online, the performativity observable in trolling represents a significant qualification to the deindividuated impression of disembodiment in CMC. Indeed, the intensity of invective prevalent in CMC suggests an intimation of authority – real or imagined – that is being undermined in a struggle for recognition that belies the experience of true anonymity.

The insulting rhetoric that obtains, while potentially frustrating to negotiate, may also result in heightened analytical reading skill. When posters in CMC are on guard for the performance of anonymity in CMC, their own as well as others, writing and reading skills achieve an acumen perhaps excelling inhibited communication offline.

Table 1. Cryptome oblique trolling strategies

Tics and Tactics	How It Works
Play dumb	No matter what evidence or logical argument is offered, avoid discussing issues except with denials that they have any credibility, make any sense, provide any proof, contain or make a point, have logic, or support a conclusion. Mix well for maximum effect.
Wax incredulous and indignant	Avoid discussing key issues and instead focus on side issues which can be used to show the topic as being critical of some otherwise sacrosanct group or theme. This is also known as the "How dare you!" gambit.
Knock down straw men	Deal only with the weakest aspects of the weakest charges.
Characterize proofs not in your favor as "rumors" or, better yet, "wild rumors"	Avoid discussing issues by describing all charges, regardless of venue or evidence, as mere rumors and wild accusations. Other derogatory terms may work as well.
Impugn motives	Attempt to marginalize opponents by suggesting that they are not really interested in the truth but are simply pursuing a partisan political agenda or are out to make money.
Invoke authority	Claim for yourself or associate yourself with authority and present your argument with sufficient jargon and minutia to illustrate you are "one who knows," and simply say it isn't so without discussing issues or demonstrating why or citing sources.
Dismiss uncomfortable facts as "old news"	Only your story and stories amenable to your story are relevant and current.
Come half-clean	Create the impression of candor and honesty while admitting to relatively harmless "mistakes" or misspeaking. This often involves embracing a fall-back position quite different from the one originally taken.
Alice in Wonderland logic. Enigmas have no solution. Characterize the controversy as impossibly complex and the truth as ultimately unknowable	Derp it up. Post absurdities as though you believe them. Avoid discussion of the issues by reasoning backwards or with an apparent deductive logic which forbears any actual material fact. Drawing upon the overall umbrella of events surrounding disagreements, paint the entire affair as too complex to solve. This causes those otherwise following the matter to lose interest more quickly without having to address the actual issues.
Demand complete solutions	Avoid issues and ignore questions by requiring opponents to resolve controversies completely before you will accept their point of view.
Change the subject	Usually in connection with another of these ploys, find a way to sidetrack discussion with abrasive or controversial comments in hopes of turning attention to a new, more manageable topic. This works especially well with companions who can "argue" with you over the new topic and polarize the discussion arena in order to avoid more key issues.
Lightly report incriminating facts, then make nothing of them	Seeds of suspicion can be harvested later.
Ignore proofs presented. Demand impossible proofs	Regardless of what material may be presented by an opponent in public forums, claim the material irrelevant and demand proof that is impossible for the opponent to come by. In order to completely avoid discussing issues, it may be required that you categorically deny and be critical of media or books as valid sources, deny that witnesses are acceptable, or even deny that statements made by government or other authorities have any meaning or relevance.

http://cryptome.org/2012/07/gent-forum-spies.htm

REFERENCES

Anderson, A., Brossard, D., Scheufele, D., Xenos, M., & Ladwig, P. (2013, February 19). Crude comments and concern: Online incivility's effect on risk perceptions of emerging technologies. *Journal of Computer-Mediated Communication.* Retrieved February 24, from http://onlinelibrary.wiley.com/doi/10.1111/jcc4.12009/full.

{Anonymous}. (2013, January 8). I was a paid internet shill: How shadowy groups manipulate internet opinion and debate. *ConsciousLifeNews.com.* Retrieved January 17, 2013, from http://consciouslifenews.com/paid-internet-shill-shadowy-groups-manipulate-internet-opinion-debate/1147073/

Bazelon, E. (2013, March). How to stop the bullies. *Atlantic (Boston, Mass.)*, 82–89.

Bishop, J. (in press). The psychology of trolling and lurking: The role of defriending and gamification for increasing participation in online communities using seductive narratives. In J. Bishop (Ed.), *Examining the concepts, issues, and implications of internet trolling.* Hershey, PA: IGI Global. doi:10.4018/978-1-4666-0312-7.ch010

Burns, M., & Blessener, E. (2013, January 22). Commenters, we want you back. *TechCrunch.com.* Retrieved January 22, 2013, from http://techcrunch.com

Coldewey, D. (2012, August 8). Romney twitter account gets upsurge in fake followers, but from where? *NBCnews.com.* Retrieved January 15, 2013, from http://nbcnews.com.

Conley, M. (2010). *Toward a rhetoric of insult.* Chicago, IL: University of Chicago Press. doi:10.7208/chicago/9780226114798.001.0001

Dibble, J. (1993). A rape in cyberspace: How an evil clown, a Haitian trickster spirit, two wizards, and a cast of dozens turned a database into a society. *The Village Voice.* Retrieved February 4, 2013, from http://juliandibbell.com.

Diener, E. (1980). Deindividuation: The absence of self-awareness and self-regulation in group members. In P. Paulus (Ed.), *The Psychology of Group Influence* (pp. 209–242). Hillsdale, NJ: Erlbaum.

Donath, J. (1999). Identity and deception in the virtual community. In M. Smith and P. Kollack (Eds.), *Communities in cyberspace.* London: Routledge. Retrieved June 14, 2013, from http://smg.media.mit.edu/people/Judith/Identity/IdentityDeception.html

eBuzzing.com. Retrieved January 16, 2013, from http://social.ebuzzing.co.uk/advertisers.

Franzen, C. (2013). Mozilla, Reddit, 4Chan join coalition of 86 groups asking Congress to end NSA surveillance. *The Verge.* Retrieved June 11, 2013, from http://www.theverge.com/2013/6/11/4418794/stopwatchingus-internet-orgs-ask-congress-to-stop-surveillance

Goffman, E. (1959). *The Presentation of self in everyday life.* New York: Doubleday.

Hess, A. (2012, October 15). Gawker outed Reddit's most notorious troll? Why isn't law enforcement doing the same? *Slate.com.* Retrieved February 16, 2013, from http://www.slate.com/blogs/xx_factor/2012/10/15/reddit_troll_violentacrez_outed_by_gawker_when_will_law_enforcement_catch.html

Hollenbaugh, E., & Everett, M. (2013, February). The effects of anonymity on self-disclosure in blogs: An application of the online disinhibition effect. *Journal of Computer-Mediated Communication.* Retrieved February 24, 2013, from http://dx.doi.org/10.1111/jcc4.12008.

Johnson, B. (2009, January 20). How Boxxy brought the web to its knees. *The Guardian*. Retrieved January 3, 2013, from http://www.guardian.co.uk/technology/blog/2009/jan/20/internet

Jung, J. (2007). Textual mainstreaming and the rhetorics of accommodation. *Rhetoric Review*, *26*(2), 160–178. doi:10.1080/07350190709336707

Lea, M., O'Shea, T., Fung, P., & Spears, R. (1992). Flaming in computer-mediated communication: Observations, explanations, implications. In M. Lea (Ed.), *Contexts of computer-mediated communication* (pp. 30–65). Hempel Hempstead, UK: Harvester Wheatsheaf.

Lee, E. (2007). Deindividuation effects on group polarization in computer-mediated communication: The role of group identification, public-self-awareness, and perceived argument quality. *The Journal of Communication*, *57*(2), 385–403. doi:10.1111/j.1460-2466.2007.00348.x

Lessig, L. (2013, June 12). It's time to rewrite the internet to give us better privacy, and security. *The Daily Beast*. Retrieved June 12, 2013, from http://www.thedailybeast.com/articles/2013/06/12/its-time-to-rewrite-the-internet-to-give-us-better-privacy-and-security.html

Lukas, P. (2013, April 24). Trolling right along: An interview with Joe Big Cock Johnson. *Uni-Watch.com*. Retrieved June 13, 2013, from http://www.uni-watch.com/2013/04/19/an-interview-with-uni-watchs-most-prominent-troll/

Martin, A. (2007, July 12). Whole foods executive used alias. *New York Times*. Retrieved January 12, 2013, from www.nytimes.com/2007/07/12/business/12foods.html

McKee, H., & DeVoss, D. (2007). *Digital Writing Research: Technologies, Methodologies, and Ethical Issues*. New York: Hampton Press.

mclol.com. (2010, August 20). Famous internet trolls who did it for the lulz. *mclol.com*. Retrieved January 5, 2013, from http://www.mclol.com/funny-articles/famous-internet-trolls-who-did-it-for-the-lulz/

Monbiot, G. (2011, February 24). Corporate-funded online 'astroturfing' is more advanced and automated than you might think. *Alternet.org*. Retrieved January 8, 2013, from http://www.alternet.org/story/150049/corporate-funded_online_%27astroturfing%27_is_more_advanced_and_more_automated_than_you_might_think

Mooney, C. (2013, January 10). The science of why comment trolls suck. *Mother Jones*. Retrieved February 3, 2013, from http://www.motherjones.com/environment/2013/01/you-idiot-course-trolls-comments-make-you-believe-science-less

Munroe, R. (2013, January 27). Argument. *XKCD: A webcomic of romance, sarcasm, math, and language*. Retrieved January 29, 2013, from http://ckcd.com.

Natsios, D., & Young, J. (2012, July 12). The gentleperson's guide to forum spies. *Cryptome.org*. Retrieved January 4, 2013, from http://cryptome.org/2012/07/gent-forum-spies.htm.

Pareene, A. (2013, January 16). Right-wing press happily allows itself to be trolled by made-up video game. *Salon.com*. Retrieved January 16, 2013, from http://www.salon.com/2013/01/16/right_wing_press_happily_allows_itself_to_be_trolled_by_made_up_video_game/

Postmes, T., Spears, R., & Lea, M. (1998). Breaching or building social boundaries? SIDE-effects of computer-mediated communication. *Communication Research*, *25*, 689–715. doi:10.1177/009365098025006006

Protalinski, E. (2011, August 2). Facebook: Anonymity on the internet has to go away. *ZDNet.com*. Retrieved January 20, 2013, from http://www.zdnet.com/blog/facebook/facebook-anonymity-on-the-internet-has-to-go-away/2270.

Sonderman, J. (2012, January 11). People using pseudonyms post the highest quality comments, Disqus says. *Poynter.org*. Retrieved January 12, 2013, from http://www.poynter.org/latest-news/mediawire/159078/people-using-pseudonyms-post-the-most-highest-quality-comments-disqus-says/

Spears, R., Postmes, T., Lea, M., & Wolbert, A. (2002). When are net effects gross products? The power of influence and the influence of power in computer-mediated communication. *The Journal of Social Issues*, *58*(1), 91–107. doi:10.1111/1540-4560.00250

Suler, J. (2004). The online disinhibition effect. *Cyberpsychology & Behavior*, *7*(3), 321–326. doi:10.1089/1094931041291295 PMID:15257832

Sullivan, A. (2011, November 29). Ask me anything: Why no comments section? [Web video log post]. Retrieved January 24, 2013, from http://dish.andrewsullivan.com/2011/11/29/ask-me-anything-why-arent-comments-allowed/

Sunderman, E. (2013, January 23). A$AP Rocky lights up the city. *Village Voice*. Retrieved January 26, 2013, from http://www.villagevoice.com/2013-01-23/music/asap-rocky-harlem-new-york/

Turkle, S. (1995). *Life on the screen: Identity in the age of the Internet*. New York: Simon & Schuster.

Turkle, S. (2011). *Alone together: Why we expect more from technology and less from each other*. New York: Basic Books.

Underwood, J., Kerlin, L., & Farrington-Flint, L. (2011). The lies we tell and what they say about us: Using behavioural characteristics to explain Facebook activity. *Computers in Human Behavior*, *27*, 1621–1626. doi:10.1016/j.chb.2011.01.012

Walther, J. B. (2007). Selective self-presentation in computer-mediated communication: Hyperpersonal dimensions of technology, language, and cognition. *Computers in Human Behavior*, *23*, 2538–2557. doi:10.1016/j.chb.2006.05.002

Walther, J. B., Anderson, J. F., & Park, D. W. (1994). Interpersonal effects in computer-mediated interaction: A meta-analysis of social and antisocial communication. *Communication Research*, *21*, 460–487. doi:10.1177/009365094021004002

Walther, J. B., & Parks, M. R. (2002). Cues filtered out, cues filtered in: Computer-mediated communication and relationships. In M. L. Knapp. & J. A. Daly (Eds.), Handbook of interpersonal communication (pp. 529-563). Thousand Oaks, CA: Sage.

Worsham, L. (1998). Going postal: Pedagogic violence and the schooling of emotion. *JAC: A Journal of Composition Theory, 18*(2), 213-45.

Zimbardo, P. G. (1969). The human choice: Individuation, reason, and order vs. deindividuation, impulse and chaos. In W. J. Arnold & D. Levine (Eds.), *Nebraska Symposium on Motivation, 17*, 237-307. Lincoln, NE: University of Nebraska Press.

KEY TERMS AND DEFINITIONS

Anti-Anonymity: The theory that 'logged-in' CMC will ameliorate invective and lessen cyberbullying.

Astroturfing: Paying posters to troll and 'agenda-monger' for undisclosed employers.

CMC: Computer mediated communication; non-'face-to-face' conversation.

Deindividuation: Loss of sense of self, as in crowds or online.

Derp: The performance of a troll who 'plays dumb.'

Disembodied Disinhibition: A sense of quasi-anonymity CMC induces that may result in exaggerated, disingenuous, or hostile CMC.

Encyclopedia Dramatica: A troll wiki.

Quasi-Anonymity: the performance of invisibility in CMC.

Reputation Systems: Community moderated chatrooms and comment sections.

Scramble for Recognition: Conley's theory that insult is often meant not maliciously but to keep people 'in check.'

Spinstorms: Troll-hijacked CMC.

Trolling: Disingenuous communication, meant to bait or upset others.

Chapter 16
Embodied Digital Rhetoric:
Soft Selves, Plastic Presence, and the Nonfiction Narrative

Nonny de la Peña
University of Southern California, USA

ABSTRACT

A new embodied digital rhetoric emerges when using nonfiction narratives built in fully immersive virtual reality systems that take advantage of the plasticity of our sensations of presence. The feeling of "being-in-the-world" as described by phenomenologists, including philosophy of mind, film, and virtual reality theorists, is part of the adaptability that humans show in their relationship to technological tools. Andy Clark's "soft selves" and our "plastic presence" merge as the high resolution graphics of the latest virtual reality goggles and robust audio captured at real events tricks our minds into having an embodied connection with the stories portrayed in these new spaces. By putting people into news or documentary pieces on scene as themselves, opportunities for persuasive and effective rhetoric arise. This chapter cites theory, psychology and virtual reality research as well as the author's specific case studies to detail the potential for this new embodied digital rhetoric that allows us to pass through the screen and become present as witnesses to a nonfiction story.

Where does the body end and the mind begin?" young Quastro asked, amid recurring attempts to fine-tune the differences between real and virtual violence. "Is not the mind a part of the body?" "In MOO, the body IS the mind," offered

HerkieCosmo gamely, and not at all implausibly, demonstrating the ease with which very knotty metaphysical conundrums come undone in VR (A Rape In Cyberspace, Dibbell (1993))

DOI: 10.4018/978-1-4666-4916-3.ch016

Copyright © 2014, IGI Global. Copying or distributing in print or electronic forms without written permission of IGI Global is prohibited.

INTRODUCTION

I have a memory of complete immersion: I was in fourth grade and, as often occurred, I had completed the assignment before my classmates. While I waited for the other children to finish, I sat on top of my book and secretly read by moving my legs aside to reveal the pages. Turning a page was slightly problematic and usually led to discovery if my teacher, Mrs. Wolfe, hadn't already noticed that I had stopped paying attention. That kind of getting in trouble was worth it, however, especially if the book was good and the alternative was boredom.

That year I was particularly fond of a novel called *Mountain Pony*, which I had picked up with my family at a thrift store. It didn't matter that I had probably already read it half a dozen times. At the moment when the protagonist and his pony are trying to cross a treacherous mountainside in the pouring rain, I was always transported deeply into the story. The sense of my physical body would disappear. While I remember little else from that year, when the annoyed Mrs. Wolfe snarled at me to hand over my book, the sensation of looking up to see sunshine pouring through the Southern California schoolroom windows instead of gnashing thunder clouds spewing crazy lightening was completely disorienting. Where was I again? Oh, yes, here. And in trouble.

Several decades later in 2007, a female-gendered avatar in the online virtual world of Second Life threatened to hit me with a baseball bat. Her avatar was completely green, wearing ice skates and dressed in an outfit resembling a jumpsuit, with long sharp points emerging from her clothes. Of course she couldn't really hit or hurt me, but as she slapped her hand with a virtual bat and expressed her anger over my use of Second Life, I felt extremely intimidated.

Her male-gendered avatar partner had just gone through the "experience" associated with *Gone Gitmo,* a digital recreation of Guantànamo Bay prison I built with artist Peggy Weil. The site was designed so that after entering a model of a C-17 transport plane, and then touching an orange panel, one's avatar would be bound in white straps and a "black hood" would drop over the "vision" of the now disabled avatar. The experience was carefully constructed using source material, including photographs leaked by soldiers, which revealed how detainees were transported to the prison (Figure 1).

The virtual "black hood" was created from video in which the camera lens was covered with black fabric that allowed only flickers of light to filter through and was intended to play as the POV of a hooded individual. Soldiers' voices, detainees' cries and jet noises were later added as the soundtrack. Once the video began, it would fill the entire screen of a participant's computer, taking away control, and when it finished – an equivalent of the hood being "removed" – the individual would then find s/he had been transported from the plane to the interior of a virtual replica of the notorious Camp X-Ray cage. Inside the cage, the body of the avatar appeared bound in shackles, a startling feeling for participants, albeit the restraints were merely visual and the avatar could actually move about freely.

The green bat-wielding avatar was put on the defensive after seeing her companion jailed in the virtual X-Ray cage even though he quickly stood up and walked around. As she began to dialogue, I directed her to the embedded videos depicting treatment of detainees at the prison camp. (Initially released by the US Department of Defense, these videos were quickly retracted due to international outcry over the inhumane conditions they revealed.) However, the images did nothing to lessen her outrage focused at me. The more she felt the site "defended" the detainees, the angrier she became.

Clearly, the experience of the virtual construct communicated something inherently upsetting to her. Equally important, the slapping of the baseball bat felt physically threatening to me, despite the fact that I was only viewing a three-inch digital

Figure 1. An avatar in a "bound position" in the Gone Gitmo camp x-ray cage

representation of myself, controlled and mediated through a plastic keyboard. We shared this deep connection to our digital selves even as the evocative content, based on a news story with a parallel in the physical world, placed us in contrary positions.

Cognitive science philosopher Andy Clark (2003) uses the term *soft selves* [italics mine] to describe the way we fluidly adopt and integrate with technologies, from pencil to sophisticated prostheses, which enhance or augment our bodies (p. 141). In this Second Life encounter, however, the augmentation was not so much about utilizing a tool until it became a natural extension of the self, but rather using the tool to carry *ourselves* into the virtual environment. The certain resonance of who we were, especially given that we felt defined by a political position we occupied in our real lives, echoed loudly. The confrontation underscored how loosely circumscribed a physical definition of what makes us "real" can be.

Clark's *soft selves* concept has become even more relevant given recent advances in virtual reality technology. There is a strong feeling of presence that comes from leaving a desk-anchored screen for freedom of movement with wide field of view virtual reality goggles, believable audio, body and gaze tracking and immersive content. These particular tools extend the *soft self* to offer something closer to Heidegger's "being-in-the-world" as described by Merleau-Ponty's phenomenology:

The theory of the body schema is, implicitly, the theory of perception… we shall need to reawaken our experience of the world as it appears to us in so far as we are in the world through our body, and in so far as we perceive the world with our body. But by thus remaking contact with the body and with the world, we shall also rediscover ourself, since, perceiving as we do with our body, the body is a natural self and, as it were, the subject of perception. (Merleau-Ponty, 1962, p. 239)

As I will discuss further in this chapter, it turns out that the sense of self, perception and presence described by Merleau-Ponty all have an unexpected flexibility. In fact, we have a *plastic presence* that allows for "injection-molding" into different spaces or different body forms. People can actually feel as if they have been transported to another place or that they inhabit a different body. This is not to say that participants entirely forget their physical world whereabouts or completely detach from the environment in which their bodies actually reside, but this secondary connection can be intense.

Importantly, these sensations of presence can only be achieved if the changes in the virtual environment happen in real time, that is, if the viewer participant is allowed to move freely while the digital environment changes visually and aurally in exact keeping with gaze, location and body position (jumping, squatting, bending, etc). This combination of virtual reality tools, including goggles and fast computer graphics, invokes a fully immersive experience that takes advantage of our plastic presence. By using both body and the *kairos* of a real time delivery to create an empathetic connection, a new embodied digital rhetoric emerges for framing persuasive arguments.

While most of us are familiar with the sensation of having our minds take us to another place, like my immersion as a young girl reading *Mountain Pony*, few people have yet experienced the virtual reality mind/body-trick that occurs when the eyes and ears are fed imagery and audio that correspond with natural head and body movements. This is rapidly changing as the technology is now reaching wider audiences through the recent advent of the Oculus Rift and other lower cost goggles. With growing possibilities for "recovering delivery" though the inclusion of the body, as Porter (2008) has deftly advocated, embodied digital rhetoric can be particularly persuasive and resonant if it draws from real, physical world stories. I have been calling the technique of placing a participant in the middle of a virtual reality recreation of a news story immersive journalism.

The encounter in the virtual *Gone Gitmo* illustrates immersive journalism to a certain degree, but when viewer participants feel that they are actually embodied as themselves, experiencing an intense nonfiction narrative without costume, role or pretense, something exceptional occurs. As evidenced through my piece *Hunger in Los Angeles*, which I will detail shortly, when participants became on-scene witnesses to a crisis unfolding at a food bank line, the powerful sensation of "being-in-THAT- world" was felt across different genders, ethnicities, ages, and computer-sophistication levels. While not privileging virtual reality over text, audio or film, it has become crucial that we strive to understand and accept the potential of embodied digital rhetoric in order to utilize (and engender critical thinking about) its ability to engage us in the important stories of our world. We should also be prepared for it to become the ready-tool of propaganda, which will almost certainly occur.

THE SCREEN, OUR EMBODIED PRESENCE

We accept that we experience text. We understand that the written word can convey meaning and engross us completely. For both novels and nonfiction, the mind constructs the meaning of encountered symbols to evoke pleasure, excitement, sorrow, and, on important occasion, to "hear" a call to action. We bring our feelings of presence, of immersion, to where that meaning takes us. We also believe that this long-accepted form of communication offers a legitimate connection, whether it be fantastical or valued as true.

With the advent of online virtual communication, our relationship to text on the computer screen has engendered debate over whether the same legitimacy conveyed to offline text and, importantly, to our physical selves should still apply.

In Second Life, the green avatar and I were not communicating with voice, only typing our replies to each other with our virtual hands mimicking the "typing on a keyboard" motion that was one of the hallmarks of the early version of the platform. Our encounter was mediated by a technology that put us somewhere between a fully text-based virtual world and a completely embodied virtual reality experience. My reaction to what she was typing/ saying, her spiky appearance and the slapping baseball bat were not so irrelevant that I could simply dismiss what was happening by logging off. She was in my territory and she was attacking me in a way unusual for Second Life, a social platform not designed for competitive or violent game play. When exu, a member of the text-based world LambdaMoo, expressed her terrible, tear-wrought anguish over her virtual rape, the debate found a stark focus. Julian Dibbell wrote of this "Rape in Cyberspace" in the *Village Voice,* noting that he found himself undergoing a transformation as he invested more time in world. "Where before I'd found it hard to take virtual rape seriously, I now was finding it difficult to remember how I could ever not have taken it seriously." This shift caused him to question his fundamental beliefs. "...[I]n fact, the more seriously I took the notion of virtual rape, the less seriously I was able to take the tidy division of the world into the symbolic and the real...." (1993, p. 14)

Dibbell was struggling with the same question asked by Quastro at the start of the chapter, "Where does the body end and the mind begin?" The Cartesian split suggests that the mind and body can be regarded as separate entities. However, film, visual media, and virtual reality theorists have long called into question this dissolution, seeking instead to find cohesion between where we are in the world and our connection to the images we see before us. Their work offers a parallel for considering how body and perception intertwine through the medium of the screen and can help elucidate why our plastic presence permits embodied digital rhetoric.

Film theory regards the audience member as a sort of whole body participant observer, using phenomenology to define how and what that may be. For example, Thomas Elsaesser and Malte Hagener (2010) believe the body's involvement in understanding cinema is crucial. They "...focus on the 'return' to the body as a complex yet indivisible surface of communication and perception" (p. 124) and use several film theorists to delineate this position. Laura Marks (2000) calls it, "...a contact between perceiver and object represented. It also suggests the way vision can be tactile, as though one were touching a film with one's eyes: I term this *haptic visuality*" (p. 12) As early as 1960, film theorist Sigfried Kracauer claimed that, "unlike the other type of pictures, film images affect primarily the spectator's senses, engaging him physiologically before he is in a position to respond intellectually." (p. 127). Most crucial, however, is Vivian Sobchack's appropriately named *Address of the Eye* (1992) and her use of the work of Maurice Merleau-Ponty. Sobchack says "...my fingers knew what I was looking at..." even before the image focused to reveal hands on the keys in *The Piano*. She considers this evidence of the necessity in taking a whole body approach to the experience of cinema, one that couples observation with participation. Sobchack continues:

[M]ost film theorists seem either embarrassed or bemused by bodies that often act wantonly and crudely at the movies... [C]lassical and contemporary film theory have not fully addressed the cinema as life expressing life, as experience expressing experience... Indeed it is this mutual capacity for and possession of experience through common structures of embodied existence, through similar modes of being-in-the-world, that provides the intersubjective basis of objective cinematic communication. (Sobchack, 1992, p. 5)

The idea is that cinema is not merely conceived by the mind via an ocular system but rather is understood through resonant feelings of presence in the world, intermingling sensory experience and consciousness.

Phenomenology has also been used to explore connection and interaction with computers including the work of Paul Dourish's *Where the Action Is* (2001). He explains, "In contrast to philosophical positions that look for a 'truth' independent of our own experience, phenomenology holds that the phenomena of experience are central to the questions of ontology (the study of the nature of being and categories of existence) and epistemology (the study of knowledge)" (p. 103). Dourish summarizes Heidegger's position as "the meaningfulness of everyday experience lies not in the head, but in the world." In fact, it is Heidegger's *Dasein*, translated as "being-in-the-world," which informs Sobchack's ideas about an audience's relationship to cinema.

Certainly, phenomenology has been taken up both explicitly and experimentally in work on virtual worlds and virtual bodies. "The Corporeal Body in Virtual Reality" (Murrays & Sixsmith, 1999) and "Corporeal Virtuality: The Impossibility of a Fleshless Ontology" (Richardson & Harper, 2001) maintain there is truth in Merleau-Ponty's claim that "My body is to the greatest extent what everything is: a dimensional this. It is the universal thing." (1968, pp. liv-lv). By considering the corporeal, authors Murrays and Sixsmith and Richardson and Harper reacted against the then prevailing Cartesian approach to virtual reality in which the mind can leave the body behind as it experiences "having had your everything amputated." (Barlow, 1990, p. 42) Instead, they argued that "such complacency neglects to consider that our body is our originary and inescapable anchorage and opening onto the world by which *all* information and knowledge is accessed and meaning generated. We live *through* our bodies…" (Richardson & Harper, 2001, p. 13)

If there is an overwhelming connection to what we are seeing on a screen, Anne Friedberg's consideration of the virtual window offers some insight. Friedberg (2003) struggles with,

"Descartes' description of a subject who stood outside the world and represented reality to him/herself." For Friedberg, the solution comes from Heidegger's world as a picture: that "the world becomes picture is one and the same event with the event of man's becoming subjectum in the midst of that which is." Friedberg's surveys the historical landscape for the frames of "that which is" and finds Heidegger's picture in the virtual window offered by paintings, photographs and our modern screens, be they television, film or computer (p. 342).

However, Friedberg finds she must return to Cartesian imagery in order to make sense of the computer's virtual spaces, with their "new 'windowed' multiplicity of perspectives [where] we can be at two (or more) places at once, in two (or more) time frames in a fractured post-Cartesian time." Where exactly do our bodies lay for Friedberg? Does "post-Cartesian" infer that the split, this time into multiple minds, creates a sheared distinction from our physical selves? For Friedberg we are still *leches les vitrines/*licking the windows, rather than achieving the "being-in-the-world" of the images we see, no matter whether we react with a desire comparable to the emotions we feel as if we are standing outside a shop front window peering in on material goods that we can imagine bringing us pleasure.

Friedberg's arguments unfortunately lose the body at what may be a crucial moment. We stand frozen at the window or slaves to our desks. This contrasts to the otherwise similar framing neuroscientist Antonio Damasio offers. Damasio (1994) writes, "Contrary to traditional scientific opinion, feelings are just as cognitive as other percepts. They are the result of the most curious physiological arrangement that has turned the brain into the body's captive audience… Were it not for the possibility of sensing body states that are inherently ordained to be painful or pleasurable, there would be no suffering or bliss, no longing or mercy, no tragedy or glory in the human condition." This quote, taken from the book *Descartes' Error*, is intended to illustrate that all perception, feeling and experience are based on an interconnection of mind and body (p. xviii).

So, what then if we are able to step through Friedberg's frame to embrace an experience more closely related to Damasio's neurobiological union? As touched on earlier, advances in virtual reality goggle technology can elicit a secondary presence that allows us to feel as if we exist in two worlds at the same time. Indeed, this "different kind of embodiment" that Richardson and Harper (2001) foresaw, in many ways offers an immersion that overlays digitally created imagery onto our mental perceptions of our physical bodies. This allows us to apply that same "biological plasticity" as described by Clark's *soft selves*. He says, "[W]e humans… are biologically disposed towards literal (and repeated) episodes of sensory re-calibration, of bodily reconfiguration and of mental extension. Such potential for literal and repeated re-configuration is the mark of what I shall call 'profoundly embodied agency'…" (Clark, p. 263, 2007)

In fact, virtual reality technology has been used to explore this flexibility of body ownership in several studies. For example, Mel Slater and his research colleagues have created a series of studies to measure RAIR – Response as if Real, which requires two critical components, place illusion and plausibility. Place illusion refers to the sense that one is in a place that feels believable. Plausibility means that the situation depicted is not so fantastical as to completely disconnect the participant from the narrative. These concepts have direct equivalents in rhetoric, as connection and believability are central to effective persuasion.

This does not mean RAIR experiences must mirror participants' perception of themselves in the non-virtual. In one experiment, grown men successfully inhabited and connected to the virtual body of an eight-year-old girl (Slater, Spanlang, Sanchez-Vives, & Blanke, 2010). Another project created an illusion in which participants experienced ownership over a virtual arm that was up to

three times the length of their normal arm, although that ownership connection weakened as the arm grew longer (Kilteni, Normand, Sanchez-Vives, & Slater, M., 2012).

In an immersive journalism investigation, participants were "put into the body" of a detainee in a stress position. While sitting upright on a stool with their hands clasped behind their backs, participants heard a binaural recreation of a real interrogation that sounded as if it was coming from another room. Throughout, participants wore virtual reality goggles with tracking so that a bound detainee seen in a virtual mirror could synchronously mimic their movements and breathing. After less than fifteen minutes, participants indicted they had taken on the hunched position of the virtual reality detainee despite the fact they were actually sitting upright (Figure 2) (de la Peña et al., 2010).

In another cogent example, researchers at the 2013 Annual Conference on Human Factors in Computing Systems in Paris presented results indicating that just looking at an avatar wearing a backpack makes participants "feel" the extra weight. A group of students who saw that a backpack was attached to an avatar that they themselves had created overestimated the heights of virtual hills. The researchers noted that this finding was

Figure 2. The virtual reality detainee in a stress position

consistent with physical world results, in which people tend to overestimate heights and distances while carrying extra weight.

These studies initially seem to support a Cartesian split wherein the mind can be manipulated to accept a body that is unrelated to the one it actually controls. In actuality, the body's involvement was crucial to all of the results. For example, in the first two studies described here, the researcher stroked the subject's actual arm while the subject, wearing virtual reality goggles, looked down or at a virtual mirror that showed a faux arm growing or placed him/her inside the virtual 8-year-old's body. In the detainee study, the experiment required participants to clasp their hands behind the back, enhancing bodily participation in a sensation of being bound and hunched over. The backpack study recalled the body through past experience, a cohesion of body and mind as described by Hume's argument that the knowledge that touching something burning hot hurts will then modify all present and future behavior.

Experiences of the body are also informed by cultural contexts and priming from implicit memory can affect "who we are." For example, identity and performance change with costume and role-play, a behavioral manifestation that has been well studied both offline and online. The notorious 1971 Stanford Prison Experiment, which recreated a prison using college students, found that the "prison guards" soon became sadistic and the "prisoners" showed signs of stress and depression. Other studies noted that subjects wearing black uniforms behaved more aggressively than subjects wearing white uniforms (Frank & Gilovich, 1988) and that subjects dressed in Ku Klux Klan robes delivered significantly longer shocks than those in nurses' uniforms (Johnson & Downing, 1979).

Similar results are found online. For example, researcher Jorge Peña (2008) found that participants' behavior was changed by the appearance of their avatars. When they were assigned avatars costumed in Ku Klux Klan outfits, they played more aggressively than avatars dressed in white

doctor coats. When Slater et al. (2006) repeated the infamous Milgram study, but in a virtual environment, they found participants had both subjective and physiological responses when they applied "shocks" to a screaming avatar they could see and hear.

Yee and Bailenson (2007) designated attractive or unattractive avatars to subjects who shared a virtual space with counterparts "blind" to the condition – the counterparts only saw an "untextured face" that was "structurally human but left uncolored." The results found that those who believed themselves to be more attractive were friendlier and moved significantly closer in the virtual space to their counterpart's avatar compared to the unattractive or average appearing avatar. In the same series of experiments, Yee and Bailenson used height as a mitigating characteristic. Subjects and their counterparts were each given two turns to divvy up one hundred dollars. If they both agreed to the split, however uneven, they were allowed to keep the money. If they could not agree, the money would be forfeited. In this scenario, the benign counterpart saw his/her avatar as being of equal height to that of the subject of the study's avatar. However, the subject of the study saw his/her own avatar as being either taller, the same height or shorter than their counterpart's avatar. Yee and Bailenson found that when subjects perceived their avatars to be taller, they tended to propose splits with higher cash values in their own favor. It seems that just slight adjustments in "self-perception" can have a significant impact on user behavior, a phenomenon Yee and Bailenson call "The Proteus Effect." (Perhaps the green spiky suit and sharp bladed skates contributed to the aggressiveness of the Second Life avatar I encountered while almost certainly enhancing my wariness.)

Our plastic presence is also reflected more generally in how societal attitudes can easily migrate and map onto online behavior. According to Nowak and Rauh (2007), virtual appearance, like physical world appearance, significantly affects how users interact with one another. They note, "Despite the obvious media differences, research suggests that the underlying process of perceiving people online is analogous to the process of perceiving people offline" (p. 1474). Nowak and Rauh also found that identifiable gender was central to online perception and conduct while sexual harassment has also been documented as part of online environments for nearly twenty years. When Bruckman (1992) decided to examine text-based multi-user virtual environments called MUDs, her research found that female players were subjected to sexual overtures as soon as they came online:

Female characters are often besieged with attention. By typing the who command, it is possible to get a list of all characters logged on. The page command allows one to talk to people not in the same room. Many male players will get a list of all present, and then page characters with female names. Unwanted attention and sexual advances create an uncomfortable atmosphere for women in MUDs, just as they do in real life. (Bruckman, 1992, p. 2)

We considered the issue for virtual worlds, and in survey data we collected of Second Life users, we found that 92% of females with female avatars reported being regularly harassed. In keeping with offline studies indicating that women regularly find a situation more harassing than men do, the data also found that females with female avatars felt much more harassed than males using male avatars, (de la Peña, Morie, Curtis, forthcoming). As one user indicated:

This is so common to Virtual Worlds of adult nature, it's going to happen. It does in both worlds, or any worlds I've been to.

While sexual coercion might not be physical in the same way as experienced offline, like Dibbell's "Rape in Cyberspace," comments offered by the women players of Second Life make clear how deeply the abuse can be felt. One player

said, [T]his time I ran across a real stinker. Not just obnoxious, but sexually violent and verbally abusive. If it had been real life, I would have had some pretty serious injuries, and I would definitely have called the cops." When asked how she responded, a player wrote, "Cried and wrote in my live journal." Another comment also exemplifies how powerful text still can be in a virtual world: "[T]he person who followed me saying he would 'rape my face,' was extremely upsetting." Clearly, the sense of coercion can be deeply felt and may have similar psychological impact to offline experiences[1].

There is, of course, a crucial distinction. Virtual world attacks that are described with text or realized through animations are not indicators that the person behind the keyboard would actually take action in the physical world. They may be more akin to someone simply shouting a threat – viscerally felt but physically bounded. Dibbell reveals the real rapist in LambdaMOO to actually be a group of male college students at the keyboard acting together, an encouraging mob most likely oblivious to and unconcerned with the actual anxiety they might be causing. (One is reminded of the Stanford university students acting in a collaboration of aggression.)

However, what would those male students have felt had they been playing as a female, using a gender-swapped avatar to act as their online presence?[2] Our same Second Life study measuring prevalence of sexual harassment found an unexpected result. When men who had swapped into female avatars became victims of sexual harassment, they found the experience significantly more harassing than women playing with a female avatar. Unfortunately, these male players were not asked why they felt more harassed, and we are left wondering what made them connect so significantly to their female avatars that they expressed such a strong reaction. Still, this data supports a sentiment expressed by a player interviewed by Turkle (1995), whose text-based gender swapping led him to have a "newfound empathy with women":

Other players start showering you with money to help you get started, and I had never once gotten a handout when playing a male player. And then they feel they should be allowed to tag along forever. Then when you give them the knee after they grope you, they wonder what your problem is, reciting that famous saying, "What's your problem? It's only a game." (Turkle, p. 222)

While a discussion about sexual harassment may seem a detour, in fact it is extremely relevant in considerations of digital rhetoric. After all, how extraordinary that individuals can connect to their virtual selves to such a degree that they have strong feelings of empathy, even when their gender swapping is occurring only on screen. This connection, a clear example of plastic presence, was also crucial for *Gone Gitmo* and our work that put the audience in the "body" of a detainee in a stress position. It is also key to understanding why *Hunger in Los Angeles* offers a successful example of fully embodied digital rhetoric.

HUNGER IN LOS ANGELES

I constructed *Hunger in Los Angeles* to call attention to the important issue in the United States of people going hungry in the economic downturn and the strain on food banks trying to help. Rather than using video or text, my intent was to put the audience *inside* the news story/documentary using virtual reality to recreate a nonfiction event. The piece, which premiered in January of 2012 at the Sundance Film Festival, reconstructed a dramatic crisis that took place at a food bank in August, 2011. A man with diabetes was one of dozens in a long line of people, desperate to obtain food. However, the wait prevented him from receiving sustenance in time to stop a precipitous blood sugar drop. He had a seizure and went into a diabetic coma, all of which was recorded with audio and photographs. That material was then used to inform the reconstruction.

First, three-dimensional models were built depicting the street and surrounding buildings. Virtual humans, both donated and purchased online, were programmed through the use of motion capture. This meant the virtual humans moved with natural human gestures instead of computer-generated animations. Audio was edited from approximately seventy-five minutes down to six and a half minutes, including reducing the wait time for the ambulance from approximately twenty minutes to two minutes. The sounds capture how overwhelmed the woman running the food bank finds herself as she begins shouting, "There's too many people!" and "Please don't push!" When the diabetic man collapses, the sounds of panicked calls to 911 and worried bystanders can be heard (Figure 3).

Wearing virtual reality goggles and headphones, the audience moves freely around a life-sized experience that places them in the middle of the scene as it unfolds. The genuine looking street and buildings, the natural movement of the avatars and the powerful audio create a striking realism, even if the avatars look slightly cartoonish or strange. When the man falls to the ground in the throes of his seizure, the impact is both startling and disturbing.

At the Sundance premiere, surveys were taken of a 155 users, whose demographics broke down to 57% male and 42% female (one preferred not to answer) and included ages ranging from 10 to 65. A variety of backgrounds were also present, mostly likely because, unlike films at the festival, the exhibit required no tickets and anyone could walk in. Participants came from a cross section of ethnicities and races, including whites, African-Americans, Latinos, Asians, with some specifically noting they were American Indian, Jewish or Middle-Eastern.

In order to measure feelings of "presence," of "being-in-*that*-world," the survey relied on the Slater, Usoh and Steed (SUS) questionnaire, which offers language to test connection to a virtual environment. A five point Likert scale

Figure 3. A composite image merging the physical world location and the virtual world build of Hunger in Los Angeles

was used, with potential responses ranging from strongly agree to strongly disagree. One of the key questions was "At times during the experience, did the virtual environment feel like reality to you?" The results came back as significant, with 109 respondents indicating that the experience did "feel like reality" to them (88 agreeing and 28 strongly agreeing). Of those, 106 also felt "frustrated" that they could not help the seizure victim. In fact, there was a clear correlation: if participants agreed the experience felt like reality, they also reported frustration that they could not help. This was true even though a peripheral view of the room was still available (Figure 4).

Participants also displayed an identifiable empathy with the scene that supported survey data. I watched in amazement as users yanked out their mobile phones to call for help at the moment the seizure victim hit the ground before they remembered that what they were experiencing was not real. Dozens of people concluded the experience in tears. Many kneeled down at the head of the virtual seizure victim, speaking aloud as they tried to comfort him while he lay "unmoving" on the ground.

Comments from participants described this connection: "The experience of the environment and the story left me feeling a very specific emo-

Figure 4. A participant tries to touch the "seizure victim" while experiencing Hunger in Los Angeles

tion that I don't believe I have felt previously. I felt the desire to help or to say something in an active voice to the characters on the street." Another participant said, "Once I felt immersed in the events, I wanted to do anything I could to help the seizure victim and the people there. Very heavy piece but it has a lasting impact..." Similarly, a third person reported, "I would say that I predict a long lasting empathic response in myself; I find myself worried about the victim and concerned about the situation in a way that I was not previously." In fact, most comments focused on the overwhelming sensation of presence and being connected to the unfolding events, "I felt a part of the scene and not only sympathized with the people online but identified with them as well" (Figure 5).

In keeping with an assertion made in the introduction of this chapter, participants' comments also described duality of presence rather than a total abandonment of the physical world. "It was not as though I didn't realize that I was in a virtual environment but as though two parts of my brain were active and conflicted about the expe-

rience," noted one participant. "I had to keep reminding myself that this was, in fact, a simulation." Another comment agreed, "It was my first experience with virtual reality and I found myself focused on both the environment and the altered awareness of self that I was experiencing." It was perhaps best put by a third participant, "Connected and disconnected at the same time." This strange existence in both worlds has been supported by research that found that when avid World of Warcraft players thought about their avatars, the same areas of the brain were activated as when they were thinking about themselves. Interestingly, in that same study, the area of the brain associated with imagination was also activated, as if the experience felt real and imaginary at the same time (Callaway, 2009).

A small group of *Hunger in Los Angeles* participants indicated they were not absorbed and the common theme in their comments was that they were particularly focused on the technology versus the content of the experience. Our limited data has thus far been unable to tease out any demographic connection with this minority of

Figure 5. A woman, who later reported that she had witnessed her own father having diabetic seizures, kneels near the "seizure victim" while experiencing Hunger in Los Angeles

participants who disagreed or strongly disagreed that *Hunger* at some point felt real. One thing we were able to rule out was that a previous robust video gaming or virtual reality experience was not shared among these participants.

An element that may have had an effect on the larger population who felt connected to and present at the scene was the possibility that they were primed to believe the story was "real." Certainly the audience was told that the audio was recorded on scene and the immersive content shared the same intent as a documentary or news piece. People often read meaning into what were simply low quality graphics. For example, I was told that the rough-looking arms of one woman made it clear she was a heroin addict. Another person noted that the seizure victim's knees were clearly marked up from falling to the ground so often. While we

had not included questions on prior experience in the survey, a number of individuals who were particularly shaken told me that they had actually been present when someone had a seizure in real life and were feeling the same anxiety as they had originally.

Despite having been built on a gaming platform, *Hunger in Los Angeles* offered little agency to the participants. They could not affect the linear nature of the narrative, which unfolded much like the real events of the day and no intervention could have shifted time or the events in the physical world from which it was captured. There were no levels, no points. This was part of the design; after all, one cannot change events that unfold in the real world. Like a news or nonfiction story, participants were simply witnesses. This lack of being able to control or affect what was happening was registered in both the survey data and noted repeatedly participants' comments. "I did feel disempowered about being unable to get help or speed up the process to getting the man help." Finally, in a comment that in many ways summarizes the overall experience of immersion, empathy and frustration, a participant said, "I did feel bad I couldn't help the seizure victim. I felt like I was really there. Made me understand what they went through..."

CONCLUSION

Humans have long been able to immerse themselves in other worlds, through oral story or novels, painting, photographs, television, cinema and pure imagination. The mind does not travel alone -- the body most certainly comes along for the ride. For example, a 2008 study found that die-hard fans have greater heart attack risks from the stress of watching their favorite sports teams. (Wilbert-Lampen, Leistner, Greven, Pohl, Sper et al., 2008) The joys and sorrows of connection are real, as also exemplified by research on sexual harassment. However, I would argue we are on the cusp of a grand shift in which the sense of bodily presence has been extended from the physical world and that a new form of immersion has arisen. This uncoupling of digital experience from the frame of the computer screen by using wide field of view virtual reality goggles and appropriate audio and content offers a new way for our *soft selves* to not just enjoy an extended body, but to also occupy space and become *present* inside a story.

While this concept of using virtual reality for realistic news or nonfiction may seem strange at first, a critical examination of the essential element of any current news medium raises similar questions. Why should the symbols of text be any more valid? Is the 2D video on a flat television or computer screen any more authentic? The lack of realism inherent in the computer graphics that engender the most criticism and deny credibility to immersive journalism is disappearing quickly.

Despite its limitations, *Hunger in Los Angeles* underscores the worthiness of building virtual experiences that incorporate some of the physicality we enjoy in the natural world in order to tell the stories that come from our natural world. The piece achieves the lauded goal for journalists to give the audience "a view from the ground," as World War II reporter Martha Gellhorn called it. While not replacing the reality of our flesh and blood on scene, *Hunger in Los Angeles* and the technology it employs offer a deeply felt being-in-the-world. It can certainly be considered persuasive expression, in keeping with traditional rhetoric.

Ultimately, I would argue that this type of immersive nonfiction virtual reality brings us closer to the Damasio's (1994) unified body and mind. The ability to move freely while having an existence in another place is specific to this technology and, as exemplified by *Hunger in Los Angeles*, an

effective "different kind of embodiment." I can even state, based on my data, that with appropriate imagery and audio, immersive virtual reality can create a "being-in-*that*-world" measured by the philosophy of the phenomenologist. In sum, Clark's *soft selves* concept and the idea of *plastic presence* merge, something that may have been more pronounced because participants understood that what they were experiencing a recreation of an actual event in Los Angeles with desperately hungry people.

Not only does immersive nonfiction deserve a respected place alongside the traditional journalistic tools of text, radio, and film, it allows a complete experience for the embodied mind. While we can start our engaged journey with text (recall my connection to the novel *Mountain Pony*), film or other visual encounter, there is a fundamental shift when the body is no longer relegated to the theatre seat or desk chair and can move within the content. The *soft self's plastic presence* goes beyond the digital plasticity of William Gibson as described by Jeremy Bailenson and Andrew Beall (2005), which considers only the malleability of presentation. Instead, we remain who we are when we travel the nonfiction story, without costume and without pretense. This manifestation of "oneself," akin to being present in the natural world, allows the world's stories to be communicated in a uniquely visceral manner. Ultimately, it also means that with the new era of embodied digital rhetoric, effective persuasion will require novel approaches as the orator must now consider the freedom of the spectator's gaze and embodied position within the content and context of the multi-dimensional story. After all, in virtual reality, looking backward no longer means one is not paying attention.

REFERENCES

Bailenson, J. N., & Beall, A. C. (2005). Transformed social interaction: Exploring the digital plasticity of avatars. In R. Schroeder, & A. Axelsson (Eds.), *Avatars at work and play: Collaboration and interaction in shared virtual environments*. New York: Springer-Verlag.

Callaway, E. (2009, 6 Nov). How your brain sees virtual you. *New Scientist*. Retrieved from http://www.newscientist.com/article/dn18117-how-your-brain-sees-virtual-you.html#.Uj9bARZL-FAs

Clark, A. (2003). *Natural-born cyborgs – Minds, technologies, and the future of human intelligence*. New York: Oxford University Press.

Damasio, A. R. (1994). *Descartes' error: Emotion, reason, and the human brain*. New York: Putnam.

Dibbel, J. (1993, Dec. 23). A rape in cyberspace. *The Village Voice*.

Dourish, P. (2001). *Where the action is: The foundations of embodied interaction*. Cambridge, MA: MIT Press.

Elsaesser, T., & Hagener, M. (2010). *Film theory: An introduction through the senses*. New York: Routledge.

Frank, M., & Gilovich, T. (1988). The dark side of self and social perception: Black uniforms and aggression in professional sports. *Journal of Personality and Social Psychology*, *54*, 74–85. doi:10.1037/0022-3514.54.1.74 PMID:3346809

Gellhorn, M. (1988). *The view from the ground*. New York: Atlantic Monthly Press.

Johnson, R., & Downing, L. (1979). Deindividuation and valence of cues: Effects on prosocial and antisocial behavior. *Journal of Personality and Social Psychology*, *37*, 1532–1538. doi:10.1037/0022-3514.37.9.1532 PMID:501521

Kilteni, K., Normand, J. M., Sanchez-Vives, M. V., & Slater, M. (2012). Extending body space in immersive virtual reality: A very long arm illusion. *PLoS ONE*, *7*(7), e40867. doi:10.1371/journal.pone.0040867 PMID:22829891

Lenggenhager, B. et al. (2007). Video ergo sum: Manipulating bodily self-consciousness. *Science*, *317*, 1096–1099. doi:10.1126/science.1143439 PMID:17717189

Macann, C. E. (1993). *Four phenomenological philosophers: Husserl, Heidegger, Sartre, Merleau-Ponty*. London: Routledge.

Marks, L. U. (2000). *The skin of the film: Intercultural cinema, embodiment, and the senses*. Durham, NC: Duke University Press.

Merleau-Ponty, M. (1962). *Phenomenology of perception*. New York: Humanities Press.

Merleau-Ponty, M., & Lefort, C. (1968). *The visible and the invisible, followed by working notes*. Evanston, IL: Northwestern University Press.

Murray, C. D., & Sixsmith, J. (1999). The corporeal body in virtual reality. *Ethos (Berkeley, Calif.)*, *27*(3), 315–343. doi:10.1525/eth.1999.27.3.315

Richardson, I., & Harper, C. (2001). *Corporeal virtuality: the impossibility of a fleshless ontology*. Retrieved from http://people.brunel.ac.uk/bst/2no2/Papers/Ingrid%20Richardson&Carly%20Harper.htm

Slater, M., Spanlang, B., Sanchez-Vives, M. V., & Blanke, O. (2010). First person experience of body transfer in virtual reality. *PLoS ONE*, *5*(5), e10564. doi:10.1371/journal.pone.0010564 PMID:20485681

Sobchack, V. C. (1992). *The address of the eye: A phenomenology of film experience*. Princeton, NJ: Princeton University Press.

Thorburn, D., Jenkins, H., & Seawell, B. (2003). *Rethinking media change: The aesthetics of transition*. Cambridge, MA: MIT Press.

Turkle, S. (1995). *Life on the screen: Identity in the age of the Internet*. New York: Simon and Schuster.

Wilbert-Lampen, U., Leistner, D., Greven, S., Pohl, T., Sper, S., & Volker, C. et al. (2008). Cardiovascular events during World Cup Soccer. *The New England Journal of Medicine, 358*(5), 475–483. doi:10.1056/NEJMoa0707427 PMID:18234752

Yee, N., & Bailenson, J. N. (2007). The Proteus effect: The effect of transformed self-representation on behavior. *Human Communication Research, 33,* 271–290. doi:10.1111/j.1468-2958.2007.00299.x

Zimbardo, P. (1969). The human choice: Individuation, reason, and order vs. deindividuation, impulse and chaos. In W. J. Arnold & D. Levine (Eds.), *Nebraska Symposium on Motivation, 17,* (pp. 237-307). Lincoln, NE: University of Nebraska Press.

KEY TERMS AND DEFINITIONS

Embodied Digital Rhetoric: Using the sense of presence that comes with advanced virtual reality technologies to create persuasive narratives.

Immersive Journalism: Using gaming platforms and advanced virtual reality technologies to give the audience a sense of presence and the feelings of being "on scene" while a news story unfolds.

Plastic Presence: The concept that we can feel ourselves present in more than one place and at the same time; that our presence itself has a malleable plasticity.

Soft Selves: A term used by Andy Clark to describe how advanced biological systems will adopt resources such as tools and absorb them into "both our cognitive and physical problem-solving routines."

ENDNOTES

[1] In the physical world, sexual harassment has been found to have a number of negative consequences. It is a worldwide problem that affects students, those in the military, people at work and at social events. As Barak (2005) notes, "Theory and research show that sexual harassment… has substantial personal and organizational costs." (p.77) It depresses morale, lowers worker productivity and … "[t]hese experiences were associated with deleterious mental and physical health conditions." (Street, Stafford, Mahan and Hendricks, 2008. p. 409) While sexual harassment can be aimed at different genders and those of different sexual orientation, women remain predominantly the target of such unwanted advances (Barak, 2005; Street, et al., 2008; Gruber, 1997; Paludi & Paludi, 2003).

[2] Much has been written about gender swapping on the internet including Bruckman's early work on text-based MUDs as well as later research by Savicki et al. (1996) and Senft, (1997). It has also been a topic in a number of books, with Sherry Turkle devoting a chapter to the issue in *Life on the Screen: Identity in the Age of the Internet* (1995), while Howard Rheingold's *Virtual Community: Homesteading on the Electronic Frontier* (1993), Stone's *The War of Desire and Technology at the Close of the Mechanical Age* (1995) and the edited volume *Virtual Gender* (2001) have all discussed the issue.

Compilation of References

{Anonymous}. (2013, January 8). I was a paid internet shill: How shadowy groups manipulate internet opinion and debate. *ConsciousLifeNews.com*. Retrieved January 17, 2013, from http://consciouslifenews.com/paid-internet-shill-shadowy-groups-manipulate-internet-opinion-debate/1147073/

Aarseth, E. (1997). *Cybertext—Perspectives on ergodic literature*. Baltimore, MD: Johns Hopkins University Press.

Acar, A., & Muraki, Y. (2011). Twitter for crisis communication: Lessons learned from Japan's tsunami disaster. *International Journal of Web Based Communities*, 7(3), 392–402. doi:10.1504/IJWBC.2011.041206

Afghanistan Internet Usage and Telecommunications Reports. (2012, 12 Nov.). *Internet world stats: Usage and population statistics*. Retrieved 19 Dec. 2012 from http://www.internetworldstats.com/asia/af.htm

Agarwal, R., & Karahanna, E. (2000). Time flies when you're having fun: Cognitive absorption and beliefs about information technology usage. *Management Information Systems Quarterly*. doi:10.2307/3250951

Alessi, J. (2008). *Games demystified: Portal*. Gamasutra. Retrieved 2008-08-28.

Althusser, L. (1971). Ideology and ideological state apparatuses. In *Lenin and Philosophy* (pp. 127–177). New York: Monthly Review Press.

Altun, S., & Büyükduman, F. I. (2007). Teacher and student beliefs on constructivist instructional design: A case study. *Educational Sciences: Theory and Practice*, 7(1), 30–39.

Amazon Mechanical Turk. (n. d.). Retrieved from https://www.mturk.com/mturk/

America's Army. (2013). In *Wikipedia*. Retrieved from https://en.wikipedia.org/wiki/America's_Army

Ancona, D. G., Okhuysen, G. A., & Perlow, L. A. (2001). Taking time to integrate temporal research. *Academy of Management Review*, 25(4), 512–529.

Andersen, R. (2013). Omens. *Aeon*. Retrieved from http://www.aeonmagazine.com/world-views/ross-andersen-human-extinction/

Anderson, A., Brossard, D., Scheufele, D., Xenos, M., & Ladwig, P. (2013, February 19). Crude comments and concern: Online incivility's effect on risk perceptions of emerging technologies. *Journal of Computer-Mediated Communication*. Retrieved February 24, from http://onlinelibrary.wiley.com/doi/10.1111/jcc4.12009/full.

Anderson, C. (2009, June). The new new economy. *Wired*. 98 – 121.

Anderson, D. (2003). Prosumer approaches to new media composition: Consumption and production in continuum. *Kairos: A Journal of Rhetoric, Technology, and Pedagogy, 8*(1), Spring.

Anderson, J. A. (1996). *Communication theory: Epistemological foundations*. New York: The Guilford Press.

Anderson, J. A., & Baym, V. (2004). Philosophies and philosophic issues in communication, 1995-2004. *The Journal of Communication, 54*(4), 589–615. doi:10.1093/joc/54.4.589

Aneesh, A. Hall. L., & Petro, P. (2012). Beyond globalization: Making new world in media, art, and social practices. New Brunswick, NJ: Rutgers University Press.

Anti-Defamation League. (2005). *Swastika/Nazi party flag.* Retrieved from http://archive.adl.org/hate_symbols/neo_nazi_swastika_flag.asp

Appadurai, A. (2001). Grassroots globalization and the research imagination. In A. Appadurai (Ed.), *Globalization* (pp. 1–21). Durham, NC and London: Duke University Press. doi:10.1215/9780822383215-001

Appelbaum, L. G., Cain, M. S., Darling, E. F., & Mitroff, S. R. (2013). Action video game playing is associated with improved visual sensitivity, but not alterations in visual sensory memory. *Attention, Perception & Psychophysics, 75*(4), 1–7. doi: doi:10.3758/s13414-013-0472-7 PMID:23709062

Arasaratnam, L. (2011). *Perception and communication in intercultural spaces.* New York, NY: University Press of America, Inc.

Aristotle, . (1984). Metaphysics. In J. Barnes (Ed.), *The complete works of Aristotle* (Vol. 2, pp. 1552–1728). Princeton, NJ: Princeton University Press.

Aristotle, . (2006). *On rhetoric* (G. Kennedy, Trans.). Oxford, UK: Oxford University Press.

Arnheim, R. (1956). *Art and visual perception.* London: Faber.

Arola, K. L. (2010). The design of Web 2.0: The rise of the template, the fall of design. *Computers and Composition, 27*(1), 4–14. doi:10.1016/j.compcom.2009.11.004

Atwill, J. M. (1998). *Rhetoric reclaimed: Aristotle and the liberal arts tradition.* Ithaca, NY: Cornell University Press.

Avital, M. (2000). Dealing with time in social inquiry: A tension between method and lived experience. *Organization Science, 11*(6), 665–673. doi:10.1287/orsc.11.6.665.12532

Bachen, C. M., Hernández-Ramos, P. F., & Raphael, C. (2012). Simulating REAL LIVES: Promoting global empathy and interest in learning through simulation games. *Simulation & Gaming, 43*(4), 437–460. doi:10.1177/1046878111432108

Bacon, F. (2011). *The new organon: Or true directions concerning the interpretation of nature.* Retrieved 2 April 2012, from http://www.constitution.org/liberlib.htm

Bailenson, J. N., & Beall, A. C. (2005). Transformed social interaction: Exploring the digital plasticity of avatars. In R. Schroeder, & A. Axelsson (Eds.), *Avatars at work and play: Collaboration and interaction in shared virtual environments.* New York: Springer-Verlag.

Bakhtin, M. (1973). *Marxism and the philosophy of language.* Cambridge, MA: Harvard University Press.

Bal, P. M., & Veltkamp, M. (2013). How does fiction reading influence empathy? An experimental investigation on the role of emotional transportation. *PLoS ONE, 8*(1), e55341. doi:10.1371/journal.pone.0055341 PMID:23383160

Barbara, E. H., & de Nooy, J. (2009). *Learning language and culture via public internet discussion forms.* Great Britain, UK: Palgrave MacMillan.

Barthes, R. (1975). *The pleasure of the text* (R. Miller, Trans.). New York, NY: Hill and Wang.

Barthes, R. (1977). *Image/music/text* (S. Heath, Trans.). New York, NY: Hill and Wang.

Barthes, R. (1977). The death of the author. In R. Barthes (Ed.), *Image, music text* (pp. 90–99). London: Fontana.

Barthes, R. (1981). *Camera lucida* (R. Howard, Trans.). New York, NY: Hill and Wang.

Baudrillard, J. (2010). *Simulacra and simulation* (S. F. Glaser, Trans.). Ann Arbor, MI: U of Michigan P.

Baumlin, J. S. (1987). Decorum, kairos, and the new rhetoric. *PRE/TEXT, 5,* 171–183.

Bazelon, E. (2013, March). How to stop the bullies. *Atlantic (Boston, Mass.),* 82–89.

Bazermann, C. (1981). What written knowledge does: Three examples of academic discourse. *Philosophy of the Social Sciences, 11,* 361–387. doi:10.1177/004839318101100305

Beauvais, P. J. (2002). First contact: Composition students' close encounters with college culture. In J. M. Wolf (Ed.), *Professing in the contact zone: Bringing theory and practice together* (pp. 21–47). Urbana, IL: NCTE.

Becker, J. D. (1988, August 29). *Unicode 88.* Retrieved from http://www.unicode.org/history/ unicode88.pdf

Bedny, G. Z., & Karwowski, W. (2003). A systemic-structural activity approach to the design of human-computer interaction tasks. *International Journal of Human-Computer Interaction, 16*, 235–260. doi:10.1207/S15327590IJHC1602_06

Beetham, H., McGill, L., & Littlejohn, A. (2009) *Thriving in the 21ˢᵗ century: Final report of learning literacies for the digital age (LLiDA) project.* Retrieved June 10, 2007, from http://www.academy.gcal.ac.uk/llida/

Bellamy, R. K. E. (1996). Designing educational technology: Computer-mediated change. In B. Nardi (Ed.), *Context and consciousness: Activity theory and human-computer interaction* (pp. 123–146). Cambridge, MA: MIT Press.

Bemer, R. W. (1960). *Commentary on survey of coded character representation.* Retrieved from http://www.bobbemer.com/PUBS-ASC.HTM

Benjamin, W. (1968). The work of art in the age of mechanical reproduction. In H. Arendt (Ed.), *Illuminations* (pp. 214–218). London: Fontana.

Benkler, Y. (2006). *The wealth of networks: How social production transforms markets and freedom.* New Haven, CT: Yale University Press.

Berlin, J. (2003). Rhetoric and ideology in the writing classroom. In V. Villanueva (Ed.), *Cross-talk in comp theory* (2nd ed., pp. 717–737). Urbana, IL: NCTE.

Berlin, J. A. (1982). Contemporary composition: The major pedagogical theories. *College English, 44*(8), 765–777. doi:10.2307/377329

Berlin, J. A. (1987). *Rhetoric and reality: Writing instruction in American colleges, 1900-1985.* Carbondale, IL: Southern Illinois University Press.

Berlin, J. A. (1992). Poststructuralism, cultural studies, and the composition classroom: Postmodern theory in practice. *Rhetoric Review, 11*(1), 16–33. doi:10.1080/07350199209388984

Berlinski, D. (2011). *The advent of the algorithm.* New York: Mariner Books.

Bernstein, B. (1999). Vertical and horizontal discourse: An essay. *British Journal of Sociology of Education, 20*(2), 157–173. doi:10.1080/01425699995380

Berry, P. W., Hawisher, G. E., & Selfe, C. L. (2012). *Transnational literate lives in digital times.* Logan, UT: Computers and Composition Digital Press/Utah State University Press. Retrieved June 1, 2013, from http://ccdigitalpress.org/transnational

Betts Van Dyk, K. K. (2006). From the plaint to the comic: Kenneth Burke's *Towards a Better Life. Rhetoric Society Quarterly, 36*(1), 31–53. doi:10.1080/02773940500403611

Bhabha, H. K. (1994). *The location of culture.* London: Routlege.

Bhaduri, S. (Ed.). (2008). *Negotiating glocalization: Views from language, literature and cultural studies.* Delhi, India: Anthem.

Bigum, C. (1995). Schools and the Internet: Reinventing the 1980s?. *Incorporated Association of Registered Teachers of Victoria (IARTV) Seminar Series, no. 47.*

Bijke, W. (1997). *Of Bicycles, bakelites and bulbs. Toward a theory of sociotechnological change.* Cambridge, MA: MIT Press.

Binder, A. R. (2012). Figuring out #Fukushima: An initial look at functions and content of US Twitter commentary about nuclear risk. *Environmental Communication: A Journal of Nature and Culture, 6*(2), 268–277.

Bishop, J. (in press). The psychology of trolling and lurking: The role of defriending and gamification for increasing participation in online communities using seductive narratives. In J. Bishop (Ed.), *Examining the concepts, issues, and implications of internet trolling.* Hershey, PA: IGI Global. doi:10.4018/978-1-4666-0312-7.ch010

Bissell, T. (2011). *Extra lives: Why video games matter.* New York, NY: Vintage Books.

Bitzer, L. (1968). The rhetorical situation. *Philosophy and Rhetoric, 1*(1), 1–14.

Bizzell, P. (1992). *Academic discourse and critical consciousness.* Pittsburgh, PA: University of Pittsburgh Press.

Black, P. J., & Wiliam, D. (1998). *Inside the black box.* London: GL Assessment.

Blog Carnivals. (2012). *Digital rhetoric collaborative.* Retrieved February 12, 2014, from http://www.digital-rhetoriccollaborative.org/blog-carnivals/

Bluedorn, A. C. (2002). *The human organization of time: Temporal realities and experience.* Stanford, CA: Stanford University Press.

Bobbitt, D. A. (2004). *The rhetoric of redemption: Kenneth Burke's redemption drama and Martin Luther King, Jr.'s I have a dream speech.* Lanham, MD: Rowman & Littlefield Publishers.

Bødker, S. (1989). A human activity approach to user interfaces. *Human-Computer Interaction, 4.*

Bødker, S. (1991). *Through the interface: A human activity approach to user interface design.* Hillsdale, NJ: Lawrence Erlbaum.

Bogost, I. (2007). *Persuasive games: The expressive power of videogames.* Cambridge, MA: The MIT Press.

Bogost, I. (2008). The rhetoric of video games. In K. Salen (Ed.), *The ecology of games: Connecting youth, games, and learning* (pp. 117–140). Cambridge, MA: The MITPress.

Bogost, I. (2012). *Alien phenomenology.* Minneapolis, MN: University of Minnesota Press.

Bogost, I. (2013). Exploitationware. In R. Colby, M. S. S. Johnson, & R. S. Colby (Eds.), *Rhetoric/composition/play through video games: Reshaping theory and practice of writing* (pp. 139–148). New York, NY: Palgrave Macmillan. doi:10.1057/9781137307675.0019

Boler, M. (1999). *Feeling power: Emotions and education.* New York, NY: Routledge.

Bolter, J. D., & Grusin, R. (2000). *Remediation: Understanding new media.* Cambridge, MA: MIT Press.

Boone, G. W. (2008). *A Burkean analysis of World of Warcraft: Identity work in a virtual environment.* (Master's thesis). Retrieved from ProQuest Dissertations and Theses. (AAT 1454169) Berkeley, CA: University of California Press.

Booth, W. (1974). *Modern dogma and the rhetoric of assent.* Chicago, IL: University of Chicago Press.

Booth, W. (1983). *The rhetoric of fiction.* Chicago, IL: University of Chicago Press. doi:10.7208/chicago/9780226065595.001.0001

Booth, W. C. (1974). *The rhetoric of irony.* Chicago, IL: University of Chicago Press.

Borgmann, A. (2000). *Holding on to reality: The nature of information at the turn of the millennium.* Chicago, IL: University of Chicago Press.

Bostock, D. (2006). Space, time, matter, and form: Essays on Aristotle's Physics (Oxford Aristotle Series). J. Annas and L. Judson (Eds.). New York: Oxford.

Boud, D. (1995). *Enhancing learning through self-assessment.* London: Kogan Page.

Bourdieu, P. (1991). *Language & symbolic power.* Cambridge, MA: Harvard University Press.

Bourdieu, P., & Passeron, J. C. (2000). *Reproduction in education, society and culture* (2nd ed.). California, CA: SAGE.

Bourgonjon, J., Rutten, K., Soetaert, R., & Valcke, M. (2011). From counter-strike to counter-statement: Using Burke's pentad as a tool for analysing video games. *Digital Creativity, 22*(2), 91–102. doi:10.1080/14626268.2011.578577

Bowie, J. L. (2009). Beyond the universal: The universe of users approach to user-centered design. In S. Miller-Cochran, & R. L. Rodrigo (Eds.), *Rhetorically rethinking usability: Theories, practices and methodologies* (pp. 135–163). Cresskill, NJ: Hampton Press, Inc.

Boyd, d. (2009, April). *Living and learning with social media.* Paper presented at the Penn State Symposium for Teaching and Learning with Technology. State College, PA. Retrieved from http://www.danah.org/papers/talks/PennState2009.html

Bratteteig, T., Morrison, A., Stuedahl, D., & Mortberg, C. (2010). Research practices in digital design. In I. Wagner, T. Bratteteig, & D. Stuedahl (Eds.), *Multi-disciplinary design practices* (pp. 17–54). London: Springer-Verlag.

Braun, M. J. (2008). The political economy of computers and composition: Democracy hope in an era of globalization. In L. Worsham, & G. Olson (Eds.), *Plugged in technology: Rhetoric and culture in a posthuman age* (pp. 95–124). Cresskill, NJ: Hampton Press, Inc.

Bredemeier, K., & Simons, D. (2012). Working memory and inattentional blindness. *Psychonomic Bulletin & Review*, *19*, 239–244. doi:10.3758/s13423-011-0204-8 PMID:22222359

Brodkey, L. (1987). *Academic writing as social practice.* Philadelphia, PA: Temple University Press.

Brooke, C. G. (2009). *Lingua fracta: Toward a rhetoric of new media.* Cresskill, NJ: Hampton Press, Inc.

Brooks, J., & Normore, A. (2010). Educational leadership and globalization: Literacy for a glocal perspective. *Educational Policy*, *24*(1), 52–82. doi:10.1177/0895904809354070

Brown, A. L., Ash, D., Rutherford, M., Nakagawa, K., Gordon, A., & Campione, J. C. (1993). Distributed expertise in the classroom. In G. Salomon (Ed.), *Distributed cognitions: Psychological and education considerations* (pp. 188–228). Cambridge, UK: Cambridge University Press.

Bruffee, K. A. (1986). Social construction, language, and the authority of knowledge: A bibliographical essay. *College English*, *48*(8), 773–790. doi:10.2307/376723

Brummett, B. (1979). Three meanings of epistemic rhetoric. In *Proceedings of Speech Communication Association Annual Convention* (pp. 1-9). San Antonio, TX.

Brummett, B. (1989). Perfection and the bomb: Nuclear weapons, teleology, and motives. *The Journal of Communication*, *39*(1), 85–95. doi:10.1111/j.1460-2466.1989.tb01021.x

Buchanan, R. (1995). Rhetoric, humanism and design. In R. Buchanan, & V. Margolin (Eds.), *Discovering design: Explorations in design studies* (pp. 26–66). Chicago, IL: The University of Chicago Press.

Buchanan, R., & Margolin, V. (1995). Introduction. In R. Buchanan, & V. Margolin (Eds.), *Discovering design: Explorations in design studies* (pp. ix–xxvi). Chicago, IL: The University of Chicago Press.

Buckingham, D. (1993). *Children talking television: The making of television literacy.* London, UK: Falmer Press.

Buckingham, D. (2003). *Media education: Literacy, learning and contemporary culture.* Cambridge, MA: Polity Press.

Buell, L. (2001). *Writing for an endangered world.* Cambridge, MA: Harvard University Press.

Burgelman, J. C. (2000). Traveling with communication technologies in space, time, and everyday life: An exploration of their impact. *First Monday*, *5*(3). doi:10.5210/fm.v5i3.733

Burke, K. (1966). *Language as symbolic action: Essays on life, literature, and method.*

Burke, K. (1966, 2001). Language as symbolic action. In P. Bizzell & B. Herzberg (Eds.). The rhetorical tradition (2nd ed.) (pp. 1340-47). Boston, MA: Bedford/ St. Martin's

Burke, K. (1969a). A grammar of motives (California Ed.). Berkeley, CA: University of California Press.

Burke, K. (1969b). A rhetoric of motives (California Ed.). Berkeley, CA: University of California Press.

Burke, A., & Rowsell, J. (2009). Reading by design: Two case studies of digital reading practices. *Journal of Adolescent & Adult Literacy*, *53*(2), 106–118. doi:10.1598/JAAL.53.2.2

Burke, K. (1941). *The philosophy of literary form: Studies in symbolic action.* Baton Rouge, LA: Louisiana State University Press.

Burke, K. (1951). Rhetoric - old and new. *The Journal of General Education*, *5*(3), 202–209.

Burke, K. (1954). *Permanence and change: An anatomy of purpose.* Berkeley, CA: The University of California Press.

Burke, K. (1961). *The rhetoric of religion: Studies in logology.* Boston, MA: Beacon.

Burke, K. (1969). *A grammar of motives.* Berkeley, CA: University of California Press.

Burke, K. (1997). *A rhetoric of motives.* Berkeley, CA: University of California Press.

Burke, P. (2009). *Cultural hybridity.* Cambridge, UK: Polity Press.

Burn, A., & Durrant, C. (2008). Media education: A background. In A. Burn, & C. Durrant (Eds.), *Media teaching: Language, audience and production* (pp. 11–25). Adelaide, Australia: Wakefield Press.

Burns, M., & Blessener, E. (2013, January 22). Commenters, we want you back. *TechCrunch.com*. Retrieved January 22, 2013, from http://techcrunch.com

Burton, G. O. (n. d.). Figures of time. In *Silva Rhetoricae*. Retrieved from http://rhetoric.byu.edu

Byram, M. (1997). *Teaching and assessing intercultural communicative competence*. Clevedon, UK: Multilingual Matters Ltd.

Caillois, R. (2001). *Man, play, and games* (M. Barash, Trans.). Chicago, IL: University of Illinois Press.

Cairo, J., Knobel, M., Lankshear, C., & Leu, D. (Eds.). (2008). *Handbook of research on new literacies*. New York, NY: Peter Lang.

Caldwell, W. B., IV. (2010, 13 Sep.). Literacy as a matter of life and death. *The Huffington Post*. Retrieved 6 Feb. 2011 from http://www.huffingtonpost.com/lt-gen-william-b-caldwell-iv/post_838_b_714906.html

Caldwell, W. B. IV, & Finney, N. K. (2011, January-February). Security, capacity, and literacy. *Military Review*, 23–27.

Callaway, E. (2009, 6 Nov). How your brain sees virtual you. *New Scientist*. Retrieved from http://www.newscientist.com/article/dn18117-how-your-brain-sees-virtual-you.html#.Uj9bARZLFAs

Canagarajah, A. S. (2002). *Critical academic writing and multilingual students*. Ann Arbor, MI: University of Michigan Press.

Canagarajah, A. S. (2004). Multilingual writers and the struggle for voice: Assessing some approaches. In A. Blackledge, & A. Pavlenko (Eds.), *Negotiation of identities in multilingual contexts* (pp. 266–289). Clevedon, UK: Multilingual Matters Ltd.

Canagarajah, A. S. (2006). The place of world Englishes in composition: Pluralization continued. *College Composition and Communication, 57*(4), 586–619.

Canagarajah, S. A. (1999). *Resisting linguistic imperialism in English teaching*. Oxford, UK: Oxford University Press.

Carnegie, T. A. M. (2009). Interface as exordium: The rhetoric of interactivity. *Computers and Composition, 26*, 164–173. doi:10.1016/j.compcom.2009.05.005

Carpenter, R. (2009). Boundary negotiations: Electronic environments as interface. *Computers and Composition, 26*, 138–148. doi:10.1016/j.compcom.2009.05.001

Carrington, V., & Robinson, M. (Eds.). (2009). *Digital literacies: Social learning and classroom practices*. California: UKLA.

Carr, N. (2010). *The shallows: What the Internet is doing to our brains*. New York: Norton.

Carter, M. (1988). Stasis and kairos: Principles of social construction in classical rhetoric. *Rhetoric Review, 7*(1), 97–112. doi:10.1080/07350198809388842

Castells, M. (2000). The rise of the networked society (The information age: Economy, society, and culture, Vol. 1). Oxford, UK: Blackwell Publishers.

Castells, M. (2005). The network society: From knowledge to policy. In M. Castells, & G. Cardoso (Eds.), *The network society: From knowledge to policy* (pp. 3–21). Washington, DC: John Hopkins Centre for Transatlantic Relations.

Castells, M. (2008). The new public sphere: Global civil society, communication networks, and global governance. *The Annals of the American Academy of Political and Social Science, 616*, 78–93. doi:10.1177/0002716207311877

Castells, M., Fernández-Ardèvol, M., Qiu, J. L., & Sey, A. (2009). *Mobile communication and society: A global perspective*. Cambridge: MIT Press.

CEFcult. (n. d.). Retrieved from http://www.cefcult.eu

Chabert, J.-L. (Ed.). (1999). *A history of algorithms: From the pebble to the microchip* Weeks, C., Trans.). New York: Springer. doi:10.1007/978-3-642-18192-4

Charland, M. (1987). Constitutive rhetoric: The case of the *Peuple Quebecois*. *The Quarterly Journal of Speech, 73*(2), 133–150. doi:10.1080/00335638709383799

Chatman, S. (1980). *Story and discourse: Narrative structure in fiction and film*. Ithaca, N.Y: Cornell University Press.

Chayes, S. (2007). *The punishment of virtue: Inside Afghanistan after the Taliban*. New York: Penguin.

Cheal, J. (2011). What is the opposite of meta? *Acuity, 2*, 153–161.

Chertoff, D. B. et al. (2008). Improving presence theory through experiential design. *Presence (Cambridge, Mass.)*, *17*(4), 405–413. doi:10.1162/pres.17.4.405

Christenson, C. M. (1997). *The innovator's dilemma: When new technologies can cause great firms to fail.* Boston: Harvard Business School Press.

Chun, W. H. K. (2009, April). *Where's the beef: Cyworld versus Faceboo.* Paper presented at the Communications Department Colloquium. Amherst, MA.

Cicero, M. T. (2001). *On the ideal orator* (J. M. May, & J. Wisse, Trans.). New York: Oxford University Press.

Clark, A. (2003). *Natural-born cyborgs – Minds, technologies, and the future of human intelligence.* New York: Oxford University Press.

Clark, H. H., & Brennan, S. (1991). Grounding in communication. In L. Resnick, J. Levine, & S. Teasley (Eds.), *Perspectives on socially shared cognition* (pp. 127–149). Washington, DC: American Psychological Association. doi:10.1037/10096-006

Cohen, D. (2006). *Globalization and its enemies* (J. B. Becker, Trans.). Cambridge, MA: MIT Press.

Cohen, J. (2006). Audience identification with media characters. In J. Bryant, & P. Vorderer (Eds.), *Psychology of entertainment* (pp. 151–181). Mahwah, NJ: Lawrence Erlbaum.

Colby, R. S. (2013). Gender and gaming in a first-year writing class. In R. Colby, M. S. S. Johnson, & R. S. Colby (Eds.), *Rhetoric/composition/play through video games: Reshaping theory and practice of writing* (pp. 123–138). New York, NY: Palgrave Macmillan. doi:10.1057/9781137307675.0017

Coldewey, D. (2012, August 8). Romney twitter account gets upsurge in fake followers, but from where? *NBCnews.com.* Retrieved January 15, 2013, from http://nbcnews.com.

Cole, M., & Engeström, Y. (1991). A cultural-historical approach to distributed cognition. In G. Salomon (Ed.), *Distributed Cognition* (pp. 1–47). Cambridge: Cambridge University Press.

Collins, D. (2011). *Is Twitter a waste of time?* Problogger, 2 June 2011. Retrieved from http://www.problogger.net/archives/2011/06/02/is-twitter-a-waste-of-time/

Columbia, SC: University of South Carolina Press.

Comninos, A. (2011). *E-revolutions and cyber crackdowns: User-generated content and social networking in protests in MENA and beyond.* (Thematic reports of the Global Information Society Watch). Retrieved from http://www.giswatch.org/sites/default/files/gisw_-_e-revolutions_and_cyber_crackdowns_0.pdf

Conley, M. (2010). *Toward a rhetoric of insult.* Chicago, IL: University of Chicago Press. doi:10.7208/chicago/9780226114798.001.0001

Connor, U. (1996). *Contrastive rhetoric.* Cambridge, MA: Cambridge University Press. doi:10.1017/CBO9781139524599

Connor, U. (2008). Mapping multidimential aspects of research. In U. Connor, E. Nagelhout, & W. V. Rozycki (Eds.), *Contrastive rhetoric: Reaching to intercultural rhetoric.* Philadelphia, PA: John Benjamins B.V. doi:10.1075/pbns.169

Conway, S. (2010). A circular wall? Reformulating the fourth wall for videogames. *Journal of Gaming and Virtual Worlds*, *2*(2), 145–155. doi:10.1386/jgvw.2.2.145_1

Cooley, M. (2000). Human centered design. In R. Jacobson (Ed.), *Information design.* Cambridge, MA: MIT Press.

Cooper, M. M. (2007). Learning digital literacies. In G. E. Hawisher, & S. Selfe (Eds.), *Multimodal composition: Resource for teachers, new dimensions in computer and composition* (pp. 181–186). Cresskill, NJ: Hampton Press, Inc.

Cope, B., & Kalantzis, M. (2000). Designs for social futures. In B. Cope, & M. Kalantzis (Eds.), *Multiliteracies: Literacy learning and the design of social futures* (pp. 203–234). New York, NY: Routledge.

Cope, B., & Kalantzis, M. (2000). *Multiliteracies: Literacy learning and the design of social futures.* London, UK: Routledge.

Cope, B., & Kalantzis, M. (2000). Multiliteracies: The beginnings of an idea. In B. Cope, & M. Kalantzis (Eds.), *Multiliteracies: Literacy learning and the design of social futures*. London: Routledge.

Cress, C. M., Collier, P. J., & Reitenauer, V. L. et al. (2005). *Learning through serving: A student guidebook for service-learning across the disciplines*. Sterling, VA: Stylus Publishing.

Crogan, P. (2002). Blade runners: Speculations on narrative and interactivity. *The South Atlantic Quarterly, 101*(3), 639–657. doi:10.1215/00382876-101-3-639

Cross, N. (1995). Discovering design ability. In R. Buchanan, & V. Margolin (Eds.), *Discovering design: Explorations in design studies* (pp. 105–121). Chicago, IL: The University of Chicago Press.

Crusius, T. W. (1986). A case for Kenneth Burke's dialectic and rhetoric. *Philosophy and Rhetoric, 19*(1), 23–37.

Csikszentmihalyi, M. (1990). *Flow: The psychology of optimal experience*. New York, NY: Harper & Row.

Cultack, G. (2013, February 12). Xbox 720 may require Kinect to be plugged in, switched on and watching you. *Gizmodo UK*. Retrieved February 14, 2013 from http://www.gizmodo.co.uk/2013/02/xbox-720-may-require-kinect-to-be-plugged-in-switched-on-and-watching-you/

Cummings, R. (2006). Coding with power: Toward a rhetoric of computer coding and composition. *Computers and Composition, 23*, 430–443. doi:10.1016/j.compcom.2006.08.002

Cuonzo, M. A. (2010). Gossip and the evolution of facebook. In D. E. Wittkower (Ed.), *Facebook and philosophy* (pp. 173–179). Chicago, IL: Open Court.

Daft, R. L., & Lengel, R. H. (1986). Organizational information requirements, media richness and structural design. *Management Science, 32*(5), 554–571. doi:10.1287/mnsc.32.5.554

Damasio, A. R. (1994). *Descartes' error: Emotion, reason, and the human brain*. New York: Putnam.

Daniell, B. (1999). Narratives of literacy: Connecting composition to culture. *College Composition and Communication, 50*(3), 393–410. doi:10.2307/358858

Davidson, C. N. (2012, January 2). A fourth 'R' for 21st century literacy. *The Washington Post*, sec. Post Local.

Dawkins, R. (2006). *The selfish gene* (3rd ed.). New York, NY: Oxford University Press.

Day, D. G. (1960). Persuasion and the concept of identification. *The Quarterly Journal of Speech, 46*(3), 270–273. doi:10.1080/00335636009382421

De Certeau, M. (1984). *The practice of everyday life* (S. Rendall, Trans.). Los Angeles, CA: University of California Press.

de Vries, K. (2009). Identity in a world of ambient intelligence. In Y. Abbas, & F. Dervin (Eds.), *Digital technologies of the self* (pp. 15–36). Newcastle, UK: Cambridge Scholars.

Deen, P. D. (2011). Interactivity, inhabitation and pragmatist aesthetics. *Game Studies: The International Journal of Computer Game Research, 11*(2). Retrieved from http://gamestudies.org/1102/articles/deen

Deleuze, G. (1992). Postscript on the societies of control. *October, 59*, 3-7.

Dennis, A., & Valacich, J. (1999). Rethinking media richness: Towards a theory of media synchronicity. In R. Sprague (Ed.), *Proceedings of the 32nd Hawaii International Conference on Systems Science* (pp. 48-57). Los Alamitos, CA: IEEE Computer Society.

Derrida, J. (1967). Structure, sign and play in the human sciences. In J. Derrida (Ed.), *Writing and difference* (pp. 278–293, 339). (A. Bass, Trans.). Chicago: University of Chicago Press.

Dervin, B. (2000). Chaos, order, and sense-making: A proposed theory for information design. In R. Jacobson (Ed.), *Information design*. Cambridge, MA: MIT Press.

Dery, M. (1994). *Flame wars: The discourse of cyberculture*. Durham, NC: Duke University Press.

DeSanctis, G., & Poole, M. S. (1994). Capturing the complexity in advanced technology use: Adaptive structuration theory. *Organization Science, 5*(2), 121–147. doi:10.1287/orsc.5.2.121

Dibbel, J. (1993, Dec. 23). A rape in cyberspace. *The Village Voice*.

Dibbell, J. (1998). *My tiny life: Crime and passion in a virtual world*. New York: Holt.

Dibble, J. (1993). A rape in cyberspace: How an evil clown, a Haitian trickster spirit, two wizards, and a cast of dozens turned a database into a society. *The Village Voice*. Retrieved February 4, 2013, from http://juliandibbell.com.

Diener, E. (1980). Deindividuation: The absence of self-awareness and self-regulation in group members. In P. Paulus (Ed.), *The Psychology of Group Influence* (pp. 209–242). Hillsdale, NJ: Erlbaum.

Dilger, B., & Rice, J. (Eds.). (2010). *From A to <A>: Keywords of markup*. Minneapolis, MN: University of Minnesota Press.

Doan, S., Vo, B.-K. H., & Collier, N. (2011). An analysis of Twitter messages in the 2011 Tohoku earthquake. In *Proceedings of the eHealth 2011 Conference*, (pp. 58–66).

Doecke, B., & McCleneghan, D. (1998). Reconceptualising experience: Growth pedagogy and youth culture. In W. Sawyer, K. Watson, & E. Gold (Eds.), *Re-viewing English* (pp. 46–57). Sydney, Australia: Clair Press.

Donath, J. (1999). Identity and deception in the virtual community. In M. Smith and P. Kollack (Eds.), *Communities in cyberspace*. London: Routledge. Retrieved June 14, 2013, from http://smg.media.mit.edu/people/Judith/Identity/IdentityDeception.html

Dourish, P. (2001). *Where the action is: The foundations of embodied interaction*. Cambridge, MA: MIT Press.

Dowling, D. (1987). *Fictions of nuclear disaster*. Iowa City, IA: University of Iowa Press.

Dyson, G. (2012). *Turing's cathedral*. New York: Vintage.

eBuzzing.com. Retrieved January 16, 2013, from http://social.ebuzzing.co.uk/advertisers.

Economist.com. (n. d.). 'From literacy to digiracy: Will reading and writing remain important?' Retrieved May 18, 2008, from http://www.economist.com/science/PrinterFriendly.cfm?story_id=11392128

Edingo, D. (2013). Re-evaluation of Nepali media, social networking spaces, and democratic practices in media. In M. Limbu, & B. Gurung (Eds.), *Emerging pedagogies in the networked knowledge society: Practices integrating social media and globalization*. Hershey, PA: IGI Global. doi:10.4018/978-1-4666-4757-2.ch015

Ellul, J. (1964). *The technological society*. New York, NY: Vintage Books.

Elsaesser, T., & Hagener, M. (2010). *Film theory: An introduction through the senses*. New York: Routledge.

Engeström, Y., Miettinen, R., Punamäki-Gitai, R. L., & International Congress for Research on Activity Theory. (1999). *Perspectives on activity theory*. Cambridge, UK: Cambridge University Press.

Engeström, Y. (1999). Activity theory and individual and social transformation. In Y. Engeström, R. Miettinen, & R. Punamäki (Eds.), *Perspectives on activity theory* (pp. 19–38). Cambridge, UK: Cambridge University Press. doi:10.1017/CBO9780511812774.003

Engeström, Y. (2000). Can people learn to master their future? *Journal of the Learning Sciences*, 9(4), 525–534. doi:10.1207/S15327809JLS0904_8

Engeström, Y., Miettinen, R., & Punamäki, R. (1999). *Perspectives on activity theory*. Cambridge, UK: Cambridge University Press. doi:10.1017/CBO9780511812774

Enos, R. L. (2002). Inventional constraints on the technographers of ancient Athens. In P. Sipiora, & J. S. Baumlin (Eds.), *Rhetoric and kairos: Essays in history, theory, and praxis* (pp. 77–88). Albany, NY: State University of New York Press.

Eraut, M. (2004). Learning to change and/or changing to learn. *Learning in Health and Social Care*, 3(3), 111–117. doi:10.1111/j.1473-6861.2004.00073.x

Ertz, S. (2012, August 26). Sony patents an interactive commercial concept. *The Upstream*. Retrieved February 10, 2013 from http://www.plughitzlive.com/theupstream/1925-sony-patents-an-interactive-commercial-concept.html.

Evans, V. (2004). *The structure of time: Language, meaning, and temporal cognition.* Amsterdam, The Netherlands: John Benjamins. doi:10.1075/hcp.12

Faculty Focus. (2010). *Twitter in higher education 2010: Usage habits and trends of today's college faculty.* Retrieved from http://www.facultyfocus.com/free-reports/twitter-in-higher-education-2010-usage-habits-and-trends-of-todays-college-faculty/

Faigley, L. (1985). Nonacademic writing: The social perspective. In L. Odell, & D. Goswami (Eds.), *Writing in nonacademic settings* (pp. 231–248). New York: Guilford.

Faigley, L. (1986). Competing theories of process: A critique and proposal. *College English, 48,* 527–541. doi:10.2307/376707

Fairclough, N. (1995). *Critical discourse analysis.* Boston, MA: Addison Wesley.

Fairclough, N. (2006). *Language and globalization.* New York, NY: Routledge.

Farrell, T. (2008). The weight of rhetoric: Studies in cultural delirium. *Philosophy and Rhetoric, 41*(4), 467–487. doi:10.1353/par.0.0018

Feenberg, A. (1991). Critical theory of technology. New York, NY: Oxford.

Feenberg, A. (1991). *Critical theory of technology.* New York: Oxford University Press.

Feenberg, A. (2010). *Between reason and experience: Essays in technology and modernity.* Cambridge, MA: The MIT Press.

Fidler, R. (1997). *Mediamorphosis: Understanding new media.* Newbury Park, CA: Sage.

Fine, G. A. (2002). *Shared fantasy: Role playing games as social worlds.* Chicago, IL: University of Chicago Press.

Fitzsimmons-Hunter, P., & Moran, C. (1998). Writing teachers, schools, access, and change. In T. Taylor, & I. Ward (Eds.), *Literacy theory in the age of the Internet* (pp. 158–170). New York: Columbia University Press.

Fleckenstein, K. S. (2003). *Embodied literacies: Image-word and a poetics of teaching.* Carbondale, IL: Southern Illinois University Press.

Flynn, C. J. (2003). *Swastikas to be banned by Microsoft?* Retrieved from http://www.mail-archive.com/unicode@unicode.org/msg20776.html

Foley, B. E. (1994). The development of literacy in individuals with severe congenital speech and motor impairments. In K. G. Butler (Ed.), *Severe communication disorders: Intervention strategies* (pp. 183–199). Gaithersburg, MD: Aspen.

Foss, S. K., Foss, K. A., & Trapp, R. (2002). *Contemporary perspectives on rhetoric* (3rd ed.). Prospect Heights, IL: Waveland Press.

Fountain, H. (2012, October 26). Yes, driverless cars know the way to San Jose. *The New York Times.*

Frank, M., & Gilovich, T. (1988). The dark side of self and social perception: Black uniforms and aggression in professional sports. *Journal of Personality and Social Psychology, 54,* 74–85. doi:10.1037/0022-3514.54.1.74 PMID:3346809

Franzen, C. (2013). Mozilla, Reddit, 4Chan join coalition of 86 groups asking Congress to end NSA surveillance. *The Verge.* Retrieved June 11, 2013, from http://www.theverge.com/2013/6/11/4418794/stopwatchingus-internet-orgs-ask-congress-to-stop-surveillance

Freebody, P., & Luke, A. (1990). Literacies programs: Debates and demands in cultural context. *Prospect: Australian Journal of TESOL, 5*(7), 7–16.

Friedman, T. (2007). *The world is flat 3.0: A brief history of the twenty-first century.* New York: Farrar, Straus and Giroux.

Fulk, J., Steinfield, C. W., Schmitz, J., & Power, J. G. (1987). A social information processing model of media use in organizations. *Communication Research, 14*(5), 529–552. doi:10.1177/009365087014005005

Galloway, A. (2004). *Protocol: How control exists after decentralization.* Cambridge, MA: MIT Press.

Galloway, A. R. (2012). *The interface effect.* Cambridge, UK, Malden, MA: Polity Press.

Gaonkar, D. P. (1997). The idea of rhetoric in the rhetoric of science. In A. G. Gross, & W. M. Keith (Eds.), *Rhetorical hermeneutics: Invention and interpretation in the age of science* (pp. 25–88). Albany, NY: SUNY Press.

Garber, M. (2012, January 31). Be better at Twitter: The definitive data-driven guide. *The Atlantic*. Retrieved from http://www.theatlantic.com/technology/archive/2012/01/be-better-at-twitter-the-definitive-data-driven-guide/252273/

Garrelts, N. (2013). The pencil-shaped joystick: A synoptic history of text in digital games. In R. Colby, M. S. S. Johnson, & R. S. Colby (Eds.), *Rhetoric/composition/play through video games: Reshaping theory and practice of writing* (pp. 25–32). New York, NY: Palgrave Macmillan. doi:10.1057/9781137307675.0009

Gasperini, J. (2000). Structural ambiguity: An emerging interactive aesthetic. In R. Jacobson (Ed.), *Information design*. Cambridge, MA: MIT Press.

Gazale, M. (1999). *Gnomon: From pharaohs to fractals*. Princeton: Princeton University Press.

Gee, J. P. (2003). *What video games have to teach us about learning and literacy*. New York: Palgrave Macmillan.

Geisler, C., & Munger, R. (2002). Temporal analysis: A primer exemplified by a case from prehospital care. In E. Barton, & G. Stygall (Eds.), *Discourse studies in composition* (pp. 283–304). Cresskill, NJ: Hampton Press.

Gellhorn, M. (1988). *The view from the ground*. New York: Atlantic Monthly Press.

George, D. (2002). From analysis to design: Visual communication in the teaching of writing. *College Composition and Communication*, *54*(1), 11–39. doi:10.2307/1512100

Gibson-Graham, J. K. (2006). *A postcapitalist politics*. Minneapolis, MN: University of Minnesota Press.

Giddens, A. (1984). *The constitution of society: Outline of the theory of structuration*. Berkeley, CA: University of California Press.

Gillen, J., & Barton, D. (2010). *Digital literacies* (A research briefing by the technology enhanced learning phase of the teaching and learning research programme). Engineering and Physical Sciences Research Council. Retrieved from http://eprints.lancs.ac.uk/33471/1/DigitalLiteracies.pdf

Gilter, P. (1997). *Digital literacy*. New York, NY: John Wiley & Sons.

Giroux, H. (1991). *Border crossings: Cultural workers and the politics of education*. New York, NY: Routledge.

Gladwell, M. (2010). Small change: Why the revolution will not be tweeted. *New Yorker (New York, N.Y.)*, (October): 4. Retrieved from http://www.newyorker.com/reporting/2010/10/04/101004fa_fact_gladwell?currentPage=al

Gleick, J. (2012, August 4). Auto crrect ths! *The New York Times*.

Gleick, J. (1999). *Faster: The acceleration of just about everything*. New York, NY: Vintage Books.

Goffman, E. (1959). *The Presentation of self in everyday life*. New York: Doubleday.

Goffman, E. (1967). *Interaction ritual*. New York: Pantheon.

Google Flu Trends. (n.d.). *Explore flu trends - United states*. Retrieved February 18, 2013 from http://www.google.org/flutrends/us/#US

Gorn, G. J., Chattopadhyay, A., Sengupta, J., & Tripathi, S. (2004). Waiting for the Web: How screen color affects time perception. *JMR, Journal of Marketing Research*, *41*(2), 215–225. doi:10.1509/jmkr.41.2.215.28668

Gottschalk, K. K. (2002). Contact zones: Composition's content in the university. In J. M. Wolf (Ed.), *Professing in the contact zone: Bringing theory and practice together* (pp. 58–78). Urbana, IL: NCTE.

Grabill, J. T. (2003). On divides and interfaces: Access, class, and computers. *Computers and Composition*, *20*, 455–472. doi:10.1016/j.compcom.2003.08.017

Graupner, M., Nickoson-Massey, L., & Blair, K. (2009). Remediating knowledge-making spaces in the graduate curriculum: Developing and sustaining multimodal teaching and research. *Computers and Composition*, *26*, 13–23. doi:10.1016/j.compcom.2008.11.005

Green, B. (1988). Subject-specific literacy and school learning: A focus on writing. *Australian Journal of Education*, *32*(2), 156–179. doi:10.1177/000494418803200203

Green, B. (2001). 'English teaching, 'literacy' and the post-age. In C. Durrant, & C. Beavis (Eds.), *P(ICT)ures of English: Teachers, learners and technology*. South Australia: AATE.

Green, B., & Bigum, C. (1993). Aliens in the classroom. *Australian Journal of Education, 37*(2), 119–134. doi:10.1177/000494419303700202

Greenhow, C., Robelia, B., & Hughes, J. E. (2009). Learning, teaching, and scholarship in a digital age: Web 2.0 and classroom research: What path should we take now? *Educational Researcher, 38*(4), 246–259. doi:10.3102/0013189X09336671

Gregory, S., & Losh, E. (2012). Remixing human rights: Rethinking civic expression, representation and personal security in online video. *First Monday, 17*(8). doi:10.5210/fm.v17i8.4104

Greitemeyer, T., Osswald, S., & Brauer, M. (2010). Playing prosocial video games increases empathy and decreases schadenfreude. *Emotion (Washington, D.C.), 10*, 796–802. doi:10.1037/a0020194 PMID:21171755

Gurak, L. (2001). *Cyberliteracy: Navigating the internet with awareness*. New Haven, CT: Yale University Press.

Gurak, L., & Lannon, J. (2007). *A concise guide to technical communication* (3rd ed.). New York, NY: Pearson.

Habermas, J. (1981). *Theory of communicative action volume one: Reason and the rationalization of society*. Cambridge, MA: MIT Press.

Hall, S. (1986). On postmodernism and articulation: An interview with Stuart Hall. L. Grossberg (Ed.). Journal of Communication Inquiry, 10(2) 45-60.

Handa, C. (2004). *Visual rhetoric in a digital world*. Boston, MA: Bedford/ St. Martin's.

Han, J., Kamber, M., & Pei, J. (2012). *Data mining concepts and techniques* (3rd ed.). Waltham, MA: Morgan Kaufmann Publishers.

Hanna, B. E., & Nooy, J. D. (2009). *Learning language and culture via public Internet discussion forums*. Great Britain, UK: Palgrave MacMillan. doi:10.1057/9780230235823

Haraway, D. J. (1990). *Simians, cyborgs, and women: The reinvention of nature*. New York, NY: Routledge.

Harding, S. (2006). *Science and social inequality: Feminist and postcolonial issues*. Champaign, IL: University of Illinois Press.

Hardt, M., & Negri, A. (2000). *Empire*. Cambridge, MA: Harvard University Press.

Hardy, M. (2002). Life beyond the screen: Embodiment and identity through the Internet. *The Sociological Review, 50*(4), 570–585. doi:10.1111/1467-954X.00399

Harman, G. (2002). *Tool-being: Heidegger and the metaphysics of objects*. IL, Peru: Open Court Publishing.

Harp, D., Bachmann, I., & Guo, L. (2012). The whole online world is watching: Profiling social networking sites and activities in China, Latin America, and the United States. *International Journal of Communication, 6*, 298–321.

Harp, S. F., & Mayer, R. E. (1998). How seductive details do their damage: A theory of cognitive interest in science learning. *Journal of Educational Psychology, 90*(3), 414–434. doi:10.1037/0022-0663.90.3.414

Harrison, S., & Dourish, P. (1996). Re-place-ing space: The roles of place and space in collaborative systems. In *Proceedings of the 1996 ACM conference on Computer Supported Cooperative Work* (pp.67-76). Boston, MA: ACM Press.

Hart-Davidson, B., & Krause, S. D. (2004). Re: The future of computers and writing: A multivocal textumentary. *Computers and Composition, 21*, 147–160. doi:10.1016/j.compcom.2003.08.008

Hartmann, T., Toz, E., & Brandon, M. (2010). Just a game? Unjustified virtual violence produces guilt in empathetic players. *Media Psychology, 13*(4), 339–363. doi:10.1080/15213269.2010.524912

Harvey, D. (2007). *A brief history of neoliberalism*. New York: Oxford University Press.

Hauser, G. (1999). *Vernacular voices: The rhetoric of publics and public spheres*.

Havelock, E. (1963). *Preface to Plato*. Cambridge, MA: Harvard University Press.

Hawisher, G. E., & Selfe, C. L. (2000). Introduction: Testing the claims. In G. E. Hawisher, & C. L. Selfe (Eds.), *Global literacies and the World-Wide Web* (pp. 1–18). New York, NY: Routledge.

Hawisher, G., & Selfe, C. (2000). *Global literacies and the world-wide web*. London: Routledge.

Hawisher, G., Selfe, C., Kisa, G., & Ahmed, S. (2010). Globalism and multimodality in a digitized world. *Pedagogy*, *10*(1), 55–68.

Hayes, T. (2011) Finding a place for Falstaff: Language and creativity in the English curriculum. In *AATE Conference Notes December 3-6, Melbourne*. Retrieved January 22, 2012, from http://www.vate.asn.au/aateconference2011/component/content/article/10-about-aate-conference-2011.html

Hayles, N. K. (2005). *My mother was a computer: Digital subjects and literary texts*. Chicago, IL: University of Chicago Press. doi:10.7208/chicago/9780226321493.001.0001

Heidegger, M. (1962). *Being and time*. New York, NY: Harper & Row.

Heidegger, M. (1982). *The question concerning technology, and other essays*. New York: Perennial.

Heise, U. K. (2008). *Sense of place and sense of planet: The environmental imagination of the global*. New York, NY: Oxford University Press. doi:10.1093/acprof:oso/9780195335637.001.0001

Herring, S. C. (2001). Computer-mediated discourse. In D. Schiffrin, D. Tannen, & H. Hamilton (Eds.), *The Handbook of Discourse Analysis* (pp. 612–634). London: Blackwell.

Hess, A. (2012, October 15). Gawker outed Reddit's most notorious troll? Why isn't law enforcement doing the same? *Slate.com*. Retrieved February 16, 2013, from http://www.slate.com/blogs/xx_factor/2012/10/15/reddit_troll_violentacrez_outed_by_gawker_when_will_law_enforcement_catch.html

Hiebert, E. H. (1991). Introduction. In E. H. Hiebert (Ed.), *Literacy for a diverse society: Perspectives, practices, and policies* (pp. 1–6). New York: Teachers College Press.

Hill, C. A., & Mehlenbacher, B. (1998). Transitional generations and World Wide Web reading and writing: Implications of a hypertextual interface for the masses. *TEXT Technology*, *8*(4), 29–47.

Hilligoss, S., & Williams, S. (2007). Composition meets visual communication: New research questions. In H. A. McKee, & D. N. DeVoss (Eds.), *Digital writing research: Technologies, methodologies, and ethical issues* (pp. 229–247). Cresskill, NJ: Hampton Press.

Hiltz, S. R., & Turoff, M. (1978). *The network nation: Human communication via computer*. Reading, MA: Addison-Wesley.

Hines, K. (2012). An in-depth look at the science of Twitter timing. *KISSmetrics: A blog about analytics, marketing and testing*. Retrieved from https://blog.kissmetrics.com/the-science-of-twitter-timing/

Hmelo-Silver, C. E. (2004). Problem-based learning: What and how do students learn? *Educational Psychology Review*, *16*(3), 235–266. doi:10.1023/B:EDPR.0000034022.16470.f3

Hofstede, G. (1980). *Culture's consequences: International differences in work-related values*. Beverly Hills, CA: Sage.

Hofstede, G. (2001). *Culture's consequences: Comparing values, behaviors, institutions and organizations across nations* (2nd ed.). Thousand Oaks, CA: Sage.

Hofstede, G., Hofstede, G. J., & Minkov, M. (2010). *Cultures and organizations: Software of the mind*. New York: McGraw-Hill.

Hollenbaugh, E., & Everett, M. (2013, February). The effects of anonymity on self-disclosure in blogs: An application of the online disinhibition effect. *Journal of Computer-Mediated Communication*. Retrieved February 24, 2013, from http://dx.doi.org/10.1111/jcc4.12008.

Horner, B., Lu, M., Royster, J. J., & Trimbur, J. (2011). Language difference in writing: Toward a translingual approach. *College English*, *73*(1), 303–321.

Howard, T. W. (2004). Who owns electronic texts? In J. Johnson-Eilola, & S. A. Selber (Eds.), *Central works in technical communication* (pp. 397–408). New York, NY: Oxford University Press.

Huizinga, J. (1950). *Homo ludens*. London: Routledge & Kegan Paul.

Hull, G., & Nelson, M. E. (2005). Locating the semiotic power of multimodality. *Written Communication, 22*, 224–161. doi:10.1177/0741088304274170

Humphrey, G. (1924). The psychology of the gestalt. *Journal of Educational Psychology, 15*(7), 401–412. doi:10.1037/h0070207

Huot, B. (2002). Toward a new discourse of assessment for the college writing classroom. *College English, 65*(2), 163–180. doi:10.2307/3250761

Intercultural Skills Develop Program (ISDP). (2013). *Duke University international house*. Accessed February 15, 2013 from http://studentaffairs.duke.edu/ihouse/trainings-and-workshops/intercultural-skills-development-program-isdp.

Interfaith dialogue (The Global Future 2045 Congress). (2012). *YouTube*. Accessed March 10, 2013 from https://www.youtube.com/watch?feature=player_embedded&v=MudSgPnqBFM.

Ironmonger, D. (1999). Counting outputs, capital inputs and caring labor: Estimating gross household product. *Feminist Economics, 2*(3), 37–64. doi:10.1080/135457 09610001707756

Ivanič, R. (1998). *Writing and identity: The discoursal construction of identity in academic writing*. Philadelphia, PA: Benjamins. doi:10.1075/swll.5

Jenkins, H. (2006). *Convergence culture: Where old and new media collide*. New York: New York University Press.

Johnson, B. (2009, January 20). How Boxxy brought the web to its knees. *The Guardian*. Retrieved January 3, 2013, from http://www.guardian.co.uk/technology/blog/2009/jan/20/internet

Johnson, D. R. (2012). Transportation into a story increases empathy, prosocial behavior, and perceptual bias toward fearful expressions. *Personality and Individual Differences, 52*(2), 150–155. http://0-dx.doi.org.lib.utep.edu/10.1016/j.paid.2011.10.005 doi:10.1016/j.paid.2011.10.005

Johnson-Eilola, J. (1997). Living on the surface: Learning in the age of global communication networks. I. Snyder (Ed.), Page to screen: Taking literacy into the electronic era (pp. 185-210). Sydney, Australia: Allen and Unwin.

Johnson-Eilola, J. (2004). The database and the essay: Understanding composition as articulation. In A. F. Wysocki, J. Johnson-Eilola, C. Selfe, & G. Sirc (Eds.), *Writing new media: Theory and applications for expanding the teaching composition* (pp. 199–235). Logan, UT: Utah State University Press.

Johnson-Eilola, J. (2005). *Datacloud: Toward a new theory of online work*. Creskill, NJ: Hampton.

Johnson-Eilola, J., & Selber, S. (1996). After automation: Hypertext and corporate structures. In P. Sullivan, & J. Daughtermann (Eds.), *Electronic literacies in the workplace: Technologies of writing* (pp. 115–141). Urbana, IL: National Council of Teachers of English.

Johnson-Eilola, J., & Selber, S. A. (2004). *Central works in technical communication*. New York, NY: Oxford University Press.

Johnson, M. S. S., & Colby, R. (2013). Ludic snags. In R. Colby, M. S. S. Johnson, & R. S. Colby (Eds.), *Rhetoric/composition/play through video games: Reshaping theory and practice of writing* (pp. 83–98). New York, NY: Palgrave Macmillan. doi:10.1057/9781137307675.0014

Johnson, N. R. (2012). Information infrastructure as rhetoric: Tools for analysis. *Poroi, 8*(1), 1–3. doi:10.13008/2151-2957.1113

Johnson, R., & Downing, L. (1979). Deindividuation and valence of cues: Effects on prosocial and antisocial behavior. *Journal of Personality and Social Psychology, 37*, 1532–1538. doi:10.1037/0022-3514.37.9.1532 PMID:501521

Johnson, S. (1997). *Interface culture: How new technology transforms the way we create & communicate*. New York, NY: Basic Books.

Johnson, S. (2005). *Everything bad is good*. New York: Riverhead Trade.

Jones, J. (2011, December). *Algorithmic rhetoric and search literacy*. Paper presented at the meeting of the Humanities, Arts, Sciences, and Technology Advanced Collaboratory (HASTAC), Ann Arbor, MI.

Jordan, P. (2000). *Designing pleasurable products*. Philadelphia, PA: Taylor & Francis.

Journet, D. (2013). Afterword. In R. Colby, M. S. S. Johnson, & R. S. Colby (Eds.), *Rhetoric/composition/play through video games: Reshaping theory and practice of writing* (pp. 205–206). New York, NY: Palgrave Macmillan. doi:10.1057/9781137307675.0024

Julier, G. (2008). *The culture of design* (2nd ed.). London: Sage.

Jung, J. (2007). Textual mainstreaming and the rhetorics of accommodation. *Rhetoric Review*, *26*(2), 160–178. doi:10.1080/07350190709336707

Juul, J. (2005). *Half-real: Video games between real rules and fictional worlds*. Cambridge, MA: MIT Press.

Kalantzis, M., & Cope, B. (2012) Literacies. Port Melbourne, Australia: Cambridge.

Kaptelinin, V. (1996). Activity theory: Implications for human-computer interaction. In B. Nardi (Ed.), *Context and consciousness: Activity theory and human-computer interaction* (pp. 103–116). Cambridge, MA: MIT Press.

Kaptelinin, V., Kuutti, K., & Bannon, L. (1995). Activity theory: Basic concepts and applications. In *Human-Computer Interaction* (pp. 189–201). Heidelberg, Germany: Springer Berlin. doi:10.1007/3-540-60614-9_14

Kaptelinin, V., & Nardi, B. A. (2006). *Acting with technology: Activity theory and interaction design*. Cambridge, MA: MIT Press.

Kastely, J. L. (1996). Kenneth Burke's comic rejoinder to the cult of empire. *College English*, *58*(3), 307–326. doi:10.2307/378714

Katz, S. B. (1992). The ethic of expediency: Classical rhetoric, technology, and the holocaust. *College English*, *54*(3), 255–275. doi:10.2307/378062

Kelley, J. F. (1984). An iterative design methodology for user-friendly natural language office information applications. *ACM Transactions on Office Information Systems*, *2*(1), 26–41. doi:10.1145/357417.357420

Kellner, D. M. (2002). Technological revolution, multiple literacies, and restructuring of education. In I. Synder (Ed.), *Silicon literacies: Communication, innovation and education in the electronic age* (pp. 152–167). New York, NY: Routlege.

Kellner, D., & Share, J. (2007). Critical media literacy: Crucial choices for a twenty-first century democracy. *Policy Futures in Education*, *5*(1), 59–69. doi:10.2304/pfie.2007.5.1.59

Kelly, A. R., & Kittle Autry, M. (2013). Access, accommodation, and science: Knowledge in an 'open' world. *First Monday*, *18*(6). doi:10.5210/fm.v18i6.4341

Kelly, A. R., & Miller, C. R. (forthcoming). Intersections: Scientific and parascientific communication on the Internet. In A. Gross, & J. Buehl (Eds.), *Science and the Internet: Communicating knowledge in a digital age*. Amityville, NY: Baywood Press.

Kenichiro, I., & Kojima, H. (Producers). Shuyo, M., & Kojima, H. (Directors). (2008). Metal gear solid 4: Guns of the patriots [Videogame]. Japan: Konami.

Kenyon, S. (2008). Internet use and time use: The importance of multitasking. *Time & Society*, *17*(2/3), 283–318. doi:10.1177/0961463X08093426

Khazan, O. (2013, June 12). These charts show how crucial Twitter is for the Turkey protesters. *The Atlantic*. Retrieved from http://www.theatlantic.com/international/archive/2013/06/these-charts-show-how-crucial-twitter-is-for-the-turkey-protesters/276798/

Kilteni, K., Normand, J. M., Sanchez-Vives, M. V., & Slater, M. (2012). Extending body space in immersive virtual reality: A very long arm illusion. *PLoS ONE*, *7*(7), e40867. doi:10.1371/journal.pone.0040867 PMID:22829891

Kimmehea, A. C., & Turnely, M. (2010). Refiguring the interface agent: An exploration of productive tensions in new media composing. In C. E. Ball & J. Kalmbach (eds.), RAW [Reading and Writing] New Media (pp. 257-273). Cresskill, NJ: Hampton Press, Inc.

Kinneavy, J. L. (1986). *Kairos*: A neglected concept in classical rhetoric. In J. D. Moss (Ed.), *Rhetoric and praxis: The contribution of classical rhetoric to practical reasoning* (pp. 79–105). Washington, DC: The Catholic University of America Press.

Kinsella, W. J., Kelly, A. R., & Kittle Autry, M. (2013). Risk, regulation, and rhetorical boundaries: Claims and challenges surrounding a purported nuclear renaissance. *Communication Monographs, 80*(3). doi:10.1080/03637751.2013.788253

Kittle Autry, M., & Kelly, A. R. (2011). A humanistic approach to the study of social media: Combining social network analysis and case study research. In *Proceedings for the 29th ACM International Conference on Design of Communication*. (pp. 257-260). Pisa, Italy: ACM.

Kittler, F. (1999). *Gramophone, film, typewriter*. Palo Alto, CA: Stanford University Press.

Kline, S., Dyer-Witherford, N., & de Peuter, G. (2003). *Digital play: The interaction of technology, culture, and marketing*. Montreal: McGill-Queen's University Press.

Knobel, M., & Lankshear, C. (2007). *A new literacies sampler*. Retrieved April 15, 2012, from http://everydayliteracies.net/files/NewLiteraciesSampler_2007.pdf

Knobel, M., & Lankshear, C. (2008). Introducing TPCK. In American Association of Colleges for Teachers (Ed.), Handbook of technological pedagogical content knowledge (TPCK) of educators (pp. 3-27). New York, NY: Routledge.

Kock, N. (2005). Media richness or media naturalness? The evolution of our biological communication apparatus and its influence on our behavior toward e-communication tools. *IEEE Transactions on Professional Communication, 48*(2), 117–130. doi:10.1109/TPC.2005.849649

Koç, M. (2006). Cultural identity crisis in the age of globalization and technology. *The Turkish Online Journal of Educational Technology, 5*(1), 37–43.

Konami Corporation. (2009, May 14). *FY2009 financial results*. Retrieved from http://www.konami.co.jp/en/ir/ir-data/meeting/2009/0514.pdf

Kreps, D., & Pearson, E. (2009). Community as commodity: Social networking and transnational capitalism. In N. Panteli (Ed.), *Virtual social networks: Mediated, massive, and multilayers sites* (pp. 155–174). Eastbourne, UK: Macmillan.

Kress, G. (1995). *Literacy or literacies: Thoughts on an agenda for the day after tomorrow*. Unpublished paper.

Kress, G. (2010). The profound shift of digital literacies. In *Digital Literacies* (A research briefing by the technology enhanced learning phase of the teaching and learning research programme). Engineering and Physical Sciences Research Council. Retrieved from http://eprints.lancs.ac.uk/33471/1/DigitalLiteracies.pdf

Kress, G. (1997). Visual and verbal modes of representation on electronically mediated communication: the potentials of new forms of text. In I. Snyder (Ed.), *Page to screen: Taking literacy into the electronic era*. Sydney, Australia: Allen and Unwin.

Kress, G. (1999). English at the crossroads: Rethinking curricula of communication in the context of the turn of the visual. In G. Hawisher, & C. Selfe (Eds.), *Passions, pedagogies and 21st century technologies* (pp. 66–88). Logan, UT: Utah State University Press.

Kress, G. (2003). *Literacy in the new media age*. London: Routledge. doi:10.4324/9780203164754

Kress, G., & van Leeuwen, T. (2001). *Multimodal discourse: The modes and media of contemporary communication*. London: Arnold.

Kress, G., & van Leeuwen, T. (2006). *Reading images: The grammar of visual design* (2nd ed.). New York, NY: Routledge.

Kuhn, T. (1996). *The structure of the scientific revolution*. Chicago, IL: University of Chicago Press. doi:10.7208/chicago/9780226458106.001.0001

Kuhn, T. S. (1962). *The structure of scientific revolution*. Chicago, London: University of Chicago.

Kurzweil, R. (2001). The law of accelerating returns. *Kurzwell: Accelerating intelligence*. Retrieved February 24, 2013, from http://www.kurzweilai.net/the-law-of-accelerating-returns.

Landow, G. (1993). *Hypertext 3.0*. Baltimore, MD: Johns Hopkins University Press.

Langer, J. A. (1991). Literacy and schooling: A sociocognitive perspective. In E. H. Hiebert (Ed.), *Literacy for a diverse society: Perspectives, practices, and policies* (pp. 9–27). New York: Teachers College Press.

Lanham, R. A. (1992). Digital rhetoric: Theory, practice and property. In M. C. Tuman (Ed.), *Literacy online: The promise and perils of reading and writing with computers* (pp. 221–243). Pittsburgh, PA: Pittsburgh University Press.

Lanham, R. A. (1993). *The electronic word: Democracy, technology and the arts*. Chicago, IL: University of Chicago Press. doi:10.7208/chicago/9780226469126.001.0001

Lanham, R. A. (2006). *The economics of attention: Style and substance in the age of information*. Chicago, IL: University of Chicago Press.

Lanier, J. (2010). *You are not a gadget: A manifesto*. New York, NY: Alfred A. Knopf.

Lankow, J., Ritchie, J., & Crooks, R. (2012). *Infographics: The power of visual storytelling*. Hoboken, NJ: Wiley & Sons, Inc.

Lankshear, C., & Snyder, I. with Green, B. (2000). Teachers and technoliteracy: Managing literacy, technology and learning in schools. Sydney, Australia: Allen and Unwin.

Lankshear, C. (1997). *Changing literacies*. Buckingham, UK: Open University Press.

Lankshear, C., & Bigum, C. (1999). Literacies and new technologies in school settings. *Pedagogy, Culture & Society, 7*(3), 445–465. doi:10.1080/14681369900200068

Lankshear, C., & Knobel, M. (2006). *New literacies: Everyday practices in classroom learning*. Berkshire, UK: OUP.

Larsson, A. O., & Ågerfalk, P. J. (2013). Snowing, freezing … tweeting? Organizational Twitter use during crisis. *First Monday, 18*(6). Retrieved from http://firstmonday.org/ojs/index.php/fm/article/view/4294/3688 doi:10.5210/fm.v18i6.4294

Latour, B. (1998). *Actor network theory: A few clarifications*. Retrieved from: http://www.nettime.org/Lists-Archives/nettime-l-9801/msg00019.html

Latour, B. (2002). Morality and technology: The end of means. *Theory, Culture & Society, 19*, 247–260. doi:10.1177/026327602761899246

Latour, B. (2005). *Reassembling the social: An introduction to actor-network-theory*. Oxford, UK: Oxford UP.

Latour, B., & Woolgar, S. (1986). *Laboratory life: The construction of scientific facts*. Princeton, NJ: Princeton University Press.

Laurel, B. (1990). Introduction: What's an interface? In B. Laurel (Ed.), *The art of human computer interface design* (pp. xi–xiii). Boston: Addison-Wesley.

Laurel, B. (2003). The six elements and causal relations among them. In N. Wardrip Fruin, & N. Montfort (Eds.), *The new media reader* (pp. 564–571). Cambridge, MA: MIT Press.

Lawn, R. (2012, September 6). Tu and Twitter: Is it the end for 'vous' in French? *BBC News Magazine*. Retrieved from http://www.bbc.co.uk/news/magazine-19499771

Lea, M., O'Shea, T., Fung, P., & Spears, R. (1992). Flaming in computer-mediated communication: Observations, explanations, implications. In M. Lea (Ed.), *Contexts of computer-mediated communication* (pp. 30–65). Hempel Hempstead, UK: Harvester Wheatsheaf.

Leccardi, C. (2003). Resisting acceleration society. *Constellations (Oxford, England), 10*(1), 34–41. doi:10.1111/1467-8675.00310

Lee, E. (2007). Deindividuation effects on group polarization in computer-mediated communication: The role of group identification, public-self-awareness, and perceived argument quality. *The Journal of Communication, 57*(2), 385–403. doi:10.1111/j.1460-2466.2007.00348.x

Lee, H. (2008). Learner agency and identity in second language writing. *International Journal of Applied Linguistics, 156*, 109–128. doi:10.2143/ITL.156.0.2034425

Lee, H., & Liebenau, J. (2000). Time and the Internet at the turn of the millennium. *Time & Society, 9*(43), 43–56. doi:10.1177/0961463X00009001003

Leetaru, K. H., Wang, S., Cao, G., Padmanabhan, A., & Shook, E. (2013). Mapping the global Twitter heartbeat: The geography of Twitter. *First Monday, 18*(5-6).

LeFevre, K. (1987). *Invention as a social act (Studies in Writing and Rhetoric)*. Carbondale, IL: Southern Illinois UP. Leont'ev, A. N. (1978). *Activity, consciousness, and personality*. Englewood Cliffs, NJ: Prentice-Hall.

Leki, I., Cumming, A., & Silva, T. (2008). *A synthesis of research on second language writing in English*. New York, London: Routledge.

Lenggenhager, B. et al. (2007). Video ergo sum: Manipulating bodily self-consciousness. *Science, 317,* 1096–1099. doi:10.1126/science.1143439 PMID:17717189

Leont'ev, A. (1981). *Problems of the development of mind*. Moscow, Russia: Progress Press.

Lessig, L. (1998). The laws of cyberspace. Retrieved from http://cyber.law.harvard.edu/works/lessig/laws_cyberspace.pdf

Lessig, L. (2013, June 12). It's time to rewrite the internet to give us better privacy, and security. *The Daily Beast*. Retrieved June 12, 2013, from http://www.thedailybeast.com/articles/2013/06/12/it-s-time-to-rewrite-the-internet-to-give-us-better-privacy-and-security.html

Lessig, L. (1999). *Code and other laws of cyberspace*. New York, NY: Basic.

Lessig, L. (2001). *The future of ideas: The fate of the commons in a connected world*. New York: Random.

Lidwell, W., Holden, K., & Butler, J. (2003). *Universal principles of design*. Beverly, MA: Rockport Publishers.

Limbu, M. (2012). Teaching writing in the cloud: Networked writing communities in the culturally and linguistically diverse classrooms. *Journal of Global Literacies, Technologies, and Emerging Pedagogies, 1*(1), 1–20.

Limbu, M. (2013). Emerging pedagogies in the networked knowledge communities: interweaving and intersecting global communities in the 21st century global village. In M. Limbu, & B. Gurung (Eds.), *Emerging pedagogies in the networked knowledge society: Practices integrating social media and globalization*. Hershey, PA: IGI Global. doi:10.4018/978-1-4666-4757-2.ch003

Lindgren, S. (2013). *New noise: A cultural sociology of digital disruption*. New York, NY: Peter Lang.

List of best-selling video game franchises. (2010). In *Wikipedia*. Retrieved from http://en.wikipedia.org/wiki/List_of_best-selling_video_game_franchises

List of best-selling video games. (2010). In *Wikipedia*. Retrieved from http://en.wikipedia.org/wiki/List_of_best-selling_video_games#PlayStation_3

List of. *Metal Gear* media. (2013). In *Wikipedia*. Retrieved from http://en.wikipedia.org/wiki/List_of_Metal_Gear_media

Little, D. (2005). The common European framework and the European language portfolio: Involving learners and their judgments in the assessment process. *Language Testing, 22*(3), 321–336. doi:10.1191/0265532205lt311oa

Lockett, A., Losh, E., Rieder, D. M., Sample, M., Stolley, K., & Vee, A. (2012). The role of computational literacy in computers and writing. *Enculturation, 14*.

Longest cutscene in a video game. (2013). *Guinness World Records*. Retrieved from http://www.guinnessworldrecords.com/records-5000/longest-cutscene-in-a-video-game/

Lopez, A. (2008). *Mediocology: Multicultural approach to media literacy in the twenty-first century*. New York, NY: Peter Lang.

Losh, E. (2011). The seven million dollar PowerPoint and its aftermath: What happens when the house intelligence committee sees "terrorist use of the internet" in a battlefield 2 fan film. In M. Nunes (Ed.), *Error glitch, noise, and jam in new media cultures*. New York: Continuum. Retrieved from http://public.eblib.com/EBLPublic/PublicView.do?ptiID=655513

Losh, E. (2012) Defining digital rhetoric with 20-20 hindsight. *Digital Rhetoric Collaborative*. Retrieved from: http://www.digitalrhetoriccollaborative.org/2012/06/25/defining-digital-rhetoric-with-20-20-hindsight/

Losh, E. (2012) *Defining digital rhetoric with 20-20 hindsight*. Retrieved July 14, 2013, from http://www.digitalrhetoriccollaborative.org/2012/06/25/defining-digital-rhetoric-with-20-20-hindsight/

Losh, E. (2009). *VirtualPolitik*. Cambridge, MA: MIT Press.

Losh, L. (2013). Foreward. In G. Verhulsdunk, & M. Limbu (Eds.), *Digital rhetoric and global literacies: Communication modes and digital practices in the networked world*. Hershey, PA: IGI Global.

Lovink, G. (2011). *Networks without a cause: a critique of social media*. Cambridge, UK: Polity.

Lu, M. Z. (1998). Reading and writing differences: The problematic of experience. In Jarratt and Worsham (Eds.), Feminism and composition studies: In other words (pp. 239-251). New York: Modern Language Assocation.

Luhmann, N. (1992). What is communication? *Communication Theory*, 2(3), 251–259. doi:10.1111/j.1468-2885.1992.tb00042.x

Lukas, P. (2013, April 24). Trolling right along: An interview with Joe Big Cock Johnson. *Uni-Watch.com*. Retrieved June 13, 2013, from http://www.uni-watch.com/2013/04/19/an-interview-with-uni-watchs-most-prominent-troll/

Luke, C. (2000). Cyber-schooling and technological change: Multiliteracies for new times. In B. Cope, & M. Kalantzis (Eds.), *Multiliteracies: Literacy, learning, and the design of social futures* (pp. 69–91). New York, NY: Routledge.

Luke, C. (2000). New literacies in teacher education. *Journal of Adolescent & Adult Literacy*, 43(5), 424–435.

Lule, J. (2012). *Globalization and media: Global village of Babel*. New York, NY: Rowman & Littlefield Publisher, Inc.

Lu, M. (2004). An essay on the work of composition: Composing english against the order of fast capitalism. *College Composition and Communication*, 56(1), 16–50. doi:10.2307/4140679

Lu, M. (2006). Living-English work. *College English*, 68(6), 605–618. doi:10.2307/25472178

Lu, M., & Horner, B. (2009). Composing in a local-global context: Careers, mobility, skills. *College English*, 72(2), 113–133.

Lundin, R. W. (2008). Teaching with wikis: Toward a networked pedagogy. *Computers and Composition*, 25, 432–448. doi:10.1016/j.compcom.2008.06.001

Lynch, L. (2012). We don't wanna be radiated: Documentary film and the evolving rhetoric of nuclear energy activism. *American Literature*, 84(2), 327–351. doi:10.1215/00029831-1587368

Lyotard, J. L. (1984). *The postmodern condition: A report on knowledge*. Minneapolis, MN: University of Minnesota Press.

Macann, C. E. (1993). *Four phenomenological philosophers: Husserl, Heidegger, Sartre, Merleau-Ponty*. London: Routledge.

MacCormick, J. (2011). *Nine algorithms that changed the future: The ingenious ideas that drive today's computers*. Princeton, NJ: Princeton University Press.

Mannix, P. (1992). *The rhetoric of antinuclear fiction: Persuasive strategies in novels and films*. Lewisburg, PA: Bucknell University Press.

Manovich, L. (2001). *The language of new media*. Cambridge, MA: MIT Press.

Marchant, J. R. V., & Charles, J. F. (1892). *Cassell's Latin dictionary*. UK: Cassell Publishers.

Marcus, A., & Gould, E. W. (2012). Globalization, localization, and cross-cultural user-interface design. In J. A. Jacko (Ed.), *The human-computer interaction: Fundamentals, evolving technologies, emerging applications* (3rd ed., pp. 341–366). London, New York, NY: CRS Press Taylor & Francis Group. doi:10.1201/b11963-19

Mardsjo, K. (1996). Interfacing technology. *Computers and Composition*, 13, 303–315. doi:10.1016/S8755-4615(96)90019-5

Margolin, V. (1995). The product milieu and social action. In R. Buchanan, & V. Margolin (Eds.), *Discovering design: Explorations in design studies* (pp. 121–145). Chicago, IL: The University of Chicago Press.

Marks, L. U. (2000). *The skin of the film: Intercultural cinema, embodiment, and the senses.* Durham, NC: Duke University Press.

Mar, R. A., Oatley, K., Hirsh, J., Paz, J., & Peterson, J. B. (2006). Bookworms versus nerds: Exposure to fiction versus non-fiction, divergent associations with social ability, and the simulation of fictional social worlds. *Journal of Research in Personality, 40*(5), 694–712. doi:10.1016/j.jrp.2005.08.002

Marshall, D. P. (2004). *New media cultures.* New York, NY: Oxford University Press.

Martin, A. (2007, July 12). Whole foods executive used alias. *New York Times.* Retrieved January 12, 2013, from www.nytimes.com/2007/07/12/business/12foods.html

Masco, J. (2004). Nuclear technoaesthetics: Sensory politics from Trinity to the virtual bomb in Los Alamos. *American Ethnologist, 31*(3), 349–373. doi:10.1525/ae.2004.31.3.349

Massey, A. P., Montoya-Weiss, M. M., & Hung, Y.-T. (2003). Because time matters: Temporal coordination in global virtual project teams. *Journal of Management Information Systems, 19*(4), 129–155.

Mateas, M., & Stern, A. (2005). Interaction and narrative. In K. Salen, & E. Zimmerman (Eds.), *The game design reader: A rules of play anthology* (pp. 642–669). Boston, MA: MIT Press.

Matias, A., & Wolf, D. F. II. (2013). Engaging students in online courses through the use of mobile technology. In L. A. Wankel, & P. Blessinger (Eds.), *Increasing student engagement and retention using mobile applications: Smartphones, Skype, and texting technologies: Cutting edge technologies in higher education.* Bingley, UK: Emerald Group. doi:10.1108/S2044-9968(2013)000006D007

Matsuda, P. K., Canagarajah, S., Ken Hyland, L. H., & Warschauer, M. (2003). Changing currents in second language writing research: A colloquium. *Journal of Second Language Writing, 12,* 151–179. doi:10.1016/S1060-3743(03)00016-X

Mattelart, A. (1996). *The invention of communication* (S. Emanuel, Trans.). Minneapolis, MN: University of Minnesota Press.

Maznevski, M. L., & Chudoba, K. M. (2000). Bridging space over time: Global virtual team dynamics and effectiveness. *Organization Science, 11*(5), 473–492. doi:10.1287/orsc.11.5.473.15200

McAllister, K. S. (2001). *Game work: Language, power, and computer game culture.* Tuscaloosa, AL: University of Alabama Press.

McClintock, A. (1995). *Imperial leather: Race, gender, and sexuality in the colonial contest.* New York, NY: Routledge.

McCombs, M., & Shaw, D. (1972). The agenda setting function of mass media. *Public Opinion Quarterly, 36*(2), 176–187. doi:10.1086/267990

McCorkle, B. (2012). *Rhetorical delivery as technological discourse.* Carbondale, IL: Southern Illinois University Press.

McGee, M. C. (1990). Text, context, and the fragmentation of contemporary culture. *Western Journal of Speech Communication, 54*(3), 274–289. doi:10.1080/10570319009374343

McGrath, J. E. (1991). Time, interaction, and performance (tip): A theory of groups. *Small Group Research, 22*(2), 147–174. doi:10.1177/1046496491222001

McKee, H., & DeVoss, D. (2007). *Digital Writing Research: Technologies, Methodologies, and Ethical Issues.* New York: Hampton Press.

mclol.com. (2010, August 20). Famous internet trolls who did it for the lulz. *mclol.com.* Retrieved January 5, 2013, from http://www.mclol.com/funny-articles/famous-internet-trolls-who-did-it-for-the-lulz/

McLoughlin, C., & Lee, M. (2008). The three P's of pedagogy for the networked society: Personalization, participation, and productivity. *International Journal of Teaching and Learning in Higher Education, 20,* 10–27.

McLoughlin, C., & Lee, M. J. W. (2010). Personalised and self-regulated learning in the Web 2.0 era: International exemplars of innovative pedagogy using social software. *Australasian Journal of Educational Technology, 26,* 28–43.

McLuhan, M. (1964). *Understanding media: The extensions of man.* New York: Signet.

McLuhan, M., & Fiore, Q. (2001). *The medium is the massage*. Corte Madera, CA: Gingko Press.

McNely, B. J. (2008). *Agency, invention, and sympatric design platforms*.

Meehan, E. R. (1986). Conceptualizing culture as commodity: The problem of television. *Critical Studies in Mass Communication*, *3*(4), 448–457. doi:10.1080/15295038609366675

Merleau-Ponty, M. (1962). *Phenomenology of perception*. New York: Humanities Press.

Merleau-Ponty, M., & Lefort, C. (1968). *The visible and the invisible, followed by working notes*. Evanston, IL: Northwestern University Press.

Metal gear solid 2: Sons of Liberty. (2013). In *Wikipedia*. Retrieved from http://en.wikipedia.org/wiki/Metal_Gear_Solid_2:_Sons_of_Liberty

Metal gear solid 4: Guns of the patriots. (2010). In *Wikipedia*. Retrieved from http://en.wikipedia.org/wiki/MGS4

Miller, C. R. (1979). What's practical about technical writing? In B. E. Fearing, & W. K. Sparrow (Eds.), *Technical writing: Theory and practice* (pp. 14–24). New York, NY: MLA.

Miller, C. R. (1992). Kairos in the rhetoric of science. In S. P. Witte, N. Nakadate, & R. D. Cherry (Eds.), *A rhetoric of doing: Essays on written discourse in honor of James L. Kinneavy* (pp. 310–327). Carbondale, IL: Southern Illinois University Press.

Miller, C. R. (1994). Opportunity, opportunism, and progress: Kairos in the rhetoric of technology. *Argumentation*, *8*, 81–96. doi:10.1007/BF00710705

Miller, C. R. (2002). Forward. In P. Sipiora, & J. S. Baumlin (Eds.), *Rhetoric and Kairos: Essays in history, theory, and praxis*. Albany, NY: State University of New York Press.

Miller, C. R. (2004). A humanistic rationale for technical writing. In J. M. Dubinski (Ed.), *Teaching technical communication* (pp. 15–23). Boston, MA: Bedford/St. Martin's.

Miller, C. R. (2010). Should we name the tools? In J. Ackerman, & D. Coogan (Eds.), *The public work of rhetoric: Citizen-scholars and civic engagement* (pp. 19–38). Columbia, SC: University of South Carolina Press.

Miller, R. (2002). Fault lines in the contact zone. In J. M. Wolf (Ed.), *Professing in the contact zone: Bringing theory and practice together* (pp. 121–146). Urbana, IL: NCTE.

Miller, R. E. (2005). *Writing at the end of the world*. Pittsburgh, PA: University of Pittsburgh Press.

Miller, T., & Yudice, G. (2002). *Cultural policy*. London: SAGE.

Mills, N. (2011). Situated learning through social networking communities: The development of joint enterprise, mutual engagement, and a shared repertoire. *CALICO Journal*, *28*(2), 345–368.

Mischler, E. G. (2006). In A. De Fina, D. Schiffrin, & M. Bamberg (Eds.), *Discourse and Identity* (pp. 30–47). New York: Cambridge University Press. doi:10.1017/CBO9780511584459.003

Mitchell, W. J. T. (1986). *Inconology: Image, text, ideology*. Chicago, IL: University of Chicago Press.

Mohanty, C. T. (2003). *Feminism without borders: Decolonizing theory, practicing solidarity*. Durham, NC: Duke University Press. doi:10.1215/9780822384649

Monbiot, G. (2011, February 24). Corporate-funded online 'astroturfing' is more advanced and automated than you might think. *Alternet.org*. Retrieved January 8, 2013, from http://www.alternet.org/story/150049/corporate-funded_online_%27astroturfing%27_is_more_advanced_and_more_automated_than_you_might_think

Mooney, C. (2013, January 10). The science of why comment trolls suck. *Mother Jones*. Retrieved February 3, 2013, from http://www.motherjones.com/environment/2013/01/you-idiot-course-trolls-comments-make-you-believe-science-less

Moore, P. (1996). Instrumental discourse is as humanistic as rhetoric. *Journal of Business and Technical Communication*, *10*(1), 100. doi:10.1177/1050651996010001005

Moor, J. (1985). What is computer ethics? *Metaphilosophy*, *16*(4), 266–275. doi:10.1111/j.1467-9973.1985.tb00173.x

Morita, N. (2004). Negotiating participation and identity in second language academic communities. *TESOL Quarterly*, *38*(4), 573–603. doi:10.2307/3588281

Morozov, E. (2011). *The net delusion: The dark side of Internet freedom*. Jackson, TN: PublicAffairs.

Morris, D. (2010). Are teachers technophobes? Investigating professional competency in the use of ICT to support teaching and learning. *Procedia – Social and Behavioural Sciences 2*(2), 4010- 4015.

Morton, T. (2011). Unsustaining. *World Picture 5*. Retrieved from http://www.worldpicturejournal.com/WP_5/Morton.html

Muir, D. J. (2013). An international perspective on mobile learning. In Z. L. Berge, & L. Y. Muilenburg (Eds.), *Handbook of mobile learning* (pp. 561–570). New York: Routledge.

Mumford, L. (1934). *Technics and civilization*. San Diego, CA: Harcourt Brace.

Munroe, R. (2013, January 27). Argument. *XKCD: A webcomic of romance, sarcasm, math, and language*. Retrieved January 29, 2013, from http://ckcd.com.

Murray, C. D., & Sixsmith, J. (1999). The corporeal body in virtual reality. *Ethos (Berkeley, Calif.)*, *27*(3), 315–343. doi:10.1525/eth.1999.27.3.315

Murray, J. (1998). *Hamlet on the holodeck: The future of narrative in cyberspace*. Cambridge, MA: MIT Press.

Murray, J. (2012). *Inventing the medium: Principles of interaction design as a cultural practice*. Cambridge, MA: MIT Press.

Murthy, D. (2012). *Twitter: Social communication in the Twitter age*. Boston, MA: Polity.

Nakamura, L., & Chow-White, P. (2010). *Race after the internet*. London: Routledge.

Nardi, B. A. (1996). Activity theory and human computer interaction. In B. A. Nardi (Ed.), *Context and consciousness: Activity theory and human-computer interaction* (pp. 1–8). Cambridge, MA: The MIT Press.

Nardi, B. A. (1996). Activity theory and human-computer interaction. In B. Nardi (Ed.), *Context and consciousness: Activity theory and human-computer interaction* (pp. 7–16). Cambridge, MA: MIT Press.

Nardi, B. A., & O'Day, V. (2000). *Information ecologies: Using technology with heart*. Cambridge, MA: MIT Press.

National Institute for Standards and Technology. (2010). *NIST Time*. Retrieved from http://www.nist.gov/pml/div688/utcnist.cfm

National Institute for Standards and Technology. (n. d.). *Unit of time (second)*. Retrieved from http://physics.nist.gov/cuu/Units/second.html

National Military Academy of Afghanistan. (2011, 2 April). *Task order request*. Nato Training Mission—Afghanistan.

Natsios, D., & Young, J. (2012, July 12). The gentleperson's guide to forum spies. *Cryptome.org*. Retrieved January 4, 2013, from http://cryptome.org/2012/07/gent-forum-spies.htm.

Negroponte, N. (1979). 1996). Books without pages. *SIGDOC Asterisk Journal of Computer Documentation*, *20*(3), 2–8. doi:10.1145/235741.235742

Neisser, U., & Becklen, R. (1975). Selective looking: Attending to visually specified events. *Cognitive Psychology*, *7*, 480–494. doi:10.1016/0010-0285(75)90019-5

Nelson, M. (2006) Mode, meaning and synaesthesia in multimedia L2 writing. *Language learning and teachnology*, *10*(2), 56-76.

New London Group. (2000). A pedagogy of multiliteracies: Designing social futures. In B. Cope, & M. Kalantzis (Eds.), *Multiliteracies: Literacy learning and the design of social futures* (pp. 9–37). London, New York: Routledge.

Newman, J. (2002). The myth of the ergodic videogame: Some thoughts on player-character relationships in videogames. *Game Studies. The International Journal of Computer Game Research*, *2*(1).

Nieborg, D. B. (2009). Empower yourself, defend freedom! Playing games during times of war. In M. van den Boomen, S. Lammes, A.-S. Lehmann, J. Raessens, & M. T. Schäfer (Eds.), *Digital material: Tracing new media in everyday life and technology (MediaMatters)* (pp. 35–47). Amsterdam, The Netherlands: Amsterdam University Press.

Norman, D. (1988). *The psychology of everyday things.* New York: Basic Books.

Norman, D. (2002). Emotion and design: Attractive things work better. *Interactions Magazine, 9*(4), 36–42. doi:10.1145/543434.543435

Norman, D. (2004). *Emotional design: Why we love (or hate) everyday things.* New York, NY: Basic Books.

Nunan, D. (1988). *The learner-centred curriculum.* Cambridge, UK: Cambridge University Press. doi:10.1017/CBO9781139524506

Nunes, M. (2006). *Cyberspaces of everyday life.* Minneapolis, MN: University of Minnesota Press. Retrieved from http://site.ebrary.com/id/10180210

Obama Singh 21st Century Knowledge Initiative. (2013). *USIEF: United States-India Educational Foundation.* Accessed March 10, 2013 at http://www.usief.org.in/Institutional-Collaboration/Obama-Singh-21st-Century-Knowledge-Initiative-Awards.aspx.

Obama's speech on drone policy. (2013, May 23). *The New York Times.* Retrieved from http://www.nytimes.com/2013/05/24/us/politics/transcript-of-obamas-speech-on-drone-policy.html?pagewanted=all

Oblinger, D., Martin, R., & Baer, L. (2004). *Unlocking the potential of gaming technology.* Paper presented at National Learning Infastructure Initiative Annual Meeting. San Diego, CA.

Oblinger, D. (2003). Boomers, gen-Xers and millenials: Understanding the new students. *EDUCAUSE Review, 38*(4), 37–47.

Ohler, J. (2008). *Digital storytelling in the classroom: New Media pathways to literacy, learning and creativity.* Thousand Oaks, CA: Corwin Press.

Ohmann, R. (1985). Literacy, technology, and monopoly capital. *College English, 47*(7), 675–689. doi:10.2307/376973

Ohmann, R. (2008). Literacy, Technology, and Monopoly Capital. In M. Sidler, E. Smith, & R. Morris (Eds.), *Computers in the composition classroom: A critical sourcebook.* Boston: Bedford/St. Martins.

Olson, G. (2002). The death of composition as an intellectual discourse. In G. Olson (Ed.), *Rhetoric and composition as intellectual work* (pp. 3–31). Carbondale, IL: Southern Illinois University Press.

Ong, W. J. (1982). *Orality and literacy: The technologizing of the word* (T. Hawkes, Ed.). New York: Methuen. doi:10.4324/9780203328064

Orlikowski, W. J., & Yates, J. (2002). It's about time: Temporal structuring in organizations. *Organization Science, 13*(6), 684–700. doi:10.1287/orsc.13.6.684.501

Oscarson, M. (1989). Self-assessment of language proficiency: Rationale and applications. *Language Testing, 6*, 1–13. doi:10.1177/026553228900600103

Ottosen, R. (2009). Targeting the player: Computer games as propaganda for the military-industrial complex. *Nordicom Review, 30*(2), 35–51.

Ouellete, M. A. (2008). I hope you never see another day like this: Pedagogy & allegory in post 9/11 video games. *Game Studies. The International Journal of Computer Game Research, 8*(1).

Ougaard, M. (2004). *Political globalization: State, power and social forces.* Houndmills, UK: Palgrave Macmillan.

Oxford English Dictionary Online. (n. d.). *Algorithm.* Retrieved from www.oed.com

Pahl, K., & Rowsell, J. (2012). *Literacy and education* (2nd ed.). Thousand Oaks, CA: Sage.

Panteli, N. (2009). *Virtual social networks: Mediated, massive, and multilayers sites.* Eastbourne, UK: Macmillan. doi:10.1057/9780230250888

Panthee, R. K. (2012). Web 2.0 technologies, cultural and technological hegemonies, and teaching design to deconstruct them in the cross-cultural digital contact zone. *Journal of Global Literacies, Technologies, and Emerging Pedagoies*, *1*(1), 38–55.

Papert. S. (2002). *Hard fun*. Retrieved March 21, 2012, from http://www.papert.org/articles/HardFun.html.

Papert, S. (1992). *The children's machine: Rethinking school in the age of the computer*. New York: Basic Books.

Pareene, A. (2013, January 16). Right-wing press happily allows itself to be trolled by made-up video game. *Salon.com*. Retrieved January 16, 2013, from http://www.salon.com/2013/01/16/right_wing_press_happily_allows_itself_to_be_trolled_by_made_up_video_game/

Paretti, M. C., & McNair, L. D. (2008). Communication in global virtual activity systems. In P. Zemliansky, & K. St. Amant (Eds.), *Handbook of research on virtual workplaces and the new nature of business practices* (pp. 24–38). Hershey, PA: IGI Global. doi:10.4018/978-1-59904-893-2.ch003

Paul, C. A., & Philpott, J. S. (2009). The rise and fall of CTS: Kenneth Burke identifying with the World of Warcraft. In *Proceedings of DiGRA 2009: Breaking New Ground: Innovation in Games, Play, Practices and Theory*. Digital Games Research Association.

Peng, W. (2008). The mediational role of identification in the relationship between experience mode and self-efficacy: Enactive role-playing versus passive observation. *Cyberpsychology & Behavior*, *11*, 649–652. doi:10.1089/cpb.2007.0229 PMID:18954275

Pennington, M. C. (2003). The impact of the computer in second-language writing. In B. Kroll (Ed.), *Exploring the dynamics of second language writing* (pp. 283–310). Cambridge, UK: Cambridge University Press. doi:10.1017/CBO9781139524810.019

Perelman, C., & Olbrechts-Tyteca, L. (1969). *The new rhetoric. A treatise on argumentation*. Notre Dame, IN: University of Notre Dame Press.

Perlow, L. A. (1999). The time famine: Toward a sociology of work time. *Administrative Science Quarterly*, *44*(1), 57–81. doi:10.2307/2667031

Peters, J. D. (2009, April). *Calendar, Clock, Tower*. Paper given at the Media in Transition 6 conference, Cambridge, MA.

Pichlmair, M. (2009). Assembling a mosaic of the future: The post-nuclear world of Fallout 3. *Eludamos. Journal for Computer Game Culture, 3*(1), 107-113. Quijano-Cruz, J. (2009). Chopin's dream as reality: A critical reading of eternal sonata. *Eludamos: Journal for Computer Game Culture, 3*(2), 209–218.

Pink, D. (2005). *A whole new mind*. New York, NY: Riverhead Books.

Plato, . (2004). *Gorgias* (C. Emlyn-Jones, & W. Hamilton, Trans.). New York: Penguin Classics.

Pool, I. (1983). *Technologies of freedom*. Cambridge, MA: Harvard University Press.

Porter, J. E., & Sullivan, P. A. (2004). Repetition and the rhetoric of visual design. In C. Handa (Ed.), Visual rhetoric in a digital world: A critical sourcebook, (pp. 290-299). Bsoton/New York, NY: Bedford/St. Martin's.

Porter, J. E. (2007). Foreword. In H. A. McKee, & D. N. DeVoss (Eds.), *Digital writing research: Technologies, methodologies, and ethical issues* (pp. ix–xix). Cresskill, NJ: Hampton Press.

Poster, M. (2012). Global media and culture. In A. Aneesh, L. Hall, & P. Petro (Eds.), *Beyond globalization: Making new world in media, art, social practices*. New Brunswick, NJ: Rutgers University Press.

Postmes, T., Spears, R., & Lea, M. (1998). Breaching or building social boundaries? SIDE-effects of computer-mediated communication. *Communication Research*, *25*, 689–715. doi:10.1177/009365098025006006

Postmes, T., Spears, R., & Lea, M. (1999). Social identity, group norms, and deindividuation: Lessons from computer-mediated communication for social influence in the group. In N. Ellemers, R. Spears, & B. Doosje (Eds.), *Social identity: Context, commitment, content* (pp. 164–183). Oxford, UK: Blackwell.

Pratt, M. L. (1991). Arts of the contact zone. *Profession*, *91*, 33–40.

Preece, J., Rogers, Y., & Sharp, H. (2007). *Interaction design: Beyond human-computer interaction*. New York, NY: John Wiley & Sons.

Protalinski, E. (2011, August 2). Facebook: Anonymity on the internet has to go away. *ZDNet.com*. Retrieved January 20, 2013, from http://www.zdnet.com/blog/facebook/facebook-anonymity-on-the-internet-has-to-go-away/2270.

Qin, H., Rau, P., & Salvendy, G. (2009). Measuring player immersion in the computer game narrative. *International Journal of Human-Computer Interaction*, *25*, 107–133. doi:10.1080/10447310802546732

Quintilian, . (1980). *Institutio Oratoria: Books I-III* (H. E. Butler, Trans.). Cambridge, MA: Harvard University Press.

Rainie, L., & Wellman, B. (2012). *Networked: The new social operating system*. Cambridge, MA: MIT Press.

Ralon, L. (2012, July 25). Interview with Carolyn Miller. *Figure/Ground Communication*. Retrieved from http://figureground.ca/2012/07/25/interview-with-carolyn-r-miller/

Ramo, H. (1999). An Aristotelian human time-space manifold. *Time & Society*, *8*(2-3), 309–328. doi:10.1177/0961463X99008002006

Ramsay, S. (2011). *Reading machines: Toward an algorithmic criticism*. Urbana, IL: University of Illinois Press.

Raskin, J. (2000). *The humane interface: New directions for designing interactive systems*. Boston, MA: Addison Wesley.

Redden, E. (2013). *Strangers in a strange land*. Inside Higher Ed. Accessed March 1, 2013 at http://www.inside-highered.com/news/2013/03/04/international-educators-consider-challenges-integrating-students-abroad.

Rheingold, H. (2003). *Smart mobs: The next social revolution*. New York: Basic.

Richards, I. A. (1936). *The philosophy of rhetoric*. New York, NY: Oxford University Press.

Richardson, I., & Harper, C. (2001). *Corporeal virtuality: the impossibility of a fleshless ontology*. Retrieved from http://people.brunel.ac.uk/bst/2no2/Papers/Ingrid%20Richardson&Carly%20Harper.htm

Riedl, M. O., & Bulitko, V. (2013). Interactive narrative: an intelligent systems approach. *AI Magazine*, *34*(1).

Ritzer, G. (2004). *The McDonaldization of society*. Thousand Oaks, CA: Sage.

Robert-Houdin, J.-E. (2009). *Memoirs of Robert-Houdin* (R. S. Mackenzie, Trans.). Whitefish, MT: Kessinger Publishing.

Robertson, R. (1995). Glocalization: Time-space and homogeneity-heterogeneity. In M. Featherston, S. Lash, & R. Robertson (Eds.), *Global modernities* (pp. 22–44). London: Sage. doi:10.4135/9781446250563.n2

Robin, B. (2008). Digital storytelling: A powerful technology tool for the 21st century. *Theory into Practice*, *47*(3), 220–228. doi:10.1080/00405840802153916

Robinson, K. (2005). RSA animate - Changing education paradigms. Accessed March 10, 2013 from http://www.youtube.com/watch?v=zDZFcDGpL4U&list=PL39BF9545D740ECFF&index=7.

Rorty, R. (1979). *Philosophy and the mirror of nature*. Princeton, NJ: Princeton University Press.

Rosinski, P., & Squire, M. (2009). Strange bedfellows: Humans-computer interaction, interface design, and composition pedagogy. *Computers and Composition*, *26*, 149–163. doi:10.1016/j.compcom.2009.05.004

Roy, A. (2001). *Power politics* (2nd ed.). Cambridge, MA: South End Press.

Rupert, M. (2000). *Ideologies of globalization: Contending visions of a new world order*. London: Routledge.

Rupley, S. (2004). Microsoft's font foibles. *PC Magazine*. Retrieved from http://www.pcmag.com/article2/0,2817,1526828,00.asp

Russell, D. (1997). Rethinking genre in school and society: An activity theory analysis. *Written Communication*, *14*(4), 504–554. doi:10.1177/0741088397014004004

Sakaki, T. (2010). Earthquake shakes Twitter users: Real-time event detection by social sensors. In *Proceedings of the International World Wide Web Conference*, (pp. 851–860).

Saltzer, J. H., Reed, D. P., & Clark, D. D. (1984). End-to-end arguments in system design. *ACM Transactions on Computer Systems*, 2(4), 277–288. doi:10.1145/357401.357402

Savage, G., & Yu, H. (2013). *Negotiating cultural encounters: Narrating intercultural engineering and technical communication*. Hoboken, NJ: Wiley.

Scenters-Zapico, J. (2010). *Generaciones' narratives: The pursuit & practice of traditional & electronic literacies on the US-Mexico Borderlands*. Logan, UT: Utah State University Press.

Schell, J. (2008). *The art of game design: A book of lenses*. Burlington, MA: Morgan Kaufmann.

Schlick, M. (1992). The future of philosophy. In R. Rorty (Ed.), *The linguistic turn: Essays in philosophical method* (pp. 43–53). Chicago, IL: University of Chicago Press.

Schulzke, M. (2009). Moral decision making in Fallout. *Game Studies. The International Journal of Computer Game Research*, 9(2).

Schwittay, A. (2011). The financial inclusion assemblage: Subjects, technics, rationalities. *Critique of Anthropology*, 31(4), 381–401. doi:10.1177/0308275X11420117

Scott, R. L. (1967). On viewing rhetoric as epistemic. *Central States Speech Journal*, 18, 9–17. doi:10.1080/10510976709362856

Screven, C. G. (2000). Information design in informal settings: Museums and other public spaces. In R. Jacobson (Ed.), *Information design*. Cambridge, MA: MIT Press.

Searle, J. R., Kiefer, F., & Bierwisch, M. (Eds.). (1980). speech act theory and pragmatics. Dordrecht, Holland: Reidel Publishing Company.

Selber, S. (2004). *Multiliteracies for a digital age*. Carbondale, IL: Southern Illinois University Press.

Selber, S. A., Johnson-Eilola, J., & Mehlenbacher, B. (1996). Online support systems. *ACM Computing Surveys*, 28(1), 197–200. doi:10.1145/234313.234397

Selfe, C. (1998, April). *Technologies and literacy in the 21ˢᵗ century: The perils of not paying attention* (Chair's address to the conference on College Composition and Communication). Chicago.

Selfe, C. L., & Hawisher, G. E. (2013). Foreword. In R. Colby, M. S. S. Johnson, M. S. S., & R. S. Colby (Eds.), Rhetoric/composition/play through video games: Reshaping theory and practice of writing (pp. xv-xviii). New York, NY: Palgrave Macmillan.

Selfe, C. (1999). Technology and literacy: A story about the perils of not paying attention. *College Composition and Communication*, 50(3), 411–436. doi:10.2307/358859

Selfe, C. L. (1999). *Technology and literacy in the twenty-first century: The importance of paying attention*. Illinois, IL: Southern Illinois University Press.

Selfe, C. L. (2009). The movement of air, the breath of meaning: Aurality and multimodal composing. *College Composition and Communication*, 60, 616–663.

Selfe, C., & Hawisher, G. (2004). *Literate lives in the information age: Narrative of literacy from the United States*. Mahwah, NJ: Erlbaum.

Selfe, C., & Selfe, R. (1994). The politics of the interface: Power and its exercise in electronic contact zones. *College Composition and Communication*, 45(4), 480–504. doi:10.2307/358761

Sener, J. (2007). In search of student-generated content in online education. *E-mentor*, 4, 1–8.

Senge, P., Scharmer, C. O., Jaworski, J., & Flowers, B. S. (2004). Presence: Human purpose and the field of the future. Cambridge, MA: The Society for Organizational learning, Inc.

Shah, N. (Ed.). (2010). *Digital AlterNatives with a cause?* Hivos & Centre for Internet and Society.

Shannon, C., & Weaver, W. (1948). *The mathematical theory of communication*. Urbana, IL: University of Illinois Press.

Shedroff, N. (2001). *Experience design*. Indianapolis, IN: New Riders.

Sheridan, D., Ridolfo, J., & Michel, A. (2008). The available means of persuasion: Mapping a theory and pedagogy of multimodal public rhetoric. In L. Worsham, & G. Olson (Eds.), *Plugged in technology, rhetoric and culture in a posthuman age* (pp. 61–94). Cresskill, NJ: Hampton Press, Inc.

Short, J. A., Williams, E., & Christie, B. (1976). *The social psychology of telecommunications*. New York, NY: John Wiley.

Sidney, D., Rice, J. A., & Vastola, M. (2011). *Beyond postprocess*. Logan, UT: Utah State University Press.

Silver, N. (2012). *The signal and the noise: Why most predictions fail but some don't*. New York, NY: Penguin Press.

Silvertone, R. (1999). *Why study the media?* London, UK: SAGE.

Sipiora, P. (2002). Introduction: The ancient concept of *kairos*. In P. Sipiora, & J. S. Baumlin (Eds.), *Rhetoric and kairos: Essays in history, theory, and praxis* (pp. 1–19). Albany, NY: State University of New York Press.

Skjulstad, S., & Morrison, A. (2005). Movements in the interface. *Computers and Composition, 22*, 413–433. doi:10.1016/j.compcom.2005.08.006

Slater, M., Spanlang, B., Sanchez-Vives, M. V., & Blanke, O. (2010). First person experience of body transfer in virtual reality. *PLoS ONE, 5*(5), e10564. doi:10.1371/journal.pone.0010564 PMID:20485681

Sleeter, C., & Tettegah, S. (2002). Technology as a tool in multicultural teaching. *Multicultural Education, 10*(2), 3–8.

Smith, A., & Brenner, J. (2012). *Twitter use 2012* (Report of the PEW Internet and American Life Project). Washington, DC: PEW Research Center. Retrieved from http://www.pewinternet.org/~/media//Files/Reports/2012/PIP_Twitter_Use_2012.pdf

Smith, J. E. (2002). Time and qualitative time. In P. Sipiora, & J. S. Baumlin (Eds.), *Rhetoric and kairos: Essays in history, theory, and praxis* (pp. 46–57). Albany, NY: State University of New York Press.

Snyder, I. (Ed.). (2002). *Silicon literacies: Communication, innovation and education in the electronic age*. New York, NY: Routledge.

Sobchack, V. C. (1992). *The address of the eye: A phenomenology of film experience*. Princeton, NJ: Princeton University Press.

Soetaert, R., Bourgonjon, J., & Rutten, K. (2011). Video games as equipment for living. *CLCWeb: Comparative Literature and Culture, 13*(3). doi: doi:10.7771/1481-4374.1794

Soja, E. W. (1996). *Thirdspace: Journeys to Los Angeles and other real-and-imagined places*. Cambridge, UK: Blackwell.

Sonderman, J. (2012, January 11). People using pseudonyms post the highest quality comments, Disqus says. *Poynter.org*. Retrieved January 12, 2013, from http://www.poynter.org/latest-news/mediawire/159078/people-using-pseudonyms-post-the-most-highest-quality-comments-disqus-says/

Spears, R., Postmes, T., Lea, M., & Wolbert, A. (2002). When are net effects gross products? The power of influence and the influence of power in computer-mediated communication. *The Journal of Social Issues, 58*(1), 91–107. doi:10.1111/1540-4560.00250

Spinuzzi, C. (2003). *Tracing genres through organizations*. Cambridge, MA: MIT Press.

Spinuzzi, C. (2008). *Network: Theorizing knowledge work in telecommunications*. New York, NY: Cambridge University Press. doi:10.1017/CBO9780511509605

Spinuzzi, C. (2009). Light green doesn't mean hydrology!: Toward a visual rhetorical framework for interface design. In S. Miller-Cochran, & R. L. Rodrigo (Eds.), *Rhetorically rethinking usability: Theories, practices and methodologies*. Creskill, NJ: Hampton Press, Inc.

Spinuzzi, C. (2013). *Topsight: A guide to studying, diagnosing, and fixing information flow in organizations*. Austin, TX: Self-Published.

Sproull, L., & Kiesler, S. (1992). *Connections: New ways of working in the networked organization*. Cambridge, MA: MIT press.

Squire, K. D. (2006). From content to context: Video games as designed experiences. *Educational Researcher, 35*(8), 19–29. doi:10.3102/0013189X035008019

St. Amant, K. (2007). Online education in an age of globalization: Foundational perspectives and practices for technical communication instructors and trainers. *Technical Communication Quarterly, 16*(1), 13–30. doi:10.1080/10572250709336575

Stagnitti, K. (2004). Understanding play: The implications for play assessment. *Australian Occupational Therapy Journal, 51*, 3–12. doi:10.1046/j.1440-1630.2003.00387.x

Starke-Meyerring, D. (2010). Globally networked learning environments in professional communication: Challenging normalized ways of learning, teaching, and knowing. *Journal of Business and Technical Communication, 24*(3), 259–266. doi:10.1177/1050651910363266

Starke-Meyerring, D., & Andrews, D. (2006). Building a shared virtual learning culture: An international classroom partnership. *Business Communication Quarterly, 69*(1), 25–40. doi:10.1177/1080569905285543

Starke-Meyerring, D., Duin, A. H., & Palvetzian, T. (2007). Global partnerships: Positioning technical communication programs in the context of globalization. *Technical Communication Quarterly, 16*(2), 139–174. doi:10.1080/10572250709336558

Stealth game. (2013). In *Wikipedia*. Retrieved from http://en.wikipedia.org/wiki/Stealth_game

Steelman, J. D., Pierce, P. L., & Koppenhaver, D. A. (1994). The role of computers in promoting literacy in children with severe speech and physical impairments. In K. G. Butler (Ed.), *Severe communication disorders: Intervention strategies* (pp. 200–212). Gaithersburg, MD: Aspen.

Steiner, C. (2012). *Automate this*. New York: Portfolio.

Stern, S. (2008). Producing sites, exploring identities: Youth online authorship. In D. Buckingham (Ed.), *Youth, identity, and digital media* (pp. 95–118). Cambridge, MA: The MIT Press.

Stevenson, N. (2011). *Education and cultural citizenship*. Los Angeles, CA: SAGE.

Stiglitz, J. E. (2002). *Globalization and its discontents*. New York: Norton.

Streeter, T. (2010). *The net effect: Romanticism, capitalism, and the Internet*. New York: New York University Press.

Stuedahl, D., Morrison, A., Mortberg, C., & Bratteteig. (2010). Researching digital design. In I. Wagner, T. Bratteteig, & D. Stuedahl (Eds.), *Multi-disciplinary design practices* (pp. 3-15). London: Springer-Verlag.

Suler, J. (2004). The online disinhibition effect. *Cyberpsychology & Behavior, 7*(3), 321–326. doi:10.1089/1094931041291295 PMID:15257832

Sullivan, A. (2011, November 29). Ask me anything: Why no comments section? [Web video log post]. Retrieved January 24, 2013, from http://dish.andrewsullivan.com/2011/11/29/ask-me-anything-why-arent-comments-allowed/

Sullivan, P., & Porter, J. (1997). *Opening spaces: Writing technologies and critical research practices*. Greenwich, CT: Ablex.

Sunderman, E. (2013, January 23). A$AP Rocky lights up the city. *Village Voice*. Retrieved January 26, 2013, from http://www.villagevoice.com/2013-01-23/music/asap-rocky-harlem-new-york/

Sun, H. (2012). *Cross-cultural technology design: Creating culture-sensitive technology for local users*. Oxford, UK: Oxford University Press. doi:10.1093/acprof:oso/9780199744763.001.0001

Sutton-Smith, B. (1997). *The ambiguity of play*. Cambridge, MA: Harvard University Press.

Sweetser, P., & Wyeth, P. (2005). *Gameflow: A model for evaluating player enjoyment in games*. ACM Computers in Entertainment.

Tamari, E. (n.d.). Hideo Kojima interview. *Konami*. Retrieved from http://www.konami.jp/mgs4/uk/interview/03.html

Taylor, B. C. (2010). A hedge against the future: The post-Cold War rhetoric of nuclear weapons modernization. *The Quarterly Journal of Speech, 96*(1), 1–24. doi:10.1080/00335630903512721

Tharpe, M. (2001). *Marketing and consumer identity in multicultural America*. Thousand Oaks, CA: Sage.

Thatcher, B. (2005). Situating L2 writing in global communication technologies. *Computers and Composition, 22*(3), 279–295. doi:10.1016/j.compcom.2005.05.002

Thatcher, B. (2011). *Intercultural rhetoric and professional communication: Technological advances and organizational behavior*. Hershey, PA: IGI-Global Press. doi:10.4018/978-1-61350-450-5

The Data Machine. (n. d.). *Homepage.* Retrieved February 5, 2013 from http://www.thedatamachine.com

The New London Group. (2000). A pedagogy of multiliteracies: Designing social futures. In B. Cope, & M. Kalantzis (Eds.), *Multiliteracies: Literacy, learning, and the design of social futures* (pp. 9–37). New York, NY: Routledge.

Thompson, J. B. (1995). *The media and modernity.* California, CA: Stanford University Press.

Thomson, R., Ito, N., Suda, H., Lin, F., Liu, Y., Hayasaka, R., et al. (2012). Trusting Tweets: The Fukushima disaster and information source credibility on Twitter. In *Proceedings of the 9th International ISCRAM Conference,* (pp. 1–10).

Thorburn, D., Jenkins, H., & Seawell, B. (2003). *Rethinking media change: The aesthetics of transition.* Cambridge, MA: MIT Press.

Toffler, A. (1970). *Future shock.* New York: Random.

Toffler, A. (1980). *The third wave.* New York: William Morrow.

Tomlison, J. (1999). *Globalization and culture.* Cambridge, UK: Polity Press.

Treanor, M., Blackford, B., Mateas, M., & Bogost, I. (2012). The micro-rhetorics of Game-O-Matic. In *Proceedings of Procedural Content Generation Workshop.* Raleigh, NC, USA.

Trimbur, J. (2002). Delivering the message: Typography and the materiality of writing. In G. Olson (Ed.), Rhetoric and composition as intellectual work (pp. 188-202). Carbondale & Edwardsville, IL: Southern Illinois University Press.

Trompenaars, F., & Hampden-Turner, C. (1997). *Riding the waves of culture.* New York, NY: McGraw-Hill.

Tsukayama, H. (2012, September 24). Facebook, Twitter and data access. *The Washington Post.* Retrieved from http://www.washingtonpost.com/business/technology/facebook-twitter-and-data-access/2012/09/24/ab8eb0a8-0655-11e2-afff-d6c7f20a83bf_story.html

Tuan, Y. (1977). *Space and place: The perspective of experience.* Minneapolis, MN: University of Minnesota Press.

Tufte, E. (1990). *Envisioning information.* Cheshire, CT: Graphics Press.

Turing, A. (1988). Computing machinery and intelligence. In D. R. Hofstadter, & D. C. Dennet (Eds.), *The mind's eye: Fantasies and reflections on self and soul* (pp. 53–67). New York: Bantam.

Turkle, S. (1995). *Life on the screen: Identity in the age of the internet.* New York: Simon & Schuster.

Turkle, S. (1997). *Life on the screen: Identity in the age of the Internet.* New York, NY: Touchstone.

Turkle, S. (1999). Cyberspace and identity. *Contemporary Sociology, 28*(6), 643–648. doi:10.2307/2655534

Turkle, S. (2009). *Simulation and its discontents.* Cambridge, MA: MIT Press.

Turkle, S. (2011). *Alone together: Why we expect more from technology and less from each other.* New York: Basic Books.

Turnley, M. (2005). Contextualized design: Teaching critical approaches to web authoring through redesign projects. *Computers and Composition, 22,* 131–148. doi:10.1016/j.compcom.2005.02.007

Turnley, M. (2011). Towards a mediological method: A framework for critical engaging dimensions of a medium. *Computers and Composition, 28,* 126–144. doi:10.1016/j.compcom.2011.04.002

Twitter. (2013). *About.* Retrieved from https://about.twitter.com/

Tychsen, A., Newman, K., Brolund, T., & Hitchens, M. (2007). Cross-format analysis of the gaming experience in multi-player role-playing games. In *Proceedings of the DIGRA 2007 Conference.*

Ulmer, G. (1989). *Teletheory: Grammatology in the age of video.* New York, NY: Routledge.

UNData. (2012, 10 Sep.). *Personal computers per 100 population.* United Nations Statistics Division. Retrieved December 12, 2012, from http://data.un.org/Data.aspx?d=MDG&f=seriesRowID%3A607

Underwood, J., Kerlin, L., & Farrington-Flint, L. (2011). The lies we tell and what they say about us: Using behavioural characteristics to explain Facebook activity. *Computers in Human Behavior, 27*, 1621–1626. doi:10.1016/j.chb.2011.01.012

Unicode Consortium. (n. d.). *The Unicode Standard, version 6.2.* http://www.unicode.org/versions/Unicode6.2.0/Preface.pdf

United States Department of Defense. (2011). *Unmanned systems integrated roadmap, FY2011-2016.* Washington, DC: Department of Defense.

Uysal, H. H. (2007). Tracing the culture behind writing: Rhetorical patterns and bidirectional transfer in L1 and L2 essays of Turkish writers in relation to educational context. *Journal of Second Language Writing, 17*, 183–207. doi:10.1016/j.jslw.2007.11.003

Van Dijk, J. (2006). *The network society: Social aspects of new media.* London, UK: SAGE Publications.

Van Velsen, M., Williams, J., & Verhulsdonck, G. (2009). Table-top gaming narratology for digital interactive storytelling. In *Proceedings of the 2009 ICIDS Conference.*

Vanhoosier-Carey, G. (1997). Rhetoric by design: Using web development projects in technical communication classroom. *Computers and Composition, 14*, 395–407. doi:10.1016/S8755-4615(97)90008-6

Vargas, J. A. (2011, February 7). Egypt, the age of disruption and the me-in-media. *The Huffington Post.* Retrieved from http://www.huffingtonpost.com/jose-antonio-vargas/egypt-age-of-disruption-me-in-media_b_819481.html

Vatz, R. E. (1968). The myth of the rhetorical situation. *Philosophy & Rhetoric, 6*(3), 154–161.

Verhulsdonck, G. (2007). Issues of designing gestures into online interactions: Implications for communicating in virtual environments. In D. Novick, & C. Spinuzzi (Eds.), *Proceedings of Special Interest Group Documentation and Online Communication (SIGDOC) 2007* (pp. 26–33). New York: ACM Press. doi:10.1145/1297144.1297151

Verjans, S., Rajagopal, K., & Valentine, C. (2009). *Online CEF-based assessment of oral proficiency for intercultural professional communication.* Education and Culture DG: Lifelong Learning Programme. Accessed March 11, 2013 at http://cefcult.eu/data/Training_material_background-CEFcult.pdf.

Virilio, P. (2006). Speed and politics. Los Angeles, CA: Semiotext(e).

Virilio, P. (1994). *The vision machine.* Indianapolis, IN: Indiana UP.

Virilio, P. (1997). *Understanding pragmatics.* London, UK: Verso.

von Neumann, J. (1959, orig. 1928). On the theory of games of strategy. In A. W. Tucker & R. D. Luce (Eds.), Contributions to the theory of games, vol. 4 (pp. 13- 42). Princeton, NJ: Princeton University Press.

von Neumann, J., & Morgenstern, O. (1944). *Theory of games and economic behavior.* Princeton, NJ: Princeton University Press.

Voorhees, J. (2013, March 8). The guy who wrote Bush's torture memos thinks Rand Paul was standing for some extreme position. *The Slatest.* Accessed March 10, 2013 from http://www.slate.com/blogs/the_slatest/2013/03/08/john_yoo_drones_torture_memo_author_sides_with_obama_blasts_paul_rand_s.html.

Voorhees, G. (2009). The character of difference: procedurality, rhetoric, and roleplaying games. *Game Studies. The International Journal of Computer Game Research, 9*(2).

Voskouinsky, A. E., Mitina, O. V., & Avetisova, A. A. (2004). Playing online games: Flow experience. *PsychNology, 2*(3), 259–281.

Vygotsky. (n. d.). Retrieved from http://psychology.about.com/od/profilesmz/p/vygotsky.htm

Vygotsky, L. (1978). *Mind in society: The development of higher psychological processes.* Cambridge, MA: Harvard University Press.

Vygotsky, L. S. (1986). *Thought and language.* Cambridge, MA: MIT Press. (Original work published 1934)

Vygotsky, L. S. (1987). *Thinking and speech* (N. Minick, Trans.). New York: Plenum Press.

Wagner, I., Bratteteig, T., & Stuedahl, D. (Eds.). (2010). *Multi-disciplinary design practices*. London: Springer-Verlag.

Walker, J. (2009). Time as the fourth dimension in the globalization of higher education. *The Journal of Higher Education*, *80*(5), 483–509. doi:10.1353/jhe.0.0061

Walker, J. et al. (2011). Computers and composition 20/20: A conversation piece, or what some very smart people have to say about the future. *Computers and Composition*, *28*, 327–346. doi:10.1016/j.compcom.2011.09.004

Walther, J. B., & Parks, M. R. (2002). Cues filtered out, cues filtered in: Computer-mediated communication and relationships. In M. L. Knapp. & J. A. Daly (Eds.), Handbook of interpersonal communication (pp. 529-563). Thousand Oaks, CA: Sage.

Walther, J. B. (2007). Selective self-presentation in computer-mediated communication: Hyperpersonal dimensions of technology, language, and cognition. *Computers in Human Behavior*, *23*, 2538–2557. doi:10.1016/j.chb.2006.05.002

Walther, J. B., Anderson, J. F., & Park, D. W. (1994). Interpersonal effects in computer-mediated interaction: A meta-analysis of social and anti-social communication. *Communication Research*, *21*, 460–487. doi:10.1177/009365094021004002

Warnick, B. (2007). *Rhetoric online: Persuasion and politics on the World Wide Web*. New York: Peter Lang.

Warschauer, M. (2003). *Technology and social inclusion: Rethinking the digital divide*. Cambridge, MA: MIT Press.

Watts, E. (2011). Ruin, gender, and digital games. *Women's Studies Quarterly*, *39*(3/4), 247–265. doi:10.1353/wsq.2011.0041

Watzman, S., & Re, M. (2012). Visual design principles for usable interfaces: Everything is designed: Why we should think before doing. In J. A. Jacko (Ed.), *The human-computer interaction: Fundamentals, evolving technologies, emerging applications* (3rd ed., pp. 315–340). London, New York, NY: CRS Press Taylor & Francis Group. doi:10.1201/b11963-18

Weaver, R. (1985). Language is sermonic. In R. L. Johannessen, R. Strickland, & R. T. Eubanks (Eds.), *Language is sermonic* (pp. 201–226). Baton Rouge, LA: Louisiana State University Press.

Weaver, W., & Shannon, C. E. (1963). *The Mathematical theory of communication*. Chicago, IL: University of Illinois Press.

Weise, M. (2003). *How videogames express ideas*. Retrieved from DiGRA: Digital games research association Web site: http://www.digra.org/dl/db/05150.07598.pdf

Wertsch, J. (1998). *Minds as action*. New York, NY: Oxford University Press.

Wess, R. (1996). *Kenneth Burke, rhetoric, subjectivity, postmodernism*. New York, NY: Cambridge University Press. doi:10.1017/CBO9780511552878

What Pakistani girls think about India - amazing video! (2011). *YouTube*. Accessed March 10, 2013 at https://www.youtube.com/watch?v=9QwvVFhplkQ.

White, M. (2009). The senescence of creativity: How market forces are killing digital games. *Loading...*, *3*(4).

Wilbert-Lampen, U., Leistner, D., Greven, S., Pohl, T., Sper, S., & Volker, C. et al. (2008). Cardiovascular events during World Cup Soccer. *The New England Journal of Medicine*, *358*(5), 475–483. doi:10.1056/NEJMoa0707427 PMID:18234752

Williams, D. C. (1989). Under the sign of (an)nihilation: Burke in the age of nuclear destruction and critical deconstruction. In H. W. Simons, & T. Melia (Eds.), *The legacy of Kenneth Burke* (pp. 196–223). Madison, WI: University of Wisconsin Press.

Wilson, T. (1896). The swastika: The earliest known symbol, and its migrations, with observations on the migration of certain industries in pre-historic times. In *Report to the U.S. National Museum for 1894*. Washington, DC: Government Printing Office.

Winner, L. (1977). *Autonomous technology*. Cambridge, MA: MIT Press.

Winner, L. (1993). Upon opening the black box and finding it empty: Social constructivism and the philosophy of technology. *Science, Technology & Human Values*, *18*, 362–378. doi:10.1177/016224399301800306

Winograd, T. (1997). From computing machinery to interaction design. In P. Denning, & R. Metcalfe (Eds.), *Beyond calculation: The next fifty years of computing* (pp. 149–162). New York: Springer-Verlag. doi:10.1007/978-1-4612-0685-9_12

Wolf, J. M. (Ed.). (2002). *Professing in the contact zone: Bringing theory and practice together.* Urbana, IL: NCTE.

Wolin, R. (2001). *The rhetorical imagination of Kenneth Burke.* Columbia, SC: University of South Carolina Press.

Wood, D. (1992). *The power of maps.* New York, NY: Guilford.

World Bank. (2012, October). *Afghanistan overview.* Retrieved December 20, 2012, from http://www.worldbank.org/en/country/afghanistan/overview

World Factbook, C. I. A. (2012). *CIA World factbook—Afghanistan.* Retrieved December 18, 2012, from https://www.cia.gov/library/publications/the-world-factbook/geos/af.html

Worsham, L. (1998). Going postal: Pedagogic violence and the schooling of emotion. *JAC: A Journal of Composition Theory, 18*(2), 213-45.

Wright, E., & Wright, E. (Eds.). (1999). *The Žižek reader.* Oxford, UK: Blackwell Publishers, Ltd.

Wurman, R. S. (2001). *Information anxiety 2.* Indianapolis, IN: QUE.

Wysocki, A. F. (2005). Awaywithwords: On the possibilities in unavailable designs. *Computers and Composition, 22,* 55–62. doi:10.1016/j.compcom.2004.12.011

Wysocki, A. F., & Jasken, J. I. (2004). What should be an unforgettable face…. *Computers and Composition, 21,* 29–48. doi:10.1016/j.compcom.2003.08.004

Xtranormal. (n. d.). Retrieved from http://www.xtranormal.com/watch/12353479/rmit-english-digital-intro-2011

Yee, C. (2002). Contact zones in institutional culture: An anthropological approach to academic programs. In J. M. Wolf (Ed.), *Professing in the contact zone: Bringing theory and practice together* (pp. 257–273). Urbana, IL: NCTE.

Yee, N., & Bailenson, J. N. (2007). The Proteus effect: The effect of transformed self-representation on behavior. *Human Communication Research, 33,* 271–290. doi:10.1111/j.1468-2958.2007.00299.x

Zaheer, S., Albert, S., & Zaheer, A. (1999). Time scales and organizational theory. *Academy of Management Review, 24*(4), 725–741.

Zappen, J. P., Halloran, S. M., & Wible, S. A. (n.d.). Some notes on ad bellum purificandum. *The Journal of the Kenneth Burke Society.* Retrieved January 10, 2013 from http://kbjournal.org/node/201

Zappen, J. (2005). Digital rhetoric: Toward an integrated theory. *Technical Communication Quarterly, 14*(3), 319–325. doi:10.1207/s15427625tcq1403_10

Zimbardo, P. (1969). The human choice: Individuation, reason, and order vs. deindividuation, impulse and chaos. In W. J. Arnold & D. Levine (Eds.), *Nebraska Symposium on Motivation, 17,* (pp. 237-307). Lincoln, NE: University of Nebraska Press.

Žižek, S. (1997). *The plague of fantasies.* New York, NY: Verso.

About the Contributors

Gustav Verhulsdonck's research is focused on the areas of rhetoric, professional and technical communication, virtual reality, human-computer interaction, interface design, video game theory and new forms of digital rhetoric created by various technologies. His research investigates how human-computer interaction develops through media, and how it can improve technical communication processes and so foster better human understanding and learning. He has worked as an information developer and technical writer for International Business Machines (IBM), has been a researcher for the U.S. Army and National Aeronautics Space Administration (NASA) and was a visiting researcher at the Institute for Creative Technologies at the University of Southern California where he conducted experiments in virtual worlds in various contexts. He has authored a number of papers for the Association of Computing Machinery (ACM) and the Institute of Electrical and Electronic Engineers (IEEE) on virtual worlds, non-verbal and verbal communication in virtual negotiations, issues of identity related to avatar interaction, and interactive narratives. He teaches at the University of Texas at El Paso's Rhetoric and Writing Program, where he is a visiting assistant professor and has taught graduate and undergraduate courses on topics such as computers and writing, technical and professional writing.

Marohang Limbu is an assistant professor in the Writing, Rhetoric, and American Cultures at Michigan State University, East Lansing, Michigan, USA. Limbu is a co-editor of *Emerging Pedagogies in the Networked Knowledge Society: Practices Integrating Social Media and Globalization (2013)* with IGI Global and a founder and editor-in-chief of the journal, *Journal of Global Literacies, Emerging Pedagogies, and Technologies* (peer-reviewed quarterly journal). Limbu's recent publications (journal articles and book chapters) address the areas of cross-cultural composition, social media and writing, teaching writing with technologies in multicultural/multilingual classrooms, networked communication, networked pedagogies, and global literacies. His current research interests include Web 2.0 tools, cloud computing, networked pedagogies and communication, intercultural communication, cross-cultural communication, second language writing, global literacies, and global indigenous rhetorics.

* * *

Mike Edwards investigates the intersections of economics, composition, and digital rhetorics in his research, and in particular explores the diverse ways in which neoclassical, Marxist, and Marxian economic ideologies account for value and its appropriation at various stages in the cycle of production, distribution, use, and re-production associated with digital texts. For that reason, his research interests also necessarily include concerns of digital materiality, authorship, ownership, and intellectual property, especially in situations where motivations other than that of capitalist market-based exchange contribute to the production and consumption of digital texts. He is currently at work on a scholarly monograph titled "Antimonopolist 2.0" that examines the economics of composing, publishing, and teaching in contexts connected to the military. He teaches courses in English and Digital Technology and Culture at Washington State University.

Julie Faulkner is a senior lecturer in the Faculty of Education at Monash University, Melbourne, Australia. She writes and teaches on matters of literacy, popular culture, identity and digital reading/writing practices. Her publications include the role of new media in curriculum innovation, the development and use of a virtual school in preservice teacher education and the role of pedagogies of discomfort in learning. She has edited *Disrupting Pedagogies in the Knowledge Society: Countering Conservative Norms with Creative Approaches* (IGI Global), and has jointly edited *Learning to Teach: New Time, New Practices* (Oxford University Press), currently in second edition. Her research areas cross areas of curriculum design, intercultural communication pedagogies, transition from school to university, critical reading practices and computer games as generative literacy learning environments.

Jorge Gomez's research interests encompass the rhetoric of videogames, environmental injustice in contemporary American fiction, and the nexus of neuroscience and art. His research also considers multimodal forms of composing in the writing classroom, and the use of social media to teach online presence, concision, and engagement. His work has been published in the Eleventh Biennial Conference on Communication and the Environment conference proceedings on Borders and Environments, and in *The Acentos Review*. Currently, he teaches Xicano/a literature at New Mexico State University, and first-year composition at the University of Texas at El Paso.

Nicholas Hanford's research focuses on game studies with a particular interest in the role of criticism in the medium's history. He is also interested in data mining, the role of the audience in games, and game fandom. He is a graduate student in the Department of Communication and Media at Rensselaer Polytechnic Institute and is the managing editor of the *Journal of Games Criticism*, an open access game studies journal.

Chris Ingraham is a Ph.D. candidate in the Department of Communication at the University of Colorado at Boulder. He received his B.A. (1999) from Amherst College, and his M.A. (2002) from the University of Chicago, where he worked with the late Wayne Booth. At Colorado he studies with Gerard A. Hauser, and is currently working on a dissertation about the literary public sphere in the digital age. His recent work has appeared in *Philosophy & Rhetoric* and *Text and Performance Quarterly*.

Ashley Rose Kelly is an Assistant Professor in the Brian Lamb School of Communication at Purdue University. Kelly's research and teaching interests are in the areas of rhetoric of science and technology, communication networks, and new media.

Meagan Kittle Autry's areas of research include rhetoric, particularly rhetoric of science and technology; genre theory; writing across the curriculum; and graduate student writing. Her most recent projects focus on how graduate students learn to write as experts in their fields, especially in the sciences and engineering, and the influence of open access on writing in the academy. She currently serves as the inaugural Director of Thesis and Dissertation Support Services in the Graduate School at N.C. State University, where she directs programming to support scholarly writing instruction for graduate students across the university. In her role, she develops and leads workshops, runs a Dissertation Institute, coaches students, and partners with groups across campus to develop life-long scholarly writers prepared to undertake the writing necessary for successful research careers.

Demetri Lallas's research focuses on the rhetorical genealogy of values and their development in the digital age. He investigates the transformation of "the good" and "the bad" in ethical and aesthetic terms as contemporary social media have de-monopolized these categories from the discourse of cultural elites. Of special focus is the manners by which popular music in particular and art in general are assessed in a post-critical world of filesharing and blogging, and how digital communities collect around shared political and aesthetic priorities, interests Lallas honed content-managing and moderating various city feeds on Steven Johnson's pioneering hyperlocal blog aggregator, outside.in. Lallas's record reviews have appeared on AllMusic.com and his fiction in *The Minus Times Collected*. His dissertation coincided with the subprime mortgage crisis and is the first study to chart "the American dream" from its 1914 coinage. Lallas has taught literature at Wagner College and rhetoric at the City University of New York's Brooklyn Educational Opportunity Center, the College of New Rochelle, and St. Joseph's College.

Ben Lauren is a PhD candidate in Technical Communication & Rhetoric at Texas Tech University. He is also Coordinator of the Florida International University Digital Writing Studio and a Senior Instructor in the Writing and Rhetoric Program, where he teaches courses in rhetorical theory, professional and technical writing, and advanced writing and research. Recent book chapters and journal articles include topics addressing contingent faculty research, intercultural communication, problem-based service-learning, photo essays, and media labs. His research focuses on connections between hybrid environments, new media, media labs, sound, and teaching. Additional interests include activity theory, thirdspace theory, usability, new media, intercultural communication, and app and website development.

Jennifer Helene Maher's research focuses on the politics and morality in software. Her book *Software Evangelism and the Rhetoric of Morality: Coding Justice in a Digital Democracy* (Routledge 2014) examines how the evangelical rhetoric of software developers encodes code within a liberal system of democratic justice that allows competing moral visions of programming to flourish. Maher is an Associate Professor at the University of Maryland, Baltimore County where she teaches in the English Department's Communication and Technology Track, as well as in the interdisciplinary Ph.D. program Language, Literacy and Culture.

Brad Mehlenbacher is Associate Professor of Distance Learning (Leadership, Policy and Adult and Higher Education), Primary Area Faculty Member with Human Factors and Ergonomics (Psychology), Affiliated Faculty Member with Communication, Rhetoric, and Digital Media (English and Communication), and Affiliated Faculty Member with the Digital Games Research Center (Computer Science) at

NC State University. Mehlenbacher is author of the CCCC's 2012 Best Book in Technical and Scientific Communication, *Instruction and Technology: Designs for Everyday Learning* (MIT Press, 2010), co-author of *Online Help: Design and Evaluation* (Ablex, 1993), and has chapters in *The Human-Computer Interaction Handbook* (Lawrence Erlbaum), *The Computer Science and Engineering Handbook* (CRC), and the 1998 NCTE award-winning *Computers and Technical Communication* (Ablex). He earned his BA and MA at the University of Waterloo (focusing on computer-assisted learning and computational text analysis) and his PhD in Rhetoric at Carnegie Mellon University (focusing on online information design and human-computer interaction).

Mª Pilar Milagros has worked at Koç University in Istanbul, Turkey since 2012. She was born in Spain but has lived and taught in other countries such as England, Greece, the United States and the Netherlands. In 2011, she received a PhD in Rhetoric and Professional Communication from New Mexico State University in Las Cruces, NM. U.S., with a specialization in Second Language (L2) writing. Her dissertation examined ways in which reflection and self-assessment activities provided L2 students with spaces to engage in negotiations of knowledge and identities. María Pilar has a varied work experience in other fields as well; she has taught Spanish Language and Literature, English as a Second Language (ESL), and Rhetoric and Composition courses in various educational institutions. In addition to her broad teaching experience, she has also worked as a computational linguist in Las Cruces, NM. As such, she translated, created and collected online learning materials and tools for lesser taught languages, such as Guarani. Parallel to her teaching career, she has also engaged in various research projects. She has presented her research work in various countries (the U.S., México, Morocco, Hungary, and Turkey), and has published in conference proceedings and in forthcoming venues. María Pilar's research interests include rhetoric, second language (L2) writing, intercultural communication, technology and new forms of digital rhetoric, and reflection and self-assessment. Her research explores ways in which technology in general and new media in particular influence L2 and intercultural students' writing and communication practices. In particular, she is interested in utilizing technology and new media and digital tools in the classroom to examine whether and how new epistemologies that are inclusive of L2 and intercultural different needs, learning styles, multiple identities (gender, ethnicity, social class, etc.) can be created and negotiated among all vested parties (administrators, instructors, and students).

Curtis Newbold's research examines the role of information design in complex contexts, including academic, professional, and scientific disciplines. Specifically, Newbold's work frequently explores how the visual presentation of information affects not only decision-making in technical, scientific, and professional environments, but also how design triggers visceral, emotional, and epistemological internalizations of information. Newbold has written and presented nationally on the intersections of creativity, ambiguity, rhetoric, art, and design and their roles in the development of ethical, engaging, and efficient communication strategies. His doctoral dissertation, *Ambiguous Science and the Visual Representation of the Real* addressed the valuable role visual ambiguity plays in the construction of scientific thought. Newbold has taught college courses in diverse communication topics, including visual communication, desktop publishing, information design, business communication, technical writing, popular science journalism, proposal writing, web design, editing, scientific writing, composition, and public speaking. He has also worked at a multinational exercise equipment firm as a technical writer and does web development and design consulting. Curtis Newbold earned his PhD in Rhetorics, Communication, and Information Design at Clemson University. He is currently an Assistant Professor of Communication at Westminster College in Salt Lake City, Utah where he teaches in the Master's of Professional Communication program.

Rajendra Kumar Panthee's research area includes of First-Year Composition, cross-cultural technology design, interface design, educational technologies, contact zone, and technological literacy. His research investigates how students from different cultural and linguistic backgrounds perceive Learning Management Systems that are used in writing classrooms. He also analyzes interface design by writing students and its relationship to student agency and invention in their digital writing and research in a cross-cultural digital contact zone situation of First-Year Composition in US universities. He has published a number of journal articles and book chapters. He won First Annual First-Year Composition (FYC) Award for Dissertations because of his study's contribution to the field. He teaches FYC, professional and technical Communication at the University of Texas at El Paso (UTEP). Prior to his PhD at UTEP, he taught at Tribhuvan University, Nepal for about 10 years as an assistant professor.

Nonny de la Peña is an Annenberg Fellow at the University of Southern California's Cinema School of Arts Interdivisional Media Arts and Practice Program and was named "One of the 13 People Who Made the World More Creative" by Fast Company's Cocreate. As a pioneer of the groundbreaking Immersive Journalism, she uses gaming platforms to offer fully immersive experiences of news and nonfiction using virtual reality gaming platforms. She is an AP/Google Technology and Journalism Scholar and has been funded by the World Economic Forum and the Tribeca Film Foundation for upcoming projects. One of her most recent pieces, Hunger in Los Angeles, premiered at the 2012 Sundance Film Festival and creates the feeling of *Being There* as a real crisis unfolds on a food-bank line. Other projects include the MacArthur-funded Gone Gitmo, a virtual Guantanamo Bay Prison; Cap & Trade, an exploration of the carbon markets built with Frontline World and CIR; Ipstress which investigates detainees held in stress positions; and Three Generations, a newsgame about the California eugenics movement that premiered at 2011 Games For Change. A graduate of Harvard University, she is an award-winning documentary filmmaker with twenty years of journalism experience including as a correspondent for Newsweek Magazine and as a writer whose work has appeared in the New York Times, Los Angeles Times Magazine, and others. Her films have screened at theatres in more than fifty cities around the globe, garnering praise from critics like A.O. Scott who called her work "a brave and necessary act of truth-telling."

Rich Rice is Associate Professor at Texas Tech University where he teaches new media, rhetoric, grant writing, intercultural communication, and composition in the Technical Communication and Rhetoric program. He directs the TTU Department of English Media Lab. His most recent book is *ePortfolio Performance Support Systems: Constructing, Presenting, and Assessing Portfolios* (2013) with Parlor Press and the WAC Clearinghouse. Recent book chapters and journal articles include topics addressing faculty professionalization, intercultural competence, teaching philosophies, mobile medicine, convergence theory, problem-based universal design for learning, photo essays, media labs, and study abroad models. His research works to make connections between new media, communication, and teaching. He is currently developing study abroad models between TTU and post-secondary institutions in India to strengthen opportunities for glocal teaching, research, service, and grant writing.

Martin van Velsen's research focuses on the use of language and language technologies to better utilize narrative in interactive entertainment, intelligent tutoring systems and educational games. He is currently lead user-interface engineer for the Cognitive Tutor Authoring Tools (CTAT) project at the Human Computer Interaction Institute, Carnegie Mellon University. Previously he worked at The Institute for Creative Technologies, University of Southern California. Before this worked on research in robotics at Carnegie Mellon University and he started his career in research on automated emotion recognition at the Delft Institute of Technology. Martin has authored a number of conference papers for the Association of Computing Machinery (ACM), Association for the Advancement of Artificial Intelligence (AAAI) and many other conferences. He is the co-author of a number of journal articles and related research papers. He is actively involved in the scientific community through panels, peer-review and through conference committees. Martin has worked on visualization and interface design and software engineering projects of a widely varied nature, some which are: neurosurgery simulations, large scale artificial intelligence architectures, virtual humans and training simulations. Martin has served as technical adviser to many leading specialists in the field of digital games, simulations and cinematic authoring.

Index

A

Activity Theory 1, 3, 16, 22-26, 154, 158, 162-163, 170
Ad Bellum Purificandum 107-108, 112
Administrative Technologies 209-210, 213, 215, 219-220, 223-224
Aesthetics 5, 44, 47, 59, 88, 258, 262, 281
Affordance 20-22, 39, 247, 265, 273, 281, 292
Agency 5, 15-16, 21, 24-25, 64, 161, 164, 166, 174-178, 184-185, 190, 194, 222, 241, 249, 263, 270, 272-276, 281, 284, 292-293, 296, 318, 324
AI 120-121, 256-257, 269-270, 272-273, 281
Algorithm 14, 62-66, 68-76, 78
Anti-Anonymity 304, 310
Artifact 8, 12, 14-16, 28, 121, 161, 233, 248-250, 252, 258, 276, 281
Astroturfing 310
Asymmetrical Power Relations 176, 179, 189
Avatar 29, 33, 115, 129, 313-314, 316, 318-320

C

Center 85, 121, 147, 154, 175-176, 189, 196
Chronos 227-233, 235, 239-240, 242, 247
Citizen Designers 174-175, 180, 185, 189
Cloud Computing 28-29, 135-140, 142-143, 146-147, 153
CMC 3-4, 10, 13, 16-19, 22-23, 27-28, 31, 34, 296-297, 299-300, 303, 306, 310-311
Composition Practices 191, 196, 208
Computation 3, 8-9, 12, 14-16, 22-23, 25-26, 28, 33, 40, 114
Consubstantiation 99, 101-102, 104, 106, 112
Continuum 1-4, 8, 12, 22, 24-27, 31-32, 40, 53, 230
Convergence 2-4, 8, 15, 22, 26, 28-34, 40, 72, 161-162, 172
Convergence Culture 30-31, 161, 172
Critical Thinking 191-192, 196, 198, 200-202, 204, 208, 315
Cross-Cultural 131-132, 135-136, 140, 142-148, 153, 156, 160, 169, 175-177, 180-185, 189, 221
Cross-Cultural Communication 140, 142-148, 153, 156
Cross-Cultural Contact Zone 176-177, 189
Cultural Literacies 144, 153
Customize 164, 177, 182-184, 189, 263

D

Data Mining 2, 97-99, 102, 104, 106-108, 112
Deep Ecology 249-250, 254, 281
Deindividuation 296-297, 299-300, 311
Democratic Platforms 174-175, 179, 185, 189-190
Derp 311
Dialectic 70, 72-73, 104-105, 107-108, 112, 141, 228, 253
Digital Literacies 29, 34, 131-135, 140, 146-148, 153, 209, 212-214, 221
Digital Media 2-3, 5-7, 10, 12-16, 20, 22-23, 25-29, 33, 40, 49, 55, 58-59, 114, 126, 227-228, 230-231, 240-242, 247, 291, 293
Digital Medium 12, 14, 16-22, 25, 27-29, 33, 40, 290, 292
Digital Rhetoric 1-16, 18-29, 31, 33-34, 40, 42, 62-63, 68, 75, 97-99, 101, 103, 105-109, 113-115, 117, 121, 125-126, 227-228, 239-242, 248-250, 258, 276, 281, 296, 312, 315-316, 321, 325, 327
Digital Video Game 129
Disembodied Disinhibition 297-299, 301, 311
Diverse Economy 218, 224
Dramatism 249, 252-253, 268, 276, 281

E

Embodied Digital Rhetoric 312, 315-316, 321, 325, 327

Encyclopedia Dramatica 303, 311
Engagement Design 41, 43-46, 50, 56-59, 61
Enjoyment 43, 46-47, 50-57, 59, 61, 125
Equipment 85, 90-91, 96, 155, 161, 169, 211, 265

F

Framed Narrative 249, 261, 263, 272-276, 281

G

global communication 23, 33, 134, 139, 146, 149, 153
Global Literacies 3-4, 22, 26, 33, 131-132, 134, 136, 139-140, 144-149, 153, 162, 205, 219
Glocalization 27-28, 155, 158, 161, 168, 172

H

HCI 13, 15-16, 23, 34, 40

I

Identification 16, 22, 68, 78, 84, 88, 94, 97, 99, 101-106, 108, 112, 251, 256, 265, 268, 304
Immaterial Capital 216-218, 222-224
Immaterial Labor 210-213, 216-218, 222-223, 225
Immersion 85, 125, 249-250, 254, 272-273, 275-276, 281, 297, 313, 315, 318, 324-325
Immersive Journalism 315, 318, 325, 327
Instrumental Communication 44, 46, 49, 54, 56, 59, 61
Interaction Design 13, 15-16, 22-23, 34, 40, 158, 163
Intercultural Communication 131-132, 144-146, 153-154, 157, 162-163, 166, 169, 208
Intercultural Competence 154-155, 157-162, 168-170, 172, 192
Interface 1, 5, 10, 13, 15-16, 19-21, 28-29, 33, 39, 129, 134, 163-164, 166, 169, 174-176, 178-182, 184-185, 189-190, 240, 254, 258-260, 264, 282, 297
Interface and its Redesign 189
Intrinsic Humanistic Design 46, 61
Invention 17, 26, 43-44, 74-75, 146, 177, 190, 240

K

Kairos 7, 12, 44, 192, 227-231, 233, 235, 241-242, 247, 315

L

Ludology 249, 282
Ludonarrative 249, 261, 263, 272-276, 281-282

M

Macro-Rhetorics 71-72, 78
Material-Technological Capital 216-217, 222, 225
Mechanics 1, 4-5, 12, 113, 115, 117, 233, 258, 261, 272, 274, 282
Mediological 25, 27, 31, 40
Mesa-Rhetorics 78
Metaphysics 82-83, 88, 96
Micro-Rhetorics 69, 74, 78
mischief 296
MMORPG 129
Mode 3, 5-7, 24, 27, 30, 89, 117, 178, 250, 252, 281-282, 286, 289, 292, 295
Multiliteracies 3, 27-28, 194-195, 222, 248-251, 276, 282, 285-286
Multimodal 1-2, 7, 26-27, 134, 205, 249-252, 264, 273, 275, 282-283, 285-288, 292, 295
Multi-Modal Composition 177, 190
Multimodality 1, 3, 12, 26-27, 33, 283, 286, 292

N

Negotiated Space 175, 190
Neutral Space 174-175, 190
NPC 129

P

Participation 30, 54, 61, 141, 143, 159, 166, 175, 184-185, 190, 192, 203-204, 235, 251, 283, 287, 316, 319
Phronesis 82, 87-88, 91, 96
Plastic Presence 312, 315-316, 319, 321, 325, 327
Player Character 118, 125, 129
Pleasure 43, 46-50, 53-54, 56-59, 61, 87, 93, 256, 263, 300, 315, 317
PMC 261, 265-266, 282
Problem-Based Learning 173
Procedurality 9, 63, 78, 249

Q

Quasi-Anonymity 299, 306, 311

R

Representation 4, 7-8, 29, 33, 76, 100, 114, 129, 175, 185, 237, 247, 250-251, 253, 256, 267, 283-287, 292, 295, 314
Reputation Systems 304, 311
Rhetoric of Rebirth 248-250, 253, 267, 282
RPG 129, 255

S

Scramble for Recognition 297, 299, 311
Second Language (L2) Writing 208
Semiotics 12, 16, 33, 295
Social Media 48, 55, 132-134, 136-137, 141, 147, 161, 191-193, 197-205, 208, 229, 235, 239, 241, 247, 250, 284, 296, 300, 303-304
Soft Selves 312, 314, 318, 325, 327
Spinstorms 306, 311
Structural Ambiguity 55, 61
Student Agency 177, 190
Substance 4-5, 84, 102-103, 112, 271
Synaesthesia 283, 286-287, 290, 295

T

Text-Centric 177, 190
Thirdspace 166, 169, 173
Tool-Being 85-86, 88, 94, 96
Transactional Learning 154, 173
Trolling 296-297, 300, 302-303, 306, 311

U

Unicode 80-83, 86, 88-91, 93, 96
Unifying Spaces 174-175, 190
Usability 41-44, 46-47, 57-59, 61, 169, 174-175, 180, 190
Usability Test 59, 169, 174-175, 180, 190

V

Virtual World 129, 263, 313, 316, 320, 322
Vision Machine 45, 99-100, 112

W

Web 2.0 48, 75, 132, 136, 138-139, 143, 178, 190, 193-194, 290
Web Online Environments 174-175, 181, 190